PENGUIN BOOKS

THE ROAD TO MY FARM

Nora Jannsen Seton grew up in Northampton, Massachusetts. She received her M.S. in agricultural economics from Texas A&M and worked in agribusiness for four years before becoming a freelance writer covering food and agriculture for trade journals, magazines, and newspapers. She now lives with her husband in Zurich.

The
Road to My
Farm

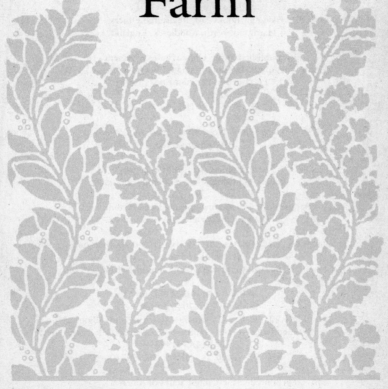

Nora Janssen Seton

PENGUIN BOOKS

PENGUIN BOOKS
Published by the Penguin Group
Penguin Books USA Inc., 375 Hudson Street,
New York, New York 10014, U.S.A.
Penguin Books Ltd, 27 Wrights Lane, London W8 5TZ, England
Penguin Books Australia Ltd, Ringwood, Victoria, Australia
Penguin Books Canada Ltd, 10 Alcorn Avenue,
Toronto, Ontario, Canada M4V 3B2
Penguin Books (N.Z.) Ltd, 182–190 Wairau Road,
Auckland 10, New Zealand

Penguin Books Ltd, Registered Offices:
Harmondsworth, Middlesex, England

First published in the United States of America by
Viking Penguin, a division of Penguin Books USA Inc., 1993
Published in Penguin Books 1994

1 3 5 7 9 10 8 6 4 2

The author has changed the names of
certain individuals described in this book.

Portions of this book first appeared, in different form,
in *Eating Reading* and *Greenwich News*.

THE LIBRARY OF CONGRESS HAS CATALOGUED THE HARDCOVER AS FOLLOWS:
Seton, Nora Janssen.
The road to my farm/Nora Janssen Seton.
p. cm.
ISBN 0-670-84514-0 (hc.)
ISBN 0 14 01.7045 6 (pbk.)
1. Seton, Nora Janssen. 2. Farmers—New England—Biography.
3. Women farmers—New England—Biography. I. Title.
S417.S44A3 1993
630´.92—dc20   [B]   92–50770

Printed in the United States of America
Set in Galliard
Designed by Kathryn Parise

*This book is dedicated to my
mother and father.*

Whatsoever thy hand findeth to do,
do it with thy might.

ECCLESIASTES 9:10

Acknowledgments

I am indebted to Texas A&M and the indefatigable Aggie spirit which embraced and nurtured me during my years in College Station. My special thanks to Ron Knutson, a true mentor, and to Carl and Peggy Shafer, who gave me the intangibles.

This book is a consequence of the counsel and encouragement of family, friends, farmers, merchants, and millers, to whom I'm very grateful.

Of course, there would be no such book were there not Kathryn, Caroline, and John.

Contents

The
Road to My
Farm

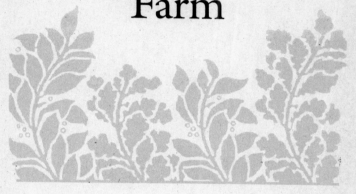

Prologue

The Own Farm Overture

"Oh, *don't* be a farmer," said a friend of mine. "Everybody's fed up with farmers nowadays. Farmers are poisoning the American food supply. And they won't give their grain to millions of starving refugees in the Sudan. I read that somewhere."

It was a perfect, crisp October day in 1988, and we had been spending the afternoon touring the autumn colors of the Vermont countryside. My friend had picked up several items along the way, toys for her young children, folk art for her living room, a gift for her mother-in-law. There were: a wooden cow on wheels with a pulling string; an old cast-iron cornbread mold with the shapes of corn cobs; a copper reproduction of an early American rooster weather vane; some note cards with colorful images of grazing barnyard animals.

Her thoughts had followed mine.

"Farms have changed," she said. "They used to be nice places full of different animals making nice squawks. Farmers were American heroes, Noble Savages, tillers of the land and all that. They raised healthy crops without all the chemicals and their cows were, you know, happy.

"But it's all over. Farming's become a different thing. Farmers are destroying the soil. They need the drug and chemical companies to keep the ground producing anything. They dope up their animals to make them grow unnaturally fast. They're polluting the national water supplies. And, I'll tell you what—they don't even let animals have sex anymore. It's all done with pipettes and tanks of frozen sperm.

"It's all different, believe me. It's not like it looks in the picture books, and it bears little relation to your agribusiness experience, I'll bet, if that's what you're thinking. I don't understand how you could just up and do this."

We had come from Woodstock and were driving southward, along fallowed fields of blond stubble and small, discrete meadows sprinkled gently with white sheep. In the autumn, New England farmland turns almost stoic. I love the monkish quiet after the exuberant blossoms of summer and before the mantling cold of winter.

"Well," I said, "we're not approaching this rashly. But we're pretty serious. I have to do some investigating first."

We passed a field dotted with grids of two-foot fir trees. This belonged to the Christmas tree business of the Northeast. Most of these saplings, after four or five years, would be spiral-bound and trucked to the sidewalks of East Coast cities. It is a lucrative business, I was thinking, particularly with older and more majestic trees, and even more so on the "cut-your-own" acres, where buyers deliriously pay extra to hack down and haul away their own trees. The cut-your-own/pick-your-own farms, I reflected, had emerged as a pretty savvy way to go.

"Vegetables might be nice," said my friend, nestling into the possibilities. "What you didn't feed to your animals, you could eat."

I sighed.

She sighed, too: "Everything looks so healthy up here. If you're going to farm, do it this way. Do it like they do in Vermont."

Vermont's got a good thing going. Anything it touches seems to turn natural shades of nice. In the 1980s rush to find healthful food products, retailers figured out straightaway that all a shelf item needed was the word *Vermont* on the label, and presto, off it went into the basket of certified organic sundries. Not just maple syrup. Not just cheddar cheese. Why constrain the Green Mountain entrepreneur? Out of the closet came Vermont coffees, Vermont salsas, Vermont champagne mustards. Sales of these products exceeded anyone's imagination—and imagination plays a sizable role in the interchange between buyers and sellers of food.

"I'll bet people up here don't use chemicals on their farms," mused my friend.

"Well, it's hard to generalize," I said. "I think a lot depends on what you're up against. Soil depletion. Livestock viruses. Crop pests."

She said, "No. I think up here, where it's not so industrialized—where it's families farming—people don't use chemicals because their kids could get hurt. Or their wells would be contaminated. Oh, look," she pointed. "There's a brown sheep over there. Brown sheep. Things are always so much more natural in Vermont."

·

My own background was not one of farming; it was barely rural. I was raised in Northampton, Massachusetts, a college town in the Berkshires, within a family whose sphere of intellectual inquiry extended into several arts and several sciences—but not those of agriculture, aesthetic as they were. My parents emphasized a classical education for all five of their children, and for me that led to Harvard University, where I stumbled through the odes of Propertius and mulled over the ancient coins of Greece. It might have been a tidy story, beginning with the liberal arts and metamorphosing eventually into some less liberal but pragmatic and remunerative career.

But my mother died as I was finishing up at Harvard, and then all the premises changed.

"I hope that this period of mourning," wrote one of my advisers, "will give way to a renewed sense of purpose." These words stand even today as one of the most important aids to my thinking. Purpose, I thought. The rebuilding of an internal scaffolding. Out of the ashes.

Several months after graduating from college, while dabbling without heart in a sequence of professional distractions, I got lucky. A swarm of hitherto unconnected aspirations suddenly collided (the Big Bang Theory of career development), and the outcome was not unlike the creation of a new private universe: agriculture, whatever that was. The idea seemed at first foreign to most of my family and friends, but they came to see that it made sense for me in terms of my interest in rural development, environmental resources, politics, and animals—cattle, primarily. When I announced that I had enrolled to study agricultural sciences at Texas A&M University, one of my sisters said, delighted, "Oh, cow college! What a great idea."

By coming relatively late to agriculture, my predisposition and academic credentials were different from those of most of my colleagues and professors. My ways of thinking about agrarian problems and achievements were considered at times heretical, at times innovative, at times useful, and at times altogether comical. My perspective matured, for obvious reasons, with more detachment than that of my peers, most of whom had grown up in the midst of agrarian communities.

As the daughter of a psychoanalyst, I suppose I would say that I developed a complex affection for American agriculture. I have admired its struggle to advance, to shed the constraining yokes of its history and the social romance that surrounds it. I once even aspired to become the secretary of agriculture, to help unknot and rebuild what I saw as a tangled and foundering entity. Even now I would hold a lingering ambition for that job, were I still as ignorant of the bureaucracy and unprogressive spirit embodied by the vast United States Department of Agriculture. But the USDA is a politically administered branch of our government and thus one whose deportment is not responsible to basic economic principles or consumer-oriented preferences; its policies are tolerated to remain in conflict while its programs grow increasingly expensive and corpulent. In my mind, agriculture is the fat and unhappy adolescent whose parents, wishing their child had turned out otherwise, pitch him more food to keep him, at least, hushed.

"You've put agriculture on the couch," said a friend.

·

Farming creeps into the American dream with surprising frequency. Most of us at one time or another have fantasized about it. Cashing in on the local mesclun market. A few chickens in the yard, like grandfather once had. Some glorious stallions tossing their silky manes around the meadow. Corn tassels as far as the eye can see. Two longhorns for effect in the front forty. And, apart from the pleasing visual images, farming has been viewed as an inherently healthy way of life, studded with moral lessons for children and good, solid work for adults. Despite modern soul-destroying realities along the lines of chemical herbicides and slaughterhouse (dis)assembly lines, this is the image that survives in the minds of America's nonfarm population, the ninety-eight percent of us 250 million whose only connection with the plough is through childhood stories and the charm of folk art renderings. We have coveted these impressions and hold ourselves above many of today's industrialized agricultural practices: "Not me. Oh, no. I wouldn't do it that way." Ultimately, however, most of us don't do it at all.

When I became involved with agriculture, I was startled by the degree of interest in it that lay simmering among friends, family, and acquaintances. It was as though I had flushed from the bush a hundred starling musings. There was a thirst for stories about the agrarian ethic, the bucolic aesthetic, the comedy of the barnyard and the miracle of calving. I probably bridled a bit; I don't remember. I have never had much patience with people getting sentimental about other lifestyles. For me, it distorts or denies the reality of those lifestyles—complex, unhappy, or splendid as they may be. What I loved about farming was the straightforward way it managed to combine the primordial chores of sowing and harvesting, and the warm-blooded conviction of animals like sheep, with the highly advanced machinery and technologies that have been steadily rattling the rest of society's bones. Agriculture makes a science of life and death, without removing a sense of either the miraculous or the melancholy.

Sometime during the years I spent in agribusiness, I became seriously interested in setting up a farm myself. My husband and I were planning to start a family, and apart from feeling pulled to farming, we thought it would be a felicitous, healthy context in which to raise children. I thought I could do it better—more efficiently, more humanely, more productively than others—and I believe a person needs to feel that way about any such embarkation. So I began to research the idea, at first with trepidation, then more forthrightly. I explored farming as plain food production, as a lifestyle, and as a source of personal meaning. I took in the myths and befriended a few unwelcome vulnerabilities. I looked at the broad picture and then I looked inside myself. This is how it looked.

Part One

Food Maker

1

The Seedstock of
the Farmer

The desire to start a farm had plagued me for years. I say "plague" because for some time it really irked me—it didn't fit in properly with my image of myself, my background, or my professional goals. What was all that education for? How could I sacrifice my career? What did I know about the rudiments of ploughing a field or husbanding livestock? Was this some sort of fleeting romance? What if it failed?

And then I heard another voice: "Why are you always fighting with yourself?"

That was my father. Eventually, it also became the voice of my husband, a man who likewise didn't cotton to my internal battles, and who liked the idea of raising crops and livestock—particularly lamb—as much as I did. It was then that the fighting stopped, and the planning precipitated and the whole journey toward starting a farm began. For me, it has been both illuminating and exciting. The process has involved on the one hand a searching backward, to find the origin of my own penchant for farming, and on the other hand a searching forward, to project myself into the modern realities of small-scale agriculture.

The farm I had in mind comprised both crop and livestock

production. I imagined a small operation, old-fashioned in the sense of raising a little bit of everything. I wanted cattle and goats and poultry, my husband wanted sheep, and we both were interested in trying our hands at raising vegetables and maybe cultivating some fruit trees. That might sound extravagant if not far-fetched, given the current propensity toward monoculture and cash crops. In fact, it is altogether conceivable.

I looked upon the venture with a great excitement about the unknown: I hoped to learn from season to season, keep a farm journal that would itself mature into my yearly guide. I daydreamed about cultivating watercress, which my mother had loved, or curious salad greens for the area restaurateurs. I envisioned my farm on the rolling hilltops of northwest Connecticut, or maybe in Virginia. If it were Virginia, I wondered, would I feel compelled to grow okra? One had to be open-minded, I kept reminding myself, not yet knowing the particular constraints of soil or community.

"Open-minded?" my husband smiled, his eyes wide. "This is indeed a pivotal moment. But bok choy, bean sprouts, hot chilies, and rabbits for meat? How open-minded are you going to be?"

"Well," I said, "within practical boundaries. If we end up buying a farm with a sizable rock ledge, say, I might expand the goat idea. If we move to Texas, I might consider the cotton option. That's what I mean by open-minded. Adapting to the land as opposed to tailoring it. I don't want to buy swampland with the intention of filling it in and I don't want to buy mountainside with the intention of blasting it into a steppe."

"I feel the same way." He paused. "With one exception. The cotton. No cotton. I've heard plenty about cotton and I just don't think I could survive it."

I had indeed been reading up on cotton and making observations to my husband about the laborious process of raising it (it is temperamental), protecting it (it is prized by several bugs), weeding it (hoeing the rows is called "chopping" and is widely recognized as rugged, nightmarish work) and harvesting it (the recipe: one good crop dusting of chemicals for killing off the foliage; one enormous air-conditioned tractor for collecting the fluffy bolls from the dried-out plants; and one medical insurance policy with a low premium). But after a few days of discussing how taxing cotton production seemed, my husband and I finally agreed we might try it.

"Okay," he smiled. "Cotton. Even the image is slightly addictive." He added sarcastically, "I have a feeling I'm going to find out why our forefathers embraced slavery the way they did."

"I'll just plant a couple of rows," I said. "You can gin it in the kitchen. What a great idea."

This change of heart over cotton really characterized my husband's and my attitude about the farm. We were curious. Everything seemed worth a chance, worth investigation. Whatever crops we might intend to sell for income, we would grow others as well just to learn. I wanted to sense for myself the rhythms of cotton and kumquats, herbs and potatoes. Our field rows would be bordered with miscellany. And then, of course, there would be the animals. The keeping of livestock—most specifically, cattle and goats—alongside our crops best embodied my farm plan. I was drawn to the Jeffersonian ideals of diversity and complementarity. The notion of a motley barnyard with its spectrum of crops and livestock appealed to me. Each species has its own intrinsic rhythm, its own season, as we all do.

Although my husband and I agreed in principle about having a farm, we didn't just quit our jobs and head for Maine. We decided to keep working to save a little extra income for putting toward the future expense. There is an old joke in agricultural circles about a farmer who won a million-dollar lottery. Asked what he would do with all that money, the farmer said, "Oh, I guess I'll just keep on farming until it runs out." We accepted the humor of this story as well as the moral, and we decided to gather information over the next few years as we waited for an auspicious moment to buy our farm.

There was certainly time to think things through, since we were living at that point in the affluent community of Greenwich, Connecticut, just over the border from what demographers aptly dub the "major metropolitan area" of New York City—a sprawl of densely populated suburbs. In a town where property values stretched easily into the millions, we were comfortably ensconced in a small guest cottage on an ample estate. We loved the coziness of the cottage—coziness in the sense of tiny, since "cozy" in the sense of snugly insulated it was not. It was a terrific place for a couple actively extending their honeymoon into a third year. For people like this, carpenter ant infestations and breezes wafting through the walls are trifling matters.

One day, after settling a second fluffy layer of fiberglass insulation (upside-down, which shows how I deal with printed instructions) along the attic rafters, I sat out on the front stoop to have a cup of coffee and wash the glass dust down my throat. We had two petite garden plots on either side of the front door. They were meticulously laid out and wood-chipped, and I noticed a lone green plant poking up willfully among the clods of bark. Presuming that it didn't belong to The Plan of the estate's gardens, I permitted curiosity its rein and set myself to an investigation. I dug down around the stem for two inches before I bumped into a knob, a tuber of sorts. It was easily exhumed along with its knotty web of white roots and surprised worms.

"Who are you and where did you come from?" I murmured, prone to animism in my solitary hours. No answer—the inevitable pitfall of animism.

"Weed," I decided, stung by what I took as its tacit indictment of my sanity. But as I examined this plant, I suddenly saw in it an analogy to my decision about farming. Here was this robust yearning for a farm, I reflected, poking up in the midst of an otherwise nonagrarian life. If I burrowed down, maybe I would find the seed of this predilection, maybe I would be able to discern the roots of the idea itself. In the end, I would at least be better informed about what farming actually entailed, what kind of lifestyle and fulfillment it might provide.

And there was one other issue of which the plant incident made me mindful: I had and have now very mixed feelings about plants. Individually, or in small numbers, I don't much like them at all. Flower gardens especially tend to make me uneasy. I expect blooms to turn to pillars of salt if I look at them too long. The fragility and silence of all that foliage and petalry fills me with apprehensions. I have no inherent way with plants, and I speculate that it is only in spite of me that a few potted ivies have ever survived my ministry.

This pathology, however, is somehow divorced in my head from farm crops. At the same time that I will flinch from a breathtaking begonia, I can envision an acre of lettuce with confident pleasure and anticipation. Unearthing long furrows of fresh red potatoes transports me, gives me the thrill of an archaeologist. Beets are borderline, tomatoes I don't like staking, but most other vegetables I can readily conceive of cultivating on a scale of acres. In short, farming to my mind is completely and favorably removed from the negotiations of a house or garden plant. There is strength for me in the image of mass. I think that a field of sunflowers, soybeans, or pumpkins is a chorus of vigor.

As for whatever green life form I had yanked out of the cottage garden, however, it was definitely not singing any longer. After my few exploratory incisions and amputations, it was drooping miserably.

"You probably pulled up the last example of a rare species of some exquisite flower hitherto thought extinct," smiled my husband that evening, as he observed the remains of this autopsied plant on the flagstones.

"I know what we can call your farm," he offered—it was always "his" garden and "my" farm. "Farmageddon. The ultimate battleground."

My husband had become an avid gardener since we moved

out of the city into the suburbs. He happily spent spring and summer weekends relocating heavy clumps of perennials to "definitely sunnier spots," and then relocating them once again as the shadows shifted. He loved to follow the directions on seed packets, to rake our clay soil into a beautiful pebbly grain (until the first rain), to fertilize and exhort and transplant and prune ad nauseam—ad meam nauseam. And it has been a complementary relationship over the years, with my enthusiasm for his well-staked tomatoes which he insists he plants only for me, and his happy solitude digging craters to shelter his cucumber sproutings.

"I love planting," he said one day. "Planting is like setting a little time bomb. You poke a seed in the ground. You forget about it. And then later, boom!"

There was only one year, when my husband broke his leg, that I was entrusted with the spring planting of the garden—his garden. In the evenings during the course of those three months, he and I would head outside with trowel, seeds, hose, and a stool. I pushed everything along in the wheelbarrow, solemnly hanging my head and giving the procession something of a funereal air. My husband would orchestrate the garden blueprint from his stool, gesturing with a crutch, while I drew a finger through the dirt to make a row for coriander and poked cucumber seeds down one inch or so. The experience brought me face to face with that hoard of deep-threaded anxieties about the delicate and unpredictable nature of plants, their noiseless lives. The days I spent waiting for signs of life from the watered soil seemed interminable. And once the plants broke surface, a series of hazards seemed to await them. There were the rabbits, deer, and woodchucks. There was, among the calendulas and tomatoes, a "five-o'clock wilt" after a day of unmitigated sunshine—it was enough to ruin my dinner. And when the arugula bolted at only four inches of height, and microscopic white worms were gainfully goring every red radish we had, I was convinced that I, as a gardener, was not Mother Nature's torch bearer.

"Oh, how satisfying this geranium bed is," cooed my neighbor one morning from across her white picket fence. She was rosily lopping off the browning blossoms and throwing Miracle Gro over the lot. "Shall I come over and help you weed?"

Weed? I thought. Which one is the weed? I looked up at her with a pair of industrial-scale vine shears dangling from my hand. She had clearly construed that my husband's beloved pole beans faced a greater peril from my hand than from the multiplicity of slugs and beetles that supped on them. So she walked over and nestled herself between the Bibb lettuce and the basil and started pinching out the aggressive threads of new grass and clover.

"This is your lettuce." She pointed. "And this is just a weed." She held up something very healthy-looking, and smiled. "You say you're in agriculture?"

I was indeed "in agriculture," I supposed. After studying agricultural economics at Texas A&M University, I had gone on to work first for a cattle genetics company, then for a grain export company, and later for a specialty beef company. These were corporate encounters of the agribusiness kind, but I think they contributed something to my interest in small-scale farming. They kept my thoughts trained on animal breeds, corn prices, and industry issues, and they kept my ear tuned to the field and to the vocabulary of farming. Above all, they made me feel cheerlessly remote from what I had begun to love in agriculture, which was the bread-and-butter of it, the daily chores.

Livestock had been the focus of most of my agribusiness career, and because of that I felt most comfortable with the idea of handling cattle, sheep, poultry, and pigs—well, pigs only if necessary. I daydreamed about proper fencing techniques, about irrigation channels and feed bunks. I subscribed to magazines that kept me updated with tips on handling calves, feeding pregnant goats, and measuring the moisture content of hay in my microwave oven. I wrote to the publishers. I said, How can I keep the flies off my calves, and What if I don't have a microwave oven, which I don't?

Fruit and vegetable crops I had only an indirect sense about, but a commercial instinct, which is why I went to work on area vegetable farms when we moved to Greenwich, and which is also why I tended to bring steel-industry tools to bear upon our little garden out back. I was an unwitting Goliath in that leafy patch. It made me irritable that everything was so petite and that I must surely have seemed more a menace to my husband's vegetables than an aide.

Yes, I'm in agriculture, I would fume to myself. I sit behind a desk each day and imagine supertankers full of soybeans and frozen pork bellies crisscrossing the globe.

The real roots of my decision to have a farm originated before my agribusiness involvement. I look back to childhood and childhood friends, to a semester off from college when I worked on a cattle ranch in Wyoming, to my unwavering interest in natural resources and to my long-standing and undernourished love of livestock. These experiences together introduced me to the multiple facets of agrarian life. These were the roots of my desire to farm, the roots of that plant I came across.

•

I grew up in the town of Northampton, Massachusetts, at a time when it was still a small college town tucked into the foothills of the Berkshire mountains and ringed by small farms of cucumbers, asparagus, corn, and tobacco. My family lived at the edge of Smith College, the oldest women's college in the country. The campus was lovely, full of green fields, gardens, huge brick and clapboard houses that served as dormitories, and a pond on which the whole town skated out its winters.

Our own home was a big yellow house just beyond a brick quadrangle of student dormitories. It was an old three-storey house that had originally been built to accommodate wealthy patricians during their recuperation from treatments at the local hospital. That was in the day when Harrison Avenue was fields and meadows. It is now a thoroughly residential street, replete with a creative variety of neighbors that bring the issues of the world literally to one's doorstep—AIDS, divorce, yuppies, affairs, even the superbly restrained vendettas waged over swimming pools, backyard fences, and aerial antennas.

My parents moved to Northampton in 1957. My father was for many years the only local psychoanalyst for the area colleges and the community at large. Psychoanalysts were a rare commodity in the 1950s. Like cancer or divorce, their work was a subject one didn't discuss. It's hard to imagine that reserve nowadays, as we have evolved into such an all-baring, long-winded culture for whom cancer, divorce, and psychotherapy are mundane and chat-worthy issues. My father suffered a further image problem by refusing to identify himself with "the Freudians" or "the Jungians," a choice that denied people a quick and comfortable laying on of pigeonholing hands. He would say that human beings are too varied to have a simple set of methodologies applied to them, that you must take each person as he or she is, complicated and conflicted.

Since the very first mention of my agricultural aspirations, my father has been delighted by the idea of a farm in the family. He remembers sharing a bivouac in World War II with a farmer from Indiana, an "extremely decent man," he recalled, with enormous and strong hands. "Look at your hands," he had said to the soldier. "You've got hands the size of a ham. And your wrists!"

My mother graduated from Smith College in 1948. She had loved the town and the college, and their images were to recur quietly and fondly in her books. Words were her métier, as a critic and novelist. She taught herself French by reading Proust, and she wanted her children to be avid readers. We all did grow to be readers and writers, although my own start was relatively sluggish. When I was in my teens, my mother was still devising inventive bribes for me to "just get through" a smattering of pages of Galsworthy per month. Even now I cannot pick up a Galsworthy novel without distress, because he has remained synonymous for me with a torturous ennui—and my failure to overcome it.

After years of treatments and remissions, my mother died of Hodgkin's disease when I was a senior in college. I was too late to tell her a lot of things. Death, I think, is an ongoing lesson in finality, and so I have had to come to grips, periodically, with The Next Thing I will not be able to tell her. She would not have guessed about the farm, though it was she who spent the summers of her own childhood breathing in the white dandruff air from the duck farms of East Moriches, Long Island, and she, I think, who had good instincts about handling all kinds of creatures that crossed her path.

My one brother, the eldest child in the family, left the house quickly and angrily in the mid-1960s. My three older sisters— a doctor, a lawyer, and an art conservator—were more vividly a part of my own growing up. I watched them mature, I attended their high school honor roll initiations, I helped to move their plants and record albums into their college dorm rooms, and I missed them when my own time came for these rites. What will they all think of the farm, I wonder. And I'm quite sure they'll let me know.

There was a lot of Ivy in my family, and Ivy became a kind of premise for me, too, although I advanced to it in many respects blithely unaware. I was an average student, "mediocre," as my high school English teacher once verified for me in her singeing way. Still, the powers of the public school system posited me in various accelerated programs along the way—a choice, I was sure, that rested on my trailing so much Phi Beta Kappa material in the form of my sisters. As early as the fourth grade, I was bused to a special classroom that seemed leagues away from home (probably two miles), and it was there that I met Barbara, a Polish girl whose family lived behind the county fairgrounds on a farm. I loved to go over to her home, a modest olive-green two-storey house which she shared with her mother (a hairdresser), a blind and markedly homely sister who, in the throes of her own private agonies, demeaned and bullied Barbara, and a grandmother and grandfather who milked the twelve dairy cows and tilled the acreage in corn. Only Barbara and her sister spoke English as a first language. Her mother stammered by to confer on hair lengths and groceries, but her grandparents spoke no English at all.

In Barbara's house, I was acquainted with exotic dishes like golumpki, pirogi, and tomatoes in sour cream. We played in the barns, and would squat quietly in the hay beside her grandfather as he milked his cows by hand. I was suffered on occasion to feel the hot flanks and udders of the cows and to try my own hand at squeezing a teat. Barbara's grandfather thought that the finest gift a child could be given was a glass of warm, fresh milk. In fact, most people will agree that warm milk, straight from the udder, is a taste acquired only by dint of strenuous conviction. Unstrained, unchilled, unseparated milk enamors one only of machine-sure filtration and homogenization. The warm cup that Barbara's grandfather would extend to me—he grinning the proud and toothless grin of a European peasant farmer, me with eyes wide and lower lip quivering—seemed like an initiation by fire. Well, and it made me feel very, very mature to put down that milk without tears. At the time I viewed it as a fair price to pay for staying overnight at the farm.

During the winters, when my mother would drive me over to Barbara's house, we would turn off one rubbly gravel road onto the frozen, rutted earth of the barnyard driveway. Three foaming and barking German shepherd guard dogs invariably jumped to alarm. They would strain forward with their teeth bared, their necks defying imminent severance by their collars, only a skimpy chain hampering them from reaching us. From eating us, we agreed. We would wait in the car until Barbara or her mother came to rescue me, and to usher me, shivering, into the house. Then my mother, shivering also, would drive home.

On such days, Barbara and I would go for walks in the half-frozen mud of the barnyard, where tractor ruts were covered with a thin sheet of ice, hiding pools of yellow-green cow urine that seemed never to disappear. We would walk into the fields, Barbara in a heavy sweater, I stumbling beside her in an awkward, bulky, and completely incapacitating orb of a snowsuit, hobbling over the snow and the blond stubble of hay poking up through it. We would visit the cows and avoid with a fuss the yellow snow they left about them. We would watch a pile of fresh manure melt an aureole about itself and show the grass bright green beneath.

Northampton was surrounded by small farms like that of Barbara's family. I have heard that the alluvial soil of the Connecticut River Valley, its loess, is some of the finest soil in the country. In the summers, many of my school friends would work for the valley farms. Some picked cucumbers and corn. Most picked tobacco under the gauzy, cream-colored nets, and hung the leaves to dry in the familiar long red barns whose vertical slats were opened in the summer for aeration. Massachusetts and Connecticut still host the largest number of cigar wrapper and cigar binder tobacco leaf growers in the nation, but their netted fields, marked by steepling red and black barns and once such a common piece of the landscape, now must be sought out with the aid of guidebooks. Highways and housing developments roll over many of the old tobacco farms, the developments having adopted names like Valley Farms, Silo Circle, or Tobacco Hill.

Northampton evolved over the years into a bustling nucleus of boutiques and bistros, wealthy young parents, and enormous malls, each with the same clothing stores and organic food markets. Gradually the town attracted an increasing number of lesbians and became known as a kind of East Coast capital for women who preferred women and preferred to let you know. The J. J. Newberry's and the McCallum's disappeared and instead you could buy Italian shoes, French unfitted sheets, and blackened redfish, lump fish, or catfish. Psychotherapists now hang their shingles along Main Street, Center Street, and all the side streets as well—so many therapists, it seems, that there is simply no excuse for staying troubled in Northampton.

I went back to Northampton last summer to visit the local Agway dealership in town. Agway is a Northeast cooperative that has spent the last few decades being bought and sold and bought again. The exodus of farming from this region of the country has taken a severe toll on businesses like Agway that supplied equipment, feeds, vehicles, and other production materials to the now-retired small-scale farms.

In Northampton, the Agway store on King Street had somehow managed to survive the town's doggedly insistent adornments of sophistication. When I drove into the Agway parking lot, I began to understand. "Somehow" may have had to do with the fact that the store was currently more apt to be selling snowblowers, birdhouses, and Holland bulbs than, say, chicken feed, pig vaccines, and $150,000 John Deere tractors.

"Feed?" said the woman behind the raised garrison of a four-sided checkout counter.

"Yes."

"Well, honey, I can give you dog feed, cat feed, and bird feed, but we don't sell no—what did you say? *Livestock* feed?"

I walked by shelves of garden spades, bird feeders, green twine, and barbecue grills.

"Seed?" she looked at me like she hadn't heard right.

"Yes."

"I've got *bird* seed, flower seed, and a few packets left of lettuce seed. How much corn were you wanting to grow?"

So I wandered outside onto their tarmac of swing sets, woodchippers, tractor lawn mowers, and wilting flats of unidentifiable blossomless flowers.

"*Tractor* tractors?" she was sighing now.

"Yes."

"Not a lawn mower?"

"No."

"Oh, honey. I think we're three for three for you today. But look here. Here's a catalogue. Anything in it you like, I'm sure we can order for you."

She heaved toward me a ponderous graying lump of an out-of-date Agway sales catalogue. I thanked her for her trouble and went to my car to regroup.

•

In my family, extraordinary emphasis was laid on semantics. We often discussed the appropriateness of specific words, the connotations and denotations of words, what words meant to a novelist or to a psychoanalyst or the fellow on his couch. One of the points that my father most stressed was how word use could define a person's sense of self. For example, he once explained to me, it's one thing if you say a person is alcoholic, but if you say he or she is *an* alcoholic—if you turn the adjective into a noun—you essentially trap and curtail that person's identity.

"People too often get named, or identified, by their symptoms," he would say. Words like *homosexual* or *alcoholic* were really descriptive adjectives instead of comprehensively identifying nouns.

"I suppose it's almost like using a synecdoche," my father said, "where you're identifying a whole association of things by one aspect." Evocative in poetry, he added, but it rarely did justice to a whole, complex human being.

So when I decided to start a farm, I couldn't help but ruminate on the question: What was the difference between being a farmer and farming? What were the connotations of being a farmer, and did I like them? I knew that my husband had contended with similar questions. He would bristle when called a banker

—which indeed he was for all conventional purposes—because he didn't like the connotations. He often preferred the nebulous phrase "I work in finance." Verbs are much more freeing than nouns.

One day a friend sent me a poem that had been published in *Harvard Magazine*. The little biographical blurb at the bottom of the page said the poet was a blueberry farmer in Maine. It made me recoil. The image seemed at once pretentious and overly coy. I wasn't put in mind of the plain hard work and bird-battling of blueberry farming; rather I caught myself connecting the words with a kind of dainty, flowery self-avowal. It wasn't a rational attribution. I knew very well how strenuous farming is. Maybe it was just the blueberries, alliterative and adorable, that seemed to ally themselves these days more with ginghams and dolls than with farmers' woes and pails.

The incident made me realize that in many ways I was bashful about the idea of calling myself a farmer. I didn't want to be identified with cute crops. I would rather have planted one of those merciless fields of cotton, I thought, than be affiliated with a farm with a corny image. You're a snob, I said to myself, and I was right. I would have bent over backward to adhere to the image of a peasant laborer before I let myself look the part of a beribboned daisy-picker. Unnerved to discover these intransigent feelings in myself, I wondered if other people felt the same way about farming and the connotations of "being a farmer." I sought out the opinions of family and friends.

"I'm going to start a farm," I would say, testing the waters. And there was a broad gamut of response.

"Adorable. When do we eat?"

"Upwind or downwind of me?"

"Do farms have posts and lintels or only ranches?"

"Wonderful," said one friend. "A good idea tastes like honey, doesn't it?"

"Mankind has struggled for centuries to release himself from that drudgery," commented another.

"You're going to kill baby sheep?"

"A fine tradition."

There's nothing like a fine tradition, I decided. But it's even better when one knows a little something about what that tradition is. It being a Sunday evening, I picked up, with interest and irony, the Bible.

According to the Old Testament, food came before agriculture in the scheme of things. In Genesis 1, God created seafood and poultry on the fifth day. Beef, bugs, salad, and fruit arrived on day six, which was fortuitous for Adam and Eve, because they also came into being that morning or afternoon.

And God said to everybody (1:22; 1:28): "Be fruitful and multiply." But to man, he added: ". . . and fill the earth and subdue it; and have dominion over the fish of the sea and over the birds of the air and over every living thing that moves upon the earth."

He went on (1:29): "Behold, I have given you every plant yielding seed which is upon the face of all the earth, and every tree with seed in its fruit; you shall have them for food." And for all of the other creatures, God provided "every green plant for food" (1:30).

Genesis 2, however, presents a slightly different chronology. Here, man appears "formed . . . of dust from the ground," after earth was watered, but before it was planted. So from this version, only after "man became a living being" did God create "a garden in Eden, in the east; and there he put the man whom he had formed. And out of the ground the Lord God made to grow every tree that is pleasant to the sight and good for food . . ."

And then (2:15): "The Lord God took the man and put him in the Garden of Eden to till it and keep it." This is the first implication that food is going to take some cultivation by Adam and his helper, Eve; but, or so it would seem by all accounts, the Garden required very low maintenance indeed.

With the expulsion from Eden, God condemned Adam to the

exertions of farming. "Cursed is the ground because of you," he said; "in toil you shall eat of it all the days of your life; thorns and thistles it shall bring forth to you; and you shall eat the plants of the field. In the sweat of your face you shall eat bread till you return to the ground, for out of it you were taken; you are dust, and to dust you shall return" (3:17–19).

Outside the Garden of Eden, food was going to be a function of man's willingness to labor. Abel became a shepherd and Cain became a farmer, among other things. And the Bible would have you believe it all went downhill from there.

There are lots of versions of agricultural Beginnings, and some greet the science of agriculture more as a blessing than as a punishment. For the ancient Egyptians, it was the wise and powerful god Osiris who taught men to farm—giving them a tidier and more reliable alternative to foraging and cannibalism. In Greek mythology, Demeter was goddess of the cornfield. She ministered not only the sowing of farm crops and the breeding of animals, but also the matrimonial bed, where mankind's corresponding seeds and eggs were, one infers, of nearly comparable importance. When Demeter learned that it was Hades who had carried off her daughter, Persephone, she cast a scourge upon the earth. As Robert Graves wrote in *the Greek Myths,* volume I: "Demeter was so angry that, instead of returning to Olympus, she continued to wander about the earth, forbidding the trees to yield fruit and the herbs to grow, until the race of men stood in danger of extinction." But after Persephone was restored to her for the larger part of each year, Demeter sent one of her priests to earth to resurrect the parched ground. "Triptolemus she supplied with seed-corn, a wooden plough, and a chariot drawn by serpents; and sent him all over the world to teach mankind the art of agriculture." When the Romans embraced the gods of the Greeks, they called Demeter's counterpart Ceres, from which name is derived the word *cereal.*

As I decided to start a farm, the mythologies of the "original farmer" became mine to investigate, just as we all negotiate our personal images within the context of images set forth by our family and culture. But it was no mere exercise in introspection—modern farming has not extricated itself wholly from ancient teachings and rituals. You can still trace the force of early religious and folklorish edict in some cultures' farming practices today. Plenty of farmers swear that one must sow upward-growing plants such as pole beans when the moon is waxing, and downward-growing plants like carrots when the moon is waning. We have visited Shaker, Amish, and Mennonite villages where antiquated farming customs are preserved. Also maintained over time were the revered, millennia-old dietary laws of the Old Testament, the Kashruth. Kashruth dictates the way kosher food must be prepared and eaten among observant Jews even today.

Whenever I have worked on farms, I have found my thoughts drifting back to the early agricultural parables, perhaps because the very nature of manual work leaves one's mind open to unhampered thinking, and perhaps because many basic farm chores today are remarkably unremoved from farm chores thousands of years old—shoveling out irrigation canals and mounding dikes, milking cows or collecting seed. Frequently my thoughts idle on the polarity between cultures whose mythologies teach that their seminal founders somehow fell from grace and were condemned to agricultural toil, and those whose lore holds that their people were honored and rewarded by the gift of agricultural knowledge. It's part of a dialectical litany in agriculture between the peasant laborer and the champion provider. Do we perceive agriculture as a chore and the burdensome province of the poorest tier of the laity, or do we see agriculture as a wisdom and the blessed inheritance of mankind? In fact, it is a little of both, as is true with most of life. Farming encompasses both the tedium of manual labor and the richness of the most elaborate science.

Then, taking the idea a step further: Might this discrepancy in founding mythologies persist through time to have any bearing on our culture's contemporary attitudes toward its agricultural sector? Suppose the original farmer really had been the fruit of a divinely convicted and penalized parentage? How else might this farmer have evolved over time, conceptually, but as the lower class, the sweated peasantry, the peon? Around him, then, the other levels of maturing civilization—the royalty, the bourgeoisie, the burghers—would be seated higher on the social ladder for not having to produce their own foodstuffs. And arranged on the rungs of a comfortably distinct ladder would be the clergy, God's servants, who would sometimes farm, sometimes procure. Historically, of course, they had their own internal hierarchies, their own sense of what, exactly, was God's work. It was typically the local proletariat who pruned the monastery orchards, for there were, after all, a lot of manuscripts to copy.

But suppose the original farmer had instead been conceived of as the fortunate heir to sacred agricultural knowledge. I had some difficulty in seeing that positive image sustaining itself over time. It could be that, ten or so thousand years ago, when the first primitive communities of the Middle East's Fertile Crescent (not recognizable today, hardly fertile, a desert of war debris) were catching on to the reproductive capacities of their grains, individuals who flaunted a green thumb were celebrated by the others of that community. The better farmers may even have been tribal chiefs of a sort—we don't know. However, by the time our informative stone tablets became clearer a few millennia later, it seemed that farmers were not ascending to the upper echelons of civic hierarchy. Wealth and power were already attaching to ownership of fertile land, but the actual exertions of farming had been relegated by and large to the lower castes, the slaves of the king or the local peasantry.

The myth of a divinely favored farmer would appear to have lost steam over the course of time, in part, I believe, because agriculture necessarily became a communal chore and not the divine calling of a few heroic individuals; and then especially in the face of farming's intrinsic grind, which is hard to dispute. All in all, I think that the instinctive ascent of civilization, with its secular structural efficiencies and its growth, organized or chaotic, has always tended to subsume the farmer's stature into some necessary, primary, and highly strenuous constituent of society. This last bit—the highly strenuous part—would naturally have impelled the more powerful segments of society to elude such a role. Farming, when possible, would be relegated, not extolled.

If I did become a farmer, I knew there would be people who would view me as someone who was without a more enlightened choice, someone to whom the food-raising chores of society were relegated. I, rather, take a divergent view and keen comfort in the agreeable image of the gentleman farmer, which surfaces periodically in our agrarian legacy. The image of the gentleman farmer recalls most precisely for me the aristocratic agriculturalists of the nineteenth century, but the concept might be used even more broadly to describe the wonderfully curious and methodical landowners who have for centuries kept records of their crops and animal husbandry and cleverly experimented with their scant sciences to improve their yields. The gentleman farmer, in my mind, is a character from a sort of secular myth —one in which elegant sciences fit comfortably alongside commonplace chores.

When I reflect on the way the complex dimensions of agricultural mythologies have sustained their lessons by word of mouth or monastery, mingled and expressed (or not) through successive centuries, I'm reminded of the way human genes are passed on, mingled and expressed (or not) through generations of families. This parallel, like a barge, carries me over the river from the propositions of parable to the propositions of biology, and I wonder what Darwinian logic would have to impart with respect to the genesis and evolution of the farmer.

In evolutionary theory, food evolved simultaneously with every tapeworm and brontosaurus. In fact, the same worm and dinosaur *became* someone else's food when their days or hours of eating were over. All evolutionary organisms spent their limited time and energies rummaging the earth's terrestrial and aquatic regions for food. Even plant life forages the air and soil for desirable gasses and nutrients as they fumble by. All the time.

For the early dedicated herbivores there was a gamut of plant life to satisfy appetites, from the tiniest algae to large, leafy shrubs. Sauropods, believed to have been the largest of the herbivorous dinosaurs (the small-headed, long-necked, round-bodied, copacetic chewers of greens, invariably portrayed in the movies as friendly types), were equipped with a sorely lacking dental set for eating the upwards of three hundred pounds of greens they are supposed to have needed each day.

For the carnivores, the basic rules of the hunt applied. Larger animals ate smaller animals. Quicker animals ate slower animals. Smarter animals ate dumber animals, and this is where many optimists think man got his leg up on the game. Today, of course, there is some sensible reluctance toward accepting the hypothesis that man is more advanced than other creatures. There is also a scaling aversion to his continued habit of eating the "dumber" others.

Eating, and hoping to do so again soon, made up the daily life of the earth's primordial creatures. Food meant survival, and survival favored the most fit of species and specimens. But food was not always easy to come by. Weather, competitors, natural scarcities, and spoilage were some of the impediments to a regular meal. This kept most animals, human and otherwise, on the move, seeking out an achievable prey or familiar plants. Hunting was a high-risk occupation no matter where you stood on the food chain, and gathering was no picnic either. When man learned how to farm, he took the revolutionary step of subduing a tremendous entropy in his existence. By cultivating crops, he tamed the haphazard nature of his food supply. He could settle down, shed the nomadic life. By the same token, he could move—take his seeds and expertise to better soils or more clement weathers. It was in this way that agriculture allowed civilizations to take root and to spread.

Whether divinely bestowed or intellectually ferreted out, agriculture has always meant the subjugation of the soil and select species for the creation of foodstuff for mankind. People who believed their god(s) was (were) responsible for this prayed gratefully through the centuries for a continued bounty. They offered to their heavens a share of the harvest—some organs from the ox, a fetus from the llama, or a bowl of fruit—to say thank you, and please keep up the good work. Other peoples have no doubt cursed those same heavens for withholding rain or sending locusts when farming already seemed arduous and profane enough. Whatever the era or locale, it is all the same agriculture, the same exploitation, cultivation, and deployment of the local natural resources toward the ongoing and increasing production of food. Human beings do it. Ants do it, too.

2

Agriculture versus Food

A bumper sticker that came out sometime in the 1960s read: IF YOU EAT FOOD, YOU'RE INVOLVED WITH AGRICULTURE. The objective was to raise the consciousness of Americans about the safety and quality of our food supplies. We had, it was suggested, become too complacent.

As I stride toward becoming a farmer myself, I think about this phrase in reverse: In essence, if you're involved with agriculture, you're involved with food. It may seem obvious, but many agricultural industries have until recently been quite removed from the food issue. They have concerned themselves with a specialized form of sorghum for processing, tomatoes for ketchup, or piglets without stress. When I reflect on the farmers I have known or known of—whether they have raised wheat or beef cattle—I would have to argue that they are not particularly sensitive diners themselves, even though they grow the raw materials.

"I don't understand these farmers I deal with," said a grain buyer and trader I met. "Here they are in North Dakota, say, heartland of America, finest producers of wheat in the world—and what do they eat out there? Junk! Wonder Bread. Canned vegetables. Canned fruit. Canned spaghetti. I say to them, 'Do you know that New Yorkers pay a fortune to eat itsy-bitsy whole grain buns with thick crusts made from *your* wheat, while you eat nothing but pasty white Fluffernutter loaves of puffed flour?' "

When I was working on a cattle ranch in Wyoming during time off from college, I came across the same (dis)respect for diet; steak sauce, Tang, imitation maple syrup, and canned peas and carrots were the staples that sat out on our cookhouse counter. Jelly on white bread was a special favorite among the hands.

The fact is, farmers don't generally go into farming because of their acute dietary discrimination. After harvesting five hundred acres of durum wheat, they don't go to the supermarket to compare quality among various brands of dry noodles. And when I envision establishing a farm, I'm not fantasizing about improving the culinary repertoire of my community—I'm thinking mainly about farming, about sourcing feeds and seeds, about sunny days and soft rains, about wool and meat and onions and so on. Still, I'm aware that if I try to sell lousy produce each year, then I'll lose my customers, lose my business. Basically, whatever I raise I would like to raise the best. So there is a voice inside me steering me toward the tenderest rack of lamb and the sweetest parsnips (the parsnips are for my father; I don't know another person who raves about them). I suspect that it is usually the smaller farm, such as the one I imagine having, that is inclined to cater to consumers' taste buds and strive for overall excellence, because larger, industrial-scale farms have to play the average. The huge commercial farms are founded on principles of bulk, volume, and the processing equipment of their wholesale buyers. They cannot pamper and primp their stock or spinach as might a small boutique farm or even a well-managed medium-size farm—the proverbial family farm. This may be one reason why we Americans have so embraced the idea of our small and family farms: we feel they respond to us, care about our food wants.

In 1988, I watched Representative Richard Gephardt, a Democratic Congressman from Missouri, the Show-Me State, show Americans how fine indeed was the country's sentimental attachment to its "family farmer." He ran for the office of president that year as a strong proponent of the political effort to "save the family farm." The legislation supporting this effort was intended to allocate the bulk of USDA crop subsidies and other like program payments to midsize farms—family farms, which have been gradually squeezed out of business by industrial-size farms and their inherent economies of scale. Family farms are a part of the American heritage, the Gephardt people told us.

But we showed Richard Gephardt that, even though we cared about the family farm idea, we didn't care enough. We enjoyed the low food prices that derived from the relatively low costs enjoyed by the very large-scale farms in this country. And so while we were tugged at by the thought of losing more family farms, we indicated to Mr. Gephardt, through an overall lack of support of his candidacy, that we wished to continue being rather pragmatic about our food production.

In fact, Americans are not pragmatic about our food production at all; we are extraordinarily conflicted about it. The very term *food production* puts a lot of people ill at ease. Most Americans, it would seem, prefer to see food production as two separate and discrete concepts: food and agriculture. Food, people like to know about, talk about, fuss with, fret over, indulge in, do without, and find cheap and without bruises. Agriculture, to the ninety-eight or so percent of Americans who are not farmers, is a discomfiting subject.

People who like to talk about food often don't like to think about agriculture. "Mention agriculture to my editor," said a woman who writes about food for *The New York Times,* "and he begins to hyperventilate." And when food-prepossessed people do turn their glances toward the silo, they frequently assume quite horrified and self-righteous poses vis-à-vis today's accepted practices for raising crops and livestock.

"I will not touch white veal anymore!"

"I heard about chickens! We're only eating fish now."

"Do you know what happens to bananas en route?"

It's difficult to blame them. Farmers have lost touch with consumers in a world where the raising of wheat and cattle is so far removed from the selling of the bread loaf and the steak. And consumers have wallowed collusively in their ignorance about the country's food production systems. It came as something of a surprise in the 1970s when we heard inklings that white veal was the result of overtly inhumane livestock husbandry practices. We were introduced to photographs of calves that mournfully lived out their mere six months in dark crates. We learned that all of those man-made crop-enriching and crop-protecting nutrients were washing into rivers and decimating marine life. And the Europeans broke into our passive daze by firmly declaring that, whether or not steroid growth promotants used in livestock operations deleteriously affected the meat yielded in those operations—*whether or not*—they didn't want that meat anymore.

Clearly, American consumers' long-standing disregard of our agriculture has borne its unsavory results (the Chickens-Come-Home-To-Roost Department). The cheap, bountiful foodstuffs that our presidential candidates have loved to stump about finally came out of the closet and suddenly our images of amber waves of grain were thrust aside. Midwestern topsoil, it seemed, was washing into rivers at a rate of hundreds of tons a day, the barren deserts of Southern California had metamorphosed into a prolific kitchen garden for the country, and the farm-chemicals egg had hatched into a broad-winged, tenaciously clawed bird.

So consumers balked—a little. We launched one counter-skirmish against the American farmer by rekindling our flirtation with the organic food industry. It came at the end of the 1980s, spurred on, I think, by our society's growing affluence and its presiding obsession with intake. But, interestingly, the rejuvenated alliance with organics was a brief one, swiftly engulfed in a deluge of mass-market foods, newly advertised as healthy and environmentally-friendly. The Campbell's soup kids slimmed down, and the plump Pillsbury Doughboy seemed temporarily whisked away to the Gulag. Green and beige began to appear on food labels everywhere, and this packaging gimmick, which pretended to some kind of certification from the Sierra Club, seemed to saturate even nonorganic food shelves. Sales of genuine organics crested after a brief missile launch into vogue.

American consumers! We're impossible. We want cheap food, unblemished food, organic food, and noncaloric dessert food. On Sunday afternoons, we want the family farm and the roadside vegetable stand manned by nice folk who do it all for pleasure. And on Monday mornings we sweep imperiously down our supermarket aisles, squarely eschewing nature's irregularities when it comes to the size and shape of our lettuce heads. We're known to rage upon discovering a seed in a navel orange. Hasn't somebody solved that problem yet? we snarl, for we are still feeling irritable about the milk carton's mere two-week shelf life and the way our bagged carrots, like our tomatoes, look the proper color and shape but taste routinely like shirt cardboards. Americans prefer to imagine that our farmers, like our doctors, work in an arena of perfect, mathematical science, an arena where outcomes are predictable and results consistent. But in fact farmers, just like doctors, operate on live genetic material and confront the vagaries of a complex, respiring code. Sometimes there will still be seeds in a navel orange, but they're working on it.

·

I saw the conflict between food and farming firsthand one year when I worked on a small vegetable farm in New England. It was composed of a hundred acres, mostly scenic hilltop, now locked in by country clubs, capacious estates, and horse-riding rings. The land was farmed by a seventy-year-old man and his son, Richie. And Richie was agitated and angry with his lot.

"Name a golf course in this county," he would growl to me.

"We used to farm it." It was Richie who eventually repainted the sign at the farm's front gate to read, LUCCO'S FARM: THIS IS *NOT* AN ORGANIC FARM.

"These New Yorkers," he would complain to me, "come up on the weekend and roll down our field road, real slow, real careful, in their fancy German cars. They wanna pick strawberries. They wanna pick out their own head of lettuce. They bring the kids. They bring the dog. They trample around the berries for a few minutes and then they ask about discounts. I say to them, 'I don't give discounts.' They tell me about their grandmother's senior citizen card—she's been sitting in the back seat of the car this whole time with the air conditioning turned up. And then they ask me why don't I go organic. 'You're probably right,' I say to them. 'Now I got work to do.' Me, without a fancy car, with two kids, just trying to make ends meet, you know? I wanna say, 'The only thing to put me outa business faster than wimpy scabby bruised-up organic produce is people like you.' "

Richie ran one of the last pick-your-own diversified vegetable farms in the region. He operated this way because he figured he came out ahead through lower labor costs, but most of his farmer friends had stopped letting people onto their farms at all.

"John, Johnny B., Frank, and Mario," Richie used to grumble, "they all go wholesale only now. They think I'm crazy to let people on the farm. One old lady trips between the rows and I'm a goner, they say. But you know, I like that folks like to come here. They think I'm happier than them for doing this, and maybe I am. I dunno. Maybe I'm just crazy. But don't forget, I grow the biggest damn beets in New England."

People did indeed like driving down the pitted dirt road to Richie's corrugated iron lean-to shed. They would park under an enormous old maple tree that was industriously toppling the shed with its slow and steady root growth. They did indeed enjoy trampling Richie's strawberry plants in search of the one perfect red orb. And most of all they loved to tell us—the farm hands—how great it felt to be "in touch with actual food." They would stand at the scales for ten or fifteen minutes, eating their berries before we weighed them and chatting with us about their feelings of disenfranchisement from food nowadays.

"This is wonderful," they would say. "You may not realize it, young lady, but you are very very fortunate to be working here."

"I'm going to bring my children back tomorrow," said one woman. "I want to show them what real food is. They honestly think supermarkets make food."

I could only smile. I understood what they were feeling. Visitors to the farm were so heartened to find produce without cellophane wrapping that they immediately ascribed to our vegetables a hoard of other delightful attributes—a healthier tinge, better flavor, nicer leaves. Spinach from the supermarket, they would grimace to me confidentially, well it just didn't taste like much of anything.

"Be sure to wash or rinse everything," I would say to the people who came by. Even though I rank among the worst offenders of this policy, I encourage others to believe in it. Richie's farm chemicals notwithstanding, the world is full of bacteria, and the schmoozing bugs and deer and rabbits that customarily gambol through farm fields are notorious carriers of filth and disease. A few omissions to the washing rule are not harmful, and there is no need to go overboard by boiling every tomato and pear you buy, but from my own background in farming I have learned to wash rigorously after leaving the barn or fields—wash both myself and Richie's green peppers.

As for Richie's customers, I agreed with them about the satisfaction of seeing vegetables in the soil. Children were invariably thrilled to find plump crescents of pea pods dangling under the thick shade of green vine and tendrils. The youngest, especially, seemed to know next to nothing about the origins of their food. Most mothers I chatted with spoke resolutely about their intentions to teach their kids how chocolate milk is produced or french fries raised, although they usually had a clause about meat.

"No," they would say, fidgety. "I don't think Stevie has to learn where his hamburger patties come from yet."

To be fair, I never rolled my eyes until after I (or they) had walked away. Furthermore, it wasn't that I expected infants to understand the horror of animal slaughter, but that, of the few terms in the English language that I abhor, *patty* is one—*hamburger patty* is another. As for knowing where your meat comes from, that's a delicate theme, and I have nothing against leaving children in the dark for years.

When I was a child, there was always a butcher stationed in the meat section of our local A&P. Aproned and stout, he was usually to be found out front by the beef case, rearranging heavy packs of hamburger and steaks. In those days beef, if it was prized, was so fatty and marbled that it tended to look a pale pink, not purple or red. Our butcher loved to fuss with the steaks until he found one he felt you truly deserved—the premium cuts, laced with yellowish veins of fat that certified the animal had been richly corn-fed. And when he was through reshuffling these packs of manna, he went back behind a big plate-glass window to his cutting room, where he would set to carving hunks of this prime beef off a massive hindquarter or forequarter. I could see the shiny metal hooks that ran on a rail along the ceiling of the bright white room, more than one weighted down by a carcass quarter in reserve; and I could see blood. I used to bend way over at the waist and twist my neck up to look at the hindquarters upside-down. Since they were hung from their hocks on the rails, I could from this angle try to imagine the full reconstruction of a real cow from these massive, detached contours of legs-plus of bone, steak, and fat. No sir, it certainly didn't look like any cow I'd ever seen. And the Northampton A&P was certainly no showcase for bloodied heads, hooves, and testicles also triumphantly displayed for sale, letting you know this was once indeed the cow you'd known. I had seen that as a child in France, where the butchers wore bloodied aprons with pride. The French were savages. They ate snails, even. *Our* cows were happy.

So I dangled my head happily upside-down by the meat case while the white-frocked butcher trimmed a roast for seven. Then, just before I went down from vertigo: "Come on now, grocery stores aren't playgrounds." That would be my mother. Off we would go to the next aisle of adventure.

The experience of today's butcher departments has become one of unsullied stainless steel meat cases and white plastic cutting boards (because wood is now considered by the USDA to be too difficult to clean and sterilize). No carcasses are hanging behind the counter, and many bright red steaks are now purple under the vacuum packing, which took place somewhere in Iowa. Moreover, what has happened in the meat case has happened throughout the whole supermarket. When I do the food shopping these days, I'm hardly put in mind of any farmer behind the works. Instead, I'm left to sort through quadruple shelves of uniform breads, identical cookies, and flawless blocks of processed cheese; even some "fresh foods" look like they were born to plastic wrapping.

"I must be from a different epoch," sighed my father one day as we shopped together for dinner ingredients. "This all looks so artificial to me." He was passing a pristine pyramid of shiny Red Delicious apples that seemed jewellike under the tinted lights of the fruit bins. We pushed our cart over to the meat case, where a bright red sign pointed to Perdue's Perfect Chickens.

"Perfection has its alienating side," he said. "A kind of sterility that belongs not to sanitation, but to rebuffing the observer." He advanced toward the lamb section.

"People seem to want their foods that uniform today," I said. "Their cutlets matching, their eggs all the same size, their chicken marigold-yellow. I think a farmer would shoot himself if he heard you complain that his produce looked too perfect."

"You know, I was raised in an era when we were moving as

far away as possible from dirt," my father went on. "In the thirties, people were still very concerned about contamination and food spoilage. There was always a lot of conversation and apprehension about spoilage, and a sharing of tips on how to prevent it. Of course, we didn't have Frigidaires and such when I was a child. It was ice boxes then.

"Nowadays, you don't hear the talk about spoiled food. Well, you've got a salmonella scare for undercooked poultry, I guess. And undercooked fish pose a worry, too, but trichinosis in pork is virtually eliminated, and the nature is completely cooked out of milk these days, and they've learned to line cans so that you can let food sit in them forever. That's a great improvement in terms of sanitation and convenience."

It was interesting to hear my father's ambivalent and, to me, relatively veteran perspective on today's food. I agreed with him about the remarkable degree of safety we enjoy in today's food supply compared with that of several decades ago; but I also agreed that food has a way of looking too perfect these days, and occasionally a bit waxy or plasticky. I sometimes miss that sense of the fragility of fresh food—the fragility that still befalls other plants, like the painted daisies and lupines in my husband's perennial bed.

When my husband and I went on vacation last year, we forgot a bunch of grapes and half a head of iceberg lettuce in the refrigerator for two weeks. Upon our return, I had some trepidation about digging them out—dreading whatever color they might have turned, whatever exotic mold they would be cultivating.

"This is men's work," I said to my husband, and pointed at the refrigerator door.

But they were fine. The grapes were just sitting there, plumpish, juicy, the lettuce still crispy when I bowled it into the garbage pail. That was not a particularly comforting feeling. It was the kind of incident that tempts you to perform laboratory tests. Knowing that fresh lettuce leaves gathered from my husband's garden would wilt in a matter of hours, I was bewildered by these stout and impervious heads that I could find daily in the supermarket. Everyone knew they had already traveled over 2,794 miles (Los Angeles to New York City) cross-country to get here. I felt like I had spun 180 degrees, back to wanting a little silt to wash off my spinach leaves.

If you ask a farmer—and farmers generally visualize food and agriculture as more closely associated than does the general public—he might tell you there was definitely dirt on those spinach leaves when they left his field. After that point, he doesn't know who does what to them. Farmers often sell to distributors, packers, or processing companies that wash, trim, butcher, package, chill, gas, box and otherwise transform raw agricultural produce into neat, inviting bundles of shelf-stable (or pyramid-building) supermarket food. There is a sizable distance between sandy spinach leaves and the washed, chopped, frozen spinach that arrives in 1¼-by-4-by-5¼-inch boxes in the freezer case—and frozen vegetables probably represent the simplest end of the processing sequence. You're really a far cry from the farmer when you eat those frozen pot pies or canned tamales. You're at the threshold of somebody's laboratory kitchen. Most of today's supermarket foods spend some amount of time in this type of kitchen after they leave the farm.

If you think about it, it's rarely the farmer making pitches to the food shopper anymore. He has conferred that job, that territory, upon those zealous food processing companies that thirst overtly for your dollars all over the nation's billboards and televisions. It is the food companies that create and embellish the food we buy, that roll with the punches of our capricious tastes and fads, that interpret our encoded cash register tapes and reformulate their packages and prices accordingly. It is the food companies that take our trending temperatures and turn around and tell the farmer to raise bigger-framed cattle, leaner hogs, redder peppers, larger grapefruits, and higher-protein wheat. If you're discontented with your food options these days, you have to bring your complaints to the General Foods, the Nabiscos, and the ConAgras—not to the farmer.

Having directed you thus, I confess you may or may not find a willing ear at the other end of the line. Some food companies view the common food shopper and his or her fickle preferences more as an aggravation than as their bread and butter. After all, these food companies had only just perfected their updated Ray Bradbury–style "retort" bags that enabled them to sell *en plein air* shelf-stable, indestructible, microwaveable dinners—a veritable "taking the hill" of the pressed-for-time 1980s—when the public mood whimsically swayed back toward fresh products and recyclable containers. This kind of shift in tastes makes a food company feel, if only temporarily, bamboozled by its Average Food Shopper—"she," as they like to say—who suddenly abandons the crusade for convenience for the morality-rich priorities of the combined food-safety and environmentalist movements. "She" is nowadays more interested in foods with less packaging, fewer additives and preservatives, less salt, less fat, and less sugar, than in those excessively predictable and neatly trayed (and under 200 calories, what with those new vegetable gums) freezer entrées.

Not an easy customer. I suppose that's why there are already some ten different versions of the common Coke. And I imagine I, too, may bump into this mercurial consumer problem one day when I become a farmer. The store manager to whom I sell my lettuces may tell me to bring only the red-leaf variety from now on; he doesn't want my green-leaf heads because his customers don't seem to go for them.

"What's the matter with your customers?" I might wail. And there I would be, driving home that night to ten acres of just-maturing green Romaine leaves. In these scenarios, the store manager acts as a kind of interpreter between the farmer and the consumer. Nowadays, this is the most basic, direct form of the dialogue between farmer and food shopper, unless the farmer can operate his own farm stand—essentially, unless the farmer can be his own retailer.

The gulf between original producer and ultimate consumer is only widening as we Americans eat more and more processed foods. When we choose breakfast cereals or prepared dinners as opposed to, say, my hypothetical red-leaf lettuces, we're thrusting an additional layer of negotiation between ourselves and the farmer. Now it is not just the retailer, but the modern food processor, positioned between the supermarket shelf and the farm furrow, who relays messages back and forth. Understanding this may help to throw light on why food costs what it does, and how the farmer's role in our final food products has so diminished over time.

Few of us relish the notion of processed foods, but we Americans continue to consume them at ever-increasing rates. To many minds, processing connotes food-manhandling, the infusion of dyes and various questionable chemicals, the pulverization and reformulation of foods in such a way as to make them appear unpulverized and unreformulated, and of course, shelf-stable. But food processing actually encompasses a broad range of activities that begin with the simple harvesting of the broccoli or the plucking of the chicken.

"I'm no snob about processed foods," said a friend. "Give me Stouffer's frozen chicken à la king any day. At least I know Stouffer's washed, homogenized, and completely sterilized the stuff. Is it true what they're saying about chickens?"

Almost all raw agricultural products are processed to some extent before we consume them as food. Snapping the tips off green beans is processing them. Boiling oats is a type of processing. My father's barber explained recently that she was preparing sweet and sour pirogi for her husband's parents. Now *that's* food processing—if it isn't food poisoning.

Processing is, essentially, preparing food for eating. A more advanced level of food processing is carried on by the leagues of food technologists and food scientists, a relatively new breed of food engineers who explore even the molecular composition of foods. They talk without emotion about flavor, texture, and content. They design foods from natural and arguably unnatural ingredients. They work in laboratories, wear white coats, and tinker with bottles of clear esters and very unkitchenlike appliances. Apples, in their hands, turn into apple fillings. Pieces of a livestock carcass that we don't even like to think about are transformed on their counters into meaty pot pies, hot dogs, and frozen enchiladas.

The obligations food technologists have taken on for themselves have snowballed in recent years. Food has its intractable properties. Fiddle with this trait, you may have to fiddle with that one. One food technology invariably leads to another. In this way, food science has evolved into an enormous enterprise over the last decade. The output of the industry's small and large companies alike now comprises a virtual Sears and Roebuck catalogue of improved-food or food-improving characteristics.

The field of food technology is only growing. Computer analyses continue to refine our understanding of what exactly food is—stirring details for a race of people that believes now more than ever that we are what we eat. What's wrong with this picture? Well, it would appear that the average commercial farmer is going to raise his crops and livestock to suit the needs of the food processors—needs corresponding to milling machinery gauges, slaughterhouse equipment, seasonal production fluctuations, etc. So remember, if you think he isn't listening to you and your preferences, it's because you aren't his buyer anymore.

•

One of the greatest pleasures in farming, I think, is experiencing the intimate connection to food—all food, even if you personally are cultivating ten straight acres of rutabagas. Agriculture used to be closer to food—literally (geographically) as well as figuratively, and for all people. It was once, and commonly so, the province of the individual family, whose food supply was a function of its members' industriousness. In colonial times, there might have been a meadow by the home, with its small stock pasture and its fenced-in vegetable garden. You sold or traded your radishes and hams to people you knew, a system which, in small communities particularly, provided sufficient incentive for the farmer to keep his quality up and his prices equitable. The tending and farming evolved toward small-scale efficiencies and specialties—the neighbor who butchered, the fellow who owned the milking cows.

Agriculture was gradually surrendered, or bequeathed, to the concise province of fewer farmers. It's outside of our city now. It's often outside of our country. This is the geographical separation. There has similarly been a figurative separation growing between foods as we know them in the market and their simple raw agricultural counterparts in the field. Grains, meats, fruits and so on, in their elemental forms, have become more rare on the common American plate. Fewer bowls of groats, more Wonder Bread. Fewer roasts, more trays of frozen beef Stroganoff. Fewer bananas, more cans of diced fruit cocktail. This persistent polarization of raw commodity and finished food product has no doubt helped to occlude the image of the farmer, and therefore a farm consciousness, from the consumer. It continues to do so, in fact, and the gaps between farmer and consumer likewise continue to be bridged by none other than that multitalented food processor.

The processing of farm products, as I mentioned earlier, is what differentiates raw agricultural yields from food on the plate. The separation has become so material that the U.S. government's traditional formulation of a combined food and agriculture policy has in many ways become obsolete. An easy way to comprehend the extent of this separation is by analyzing the cost of an agricultural product within the price of the final food item—for instance, the cost of the wheat used to make a one-pound loaf of bread or, put another way, the price paid to the farmer for his wheat used in that one-pound loaf. The Department of Agriculture, a bastion of numerical harvests itself, calculates what it calls the "farm value share" of a consumer's dollar. This is the portion of the dollar you spend on food which goes to the farmer. Naturally, the more highly refined or processed the food, the smaller the percentage of its price will be pocketed by the farmer. For example, USDA estimates that if you spend one dollar on a loaf of white bread, only about eight cents of that goes to the farmer for his wheat. Whereas, if in a burst of baking fever you buy one dollar's worth of wheat flour yourself, the farmer's share of your dollar will be approximately thirty-two cents. Less processing means a larger percentage of the ultimate price will go to the original farmer. If you spend one dollar on a box of eggs, the farmer will receive about two-thirds of that. Eggs don't require painstaking processing. Primarily, they need washing, sorting, and boxing. Whereas, if you buy one dollar's worth of corn flakes, the corn farmer gets six cents.

Naturally, if I were to become a corn farmer, I would only concern myself with how much I received per bushel. That's where my cost-benefit analysis would take place. I would compare the expense of land, fertilizers, seed, and so on, to the price I was receiving for my yields. A farmer can't be haunted by the potential profits yielded down the processing road by Kellogg's popping and flaking machinery in Kalamazoo, Michigan. He cannot collate his field costs with the price of a highly formulated, value-added food item.

There are definitely ways, however, by which a small farmer can capture a larger share of the consumer's food dollar. There are ways of adding value to my farm yields without necessarily expanding into the elaborate and expensive strata of food processing. First, I would say to myself, don't plant corn if you want to get rich. That just isn't the kind of crop for a small farmer to stake his pension on, much less his hopes for a bigger car. Corn is a crop that makes money in volume: "It's in the margins," one farmer said to me. And there are a few other crops that fall into that category—the world's staple grain crops, for example, or sugar. Instead, to increase the value of my farmland, I would head toward the more exotic items. If I intended to establish an orchard, I might try planting apple varieties that seemed to command a premium in the marketplace—Fujis, Jonagolds, Empires, or even more unfamiliar types. Some farmers I know raise curious herbs, yellow raspberries, striped peanuts, goats for milking, ducks for egg-laying, or sheep with unusual wool in order to get better prices for their goods.

The wife of a turkey farmer in Massachusetts started baking fresh turkey pot pies from their home, and within a year the demand for her pies induced her to start her own business, a complement to her husband's fresh turkey trade. I thought this was an interesting example of basic agricultural products and value-added food products being marketed side-by-side. They were earning close to a hundred percent of the farm share value for each retail turkey, and probably fifty or so percent of the farm share value on their pot pies. Their little farm operation seemed like a good argument for selling directly to the public.

"I can just see you handling the customers now," my husband said to me one day as we considered the option of a farm stand. "One funny look at your tomatoes and you'll tear them to pieces."

"Well," I said. "Why should they look funny at my tomatoes? Anyway, I'm not going to sell tomatoes. Everybody sells tomatoes."

"Eggs, then," he argued. My husband was the virtuoso on his high school debating team. "If they only want half a box, if they break one by mistake and want you to replace it, are you going to be civil?"

"Civil?" I asked.

"You're not going to bellow if they don't like our rosemary-fed lamb?" he pursued.

"I'm in the farming business," I protested, "not the food business. No farm stand. No customers."

He thought a minute.

"I know what we can call your farm," he said. "Farm from the Madding Crowd."

You could see the problem.

3

The Death Scream of the Tomato

It's a habit of mine to listen to National Public Radio's program "All Things Considered" as I snap green beans, stir onions, or devein shrimp for the evening meal. Unfortunately, I once missed a segment on livestock production and only learned of it—and its graphic details—days later, when the news commentators read a number of listeners' letters responding to the report. The tone of the letters was in concert:

"Disgusting!"

"Outrageous!"

"I shall never eat pork again."

"The pig-killing was gratuitously conveyed!"

"I cannot ever again feel safe listening to your radio program when my children are in the room."

Makes you want to be a farmer, doesn't it?

No longer do you hear the public thanking farmers for good-quality, cheap pork chops and bacon. Agriculture now appears to curry the kind of media favor that countries like Bolivia enjoy—a little news now and again, and then not very positive. We hear that our cattle are destroying acres of rare and indigenous vegetation. Our cropping methods are poisoning aquifers. Our broiler operations share a borderline with inhumanity. Indeed, American agriculture could benefit from a bright and maverick new leader to overhaul its obese, indolent, and entrenched systems (I'm referring congenially to the USDA), and to improve public perceptions, if only temporarily.

I particularly wish I had caught the segment on the radio, because the slaughter of animals for meat in this world is one of the most sticky, objectionable topics for many people to contemplate. Moreover, if you are going to raise livestock on your farm, and unless you are planning to study natural senescence in sheep, you have to confront slaughter head on. Slaughter is the bridge between animal and meat.

The British and Australians call a slaughterhouse an "abattoir," and this is indeed a relieving, euphemistic substitution of terms for those who have no knowledge of French. In the States you hear about "packing plants" and "meat packers." It is still "the slaughterhouse." Livestock are "sent to slaughter." There they spend time on the "kill floor." All in all, it is not a nice language, and in off-farm company the terms connote a pretty savage bloodbath.

What I find so disconcerting about modern slaughterhouses is not that live animals go in and packages of steak come out, but that thousands of animals go in every day and tons of meat, tallow, and offal in various wholesale configurations come out. I really believe the numbers make it bad. The numbers. The numbers of us that have resulted in the numbers of them— animals for burgers. We are so many, and so wealthy and so hungry. We expect meat on a daily basis, more than once a day. We like it cheap. We want it prepackaged and marinated if possible. Because we are so many, we create a demand that only big and efficient slaughterhouses can feed. And they do feed that demand. They kill and skin and disembowel and butcher tens of thousands of animals each day, and that very act of magnitude, that amplification, necessarily turns slaughterhouses into places not a little gruesome.

In packing plants you will find the commonness of death

spattered all over the floors and walls, the thick and sickening smell of it, the heavy mass of spiritless flesh and wastes. Gone is the reverence man at one time felt for his stock. Gone is ritual. Gone is myth. Present are the faces of America's rural backwaters, the inbred, the poor, the transient, the illegal worker, the idiot. These are the people who kill and gut by the hour, removing the rest of us just that much farther from a basic visitation with life—and death.

The more vehement vegetarians and animal rightists would have you believe that abattoirs are second only to the World War II concentration camps in terms of genocidal brutality. If you have the opportunity to visit a slaughter plant, you will decidedly be glutted by a landscape of deep rivers of sticky hot blood, spasmodic hides and organs, butchering and the concomitant odors of death. I don't recommend it, but then, I think there is a lot in life worth missing.

·

I was employed in the beef business when some close friends had their first baby, a boy. I went to visit with them one afternoon, and we all settled among the toy animals that littered the living room floor. We were talking about my work with cattle when Mark, the father, said, "Well, you know, we don't eat that much meat anymore." He said this into his cup of coffee.

The remark, I suppose, was meant to soften some larger unspoken indictment of beef companies. People who have remarked to me, "We don't eat meat," often look at me with eyes that say "You bump off guileless cows." I thought about Mark's statement. He seemed eminently relieved to have made the avowal.

"Is this a new decision?" I asked. There was a contemplative pause.

"Well," he said, "when you have a baby, it's as though you're suddenly vulnerable to all the hurt around you in this world. I know it sounds crazy, but even hurting cows—killing them and cutting them up and eating them . . . When you have a baby, you can't think about eating another animal's meat. Do you see what I mean?"

I hadn't had any children then, so I was certainly being set up to say "No," or "Maybe I'll understand when I have a baby, too." In general, I take no issue with vegetarianism, but I noticed my feathers were slightly ruffled by Mark's explanation. Many vegetarians take enormous pride in moralizing their choice, in saving savannahs worldwide, in eating a diet that is incontrovertibly closer to the gods. But here was a new angle: becoming a parent makes you an infinitely more sensitive human being, to whom red meat suddenly chills you as would violence against your own infant.

"That's interesting," I said.

Defending the slaughter of animals is not a position in which I like to find myself. I have had the chance to tour many slaughter facilities, and none is likable and I harbor an innate distrust of the employees. It is mechanized, large-scale butchering, an assembly line of disassembling, a factory whose waste is still-warm plasma and clumps of feathers. It is a form of food processing that some people argue is no different from the ripping of a plant from the soil, though I would disagree.

If you are going to raise livestock, you have to give this phase of the farming a good, hard look. My own comfort with or rationale for the modern abattoir comes from appreciating the setting of slaughter on a broad scale—how all animals treat one another in their particular "wilds." You might also find some small consolation in the fact that the killing of animals for meat has gone on for years, millennia even. Civilization has not climbed up some lonely pantophagous mountain to arrive breathless, in this brilliant twentieth century, at the villainous pinnacle of eating other earthbound animals. It's been going on, interspecies, for some time.

You might have a look at George Stubbs's eighteenth-century paintings and lithographs on the theme of the horse and the lion in the wilderness. The *White Horse Frightened by a Lion* series—even its name alone—is enough to underscore my point. The *Horse Attacked by a Lion* will drive that point home. And the *Horse Devoured by a Lion,* metaphorically or literally speaking, carries the full flavor of animal-to-animal relations. These paintings are startling to see, full of action and the idealized allegories of the animal kingdom that were in Stubbs' time the vogue. But the story is not far from an accepted truth. Animals are not what we would term chivalrous with one another in the wild. Cattle, when they have been left to fend for themselves in the wilderness, have not historically met a comfortable demise. A domestic chicken of today wouldn't survive a Boy Scout camp-out. (Its cousin, however, the wild turkey, might still give you a sense of the chicken's physically deft ancestors and their ability to survive the night alfresco.) Feral pigs are thin and fierce and perish not infrequently during their ravenous, unprovoked charges against animals much larger than themselves. Even among species beyond those we traditionally think of as livestock, there is rarely anything like "ripe old age" in the wild. Maybe that's an element in mankind's (and here I leave myself out) fixation with the Loch Ness monster. If we don't harpoon the thing, it might actually testify to its natural lifespan. Even we don't do that anymore; we outlive ours.

"My mother lives in Hilton Head and had an alligator living in the pond behind her house," said a friend of ours. "I guess the rule is that when they grow to be twelve feet, they're moved."

"Moved where?" I asked. Not here, I hoped.

"I'm not sure," she said, wrinkling her nose. "But they decided to move my mother's. They lured it out of the pond with a trail of—you won't believe this—marshmallows. A trail of tiny, fluffy white marshmallows. And sure enough, they got him.

"Actually," she added, "they finally had to shoot him because he didn't respond to about ten huge tranquilizer darts. And when they opened him up, they found a bunch of dog collars, horseshoes, and even some leather reins. It was horrible. My mother said the sheriff said these alligators drag their prey down into the water until it drowns and then they can eat it at their leisure. I said to my mother, 'Didn't you hear anything? You must have heard *something*. This alligator ate a horse right outside your bedroom window.' "

I mention this anecdote to reiterate that slaughter of livestock must be viewed in fair context. The modern abattoir can emerge as a relatively humane institution, I think, when compared to the full-scale carnage born out by one animal against another in their natural environs.

Still, the jitters of farm slaughter may not be entirely behind you. We have all grown up on grisly stories of chickens, freshly beheaded, running around the yard. Killing and butchering animals has some raw truths that take ingesting and it is also extremely strenuous—in case you were ever thinking of doing it yourself.

Assuming that slaughter isn't a task I plan to experience, raising livestock in an area remote from any public or private facility is a recipe for anguish and mayhem. I would have to hope there were individuals around who would do "that kind of thing" for me. There might be deer hunters, retired butchers, other farmers. There might even be services that haul off your animals and, a day or two later, return a nicely bagged, neatly cut-up oven-ready roast to your doorstep. Comforting. Just like the supermarket.

Some people feel, however, that one is not whole if one does not slaughter, clean, and process one's own livestock. For this sect, the USDA Cooperative Extension Service has bundles and bundles of brochures and booklets that teach the proper methodologies of slaughter. One of the publications they sent to me even highlighted the story of a young boy "dressing" (an industry word for killing, cleaning, and preparing) a mature chicken. It may be bolstering to other budding farmers to know that 4-H kids do this all the time. I found it rather intimidating.

If I were responsible for slaughtering my livestock now and

then for food, then either they or I would be senile before it happened. Guns and knives are not my forte. That's a project for the professionals at the local packing plant—if you can find them.

Twenty or thirty years ago, before cities and their suburbia consumed so much of America's rural acreage, the local packing plant was a fairly routine sight. It was often a small, unembroidered, white-washed cinderblock set back from the road. But local packing plants are hard to come by now. At the same time that developers were siting condominium clusters next to quaintly crumbling silos, the USDA started to crack down on the small slaughter operations. Upgraded sanitary and operational codes were imposed. Coolers were remodeled, pipes rerouted, walls repainted, workers retrained. Yet, in spite of all of these modernizing permutations, residents of the new condominium warrens still complained of animal sounds and smells, so many local slaughterhouses were promptly boarded up and padlocked. The ascendancy of big packing houses, such as Holly Farms or Iowa Beef Packers, with their nationwide distribution efficiency, was also a factor in the demise of the rural packing plant. These companies were just too successful at distributing cheap meat nationwide.

Wherever we establish our farm, I'll be able to locate the nearest slaughterhouse facilities by calling the State Department of Agriculture. They keep a list. I could also query my downtown butcher; sometimes these fellows custom-slaughter livestock on the side. And if we ended up in an area where deer, bear, or duck hunting is permitted, I might just ask for names from the waitress at that diner that opens at four a.m.

You might be thinking, "No thanks, I'll just stick with plant life and cropping. Harvesting a live kohlrabi is something I can do." Fair enough. Cutting roots and stems is easier to stomach than cutting jugular veins. And people generally grow less attached to individual plants over the growing season—they will more readily take scythe and tractor wheel in hand. I should add that the harvest was not always perceived in so benign a way. I've read some wonderful histories of the common tomato plant, which early botanists classified as a cousin of the deadly nightshade family. It was thought, centuries ago, that a tomato plant when pulled by its roots from the soil shrieked mercilessly in the throes of its death.

"Imagine if plants really screamed when they were harvested," said my husband. "You just couldn't live with the noise. Having a garden would be horrendous."

"In three hundred years," I said, "scientists will probably tell us that plants do scream on some heretofore inaudible frequency. What will the vegetarians say to that?"

I mused, "If it really were a high frequency, wouldn't dogs be able to hear it by now?"

"Dogs already perceive us as inhuman," my husband said.

·

"I'm not so adept at dealing with death," I said to my father one day. I was thinking about my mother, about a friend from college days now dying of AIDS, and also about my work in livestock agriculture.

"Hmmm," he said. "You're in good company. Not many people are."

"I hope I go quickly and painlessly myself," I said.

"That seems reasonable."

"Sometimes I think I would even like to die young," I added. "Miss some of the infirmities of old age. Is that cowardly?"

"Cowardly?" he considered. "I think not. Human, maybe."

Agriculture has shed new light for me on mortality. Farming's rhythm of birth and death distills the pattern of our human lives into the space of a year or two. It is an exemplar, I find, for the final meaninglessness of one's own existence—unless one acts tenaciously to make something of life either for oneself or for others. I have never felt that I had some predetermined purpose in being, other than what purpose I could construct for myself.

I am an organism, much like the others on the planet, preoccupied with mating and surviving and dying. I feel lucky not to have been a cow (although some people have told me that I already was a cow in a former life), but of course as a cow I would have been, and gratefully so, spared this cast of melancholy philosophical speculation. Listening to the news lately, I also feel fortunate not to have been born in Croatia, or Somalia, or Japan. I have enjoyed the creature comforts of being a Caucasian in America, and through the providence of that path I have been educated sufficiently to humble myself entirely.

Dust to dust. Fallow to harvest. Breeding, calving, and slaughtering. Plough under the winter rye in spring so that it may decompose and nourish the soil. I am: formed through the magnetism of molecules, the thirst of atoms for harmony, the horse-trading jumble of genetic codes, the blind pluck of the vigorous sperm. Farming brings the cycles of life home to me. Maybe that's what ultimately seems so satisfying. A small farm is not far removed from the basics of existence—the need to eat, breed and die.

"Perhaps it's because I am afraid of dying that I want a farm," I said to my father.

I was sitting in the grass while he worked in his garden—his "plantation" we affectionately called it—in Northampton. He was busy stringing twine from corner to corner, from high to low, side to side, in an eventually dense arrangement that articulated something like universal entropy. When he ran out of twine he gathered some fallen branches and poked them through the network, just so, here and there, in a pretty menacing array. This was in fact an annual ritual for him, like the autumn broadcasting of vast quantities of lime. Each spring he would create this absorbing maze—his Maginot Line, he would write in his letters—the front-line shield to protect his "crops" against the neighborhood cats.

"Well," he said, straightening his back for a moment, "that's probably more useful than creating an afterlife for yourself."

He recalibrated a branch just so.

"Tell that to Saint Peter," I brooded. "If I meet up with him at the gates, he's going to send me directly south for not believing."

My father wiped his forehead with a handkerchief. We both watched as a tiger cat wriggled through the side yard hedge and surveyed this weird architectural barrier of twine and twigs with obvious derision.

"You can tell Saint Peter you've already been there," said my father. "Farming is hell."

Part Two

Tiller

4

Le American Farmer

I will be an American farmer. American agriculture is one of the few things that still makes me proud of this country. It has not been trivialized or forsaken. It has been assaulted, slightly corrupted surely, but it nonetheless remains unparalleled throughout the world.

"Why an American farmer?" asked a friend. "Why not be a European type of farmer? That seems very painterly. The farms there are small, everything well kept—you'd feel right at home."

Sure, I thought, small farms with big subsidies and considerable instincts for self-preservation. Only a year before, my husband and I had traveled in France and observed several of their charming farmers ploughing up median strips between *les superhighways* and planting corn only French centimeters from airport runways. More recently, these enchanting agriculturalists of Europe have engaged their tractors in blocking roads instead of ploughing fields. They have been protesting the few proposals that have managed to squeak through the otherwise stymied GATT (General Agreement on Tariffs and Trade) negotiations—the Uruguay Round, which began way back when, when there were still two Germanys and one cholesterol, but which nonetheless marches on as I write, into a maturity with no graceful conclusion (just like mankind's), the continued subject of obdurate international griping and protest. This round of GATT would go down in a blaze of posturing and pettiness, I believe. *Vive le small farmer*.

"It's a question of identity," I said. "American agriculture is a piece of mine."

"I don't know. I could see you in seven aprons and a babushka."

"What do you have against American farmers?" I asked.

My friend said, "I like what they were, not what they are."

"What the American Farmer was" is a knotty national myth with deeply embedded and entangled roots. Farmer-pioneers posed at one time a plausible exemplar for the American personae (one of them, since several such personae haunt the melting pot) as the nourisher of a young nation, the valiant pathblazer, ground-tamer. How pleasing to believe that farmers are, and have always been, custodians of America's rich indigenous resources, stewards of the soil, heroes because they have made us all fat at relatively low cost.

"Not anymore," remarked my friend. "Not the big guys out West. The only thing they're custodians of is their unnumbered Swiss bank accounts full of taxpayer monies, not that I could blame them. Does the USDA help farmers set up their Swiss bank accounts?"

I said, "You think I fit the image better of a small-time Yankee farmer—"

"Maybe I'll go visit the USDA . . ."

"—spending pennies to patch my shoddy barn, steadily refining my expertise in bankruptcy law?"

She said, "Yes. That's definitely you."

A lot of our friends, when questioned, asserted that prominent differences existed among farmers and farming from one region of the country to another. Interestingly, New England farmers got a reprieve from the otherwise grievous accusations leveled against a big, impersonal agriculture "out West."

"You need a degree in chemical engineering to farm in Kansas nowadays," said one.

"I get sleepy just thinking about Nebraska," commented another.

"New England has to be more ethical about its farming," added a third. "We're packed too tightly together up here. If somebody dusts calcium arsenate over schoolyards during recess, they'll be caught."

I heard a lot of emphatic and questionably accurate refrains extolling the patrimonial virtues of Northeast farmers, sometimes generously extending down to a few Pennsylvanians. It would seem that one part of the Union possessed a lien on some ethically spotless route through agricultural history. I was surprised that so many New Englanders I spoke with distrusted the farm practices of other parts of the country, while the Yankee farming traditions remained revered. It persisted as a curious bias—the more so, I thought, considering the quick pace at which these densely populated New England states have year after year been squeezing their beloved farmers out of existence by licensing endless suburban growth. It was my own experience that while agriculture changes from one region to another, farmers by and large don't.

As an American nonfarmer of the moment, I resolved to upgrade my understanding of the American farmer, or rather the pan-American farmer. And I began my investigation at the library.

"That's a lot of books," remarked my husband observing his dinner table under siege by the various volumes. "Are you going to plant them?"

•

If you go back to the initial farmers of America, those who moored their boats off the Carolina shores in the sixteenth and seventeenth century, then they actually did have some resemblance to me. After all, they weren't farmers at all and it seems they didn't disembark from the *Tyger* prepared to cultivate their gardens. They came looking for pearls and spices, fully anticipating that food would be sent from the larder in England or gratefully supplied by the local Indians. Not many of the first colonists survived.

"Lucky for me," I said to my husband. "Even if I fail miserably with the farm, I can still drive over to the A&P and buy groceries."

He said, "Ah, now I'm beginning to see my role in this farm more clearly: I keep my job at the bank."

I have always been drawn to the stories of the early colonists, and in particular to that of the "Lost Colony" of Roanoke, because since I was an infant my family has spent a part of its summers on the Kitty Hawk shores just a few miles away from where those first boats landed.

Kitty Hawk proper lies on the reedy peninsula of the outer banks of North Carolina, along the Atlantic coastline, south of Duck and Corolla, north of Kill Devil Hills (where, to set the record straight, the Wright brothers actually first flew) and Nag's Head. It's a very thin strip of land, a virtual sandbar, with the ocean on one side and the Albemarle and Currituck Sounds on the other. From many points along the dune crests you can overlook both bodies of water at once.

There were few houses at all here in the 1960s, and most of those looked remarkably alike—cinderblock matchboxes painted in garish pastels, every window shaded with a bleached-out canvas awning. The driveways were sand and the main road, too, turned to sand just yards from our house. In the first years of our southerly pilgrimage, my mother would go to retrieve buckets of fresh water from a pump at the end of the concrete road. The local telephone was miles away at the edge of "town," in a booth in front of Anderson's Trading Post. At Anderson's was the gasoline pump, stamps, and last week's newspapers with a growl from Mrs. A. The grocery store, Winks, was eight miles away, and it, too, was a tiny pink cinderblock building with big awnings out front.

As a child, I was always surprised that the colonists had had the wits to sail beyond this sandy beach into the Pamlico and Albemarle Sounds. How did they know to go further? Well, and it was a good thing they did, I decided then, because past the hot sand dunes and their rippling densities of golden sea oats—in no way predisposed to farming—was a serene and fertile mainland, with cornfields, jam stands, and watermelon patches.

Each summer my sisters and I would plead with our parents to see *The Lost Colony,* an evening outdoor theater production in Manteo, across the sound from Nag's Head. My mother usually surrendered herself to the chore, year after year able to recite more of the play by heart. As she drove us across the bridge onto the mainland, I remember the earth suddenly changing into pine forest and peach groves, cucumber patches and soybean fields. From the back seat of our station wagon, I would gaze out, speculating that this area had offered the first colonists the best of both worlds—a beach for floating in their inner tubes, and right across the waterway, a farm where they could buy fresh tomatoes, just like we did. Each year this trip to see *The Lost Colony* seemed equally magical and mysterious, and I felt *anybody* would get lost in that pine forest at night, the small paved road almost lost to shifting sands and pine needles, and with no street lights to boot.

We slapped mosquitoes as Sir Walter Raleigh authorized the building of the first fort, and we turned our attention from the night sky's shooting stars when Agona, the comic Indian squaw, finally arrived on the stage fat and moaning and scouting out a suitable brave—lips pursed and rouged, eyes wide, corn husks shshshing from her primitive clothing and feathers drooping from her hair.

"Not a particularly attractive rendering of the Indians," sighed my mother as we drove home afterward. And indeed, there had been a lot of angry ones, whooping war cries and torching the British settlements. In recreating a moment in history about which there is scarcely any information available, this play had proffered a distinctly biased point of view.

"Maybe you should call your farm The Lost Colony," my husband suggested, "as a kind of memorial for those early farmers and settlers."

"That doesn't seem very propitious," I said. "Besides, I'd probably be sued for attempting to arouse anti-Indian sentiment."

"Mmmmm," he ruminated. "How about calling it A Maizing Grace."

The American farm did ultimately grow into a preserve of the rumored abundance. Forests were pushed back and kept at bay. Breeding stock was imported. Ploughs were refined. Corn and tobacco were exported. Corn and tobacco are still exported, and in profusion.

Tobacco, for all of its ills, always struck me as a kind of celebrity commodity within a peculiarly American heritage. The fields covered with cream-colored gauze netting and the slatted drying barns must be homey images for anyone raised in western Massachusetts—even those who don't smoke.

My grandfather worked as a young boy in a cigarette factory in the Bronx. The factory was housed in a five-storey building, and there were large holes cut in the floors from one storey down to another. The finest cigarettes, he said, were manufactured with the best tobacco on the top floor. The stray leaf shavings that fell in the normal course of business were periodically swept through the holes in the floor and rained into the leaf bins of the storey below, where lesser grade cigarettes were rolled. From floor to floor the sweepings fell and the quality slipped, and on the ground floor workers were allowed to grab handfuls of the cheapest cigarettes to take home each evening.

It's a marvelous image. When I think about tobacco today, however, it is in connection either with smoking, which is a filthy habit no matter how charming cigarette assembly ever was, or with lung cancer, which has played a fatal role in America's ugly litigious streak. So I called up the Department of Agriculture to find out what was doing with tobacco as a crop these days.

"Tobacco is the sixth-largest cash crop in America," beamed a USDA expert (between puffs, I imagined) on the end of the line. "We're still the world's major exporter."

"Terrific," I said.

"Well, of course, tobacco production is supported by the government," he said.

"I see," I said. "You mean we subsidize tobacco production, and then our Secretary of Health says 'Don't smoke, it'll kill you,' and then people die from lung cancer and we pay their lawyers to lose battles with the big cigarette companies."

(Puff, puff)

Me: "That's the American way, I guess."

He sent me a pamphlet full of charts and numbers and projections. It had a glossary in the back which gave me a richer impression of tobacco farming, in the same way that studying any language gives you a better sense of a culture (German being adjective-impoverished, for example). As I glanced through the glossary of terms, I developed a more elaborate image of tobacco's agriculture—the three dominant varieties of snuff, the "tipping" of the leaf to remove unwanted stem. "Prizing," I learned, refers to the packing of tobacco into "hogsheads," large, round wooden casks that store about one thousand pounds each of tobacco leaf for aging. Many of the terms retained a kind of colonial resonance to them, as though high technology had somehow bypassed the tobacco leaf; but interspersed, of course, were telling modern expressions like No-Net-Cost Act of 1982 or Price Supports.

Several elements of America's tobacco story echo elements of our broader agricultural background. Tobacco was a modest crop, for instance, before the colonists found a variety, the Orinoco, that was greatly preferred in the European markets. Suddenly every colonial farmer wanted to share in the windfall. That's a healthy capitalist urge. Exports exploded. Ships sagged. In 1616, so many farmers were planting tobacco that the governor of Virginia had to order the planting of at least two acres of corn to ensure adequate food stocks for the domestic population. It's not de facto that Americans always dash to extremes (although I wouldn't deny it), but perhaps that we have historically been an industrious, entrepreneurial lot.

Supply and demand. Subjugation of natural resources. Wringing profits from an often begrudging wilderness. This is the tradition, I have mused to myself in quiet moments of doubt, that I will perpetuate. These are the footsteps of exploitation that I will advance.

But of course there is a wonderfully ingenious and inventive side of that tradition, too. There were individuals for whom commercial instinct was tempered by loftier sensitivities. There have been farmers with ambitions to improve the national agriculture, to invent better farming equipment, or to ameliorate the agrarian situation. Thomas Jefferson is an easy example to cite. He researched and promoted better sheep breeds, he experimented with new crop strains, he designed more effective tools—then he wrote it all down. He kept meticulous records of his daily farm chores, harvests, weather, costs, and concepts. It can't be overly stressed that such journals were key in developing American agriculture. It flourished as much by dint of clever observation as it did by dint of physical domination.

"I guess this is where you and farming part ways," said my husband. "You're not big on recordkeeping." He looked up at me as if to punctuate the gravity of this character-based obstacle.

"I have a very intuitive side," I said, jocular, trying to avert a discussion. I can't stand these self-reforming discussions. I come from a family in which improving oneself was a pastime.

"Keeping up a good journal is critical," he pursued, "if you're going to take this farm seriously."

Did he say "seriously"? Outrage. I stifled a caustic observation.

This interchange warrants a brief digression from the subject of farm journals, I think. I have always tried to look benignly upon constructive criticism, and it might be said that I ordinarily fail. That is, I hear and mostly accede to reproof, but I don't always do it with a smile. If I obliged myself a defense, it would be that constructive criticism does tend to arrive at the most inopportune moments in life, when one, in the height of a lost humor, has done something correspondingly inferior and thus invited somebody's (a witness's) enlightening suggestions for rehabilitation. Thank you, I would like to say. Thank you for caring so much about me as to concern yourself with the fine-tuning of my dedicatedly narrow-minded wrongdoings.

Aaahh. What a good farmer I shall make, immune to all propositions of change.

I say that with humor, since farmers are not so immutable as nonfarmers like to believe, and since for a budding farmer constructive criticism is indeed not only invaluable but desired. When I become a farmer, I will be a maladroit beginner again, soliciting tips whenever possible from the already entrenched. Criticism in such instances is not denunciation, but guiding analysis. It took farming for me to want to be a beginner again, to want to start all over, like a child. I am grateful for that liberty since it is self-renewing. Do we all have a place, I wonder, where the old defenses dry up and drop off and where one feels the glorious side of Vulnerable?

Having said that, I can admit my husband was perfectly right that I am no natural recordkeeper. I might even let him know it, though his criticism in no way came on the wings of loving intonation. Mmm-hmm, he will certainly be surprised to see the zest with which I maintain a farm journal. One cannot know where Possibility lies in another.

To probe and to prepare, I took a copy of Jefferson's farm journal from the library one afternoon to see how he had arranged it.

"March 28, 1771: planted 5. grapes from N. Lewis's on S.E. edge of garden."

"March 24, 1803: a considerable snow on the blue ridge."

"May 28, 1811: artichokes come to table. The last dish is July 28."

"I'm going to need a lot of pencils," I smiled to my husband. "Just so that I don't miss a thought, you know, between feed bunk and stall for instance."

"We could set up a laptop computer in the barnyard," he said. "And everytime you walked by you could type in your notes: chicks still fairly cute this morning; tell Chuck to feed animals before going to bank; went to Stop & Shop to check out lettuces of competitors—depressing—came home and talked to goat."

•

I met a man who said he had introduced turkeys to Switzerland, or rather, had introduced the Swiss to turkeys. Well, and before that he had spent a couple of years on a sheep farm in New Zealand, and after that he had spent a year on a pig farm in southern England. He had even worked on dairy farms in Switzerland before getting a degree and moving into the food business. There wasn't much about farm management that would surprise him, he said. One day he told me about pigs from Mongolia with four inches of coarse, unmarketable hair, and when I said I had never heard of such a thing he said, "And you say you're in agriculture?"

His name was Martin and he was a Swiss man with a penchant for untangling the manure problems of farmers in the Alps. But when he was finished with that, well, he didn't know what. Maybe he would help the American farmers solve their problems.

"I am quite through with turkeys," he said. "Now everybody knows. They know a turkey."

I told Martin about my farming intentions.

"Maybe I could raise those longhaired Mongolian hogs," I smiled.

I was genuinely interested in less run-of-the-mill breeds of stock, even if that meant pigs. Secondary breeds—cattle deemed too small, sheep that mature too slowly, chickens whose breasts are not enormous—several minor breeds have been pushed toward extinction by modern agriculture's pragmatic inclinations to streamline and standardize. Threatened farm animal breeds have suffered the added disadvantage of being overlooked by most animal protection groups. I'm not sure why. There are resolute environmentalists who will lie down on train tracks for a Dutch salamander but who think of rare livestock breeds as an altogether other sphere. I remarked to Martin about my specific interest in minor breeds and I asked him to let me know when he came across other unusual illustrations.

"It is good," said Martin, "to raise the older breeds on your farm. It is good, this idea for a small operation. You just keep ten percent of your animals in the barn and ninety percent in the freezer."

"In the freezer?" I asked. I knew what he was aiming at, but his delivery made me incredulous.

"Yah, naturally," he said. "You must breed your animals, take their embryos, put them in the freezer. Everyone in America does it, I think. You need one barn, one freezer. It is very efficient. One barn, one freezer."

Embryo transfer is an interesting if not wholly reliable practice. It is still considered by some to be one of biotechnology's many infants, with all the flaws and doubts and questions accorded as a rule to infants—with the exception of human babies, who, if you ask their mothers, are indeed flawless. Embryo transfer is, however, a quick and effective way of introducing animals to foreign environments. A cattle embryo with considerable genetic value can be transplanted into a recipient cow in Burundi, say, and the calf during gestation will take on the diverse disease immunities of its local mother. A Mongolian long-haired pig embryo implanted in an agreeable pink York-shire sow . . . And embryos frozen in liquid nitrogen are infinitely more portable than a herd of livestock. It's logistically advan-tageous. One sleeps easier not having to figure out how to supervise a 747 jumbo jet packed with nervous pregnant heifers, quarantine here quarantine there, then onto the trucks without the springs and over the roads without the pavement to some rural bovine research facility deprived of electricity as we know it and certain supplies of hay as we like it, and crowing with new bugs—the ones you do see and the ones you don't.

"Good concept," I said to Martin. "Embryos are quieter, too."

"Yah," he said with a face that showed he didn't get my joke. It's hard to get jokes in other languages. There's been some controversy, too, about the genius of my jokes in general.

I said, "I'll have to find myself a willing veterinarian with liquid nitrogen on tap."

"Yah," Martin agreed. "In fact you should have your freezer there. It is more efficient."

He added, "You don't need a big American freezer, you know. A smaller model—I show you—is energy-efficienter."

"I would worry about electricity however," I mused. "One shortage, one circuit overload, and I'll have killed hundreds of seven-celled cows and goats."

"Yes, alzo," said Martin, never at a loss for solutions, "you need to keep things separated. For safety. In case the electricity breaks or so. You should have your freezer somewhere else. Or two freezers is maybe best. Two barns, two freezers."

Two barns, two freezers. Two refrigerators for all the phar-maceutical paraphernalia. Two ovens to boil the water to sterilize the instruments. Two vets to ready the cows to synchronize heats to accept the embryos . . . This was not what I had had in mind.

"Just think," said Martin. "The bigger your freezers, the

smaller your farm has to be. Land is expensive. It is a very efficient way to carry on."

·

Mongolian pigs with four inches of coarse hair are probably not in the cards for me. Pigs, overall, are not my favorite barnyard residents, although I have always enjoyed visiting other people's pigs. When I was a student of agricultural economics at Texas A&M, I used to visit the university farm centers in my free time and watch the students perform their research or husbandry chores.

At A&M, the world of agriculture is neatly aggregated across acres and acres of rolling farmland. There are cotton fields that seem to bloom snow in the autumn. There are peanut fields that yield maroon-and-white (the Texas Aggie colors) striped peanuts for insatiable alumni. There are sorghum fields where scientists make incursions into the problems of lodging (toppling over) stalks. There are poultry houses and a dairy where, I'm told, the real live Borden Milk's Bessie, a Jersey cow, plods out her productive days in between show appearances. One of my favorite excursions was to the Swine Center, where I could walk through the farrowing barn and see the sows flouncing around beside their umpteen blind and squirming piglets. They certainly weren't worried about any final exams.

Usually a group of students would be chatting in the anteroom of the little administrative building. They all wore coveralls and Texas Aggie baseball caps. (Soon, I thought, they would be wearing smart new caps sporting the logos of various swine pharmaceutical firms.) This small office was crowded with metal desks and filing cabinets, the ubiquitous coffeemaker, a water cooler, and a coat rack with white lab coats and plastic boots for visitors with shoes worth saving. The walls were adorned with humorous pig posters and Texas Aggie sports calendars. The students came to recognize me after a while, and would wave me on through the door to the barns. They enjoyed their work and swine research, but they thought it was hilarious that I would come to the center—and more than once—just to look around.

"Where you from anyway?" they would ask, their young, earnest faces tipped up under their caps. Altogether, they were a most good-natured and bright group of people. They became part of my pleasure in visiting the Swine Center. I found that after weeks of studying U.S. farm policy and its corpulent, inbred bureaucratic programs, I was invariably refreshed to see these students, with their enthusiasm and spirited outlook, learning the ropes of farm management. The same could be said for the rosy-cheeked group that worked out at the Dairy Center. This was the next generation of American farmers, and it was heartening.

Beyond the students' office was a hallway that led to the pens.

"They still look the same," a voice would call after me, laughing.

And then another, "Give the girls my regards."

Then came a helpful remark, "Pen thirteen farrowed last night."

Once I shouted back, "Oh my gosh, what happened? Where are all the animals?" It produced the desired stampede. "Just kidding," I smiled, as four panting bodies spilled into the barn behind me. So, truce, laughter, the end of traded quips. I was offered a coffee and I drank it as though puffing on a peace pipe.

Before walking through the long farrowing barns, visitors were required to step in a plastic pail of iodine, a "dip." It sat by the doorway, looking as innocent as turtle soup while it ruined one pair of unsuspecting shoes after another. Straight ahead lay long lines of farrowing pens separated by cement walkways. Cement, for all of its plain ugliness, has become extremely useful to farmers. It is easy to hose clean, easy to drive vehicles over, and terrific for anchoring iron posts. The larger the farm, the more critical seem its advantages.

Each small farrowing pen was divided in two with a piece of widely slatted iron fencing. In one half lay the sow—enormous—on her side, with her front hooves splayed forward in front of her snout and her rear legs stretched taut and vertically downward, like a ballet dancer's, toes ever so lightly grazing the pen wall. Less graceful were the occasional grunts, the snout that, even in slumber, seemed to be rooting through the straw-covered flooring for a stray turnip or truffle. This was Mom, to a litter not infrequently of over twelve little piglets that were sequestered for their own protection on the other half of the pen. They could reach readily through the iron slats for one of her many paired teats, but she could not roll over onto them in her soundest sleep and unwittingly suffocate the lot—as sows are known to do handily. So it is not uncommon on pig farms to find divided farrowing pens. On the one side lies the sow with her teats exposed; on the other side a pink brawl of siblings, blind at birth and relying on their wonderful noses to detect a promising source of milk.

Baby pigs, piglets, are unusually adorable. They call out to one's most rudimentary instincts to be held and murmured to. Warm, nuzzling, smooth, soft and uttering improbably endearing noises. Mankind would become an absolute slave to piglets if only they didn't grow into pigs (thus are we saved). I heartily recommend a visit to a pig farm for anyone not yet exposed to the scene of fourteen two-day-old piglet siblings fast asleep on top of one another, settled into a sweet pink heap of communal breathing that can only be likened to a napping rugby scrum. However, cast your glance then a little to the left and you will likely be introduced to their gargantuan mother, perhaps six hundred pounds of her, in a less endearing hide—a sight which, though a rude shock, may be considered sensibly bracing. It's a question of temperament.

I'm not drawn to hogs, although some of the smaller breeds have caught my attention lately. I have heard that they are surprisingly bright, like to stay clean, and make great pets. The more exotic breeds are growing fastest in popularity. There is a flourishing pet market in the States, for example, for the Vietnamese potbellied pig, a very small, very round pig that has captured the hearts of many wealthy pet lovers apparently bored with the usual cat-and-dog fare.

"We were going to get one of those Vietnamese pigs," said a neighbor of ours in Greenwich. "But we went over to some friends' house—they have one—and honestly, there was the pig, this fat, round thing, sitting on the couch with their kids, watching TV and eating grapes. And when the thing got bigger, you could barely see its eyes for the big folds of fat that hung down over them. You'd have to have these . . . these eyebrow flabs surgically held up or I don't know—the thing would be blind. All I can say is that the thing loved peanut butter."

The thing. That was certainly not a hard sell for anyone window-shopping the pet pig markets. I follow neither the pet pig markets nor the commercial hog markets. The image of pork belly futures trading or frozen pork bellies traveling cross-country on our railroads seizes my sense of comic whimsy, but the business itself holds no allure. Apart from pickled pig's knuckles, which I rightly or wrongly associate with Jewish holidays, pigs and pork are for me a thing of Chicago and the Midwest. And not a sanguine thing. I come across swine-industry articles in my stock magazines that shed some light for me on the modernization of the pig industry. It seems that pigs lend themselves to certain industrialized efficiencies and needs that mean fewer farmers, more cages and microchips. It sounds not unlike the poultry industry.

On the efficiency side, I have heard of farmers stacking pigs in slightly tipped battery cages—similar to what is now done with laying hens. The pigs are kept thus raised and confined for their few months before slaughter, and the handling of the cages is easier for farmers than the handling of live loose pigs. Such confinement systems are always designed to give a farmer more control over the animals and their environment, and to reduce his demand for labor. One farmer can husband hundreds of pigs by himself, but I would add that it is rarely referred to as animal husbandry at that point—rather, it is farm industry management.

On the matter of needs, pigs are relatively demanding. They require strict temperature controls. They cannot survive lengthy periods of strong heat, for instance. Pigs do not sweat and this is why you often see them immobilizing themselves in mud puddles or sinking like a plug into their own water troughs during the hot summer months. And pigs have similar luck with extended months of cold.

"In the wintertime," said one hog farmer, "I use hot-air blowers in the barns, but even that's not enough. I put down a bed of straw that's about thigh-high—no funniness here—and the pigs just burrow in there to get warm and you might as well think you didn't have any pigs around at all. You might be raising a barn of two hundred hogs but when you look inside, all you see is straw. You got to wait till spring if you want any ham. Fortunately, o'course, that's about when Easter happens."

I was told that another meaningful aspect of the pig industry is that it is essentially a traffic in minors.

"Market hogs are all very young," explained a veterinarian to me. "They're usually a matter of months old when they're shipped off. And so they are extremely susceptible to child contagions."

Child contagions, I thought. It had the ring of child labor. I asked if this were the reason for the iodine tubs at Texas A&M's Swine Center.

"It was not so much for you and your shoes," the vet said, "but for visiting hog farmers who may be carrying on their shoes the parasites or bacteria from farms with pigs not immunized or not genetically secure from these infant diseases."

I have watched market hogs, their snouts constantly sweeping along the grubby ground of their pens in search of some savory curiosity or overlooked scrap of lettuce. It was clear they were putting themselves in harm's way. But *children*, I kept thinking. I couldn't rinse the image from my head.

I would add, lastly, that pigs have proven problematic on the farmer-friendly concrete floors that garnish so many modern-day stock barns. Because of the anatomical inflexibility of their little hocks, their bodies take a beating on the hard surface and they develop what is called porcine stress syndrome, or PSS. PSS can lead to various degrees of injury. I have heard of prize boars sold at auction who are discovered later to be useless because they cannot mount a female—poor back legs. I have heard of paralysis and malaise. Moreover, pigs suffering from PSS often yield inferior meat with visibly detracting properties. PSE stands for pale soft exudate and it refers in no euphemistic way to the runny fat that can characterize the meat of pigs afflicted with PSS. It looks rank.

Instead of surrendering the convenience of concrete, many pig farmers buy floor-surface coverings of slatted or punctured plastic, equally easy to clean and sanitize but billed as more sympathetic to the hoof and hock. This is the way of all farming, I think—the growth of technologies that, whether in the right direction or the wrong, escalate and become mutually dependent. They turn a farmer from husbandman to businessman and they focus his concerns on questions like: In stacking my battery cages four instead of three high, what is the marginal profit? Do I need to switch industrial cleaning agents when I use green plastic flooring instead of plain concrete? The cleaning agent specially designed to clean this green flooring has an overpowering hygienic scent; do I need to improve my ventilation system to ensure my pigs stay healthy after I clean? This farmer is taking logical, maybe profitable steps. They develop, however, into a type-A bureaucratic snowball.

This technology-avaricious behavior is not exclusive to the swine industry. Consider the case of a poultry farmer. It used to be he sold Grade AA large white eggs in the local markets as fast as he and his wife could collect them and box them. In

1982, however, cash-register receipts analyzed by the grocery store's Profit-Center-Management-Information system (a computer) were indicating that he had to switch to a flock of brown-egg layers to keep his consumers satisfied, although it is widely known that there is no difference between white and brown eggs apart from color. So he found a "cross" (a hybrid hen) in Ohio that suited his needs, and replaced his entire flock—old hens to the soup pots, new pullets (female chicks) to the roost. Then egg consumption dropped off because of cholesterol worries, and he had to switch breeds again, this time to some layer cross shipped out of Missouri with a name that looked like a license plate—but a hen from whom he could get at least two dozen more eggs per year than out of the former breed, which meant he could cut his total flock by maybe twenty percent. He condensed barns, lay concrete for a shipping dock, installed conveyor belts and dust control systems along the walls. When times kept getting tougher in the egg business, he found that by substituting battery cages four high in lieu of his floor system (this meant moving the whole dust control system, which is a critical component of poultry operations, to ceiling connections), he could let go his last hired hand and manage the whole operation—electrical gadgetry willing—by himself with help from his wife.

What will become of my small farm? And me without a wife.

5

Ploughshares and Microchips

A ranch hand I once worked with told me, between spits of chewing tobacco juice, that I looked grrrreat on a tractor. What I replied doesn't bear the vituperative spelling out. What I felt was fury. I had faced sexual innuendo before, in office jobs, in school, on public transportation—most women do—but to find it on this ranch, in the midst of my workday, while I was in layers of filthy blue jeans and sweatshirts and struggling to put an old John Deere 435 into third gear, completely galled me. It made me venomous.

My anger came not so much from an assault on my feminist self. I am, as my mother once said of herself, a "flawed feminist." My anger came from the unsolicited intrusion of a profound, corrosive element to my state of mind *à la ferme*. Don't you ruin my agriculture, I was smoldering with your trite, invasive remarks.

I had found such a welcome respite from sexual concerns in ranch work, a peace in the manual labor, the pulling of irrigation lines, the rewinching of barbed wire fences, or the hauling of kitchen orts out to the pigs. I was certainly not as strong or mechanically adept as the other hands who were male, but I had my own chores and I could manage them alone. After this comment, it was hard for me to get up onto the rusting old John Deere without feeling self-conscious. Had I tucked in my several layers of shirts? Should I have? What was playing into his hands and what wasn't? I resented this burden, and I found it especially nettlesome since driving old tractors is rarely either comfortable or easy. On that 435, for instance, one had to wear earphones to cope with the roar and rattle. The exhaust pipe, with its cap flapping over the furrows, sent diesel fumes like champagne spume to the nose, throat, and eyes. The springs, as capable as ornament, tossed one's body up and down and left and right across the hard, molded leather seat. I used to have to hang onto the steering wheel to keep from being hurled off. How, I wondered, could that be a prrrretty sight?

I remembered this incident as I was trying to think back to what exactly the ranch had used its crumbling collection of tractors for—I was wondering whether I would need a tractor on my own small farm. Well, we had used them to pull the aluminum irrigation pipes from one alfalfa bay to the next. We had used them to haul the manure-spreader out onto the cultivated fields. And we had used them to pull other ranch vehicles (including the other tractors) out of the mud or snow. I polled my husband.

"Do you need a tractor," he contemplated. "That's a good question because, as you say, it's a function of what they're needed to pull or push. If you're not cultivating crop land, I guess you can get by without. You certainly don't need one for a garden." And here the eyebrows fluttered up and down suggestively. "But it would be great fun."

My husband is not as machine-averse as I. Tractors. All I could imagine was their noise.

"Maybe we could borrow or rent one," said my husband, "at the beginning, to help set fence posts and things like that."

This seemed sensible. Depending on how small a farm is, tractors may not be crucial for day-to-day operations. I could traffic square bales here and there in the bed of a pick-up truck—and since I already owned a small one, I felt, smugly, entirely ready to start buying livestock. I also had in the back of my mind the advice of several farmers. Above all, they have cautioned me, the biggest mistake new farmers make is to run out and buy everything first. Most of them agreed, too, that buying new equipment was almost always money down the drain. There's always a good used tractor, a good used plough-share, a good used hay wagon to be found. One farmer I knew in Danbury made this point and then pulled a long white sheet of paper from the glove compartment of his truck. It was the *Connecticut Agricultural Marketing Newsletter,* and it contained three long columns, thinly fretted with advertisements for land, machinery, animals, and help. It was farmers talking to farmers. Tractors, combines, electric fencing, silage choppers, whole farms, Toggenburg goats—the future seemed to be availing itself to me, weekly, and for extremely moderate prices. I sub-scribed.

The issue of tractors is a simple and economic one. Either the farm is so small you don't depend on one, or the farm is—grows—large enough that you need the help. Labor is expensive. We'll do what we can by ourselves and when ourselves are inadequate we'll look to machinery to assist us before we look toward hiring employees. The tractor purchase would wait. It was with this patient, head-screwed-on-right feeling that I would occasionally browse through farm equipment dealerships to see how tractors were evolving and to get a better sense of what horsepower—that wholly mysterious and ironic word—meant.

"I don't mean to butt in, hon," a Kubota tractor dealer in New York said to me, "but I think you're making a mistake. In all honesty, I think you've got things backward."

I had been perambulating his outdoor exhibit of small trac-tors, an acre or more of husky orange just-over-lawn-mower-size models set up so that you had to slalom in and out between thorny cultivating and planting attachments. I had told him no, I wasn't needing anything yet. My farm wasn't even established.

"In my mind," he went on, "a tractor is about the very first thing you *do* want to buy, and a solid one, too. Tractors aren't just a way of hauling hay, you know."

"You're probably right," I said, not because I thought he was but because this usually quiets salesmen. He was immune.

"Ask me your questions," he pushed. Obviously the Japanese were now schooling their American sales forces to get cozy with customers. "Tell me what's holding you back."

The Psychiatric Approach to Tractor Selling, by Yuki-san Moto Kubota.

"Well," I said, scanning for a question that might be hanging around the right side of my brain. "What I would really like to know is why tractor dealers and farmers keep their equipment outside in all weather? Aren't you people worried about rust?"

"Rust? Why our Kubotas are practically invincible. You're looking at layers and layers of paint on every part of the body. Layers and layers."

"You would want me to keep this in a barn or garage, wouldn't you?" I asked.

"Well," he said, "yes, naturally."

"Hmmmm," I ruminated. Question dodged. I was getting a little edgy, feeling engulfed in a profusion of identical pygmy tractors. It was like a lawn full of matchbox cars—for Goliath. Every tractor was bright and gaily colored, the wheels jet black with rubber polish—all a little big for under the Christmas tree, but panting to be played with. I imagined an *Alice in Wonderland* tag on a steering wheel: START ME.

Most other people circulating through the outdoor showcase seemed to be there for the sunny-day fun of it, or because "he" just can't stop buying machines. "It's a disease," I heard one wife say, beaming happily in the shadow of such buying power. I couldn't spot anyone there that looked like a farmer. Everyone was neatly dressed in polo shirts and khakis, the uniform for Sunday shoppers in upper Westchester County.

"When the time is right, I think I will be hunting up something a little larger," I finally said to the salesman, who had been dogging me, his hands constantly smoothing his hair. He was not going to give me up for anything. These other shoppers, well, they were there to buy. They could wait. But me, I was going to be trouble.

So I reiterated, "In any case, I'm not going to buy anything today. I'm just here to see the alternatives and the attachments."

"Honey," he said, "I can tell you right now that these little babies are twice as powerful as any midsize Case or John Deere you're ever like to find. We have got performance figures that completely blow them out of the water. These Kubotas are bona fide nuggets of power."

The "bona fide" caught my attention. I love to hear the unexpected words that turn up in various vocabularies.

I said, "Hmmmm."

He said, "You wait right here a minute, hon, and I'll run inside and get you some of our brochures. You'll be able to read the figures for yourself. Or," he paused with something akin to a leer, "would you like to test drive one of these girls?" He waved his arm in a broad arc across his amber field of engine blocks and wheel shields. He thought he had me now. "Hon" on one of the "girls."

"No," I said. "I appreciate the offer. To tell you the truth, I'm pretty confident I want an American tractor." I smiled. "We all draw lines in funny places, don't we, fella?"

•

Thomas Jefferson was, among other things, a serious student of plough design, and he had tried to budge American farmers of his time from their complacency with ineffectual implements. The early ploughs had been made of wood and often owned not by the farmer but by an independent ploughman. This ploughman would bring his plough and oxen over to your farm under contract, but since all farmers in a region do their sowing and harvesting around the same time, they must have vied strenuously to get his assistance before seed rotted, rains came, or harvests spoiled. I told my husband about this snag. He loves these sorts of stories.

"That probably marks the birth of extortion in America," he said merrily. "And what a big day that was."

The day of the independent ploughman was short-lived, with obvious reason. By the time Jefferson came along, the farmer owned his own plough, useless as it might be. I usually close my eyes when I see mechanical drawings, graphs, charts, and the like on a page, but I became interested in Jefferson's plough sketches because they were so simple and graceful, and they provided me with an elemental grasp of the concepts behind farm machinery, which I otherwise would have tried to ignore. The high-technology engines that combust down modern-day farm rows completely cow me, and I suspect I could not hope ever to grasp the theories behind their formulation. If you look at early farm implements, however, you can begin to comprehend the purposes and problems of their design. You can grapple at least in theory with the basic ideas of strength, durability, precision, and handling. From there, I infer, even if you add a few fuses, catalytic converters, hydraulic adjusters, digital analogs, and air conditioning, you can still recognize in today's high-tech tractors and combines some antiquated threads of basic engineering objectives that have steered the course of modernization since the earliest unavailing apparatus.

Among the first ploughs used to turn up American soil were the "bull ploughs." It took two men—one behind the plough, one leading the oxen—and often four to eight oxen to prepare a field. These early ploughs cut perhaps three inches into the soil, and the arduous process, accented by frequent pauses for repairs, resulted in an average of only one acre ploughed per day. One acre. Well, and any gardener can tell you three inches is not very deep when it comes to cultivating the ground. My husband and I faced this problem when we first set up a vegetable garden in our Connecticut backyard.

"We recommend you turn over a foot if you can," said our local nurseryman. "You got a rototiller?"

"No," I replied.

"Yah, well, can you get one?"

The point was being made.

"Let's suppose I couldn't," I said. "How deep now?"

"Is it sod?" he asked.

"Yes."

"For how long?"

"I don't know."

"You don't know?" There was silence. "You know, sometimes it gets kind of compacted. We recommend you get it rototilled."

"I've got a fork," I said. "About how deep?"

"About a foot."

We did eventually get the plot turned over by hand, and later our neighbors expanded it substantially with their stout little tractor and its rototiller attachment. We compared the small garden we had prepared ourselves to the larger plot of tractor-tilled land. The hand work had been far less successful in terms of aerating and breaking up the clay clods in the soil, and it had brought home all the more the difficulties of clearing new land. We, at least, had had the advantage of steel forks and shovels. The early farmers effectively had only wood.

Our interest piqued, we drove over to a farm museum in Stamford to see some such wooden tools. We walked by walls of ash, hickory, and chestnut pitchforks that showed the meticulous craftsmanship of colonial woodworkers, who sought to provide the least resistance and the most strength to the wielder. These forks were beautiful and fluid, but they seemed incredibly fragile and sometimes cumbersome for their long handles. The young woman at the museum explained that the longer handles were used to gain leverage on rocks and roots.

"They bent," she said. "They were very useful."

We were skeptical.

Iron, like a godsend, became more accepted among agricultural implements after the Revolutionary War. Ironic, I think, the way war historically seems to spawn a kind of inventiveness that assumes a benign form for gutted populations in its aftermath. Farmers would take their wooden tools over to the local blacksmith, who would attach pieces of iron sheeting, for reinforcement, to the ground-cutting surfaces. I relate more to the farmers who, I learned, desperately nailed old horseshoes, scrap-iron bits, and used hoe blades onto their ploughshares— anything available to fortify the edge and slow the wear and tear. Plain wood shares against a dense grass or clay or compacted soil were nearly futile—not unlike those little plastic knives the deli will give you to do combat against their steak sandwiches.

The plough predicament was critical, and it was exacerbated by widespread sentiment among farmers that cast iron infected the soil and fostered weeds. With perceptions such as these, it's not surprising that American farmers missed the agricultural revolution that occurred in England in the eighteenth century. But they were not too far behind. In 1837, an Illinois blacksmith by the name of John Deere picked up the used blade of a worn-out mill saw. It was made of tough Sheffield steel. Deere engineered this blade into a functional plough that was able to make quick work of the thick and claylike prairie soils. Under this plough, American farmland blossomed.

As a prospective American farmer myself, I hope I might operate with less resistance to change than some of these early farmers—but then, as a small farmer, I suspect there will be little high-technology instrumentation beating a path to my barn door.

·

When it comes to farm equipment and machinery, there are definitely ways to stay ahead of the pack. Computers offer a multiplicity of labor-substituting or labor-facilitating options suitable for many of the short-distance, regular-interval chores that take place inside a barn. The daily cadence of these chores lends itself to computerized *systems,* and we are truly a culture spellbound by systems and systems management.

I adore systems, probably more than the next guy. I loll in the familiarity of routine. When my day is ordered, it assuages my sense of internal chaos and I sometimes think I would be the last to grumble if all days were thoroughly alike. This is anathema to my husband, who flourishes within the tactical confines of computer systems, but for whom eating chicken twice in one week is a surrender to life's encroaching monotony. He will be the one to put lighting timers in the barn, and he will be the one to take DOS by the horns and fashion some wonderful farm-budget and livestock-performance programs for me on the computer.

"Think of the Lotus spreadsheets we can make," he said enthusiastically one evening. "Column after column after column on your sheep."

"I'm actually better with paragraphs than columns."

"You'll get the hang of this in no time," he continued. "And once you've got everything in Lotus, I've got a program that turns it into terrific charts and graphs. It's incredible."

"I can't read bar charts," I mumbled. "Did I ever tell you that? Besides, who's going to want to see charts on my sheep?"

That gave him pause for reflection.

"Your dad?"

I shook my head.

"We can tack them on the stall walls and encourage all the animals to strive for greater performance," he grinned. "But first, you're going to have to teach the sheep to read left to right."

Basic computer systems function in a wonderfully dry, binary way. Either this or that, they say. That, you program. Either this or that, is the follow-up question. That, again. A lot of American farmers immediately saw the advantages of computers. They programmed lighting in the barns, feed onto conveyor belts into the pens, heating, watering, and so on. I've been in eighteenth-century barns outfitted with a wall of blinking lights and buttons that hum as they command the farm. Moreover, computers are more reliable than human beings when it comes to flipping switches at certain moments in the day. On a farm, this is a real consideration. Livestock appreciate routine almost as much as I do. Chickens respond dramatically to the steady number of daylight hours they receive. And as for heating, don't ever forget how forlorn pigs look when they shiver.

On farms that offer you the peak of technological performance systems, you can bet that the next barn over is likely a garage. It houses all those air-conditioned, stereo-accoutered, laser-guided, petroleum-quaffing tractors that rumble down the furrows with a princess's sensitivity and disposition to minor maladies. For me, this has crossed a technological line into something quite overwhelming and even a bit alienating. This is not the stuff of a small farm. The equipment you generally find lying about small farms has (a) probably been lying about for no inconsiderable time, and (b) may well have been purchased in a similarly shunned and modest condition. Small farms are modest, gerry-built. You're more apt to find wood than iron, on the pithy assumption that any fool can nail two pieces of pine together with the objective of effecting a stockade of sorts. Nothing looks really impregnable, but then the animals, too, generally have a less harassed air about them due to more liberal confinement systems and more relaxed routines.

On small farms, hay gets stacked in the barns neither with houndstooth precision nor to fantastic height. It has to be accessible. It can't soar to the rafters screaming out for an elaborate fire control system. The tractor ("It's somewhere outside, isn't it?") is a spindly-looking thing. Its skinny wheels sport no colorful hubcaps. It has no interior cab. From certain angles you can see through the engine to the corn fields beyond. When in action, with spiky attachments pinned to the rear axle, it rolls over the sod doing exactly what its high-tech cousins do—

ploughing, harrowing, cultivating, tilling, seeding, harvesting, whatever.

I tend to think that, whether you own a dinosaur Deere or the latest digitalized Dolby stereo tractor with all the works, farming is pretty much the same old job it always was. Until we finally move the planted acre into the laboratory and replace soil as the growing medium with agar gel in petri dishes, the farmer's job and struggles will continue to maintain their antique profile.

I once tried to convince an acquaintance that agriculture was fated to remain singularly embedded in its ancient roots; that one needs land, that ploughing, cultivating, seeding, and harvesting were the unavoidable staples of the trade.

This woman worked for an automobile-industry chemicals import firm. She didn't go along with that, she said. Farming, she felt, was no less modernized than any other business.

I said, the tools and machinery were updated, certainly, but the anatomy of the relationship of farmer to land and to nature was still quite unassuming, simple.

No way, she said. The farmer is a modern businessman with the constraints of all beltway businesses. He worries about things like Communism just like everyone else. He's got a telephone tie-up with the Chicago Board of Trade.

They don't trade lettuce on the CBOT, I murmured.

She added, Anyone can farm today, if they can read the label on fertilizer packages and drive a car. Actually, tractors are easier to drive than cars. It does make the point though. I mean, forget about seeds; the modern farmer is just another guy down the food chain that knows his income is somehow dependent on petroleum prices.

I thought, Yeah, just like a woman who fills out customs applications so that a car mechanic in Idaho can repaint a Honda four-door sedan with a chemically formulated tint of red that kills all life forms it inadvertently touches.

I said, These big guys can mechanize and computerize until

the whole world runs off one megabyte, but someone still has to plough up the dirt, drop an appropriate seed in it, react to rain, react to no more rain, and harvest at the right time.

If they can send monkeys into space, she said, they can teach monkeys to plough a field. I know. I've been to EPCOT.

6

Drugs and
Felicitous Bugs

One of the first questions people ask me when I mention my interest in starting a farm is: will I use chemicals? This line, delivered in varying intonations with raised eyebrows and miens of horror and condemnation, invariably leaves me flustered. I want to respond: Look, wait, this is a complicated subject and if you really want an answer, I'll need to back up a minute and give you some background and balance out your eminently evident predisposition. But usually I just say, gently, "I might."

Anyone who has ever had a garden, or tried to cultivate flowers, fruits, or vegetables, knows the agony of watching the foliage turn crusty brown, the leaves become lacy with holes, the stalks droop, the buds rot, the plants forcibly transposed from your own property to that of a robust colony of oddly striped beetles. You can be overwhelmed by a feeling of helplessness and gloom. It is with this in mind, that I muster a good deal of empathy for crop farmers in their impasses with insect, weed, and mineral depredations. I can see them reaching for their proverbial guns—and for the farmer, this refers to a virtual armory of undiluted chemical canisters stockpiled in the barn. Likewise, for farmers who witness their livestock listless from disease or depleted by parasites, there is an obliging arsenal of chemical—medicinal, pharmaceutical—remedies dispensed by the major drug houses or local veterinarians.

In instances such as these, I see the rationale behind the development of agricultural chemicals in a succinctly positive light; as part of the effort to keep stock healthy and fields unscourged. But development didn't stop there—and these days little in life is restrained from its potential for inborn extremisms—and the farm chemical industry marched on at full tilt to mature into a highly specialized array of soil conditioners, pest-specific insecticides, prophylactic feed supplements, synthesized anabolic steroids, apple ripeners, etc. So when I think about agricultural chemicals in general, and when I think about using them on my own farm, I find a thousand points of hesitation flooding into my brain.

"You can't just stop using chemical inputs," said one rancher to me. "They're integral to all farming industries now. Take out the chemicals, and the whole structure of the cattle business and the grain business and the cabbage business, for that matter— it'll just fall apart."

This perspective seemed to me a mix of resignation and boast. It echoed the sentiments of the whole American agricultural establishment, which appears to be aggressively wed to its chemical inputs with little opportunity for negotiation. Production agriculture would indeed undergo substantial structural changes with the elimination or reduction of many chemical inputs, just as it underwent immense change with the arrival and infusion and bloom of those chemical inputs in the first place—in the 1950s, the 1960s, and beyond. Is change so threatening, I wondered?

"Yes," said my husband. "Unfortunately."

I believe that much of the national farm lobby has affixed itself to the status quo of modern agriculture. So, gainfully, have the chemical and pharmaceutical lobbies. These groups share an interest in maintaining the current structure of farming—the dependence on man-made inputs, the monoculture, the densities of livestock feedlots—and they have become as expert in the art of politics as in the science of agriculture. They have given Congress and the American people a sense that there is no in-between—chemicals or no chemicals. But of course, there is an in-between, a kind of demilitarized zone of moderation that awaits some management and vision.

"Monarchies have their alluring aspects," my husband grinned at me as I was bristling about the poor agricultural leadership in America. "You could certainly effect change more quickly as a queen."

But could I, in fact? First, could I actually effect material changes in agriculture if granted monarchical powers for a period; and second, what would I try to change if I had the chance? The first question I quickly sized up as a philosophical morass. Having read Zhores Medvedev's book *Soviet Agriculture* (W. W. Norton, 1987), I did have the feeling that, though policies might change, peoples don't. So essentially, I didn't think that, even with a brief stint as agricultural potentate, I could execute or secure major changes in America's farm economy.

"Italy will always be anarchical," a friend once said to me, "and that's part of why it's so wonderful."

And Americans will likely cavort within the same capitalist, self-enriching ethic that arrived on the *Niña,* the *Pinta* and the *Santa Maria,* and which the authors of *The Federalist Papers* tried to rein in. So while I would hanker for the chance to revise a few of our agricultural policies—the crop price support programs or the antiquated milk pricing systems—I have a sense that the American pursuit of wealth and security would ultimately prevail. I could imagine the unfolding of events: I would cut one program, take a little of the federal welfare system out of agriculture, say, and immediately the congressional bureaucracy would well up around me with new, compensating legislation and support mechanisms, and wash away, like the waves, any hole I had dug in the sand.

As for the second question, about exactly what I would try to change, I think I would focus on the issue of chemical inputs to production agriculture. Here is where our American liberalism, in my mind, has given way to some serious abuses. Samuel Johnson once said: "Man's chief merit consists in resisting the impulses of his nature." I believe that when it came to farm chemicals, Americans did not resist the impulses of their natures. Chemical use in production agriculture has been excessive. I don't know anyone who would dispute it.

I telephoned my sister the doctor.

"Do you really wash all your fruit?" I asked with a whine that no doubt betrayed my own lethargic attitude.

"Yes," she said dogmatically.

"But is that enough then? Not all the chemicals are on the outside, you know. They get inside, too."

"Oh!" she sighed, tired from a day of hospital rounds. "Don't bother me with the details."

She said, "Are you reading those books again? Don't. It'll paralyze you."

My sister had spent a few years running a public health clinic in Osceola, Arkansas, on the bank of the Mississippi River. She lived in the midst of soybean country—in fact, one of America's biggest margarine moguls lived right down the street. My sister remembered vividly the many times she dealt with crop chemical emergencies.

"One day," she said, "they rushed an old man into my clinic who was driving down the main road while the farmers were all out in their yellow crop-dusting planes. He opened his window, he said, to get the bad smell out of the car. Heart attack. We have him in the intensive care unit for a week. He gets out of the hospital, he's driving down the main road again, this time on his way home—another plane. Smells bad. He opens his window. Heart attack.

"Apart from that, we got people all the time with their hands burned up from chemicals, funny cancers, kids with acute leukemia, families vomiting for days because they ate vegetables from their own gardens. . . . Nice business, these farm chemicals. Nobody needs to bother with a gun when you can buy poison at the supermarket."

She added, "So wash your fruit and vegetables."

Some days it seemed like the healthy tinge was draining out of farming as through a sieve. I never imagined having a farm that was large enough to warrant aerial dustings of pesticides or defoliants, but I hadn't completely ruled out the application of specific chemicals in my cropping, either.

"Just as a for-instance," I said to my sister, "getting away from the food angle. Supposing I had a farm, and supposing I were professionally trained to apply certain agricultural chemicals like pesticides, say, and supposing I wake up one day to this apocalyptic mealyworm infestation—don't you think it would be worth the risk to go out and spray? I mean, are the risks so high?"

"Yup."

This was sobering news indeed.

•

My husband is the ingredient-reader of the family. It's worthwhile not taking him to the drugstore. He's apt to stop dead in the aisle, somewhere between bunion remedies and shaving creams, his jaw dropped, reading the ingredients of my shampoo. It is mortifying.

I'll say, "Okay, okay, let's get along."

"I've only gotten through the nonactive ingredients," he will mumble, in shock.

I say, "Look, all shampoos are composed of the same stuff. People buy one or another for the scent."

He doesn't hear me. His head is shaking. This has deeply disturbed him. He looks down at his hands.

"I can't believe they haven't dissolved," he will whisper.

We live with an extraordinary amount of chemicals in our

day—on our scalp, in our food. I would rather not farm with chemicals, although I sometimes wonder, with today's apple and potato varieties, whether that's possible. So many fruits and vegetables have been bred to complement certain herbicides and pesticides.

My husband and I believe in a sustainable agriculture. We believe this world flirts with ever-larger Malthusian correctives, and we also think a farm run sensibly (in our mind, ethically), without a substantial chemical dependency, will be a satisfying challenge. Further, we will have the experiences of the last couple of decades to draw on in determining which methods of cultivation and irrigation are most successful, which grains provide how much protein, and what kinds of chemicals are least toxic, most effective, most readily applied, and so forth.

When I have spoken to farmers about circulating proposals for "environmentally friendly" agricultural practices, they have often responded contemptuously or defensively. Many felt assaulted by the first wave of environmentalist fervor rather than courted by the kinder, gentler, and potentially profitable new methods of operation. Many, in their tucked flannel shirts and chemical-company-issue baseball caps, felt they were being preached to by a body of environmentalists, Native Americans, and first-time East Coast mothers. What did this coalition know about farm economics? And that describes in good part the controversy. Proponents of chemical-free agriculture are battling for chemical-free food. Farmers are battling for their livelihood. You can't win arguments when you're arguing about different issues.

I don't side with the farmers necessarily. I, too, like my food to arrive without warning labels. But there's a particular facet of the farmer-chemical subject that piques my interest. It's little discussed because there's essentially no such profession as agrosociology. And thank goodness.

I think that what wedded farmers to farm chemicals (apart from the latter's effectiveness, convenience, and economics) was that chemicals affirmed them as members of a modern-age professional culture. The people from Dow and Dupont and Monsanto gave farmers a new kind of stature, addressed them like honorary scientists, distinguished them in new four-color trade journals, scooped them up from the dusts of Oklahoma and posited them in the ranks of mutual fund stockholders—the au courant of today's financial bystanders. Computer technologies, following on the heels of the chemical revolution, plopped fittingly into this new professional lap.

It's a question of image, which for most people runs deeper than rationale. As for me, I shirk this image of the modern farmer. I don't want to feel a kinship with everyone who chooses office work and watches reruns of "Dallas." I prefer windows that open, heat in summer, and cold in winter. If farm chemicals were my bridge to the corporate experience, I would definitely turn them down. Even so, I have a compassion for the other side, the desire of the erstwhile Okie to reach for a higher stature.

How alike we will all soon become, I sometimes think.

So, there will be little or no chemicals on my farm. I shall try to be clever and resourceful. We have read up a lot on integrated pest management (IPM) principles, whereby benchmarks of infestations must be reached before any retaliatory action is needed. I'll couple this with crop rotations—corn one year, for example, barley the next, carrots the next, and back to corn. Crop rotation prevents the entrenchment of pests particularly keen on certain crops. It is a simple strategy and it's even suggested for your backyard garden. The experts will tell you: Never never plant your broccoli in the same place in consecutive years.

I'm also keeping informed about the positive and time-tested results from "biological controls." Biological control piggybacks on nature's own habits of predation. But who do you call? I wonder. No one is listed in the yellow pages under "Sale and Spraying of Sterilized Male Cutworms," or "Procurement of Suppressing Bugs and Natural Enemies." Moreover, there are a few biological remedies I would like to be protected from myself—blackflies, for instance, and I don't care if they are partial to aphids.

In New England, many rural properties are equipped with bat houses because bats adore eating mosquitoes and don't bother people, much. One Connecticut farmer I met kept a flock of guinea hens on his land because he said they ate the ticks that carried Lyme Disease. These control systems may have a limited efficacy. They may also have their charmless repercussions. Too many bats hanging around, so to speak. Too many fat black flies for your liking. Too many frogs once the flies are gone, and so forth. Keep the cycle going, and you'll recreate the plagues of Job in your own backyard.

•

The conspicuous alternative to using agricultural chemicals, in a black and white world, is to farm organically. No broadly accepted definitions exist in the trade to help the budding farmer understand exactly what categorizes certifiably organic practices. Facing this void, I have felt the best thing to do as part of my investigation was to speak with organic farmers and nonorganic farmers, and to clarify my own sentiment regarding organic and nonorganic food. Food is, for many people, the conclusive issue.

"I dun like the extra chores," said one organic farmer from Pennsylvania to me. "But I cannuh eat ta other."

The term "organic farming" encompasses a set of crop and animal husbandry practices that rely on naturally occurring inputs to production (no man-made chemicals), and that seem to emphasize the replenishment of the soil in an ecologically sound way. Composting, mulching, and the use of natural fertilizers, herbicides, insecticides, and fungicides, are considered the three fundamental and interrelated building blocks of organic farming. When organic farmers need to apply nitrogen to their soils, they look to such mineral-rich sources as blood meal, cottonseed meal, fish meal, and manure. They may mulch the ground between crop rows with newspaper or wood chips to suppress weed growth, or they may hoe. Wood ash, they know, will supply their soil with needed potassium. Marigolds, with varying degrees of reliability, are expected to deflect nematodes, and so on.

Organic farming suits people who feel a particular way about their land and their food. It puts farmers in closer touch with the spontaneous regeneration of their soil, the palpable vitality of their foliage, or the natural resilience of their animals. These farmers choose to work very intimately with the natural cycles and paces of their plants and livestock. They try to find within nature the nourishment or predatory checks that keep a barnyard healthy. This approach is philosophically at odds with the methods of most modern, larger-scale nonorganic farmers, who customarily depend upon the efficacy of chemical inputs to provide their soils with vital nutrients, their plants with blanket protection, and their animals with boosted vigor. Moreover, nonorganic farmers I have visited tend to maintain that corn is corn, meat is meat, and food is food is food. Organic farmers, alternatively, seem to look more dotingly on their produce, to encounter within each orange or zucchini the miraculous universe of the aboriginal seed. There is a sense of pride among many organic farmers I have met, that their yields are derived without artificial means. Does organic produce truly taste better than nonorganic produce, or even different? Is it worth the typically higher cost? These are among the fiercely disputed controversies of the field.

A couple of years ago, I had the opportunity to visit with a celebrated chef from the Plaza Hotel at a luncheon that featured only natural, or organic, foods. He looked up at me from some delicately seasoned flageolets and said, "You know, the problem I have with this organic food stuff is that only the rich can afford it."

Everyone at our table looked down at his or her plate. Yes, there was an all-organic spinach pasta at five times the price of a regular box of durum noodles. It was coiled attractively next to a portion of pond-raised salmon flown in, we were told, from Washington State's "spring-pure" waters at a cost that would make one faint. The meal was to be accented with a champagne from vines untouched by human chemicals, and a salad of miniature vegetables adoringly sprouted without the aide of fertilizers, pesticides, fungicides, or other zesty toxins.

As we nibbled appreciatively on this kingly fare, we were treated to "a few words" from more than a few people in the organic food industry. We might have to pay a little extra, they told us, but natural, chemical-free foods were worth it. They were better for the environment and better for us. They were going to become, these spokesmen said, the new gourmet foods of America. The Plaza chef turned to me.

"Bean sprouts of the rich and famous," he said with some derision.

America spends less of its income on food than any other country in the world. Our food is cheap—that's always been the goal of the USDA—and its quality ranks among the highest anywhere. Things were pretty dandy until the 1980s, when our intensifying national preoccupation with health and diet induced us to make top-gun scientists of nutritionists and other food interpreters. Immediately, eggs went down in a blaze of fat and cholesterol. Beef was crippled by early allegations of its intimate association with heart attacks. Pesticide residues, it seemed, were turning up by the teaspoonful on every green leaf and grape. It was like a period of McCarthyism in the supermarket, only the villain this time was not Communism, but rather our country's mainstream agricultural dogma. In the midst of this fever, organic farming logically thrived.

It was a new generation of organics this time, however, a shade more sophisticated than the 1970s variety. Natural food stores turned into hot properties. They became chic, well-lit, well-stocked, and staffed by clean and knowledgeable clerks. This time around, organic foods were very à la mode. Blood oranges replaced regular oranges. Purple peppers replaced the traditional green ones. Such a trendy approach to food retailing appealed to new audiences, particularly to young and affluent professionals who had become even more discriminating about their intake and bored with the usual fare. Why eat green beans, after all, when you can simmer those diamond-hard little flageolets for six hours?

Meanwhile, the news media inundated our television screens and nonrecycled front pages with stories of environmental damage done to natural resources by agricultural enterprises. A dirge was sung for the Chesapeake Bay. Cattle relieving themselves of gas, discreetly or not, were indicted for furthering the destruction of the earth's protective ozone. We were all encouraged to "eat natural," but the truth was, we couldn't all afford it. Food stamps, for instance, don't go a long way on organic fruits and vegetables. So some people worried about whether we had essentially relegated low-income populations to low-quality food.

I don't think so. The American food supply—organic and nonorganic together—continues to rank in a category of premium quality. Chemical use is stringently regulated in this country, in spite of exaggeration to the contrary. Furthermore, it's highly unregulated in most developing populations throughout the world (to whom we continue to export our most lethal agricultural toxins, and from whom we continue to import produce; so, well, okay). Many agricultural specialists believe that it was because chemical use could not be sufficiently policed in Europe that the EEC banned used of livestock hormones altogether.

America's poor, through welfare programs designed to maximize their independence, are in fact in a position to consume high-value foods—breads, pastas, vegetables, fruits, milk, cheese, poultry, and so on. I gather, however, that food stamp purchases persistently reflect preferences for low-value foods—potato chips, candy, soda—and for foods that are relatively expensive: frozen dinners, for example, or precooked canned entrées and side dishes. This leads me to believe that lousy nutrition among America's lower classes is not simply a failing of food stamps or a problem of poor-quality foodstuffs, but rather a more profound issue involving education, employment, and our welfare system.

All said, the chef from the Plaza had a valid point. Organic food is considerably more expensive than nonorganic food— largely because it costs more to produce. It requires more labor, as it did in the old days, to cultivate one's organic furrow. It takes more time to check for and do battle with insects, and people are less efficient than aerial dustings of poison in dispatching bugs or weeds. Moreover, organic methods often yield less per acre than pumped-up, super-fertilized vegetables or correspondingly pumped-up, super-fed animals.

Organic farms also sacrifice many of the conveniences of large-scale nonorganic farming. For instance, because insects will prosper in the monoculture of vast, single-cropped acreage, organic farms seem to manage best if the terrain is divided into relatively small plots, perhaps only one-quarter acre in size, with crops interspersed among one another, and with all crops rotated year after year. This tends to render impractical most modern farm equipment, whose complex systems of adjustment and navigation become extremely clumsy in the compact and diverse plots. Some experimental technologies are currently emerging to allow for large-scale organic monoculture. These have included: the industrial vacuuming of insects from crop rows; searing fields with tightly controlled flame jets just above plant height; and crop dusting with hoppers full of good bugs ready to eat the bad bugs. Such new technologies are gradually being refined, but may still suffer the disadvantages of high energy cost, ground compaction, the inadvertent decimation of good as well as bad bugs—not to mention an occasional charring of the foliage.

"What's your view on organic produce?" I asked my father.

"Well, I think I do prefer the idea of organic," he said. "On the other hand, I realize it's sometimes impractical. Sometimes soils are so depleted that I expect you need to use chemical supplements to regenerate them. As for taste or cooking, I can't tell the difference."

A lot of the small farms in the Northampton area, farms whose stands now form the bulk of my father's Saturday morning farmers' market, are organic. When I shop with him, I notice that all the farmers are young, as though it's a whole new generation taking up and redefining the region's agriculture. It is heartening to see younger farmers at all these days—one of our nation's most serious agricultural concerns is that the majority of our farmers are nearing retirement, with only a meager legion of younger farmers ready to succeed them. Indeed, this void has in itself contributed to a quicker pace of decline in farm numbers. Elderly farmers, seeing no interested successor emerge from either their families or their communities, have more readily accepted buyout offers from real estate developers and government production-reduction programs, such as the 1985 Farm Bill's dairy herd buyout.

"I'm thinking back a minute," said my father. "I think I was first introduced to the idea of organic farms when we lived in Stockbridge in the 1950s. A woman next door came over one day and gave us a puppy. She insisted that we only feed it milk from an organic dairy farm across the border in New York State. Well, we thought she was just crazy."

"Crazy?" said an organic dairy farmer to whom I related this story. "Well, he was probably right. She probably was. And me, too. You gotta be nuts to go into the milk business, and completely wacko to do it organically." Which he himself had done. "Well, I did. And the reason being," he said, "because my wife here wants to sell organic veal. And I'll tell you, you can get a fine premium for organic veal in the markets now, but you canna get nothing fine for organic milk—in fact, I think folks shy away from organic milk a little to tell you the truth. I think when it comes to milk, folks prefer their cartons extra-bleached-out white, double and triple homogenized, if you catch my meaning.

"So I say, okay, to my wife, then I'm gonna hafta make this a kosher dairy, acause organic alone wull not pay me for my troubles. Rabbis in black nightgowns and the whole nine yards. And she just looked at me, jaw-dropped and all. And then she said, okay. And you can get a mighty fair premium for kosher milk nowadays, us being next to the New York City markets especially. We allays got a couple of rabbis living up in that trailer on the hill, and they're nice enough folk. Not too talkative, if I may say."

This farmer told me the biggest obstacle he faced in going organic was raising and procuring organic feeds for his dairy cattle. The first couple of years without chemicals, his pasture was poorer. His cost for supplemental organic feed corn was over thirty percent higher than in earlier years, before the switch to organic. He had to hire two extra men part-time to help him with the chores, because without the facility of chemicals, plant and animal health required more personally involved care. His bill for fertilizers, pesticides and herbicides, however, had dropped to nil.

"It's a funny thing," he said. "In the beginning I thought, by God, I'll never last. I wull lose this farm. But. It dunna whork that way finally. It whorks out fine. Ya couldn't pay me enough to go back to chemicals."

Some people seem to think that a lot of farmers switch to organic simply to capture the financial premiums accorded to all-natural produce, but I think it's clear that the extra hard work involved in organic farming would push to the limits anybody's endurance, patience, and greed. In many ways, "going organic" is going back to the early, labor-intensive practices of farming. It means you gather, haul, and spread that wet, stinky, heavy manure on your fields instead of reaching for the handy dusting gun. It means you get the hoe out, and not the blue canister of herbicide (anyone who has hoed knows well the tedium and muscle strain that herbicides promise to relieve). And for some people, going organic means you sell that eight-year-old Deere tractor and buy, for more money than that Deere netted you, a pair of Norwegian fjord draught horses plus the hardly run-of-the-mill paraphernalia that correctly links them with any farm equipment—harrow, plough, etc. After all, if you intend to farm organically, doesn't it imply that tractors are out? Wouldn't the exhaust and inevitable oil drips nullify your otherwise impeccably noncontaminating methods? The jury is out.

"I could envision using draught horses on the farm instead of a tractor," I mused one day to my husband.

"That's an interesting idea," he said.

Then he said, "You know, they're pretty big animals."

"You think they would be too expensive to feed?" I asked.

"I mean big—tall," he said. "A lot taller than you. Do you think you could sling the reins and yoke and everything over their heads?"

"It might take some doing," I smiled. "They'll have to be very good-natured. Do horses have senses of humor?"

On a small-scale farm, I think I would enjoy using draught horses at least some of the time, regardless of whether I farmed strictly organically or not. It would be a part of the pleasure of farming—part of the pure pleasure and part (remember that tractors are the alternative) of the quiet. There are other aspects of organic agriculture that strike me as definitely less agreeable. Among the worst is having to endear yourself to a host of insects. All farmers need some smattering of basic entomology in order to distinguish the good bugs of the farm world from the bad. Organic farmers, however, commonly cultivate populations of preferred bugs in order to obliterate (naturally) a menacing community of the bad. There are hoards of books and a few magazines that can help to guide you in this effort—not to mention the brink-of-extinction breed of County Extension Agents whose entomological colleagues are ably trained to provide assistance—but literature may be far less appealing than insecticides when you notice a blushing infestation of ravenous beetles shredding your tomato field.

For me, a prospective farmer with an environmentally conscientious nature, one of the biggest obstacles to organic farming has always been the proponents—the holier-than-thou or overly folksy timbre of their literature and arguments. I once bought my husband a subscription to *Organic Gardening* magazine, and the manner of many articles irritated us even when the information was useful. One article, a "Guide to Beneficial Insects" (May/June 1991), began with this childlike dramatization:

> The aphid with the amazing appetite may have finally run out of luck. A delicate green lacewing and its ugly, ravenous larva seem to be glancing in its direction!
>
> No, the larva is either unseeing or full, and the pretty parent is flying away on those glistening emerald wings. The aphid begins to let out a tiny bug sigh, but stops as an even more tenacious foe, the armored ladybug, hovers into view!
>
> In a blind panic, the aphid scampers away as quickly as its stubby little bug legs will carry it. Just a little further, it thinks, and it will be safely hidden . . .

Exclamation points and tiny bug sighs aside, I just don't like being talked to that way. I support organic agriculture but I don't identify in the least with the readers and writers of that magazine.

The above-threatened aphid, after an extended and melodramatic flight, bought it, as they say—"*CHOMP!*"—which is from my perspective a positive ending for the story, although it doesn't quite work the magic of making me disposed to buy cartons full of praying mantis eggs and predatory thrips—the militialike insecticides of the organic farmer. I would hasten to add, moreover, that a good thrip in the eyes of one farmer may be a threat to the crops of another farmer. This kind of complication is not what I would want to cultivate on my small farm.

I once worked alongside a young woman who was an ardent organic gardener, and she found enchantment in hatching lady-bugs (widely considered good bugs) and sprinkling diatomaceous earth on her plot of summer vegetables.

Diatomaceous earth, she explained to me, was a fine dust made from the shells of millennia-old one-celled diatoms. Insects and worms ingest it, and its silica structure wreaks havoc on their respiratory and digestive systems, ripping up their miniature internal tracts and at least maiming if not killing them. The image was enough to make me side with the bugs. I wondered if someone had told the animal rights' people about this all-natural powder.

"Very effective," the woman said, nodding her head knowingly.

"It sounds it," I grinned. "No skull and crossbones on the side of the jar?"

What's a nice girl like you doing savaging these bugs? I thought.

·

I had heard that diatomaceous earth and bug therapies have been successfully used on organic farms of considerable size, but I wasn't sure that I could wholly embrace this kind of agriculture myself. I went to visit an organic farmer near Salisbury, Connecticut, in the northwest corner of the state ("It's not hard to find; you'll see a fork in the road, take that left, keep driving till you see a green barn—that's ours . . ."), to learn about his methods and their proficiency.

"Fine, glad to have you come by," he had said over the telephone. "We just got recertified by the team from Cornell, so we're in good spirits here, too."

This was a gorgeous old farm, nestled in the bottomlands of a Berkshire foothills valley. It had belonged to the family of this man's in-laws for hundreds of years, and he had finally left his job as a science professor to farm it himself. Organic farms don't look different than nonorganic farms. I pulled up to the usual sights: an old barn painted green and hankering for some simple repairs, a couple of tractors left to rust outside, tires flung about, layers of cobwebs like cottony felt across the chicken wire of a small chicken coop, broken stairs leading to the lower floor of the barn, small paddocks of curious geometries, and the smell of fresh manure. Mr. Keats walked out of the darkness of the barn to greet me. He wore a bandanna over his head, and on top of that a straw hat. It was a hot summer day, but even in trousers and a long-sleeved shirt he seemed to be staying cool.

"Hello there," he said, holding out his hand for a warm handshake. "Keats. Glad to meet you. I'm afraid I don't have too much time today. We've got to get haying, you know, but let me show you around a bit."

We walked into his barn. It was built on a small hillside so that, depending on the direction you were coming from, there was a ground-level entrance into one of two floors. From the street side, we entered the main chamber of the barn. A tractor sat idle in the shadows. A table with a picnic cooler stood by the door and a cardboard sign leaned against the cooler indicating fresh eggs inside for sale: "Please leave one dollar per dozen." A chicken coop had been built into the far corner, and the resident hens and ducks intensified their workaday pandemonium in response to my unannounced appearance. Keats showed me a well-charged electric wire he had strung at the foot of the coop's fence.

"I was forced to," he said. "Have you ever dealt with raccoons? They are unbelievably persistent—I am tempted to say astute. Every night, it seemed, they would get into my coop and make off with a few birds. I would come in the morning and find holes cut in the wire—in the *wire*—or barn boards wrenched up just enough to let them in. No fence was high enough. They were single-handedly destroying my barn. And I'll tell you something else: Raccoons are not nice to find. You don't actually want to catch them red-handed unless you're good with a gun, which I'm not, but I'm getting there."

He kicked the wire and a sizeable spark jumped out.

"This works all right," he said. "It doesn't kill anybody, but it's a discouraging shot. Watch yourself down these steps," he said, and he led us down to the dark and cool lower level where he kept his cattle.

There was great variety down there. Guernsey. Hereford. Jersey. A Scotch Highland steer. A few pigs. Two new Holstein calves. A young Angus bull. The bull immediately sauntered over to us and I really felt the hairs on the back of my neck tingle. I tried to hide my terror but it must have been plain in my facial contortions.

"Don't be frightened," Keats smiled, scratching the furry black forehead of this stout bull. A short chain hung down from the bull's nose ring and swayed as the animal nuzzled Keats's side. "I raised this fellow myself, from the bottle up. It's a myth that you can't leave bulls loose, can't enjoy them this way. People just treat them so poorly—then they end up with a nasty-tempered animal. It's no surprise. It's the same with human beings."

We walked past his pig pens. I could hear the jingle of the nose ring and chain following behind us. I was so busy trying to pretend I didn't that I don't remember a thing about Keats's pigs. I think they were mostly pink Yorkshires, big and with erect ears. And there was one spotted Poland China, a smaller pig with black and gray spots on a white hide. We parted from the jingle by dint of a charged wire fence and entered an area of the lower barn that Keats had earmarked for grain and silage storage.

"Now here's a good illustration of farm life," he said. "I'm no wizard. When I decided to make my own silage I bought a few books, took it all in, tried it out—nothing. Rotten, over-fermented nothing. So I experimented for a few years with more or less moisture, different ingredients, until I got a good mixture for myself. My mix probably wouldn't work well for the next fellow, but it's perfect here. Now I don't even think about it.

"Farming's not so hard. There aren't any mysteries. You have to blunder through this or that aspect, but then you don't again. I've got lousy land here," he waved toward the valley beyond the barn. "We flood almost every year. It looks beautiful today because we're in the midst of a terrific drought, but normally one-half of my land is a swamp." He smiled. "So you do what you can. You farm here and there. You switch varieties. You seed a new meadow. What's wonderful about farming is that it's open to your tailoring. No hard rules. You scrap along with new ideas, you buy another used tractor from another guy going out of the business, you find baby lambs on your doorstep one morning from the farmer down the road. The only hard piece of advice I have for you is not to run out and overcapitalize yourself. Start simple. Things come your way. A lot of farmers in this area will tell you the same thing—in all their years they've never bought a new tractor."

We walked outside and watched the Canadian geese wander freely through the cattle pasture picking undigested bits of corn from the manured ground. I realized that, for midsummer, Keats's black fly problem was very low. This piqued my interest, because I sometimes wonder whether black flies are the one central obstacle standing between me and my farm. I hate them.

"Nice of you to notice," Keats said when I mentioned the flies. "Well, we work at it. We keep moving our manure. We try to keep it dry, spread, less of a breeding ground. I used to buy traps but I haven't found a one that really solves the problem. I keep a few still in the barn, to relieve the animals. Me, I've gotten used to the flies at this level. But we have our house up on that hill across the valley, so we're fortunate not to live directly beside them. My wife would curse them in the house."

"Does your wife help on the farm?" I asked.

"No, she works in town, and she takes care of our daughter.

Taking care of our daughter is full-time work in itself," he laughed. "But she's a spinner, too, and a weaver, so she makes things from our wool—place mats, scarves—that we sometimes sell at the farmers' markets.

"Farming's a habitual life, but it's an individual thing—you make your own routines. It can be lonely, too, depending upon your impression of animals. I find great interest and amusement in animals, and I would say that after fighting in Vietnam, and after years of Peace Corps work in China, I find civilization a thin veneer. Human beings are not so far from other animals as we like to believe."

He looked up at me to see if I would be surprised, but I wasn't. I also think that "civilization" must be constantly aspired to, and that human beings come gutturally close to mimicking the brutality or pure dumbness of many other animals. Are the incidents of destructive ferocity between modern-day nations or tribes any less barbaric than intraspecies violence in the wild? Is there an animal that shows itself as small-minded and preening as America's Senate Judiciary Committee? (Just consider the Clarence Thomas Supreme Court nomination hearings.) When I am herded onto an airplane, am I shuffled forward with any more dignity than a cow?

"Livestock," I said to Keats, "at least don't have pretenses of a more genteel breeding. They're probably less introspective, but I don't find them less gracious than many people on the street."

Keats laughed. He said, "I find great satisfaction here." And he cast a long look across his valley, from the far hill where he kept sheep, to an old shade tree in the field under which several cattle were resting, and over to his brand-new towering navy blue silo that seems like a modern day badge of success for farmers nationwide. "Even in our toughest times, in the early days of righting this crumbling old farm, I found a great peace in the raw chores. In farming, your aspirations have to be within the chores themselves. You have to want to work with and be interested by the earth, when it's mud, when it's ice, when it's swamp, or when it's wildflowers. It's not nearly as comfortable or lucrative as my school job was. I sometimes have to remind my friends of that—these are people who earn hundreds of thousands of dollars every year in banking or business and who think my way of life seems somehow preferable. Well, it is preferable to me. But I don't think they'd like it very much, not at all.

"It's very humbling, farming is. You find there's not a lot a man can bring to it all, other than some management. Animals are pretty capable when it comes to taking care of themselves, and frankly, without us they'd probably have evolved into better specimens than they are today.

"A small farmer like me doesn't grow tired of the basic miracles of seeds and newborn calves. Sure, I get tired of waking up at three a.m. every Saturday morning to drive to the New York City farmers' market, but I don't get bored with my work here on the other days. I'm never indifferent to the growth of plants, the way hay dries, the interactions of these animals. A farmer sees miracles right in front of himself. I'm not religious, and I probably shouldn't use the word *miracle*—but farmers I know are just open to the wonderment of it all. It's nice, that, in such a jaded society."

I spent a couple of hours with Keats, who, I learned, had been a Harvard graduate within a distinguished family of "Princeton men" before settling on this old farm. It explained his eloquence, of course. And it ratified for me, in my own language, my own choice.

·

I had a close brush with organic agriculture when we lived in Connecticut. I took an opportunity to work for a small farm business that produced gourmet, specialty, all-natural organic meats—beef, primarily, but some chicken, too. It was a family operation, heavily subsidized by inherited family money and entirely run according to puzzling family ethics. The "husban-dry" was founded on a singular mixture of ancient Chinese nutritional theory, a handful of American Indian iconologies, and ultramodern computer systems. Unfortunately, while these unusual building blocks were always chatted up with a kind of conceit—the pride of knowing who among mankind was and is actually right about everything—they had never quite been put into service during the several years before I arrived, during my tenure there, or thereafter.

In the beginning I used to say to myself, "Well, some people are more patient than I when it comes to effecting their dreams." Later I grew more suspicious. It was an instructive if disheart-ening experience for me. The owner of this beef operation was terribly rich, and one might rightly suppose, "Ah, then you truly can afford to execute this elaborate plan, because the money it will cost is astounding." But sometimes it is the rich who have the most trouble making life real, realized.

The meat from this farm was organic and it was not. It was organic because the cattle and chickens were fed no medicated feeds, injected with no steroids, and otherwise cloistered from veterinary care. Indeed, these livestock were fattened on things like garlic, sweet potatoes, and dandelion greens—things it was difficult even to call fodder, livestock fodder. How much more natural can it get than to have cattle rely upon garlic bulbs for their unfailing health?

Well, in fact this operation was never and would never be certified organic by the prevailing self-appointed certifying bod-ies of the time, because the feeds used were not certified organic feeds. The sweet potatoes came waxed and dirty from the Car-olinas via the Bronx's notorious Hunt's Point Market. The garlic came from Chile, California, wherever. The other greens, a con-fidential composition of sure-to-surprise-you grasses and vege-tables and fruits, also came from regular market channels. This is taboo among organic circles, where feeds must be verified organic for the ultimate meat to be called organic.

For me, these lapses in orthodox organic statute are no major issue. I'm wishy-washy enough about most food-related fetishes that any faux pas committed along the extremist fringe don't rattle me. The meat from this farm was delicious, normally, if entirely inconsistent. And if the hay had been grown with fertilizers, it didn't matter to me. If the garlic came from South America, no problem. No problem for me, I should clarify, but once a severe problem for several hundred chickens. One truckload of particularly piquant Chilean garlic, I was told, devastated the combined intestines of the chicken coop for a week.

While I worked for this tiny beef company, I rubbed shoulders with organic enthusiasts and those who went along with the organic party line ("It's a job"). It was a community in which radical and emotional convictions about pure and unadulterated foods were the accepted cant. There was a kind of shrillness to the argument, I felt. It reminded me of being in a movie theatre: at first the sound system booms extremely loud, bites into you, and you think you will not last the whole film—and then you acclimate. After a few months of working in the organic foods realm, I became inured to the din of the partisan throng.

I had not just taken a job, however, I had bumped into a way of life, an ideology every bit as bullying as . . . as every other ideology. Everyone needed a water purifier (did I mean to drink bilge?), no one could eat veal (did I know where that came from?), and bodies were naturally temples. I was inundated with propaganda detailing the good, labyrinthine processes of organic food production versus the bad and less labyrinthine processes of our drug-addicted modern agriculture. One of the aspects I found most nettling was an underlying accusation that nonorganic farmers were lazier, always looking to take the easy route out with regard to everything from field tilth to plant yield to livestock viruses.

All told, I remain an ally of organic farmers, who, as it often happens, tend not to be themselves the kind of fringe activists that their industry lobbyists would have you believe. Fresh spirit was breathed into the organic food business at the end of the 1980s, and I think it has proven to be a healthy thing because it has brought new voices and persuasions into a fairly traditional industry. How far I take the organic principles on my own farm will only be determined over time. After all, I'm married to a man who maintains that the person who invented sour-cream-and-onion-flavored potato chips deserved a Nobel prize in chemistry. We are not witlessly chemical-averse.

My husband and I both believe in setting up a farm on a pragmatic basis and taking nonchemical measures as far as we reasonably can, but we don't want to sacrifice our crops and stock to the organic cause. We need to be coldly realistic—take in everybody's propaganda and vilify it all. We are loath to engage in chemical warfare against the ground and its bugs, out of the same subconscious aversion we have to taking pills—not a particularly reasoned response, but firmly felt. The hazards inherent in the application of insecticides, and our awareness that residues survive and survive in every clump of dirt or feeding trough, have gone a long way toward persuading us that some organic methods are worth a try.

We know a couple from New York City who grow apples espalier-style on their estate in Long Island. Well, it is the husband alone that cultivates the perfect tendrils and fruiting. Every weekend he can be found out on their Hamptons lawn, having molted his tailored suits, snipping and spraying away in a roomy coverall and work boots. He drags tanks, sacks, and spray-guns of chemicals happily between the rows of his leafing artistry, dousing the foliage much as one might retouch a painting. His wife, however, who worries for the health of their children and their two short-legged dogs, is threatening to buy a separate washing machine for the exclusive purpose of detoxifying his gardening clothes. She cannot bear the bags and canisters of fungicides, fertilizers, and pesticides that lie stacked in their garage.

"Can't you do this without chemicals?" she once asked him.

"Isn't there such a thing as organic espalier?" I piped up.

And he replied theatrically, as though quoting Shakespeare, "Nope."

I hope I am not so tied to the market basket of agricultural chemicals when I start my farm. Still, insect infestations and fungus spread may indeed pressure me into reconsideration. And where I do already and fervently see the need for a chemist's hand is in the occasional treatment of unhealthy animals—in pharmaceuticals. It is painful for me to think of orthodox organic farmers who stint on the comfort and treatment of their animals in sickness. I wouldn't play around with herbal remedies if a ewe or kid were taken ill. I would call the doctor.

"So," I said to my father one afternoon. He was busy tying the drooping limbs of his frail six-foot Japanese maple to the fence behind it. He had gotten a little discouraged when an itinerant goldfinch landed on one of the branches for a rest, and the branch had bowed, bowed, bowed down to the ground with this added weight. "A candidate for some injectable mineral pith-acceleration supplements?"

"Hmmm," he sighed. He seemed pretty demoralized. "Maybe I'll go to Agway and see what they've got. Does Agway have an emergency ward?"

"It's not that bad," I said. "It's adolescence, gawky adolescence."

"If you weren't around," he said, "I'd pull out my big guns."

"Big guns?"

"Japanese maple steroids," he teased.

"You've got me all wrong, Dad. I'm undecided on the organic orthodoxy. I'm trying to find out where the balance of sensibility lies. Who knows? I may be Miss Medicine Cabinet in the year 2000. I may have your Japanese maple hooked to an intravenous protein drip."

"Oh, I know that," he said. He did.

He mixed some Miracle Gro into a watering pail and splashed the base of the tree. The trunk was as thick as my wrist and my heart went out to him. What could be done? I would certainly not be so pious as to swear off fertilizers in the face of such a tree.

"So," I said. "Are you going to come over to the farm now and then and give my guys a shot of penicillin?"

"Natch," he said. He set down the watering pail. "And you, too."

Part Three

Tender

7

Orchards, Groves, and Furrows

If you take Route 66 out of Northampton, due west, you run quickly into farmland that has been converted into suburban neighborhoods. That must surely be the refrain of the 1990s—a mass lament for memories of open space and wilderness that we all still have and that our children will not know. I hope my children, when they are thirty, will be saying: "You know, Mom, that valley used to be filled with tasteless homes and swimming pools, and now it's all prairie." It sounds inane. It would only work, anyway, if I and everyone else *didn't have* children, if the population of our world were to shrink to sound numbers and humanity could take hold again.

Route 66 was piney, twisting, and exciting—so perceived from my ever-alert traffic control station in the backseat—for its steep hills. During the warmer months, my mother would pack us four girls, aged four to twelve, into the car and we would head out along the bumpy road for an expedition. Twenty minutes would get us to Clear Falls, a lovely lake that has since become private because of all the buses that began to turn up. Thirty minutes took us to Outlook Farm, where they used to grind up peanut butter as we watched and where fresh-cured hams and slabs of white bacon hung from the ceiling. (It's quite different now, since the USDA began cracking down on such homespun establishments; today Outlook Farm will sell you stinky potpourris and quaintly packaged jams from God knows where.) Forty minutes would find us at Lake Norwich, where we fished along the silty bottoms, baiting our stick-and-twine rods with scraps of yellow napkin. We used to catch little golden sunfish by the dozens, carefully liberating them from our hooks with a cautionary scolding not to fall for yellow napkins again. It was no doubt during these summers that I acquired my unlimited lack of respect for fish. And so, while aquaculture is nowadays an accepted segment of agriculture, you won't find mention of Tilapia fry tanks in any index of mine.

The first part of Route 66 was always the same. We passed woods, horses, cows, apple orchards, hay fields, and an old chicken house. We four nondrivers bounced up and down on the worn seat springs of the station wagon as we drove over the wells and dips of the pavement. We got to love the familiar sights along this road, our landmarks, ticking them off one by one, and announcing competitively which the next would be. The most harrowing part of the trip came when, after curling through the shadowy hollow of a pine grove, we would suddenly find ourselves hurtling downhill at a rate of thirty miles an hour toward a tiny stone bridge that we knew would only fit one station wagon. Ours. *Waaaaaah!* came the hysteria from the backseats. Did our mother want us all killed?

Sometimes I drove out with my mother to pick up my older sisters after their horseback riding lessons. The lessons were held in an old barn full of big cats with a fortunately benign disposition. I loved cats, and they seemed like especially good playmates for a four-year-old who was not much bigger than they when everybody was standing tall on two legs. It was never easy to chase one down, however; they must have had a different sense of what playing with me would be like. So I would usually get some assistance in the catching—one of the riding teachers would settle a miserable gray tom into my ready, affectionate hug—and I would take it for a walk to see the horses with my arms clasped tight around its shoulders, its front paws squeezed into a limp X in front of its face, its back legs dangling down to my red Mary Janes. Even today I remember those barn cats with both a child's happy zeal and an adult's apology. When I see a little child trying to cradle a cat or small dog, I am amazed at the animal's forgiving grit as its limbs are pulled and twisted and heartily reorganized to gain a better purchase. Cats must have very versatile stomach compartments.

One day, as we were driving out to the horse barn, my mother stopped the car by the roadside and stepped out. She smelled the air and smiled broadly.

"How would you like to pick strawberries?" she said to me.

Strawberries. What an adventure, I thought. Wouldn't I have something to tell my sisters. I bundled out of the car while my mother produced, magically, two bowls from our kitchen. From our kitchen! I thought, now this is really something dazzling. We walked up a small incline into a rolling meadow. The grass disappeared suddenly, no longer tickling my legs, and I looked down. Bright red tiny strawberries were bobbing everywhere under green leaves.

"Here's a bowl for you to put your berries in," said my mother. She spread out a blanket from the car. "Strawberries can be pretty prickly. If it stings, you can sit on this."

They were wild strawberries we picked—tiny, each the size of a little fingernail, growing like a dense ground cover, dark red and very sweet. The air was redolent with them, and with each breeze we would push up our noses to catch the full drift. My mother hummed Edith Piaf tunes.

"It smells like a peanut butter and jelly sandwich," I reported. "Only without the peanut butter."

"We are very lucky people," she would say to me between verses. She was not unwont to cite the impoverished curbsides of Rangoon on such occasions. And when I lost interest, having collected probably five or six sandy berries along with their malicious leaves and pinched them to juice en route between ground and pot, she would gather me in her lap and tell me about her summers in East Moriches—walking among the duck farms, the raucous quacking, the choppy sea of long, tall necks in an upward-swirling cloud of white feathers; or dressing up as Romans in the backyard, with bed sheets for agora wear, and long tendrils of grape vine from the arbor that spiraled down about the head and shoulders.

I have indeed been lucky to possess both my own memories of rural pleasures and some of my mother's. What a different world that was, that entertained not only an unlicensed patch of berries but also an ungoverned welcome for the chance passerby. The next time a similar experience came my way, I was thirty years old and astounded to find wild blackberry bushes pleading for disencumberment along a roadway—but that was in South America.

You can still pick strawberries and blueberries along Route 66 west of Northampton. It won't happen on a lark on a sunny Wednesday morning, but picking hours will be conveniently advertised in the *Daily Hampshire Gazette* when the fruits are ripe. You won't be alone, but there will be plenty of branches and bushes for everyone to denude. And you can't bring a bowl from your own kitchen unless you remember to stop in the proprietor's shack and get it weighed first.

This is the famous pick-your-own concept that has seemingly revolutionized New England's small fruit and vegetable operations, giving farmers the chance to keep planting without having to pay harvest-time labor. I always thought the idea would have holes. I have watched people eat their way through apple orchards and raspberry hedges. I have seen them try none too surreptitiously to shove beets back into the ground after they have pulled up a sphere not to their liking. I have found whole stalks of corn dragged to the ground in order that someone could reach that perfect ear at the top. Even so, say some farmers, it pays. And pick-your-own farms are beloved by today's consumers, if you can judge by the growing number of farms that offer the latitude.

"People just love—they just love to root around in the dirt," said one Connecticut farmer I spoke with. "They whip up here on weekends from New York City like they're gonna see the very last red tomato ever to go ripe on God's earth. They pull up our lettuces and say, 'My God! These things have roots too. I never knew a head of lettuce had roots. Look, Sarah.'

"Ah, well, there're always a few want to know if I'm growing organic or not. I used to say no, I don't, but I'm seventy-two and I been eating my own peas for over sixty years. Now I just tell 'em where the closest organic guy is, about a half hour east of here, and I watch 'em weigh out the extra miles against their organic principles, you know. Usually they sigh, real big. And then they look at me like I put 'em in a real tight spot—a rock and a hard place—and I should feel real, real bad. And then they ask for a picking box like I should beg 'em to take what they want for nothing. Oh! the way they will stare at you. I wanta say to these folks: 'Don't forget to scrub your tomatoes real good when you get home. I gotta lotta poison on 'em.' "

But pick-your-own is not for me, not for my farm. I don't want to deal with the cars, the families, the trampled produce, and the seeming frenzy to get more than you pay for—I don't want to watch it in my fields. On that basis alone, I may be ruling out tomatoes, bulk green peas, strawberries, and other crops that are demanding to harvest, but for me it's worth it. I can find crops that are more readily manageable from the standpoint of the harvester—me. That includes: pumpkins, lettuce, zucchini, beans, herbs, cabbage, leeks, and more. If I plant for private consumption plus a little extra for family and friends, then no fruit or vegetable is out of the question. If I expand to sell to local groceries or set up a farm stand, then some varietal sacrifices may have to be made.

My husband is more interested in the horticultural side of a small farm than I am right now. He would like to raise dwarf fruit trees—pear trees, above all. If possible, he would like dense hedges of raspberry and blackberry bushes to border the property. And then, behind the house perhaps, a wildflower meadow—not too big, not too small.

"You'd better be nice to me," I have told him, "or I'll let my goats and sheep loose in your wildflower meadow." This, I thought, had to be the ultimate threat.

"I see," he said. "That's fine. Just remember to fire up the grill for all the fresh kebabs we'll be eating at dinner that night."

A standoff.

He said, "We can call your farm Parchment in a Pear Tree."

Parchment, of course, comes from animal skins.

·

"To raise crops or not to raise crops," sighed a friend. "That's a good question. Whether 'tis better to have winter vacations, or no vacations at all—the latter being the livestock scenario, by the way."

"You make a persuasive argument," I said.

"Why wouldn't you at least start out with crops?" she asked. She was wearing one of those expressions of the Terminally Reasonable.

"Whether I raise crops or animals is not a question of how to get my feet wet in farming," I said. "It's a question of whether I want to plant plants, sell plants, and plant more plants, or raise animals."

"You don't need to hunt up a veterinarian for tomatoes."

"True."

"You won't need to fight the county's nuisance laws because of unbeloved barnyard noises and smells."

"True."

"And you do not have to castrate squash."

I could see she had been saving that last remark for her finale.

"Look," I said, "I fully intend to do some cropping. We're

even looking forward to it—the draught horse I'm going to get and I."

I have a feeling that many people think that if you have success growing basil (a virtual weed) in a comely ceramic pot from Tuscany, then you can start a farming operation. There is, however, a deviation well beyond the geometric multiplication of: more basil seeds, more water, more lovely painted pots. I'll leave the issue of greenhouses and a saturated market for pesto aside for the moment. Foremost in my thinking is to convey, or remind, that all life's pleasures and hobbies are transfigured when you approach them as a business, as a livelihood. A painter, when he has to sell his canvas to buy food, will necessarily approach a subject differently than when he paints for pure enjoyment and self-exploration. People who start a nursery enterprise because they have always loved red poinsettias at Christmas will be, and abruptly so, saluted by a series of business decisions that have nothing to do with whether a poinsettia looks better on the piano or mantelpiece. It is the same for me in agriculture. The closer I come toward making my first farm purchase, the more my eyes narrow, the more I discard that wonderment-of-it-all foliage and hone in on practical economic considerations. Observing that change has been an interesting experience for me. My pleasure in the field has been completely undiminished within this evolution—in fact, I think it has grown. For one thing, it has allowed me to entertain the concept of vegetable cropping with relish, as a business, far removed from the threatening delicacies of those African violets I encounter—potted irritability flung into the house around birthday time like haphazard galactic debris from the orbit of peripheral friends.

I smiled to my friend. "I'm just scouting out a few plant varieties that will withstand my supervision. I'm waiting until the biotech companies come up with a Nora-resistant carrot. The way I see things right now, as to a verdict on crops or livestock, the question of what to raise revolves around what will best pull through the first few years of my maladroit husbandry: Bump into a cow and she may grunt, but bump into a corn stalk and it's all over. I don't like those kinds of odds. I'm clumsy by nature."

"That's why you plant a lot of everything," she said.

Crop farming as opposed to raising livestock may suit a budding farmer for several reasons. Many people are intrinsically drawn to the aesthetic of orchards, groves, and fieldrows instead of hooves, snouts, and squawks. I certainly do mean to devote a few acres to a rotation of vegetables, and perchance some cantaloupes. Already my husband and I have sat down with clean pads and pens to design clever cropping schemes and to estimate our workload and expenses. It can be a fun exercise. The analysis involved in starting a small-scale cropping enterprise is relatively straightforward. The basic cost structure of planting is logical, and one can make rough calculations for each crop year. Figure what the cost of your overhead is: land, buildings, taxes. Add together the cost of your inputs: energy, seed, labor, fertilizers, insecticides, fungicides (diatomaceous earth, lady bugs, and whale oil soap for the organic vanguard). Include the cost of your equipment: tractor, planting and harvesting and hauling attachments, maybe a computer, too. A little Total Cost addition, followed by a little Price Per Unit division (long addition but not Long Division—ask your children) goes a long way toward sketching out the general financial landscape. This is true whether it is a pound of peppers or a box of Bing cherries that you would like to sell.

Will you be selling your produce as is, or processed? I would only be selling raw agricultural produce—a bean off the vine or a pear off you-know-whose tree. But there is definitely money to be made by making forays into further processing. I know several people who don't blanche at the idea of "putting up" tomatoes and peaches for the winter. "Some of my best friends make their own jam," I am tempted to sing, lying outright to assuage the fears of the novice. In fact, for me, the prospect of processing farm yields is a notion that automatically triggers panic sirens in my brain. Suddenly all I see are federal inspectors combing my kitchen and wiretapping the dishwasher, checking that the temperature is set on Jumbo High, that no breadcrumbs lurk under my counters, that I have magnificent pension funds and workers' compensation plans for all my employees, of which there are none. Visions of blank applications and misspelled form letters flicker before my eyes. It's an incurable reflex.

Most crop farmers I have met started out with a simple recipe for growing and harvesting their produce. For many, some level of processing did arise later, the conduit usually being a wife with a knack for chutneys, pies, or breads. It's only sensible to get comfortable with your crops—the level of quality and output—before stepping into the "value-added" arena, where, to be sure, profit lies.

An attractive element of small-farm cropping is the procurement issue. Seed comes through the mail, often pretreated for diseases and common predators (prepare yourself for chalk-pink cucumber seeds). Fertilizers and pesticides are readily obtained. Rudimentary tractors and ploughs are easy to come by, or you can buy yourself a couple of handsome draught horses—but then, plainly, you're tossed back into the livestock scene. No, stay with the used tractor and keep your arithmetic simple. Then if you have a truck, a strong back, and a penchant for doing battle with cutworms, you're practically there. If you find reward in stout leafy growth and soils that may whimsically turn to brick under the summer sun—don't hesitate any longer.

Economically speaking, to survive as a small-scale vegetable farmer these days, the key seems to be (paradoxically) consistency and diversity. Supermarkets demand the former; they prefer leek bunches of identical length and nectarines of identical configuration for easy stacking. Roadside shoppers prefer the latter; they like to pitch through a crate of variously apportioned onions for The One—The Onion that calls out for nothing less than an autobiography. As a new farmer, you would do well to single out your audience, wholesale (market) or retail (consumer), and build along one of those lines. If you have huge allotments of cultivable land, you may be able to enter both markets—but then your wholesale business, where consistency of supply is next to godliness, must become a priority.

I think I would like to start cropping on a very small scale and gradually build up to modest wholesaling only when I am very comfortable with or rather proud of my yields. As a crop farmer, I know I can look forward to: bickering over cheaper supermarket prices; throwing up my hands in the face of unpredictable weather and natural predators; and coping with unsympathetic wholesale buyers as well as with organic activists, if I choose not to become one, or with furious new and unfamiliar infestations, if I decide to farm without chemicals.

That's not too bad an agenda when you compare it with animal husbandry and its own distinctive tribulations. Where do I get hay anyway? Will this truckload of corn fit happily in our garage? Why do they lamb in the middle of the night? Who's going to slaughter my hens? Can you milk my herd while I'm in Paris? What are those pink larvae around the eyes? How do I camouflage these alps of manure?

Cropping can resonate like a thoroughly benign form of farming. When you feel overwhelmed by the multitude of diverse plagues circulating through your orchard and furrows, just imagine a barnful of ailing cows and pregnant goats. When, somewhere in between the depredations of deer and woodchucks, you begin to contemplate seriously the good to be derived from nuclear arms, check yourself, and go watch a sheep farmer trying to deworm his flock. You'll feel like you made the enlightened choice.

·

There are a lot of agricultural consultants jetting around the globe these days—squarely in the business of helping farmers and politicians make all sorts of agricultural choices. I had the opportunity to meet one of them in a posh office overlooking midtown Manhattan. He had just returned from a long stretch in Eastern Europe and was finding gainful self-employment by cautioning client companies not to invest there just at the moment.

"It's a funny thing," he said, taking a deep tug on his fat cigar, "most of consulting is just common sense. I was hired by the Agriculture Ministry in Poland—or whatever the hell they're now calling their agricultural *Zentrale*—to help them solve their overwhelming farm problems. The screaming started straightaway. They said, 'By God, we are sitting under an avalanche of potatoes. Our potato processing plants are working already to capacity making frozen potatoes, french fried potatoes, mashed potatoes, canned potato soup—for Poland and half of Europe. Our storage bins are full. Our export markets are saturated. The prices for our farmers are dropping every year. They are worrying us with talk of strike. Every year we have such a crisis,' they said. 'What should we do?'

"What should they do?" He stubbed out his cigar. "I said to them, 'Stop planting so goddamn many potatoes!' "

Polish farmers were, of course, fighting against more than their common sense. They were confronting years of poor farm policy, Communist coercion, and repression. It takes a longer time than the observer likes to admit for a country, or for that matter a person, to change a status quo or to think fresh, outside a set of boundaries that have become curiously comfortable even if not optimal, even if not hospitable. It will take a longer time than I think many people expect for the old East and West Germany to feel *confrères* within one collective Germany. It will take a long, long time for once-Communist countries to embrace democracy in any depth.

Individuals, like nations, also become wedded to situations that may not be progressive or beneficial for them. There is a lot of comfort to be taken in the familiarity of "the old ways."

Farming probably lends itself to this tendency more than many other professions. The work is habitual, seasonal, rhythmic, manual. Change must be inserted from the outside. It doesn't sit naturally in the table of contents.

The agricultural consultant I met took full credit for turning the attentions of Polish farmers toward other crops.

"It was incredibly tough," he explained. "Farmers want to plant this spring what they planted last spring. What is it with farmers?"

However, he added, he had managed to catalyze substantial crop diversification. The apple and apple juice industries, for instance, were expanded. Had I ever tasted Polish apple juice? he asked. Well, in fact I couldn't have because it has never been exported, and, he would have to be frank with me, there is no other apple juice in the world that comes close to Polish apple juice. It is nectar.

I had heard conflicting stories about farmers as "risk takers," farmers as flexible entrepreneurs, as ready to plant carrots as kohlrabi depending upon their soil and economic incentives. In China, it seemed that as soon as the government loosened its control over agricultural production, farmers in the country-side began to produce new, higher-value crops—celery, for instance—to capture the profits allowed through greater economic freedom of choice. In Russia, however, farmers have shown themselves fundamentally less inclined to alter cropping patterns in this revolutionary new era of disassembling and re-form. There is widespread skepticism that the new free-market systems will last. And for those entrepreneurs wanting to take advantage of the freedoms offered, there is no system to assist them; machinery, distribution networks, storage facilities, even roads are in disastrous disrepair. Lack of infrastructure is one reason, I've been told, why Russia's black market gardens, those borderline-illicit quarter-hectare backyard plots that spawned flourishing economies within other once-Communist countries, seemed always beleaguered and fruitless. Another reason was Russians.

Apart from cultural *mentalité* and market access, there is another central impasse that keeps a farmer or a whole country on a rigid diet of potatoes and cabbage, years after the Potato and Cabbage for All laws have been abolished. There are long time lags and unknown risks involved in transforming one's agriculture. Moving from crops into livestock is particularly formidable, since building up a herd is expensive and can take untold years of breeding. Simply switching from one crop to another is an undertaking. Deciphering the growth cycles of new plants is a major task, the more so when you have to take into consideration each ancillary insect, disease, and nutrient need of the unfamiliar biology.

A lot of people insist that farmers are sluggish in the flexibility and modernization department, and as an ardent generalizer myself, I'm reluctant to contest the matter. The fact is, maybe that's one of the things that draws me to farming—that vast plain of unbudgeable routine, that truly bovine, unrushable pattern of sowing, shearing, feeding, breeding, cutting, drying, wintering, fallowing. In farming, there is a rigid set of limitations governing one's versatility. Farmers can't move their land to a more desirable climate. They can't manipulate the rhythms of seasons nor forfend against freaky climatic extremes. Farmers don't switch sheep breeds as a consequence of what fashions sway down the Paris runways. They can't plant extra acres in corn so as to afford the new "must-have" Range Rover. They don't get paid extra for working late, and they call their own shots on sick days.

Friends of mine who have become eminently successful within the financial swirls of Wall Street are often the first to say they wish they could do what I am doing. They will sigh, feet on the desk, thumbs under the suspenders, eyes on the city traffic forty storeys below. They seem tired of having to keep up with society's glamorous, endless spewing of new trends. Tired but not released. Ah well, urbanity is a little addictive. I have watched these friends mark the seasons with changes of clothes and home decor. They adjust themselves continually and intemperately to keep up with modern times. They complain of being over-worked, constantly in demand. To relax, they mass in obscure seaside spas and have their eyelashes dyed. They rail about the fatuousness of other people's conversation, the emptiness of other people's lives. And then they file into therapy, one by one, to find out why they themselves feel so empty in spite of their pots of gold.

Perhaps I, too, will feel empty after years of farming. After all, farming is not *more* of a way of life compared to other professions. It's just different. I wonder often what will become of me as a farmer. I hope it isn't unrealistic to think about reading in the evenings, or writing. Limberness can gel. Will I become one of those inflexible, tied-to-her-eggplants farmers? Spinster-like qualities can creep into lives of unmitigated routine and worry. Will I make myself a relic after years of struggling to participate in society? Resenting the luxuries of other lives must have to be a possibility. I wonder. Will I long for a more monied lifestyle?

No. I don't think so. First of all, I have always found the status quo unsettling. It's not my strongest point, and I have a history of seeking out a steady daily routine and then deftly toppling it; but perhaps that will protect me from premature hardening of the brain synapses. Second, I could never become a recluse. Who would I talk to if I were a recluse? And third, I don't find today's wealth so glamorous or seductive. It seems to be concentrated in the hands of the classless. The affluent appear to me to be an unreflective, extravagant, and intellectually hollow lot. Just think about Nancy Reagan. Just look at the Trump clan. No thank you. The data is there. Money must surely pervert one. Besides, I never wanted a yacht.

"Although," said one of my sisters, "I think you might have been perfectly radiant as a rich and warring Medici."

It was true.

•

One summer I helped Cal, a farmer in Connecticut, plant his annual agenda of vegetables. Cal's foreman had disappeared suddenly after a drunken driving accident and left Cal short-handed in the middle of sowing season. When I joined him, he was preparing to transplant his tomatoes. He had grown three varieties of tomato in his greenhouses in the valley—Celebrity, Early Girl, and Beefsteak. By early June the seedlings were be-tween eight and twelve inches tall in their little peat pots, and it was time to move them out. The ground was warm enough. Tomatoes love warmth. "Summertime, and the fruiting is easy," they hum. But by June it gets so hot in a greenhouse that even tomatoes can feel a little sluggish, lose their stiff, upright pos-tures, and complain illustratively of suffocation.

The tomatoes had been started in peat pots arranged in flats, the ubiquitous plastic trays that nurserymen use to hold sets of flowers and lettuces and so forth for retail customers. They are maddening things. Nothing could be better suited to standard-ization than those flat, low-lipped, rectangular plastic trays for holding sets of smaller plastic boxes of seedlings for transplant. But are they? No. Every inspired American plastic tray manu-facturer wants to put his signature on the design. As a conse-quence, after every growing season gardeners and nurserymen alike wake up to topographical knolls on their property com-posed of hundreds of slightly uncomforming—flexible and non-flexible, grooved and nongrooved, this one too squared, that one too shallow—perfectly unstackable black, green, and gray flats. Simple in design, they seduce you with images of lavish practicality. It's hard to throw them out, although since they don't stack or fold they tend to take up inordinate amounts of storage space. They are uglier than powerboats when they sit in your driveway (they're even more abhorrent in your neighbor's driveway), poking up through the first snow, feebly suggesting a higher purpose, nonbiodegradable and finally begging to be delivered to the hazardous waste dump. Plastic garden flats will outlive us all.

The tomatoes I was to transplant for Cal sat in their hothouse flats in varied arrangements. They were growing in peat pots, which also defy sensible uniformity and turn up round and square, two by two inches or three by three, stiff or crumbly. The whole dirt floor of the greenhouse was covered in these rich green tomato seedlings, densely aligned and pungent in the humid interior air. When these were gone, the greenhouse flaps would be taped open to let breezes through, and the dirt floor would be given over to portulaca and dahlia cultivation.

Cal had already ploughed furrows up at the farm and laid down a sprinkling of fertilizers. Early on a Thursday morning, we loaded his ramshackle old truck with hundreds of tomato flats and headed, literally, for the hills. The farm unfolded on the crest of a Berkshire foothill. It was divided into irregular plots by unruly hedgerows and tractor paths. Altogether there were eighty acres available for sowing. It was cropped normally in sweet corn, beets, peas, peppers, tomatoes, lettuces, spinach, strawberries, and cauliflower, but because of poor weather conditions that spring, only half of the total acreage was suitable for planting, and only in tomatoes, peppers, and a smattering of corn. Drought was forecast throughout New England that summer, and Cal had no irrigation systems set up to compensate. Farmers in that area had traditionally relied on natural rainfall.

It was hot and dry the day we hopped off the truck. We were: two illegal farm workers from Puerto Rico, Sammy and Honario, together with their coolers full of whiskey, cigarettes, and packaged bologna; Maria, a round seventy-year-old Polish woman who had lived successfully in the States for forty years without once learning a single word of English; myself in shorts, work boots, and sunglasses engineered to protect one from the worst of alpine ultraviolet rays; and Cal, the boss, who stood inside the shade of the rickety truck and handed flats of tomatoes to us one after another. We made quite a crew. Sammy and Honario chatted constantly in rapid-fire Spanish about their brothers and cousins back in Puerto Rico. Maria sang unknown, uncomposed songs to herself. She had a habit of giggling wildly when someone said her name, a reflex that the Puerto Ricans noticed and which they periodically exploited as a distracting game. Cal smoked, inventoried, and remained quiet.

I was going gangbusters for the first couple of hours, skipping across the furrows with my heavy (just watered) tomato flats, bending, straightening, bending, straightening, dropping individual plants onto the pink and white fertilizer crystals in the rows. We took a break at ten for a Coke, which was a mistake since sodas make you thirsty. And from there it just got bad. The sun was rising higher. A breeze cropped up. It whisked the dry silts of one ploughed field into another. Silt can be like talc against your skin, soaking up the perspiration and then sticking around, coating you. The tomato seedlings must have felt the same way—parched by the sun, pushed by the breezes, and finally shrouded in a fine, powdery soil. What a shower wouldn't do for me, they affirmed in unison, picturesquely drooping as proof.

My sunglasses were falling constantly off my face and into the soil. They would slip forward slightly from the perspiration, and then plunge down the cliff of my Roman nose—a genetic liability for glasses-wearing people in the most unoffending of climates. By eleven o'clock my boots felt like a pair of thirty-pound barbells. I couldn't seem to lift my feet high enough to clear a furrow ridge. Smack, smack, smack, I went along, kicking more dry silts into the air and gradually destroying the aesthetic of Cal's evenly ploughed rows. I felt like one of Rommel's soldiers in the middle of the Serengeti, dying of thirst before the enemy even got close.

"Rommel was on the wrong side," said my husband. "First. And second, he wasn't in the Serengeti, he was in North Africa."

I was stepping out of a Siamese hot box along the River Kwai, thrusting each deadened foot forward after days of starvation and intense tropical heat, proud in front of my soldiers, mum to the enemy interrogators.

My back ached and the backs of my legs were throbbing. I glanced over at Maria, fresh and patient, forcing open the knotted roots of each plant before dropping them into the furrows. She was singing the same entropic assortment of notes. I saw Sammy and Honario, quieter now under the almost rhythmic pulse of sun, but smoking, lithe.

Kalahari, I was saying to myself. Kalahari. Water. Hey, Cal, did you bring any water?

No, but I got a Coke here with your name on it.

Show me a hospital cot with my name on it.

Ultimately, I made it through the day, but I looked like I hadn't.

"Do you have to go back tomorrow?" asked my husband. He was worried. "You look awful."

"Thanks," I said. "I haven't had enough exposure to peasant farming yet. But tomorrow we have to put the stakes in for these tomatoes and Cal needs to fix some of the fencing that rings the vegetable fields. He's having deer problems. I said I'd be there."

The work became easier each day. My energy improved. My endurance grew. My muscles tightened. Farming seemed to pull each part of me in alternation—the backs of my arms, my wrists, my calves, my stomach, my thighs. Every sinew was suddenly gainfully employed. The drought continued, but I was thriving.

We staked the tomatoes, harvested the lucky spring peas and strawberries, planted green peppers that we knew wouldn't survive the heat and dryness. Cal had a friend that filled people's swimming pools with fresh water from his truck. Once in a while, when he was free from the demands of pool owners—

usually at around nine at night—he would come by the farm and spray water over the fields. It made little impact on the wilting plants.

Then came the deer, the woodchucks, squirrels, possum, and raccoons, creatures likewise suffering under the drought and deprived of their usual food supplies. They seemed to be gathering in greater and greater numbers in Cal's fields, eating by night the few plants that we managed to keep alive through the day.

"I may lose this crop year to God," said a miserable Cal one morning. "But I sure as hell am not going to lose it to a pack of four-legged forest-rats." That's what he called deer.

So Cal upped the charge on his electric fence, strung a strand of barbed wire along the top of his wooden fence, and brought a sleeping bag out to the farm shed to keep guard in person.

"*Loco,*" said Sammy, gesturing toward Cal. Sammy and Honario were these days busier clearing deer carcasses from the perimeters of the fields than cultivating crops. There was little work for me, but I would drive by now and then to check in on Cal. The fields had turned to dust. I would find Cal sometimes oiling and cleaning his tractor, sometimes oiling and cleaning his rifle. Drought clobbered farmers throughout New England that year. Cal sold off a piece of his hilltop farmland to a developer. The following year the weather was favorable and he had a bumper crop on his seventy-seven and a half acres.

Farming.

You have to expect with cropping that a lot of fauna in this world will be as excited about your plants as you are. Predators for your wheat crop may be locusts, for your tomatoes may be beetles, for your cabbages may be worms, for your celery may be deer. The deer that daily take their salads among our beans and tulip petals—your garden-variety deer—are growing rapidly in numbers throughout sections of America. Restrictions on hunting have allowed regional populations to flourish, butting up against our own (human beings') intensive urban and suburban population growth. They are ingesting beloved shrubs, pulverizing the windshields of expensive European cars, and so arousing fewer whimpers as their outstretched carcasses lie in larger numbers along the breakdown lanes of not so country roads.

Many crop farmers will keep old rifles around for scaring deer off, if not for liquidating one or two. A farmer I know in Fairfield keeps something like a vintage blunderbuss well cleaned and oiled in his field shed. He is seventy-two and nearly blind, and people who know about the gun find the whole image rather disconcerting.

"The only thing I hate more'n deers is deer lovers," he once growled to me.

I knew another farmer in Massachusetts who sustained a similar hatred for moles. His zucchini and lettuce fields were a bas relief maze of holes and ridges sculpted by dint of a zealous population of these burrowers. Although he had been farming organically for years, he finally gave it up so that he could gas the tunnels. He used a rifle, too.

"Maybe they'll start selling twenty-two-gauge shotguns next to the hoes at Agway," I said to my husband.

He said, "Target practice will become a mandatory class at all the agricultural schools."

•

When we lived in Connecticut, the garden was my husband's greatest spring pleasure. He, who had never been a notable early bird, would be up at six in the morning on weekdays to fit in a little hoeing or planting before going to work. The amount of tending that this garden demanded would fluctuate radically from day to day.

"Oh dear. It says we have got to put the spinach in today at the latest," my husband would grumble, leafing through his manuals.

"I see here that the last frost for our area is April one," he would report.

"We absolutely can't put the lettuce where it was last year," came his fiat.

The garden demanded a lot of work, alongside his job. Occasionally he would, with the proper amount of fear in his voice, ask for my help. It usually meant weeding or reseeding somewhere.

"Where exactly?" I would ask (thunder).

Around the calendula, in between the tomatoes and the cabbage, at the end of the cucumber circles.

"Cucumber circles?" I smiled.

"You'll see them at the end of the rows, close to the woodchuck hole—I've planted them in little craters, in a circle."

"Are you sure I'll know a cucumber sprout from a weed?"

"Oh yes," he would say. "Cucumbers have two fat round leaves. They look . . . attractive. And there will be three in each crater. Whereas the weeds will be everything else. Actually," he sighed, "the weeds will probably look more robust."

"I really don't want to take chances with your cucumbers," I said. It was true. I don't like being set up for an unintentional kill.

"Don't worry," said my husband, "you can't miss them."

"Okay," I would whistle, tying up the laces of my steel-toed work boots, slipping my hands into farrier's gloves, and ambling out to the garage to select some monster tool with which, I imagined, in two broad strokes I could make child's play of this weeding marathon. "Noooo problem."

"I really appreciate your help," my husband would say, obviously hesitant to leave.

So out I went to the garden, a few things like saws, awls, and vine cutters over my shoulder, and I set to work. One glance toward the cucumber craters and I decided to leave them until last. The craters were thick with weeds and stinging nettles. A lot of things seemed "fat" and a few even seemed attractive. There were little purple and white blossoms everywhere. I would kick off my search-and-save mission in a bit, I decided, once I had had some practice with the more defined lettuce rows. Maybe I would have to buy my husband a tractor—get away from this Lilliputian nightmare.

Inevitably, it seemed, when my troubled head made one of its rare appearances among the harrowed rows, our over-the-hedge neighbor would find me and hail me. She was a beautiful Cuban woman married to the president of a huge mining corporation, and she was president herself of a local garden club. She was often to be found out on their broad lawn, pruning bushes and cutting fresh bouquets for their house. When she would see me in the garden, she would trot over smiling. She looked at me with an evangelist's eyes.

Then, "Deer!" she nearly spat that morning. This kind of vehemence was highly unlike her.

"Are they troubling you?" I asked. In the back of my mind I wondered whether our well-fed woodchuck wasn't actually at the root of her rancor.

"Don't you see?" she screamed—in a friendly way. "Hoof-prints everywhere. Why, they have been holding conferences and board meetings in my impatiens bed. You really must now put fences around your garden. High, high fences. After all your work, I would hate them to eat your vegetables. Oh and look!" She cast a glance toward the ground. "Your cucumbers are doing so marvelously!"

I dropped my saws and ran over to her.

"Where?"

8

Sacred Cows

"Who doesn't love a cow?" said a friend of mine.

I gave the question some thought. It has been my experience that the only people who don't coo about cows are ranchers. Talk to ranchers. Some of them just can't stand cattle. "So stupid," they will grimace. "So so so stupid." And this considered opinion comes from years of involvement—gathering herds from the range, running them through chutes, testing them for pregnancy, impregnating those that require it, finding lost calves on the range, regathering herds for shipping, loading frightened steers onto trucks, and so on. All of this might be less cumbersome if cattle were brighter, is the cowboy's theory. Brighter, but not brighter than cowboys.

My first introduction to ranching came with a semester off from college in 1980. I took the opportunity to work for a beef cattle company in Casper, Wyoming, where a friend of my sister had also once been hired. The owners of the ranch, the Lazy X, were brothers. They had taken over an old sheep operation and converted it to handle about sixteen hundred head of Angus and Hereford cattle. The conversion had been simple. It necessitated some fence repairs, fresh barn supports, and the dislodging of several layers of sedimentary sheep manure from some of the paddocks. The brothers had borrowed a huge Caterpillar backhoe to accomplish the last task, so compacted were the years of manure; within the layers they had found old shearing tools and whiskey bottles.

"Nope, farming hasn't changed much at all," one of the brothers had remarked, referring to all the liquor bottles he had excavated.

When I first arrived at the Lazy X, many of the old tools and bottles had been hung, unwashed and still encrusted, for decoration in the bunkhouse. I thought, after some months at the ranch, that these filthy relics were a good illustration of the ambient aesthetic and the parsimonious nature of the brothers. It was a neglected place. It conveyed the near impossibility of restoration without first committing to demolition.

I spent most of my first weeks inside the dilapidated barns, checking one pen of heifers (first-time mothers) for pregnancy, helping another set calve. There were birthing problems every day. Calves got twisted in the umbilical cord, or had turned themselves around backward, or would hook a shoulder or hoof on the way out. In these instances the farmhands had to help with delivery to keep the calf from being severely injured. "Helping" started with tying down the frantic and bellowing mother cow, since she didn't think she needed help. There is a trick to this, the crooking back of one front leg, and then if necessary, the disarmament of a defensive rear leg. Someone explained to me that cows need both front legs to get up, so if you can get a purchase on one . . . Of course, that leaves wide open the issue of getting them down on their sides to begin with, and on this Casper ranch, depending on what time of night everyone had been roused, that sometimes translated into an intemperate kicking of the cow and belting her with a two-by-four block of wood. At the time I found no justification for this behavior from the ranch's foreman and owners, and I cannot now.

Oddly enough, in spite of the violence with which some of those calves came into the oxygenated world, the births still gave me that precious sensation of miracle. One calf would gush out in a river of blood and placenta, shiny wet, pitch black, blinking, face first into the golden straw. We would set it up near its exhausted mother and she would begin to lick the tissue from its shaking body. I would bottle-feed colostrum to the sick, weak-legged, or rejected calves, and I thought that there was nothing in the world so wonderful as the warm and butting head of a seeking, hungry calf. I still think there is little that is *more* wonderful.

I reflect with a sense of gratitude on my months at this crude ranch. My love of the work and of the place itself surpassed my dislike of the management. I was forever captivated by the seasonal changes in that unfamiliar landscape. Casper offered striking vistas, markedly lunar in one direction, Mediterranean in another. The ranch was situated in a kind of vast, flat basin that allowed the uninterrupted furor of periodic storms to gather momentum as they swept across the broad skies. The weather was never gentle, the winds were unmitigated, and the ground seemed as hardened as the bleached, bleak skulls of antelope that littered it.

"Be prepared for blizzards through June," they had cautioned me. Indeed, it was toward the end of May when a stunning force of snow whipped through the Casper basin and buried cattle and vehicles under ten-foot drifts in a matter of hours. We had gone out on horseback to drive whatever cattle we could find from the draws—the nearly crevasslike cleavages of eroded earth that seemed to drop everywhere, out of nowhere, throughout the spread of the ranch. The snow was swirling so densely and shrilly around us that we often lost our bearings. At times we were literally blinded. We couldn't hear one another over the winds, and we relied on occasional glimpses of horse and rider to ascertain the strategy, success, or despair of the other hands. Then, as quickly as the storm had come, it was gone. And the earth was not savage, but crystalline and beautiful and somehow innocent as the snow dripped and melted and formed rills that carved deeper against those same sheer draws.

We lost some cows and calves in that storm, and they were frightening to find—rigid with cold and rigor mortis in contorted positions of frantic flight. We sequestered the carcasses in a remote gully, making a rubble heap of mangy hides pronged with taut dead legs and hooves. It became a grand feast for the coyotes, wolves, buzzards and prairie dogs that lived in the forsaken reaches of the ranch.

Come late spring, the earth was transformed into a knee-deep mire of slick mud. Day after day, tractors would get stuck in the wet clay as they tried to pull other, already embedded trucks and tractors out of it. Sometimes work would wait upon twenty-four hours of gray skies and rainless wind until we could finally drive the fleet of sunken, mud-encumbered vehicles out of the slowly solidifying ground. No one cursed the rains, because the ranch's alfalfa cultivation depended upon every drop that could be garnered, stored, channeled, or absorbed before summertime.

By July, the rainfall ceased. The air cleared of storm clouds, a dry wind blew, and all the ranchers in the area would drive out to inspect their irrigation dikes and clear the ditches of tumbleweeds. In the Western states, landowners rely on their privately owned water rights to obtain a continuous flow or trickle of fresh water throughout the dry summer months. The Lazy X was fortunate to hold first water rights to Barretts Creek, an unimpressive but vital flow of water that wound through the Casper basin. This last bit of water gave the ranch a significant edge on local alfalfa hay production, and it allowed us to graze animals further into the arid season before driving them onto higher ground.

The dry-weather season would arrive as quickly as those freakish spring blizzards. It immediately parched the ground, which had been ripped up into violent seas during the wet season, and which now hardened overnight into sharp peaks and pitted ruts that punctured our vehicles' tires and injured animals each day.

"It's pure adobe," said the foreman to me as he kicked brick-hard spikes of earth from sections of the farmyard. "Straw, water, and clay."

The ranch gradually whitened over the summer—a kiln-fired white. My morning chores kept me around the barns, where I could look out, from a slight rise in the earth, onto miles of parched land peppered by the black dots of distant Angus cattle foraging for the spare bits of grass, or the gray green of sagebrush and the aimless, atomic circling of tumbleweeds.

This is the land that steaks come from, I mused—not the fancy, corn-fed, perfectly marbled steaks of Omaha reputation, but a volume of tougher, leaner steaks (in an era when lean was not so preferred), chuck roasts, and hamburger that sustained a large portion of our nation and populations across the world. At that ranch, we also ate our own meat, fresh meat only hours old. It came not from young steers that we herded across the gullies, but from old cows that were no longer reproducing.

"Them's the Eat-ums," explained the foreman to me as we pitched hay into a pen of about eight five-year-old Angus cows. I had thought at first he said "Edam," meaning that these were a novel breed of cattle from Holland. Fortunately, I asked no betraying follow-up questions, and later on during my stay there I was informed in clear terms about their fate. Sure enough, as the months passed, the population in the pen diminished. A local man came by the ranch every six weeks or so to shoot and butcher one of them. He would hang two hot sides of beef in our cooler, where they were left to bleed down and "cure." I thought the eat-um meat tasted awful, fresh or frozen, but I suspect this had to do as much with my aversion to slaughter at the time as anything else.

"I only like the first half of husbandry," I wrote home to my mother. "The raising half."

•

The lifestyle of a livestock farmer is a frequent subject for consideration. One has to enjoy the daily chores, since one faces them 365 days of the year. My husband and I have had to come to grips with the fact that neither beef cattle nor dairy cattle take holidays. Beef cattle may, under profoundly desirable circumstances, offer up periods of virtual self-sufficiency, in that they can pasture fairly well. That is, they may be left to graze for weeks in open grasslands with a trifling amount of consultation. On a working ranch, cowboys will set out salt licks, molasses blocks, or supplemental feeds, but the actual tending of the cattle could be light. During these stretches, fences are repaired, barns built, grains or grasses cultivated, and feedlots contracted. It's actually a busy time for cattlemen, a time to catch up on long-neglected problems. And for the small stock farmer lucky enough to have a rambling range of a backyard, this may be a pleasantly quiet time of the year or breeding cycle. It is, unfortunately, not the perfect interval to jet to Bermuda unless you have hired someone else to look, now and again, over all those bovine shoulders for a sign of imperfect behavior—someone who knows what to do with stampeded fences, very pregnant cows, sick cows, or cows that have wandered into an alfalfa field and pretty well exploded.

With dairy cows, business is particularly ruthless in its effect on vacation plans. Dairying demands your full attention, every day of the year—once, twice, or even three times a day. When you have one cow, you can manage this by hand. I am told that beyond five cows, hand-milking is akin to self-flagellation with no sublime laurels on the other end. What happens to many farmers is that they purchase a milking machine for their ten cows or so, but then the milking goes by so quickly that they decide to buy a few more cows. Sound economics—and it helps to amortize that infernal machine. So, with a herd of twenty or thirty cows, the day seems full. But maybe a little too full, since each time a farmer finishes milking he must assiduously clean all the machinery. Dairy parlors are hotbeds of bacterial achievement and are therefore well monitored by state and federal inspectors—so sterilizing equipment becomes a significant portion of a dairyman's day. Not only can you find yourself desperate for a vacation, but you will wonder how it is you got into the agricultural machinery and sanitation business.

With dairying, I think it is particularly important to deliberate over the issue of scale. The difference between managing five cows and twenty is not geometric, but exponential. In the first instance you have taken on a chore that brings you fresh warm milk and some sort of satisfaction. In the second instance you have taken on a business that involves cattle, cattle breeding, machinery, a parlor complete with stalls, and, hopefully a competent cooperative milk pool with its own hauling system somewhere in the county.

I'm reminded of a college friend who started a brewery in Boston. He told me that when his company was small he was able to concentrate full time on his beer recipe. As the company grew larger, he felt he had become manager of a bottle cleaning and recycling operation, with beer production as a trivial sideline. I heard a parallel story from an innkeeper who expanded his Vermont lodge. In retrospect, he said, he had quit the inn business and found himself in the linen-laundering business. I think that with dairying you run something of the same risk. The labor demands shift with size, as does the amount of time you spend in front of a computer, as does the equipment you will be required to purchase. Once you subscribe to any significant scale of operation, you had better bone up on your sciences. You will need to know which detergents are safe, what temperatures are best, how suction milkers can be most efficiently managed, and what iodine dips can and cannot prevent.

I keep this in mind always as I plan for a small farm. Small it will start, and small in many ways I expect it will stay. My objective is not to gain some scale whereby I can hire extra help and buy heavy machinery—it is to do the farming myself, to enjoy the farming itself. I happen to love the work. I have to love the work, I believe, because a farmer's day-to-day options for reneging are few and his struggles are legion.

You have to have a clear objective before you get into the cattle business. There will always be that person whose daddy was a rancher, and his daddy, and his daddy's daddy . . . but if you are going to take up the saddle or the milk pail with no ancestral inclinations to speak of, then I believe you need to want something at the other end. Badly. I guarantee you will need a strong scaffolding of purpose to hang on to on the lousy days.

Possible pitfalls need mentioning, if only briefly. Otherwise they might come on you fast and furious, and you would feel inundated with irreconcilable problems, guilty feelings, maybe even frostbite or a strained back. You might thrust about looking for someone to sue under the Agricultural Hard Truths in Advertising Act, and in a burst of frustration, you might even decide to sue me under the Misleading Fun on the Farm Publications Clause. But if you feel adequately warned about those black flies and humid days, you can skip the next few paragraphs and never bemoan them.

Whether you decide to raise beef or dairy cattle, there are times when trials seem to arrive by the busload. Your feed supplier turns unreliable in the middle of winter. An unusual virus seems to be sweeping through your barn. Two weeks of deluging spring rains have made a marsh of your pasture, rotted your haystacks, and weakened your calves. And here in the middle of summer, black flies have made your air opaque. I don't like to enumerate these hapless scenarios, least of all to myself, but if you come upon them without warning you might feel singularly hapless—as I have at times. Working cattle just has its days. I keep alive for myself some nettling memories of cattle husbandry in order to stay honest and candid about my own expectations.

Consider those moments, I reflect, of trying to move cattle. Only man bests cattle when it comes to preferring the status quo. But when you weigh nine hundred pounds and you have no inclination to head to higher pastures, the wealth of prerogative would seem to be on your side. Pity the poor cowhand who rises at three thirty in the morning to begin the cattle drive to summer ranges. It is still pitch black as you ride your horse out onto the range. Gradually your eyes grow accustomed to the dark. Valleys and hillsides sprinkled with the stationary black figures of sleeping cattle grow clearer. Cattle drives traditionally commence this early, removed from the heat of noon, and calmly, so as not to spook the animals. You gather the cattle on horseback and gently nudge them along a path they know— cattle remember the trails surprisingly well from year to year. Without much fuss, calves to their mothers' hocks, they file along. This makes for a homey picture until something a little out of the ordinary comes up—you have to cross a roadway, there is a steep incline, the head cattle are startled by a coyote, or you have just pushed too far at one time. Uh-oh.

Suddenly an active yeast of dissension seems to be fermenting in this river of black hides. The usual cacophony of intermittent bellows and *maaaaa*s (the calves looking for their familiar udders) is working its way indisputably into a crescendo. From behind the herd, you watch the surface energy of black backs grow turbulent. The momentum is no longer forward. Shoulder is butting against shoulder. There is a bottleneck up front for some reason, a refusal to dare forward. Black heads shove their wet noses above the black horizon as they get squeezed from back and front. A whitecap of cattle froth is caught by the wind and sent drifting through the air. The diarrhea starts.

They are agitating up front in an old irrigation ditch along the side of the highway, which must be crossed. The fence is open. There is no traffic. But the ditch sides are perhaps a little sheer for these exquisite hooves. And then, before you can do anything else (or your partner either, and you should have one), the dam breaks and black hides swim backward beside you, not in stampede but with the assured gusto of a declined invitation. You are only lucky this didn't happen on the road itself, on the slippery (to hooves) asphalt, with a line of uranium miners in their Dodge trucks heading to work the five a.m. shift while a seeming gusher of black bodies—those not splayed across the tarmac—spill into the grassy channels between road and barbed-wire fence in a frightened frenzy.

You think, I only need one bullet.

There is another cattle-related incident I recollect on a small New England feedlot where I once worked. A large black Saler steer, unhinged after weeks of rain, escaped onto the concrete walkways between the cattle pens. He had bounded over the railing, which should be a reminder to aspiring cattlemen that their wards are actually adept at leaping. Finding himself all alone on the wet and manure-slick concrete, this steer panicked. He charged off in one direction that incidentally led to the feedlot's big manure pit, which, after those weeks of rain, was in a disagreeable state of foment. The steer, taking his bearings on the run and suddenly spotting this soupy brown pond, put on his brakes. Four wet steaming hooves ground to a halt—but not the steer. He had been running too fast to let the mere suspension of his stride interrupt his progress. Those four enchanting hooves danced, skidded stylishly past the last pen, past two unbelieving feedlot employees, past the hay bales, and then painfully down down down the slippery ramp into the manure pit, with what can only be called a "slurp."

The steer survived. He was eventually roped and hauled out of the wet manure by five stunned and recoiling men. I had never seen a steer look miserable before—much less humiliated.

I remember, too, helping out one winter day with a pregnancy testing program on a Wyoming Hereford ranch. It was way below zero that morning, and dark. We were stationed in a small barn where a long and sinuous cattle chute led in from outside and wound to a halt, its iron-levered "squeeze cage" before us. The squeeze cage was basically in the form of a V, which clapped tight and reopened to hold and then release an animal within. Cows and heifers from a corral behind the barn were being fed gradually into the chute. Each would be retained in the iron cage while checked for pregnancy; then the cage would be opened and the cattle let loose into another corral in front of the barn.

Cattle don't like to be separated from the herd. They like even less being prodded into narrow passageways, to the hooted urgings of cowhands, along a dark and unfamiliar path toward dim lights ahead. It was clearly a gross ordeal for these two- and three-year olds as they bellowed through the chute, their eyes bulging open to show white and rolling unnervingly backward. Every now and then one tried to turn herself around and got inextricably wedged—nine hundred pounds of muscle forcibly thrusting itself into a knot in the middle of a thin steel corridor—halfway down, while another frightened and snorting heifer was careening down the chute only feet behind her.

"Imagine a snake," I said to my husband, "with one elephant caught in its throat and another just swallowed whole."

As each animal barreled down the chute toward the squeeze cage, one of the gathering cowhands would warn us with a "Heifer!" or "Cow!" Standing by the open squeeze cage, another man waited until the animal's whole body was clean within the confines of the frame. Then he would yank the lever down slamming two iron panels up against her flanks. A leather brace clapped the cow's neck and left her pretty well immobilized, bawling, hooves often off the ground. The impact of the squeeze chute could be extremely powerful.

"So," I had smiled to the cowhand at the squeeze cage, "ever break any ribs?"

"Dunno, lady," he muttered.

His was not the preferred job. It is a fast rule of these operations that the chute cage becomes coated with the runny manure from one apprehensive cow after another. Cattle are quick to flush their loose bowels in a moment of alarm, so the walls of the entire squeeze chute were promptly caked and steaming with hot manure. Few of us escaped the morning unbedecked.

My job as I stood freezing in that barn was to check off the identification numbers from each animal's ear tag and make a note of whether she was pregnant or not. Those not pregnant were administered a hormone shot to start them on their heat cycle again. I jotted down the date so that the hands would know when later to re-inseminate.

By ten in the morning I had lost feeling in both my feet and was stomping across the straw-covered wood boards to revive any sensation. Our only heat was emanating from two bare bulbs that hung, one above a small table full of charts, hypodermic needles, and assorted medicinal vials, the other above the terminus of the squeeze chute where a local vet was repeatedly plunging his arm into the rectum of each Hereford female to check her ovaries. He wore a long manila rubber glove, which he hosed off from time to time with what must have been nearly freezing water.

"Gotsta hopes," he grinned at me once, his arm lost inside a heifer, "she gets the runs on the ways ins. I hates when they gets their die-harreas bys me here in the squeeze."

·

I do have dreams to carry me through the less attractive hours of cattle tending. There are two, in fact, that I have been nursing along with respect to my small farm. The first answers a fundamental question of purpose, the second responds to something even deeper.

The first dream (which, as I get closer to owning my farm, must assume the stature of a tangible objective) is to breed rare and old races of animals—to create a kind of livestock seedbank. I have heard of people doing this on a small scale, raising some peculiar breeds of poultry and cattle that had no coveted market traits and so have been gradually forsaken by commercial farmers. I, too, would like to raise and protect the old breeds. I think mankind has been prodigal with its agricultural resources, both plant and animal, too short-sighted in its self-appointed government of species and too willing to jettison entire breeds before we can even be sure what they can offer. Species extinction, oddly enough, doesn't seem to quicken a lot of pulses. I suspect that's because its consequences cannot be quantified or adequately envisioned. We occasionally hear about a smallish monkey or a largish bird on the verge of vanishing completely—only five dispirited specimens between that species' continuance and another color illustration in the history books. They tend to be in countries we never visit, in puddles we never look into. They tend to resemble every other monkey or blackish bird that we have had the luck to see. If there were so few anyway, we mull, maybe they were just gradually dying out in proper Darwinian fashion. A kind of owl in Vermont. A kind of minnow in Utah. Look, we add, we can't spend millions resuscitating an owl when we have so many social problems to address.

In agriculture, many breeds of animals have been neglected or even crossbred out of existence in attempts by man to beget specific traits. This worries a lot of people who think that if your genetic base is too thin you risk an unknown scourge—a virus or cancer, for example—that could wipe out an entire animal population. Others suggest that, with climatological changes such as are proposed by the greenhouse effect, our entire agriculture will change, and the few breeds we currently rely upon will become impractical overnight. It's not difficult to discern the tinges of extremism here—but I do agree that we human beings have lost an appreciation for the variation that used to abound. We are forsaking the broad and fabulous reverberations of hybrid vigor, and supplanting them with precise methods of gene trading.

"Ridiculous!" said a cattle breeder to me. "There's still plenty of hybrid vigor among today's breeds. Do you know how long a strand of DNA is? My god, that's just feet and inches full of variation."

Yes and no, I think. There are a lot of minuscule variations among computers, too. The fact is that most of the dairy cows in America belong to one of two breeds, and I have heard that eighty percent of these cows are artificially inseminated by a semen pool collected from around twenty bulls, most likely all of whom are now deceased. Variation? It's moot.

I think we will discover very late in the game why genetic diversity among livestock is still critical, and how some of the bygone breeds might have imparted worthwhile traits.

"My farm will teem with unmarketable breeds," I said to a friend one day. "The too-small cattle, the ones that don't give enough milk, the ones best suited to draught work, which is nobody's interest in this industrial world."

"You don't shock me," said my friend. "I was sitting next to you when you tried to flunk economics at Harvard. Still, if you could find a breed that didn't moo too loudly or that produced only prime steaks, then you might have something valuable to sell."

My farm may be a repository of information about the older races, and I could be a source to both biologists and breeders. My notes will be tight, my observations useful to the cattleman. And would there be a market for the semen from these bygone breeds? I have wondered whether modern breeders would find any interest in crossing their fine, towering dams with my curious stock. I have a sense there would be some interest. After all, breeders are constantly having to modify their lines to gratify changing consumer tastes—making the average entrecote smaller or larger, for example, to suit the current household size—or to suit different geographical markets. There is also the chance that environmental flux and environmentalist fervor may force livestock producers to rethink their practices and their "ideal" animals. In times of transition there is always a renewed interest in fresh input. In the livestock business, that means fresh genetic material. Maybe, if I were to keep such a storehouse, I wouldn't have to lose so much money after all.

"Can we use conventional barns for these ancient breeds?"

my husband asked with humor. "No dinosaurs in the dell or anything?"

"No dinosaurs," I said. "Actually, most of the unfashionable breeds are small beast material. Good for parties. Won't threaten the neighbors. Dishwasher safe."

"I've got a great idea," he laughed. "We could open up a restaurant. I'd man the grill, of course. We'd serve only steaks from old, old breeds of cattle. Tuesday could be Neanderthal Night. It's getting clearer now. And down the road, ice cream from the milk of some ancient race of cows . . ."

I said, "I get your meaning. But it sounds a little macabre, no?"

He said, "We can call your farm Nora's Ark."

I was content enough with the aim of raising the older breeds on my farm. But there is another dream I have been nursing along and that I still hope to braid into my cattle operation. I want to make my farm accessible to physically and emotionally handicapped children. I want to give these children the chance to put their own foreheads against the hot flank of a milking cow, to poke their fingers down an amazing four inches into the greasy wool of a ewe. Tending livestock, in my own life, tapped into a profound internal well. It gave me a unique and precious province which was my first real autonomy from the broad-reaching specialties of my siblings and parents. It also broke into a long-standing loneliness that had begun to enfold me at ten, when my mother became ill, and had gradually wrapped its strangling self in layers around me by the time she died, eleven years later. Handling livestock turned this loneliness into a hospitable aloneness. I have dreamt ever since of providing a similar opportunity to troubled children—not anticipating a remedy for them, but perhaps offering a little succor along the road.

"It's a wonderful idea," said my husband. "Just make sure everybody signs a waiver at the gate."

9

Wool, Milk, and Company

Route 9 runs between Northampton and Amherst.
It was for most of my youth a two-lane road with
farms on both sides. But this changed quickly in the 1970s,
when the University of Massachusetts underwent its fantastic
expansion and created a virtual metropolis in the middle of the
corn fields. Route 9 became a series of malls, minimalls, chain
restaurants, gas stations, pizza parlors, motels, traffic lights, and
traffic jams. The town of Hadley, through which this unsightly
stretch of roadway now goes, was clobbered by ugliness.
Bumper stickers were printed that read: HADLEY'S GOT YOU BY
THE MALLS.

"Didn't we go somewhere around here to pick pumpkins?" I
asked my father one October day as we were driving to South
Hadley to pick apples. This was my first trip back to Northampton since the perturbing experience at the Agway.

"Yes," he said. He looked to his left. "Oh. They've made it
part of the parking lot for that set of stores."

"Mall."

"Yes, I guess it is a mall. Well, that paved area, behind it,
that's where the pumpkin field used to be."

"You know," he added, "the asparagus never came back to

this valley. I hear the fungus problem stays dormant in the soil."

Ever since I became involved in agriculture, my father has taken up the subject with a fervor. He reports to me on what he finds at the Saturday farmers' market in town. He cuts out relevant articles for me from *The New York Times*. He interrogates orchard owners, livestock producers, and specialty mushroom growers whom he finds along his path. I took him to a sheep festival one weekend, and apart from the excessive bleating he had a good time. He even bumped into people he knew that he never realized had sheep.

I know my father worries about whether the farm will "be enough" for me, whether it will challenge and satisfy me sufficiently. He has identified me differently for so long: as a businesswoman, and as a writer and poet. But he is still ready to get excited with me about this farm, and he is already thinking out new recipes for the yields.

Of course, I also have the spirited encouragement of my husband, who, like my father, thinks of farming and grilling in one breath. While my father is open to whatever animals and crops (parsnips, please) I choose, my husband has shown some distinct partialities. He has a penchant for sheep, a penchant that comes from we know not where. He likes their habits and attitude, and he regularly champions the practical aspects of their size— compared to, say, a thousand-pound feedlot steer.

"Now think about it," he said one day as we watched the bison herd at the Bronx Zoo tear apart their morning ration of hay bales. "Could you throw a steer in the back of the pickup if you had to move him? Take him to the vet's? But a sheep, well, I just wouldn't have to worry about you. They're a good size for you, I think."

I took my husband to a sheep festival in New York State and he nearly bought four breeding ewes at the auction. I was grateful, for both his enthusiasm and his restraint. We looked over a variety of breeds, and we both prefer the Suffolk. Suffolk sheep stand tall and muscular, with a beautiful spring of girth and a graceful line to their legs. We were also taken by their black faces, the Roman noses, and the quiet temperament of the Suffolk ewes we saw in the show ring.

There are some less charming aspects to consider with sheep. They require constant worming, for example. They graze very close over the grass and often too near to their own droppings, and to my mind that bespeaks an animal with a virtual partiality to infection. Among most breeds, religious "crutching" of the breeding ewes is imperative. Crutching refers to the shearing of the wool from their back quarters and teat area to make suckling more manageable and hygienic for the newborn lamb. Moreover, sheep tend to pull grass up by the roots, so pastures must be assiduously managed. Some neighbors up the road once asked me to find them some sheep to "warm up" the meadow behind their house. These were sheep, not for eating, but for entertaining. I made a few inquiries, but the project was instantly halted when my neighbors were informed by a friend that sheep would ruin their lovely lawn by grazing it too short.

Many people show a fondness for and satisfaction in the greasy, dirty, lanolin-thick wool. My husband adores the voluminous angelic curls of a Rambouillet's fleece. We have been amazed to watch these long-haired varieties get sheared—out of a sumptuous mantle of oily, yellow-white wool steps a skinny, forlorn pink body. Still, I have been undecided about keeping a significant number of sheep on my farm, and I realize that some of my hesitation comes from having visited lambing enterprises where the animals were poorly cared for. There I have found sheep mired in mud and, overall, a grubby lot.

"We don't have to do it that way," coaxed my husband. "I've seen clean sheep . . . well, relatively clean sheep. But we won't have to worry about washing the wool anyway. We'll be shipping it off for processing, won't we? We can just worry about the racks of lamb."

I accused him of being a lobbyist.

"You'll be glad I was," he said. "You won't be able to resist my sheep."

"Your sheep?"

"You're already jealous," he said.

I had to admit there were some fine points about raising sheep. They were not smart creatures, but they were agreeable enough. Easy to handle. Not too noisy. Not too aggressive. As a knitter, I liked the idea of producing wool, and my husband was obviously committed to enjoying his lamb. If we started with a flock of four pregnant ewes, I reasoned, we would have a few months to feel out the husbandry before their offspring started arriving. Moreover, ewes customarily twin once or twice a year, which is a producer's dream. Even so, I thought, the advantages of their fertility are slightly offset by their begrudging instincts for motherhood. Ewes often have to be trained first to acknowledge their own lambs and then to express any maternal attention whatsoever.

Are sheep cute? In my mind, yes, just after they have been sheared and they stand pink, naked, and miserable. And yes, newborn lambs are pretty ingratiating. Are they smart? Well, sheep breeders wriggle a little at that question.

"Smart in exactly what way?" They will probe you.

"Do you mean will the females exhibit a motherly inclination toward their lambs?" They will groan.

"Do you mean will this ewe seek shelter from the rain?" They will squint.

"Do you mean does this breed know a Border collie from a car?" They will kick at the gravel.

I spoke with one woman who said she had switched her flock over entirely to a breed called Montadales. They are short, stocky, wool sheep—as opposed to the larger, heavily muscled Suffolks, say, which are considered meat sheep—and she had both white and dark brown ewes to show at the sheep festival. The wool from Montadales has a lovely silky feel to it, and the yarn she had spun was more delicate, thinner than most. But the reason she chose Montadales was that they have, as a breed, little lambing difficulty, and they make good mothers.

"I work a full-time job during the day," she said. "I can't be rushing back to the barn every fifteen minutes to check for birthing problems. Montadales are very resourceful."

That remark really caught my notice. I had known that some breeds of sheep and cattle are notorious for having difficulty delivering, and I wanted to be sure I wasn't asking for that kind of trouble on my own farm. So I took a second look at this woman's Montadales, and indeed, they were pretty beguiling.

Montadales are a bit funny-looking. They have long, skinny faces nesting incongruously at the fore of a dense wad of wool. This wool creeps up their necks and comes to a dead stop just behind their ears, looking like an oddly ill-fitting turtleneck sweater. Their ears bolt out to the sides like airplane wings, and they will look at you with such bored glances, the ends of un-chewed grass sticking out from their mouths. "Ahhh," they chew at you, "so why don't you wanna be a sheep?"

My husband's enthusiasm has been contagious, if not plain persuasive. He tells me he has already planned "a perfect pad-dock" with an ample shed to protect the sheep from the weather. He has proposed setting up a new kind of charged wire fence that he read about. It is apparently both effective and easy to move for shifting sheep from pasture to pasture.

"It's from New Zealand," he beamed. "Now they should know."

He has even offered to plant a bountiful herb garden near the shed. "A few days before we send off a lamb," he strategized, "we can feed it nothing but rosemary, tarragon, and a little garlic . . ."

"I don't know if marinating works that way," I replied.

"You'll get to love them," my husband said.

He said, "We can call your farm Bleating Hearts."

The idea of having sheep around was winning me over. When

you have a farm operation—raising heifer calves, for example, or propagating rare livestock breeds—it's easy enough to keep a few extra sheep on the side. And there's always the possibility that what starts out as a farm sideline may mature into a whole separate enterprise. It's not difficult when you already have the barn, the hay source, the corn source, the pens. It's not inconceivable, I supposed, that I could even grow to find sheep enchanting. A pig farmer I met said he used to have an egg business—five hundred laying hens—and that he had always kept a few hogs around for the family. In 1987, when his egg business was suffering from prevailing cholesterol concerns, he had sold off his hens and bred his two Hampshire sows. Within two years, he had developed a healthy pork business. He gave me a tour of his barns, where hundreds of pink and striped and spotted pigs at various stages of development were padding around like happy busybodies.

"Well, I try to keep an open mind," I told him, "but I don't think I could get excited about keeping pigs."

"Only a farmer and a sow can love a pig," he said, tenderly scratching the grizzled hairs on the head of his young Duroc boar.

.

A wealthy friend of mine, Murray, once bought an incorrigibly lovable English Border collie for his daughter. Few people can dispute that affectionate puppies have some magnetic pull, and since Border collies are notably bright, their assault on the average human senses is overwhelming. This puppy was delivered to Murray's estate in New Jersey to the tune of much delighted screaming and hugging. But that didn't seem enough.

"It would be a tragedy," Murray explained, "to have this magnificent dog and not allow it to flourish within its natural instincts."

So Murray, to satisfy some internal reality, bought eight mature pedigreed sheep from a farmer in New York.

"To train the puppy," he said. "I've got some cassettes, a collar, and a manual, too."

Murray handed all these training materials over to one of his estate hands and pointed toward the sheep. I was lucky to have the chance to see these sheep when they arrived. They were Corriedales, considered a good dual-purpose breed—the lambs grow quickly, and the wool from females has a respectable value among the New England wool pools. Sure enough, they were beautifully conformed. Sheep, as I have mentioned, can rarely be found in any condition bordering on cleanliness (except in the show ring), but it was easy to see the quality in their frame and muscling. There were six females, all around two years of age, and two rams that were several months younger. It was a sunny April day when I watched them investigate their new environs at Murray's place. They were installed in a small pen beside his garage with a huge round bale of hay to nibble on.

"I buy only registered animals," Murray whispered to me in confidential tones. "Let me give you a piece of advice. Never, never buy an animal without papers. Never."

These eight sheep spent a few months browsing down through the mountain of golden hay as summer blossomed into a blaze of heat and flies. Once or twice a week, they would be led into a meadow behind Murray's house with the no-longer-such-a-puppy. There they were repeatedly harassed from fence post to fence post for an hour or so with no apparent motive on the part of the dog. Eventually Augie, the collie, would become bored with this game and leave his eight sluggish play-mates to graze in tenuous peace. I observed these peculiar training sessions over the course of July's steamy afternoons, and I wondered for whose benefit this exercise was being carried out. One day as I watched, Murray sauntered outside and leaned beside me on his comely split-rail fence.

"I don't get it," Murray said. "I think the guy that sold me those sheep was a crook. Registered junk is what they are. Do you see them out there? Here I've got this magnificent Border collie trying to herd eight heaps of wool. It's a tragedy," he said.

Murray's man was having a cigarette under a tree. The collie was barking and nipping at the hocks of the sheep who were grazing and stumbling forward now and then to escape the noisome harangue. I watched for a while and then turned to Murray.

"You know, Murray," I said, "I don't mean to intrude, but don't you think it's time to shear those poor sheep?"

"Shear them?" he asked. "Already? I just bought them."

"Yeah, I see your point," I mumbled, thinking, oh my God. It so happened that Murray was, in my book, not a man whose judgment one could lightly censure.

"But I think they're about to fall over dead from heat prostration, Murray. They're wearing about four fat inches of greasy wool and it's over eighty-five degrees outside."

Murray thought a minute.

"Maybe I should call the crook I bought them from," he said. "Tell him to take them back."

"My sense is, Murray," I said, "that your sheep are basically sound, but that in this condition they're not going to give Augie much of a challenge. I mean, that dog is really what it's about out there, isn't it?"

He thought back a well-groomed moment. "Of course," he replied.

"So maybe you could get one of your men to shear those unhappy bodies?"

"Maybe you're right," Murray said. His face furrowed a bit in thought. "Know who'd want to buy my wool?" he asked.

"No," I said. I wished I could have said yes. Murray went quiet.

Then he said, "Know anything about shearing sheep?"

The next time I visited Murray, the sheep were gone. Augie was out entertaining himself in the pachysandra patch, much to the chagrin of Murray's live-in groundskeeper.

"What happened, Murray?" I asked. "Where are your sheep?"

"Sold them," he said. "For next to nothing. And to the same swindler that sold them to me."

He sighed. "It's a tragedy. Those sheep were just pitiful—tired, sick, full of worms. Their hooves were rotting! Not as billed, you know what I mean? I should've looked more closely at those papers. I'm too naive. I trust people too much. I didn't expect that kind of double dealing from a farmer."

To me, Murray never made ignorance look like bliss. He made it look pretty objectionable. I was well aware that keeping a small flock of sheep was relatively effortless, and his inability to manage it made no mark on my determination to do so.

Sheep get along with rudimentary shelter, and you can get along managing them with a few pieces of practical equipment. Sheep don't require the constant pampering that horses may. They won't savage each other like chickens. They're not too big to handle in emergencies, and what's very convenient is that they're not difficult to find when you want to buy some. When I started looking around, I found a lot of small-scale sheep operations tucked within nearby suburbs and woods. For me this was a big advantage. Not only would it be easy to find ewes, but I had ready access to a local bevy of schooled farmers. I am a firm believer in talking to people in a business before I engage in that business myself. I know I'm not the first person to confront a new or problematic situation, so I like to hear what others before me have encountered and concluded. So many typical mistakes lie along a solitary path; my feeling is, even when I want to be a lone cowboy, I don't want to be a typical lone cowboy.

Farmers tend to be open about their experiences, their good luck and bad. They are the preeminent sources for information on how different breeds fare in your area, where to purchase your feeds, and which feeds are most reasonable. They can tell you where they bought their fencing and why they chose wood, say, over wire. They may recommend a vet in the region or a particular worm dip that seems the most successful. On the whole I think it puts you in better stead to introduce yourself early, let them know you're going to be raising a few sheep yourself, and ask their opinions on a thing or two before any paddock emergencies materialize and you're forced to introduce yourself panting with distress at their farmhouse door. It's common courtesy.

"So you wanna raise sheeps, do ya?" said one Maine sheep farmer to me with a big grin. "For meat or for wool?"

"I'm not sure yet," I said, preferring to sidestep the rare-breeds concept altogether.

"Well," he said. "I kun tell ya it ain't easy."

"I think I'm expecting that," I said. "But I'm going to do it anyway. How long have you been raising sheep?"

"Me? Me? Well, lemma think. Mebbe near on forty year or so. I kun certainly tell ya a thing or two, if ya was interested."

"I very well am interested," I piped up. "I'd really like to ask you a thing or two."

"Ah, would ya?" he said. He had very thick scraggly eyebrows that lifted with surprise momentarily off his eyes.

"I'd like to know," I smiled, "for instance, why you're raising Suffolks here. And I'd really like to know what you feed them."

"Ah, so, would ya?" He thought a minute. "Well, me, I got inta Suffolk for meat. I kunna get enough money from wool up hereabouts. People don't wanna trouble witht anymore, and I kun understandt. As for feed, well t'all depends on where ya farmst. For me, I got a fella down the road here, with a big, big hay operation. And I got my protein comin' from Bangor."

"Corn?" I asked.

"Yuh corn," he said. "Sommat beans, sommat pellet, sommat oats. Come on here, I'll show ya my barn."

We walked together into a huge wooden barn that had a cool, cavernous feel. I did a quick cross-check for bats and saw cobwebs dangling from the ceiling like stalactites. There was a pathway down the middle. On the left, three large paddocks had been set up using low wood fencing. Here were the market lambs, segregated by age and marked on their rumps with a splash of red, green, or blue to identify their sires. On the right was a work area complete with shearing machine and tilt squeeze, and behind it a sea of tiny lambing pens. In these small pens the farmer kept his breeding ewes and what he called his "mother-pens." We walked along the thin corridors between the pens and saw pregnant ewes panting, newborns groping for a teat, twinned and triplet lambs sleeping deeply in curls beside one another. Then we came back toward the tilt squeeze, which was painted bright red and seemed new.

"Do you have much occasion to use the squeeze?" I asked.

"Nuh," he said, and waved it off. "But muh vet, wall, he wuldna touch a ewe w'out. Just took the sheet offt yesterday, while muh vet comt today ta look uver a mum da kunnot stand."

The tilt squeeze is a sheep-size piece of equipment used for examination or treatment of an animal. In its simplest form it consists of a plywood board on one flank and an adjustable steel barrier on the other. Farmers sandwich the sheep snugly and can then rotate or tilt the contraption so as to have better access to the animal's hooves, for example, for trimming. Many sheep raisers I met owned one of these tilt squeezes, but few used them regularly. Sheep offer you the remarkable dexterity of standing still for handling, now and then.

"Nuh here's a fine dam," said the farmer, bringing us to a stop beside one of the mother-pens. "Gut a call frum a mun in Vermont, wunts me ta embryo transfer this 'un. Wunts to buy all the females. I think it over, I tell this mun. But I wun't."

"Why not?"

"Dun't wunt to charge her," he said. "She's dun enough. She dun't need no shots and flushin'. She's a good mum."

There were feeders of varying homemade construction styles scattered about. They were rudimentary V-shaped racks filled with hay and grain and pelleted feeds. The sheep stood beside them, poking their noses through the slats to pull out mouthfuls of this or that. Also dispersed around the corrals were mineral blocks and long, galvanized iron water troughs set up on legs. I had read that sheep drink around two and a half gallons of water each day, but most of the animals in this barn, I noticed, were contentedly gathered around the feed troughs.

Outside the barn was another paddock with three rams pacing around. This paddock was connected with a series of fenced meadows by means of portable, maneuverable "cutting chutes." Cutting chutes are just fenced pathways wide enough for a single animal abreast; they are used often throughout a farm to move and sort animals one by one. This farmer had the chute arranged so that he could drive his rams into specific meadows at breeding time. It was a neat arrangement.

"Now what's that?" I said, pointing to an isolated, oversize cement trough on the side of the barn.

"Muh dip," said the farmer. "But it's nah dry as bone now. Havnt dipped since, ah, then, two month or so. Hate to dip. Allas a mess."

The dip or dipping vat is a primitive but effective way to treat sheep for lice, ticks and other assorted bodily bugs. Farmers fill their vats with water mixed with medication and send the sheep through, splashing, one at a time. It's not considered an amusing chore and many farmers prefer spray guns loaded with the proper compounds to this bathtub technique for delousing their herd.

"I kun recummendt you," said the farmer, "thut you keep yere barn clen. I wuld have to say, wall, dippin' is a most ent-terrible task."

·

My strong inclination toward goats is well known among my friends. They find it eccentric, I notice, because they feel goats offer up no marketable products for today's society—goat's milk and *cabrito* having no distinguished star within the red Michelin—and they think goats have diabolical eyes. Still, they say, they have been willing to overcome their countless reservations and are always on the lookout for me when it comes to farm-related goings-on. Such a friend of mine, who lives in New York City, telephoned one day to recommend that I visit the Central Park Zoo.

"I'm sure I saw some goats there," he said. "Unless I was dreaming it. But goats aren't the kind of thing I usually dream about. Girls I dream about."

"Do you want to come along?" I asked.

"No thanks," he said. "I actually prefer dreaming about girls."

I made a trip to the park to find these goats and to see if the zoo had procured some unique breed for their exhibition. The Central Park Zoo, narrowly rescued amid New York City's recent budgetary crisis, was given a radical facelift a few years ago. It now boasts lots of wood and glass, carpeting, and unobtrusive walkways, reproduction tropical rainforests, pleasant open-air spaces, and opportunities to draw near to various animals. You can watch ants underground, seals underwater, and monkeys undercover.

Walking down Fifth Avenue toward the Sixty-fourth Street entrance, I began to pass by some zoolike (or miniature golflike) configurations on my right, beyond and below the brick wall that keeps you out of Central Park and gives the city's homeless at least one of four walls by which all human beings gauge a home. The brick wall was stained with urine and appropriated by intermittent bundlings of soiled blankets and ruined clothes—with warm bodies underneath. Homeless human beings left to live at the curb of a zoo created a compelling juxtaposition for me. At least those lions and tigers, I thought, have food and shelter from the weather.

I looked over the Sixty-sixth Street wall onto a strange pastel-colored concrete igloo, oversize, with several cement outcroppings. Beyond its railings were a cement whale poised in no water, and cheerful little kiosks that were empty, offering information to no one.

"This was the old zoo," a passing policeman informed me. "I don't think anybody uses it anymore." He glanced over the site. "No, I don't think so."

It seemed deserted. Its pastels and fairy-tale creatures suggested a happier time, like the now hushed pathways of the old World's Fair grounds. VISUALIZE COMPLETE ABANDONMENT, the bumper sticker would say. I was reflecting on this stark emptiness, disheartened, when suddenly three small goats appeared from behind the pink cement igloo. They were pygmy goats, short, dark-haired and friendly, and they jumped up onto the concrete bulges of the igloo wall as if they were scampering along the Matterhorn. They were an image of gaiety and self-contentment within this ungracious setting. I watched them play together—something goats do affably—and reexplore their cramped space. They sniffed without prejudice at the stray flotsam of Fifth Avenue and kept their hooves nicely trimmed by scampering about their lumpy concrete confines.

Goats are bright, gregarious, and engaging. They will wilt if left alone, but can manage very well with a companion of their own species, or a sheep, or a dog, or you. The goats in the Central Park zoo did not cry out at passersby for attention or deliverance, but rather chewed their feedstuffs in a copacetic manner in the midst of these hideous surroundings of cement and street litter. This reminded me of the way wildflowers buoyantly grow out of rock crevices.

In the goat vernacular, there are does (females), bucks (intact males), wethers (castrated males), and kids (goats under six years of age). Wethers make wonderful pets—not the kind of pet you want to jog with on the beach, but the kind that offers company, follows you as you tend the lawn, eats your grass clippings, nudges you in the side for an occasional break of stroking and scratching. Male or female, goats are experts at getting out of gates, into feed sacks, onto car roofs, and over fences. My favorite goat, a doe on a dairy farm in New York, was killed when she found some rat poison bars while climbing around a hayloft. Goats are naturally inquisitive and they are often smart enough to satisfy their curiosity, even when it's dangerous to do so.

Bucks are typically kept in a separate corral on goat farms because of their disposition, or lack thereof. Bucks with horns can be dangerous even without intending to be. And bucks have extraordinarily pungent pheromonal blast furnaces that keep them smelling just like an overripe chèvre. While it must drive the does to near distraction, it is not equally enamoring to the farmer.

Goats bond well with human beings. They can be greedy for petting and nuzzling. They tend to browse on all sorts of leafy and prickly plants and shrubs that no one else in the barnyard will touch—including poison ivy. But goats eat more than thistles and scrub greenery. Many past owners of goats will rage at you. "I had goats!" they will curse. "See that meadow? Used to be fenced in. They ate down the fence and then they went after my apple trees."

The characteristic investigative palates of goats are celebrated in those terrific stories of devoured tin cans, tires, and little girls' dresses. In truth, a goat's curiosity may occasion a sniff or nibble, but neither their jaws nor their stomachs could manage such items. The story of the tin cans has more to do with a goat's predilection for the glue that binds a can's paper label than with the can itself. However, the appetite of a goat can in fact tackle a tree. It just takes time. It takes patient and determined gnawing. Goats will chew away a ring of bark and wood about the height of their comfortable nuzzling, and few trees can survive this girdling procedure. That, finally, is how goats will "eat" your trees.

If you want conversation on your farm, buy goats. Goats you can talk with about subjects ranging from the Reagan administration (which in retrospect probably gave older goats a bad name) to the quantities of hay that you are offering on any given day. Goats will hear you out about your most personal grievances, too, like your friend's inability to control her child or your family's reluctance to see you as other than an infant. I have felt silly talking to a lot of animals—even cooing to them at times—but with goats I always feel adequately heard. They remind me some of dogs, intelligent dogs, usually those medium-size mongrels that stray into your life now and then to keep you balanced.

I nearly bought two wethers one day from a convent not far from our cottage in Connecticut. The convent was perched on the top of a broad and scenic hill, and at the foot of that hill the nuns had built a modest farm from which they produced enough meat, milk, and eggs to satisfy the whole convent and then some. Within the small barn area, mapped into carefully prescribed and managed paddocks for the various resident species, Sister Margaret and Sister Lucy kept five dairy cows, ten sheep, five goats, one buck, more than thirty laying hens, and probably a matching number of barn cats and kittens. I used to drive over now and then to watch the animals. It's great to be able to visit other farms and enjoy someone else's animals. It's like being an aunt—you get all the pleasures with none of the ultimate responsibilities. I haunted the convent also to find out what the sisters were offering by way of seasonal feeds, shelter, breeding, and day-to-day attentions. I admit I was intractably predisposed to think these nuns would make the best farmers. It wasn't because they were women, but because they seemed like such a placid and do-unto-others lot. They were also, it was clear, hefty and fit enough to take on any of the larger animals—not that one is normally pressed to "throw" a dairy cow.

The goats there were of mixed parentage. They were tall, not the pygmy variety that I have often found in the Northeast—in light, I suppose, of space constraints. These convent goats reminded me of giraffes, in that they had long skinny necks springing up from a central, horizontal nucleus of stomach and ribs. Four disproportionately skinny legs wobbled underneath, looking deceptively weak. As they walked, this central expanse of chest-to-rump swayed like a flirtatious pair of hips, side to side. Then they would stop, stomach to one side, posed like Baroque angels in the idealized S-curve of a seventeenth-century triptych.

But there was more to that barrel-vaulted torso than grace. These goats adored attention and had a habit of strolling up to you and then shifting their weight suddenly, so that the whole horizontal force of stomach, muscle, and balance came slamming, affectionately, into your own imperfectly constructed (only two feet) verticality. Over you went unless you were accustomed to their ways. I think I could have invented the wrecking ball or the battering ram, way back when, by observing this effectively leveraged swing of the goat.

The taller breeds of goat are quite elegant. They have elongated necks, a stately upright posture—goats never slump—and an affinity for staying clean. The bucks, with their sage's beards and lofting backward springs of horn, act like reserve princes of the barnyard even though they are often penned in small, removed quarters due to their strength and the strength of their incredible fragrance.

"When you handle a buck," said Sister Margaret with a beatific smile, "you will smell of chèvre until Sunday."

I told my husband.

"We may have finally found something that clings worse than cigarette smoke," he said. "You'll have to stay off public transportation for a while, but we can certainly plan our vacations around your goat breeding cycles."

He said, "Tell me about this odor."

"No," I muttered.

"Maybe," he grinned, "it is more aptly termed a reek, or a stench even?"

I said, "It's a bouquet."

"We should bottle it then," said my husband. "I'm sure food

scientists could use it, if not the special forces of the U.S. Army."

Thus was my frame of mind vis-à-vis goats when kidding season at the convent farm began. It was a heyday for me, since there are few things so delightful as a baby goat; they are perky, approachable, more antelope than barnyard stock. I became happily attached to two twinned wethers whom I named Bob and Camel.

But Sister Margaret told me one morning that the convent couldn't keep all the spring calves, lambs, and kids, and that they planned to sell what animals they could to area farmers or families. I telephoned my father.

"Bob and Camel?" asked my father.

"Yes, and the nuns can't keep them," I said. "They're going to sell them. You want two goats?"

"Hmmm," he said tactfully. "I don't know how I could. I'm away too often. And I would worry about neighborhood dogs."

"Yeah, I understand."

"And I couldn't milk them," he added. "I think you need a stronger back for that."

I said, "Bob and Camel are men."

•

One year I drove up to the Vermont State Fair in Barre. It was being held in what appeared to be a high school complex up on a hill in the middle of town. In one building that looked like a surrendered gymnasium were all the tractor and equipment dealers with their shiny new models—"a must for every farmer," not to mention "the incredible trade-in values I can offer you . . ." In the school itself, which would never smell the same again, were all the various farmers with their prize yields and livestock. A maple syrup contest spanned the whole first floor, and was hard to pass by. There were maple syrups from amber to dark, maple cream, maple candies, maple cookies, maple bread, maple pies, and maple milk. There were maple syrup makers conferring on the habits of their trees, the running of the sap that spring, the proper temperatures for candy production, and of course the sorry prices for their syrup in general.

Following my nose, I headed toward the basement. The odor of straw, hay, and manure got stronger with every turn of that inimitable public school staircase. I had forgotten how hard it used to be to want to learn in those drab, institutional schools of the 1950s. The goats and sheep I found down the stairs seemed equally nonplussed.

There were three Nubian milking does standing comfortably but still in a makeshift iron-bar pen. Half a bale of hay sat behind them, falling open little by little at the edges like a toppling deck of cards. A handful of bright orange carrots lay untouched on the straw. The goats occupied their space with reserve, thought-fully chewing cud and looking out at the visitors to the fair—observer observed. One sensed that they felt the walls of their alien pen were not sufficiently dependable to protect them from the primitive hordes walking by. MILKING AT 3:00 P.M., read a hand-scribbled sign on the wall behind them. It had been taped to the painted cinderblocks, and now hung—since tape has no adherence to these surfaces, and the frustrations of elementary school art classes came flooding back—limp, curling, and askew.

Nubians are one of the larger goat breeds, and they have a proud stature. The ones at the fair were cream and white colored with a patchy, mottled mix of the two shades and a hint of tan.

"You interested in Nubians?" said a cheery woman behind a card table. She had been serving up fresh goat's milk to passersby in the tiny plastic cups that doctors use to dish out pills.

"Yes," I smiled. The goats slowly swung their heads in my direction with a weary "and-who-are-you?" expression.

"Should be!" she said. "Nubians are the queens of goat breeds. Don't give as much milk, maybe, but the butterfat content's always higher than the others. Here, try some of our milk."

I took a sip of the cooled, sieved milk, and caught my breath. It tasted awful. Bitter, thick, not right. I couldn't seem to swallow it. It hung in the back of my mouth. My throat was saying *Non, mais absolument non*. I had to use all the coercive, rational powers of my brain to get it down.

"Thank you," I must have coughed, trying my best to be courteous and holding onto the tiny cup as though I fully intended to indulge myself in another sip.

"It's not a taste for everyone," she said, gaily ignoring my efforts. "Do you like goat's cheese, though? We've got some for sampling that we make ourselves."

"That would be wonderful. How old are your goats?"

"These does are all two years old," she said. "Frankly, I think it was a big mistake to bring them. The older does do better at these sorts of fairs—not so put off by all the people. These girls won't eat until everyone goes, which, you know, is kind of late. I asked my partner to go get some oats and molasses, see if we could get them to eat treats. He should be back soon. It's always like this at shows. There's always something you plan wrong."

I inquired about her farm.

"We've got over sixty acres in pasture and hay production just southwest of here. Goats are ruminants, of course—did you know that? Good. Well, we produce all our own roughage and buy oats or corn or soybeans for protein. The usual stuff. We've got about sixty does milking at any one time, and maybe fifteen drying off. It certainly wasn't like this a few years ago. I mean, we started out pretty small, but goats have twins more often than not, and lots of our does are having triplets, so we've grown faster than we planned.

"It's okay, though. We worried about having too much milk and where would we sell our kids and you know, but it's worked out okay. There's a lot of people around interested again in goat's milk for ice cream or for their kids. We got into cheese ourselves, not knowing what else to do with all the milk, and cheese is where the profit is with our herd. We're not fancy breeders or anything. We've got no purebreds to sell, no semen from our bucks. Our cheese, though, gets better every year."

"It's delicious," I said. It was. I wondered who might be selling baguettes and wine at the Vermont State Fair so that I could round up a nice picnic for myself. Vermont wine? I wondered. It was a chilling proposition.

I asked, "Does cheese-making involve a lot of new equipment and overhead?"

"No, not for us. Not yet." She paused. "Well, we haven't got into all the fancy machines. But since we already had a dairy parlor and sterilizing equipment, the added mechanics weren't to speak of. Where we really needed help was know-how. We didn't know the first thing about cheeses, other than how to unwrap them from the store. If you're interested, there's an old guy up in Saint Albans that taught us how, still gives us tips from time to time and even showed us how to shape the pyramids and ash the cheeses. He was incredible. A French guy. You should meet him. But don't talk to him until you've tried yourself a time or two. He can be kind of impatient unless you know what you're trying to do."

She gave me his name and address and I said I looked forward to the opportunity to be snapped at.

"By the way," I said. "What do you feed your goats besides hay, carrots, oats, and molasses?"

"Well." She took a big breath and launched into a discussion of the proper balance between roughage and protein and kitchen scraps and feed supplements, pounds of energy per lactating doe versus pounds of energy per dry doe, today's cost per pound of corn and soybeans, and so on.

Wait a minute, I thought. Somebody talk bales to me.

Over by the sheep pen a crowd was gathering, so I finished up chatting with this woman, thanked her, and walked over to have a look. Three sheep, all Rambouillet ewes, were ambling around an unglamorous pen erected from old wood planks while three infant lambs slept in the straw. The lambs were offspring from one of the ewes, who was identifiable from her cleanly crutched rear end. The farmer who owned these animals had just stepped into the pen to give a hoof-trimming demonstration, and I could see from his face that he rued this commitment. The sheep were altogether discombobulated by the fair, the lights, this temporary dormitory, and the milling crowds. "On any other day," was the edict of their agitated tramping, "but my hooves stay on the ground this morning."

The farmer stood still a while watching the ewes scuttle about. I imagined he was trying either to calm them or to calculate his chances at snatching one as she trotted by. Suddenly, he lunged forward and tried to collar a passing hock with his hand. *Blaaaaaah,* came the response, plus two sharp tugs of her leg and she was gone. And she was not, definitely not, going to circle by him again. And she was recommending to her friends, through a long series of loud bleats, that they follow her example. So nestle they all did against the opposite end of the pen.

Most of us watching this exercise, and enjoying it, thought the farmer had an easy shot now. Three fat woolly ewes cramming up against one another in a fairly tight space—all he had to do was catch one. He walked slowly over toward the ewes, working no magic but, on the contrary, bringing them to a pitch of sheep alarm. They broke, darted. He bent and reached. But before his arm had finished its swing they were behind him.

"More people should see this," said a man next to me. "Sheep will make you insane. I can't watch this anymore." And he shimmied backward out of the crowd.

Now the farmer was making low, soothing clucking noises—soothing to sheep, apparently, because they lowered their decibels and stood idle and examined him, their mouths relaxing into an indolent chew of cud. The mother ewe sauntered over to her lambs and poked one, as ewes will, exhibiting no tenderness but instead a kind of self-assertive reaffirmation. She watched, we all watched, as the farmer pulled a pair of pruning shears from his back pocket. Then he walked right up to her, squatted by her rear haunches, and picked up a hind leg. She complied.

"Sheep love foreplay," came a voice next to me. "But that's all they love."

The farmer straddled the ewe's upturned leg and gave the crowd a view of it. It seemed overly padded and had obviously grown outside the bounds of the original form. The farmer used his pruning shears to trim off slowly the areas of hoof that looked curled over. Then he took a knife from another pocket and began to shave downward, heel to toe, the rounded bottom portion of the hoof pad. Chunks of hoof were dropping into the straw. The farmer pulled back finally and showed us a tidy, trim, pinkening foot. "Well done"s and "There, he did it fine"s were circulating through the audience. Our farmer-performer put down the ewe's hoof and straighted his back, not without a wince.

"If anybody's got a question . . . ," he said.

But no, we'd seen enough.

•

Goats are the only farm animals that for me enter the gray area between livestock and pet. When I think about goats, the corners of my mouth curl up and my eyes drift skyward and I detect all sorts of words issuing forth from my mouth that I normally try to steer clear of—words like *cute, sweet, frisky, snuggly, fuzzy, nuzzly* (a word, even?), *cuddly,* and the like. This kind of jargon, apart from being really soupy and brainless, exposes me, the budding farmer, in a high-risk category—High Risk Of Not Being Able To Differentiate between barn and home, between Angus dam number 82 and Pheephee the house cat, between animals for food and animals for companionship. The dividing factor, of course, is the packing plant. We Americans don't eat dogs and cats. We don't eat much *cabrito* (goat meat) either, but we don't have many friends with pet wethers and does. All of us draw our curious lines, and we usually have good reasons for it.

On my farm, goats will largely be guests, in that I don't intend to support the local specialty meat market, the local goat's milk ice cream market, or the local mohair wool market (mohair comes from Angora goats). That said, I may be willing, every so often, only at the behest of the best of friends or family, and with reluctance, to have a male kid allocated for meat. I would also consider milking a small number of goats, were there an expatriate Frenchman in the neighborhood with a passion and an extraordinary genius for making fresh chèvre and an un-Frenchmanlike generosity of spirit that embraced a cheese-for-milk barter arrangement. And, in spite of the fact that Angora goats are renowned for their nasty temperament, I might keep a few around for the sake of a discourse in varietals.

Angora goats grow to just midthigh (mine) height. They are a spectacle in their full-length coat of crinkly white hair. Many breeders I have watched will lead their Angora goats into the show ring by grabbing them by the short curl of horn and then practically dragging them across the straw and dirt to position. It's a comic scene: twenty or so breeders between the ages of eight and fifty-eight, all decked out in cowboy boots and bandannas and each crooked over at the waist with two hands firmly wrapped around one horn of a contrary Angora goat—the goat, spanking clean and shimmering with its just-shampooed mohair locks, with four trimmed hooves bolted into the dirt and an expression of convincing opposition that could only come from genetics.

Something there is, for me, that loves a goat. But I watch myself closely with goat conversation. I try to monitor my language carefully. I try to expunge most of the "adorable"s from my sentences. And this is not just because I am busily training myself to the proper imprint of a farmer; I have always been uncomfortable with things considered "cute."

"Repressed," said a friend. "Repressed about things that are cute. You should know that, of all people. You're the psychiatrist's daughter."

"Psychoanalyst," I said, deadpan. I am tired of the "psychiatrist's kids" quips after all these years; I tend to think most everyone carries with them both the banners and the baggage of their parents.

Nevertheless, cute things introduce a level of discomfort into my life. I grew up equating cute with fatuous, cute with intolerable triteness. I can't stand Hallmark cards. It makes me uptight to watch people make overt flurries over kittens, puppies, and other infant species that normally draw out the cuddling instincts in one. When I was a child, people still avoided "scenes" or "making a scene"—which certainly dates me in the face of America's current day utterly unrestrained codes. And within our household, to indicate a partiality for the color pink was to risk excommunication from the family.

Everyone grows up under the doctrinal cudgels of their parents' and their society's moralities. I wear the expected dents about me. I hope I carry a smaller cudgel. Today I am immeasurably grateful for having been shepherded through my childhood to grasp education as my first priority. It was indeed the scholarly canons of my youth that taught me how to continue forward and greet life during my mother's long illness and after her death.

But it is farming that is my balm. It is the unceremonious work of the hands and spine in a day-to-day continuum that brings me repose. A graduate student from Georgia once said to me as he led me through his Texas A&M groundnut research plot: "You know, peanuts are truly a tonic." I suppose that, for myself, farming is truly a tonic. And of course, with respect to goats, I'll be able to find them wholly cute and adorable within the privacy of my own barn.

10

The Fine Feathered
Cannibals

"Would you mind terribly if I didn't read your chapter on chickens?" asked a friend one morning.

A curious question.

"I'm just sick to death of hearing about them," she said. "One horror story after another. Salmonella. Inhumane farms. Do you know I've switched butchers twice because of chickens?"

"No," I said. "And I don't mind." Thinking, I don't really mind, but isn't it funny how people have to make these public avowals. We were quiet for a moment.

Then I proposed, "I bet a lot of people feel the way you do. Maybe I shouldn't include a poultry chapter at all."

"What? Of course you have to. Every farm has chickens and turkeys wandering around. That's what gives a farm"—my friend considered—"proper farm atmosphere."

She added, "Besides, you've said you're already short-changing pigs—"

"Swine," I corrected her.

"You can't just keep leaving animals out. Why don't you write a short chicken chapter, and while you're at it throw in a little something nice about pigs for other people. Try to be dip-lomatic."

"Once upon a time there was a pig sty and a chicken coop," I said.

"Exactly."

I said, "Actually, I've been thinking a lot about chickens recently."

"Good attitude."

"About why we are so untroubled by slaughtering them."

"Oh God."

I had happened to be reading one of my husband's war history books at the time. In it the author proposed that it was easier to do battle with—that is, to kill—a person who looks least like you. Came the theory then, and I'm sure it was not unprecedented, that it was easier for Americans to war with the Japanese in World War II or the Iraqis in 1990 than it might be, say, to fight another Western culture. I can't argue with that line of reasoning. People, like countries, have an innate element of nationalism that stems very deeply from an internal sense of familiarity and community. Persons who look significantly different from us are more vulnerable to our instinctive tendency to find a safe and protective distance for ourselves.

"This is where I expect the NAACP to take a less than genial interest in your farm views," said my friend.

"I was trying to relate this to chickens," I said. "No chicken nuggets eater cares what color the original hen's skin was—although I guess you could argue that one should."

She said, "Oh, do they really make chicken nuggets out of chicken these days?"

For some reason, I think, it has been easier for Americans to accept the killing and eating of chickens than the same treatment of other livestock—calves, for example. Ah well, you're saying, calves are babies, and nobody wants to eat a baby. Okay, I'll say, suppose you're right, and let's forget the issue of eggs or lamb; my point is that human beings seem to be better able to distance themselves from birds than from other mammals. Put that way, it makes a lot of sense. Speciation. Birds are small, armless, fluttery, jerky creatures, with none of that big brown eye stuff in their favor. They are rarely approachable, they make curious squawks, and their standard of hygiene is less than we like to imagine. They grow to adulthood in a matter of weeks, they aren't particularly precocious, and you can't pet them with satisfaction.

For all of these reasons, I think chickens are more readily taken into the pan than into the heart. The entire chicken industry has survived many a discouraging word over the matter of salmonella, chickens' dietary habits, their cannibalistic propensities, and the densely packed grow-out barns in which they're raised. None of the mud seems to stick. Chicken consumption rose at a stupendous rate in the 1980s in spite of searingly bad press. I should like to be so popular as a 1980s chicken.

"I still don't see how you can translate that war theory into chicken consumption," resisted my friend. "Especially since human beings don't look much like cattle either. Well," she considered, "at least I hope I don't look much like a cow. Some of the people you see on the street, however. . . ."

"Hold on," I said. "Listen to this." I had been flipping through a textbook titled *The Meat We Eat* (Interstate Printers & Publishers), and I found a section in the poultry chapter called "Handling Previous to Processing." It began: "Birds, like animals, should receive careful handling to avoid bruises, abrasions, and broken limbs."

"At least I think birds are animals," I said.

·

I like to watch chickens. I notice also that chickens don't mind being watched. They have a kind of feline independence to them. Their world is manageably circumscribed and you, other than around feeding time, are on the Outside. Within a microcosm of wood chips, lettuce leaves, and of course chicken wire, come the contenting patterns of their day—the laying of the egg, the scratching for the beetle, the roosting on a convenient branch, and the hunting up of a little more sunshine.

In 1989, I became acquainted with chickens while I worked on a small farm in Connecticut. It was mainly a beef cattle operation, but there were also sheep, poultry, pigs, and the seasonal duck. No one there liked chickens except for me. The other farm hands considered birds filthy, and moreover very filthy. I, however, was mesmerized by my first box of chicks and became completely attached to these birds by the time they became full-time egg layers or big-breasted broilers. The more I learned about them, the less charming they became in my mind, and the more amazing. I used to watch chickens during my coffee break, watch chickens as I thought through my reports, and watch chickens before I went home at night. They were bewitching and they were comic. They were curious about human beings but considered themselves smart enough to keep a safe distance from you.

One of my favorite moments of the farm day came every morning at ten o'clock. The laying flock was let out into the back meadow to spend some hours in the sun scratching the dirt for pebbles and bugs. The hens had finished laying their eggs in the nests (boxes built against the walls of the barn). They were ready to stretch their legs, and this interlude gave the farmhands time to collect warm eggs from the hay inside the coop.

This airing of the hens and roosters was a methodical routine interrupted only by sharp drops in the temperature, blizzards, rain, or hail. Chickens take well to schedules, to laying in the mornings, to wandering about during the daylight, to heading home at dusk. But in spite of the consistency of this daily custom, one step along the way invariably provoked alarm throughout the flock. This was the actual passage out of the barn through a tiny, bird-size door in the far wall of the coop. This little door opened out onto a ramp fixed to the rear of the barn. The ramp took the chickens down one storey to the ground and meadows beyond. Perhaps the problem was that the ramp ran parallel to the barn wall instead of jutting straight out perpendicular to it. This meant that the flock had to exit the coop and take a sharp right down the ramp. If a bird marched too far forward, it would have to do some flying—not something domesticated chickens are keen for.

So it was that when the little latched door of the coop was opened each morning, consummate havoc erupted. Hundreds of buff and white chickens, fussed at impatiently by those behind and pecked at by the member roosters, would begin shoving and bursting through the barn wall onto the ramp outside. Because the ramp was fairly slim—just wide enough to endure two fat chickens comfortably toddling side by side—each bird as it was pushed or crowded through the little door would suddenly panic as it greeted the sheer five-foot drop straight ahead. Every morning.

Chickens still do come with wings in these modern times, and yes, they can use them to buffer any free-fall. Even so, the march of the hens each morning amounted to ten minutes of unadulterated chaos and terrified squawking as the river of orange and white birds raged, surged, and spewed forth from the coop into the precarious sunlight. Most hens did manage to walk or be shoved down the wooden ramp, but a few inevitably got thrust off the side and would fall, not gracefully, to the ground. The air resounded with chicken umbrage and the minor thuds of birds landing abruptly on their breasts or rumps. Nothing was bruised, as it is said, but a modicum of dignity. The unfortunates would bounce up quickly, affronted, and forget the incident within seconds. Chickens, I think, have enviably small memory lobes.

"The brains have been bred out of 'em," said one chicken farmer to me. "It's easier to deal with 'em without brains."

I guess that would be true. It would be tough to be the warden of a wily freedom-seeking bird.

"Chickens weren't always so dumb and defenseless," he added.

"Used to use their wings more. Used to run faster, think better."

The road to the better meat and egg-laying bird was not parallel to the road to the fittest chicken. Sometimes I imagine the two trends are inversely related. If we were to let chickens revert, live freely in the wilderness, would we see a gradual return of their former cleverness or habits? Would they begin to bear offspring with a more astute and aggressive nature? And, I have wondered, would we ever see the gradual differentiation of the species back into its ancestral variations?

This is an important issue for me, since I hope to raise some of the older poultry races. I am nagged at by the thought that these races simply don't exist in any purity today, that we have only mongrel material on the hoof (on the claw, in this case), and some antique lithographs that reveal to us what a certain breed used to look like.

What's done, with chickens, is done. I think people kid themselves when they try to breed backward to the original, parental genetics, to what Darwin called the "aboriginal stocks." By raising a few of the older races, however, I hope to preserve at least some segments of the early genetic codes, and perhaps a few traits that, expressed or not in the remaining individuals, may continue to be passed along through careful breeding.

But whether you want minor breeds of poultry or major, ducks or chickens, you may be delighted to learn that they are relatively easy to come by. Modern day hatcheries will send you glossy catalogues with a wide selection of full-size chicken breeds, bantams, turkeys, water fowl, and guineas. You telephone in your order, tell the ladies what kind of chicks you want—if you want all pullets (females), cockerels (males), or a "straight run" (unsexed mix). Straight runs tend to be slightly less expensive. Then you must let the ladies know whether you want your day-old chicks vaccinated and/or debeaked. You should know that debeaking at this early stage is only effective for the first few weeks. Beaks keep growing, and if you plan to keep chickens in tight confinement then you may have to redebeak them some day yourself. Also, debeaked chickens can be a thoroughly woeful sight.

Depending on the hatchery, the type of poultry, and the number of chicks you order, the cost per chick can run from around forty-five cents to a couple of dollars. Exotic breeds naturally are the more expensive. Vaccination and debeaking will add another five cents or so to the cost of each chick. Visa and Mastercard numbers are often accepted over the phone.

At this point you should have your chicken starter and warm lights ready. A perforated cardboard box full of fluffy white or cream-colored chicks will arrive by overnight mail at your local post office, cheeping like crazy and straining the nerves of employees reared on mute parcels and backroom humdrum. The postmaster will call you up and let you know your chicks have arrived. Pick them up right away and get them to food and water. Baby chicks ingest enough of the egg's nutrient-rich yolk to last them about twenty-four hours after hatching, but then they need some care.

"Amazing," murmured a friend. "Chicks by mail order. I'm going to look differently at my L. L. Bean catalogues now."

·

People love eggs that get properly pipped, fractured, and pushed apart by a wet-feathered scrawny chick inside. They don't, anymore, love eggs that get rapped bowlside, cracked in two, and loosed into the frying pan. Conjuring eggs as carriers of salmonella, cholesterol, or unwanted calories, Americans over the last several years have been demanding more pipping and less rapping.

The egg business became a lousy business to be in during the 1980s—demanding, industrial, and ever under fire from book-writing nutritionists. It's still demanding and industrial, but there are signs that the nutritionists have retreated some. They appear to have a jungle war mentality, and, having laid waste to a few treehouses, they are on the lookout for booty in other precincts—waffles, perhaps. Yes, waffles have not yet been pilloried. In the meantime, I was surprised when a series of favorable egg episodes, egg interludes, happened along my path.

The first story arrived with a friend from New York.

"You have got to see the new exhibit at the Whitney's Forty-second Street gallery," she said. "It's all tempera painting. Tempera is in again. Everybody's into mixing up their own paint pigments and separating out the egg yolks . . ."

A rash of tempera painting alone was not going to revive the egg industry, but it was a modest effort. I called my sister the art conservator.

"Oh!" she said. "It'll never last. It's painstaking. You mix your pigment with egg yolk for binder. The effect on the canvas is unusual but it's hard to work with. It dries very fast."

Soon after, I was looking for inspiration in a craft magazine and I came across an article on herb-decorated boxes. Dried herbs could be applied to wooden boxes with egg white, then the whole thing lacquered. I tried it because I wanted to make my husband something special to commemorate his prodigious herb garden, and I was intrigued to see what an effective neutral glue the egg whites made.

On balance then, yolks to the pigment-binding, whites to the clear adhesives.

That same week, I went to visit Miss Card at the local nursing home. Miss Card was one hundred and two years old, the last surviving member of a family of nine children. She had grown up on a farm in Ontario and each week credited her ongoing longevity to the healthiness of that arduous but wholesome childhood. When I visited with Miss Card we spoke typically about her farm chores as a young girl. On this particular visit, watching the trees bud outside her window, she recalled the way her family would make maple syrup each year.

"We always used to tap our trees," she said. "We had big caldrons boiling with sap, first the one and then into another. We kept them outside, in the bush. And when the syrup was still hot, we poured it through sieves to strain out the larger impurities. Then my mother mixed up some milk and egg and stirred it into the warm syrup. The mixture cooked in the heat of the syrup and rose to the surface, taking all the rest of the impurities with it, and we could just spoon it off the top. All the dirt and dusts attached to the egg and we could lift it off with our hands."

I was beginning to look at eggs quite differently by now, seeing them not just as the province of breakfast and baking but as fundamental apparatus throughout the home. It was then that my mother-in-law said, while sipping on some of my coffee, "The best coffee I ever drank was in Texas. I had a friend, Ann, and she had a pot made out of, well, the material that lines ovens. The blue and grey lining? Ann mixed the coffee grounds with hot water and then she always threw in a couple of egg shells. The shells brought the grounds to the bottom and the coffee on top was absolutely wonderful!"

"The egg shells brought the grounds down?" I laughed. "Surely that's a little Southern witchcraft."

"No," my mother-in-law said firmly. "It worked that way. I don't know why but it actually worked."

I believed my mother-in-law (one must), so I telephoned the American Egg Board in Chicago to ask them why this short-of-kitchen-miracle reaction would happen.

"Hmmmm," came a voice on the other end of the line. I noticed this woman also had a Southern accent, so I was sure I had reached the qualified party. "Egg shells in coffee," she said slowly in her drawl. "I'm just writing this down. Do you mind if I put you on hold one second?"

I didn't. She was not long gone.

"Just the shells?" she asked.

"Yes," I said.

"Do you happen to know whether they were crushed or intact?"

"No, I don't," I replied. "I hadn't thought to ask."

"Of course not," she said soothingly. "Do you mind if I put you on hold again?"

"No," I said. I hummed to their country tunes.

"Honey, you still there? I can honestly tell you I have never heard that egg shells bring down coffee grinds, but I'm sure if your friend said so then that's true. You know, eggs are truly marvelous things . . ."

I was beginning to feel the same way, I was going to say. Eggs were growing in stature in my mind, too, but I don't have a lot of patience with trade-group pitches, so I asked her to send me some materials and rang off. Enough of this omelette business, I was thinking. People should be able to buy eggs at the hardware store. You wouldn't need to worry about fat, cholesterol, and food poisoning when you used the egg for general purpose home maintenance.

This flurry of new ideas for egg use made me think more about all farm yields as perceived in the past. There used to be more one could glean from a carcass, more one could accomplish with an egg, more ways one could look at a plant. I was reminded of a history lesson way back in elementary school. We read thick, disintegrating text books describing how the Indians of the Great Plains killed only as many buffalo as they needed to survive. The meat they ate. From the hides they made clothes and teepees. From the skeletons they fashioned weapons and implements. They made thread, for sewing those clothes and teepees, from the sinews, and they made needles for sewing from the bones. This was one of those Good Indian lessons, you realize, to be differentiated from the more numerous (in my day) Bad Indian sermons about gratuitous scalping and innocent-settler slaying.

And now I was amazed to hear of a few innovative things to do with an egg—so far am I from having to be creative, so provincial am I about my foodstuffs. Today both producers and consumers of food share a very restricted approach to food production. We breed hens specifically for egg-laying or meat yield. At the end of their productive (and hopelessly unattractive) life—eggs adjourned, meat packaged—their remains are fit only for the U.S. Army's massive soup tureens, in which the vestiges can be safely dissolved without imparting too much flavor. The remnant feathers, bones, and entrails are sometimes metamorphosed into chicken feed themselves—a nicely circular if distasteful route.

Well, at least we Americans are not wholly prodigal. We may not use all parts of a livestock carcass to full therapeutic advantage, but we certainly don't waste what we don't directly eat. Very little, in fact, is wasted in the modern packing house. All the organs, bones, fat and blood that consumers won't buy get recycled into processed foods, animal feeds, medical and industrial uses. Many of the edible parts that you wouldn't think of selecting outright will turn up, in plastic, in the refrigerated meat section of your supermarket—diverted into processed food products you will indeed buy. Nay, pet food is not the only end of the line for unsavory organs.

There are plenty of industries that take the beef fat, grind up the chicken feathers, tan the hides, and otherwise dispose of the less edible portions of a carcass. It's an efficient way to deal with the plain tonnage of detritus left after the valuable meat cuts are removed, but it's not a system that can be sensitive or creative with specific bodily by-products. Feed manufacturers and not coffee connoisseurs want the world's waste eggshells, the mass flotsam from big egg processing factories.

The number-one unpleasantness in coping with mass in general, I think, is that it forces you to ignore the value of individual components. It compels you to average, to dilute, to compromise excellence with poor quality and to neglect the merits of constituent parts. This happens within our enormous chicken processing industry and it occurs throughout our society today in a multiplicity of areas. Our own population has grown so large that government policies and doctor's offices and airplane companies are forced to deal with us as one immense herd of kindred cattle. We are all processed daily, issued new client numbers, gathered, and moved. In the modern livestock industry, so many animal carcasses are pushed through the slaughter plant each day that the waste is much easier dealt with as one manageable heap than as a gross accumulation of exclusive and serviceable parts. Burn it.

Perhaps the only other nonfood industry that has made aggressive forays into the American refrigerator is the cosmetics industry. They're interested in egg yolks, too, I notice, but they haven't cramped themselves within any one food group. Advertisements tell me that I can buy soap with oatmeal in it, shampoo with wheat germ and honey lurking inside, avocado and cucumber facial masques, or beer and lemon elixirs for my hair. It makes me uneasy to think that people who someday buy my farm produce might be going home to a mortar and pestle and shower. I don't like the notion that I might end up supporting any self-beautification craze.

I talked with one of my sisters about the many forgotten uses of different carcass parts, and she instantly burst into laughter.

"You've got to have a kind of prairie-days mentality to look to food wastes as an arts and crafts reservoir," she said. "Please, don't tell me: You're going to ask your butcher which cut of lamb would be better for staining dining room chairs. Well, I'm not the one to talk to, Nora. Just looking at a cake of yeast makes me edgy. And, well, eggshells in my coffee?"

I couldn't tell her she had slipped irreparably over the precipice into drab modernity. Or if she had, I was skidding downhill beside her. The fact is, while one can be intrigued to learn the various and diverse merits of common farm products, it's not easy to incorporate many of them into contemporary life unless seized by a sudden fit of "green" ingenuity.

"If you want everything *but* the steaks from your farmyard," my sister went on, "be sure to let me know. I *only* want the steaks, so that's fine." She giggled.

"Oh, God, Nora," she said. "Are you going to raise eye-of-newt next?"

·

"Exciting news in the turkey department," I said to my husband one afternoon. I had been flipping through some mail and poultry magazines while he was assembling elaborate radios piece by piece on the kitchen table.

"Hold on a minute," he whispered, his nose among the curious array of little leather Mickey Mouse ears and color-banded knobs that he fuses into circuit boards. He finished a presumably exacting maneuver and then straightened his back. The strain of this operation, which he calls a hobby, was obvious.

"Try breathing," I smiled. "Is this a radio for my chicken coop?"

"Do birds like music?" he asked, eyebrows raised high with mistrust.

"When you find their ears, I'll tell you if they like music," I said.

"Okay," he laughed. "Now what's this about turkeys?" He is markedly patient with my outbursts.

"Dad sent me a flyer from a butcher shop announcing the sale of Bronze turkeys, and then by coincidence I just found an article in one of my journals which says they're gaining in popularity."

"Bronzed turkeys?" He crinkled his face. "This sounds like some nasty offshoot of the group that gold-plates baby shoes."

"No, no," I said. "It's a breed. It's a color."

"I see," he said, nodding. "That's terrific, is it?"

"It's terrific," I replied. "Why don't you solder a bit while I go downtown and check out our local butchers." I called up a friend of mine and we went together.

The Broadbreasted Bronze is steadily making a commercial comeback. With hindsight, I can say I should have expected as much. America's bored and affluent baby-boomers have made such an elite sport of uncovering every conceivable curious food on the planet—white asparagus from China's conical mountains, yellow raspberries, alligator meat, and so on. Their parents strove for the perfectly white bread, but this generation will only eat stone-pounded, gritty brown loaves. For their parents, turkey producers nationwide switched over to a white-feathered bird so that every Thanksgiving roast would have that perfect translucent skin. It was only time, I guess, before the kids said, "No thanks. Show me those dark-feathered turkeys that I see on the greeting cards. Show me a roast with black pin feathers."

"Now, tell me again, why do I want black pin feathers?" asked my friend as we drove downtown. "And what are pin feathers anyway?"

I had appointed myself her food fashions coach.

"Not to worry," I said. "Tiny tiny feathers that may still be lodged under the skin. You rarely see them on white-feathered birds, and if you did, well, they pretty much burn off in the oven anyway."

"I hope I have never eaten a feather!" she said. She was from the South. Northerners would probably eat feathers if they were properly promoted.

It's good to be warned about dark-feathered birds. Their appearance can be startling the first time. You might suspect even the most highbrow butcher of an egregious transgression when you spot a Bronze in his meat case—a massive ready-to-roast bird covered with dark needle-pricks and inky stains. In spite of forewarning, my friend's jaw fell open when we arrived at the butcher's and she hung out a limp finger in the direction of the glass case.

"You're trying to poison us," she said to the butcher. "This bird died of scrofula or the Black Plague or something."

The butcher rolled his eyes with that kind of reverse snobbism that seems to make Bergdorf Goodman clerks so prosperous.

"This is a turkey that had, when it was alive, brown and black feathers," he explained. "It is called a Bronze, and the bronze turkeys are very much in vogue." He sniffed. And he remarked for emphasis: "I'm told that Lidgate's, butchers to the queen of England, carry the Bronze."

My friend turned to me. "Very worldly, the butchers around here. But do you think the queen of England really eats turkey? I mean, she may as well celebrate Thanksgiving. You tell me the queen of England celebrates Thanksgiving."

The butcher was sighing. He had no other customers to wait on, but he was clearly a time-is-money guy. But my friend and I were impervious. We both were interested in trying out this aberrant bird.

"Well," I smiled, "what's good enough for the queen of England is good enough for me. Besides"—I turned to my friend who was still squinting and rubbing her chin over this provocative turkey as though she were waiting for it to pale—"we can't just let this moment of culinary euphoria pass us by."

"Okay," she finally said. "This is very avant-garde for Ed and me, and"—she looked up at the butcher sharply—"I'm not entirely convinced." She was tough, this one. "But I'll take one, too."

He started to wrap up the turkeys.

"Wait a minute," snapped my friend. "What about its taste compared to, you know, the dry, white, routine turkeys that normal people eat?"

"The same or better," said the butcher.

"And cooking time?"

"The same."

"And stuffing?"

"The same." He looked weary.

So we purchased our Bronze turkeys, feeling, as the paparazzi do, a little smug and ahead of it all. Really, we rehearsed remarking to our astonished guests, white turkeys are just a bit passé.

The Broadbreasted Bronze is in fact what most people imagine when they think of turkeys. It is one of the largest strains of domesticated turkeys. Toms grow to as large as thirty-eight pounds, and hens tend to peak at about twenty-two. Their plumage is copper-bronze, with brown and black feathers in striation. Their wattles and caruncles (those bright red flaps and nubby protrusions along their necks) are thick and full. Broadbreasted Bronzes are stately birds, the "peacock" of the turkey breeds, with their magnificent fan tails and metallic sheen.

I hope to keep some Bronzes on my farm. I would like to raise turkeys in some shape and form for Thanksgiving and Christmas presents, and I'm not so keen on the white turkey—the vernacular of commercial operations—because they are a little ghostly-looking to me. The ones I've seen are all-over white, with pitch-black opalescent eyes and skinny sinewy necks and eerie rose-colored skull caps for heads. Bronzes, on the other hand, maintain a sovereign air in the middle of all that fluff and strut.

I have read that turkeys can be unexpectedly good company when raised in a conducive environment. One woman who kept a small flock of turkeys claimed they made wonderful companions and watchbirds, gobbling furiously at the sight of strangers (actually, only toms gobble—hens cluck). They will quite happily follow you about the yard, she wrote, and run to greet you in the mornings.

"This I have to see," said my husband.

Then I read him an account of one turkey farmer who said her birds liked to play with a rubber ball on the lawn.

"No. Stop," he said. "We must be thinking of two different animals."

There seem to be several turkeys out there to choose from. I have read about Black turkeys, Slate Blue turkeys, and Narragansett turkeys with deep black and gray feathers and salmon-colored legs. There are the Bourbon Red and the Beltsville Small White, the Crimson Dawn and the Royal Palm. Domesticated breeds of turkey throughout the world originate from our North American wild turkey, a truly national bird. This is one reason why Benjamin Franklin proposed the turkey as the official bird of the United States—"a much more respectable bird," he wrote to his daughter, than the bald eagle.

I pulled out my Murray McMurray catalogue to see what they were offering. Murray McMurray, a hatchery in Webster City, Iowa, has been around for most of this century selling and shipping poultry stock around the nation. Conveniently, they also merchandise equipment useful in poultry operations: incubators, infrared heat brooders, quail waterers, egg washers, manuals, and so on. It's one-stop shopping for many poultry enthusiasts, no less inviting for the toll-free telephone number.

I found turkeys toward the end of the catalogue, way past the bantams, past the heavy-breed chickens, past the ducks and pheasants, even past the guinea hens—those queenly polka-dotted barnyard busybodies strangely reminiscent of something from the pterodactyl era. So it was that I learned, on my way to the turkeys, that you could acquire Buff, Purple, Coral, Lavender, White, and Pearl guineas. I had only known the Pearl guineas before—black birds with a remarkably exact print of white dots across their feathers.

Guinea hens are terrific farm animals. Although these birds are noted for their meat, I know few people who would ever eat from their flock. The hens are hilarious to watch, and awfully captivating as they spend their days together, foraging your lawns for ticks, weed seeds, and the odd delectable bug. From a distance, they look like black footballs: a covey of black footballs racing at full tilt across the driveway, black footballs sitting comfortably in the sugar gum tree, black footballs *en pointe* on the stone wall, black footballs shrieking bloody murder at anyone they don't recognize. I was intrigued to imagine guineas in different colors. It was going to be hard to wait.

For turkeys, Murray McMurray was offering Broadbreasted Bronzes, Giant Whites, wild turkeys (the Eastern strain, I note for the interested aesthete), and Bourbon Reds.

"There's no denying it," I said to my husband as I scanned the page. "There is something of the buzzard in this bird."

Maybe it's the featherless head, or the blood-red cascade of wattles that dangle about the neck like primitive remnants of an entrail perhaps more judiciously left inside the body. A Darwinian oversight, in my book. McMurray's only sells turkeys in "straight run," males and females in the proportions by which they arrive. Even in this world of mankind strong-arming nature, a straight run will add up to about a fifty-fifty mix of males and females.

Having heard so much about wild turkeys, I was tempted to get a few. In the catalogue they were described as "very hardy and of course very colorful," which was compelling; and then, not "as big as the domestic turkeys but are good flyers." Did I want good flyers? Maybe another time. The Bourbon Red turkeys though, were unexpectedly alluring. The picture next to the blurb had a male and female strolling in a green meadow. It is frequently so with agricultural trade "art," that the animals depicted exude personality. He only lacked a top hat, and She was wanting her parasol. It was Sunday in the park with Tom and the little clucker. Both were deep chestnut-colored, with bold white accents on their wings and tail feathers—none of that misogynist color allocation so rife in the aviary world, where males of brilliant hues are paired with females of motley duns and grays that only ornithologists call subtle. In the turkey world, it would appear, females have plenty of rich color and equally jazzy caruncles of which to boast.

•

"A duck pond would be nice," said my husband one afternoon.

"In the wildflower meadow? Between the pear trees?"

"It would have to be covered," he said. "I don't want any Canadian geese to see it. I would have to shoot them, and the county would put me in jail."

"It's for a good cause," I said.

Canadian geese have become the bane of New England ponds, lakes, farms, and golf courses. They have proliferated during the past several years of legislated protection and, like deer, lost their favored-creature status for many Americans. I have heard from people living along the annual flyways, very civilized people who read books and prefer Mozart, strangely vicious words issuing from their lips—words like *strangle, shoot, murder, destroy, decimate*—words more at home in an angry rap tune or the Metro section of *The New York Times* than on the flagstone patio of a spacious Colonial-style house.

Flocks of Canadian geese yearly enveloped the manure piles on a farm where I once worked. They nosed out and ate undigested pieces of corn from the manure. It was a disturbing inclination. In so doing, they cleverly foiled any interest a person might have had in catching and eating one of them. I wonder if that's a Darwinian attribute. Survival of the most iron-coated stomach.

But ducks I'm fond of, and ducks we shall have on the farm. I learned from the American Minor Breeds Conservancy that the Khaki Campbell duck and the Rouen duck were considered threatened species, so I resolved to get a few to raise. And I had seen pictures of Fawn and White Runners, which are wonderfully vertical ducks with attractive (and aptly named) coloring. Those I would enjoy having around. They supposedly don't waddle, a commentary I found completely winning, and with intimations of some higher duckish gentility. Still, I don't plan to devote myself to ducks. No, the ducks, I reckon, will be largely on their own.

"You can't throw yourself into every species of livestock that the world wants to wipe out," said a friend gingerly.

"I'm not throwing myself into anything," I said. "I'm no agrarian martyr. This farm is entirely a response to my own selfish, narrow-minded, psychopathic desires. I like ducks and I like duck ponds. But ducks should be able to take care of themselves, shouldn't they? Given some food and a shoreline duck house and a second home somewhere in the Catskills."

"With that," my friend said, "I could certainly take care of myself."

I had thought little more about the duck issue until one day I went to visit the Bridgeport Zoo. Bridgeport is a city besieged. It has the garbled honor of having filed for bankruptcy as a municipality. It has a reputation for collecting the worst of inner-city problems and in no way compensating, in spite of a lovely geographical bedrock. So I felt lucky to get to the zoo before any padlocks arrived.

The zoo sprawls across a hilltop park overlooking the beautiful Naugatuck River. The usual suspects are there: wolves, deer, peacocks, bears, cats, llamas. I walked up to a kind of farm area that had a terrific mob of goats, some poultry, sheep, and a porcupine sleeping in the crook of a very young tree. Just past the snoozing porcupine was a little cement demipond, and it was there I found the most enormous duck I have ever seen. It was huge. It was beyond all duck proportions. It was swimming around in the waterweeds, probably remarking to itself that the food and the neighborhood had recently gone to hell. From the best I could make out—because all sorts of fowl were running (flapping, swimming, and waddling really) around together in the same cordoned area, and because the zoo's random explanatory placards had me completely stumped—it was a duck from China. I came home breathless.

"Have I got a duck for you!" I said to my husband. "You wouldn't believe the duck I saw today. It was gigantic—for a duck."

I had my arms open wide in narration. My husband was unmoved.

"We only have a small grill," he said.

I said, "You're missing the point. This is a fantastic animal. This guy could eat a cat for breakfast. We should really think about raising this bird."

"Well," he said, "what kind of duck is it?"

"That's the problem. I couldn't find anyone there who could tell me. The sign seemed to indicate it was from China."

"Mmmm." He frowned. "I don't want inscrutable ducks."

Part Four

Reaper

11

A Chair in
the Barn

I followed the hostage crisis in the Middle East with determination, interest, and sadness. It seems quite true that several other cultures put less value on a human life than we do in America. Well, and if the population of the world is going to reach 300 billion early into the next century, then I bet I'll put less value on a few lives, too. I already notice a black corner in my soul where the arguments in favor of capital punishment feed and thrive. There is something so dehumanizing about having so many people on this little planet that I think I have come to look upon weeding out the bad ones as a kind of sensible garden management.

Who are "the bad ones"? Who am I to judge? Quite reasonable questions, I agree. But while at one time I might have seen them as rhetorical show-stoppers, now I am apt to reply with a few candidates for culling and the acknowledgment that I am not the judge, which is the terrific luck of a lot of felons and idiots out there.

The last British and American hostages in the Middle East were finally released in the winter of 1991–1992. It seemed that, once again, so much misunderstanding, so much of the terrorists' primitivism and so many layers of confused political sediment, were responsible for the whole ordeal. Compassion mixed with my joy when I read accounts of the last men flown out of the Middle East to recuperate in Wiesbaden, Germany—not only because they had evidently suffered a good deal, but also because reintegration would be so trying. I was moved by the interview with Terry Anderson, released after a lovingly tallied 2,455 days of captivity. I read in the *International Herald Tribune* (December 7 and 8, 1991): "He told of the relatively good times, of the rich friendships he developed with fellow captives, the courses his friend Thomas M. Sutherland taught him in genetics, statistics and animal breeding, and the elaborate plans he made to start the perfect newspaper or set up the finest farm."

The finest farm, I thought. The perfect newspaper. To survive and to communicate. It was a stirringly guileless image of a soul.

The finest farm is something most farmers strive toward, most would-be farmers plan for. To some it means the highest productivity per acre, to others the most humane husbandry practices. The criteria have always been varied and contested. I have read a lot about agriculture in scientific, trade, and personal literature, and a set of definitive rules articulating the ideal husbandry has proven elusive. Instead I hear, as within a musical passage, the guiding rhythms of common sense, the cadence of seasonal changes, the bass-like beat of the basic diurnal chores.

Good agricultural reading is not easy to come by, and I rely on the trade journals for current news. Some of the magazines I have found most helpful are *American Agriculturist, Milling & Baking Weekly, Farm Journal,* and *Drovers Journal.* The USDA has a bounty of printed materials that one can summon through the Government Printing Office or state departments of agriculture. I read the newspapers and find random snippets of information. When I have sought out books about farmers and farming outside the confines of agricultural college campuses, the pickings are thin. The farm-oriented books that exist in my local library are scattered like dandelion seeds among the gardening shelves, corporate industry shelves, state history shelves, and pets shelves. Most of the literature about farmers—apart from the this-establishment-is-murdering-us ilk, or the thrillerlike tales of multinational agribusiness stratagems—seems maudlin to me. There are several books that treat farmers like a dying race of pre–Bronze Age heroes, painting them as stoic, strong, private, often Germanic (post-Bronze, these) men; a reader can almost hear the anguished sigh of the author as each page turned brings one closer to the end of the idyll.

I have found in the general farm literature a bastion of sentimentality, and it seems curiously counterpoised with the distinctly ruthless tone that characterizes what I find in most media reportage outside of the agricultural trade journals. Literature would seem to be the repository of agrarian nostalgia, whereas today's newspapers and television coverage guarantees itself a faithful audience by depicting with no measly bias the outrages of the American food production system.

When you decide to become a farmer, no matter on what scale, you're automatically jumping into the fray. Romance battles with reality. Will you do things the nice old way? Or will you partake of the modern agricultural machine? Of course, there is plenty of gray area, and you can certainly blend the best of both codes. The middle road is typically recognized as the moderate and sensible one—although it can also mean you come under fire from the woods on both sides.

If you are romantically inclined about agriculture (I hesitate to use the word *histrionic*), I think you're through as a farmer. It's easy to find delight in sheep, to find satisfaction in well-ploughed soil, but farming is a business for most people. There is money to earn and muscles to injure. There are improvements to make. There are input and output industries that push and pull upon your decisions. There are crises. There are inequities.

I wish for Terry Anderson the finest farm. He who has suffered plenty at the hands of twentieth-century primitivism, and who bore it and survived to gain an unenviable knowledge of raw human spite and transience—may he find peace on his farm. May he find the inequities of farming wonderfully banal.

·

Wherever we site the farm, there are two questions that need addressing straightaway: Can I farm, and may I farm? Indeed, it's a little late in the game for me to ask myself "Can I farm?" I've already put aside any incertitude about my own health— my allergies to alfalfa in full bloom, a physical aversion to large spiders and snakes of any size (a reaction my doctor considers entirely sound). Persisting will be the delicate issue of the health of my farmland—the quality of the soil, the inherent character of the terrain and its tenacity under seditious weather conditions. Lousy weather I regard as seditious.

As for the land itself, the first thing to do is to have the soil analyzed. One must be wary of buying land with a poor soil profile. That rings self-evident, but plenty of people do it. This contingent may be comforted by assorted success stories of land rehabilitation after the most monstrous scenarios of hazardous waste dumping and infertility. To me, the risks seem high.

A soil profile will also help me decide where to plant what, and how to fertilize, be it with chemicals, manure, cover crops, or eggshells. In the past I have enjoyed browsing the soil-sample analysis kits that they sell in hardware stores. These will alert you to the nitrogen (N), phosphorus (P), and potassium (K) levels of your ground. I prefer those boxes jam-packed with literature and 800 telephone numbers, and I steer clear of those with step-by-step printed instructions that treat you like a dummy. It's one of those mundane reminders that illiteracy in America is blooming.

N, P, and K lay the foundation for most crop fertilizers, but scores of other micronutrients are also critical in plant nourishment and soil tilth. I first learned about micronutrients in a course at Texas A&M. It was an introduction to soil sciences taught by the "marvelous Murray Milford," who sported a Marine haircut, biked to work each day on a one-speed bicycle, and learned the name of every student (a couple of hundred) in his class by the second week. He began his opening lecture with two requests: one, that baseball caps find themselves a hook outside of the auditorium, and two, that spitting (many students chewed tobacco) be suspended until after class. You could swallow in class, but you couldn't spit.

For this course, we were asked to collect a soil sample, either at random from the area or from Daddy's ranch, and to create a hypothesis with regard to it. I scooped up some dirt from the shore of nearby Lake Somerville one afternoon, having biked out there to swim, having found no living thing either in the water, of which there was little, nor some distance up the slate-colored beach, which was broad, and having thus decided that I would also not introduce my living body to the lake. I ate my yogurt, washed out the container, and scratched a quantity of this kind of shale particulate into it—it gave a new meaning to the word *beach*.

When I got back to the university, my laboratory instructor, Duane, asked me to think up a hypothesis.

I said, I just drove down to Texas two weeks ago. You tell me what you grow here.

Duane sighed. Northerners.

I said, Okay, how about I want to start a peach orchard in the vicinity?

Duane looked into my yogurt cup.

He said, You might better drill for oil.

We analyzed our soil samples for three months, and the results were as expected. No orchard. Along the way I had a wonderful time acquainting myself with the universe of nonorganic chemicals and organic matter and their interactions with water and air—from bedrock to sand, silt, and clay. Now I think about soil micronutrients with the same enthusiasm that I usually reserve for a full spice cabinet. It's not, however, a joy easily shared.

My father applies lime to his garden in the fall, out of habit now, and broadcasts his 10-10-10 fertilizer each spring. A 10-10-10 fertilizer contains ten percent nitrogen, ten percent phosphorus, and ten percent potassium.

"Which micronutrients do you suppose you have trouble with in Northampton?" I asked my father one day, my nose in a book about loams.

"Yes," he said.

"Me too," said my husband, who overheard.

Not all farmers are so abreast.

•

The second question—May you farm?—has to do with local ordinances, federal law, and environmental protection. Are there wetlands on the property? Has there been a recent sighting in your pine tree of some inexorably rare redwinged, black-billed songbird from the former Yugoslavian republic? A market basket of commercial statutes will no doubt pertain to your modest proposal to farm, and prospective farmers can begin to plumb the depths of awaiting bureaucratic stipulations with a telephone call to their community's planning and zoning commission. I did this once as an exercise when we lived in Greenwich. I called the Town Hall's Planning and Zoning department to find out how one might go about starting a farm on one's property and I was informed with firm politeness by a secretary there that such questions were the province of the local health department, to which she abruptly transferred me.

"Hmmm," said a female voice on the end of that line. "Isn't that Planning and Zoning's department?"

"One would think," I said.

She said, "Well, all I can tell you off the bat is that your animals have to be separate from your living quarters."

No cows in the house. I could accept that.

"Let me get the code out," she said. "Animal controls . . .

owners keeping or harboring more than one animal . . . no person shall build or maintain a stable or kennel within fifty feet from any house and one hundred feet from a well or watercourse or two hundred feet from a public water supply.

"Hmmm," she read on. "You have to clean the manure."

"I have to what?" I asked.

"Clean the manure, it says, so it doesn't harbor any debris. That doesn't make a lot of sense, does it? I guess it means you have to dispose of it properly, somehow. Is it dogs you're raising? If it's dogs they have to be secured, and leashes can be no shorter than ten feet in length."

"No," I said. "No kennels."

"If it's horses and you wash a horse, you have to dispose of the water somehow outside of the building." She paused. "I think that's it, as long as you keep clean—the animals I mean."

I thanked her and asked to be transferred back to planning and zoning. No one picked up the line there. Next I called the tax assessor's office.

"There's no such thing as agricultural zoning," said one of the town assessors, slightly snappish. "There's what's called farm classification. But you can't just go out and start a farm. You have to ask for a special permit for farmland from the planning and zoning commission.

"Most property," he explained, "is taxed at the rate of seventy percent of market value. To get farm classification, you have to prove to our office that you have a working farm. You have to be able to show on your Internal Revenue Service return that you got farm income. I would have to go observe the so-called farm personally."

"So," I said, "I couldn't get a tax break on my property until the farm was earning enough money to show up as income on my IRS statement."

"Correct."

"So," I said, aware that housing tracts in the community were marketed for upward of a quarter of a million dollars per acre, "it might be a few years of initial capital expenditures and overhead and no break on the property taxes."

"Correct," he said. "But it's worth pursuing. Under the 1979 valuation, a farm acre was valued at seven hundred dollars, and that value is still on the books today. It's a considerably very good deal."

It was now 1991.

"Are we still taxed under the 1979 codes?" I asked.

"Yes indeedy."

Many states have such considerably very good deals as part of an effort to preserve farmland for the public weal. There may be property-tax reductions, conservation programs, and "development rights" purchase programs whereby the state or federal government will purchase from the farmer the right to develop all or a part of that farmland into perpetuity.

I next telephoned the Connecticut Department of Agriculture in Hartford to find out where there were county extension agents who might help me through the preliminary regulatory procedures for establishing a farm. The extension service is mostly quartered in Storrs, at the University of Connecticut campus, but there are also agents working out of scattered field stations. I wasn't sure whether Connecticut even had farm management specialists. I heard that they had a spectacular horticultural department, for example, but I was nervous about their animal-science commitment.

The woman I telephoned in Hartford was in a marketing division. She had already sent me an annual report called *Connecticut Grown,* which catalogued the agricultural production statistics for the state. It was dated 1988.

"Do you have any more recent numbers than these?" I asked.

"You have 1988?" she responded. "No. Well, we've got a few numbers now for 1989. I could Xerox the sheet and send it to you . . ."

I inquired about farm management agents.

"That's a tough one," she said. "Well, we've got specialists in Bethel, for example. If you wanna grow strawberries, say, they can help you. They can tell you how far apart you plant them, okay? If you wanna grow beef, say, well they can probably help you, too."

"Yes," I said, "it's beef I'm intending to grow."

•

I am no fatalist. I used to grapple fiercely for control over my self, my life, and lose punishingly the fights I picked. Now I think less in terms of control than of a greater range of response and flexibility. I have striven to mitigate my instinctive pattern of locking all internal doors when the sirens blare, and throwing up a few impenetrable dikes. As my father once said, one is better off pursuing autonomy than autarchy. I agree with that, and I have tried.

This maturation of philosophy will be useful when I start my farm because I foresee the daily undoing of my *systems*. These are not *systems* of the technological wunderkind type, but rather concoctions of self-discipline and order within a day that is completely stripped of external blueprints. There is no how-to manual for farming. That's precisely why someone like me becomes an advice monger for years, accumulating everybody's experiences and opinions in a kettle in order to make, ultimately, my own stone soup. Comes that morning then that I wake up beside a different window, with the sun in no way bursting forth its bright encouragement but rather glowing bemusedly, waiting to see what I make of the new piece of earth I care for. Maybe there will already be a couple of sheep in the barnyard. Maybe there will already be a rooster around, rustling in his straw and preparing for another big day of mating and squabbling.

What have I gotten myself into? I will wonder in those dawns when unremembered dreams leave me beaten in my nightgown.

What shall I do first? is the better question, whether you are feeling cheerless or merry. I have learned that it is a must simply to get moving—especially so on those mornings when depression has you pinned to the mattress. Moving helps. It is a way of pushing forward that, though it sounds purely physical, seems in fact to act as a revealing metaphor for your psyche. It is as though one's body can blaze a trail forward through the huge inertia that the mind entertains.

On mornings when I feel strong, relatively doubt-free about this decision to farm, I will still need to arrange my day. I will be governor of this farm, head honcho of the hacienda, tyrant of the keep—with the usual related responsibilities. So, as a lover of patterns, I am always looking for a workable quotidian *system* that I can fall into. Suppose:

1. Feed the chickens first.

2. Feed the sheep and goats.

3. Check the cattle on pasture.

4. Fix the laying boxes.

5. Stack the new corn sacks.

6. Let the hens out and collect the eggs.

7. Clean the shed.

8. Order spring seeds.

9. Fix the south fence of the north meadow.

That makes for a good Tuesday, say, and I am such that I would enjoy the same sort of thing for Wednesday. By Wednesday, however, the corn is stacked and the vegetable seeds are already ordered. The pattern remains intact only insofar as the animals daily require feeding. What shall I fill the gaps with? No problem: four sheep need crutching and I have to get soil samples from one field to send to the extension service for analysis.

No problem. Wednesday will be great. Until, comes Wednesday morning and I find one rooster died overnight from some mysterious cause. Or maybe I notice some rats near the hay. And something is smelling odd in the goat shed. Instantly the day takes on its own momentum, overrules my *systems,* and throws me into a whirlwind of prophylactic measures. Toss those patterns out the window for today, I think. Seek them, enjoy them, and don't forget to feed the goats even on those days when the prototype fails. Try to safeguard your routines for your animals' sake—they like habits, too. And keep your sense of humor when chaos creeps like Gollum into your day.

Such is the give and take in farming. Broad patterns of routine mixed with the unpredictable particulars of mayhem. So put, farming is just a cameo for all of life. And so on the order of life's mayhem came the news one day, via my husband, that he had seen a For Sale sign that might interest me.

We had been spending some of the summer with my husband's family in northwestern Connecticut, a region we prized not so much in the 1980s when Manhattan's surplus millionaires were spilling into the area with undammable passion, but rather in the 1990s, when the money evaporated and the love affair showed its transparence and ultimately its mortality. There is beautiful farm country in this area. There are long, straight, single-lane paved roads that lead to crossroads where tall solitary oak trees stand shading old yellow houses. There are hills that pour into valleys of corn that swell into hills of grass. There are milk cows grazing—Holsteins mostly, with their imperturbable tranquility—and the colorful shingles of Black Angus breeders hung out along the road. Greenhouses are scattered beside barns, conveying that vegetable farming is taken seriously here in the land of May frosts. A man just over in Torrington raises goats I'm interested in, and I know a dairyman in Hillsdale who always shares some tips with me.

We had certainly looked at farms in the area before—picture-perfect, nestled just so, white clapboard farmhouses surrounded by meadow and two pristine barns painted red. In the last decade, those especially quaint ones were often sold to antique dealers who, with no use for the extra acreage, sold it for development—that irreversible, uncomely token of what Congress calls a healthy economy.

I found these farms as a rule spruced up and attractive, especially when I stayed in the car, way up roadside at the turnoff to the driveway. But you could tell that the woods had been creeping in without resistance for a few years, or that the little circumscribed fields of wildflowers were actually cradles of cattails, which meant marshland. A closer peek revealed the hole in the roof, the tilt of the barns, the compaction of the soil. If they were expensive to buy, they still required riches to recondition.

"I think you'll like this," said my husband, driving us over to the For Sale sign.

He handed me a newspaper clipping.

"I think you'll like this," he hummed.

Farm. Must sell. 36 Acres plus Buildings. Current lease to corn/hay production. New barn with double open stalls. No silo. Small pond. Livestock and equipment negotiable. Five minutes to railroad.

"Very tantalizing," I said. "I love distressed properties."

At the crossroads take a right, go all the way along the ridge, out of the forest, a pond is on your left, you can see Massachusetts on a clear day. We slowed. A trim little wooden sign had been staked and driven into the grass just off the road. FARM FOR SALE 36 ACRES. There was a cattle guard across the entrance. We stopped the car and stepped out to look around.

It was dead quiet up on the ridge, a Berkshire foothill. A thin pine forest to the left shimmied discreetly down the other side of the slope. Intermittent summer breezes whispered through the pines and across our ears. A katydid. A loose pebble was lifted onto the asphalt and tapped out two metallic measures of syncopation before stopping. On the right was a wooden fence that seemed to run the perimeter of the farm. It was mostly gray with age, but new brown posts here and there indicated that it was being maintained.

"I like a place that's been cared for," said my husband.

We got back into the car. There was plenty of Connecticut to see from this hilltop but the farm itself was largely invisible, tucked just over the crest.

"I love a house you can't see from the road," he said.

We drove across the cattle guard and over the rise. A serene valley stretched out below. The road curved right and downward toward a cluster of birch and copper beech trees. There the pavement petered out into a dirt farmyard, an ample circular green in the center completely shaded from the sun. The driveable path formed a circuit from farmhouse to barn to paddock and back out.

"I love shade trees," I heard beside me.

We pulled up at the house. It was a modestly proportioned, two-storey brick structure, with white shutters and nongrandiose flourishes like stone slab lintels and stone slabs under each window. There was a small porch, and the eaves of the roof seemed generously broad. I really love fat eaves. They let you keep the windows open when it rains. We wandered to the side, where we could see that the original house had been gradually added on to, chunk by pleasant chunk, guest room by kitchen by pantry, nothing too recent and mostly in white clapboards but all in concert with the initial home.

"Houses were made so sensibly then," murmured my husband.

"Hello?" I called out. I knocked on the front door but there was no answer, so we decided to make a small tour of the farmyard. The barn, painted a deep forest green, was about the same size as the house. It had a simple, lofting shape. The fronting doors to the barnyard were enormous and bolted, but a side door meant only for man and animal was open. We peered into the dark, cavernous interior. There were two double rows of stalls on each side with a walkway down the middle, and storage overhead on two lateral floors that made ceilings for the stalls but kept the center alley open to the rafters. The proportions were so modest that I had to wonder who built it all. It had a kind of European petiteness. The doorways were a perfect height for me but would have required everyone else to stoop —save the four-legged. I didn't mind that particularly. Like the brick house, from the perspective of five feet and two and three-quarters inches, it felt pleasantly sized.

A stairway down and up was at the opposite end of the barn. We could hear gentle stamping below.

"Didn't you want a barn built into a slope?" asked my husband.

"Have you already bought this place?" I asked in return.

We walked around the barn and then over to the paddock. It too was in good shape, but empty. I looked out beyond the split rail fences, beyond the inner keep of barn and house, to hayfields, some sort of vegetable rows in a flatter tract, and the remnants of stringing stone walls that relaxed and toppled against the curvatures of the slopes. It was clearly a beloved farm. I wondered who the farmer was.

My husband went to retrieve his camera from the car as I walked down into the lower storey of the barn. From the rear, hillside, it was open to the air but pitch-black inside from shadows and emanating a damp, cellarish cool. I crossed the categorical line from sunshine to shadow, from blanched, dry manure and silts to black invisible earth. Such crossings are uniquely unsettling. It's like undergoing a sentient blackout— no swooning. It tests the memory and the mettle. Where are you standing? On what?

As my eyes got accustomed to the dark, I stood hoping there were no playful bulls inside unchained by ordinance of the devoted owner. There were certainly noises, the quick *hrumph hrumph* breathing of a cow or pig. No, it didn't smell like pigs. My eyes were focusing gradually and I began to see her, them.

A chestnut-brown Jersey cow was sitting out the summer heat in a bed of straw. Two trimmed Rambouillet ewes were lying next to her chewing quietly, and another younger Jersey heifer was tethered to the side wall.

"Howdy," I said aloud.

Grunts.

A few metal milk cans were glinting from back in the shadows. It was a surprisingly large space and not cut up by walls but neatly segmented by the load-bearing timbers.

"So where's the guy that runs this place?" I said. As my eyes were adjusting, I stepped deeper into the black, chatting, commenting, and enjoying the smells. This brood looked at me with glances that said they'd heard it all before, and couldn't one have peace and quiet on a hot summer day? Rusty hand tools hung on the inner walls and a few rakes and pitchforks leaned like old stray shards around the dark crevices of the barn. There were no spider webs encasing them, though. Things were used. Basic tools forever avail themselves.

"Tell me you guys take care of yourselves," I said.

A big black rubber water bucket was sitting on the stairs that led up into the main division of the barn. I turned it over and set it in the straw by the sheep. It made a dependable, not uncomfortable chair.

"Where are your buddies? There's a lot more corn stacked upstairs than you four could eat alone—not to underestimate you, of course."

A sheep nose wandered over to my knee and investigated. Never was a knee so casually rejected.

"You'd have me believe this farm was abandoned two months ago and you've been taking care of it yourselves."

Suddenly a lamb appeared from behind me and sauntered around one ewe to the other. It bent down and butted her udder, and the ewe without budging suffered it to feed. Proper sheep behavior. I looked over my shoulder to see if there were others following behind. Indeed I could now make out a small enclosure in the rear, and I thought I spotted several young lambs curled up in the straw.

"You're really bringing out your big guns now," I said.

Loud sucking noises.

"Okay, okay, I give in," I said. "Tell me what price you're offering for this place. I can't bargain anymore."

Chew, chew, chew.

"Okay, throw yourselves in and take the price down a few pegs," I said. "Just kidding. Throw yourselves in and raise the price, let's say . . . not that I wouldn't guess you're all pedigreed, but factoring in that I don't care so much, maaayyybeee. . . . Okay, maybe it's better not to talk money among friends. Why don't you just adopt me. I try never to tell the same story twice."

We sat and breathed together for a while. Then I heard my husband's voice somewhere outside. He was calling my name. I looked at the others. Men, we thought.

"Well, I should probably be going," I said.

And then I heard his voice suddenly much closer. "I saw her disappear somewhere down here."

Two tall forms appeared as silhouettes in the open entrance.

"Nora?" my husband queried the shadows.

"Yes," I said.

"Come meet Mr. Randall, the owner of the farm. There she is, Mr. Randall. I think I can just make her out. What are you doing in there, Nora?"

What could I say?

"I found a chair in the barn."

Epilogue

Very little stood between me and this farm, if you discount all the local bankers, mortgage agreements, title searches, and tithes paid to every bureaucrat and functionary who lands during this process at the desk in front of you. We spent the next few weeks considering other farms with mild interest, just to be sure, but each proved too worn, or too sterile, or too big or too remote.

I could see in this Connecticut farm a reflection of my own desire for who I might be. It was removed, but not lonely. It lacked those perfect paddocks and flawless furrows, but it expressed some lovely, empathetic gradient of wilderness restrained. The barn had a simple aesthetic I had always adored. The forest green paint on its timbers was weathering into something effortlessly beautiful and unprimped. The old house already seemed to promise a wonderful sanctuary. I envisioned it warm with music, and having a library that would rinse the day's fatigue from a reader's shoulders. The welcoming barnyard— half garden, half utility area—would allow me to be both farmer and poet. We could keep a bench there, maybe a swing, maybe take a drink out under the trees and talk about silage, apple varieties, housing for the homeless, Dickens, deworming techniques, and George Bush's acute brand of cynicism.

This farm had a kind of vanity that I liked. I say that with some reticence, because vanity is one of those major biblical sins and turns up also throughout the history of painting in horrendous allegorical apparitions. But there is to me a benign side of vanity that is not vain, that has to do with tucking in your shirt and presenting yourself with dignity.

I have learned to befriend vanity cautiously over my short lifetime. I began to see a different side of it as I watched my mother in and out of remission from Hodgkin's disease for so many years. When she was ill, her self-image slipped away into the immaterial and her vanity disappeared. She was wan, sapped, queasy. She lost her hair from the treatments. She lost her color.

Those were the years of sickness. In the intervening years of health, she would rediscover an interest in a pretty blouse, a Liberty print. She would wear her jewelry, find a new shade of lipstick. My mother was not a showy dresser, but she always aspired to a level of elegance. It was good form to dress well, she felt, however modestly, to present oneself properly. It was part of having manners, of behaving oneself in public.

"You're the only person I know," I would say, flopped on her bed in the mornings as she pulled a handkerchief from her bureau or a belt from the closet, "who overflows with understatement."

In those years when the cancer seemed defeated and her interest in the day was revived, I saw a wonderfully sound side of vanity: the smile tested in the mirror, a new pair of stockings. I carry with me, without my mother now, a sense of vanity's rubicund angles. And I felt invigorated on this Connecticut farm, which had a character that responded to my own bashful vanities.

"It will look even better when I plant banks of yellow tulips out front," I assured my husband. But he needed no reassuring.

·

So my husband and I moved through the most preliminary of official processes, and I explored an exhilarating sensation of hope and fulfillment combined. My husband's work was going well and we were altogether feeling as if we inhabited a providential oasis within the prevailing national climate of economic decline. The world outside seemed rife with mayhem, with unnegotiable obstacles and unremarked tragedies. I was surprised, then, one evening when mayhem innocently walked through our own front door.

"Something big happened today," my husband said, setting down his briefcase and settling himself on the couch.

"Good, I hope," I smiled, trying to coax his ambivalent face into something more encouraging.

"Well," he said, "they've offered me a job in Zürich. Switzerland."

I was quiet.

He said, "It sounds like a very good job."

I was having trouble speaking. If I opened my mouth, I thought, something like a primal scream would leap out before I could say anything. I pulled a jacket from our coat rack and held it to me as I remained standing in the corner by the door.

"I think we should talk about this," my husband said softly.

"Maybe I should just take a walk first," I replied. "You know." He knew. I needed a moment to collect myself. I was trying to be sensible, to prevent the outburst that was awaiting its genetic expression in every blood cell. If we talked now, I wanted to say, I'd just end up apologizing for it all later.

"But before I go," I said, "and I won't be long, I want you to know that I'm really really proud of you and of course I know you earned it." In the shadows of the corner I smiled as tenderly as I could while the tears started rolling down my cheeks.

When opportunities fling themselves in my direction, I usually acquiesce. They are not without roots, after all, in my own doing—opportunity sprouts along the path one tramples into pathdom. As for Switzerland, I was fully aware of my own contributions to this sequence of events. Living abroad had always been a dream of my husband's and mine. We had often spoken of such a chance as exciting and enriching. In a way, I suppose, there was never any question but that I would agree to go.

I cried a lot on my own time. I saw my farm suddenly slip off to a distant hill and all that went with it—the pleasures, the peace, the labor, and the struggles.

"The farm will be there when we get back," said my husband. "We will do it. I really want to see you do it." He did.

A part of me wanted to burn all the notebooks, forget the whole farm idea, and make of Switzerland a new direction to follow. I felt somehow that I had been thwarted, repulsed from agrarian life like an invader at the foot of the wall. Boiling oil and arrows from the turrets. Go home.

And home for me was perhaps the fundamental puzzle. Where was it? It was as much in the cosmopolitan cafés of Zürich's Bahnhofstrasse as within a breezy barnyard in the Berkshires. I had still spent more of my life within the comely sanctums of museums and languages than I had in the damp straw of a corral.

So many longings in life are these dull tugs from somewhere inside you. You try to identify them, you try to sate them. They are tricky to diagnose. They are like pains in the head, with their source above the left ear and their expression beneath the right eye. Depression can be such a tug, and when we get depressed we go rooting about on all different levels of our selves; we wonder whether our professional life is empty, we wonder if our spouse is unhappy, we wonder why our parents felt so emphatic about such and such. And when we find something that even remotely fits the bill—Ah yes, *that's* what must be getting me so down!—then we lunge forward to remedy the situation with the dedication of all good soldiers, with "extreme prejudice."

My longing for a farm of my own was such a dull tug. I had researched the idea for years to assure myself that this farm was really what the tug was about—if it were not at the same time a composite of so many yearnings. Having raced down many a dead end in my life, solution-seeking, I wanted this time to be more certain. And after all the inquiry I was convinced of two things: that there were no simple solutions to the inner tugs, and that I was indeed cut out for this farm, for this working preserve of the minor breeds. Moving to Europe even confirmed that for me.

That's the point at which, I think, my story became a woman's story. Women are faced throughout their lives with changes, both deliberate and unavoidable, bodily and external, that affect their whole identity. I have learned to take pride in being flexible and adroit in adapting to the next transition, although the pattern of periodic upheaval can get fatiguing.

Waiting for my farm was not something I was going to do idly in Zürich. I picked up some other threads in my basket and wove them not incongruously into my tapestry—a tapestry which, neither young nor old, is multicolored and curiously harmonious.

"You're actually pretty lucky that this move to Switzerland came before the farm," I said to my husband one day as we were enjoying an alpine view. "Moving over here would've been a difficult transition for the sheep."

He looked at me out of the corner of his eye.

"The steep slopes?" he ventured.

"The language."

He took that in. Then he said, "You imply it wouldn't have been as tough on the goats."

I sighed. "They would have refused to come."

FOR THE BEST IN PAPERBACKS, LOOK FOR THE

In every corner of the world, on every subject under the sun, Penguin represents quality and variety—the very best in publishing today.

For complete information about books available from Penguin—including Pelicans, Puffins, Peregrines, and Penguin Classics—and how to order them, write to us at the appropriate address below. Please note that for copyright reasons the selection of books varies from country to country.

In the United Kingdom: For a complete list of books available from Penguin in the U.K., please write to *Dept E.P., Penguin Books Ltd, Harmondsworth, Middlesex, UB7 0DA.*

In the United States: For a complete list of books available from Penguin in the U.S., please write to *Consumer Sales, Penguin USA, P.O. Box 999— Dept. 17109, Bergenfield, New Jersey 07621-0120.* VISA and MasterCard holders call 1-800-253-6476 to order all Penguin titles.

In Canada: For a complete list of books available from Penguin in Canada, please write to *Penguin Books Canada Ltd, 10 Alcorn Avenue, Suite 300, Toronto, Ontario, Canada M4V 3B2.*

In Australia: For a complete list of books available from Penguin in Australia, please write to the *Marketing Department, Penguin Books Ltd, P.O. Box 257, Ringwood, Victoria 3134.*

In New Zealand: For a complete list of books available from Penguin in New Zealand, please write to the *Marketing Department, Penguin Books (NZ) Ltd, Private Bag, Takapuna, Auckland 9.*

In India: For a complete list of books available from Penguin, please write to *Penguin Overseas Ltd, 706 Eros Apartments, 56 Nehru Place, New Delhi, 110019.*

In Holland: For a complete list of books available from Penguin in Holland, please write to *Penguin Books Nederland B.V., Postbus 195, NL-1380AD Weesp, Netherlands.*

In Germany: For a complete list of books available from Penguin, please write to *Penguin Books Ltd, Friedrichstrasse 10-12, D-6000 Frankfurt Main 1, Federal Republic of Germany.*

In Spain: For a complete list of books available from Penguin in Spain, please write to *Longman, Penguin España, Calle San Nicolas 15, E-28013 Madrid, Spain.*

In Japan: For a complete list of books available from Penguin in Japan, please write to *Longman Penguin Japan Co Ltd, Yamaguchi Building, 2-12-9 Kanda Jimbocho, Chiyoda-Ku, Tokyo 101, Japan.*

Tourism and Transport

ASPECTS OF TOURISM TEXTS
Series Editors: Professor Chris Cooper, *University of Queensland, Australia*
Dr C. Michael Hall, *University of Canterbury, Christchurch, New Zealand*
Dr Dallen Timothy, *Arizona State University, Tempe, USA*

Other Books of Interest
Codes of Ethics in Tourism: Practice, Theory, Synthesis
  David A. Fennell and David C. Malloy
Cultural Tourism in a Changing World: Politics, Participation and (Re)presentation
  Melanie K. Smith and Mike Robinson (eds)
Festivals, Tourism and Social Change: Remaking Worlds
  David Picard and Mike Robinson (eds)
Film-Induced Tourism
  Sue Beeton
Histories of Tourism: Representation, Identity and Conflict
  John K. Walton (ed.)
Learning the Arts of Linguistic Survival: Languaging, Tourism, Life
  Alison Phipps
Music and Tourism: On the Road Again
  Chris Gibson and John Connell
Nature-based Tourism in Peripheral Areas: Development or Disaster?
  C. Michael Hall and Stephen Boyd (eds)
North America: A Tourism Handbook
  David A. Fennell (ed.)
Shopping Tourism, Retailing and Leisure
  Dallen J. Timothy
Tea and Tourism: Tourists, Traditions and Transformations
  Lee Jolliffe (ed.)
The Global Nomad: Backpacker Travel in Theory and Practice
  Greg Richards and Julie Wilson (eds)
The Tourism Area Life Cycle, Vol.1: Applications and Modifications
  Richard W. Butler (ed.)
The Tourism Area Life Cycle, Vol.2: Conceptual and Theoretical Issues
  Richard W. Butler (ed.)
Tourism Development: Issues for a Vulnerable Industry
  Julio Aramberri and Richard Butler (eds)
Tourism, Recreation and Climate Change
  C. Michael Hall and James Higham (eds)
Tourist Behaviour: Themes and Conceptual Schemes
  Philip L. Pearce
Tourism Ethics
  David A. Fennell
Tourism and International Exchange: Why Tourism Matters
  Gavin Jack and Alison Phipps
Tourism in the Middle East: Continuity, Change and Transformation
  Rami Farouk Daher (ed.)
Wildlife Tourism
  David Newsome, Ross Dowling and Susan Moore

For more details of these or any other of our publications, please contact:
Channel View Publications, Frankfurt Lodge, Clevedon Hall,
Victoria Road, Clevedon, BS21 7HH, England
http://www.channelviewpublications.com

ASPECTS OF TOURISM TEXTS
Series Editors: Chris Cooper (*University of Queensland, Australia*),
C. Michael Hall (*University of Canterbury, New Zealand*)
and Dallen Timothy (*Arizona State University, USA*)

Tourism and Transport
Modes, Networks and Flows

David Timothy Duval

CHANNEL VIEW PUBLICATIONS
Clevedon • Buffalo • Toronto

For Madeline

Library of Congress Cataloging in Publication Data
Duval, David Timothy
Tourism and Transport: Modes, Networks and Flows/David Timothy Duval.
Aspects of Tourism Texts
Includes bibliographical references and index.
1. Transportation engineering. 2. Transportation–Passenger traffic. 3. Tourism.
I.Title. II. Series.
TA1145.D88 2007
388'.042–dc22   2007000284

British Library Cataloguing in Publication Data
A catalogue entry for this book is available from the British Library.

ISBN-13: 978-1-84541-064-3 (hbk)
ISBN-13: 978-1-84541-063-6 (pbk)

Channel View Publications
An imprint of Multilingual Matters Ltd

UK: Frankfurt Lodge, Clevedon Hall, Victoria Road, Clevedon BS21 7HH.
USA: 2250 Military Road, Tonawanda, NY 14150, USA.
Canada: 5201 Dufferin Street, North York, Ontario, Canada M3H 5T8.

The policy of Multilingual Matters/Channel View Publications is to use papers that
are natural, renewable and recyclable products, made from wood grown in
sustainable forests. In the manufacturing process of our books, and to further support
our policy, preference is given to printers that have FSC and PEFC Chain of Custody
certification. The FSC and/or PEFC logos will appear on those books where full
certification has been granted to the printer concerned.

Typeset by Saxon Graphics Ltd.
Printed and bound in Great Britain by MPG Books Ltd.

CONTENTS

ACKNOWLEDGEMENTS

Special thanks to the series editors, Mike Hall, Chris Cooper and Dallen Timothy, as well as Mike Grover at Channel View, for their support and encouragement. Mike Hall and Tim Coles were constant sources of encouragement and support – a debt of gratitude is indeed owed. Both Chris Cooper and Mike Grover provided useful feedback and advice on a first draft – the book is clearly better for it. Thanks also to, in no particular order, Ewan Wilson (founder of Kiwi Airlines International in New Zealand), Mike Swiatek, Stephen Jones and Rachel Gardiner at Freedom Air (New Zealand), Adam Weaver, Paul Peeters, Amanda Mabon, Paul Wilkinson, Bill Found, everyone in the Department of Tourism at Otago (Monica Gilmour, Diana Evans, James Higham, Richard Mitchell, Brent Lovelock, Hazel Tucker, Neil Carr, Anna Carr, Kat Blumberg), Micha Lueck, 'ntd-devsys', Sarah Todd, David Buisson, Alan MacGregor, Rosalie Rissetto and Mike Tod at Air New Zealand, Martin Montgomery, Jan Schlaefke, and Achim Munz. Thank you to everyone in the Commerce Division Office (Amanda, Kate, Bronwen, Kathie, Lauren, Clint, Kirstin, Sarah, and Karen) for making 2005 and 2006 smooth and enjoyable. Over the years, various students from my Tourism Transport Management course at the University of Otago have had a significant input into this project, whether they knew it or not. For his encouragement and insightful discussions I want to particularly thank Ayudh Nakaprasit, a former student of mine who, as at July 2006, is working as an Aviation Analyst in the Strategic Planning Division at Nok Air in Thailand.

I was fortunate to have a team of very capable Research Assistants over the course of this project, including Trudie Walters, David Purdie, David Scott, Paul MacDonald (for reading a final draft and offering excellent suggestions), Martine Baastians, Simon Rowe and Sarah Nicolson. Thanks to everyone at Channel View for their patience and support, particularly Sami Grover (good luck, mate), Sarah Williams, Ellie Robertson, Jonna Gilbert, Ken Hall, Kathryn King, and of course Mike and Marjukka Grover.

Background sounds courtesy of Andy Bell, Vince Clarke, Dave Gahan, Martin Gore, Andy Fletcher, Alan Wilder, Ralf Hütter and Florian Schneider, Eric Mouquet and Michel Sanchez, Client, William Orbit, Leftfield, Neil Tennant, Chris Lowe, FGTH, New Order, Pitch Black, John Digweed, and Marcus Lush in the evenings on Radio Live. Finally, I want to especially thank my wife and, indeed, pillar of support, Melissa, for both her presence and tolerance.

David Timothy Duval
Opoho, October 2006

PERMISSIONS

Thanks to the following individuals/organisations for granting permissions to utilise/reproduce materials presented herein:

- David Fossett, for permission to base Figure 4.4 on his own map.

- www.cruisejunkie.com for permission to use data on cruise line environmental infringements.

- Jean-Paul Rodrigue for permission to base Figure 6.2 on his original figure (http://people.hofstra.edu/geotrans/).

- Elsevier for permission to reproduce Figure 2.2 and Figure 7.1.

- Air New Zealand (particularly Rosalie Rissetto) for Figures 8.1 and 8.2.

ABBREVIATIONS

AA	American Airlines
ACCC	Australian Competition and Consumer Commission
ACI	Airports Council International
AIF	airport improvement fee
ASA	air service agreement
ASA	Advertising Standards Authority
ASK	available seat kilometre
ASM	available seat mile
ATW	Air Transport World
BAA	British Airport Authority
BBC	British Broadcasting Corporation
BTS	Bureau of Transport Statistics (US)
BWIA	British West Indian Airways
CAA	Civil Aviation Authority (UK)
CAC	command and control
CBC	Canadian Broadcasting Association
CEV	Crew Exploration Vehicle
CFC	chloroflurocarbon
CLIA	Cruise Lines International Association
CLV	Crew Launch Vehicle
CRA	Customs and Revenue Agency
CRS	computer reservations systems
CTO	Caribbean Tourism Organization
DESA	Department of Economic and Social Affairs (UN)
DoT	Department of Transport (US)
DPRK	Democratic People's Republic of Korea
DSEC	Statistics and Census Service (Macau)
ECAA	European Common Aviation Area

EIS	Environmental impact statement
EPA	Environmental Protection Agency
ETEZ	Effective Tourism Exclusion Zone
FAA	Federal Aviation Administration (US)
FDPS	flight data processing system
FIT	free and independent travellers
FSA	full service airline
GAO	General Accounting Office (US)
GE	General Electric
GDP	gross domestic product
GDS	global distribution systems
GhG	greenhouse gas
GIS	geographical information system
HACAN	Heathrow Association for the Control of Aircraft Noise
IASA	International Aviation Safety Assessment
IATA	International Air Transport Association
ICAO	International Civil Aviation Organisation
ICCL	International Council of Cruise Lines
IDP	International Driving Permit
IEA	International Energy Agency
IMO	International Maritime Organization
IOC	Intergovernmental Oceanographic Commission
IPCC	Intergovernmental Panel on Climate Change
ISS	International Space Station
IT	information technology
ITA	Office of Travel & Tourism Industries (US)
JAO	joint airline operation
KTX	Korean Train Express
LCC	low-cost carrier
LCLF	low cost/low fare
LIAT	Leeward Islands Air Transport
MEAS	Macau Eagle Aviation Services
MEP	Maritime Environment Protection
MICE	meetings, incentives, conventions, exhibitions
MSD	marine sanitation device
NASA	National Aeronautics and Space Administration
NCN	National Cycling Network
NGO	non-governmental organisation
NSCR	North Sea Cycle Route
NZCC	New Zealand Commerce Commission

OACC	Oceanic Area Control Centre
OECD	Organization for Economic Cooperation and Development
PATA	Pacific Asia Travel Association
PERC	perchlorethylene
P&O	Peninsular and Oriental Steam Navigation Company
PNR	passenger name record
PRC	People's Republic of China
RCEP	Royal Commission on Environmental Pollution (UK)
RDC	Democratic Republic of Congo
RMS	revenue management system
RPK	revenue passenger kilometres
RPT	regular passenger transport
SAA	strategic alliance agreement
SAM	single aviation market
SAR	special administrative region
SARS	Severe Acute Respiratory Syndrome
SUV	sports utility vehicle
TSA	Transportation Security Administration
TTMRA	Trans-Tasman Mutual Recognition Arrangement
UNCCD	United Nations Convention to Combat Desertification
UNEP	United Nations Environment Programme
UNFCCC	United Nations Framework Convention on Climate Change
UNWTO	United Nations World Tourism Organization
VAA	Virgin Atlantic Airways
VBA	value-based airline
VFR	visiting friends and relatives
VLCV	very large cruise vessels
VOIP	voice over internet protocol
WMO	World Meteorological Organization
WTI	West Texas Intermediate
WTO	World Tourism Organisation
WTTC	World Travel and Tourism Council

CHAPTER 1:

INTRODUCTION: MANIFESTATIONS OF TRANSPORT AND TOURISM

LEARNING OBJECTIVES

After reading this chapter, you should be able to

1. Understand the complex nature by which transport is tied to tourism and tourism development.

2. Assess and describe the scope of transport operations worldwide, particularly as they relate to travel flows and tourism development.

3. Distinguish and draw correlations between modes, networks and flows and their role(s) in the development of transport networks.

4. Outline the top issues facing transport provision in the context of tourism.

5. Discuss the role of the mode and type of transport in the context of decision-making systems.

INTRODUCTION: A SITUATION ANALYSIS

Transport has emerged as one of the more ubiquitous and complex global economic sectors. It forms the backbone of national and international commerce by acting as a mechanism for the movement of freight and people. As a result, growth in transport systems share synergies with growth in tourism, and vice versa. The global reach of tourist activities has, in part, been facilitated by the increase in accessibility of tourist 'places' on a global scale, and the popularity of holidays in western countries that make use of personal transport surged throughout the 20th century, thus spawning consistent demand for accessibility. Importantly, externalities that affect the viability of tourism at varying spatial levels (e.g. attractions, destinations, regions, global) can have flow-on effects to transport. As well, externalities that affect transport provision can impact on tourism demand and tourism development. Indeed, the events of 11 September 2001 in the United States demonstrated the fragility of the global tourism sector and associated transport industries.

Global tourism has grown significantly in the past few decades (Figure 1.1), and even over the past century. The stagnant growth in global tourism between 2001 and 2003 seems to have begun a renewal beginning in 2004 and carrying through to early 2006 (UNWTO, 2005a, 2006). The scope for international travel, according to the IATA, is positive in some regions (e.g. Asia and Middle East) despite overall setbacks experienced in 2005 due to increased costs for fuel spurned by rising oil prices (IATA, 2005). With UNWTO predicting almost 1.6 billion arrivals by 2020 (UNWTO, 2005a), and with several airlines (e.g. Qantas, Emirates) purchasing next-generation aircraft such as the Boeing 787, the Airbus A350 or the A380, the importance of transport provision becomes clear. Developments in transport can, and will, have an enormous impact on people's mobility, and tourist motivation and demand in general already has significant impacts on the *way* people travel (Hall, 2005). As Hall (2005: 37) notes, tourists have benefited from the introduction of new technologies in transportation, which have been developed as a direct consequence of the rise in demand of travel:

> The cost and time of moving commodities, services and people have dramatically reduced in recent years. The real cost of travelling internationally has fallen sharply, as has the time it takes to travel long distances…In the first decade of the twenty-first century marginal increases in the time saved may be achieved but, more significantly, the same flight will be undertaken by double-decker jumbo jets carrying almost twice as many people as the 'traditional' jumbo jet.

The Department for Transport in Great Britain established a baseline index from 1990 and plotted the movement of distance, time and number of trips using the National Travel Survey. The result is that the number of trips has decreased steadily since 1990 while distance has increased (Figure 1.2). The amount of time spent travelling (including all forms of travel, not just tourism) has slightly decreased.

A 20-year outlook for commercial air travel produced by Boeing (2005) suggests passenger traffic between 2005 and 2024 will increase by an average of 4.8% per year, and cargo traffic is predicted to increase by an average of 6.2% across the same period. Boeing also predicts the global fleet of aircraft will double by 2024 to over 35,000 commercial aircraft (including both cargo and passenger). Airbus, a competitor, produced its own market outlook report (Airbus, 2005) with similar predictions of growth. Airbus predicts that the number of passenger aircraft in operation will double from almost 11,000 to 22,000 between 2003 and 2023. Airbus is also predicting a doubling of frequencies on existing routes, but only an increase of 20% of the number seats on aircraft.

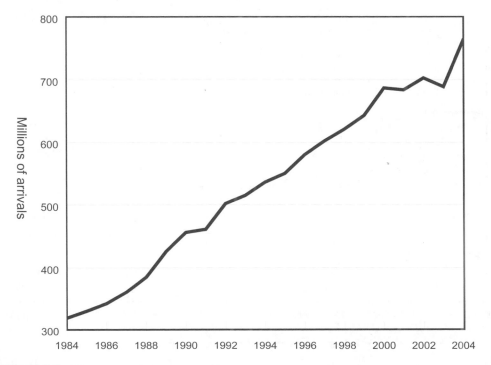

Figure 1.1 World tourist arrivals (millions)

Source: ITA (US) (2005), based on U.S. Department of Commerce, ITA, and UNWTO

ABOUT THIS BOOK: POSITIONING MODES, NETWORKS AND FLOWS

The broad purpose of this book is to map the key elements that comprise the complex relationship between transport and tourism. A framework of modes, networks and flows, as primary elements that help explain the transport/tourism relationship, is utilised. This framework has largely been adopted from the geography of transport studies literature (e.g. Hoyle & Smith, 1998), although other disciplines such as management, marketing and economics have also utlised similar approaches. Modes, network and flows can be defined as follows:

Modes: Following conventional definitions used in the business management literature with respect to categorising transport operations (see, for example, Gubbins, 2004), transport modes are manifested in three ways: ground transport, air transport and marine transport (a future mode, space transport, is considered in Chapter 9). A particular transport 'type' shall refer to the actual means of mobility realised within a particular mode. Thus, cruise tourism can be considered a type of transport that would fall under the marine mode of transport, and low-cost airlines, charter carriers and 'legacy carriers', to name a few, can be classified as a type of air transport (differentiated from other carriers

3

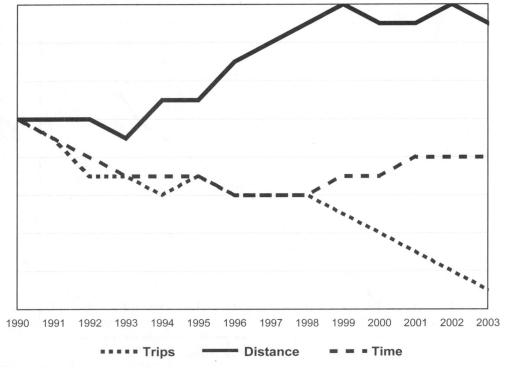

Figure 1.2 Relative change of time, distance and number of trips (all types) in Great Britain using a baseline starting point of 1990

Source: Department for Transport (2005) based on the National Travel Survey

on the basis of the business model and network served). While somewhat autocratic and rigid in its function, this classification system allows for consideration of the importance of tourism to each and to showcase useful examples of integration and importance.

Networks: If modes broadly represent the means of travel, then network structure underpins the ability of a mode or type of transport to profitably provide service and facilitate mobility. Hoyle and Smith (1998: 14) summarise the importance of networks succinctly:

> A pattern of links and nodes produces a network, a physical arrangement of transport facilities; and the design, development and management of that network requires a multifaceted transport system, which is ultimately both a response to demand and an expression of technological capability and economic resources.

Flows: Understandably, the profitability of networks depends on parameters of demand, externalities and competition. Networks are integral, therefore, in positioning modes and flows in the context of tourism such that they help explain how each work together to shape international (and regional/national) tourism. Traffic flows across networks represent the tangible measures of accessibility; they are captured in arrival statistics, load factors and demand models, and are governed by ability of modes and types of transport to service demand for traffic flow. Flows are therefore influenced by factors such as motivation and demand (incorporating economic and social variables) as well as supply.

When viewed as a wider system of variables that influence the transport/tourism relationship, modes, networks and flows can be seen to have a substantial impact on the structure of global tourism. Indeed, it can be argued that there is a significant degree of positive correlation and dependence between each concept:

1. *Networks determine flows and flows justify networks*: The spatial layout, and subsequent linkages established, of transport networks govern the flow of passengers. Thus, the ability of an airline to offer services to a particular destination, for example, plays an integral role in tourism development as it is the vector by which some tourists will arrive. This also means that, if flows are hindered by externalities such as market economics or simple demand, the scope and size of networks can change. Operators of modes of transport are therefore constantly reviewing the viability, in financial terms, of their networks. Rail providers may elect to cease services where demand is muted due to the introduction of air services, and airlines may alter their own network structure in response to decreasing demand along one or more network segments. Not surprisingly, significant investment in capital and infrastructure is required in order to maintain global networks as conduits of flows. What this can often mean is that the cost of entry can be prohibitive to the point that provision can often be concentrated in the hands of a few providers. For example, as of 2004 the top five airlines in terms of operating fleet size account for over 2400 aircraft (Table 1.1).

Table 1.1 World's top five airlines by operating fleet size (2004)

	Airline	*Number of operating aircraft*
1	American Airlines	709
2	Delta Airlines	495
3	Northwest Airlines	433
4	Southwest airlines	424
5	United Airlines	418

Source: ATW (2005a)

It is interesting to note that three of the top five airlines (American, United and Delta) have experienced fluctuating profitability problems since 2000 (see Chapter 6). Thus, while the scale of transport, particularly air transport, is massive, the fragility of the provision of services cannot be underestimated. The servicing of networks is perilous and subject to numerous externalities, including, but certainly not limited to, war, terrorist, natural disasters and economic malaise. These consequently affect cost, demand and supply. Equally important to note is that networks are not only global in scale. Regional and even national networks (for example highways or rail transport) can also influence movement and mobility at that scale, but even these can be subject to global and regional economic conditions.

2. *Patterns and intensities of flows determine the viability of networks.* Tourism is a fickle economic sector in that it relies upon the management of image, yet at the same time is vulnerable to similar externalities as transport (Hall, 2005). When image and perception change to the extent that demand is reduced, the viability of a transport provider's networks may be threatened if the pattern and/or intensity of flows is diminished. The correlation between patterns and intensities of traffic flows and the financial viability of network is therefore positive. It is for this reason that transport providers often have a financial interest in ensuring a destination is marketable and thus attractive to tourists.

3. *Regulations govern modal operations.* Despite movement toward deregulation of some transport modes (e.g. passenger air transport), transport remains a highly regulated economic industry. According to Forsyth (2006: 3), liberalisation of some air transport sectors has helped to fuel tourism growth: 'Tourism demand is quite price elastic, and aviation liberalisation has brought down fares, thus increasing tourism overall, and often, altering patterns of tourism." Despite liberalisation, however, the provision of transport services is still governed by policies and laws relating to safety, operations and competition (see Chapter 7).

4. *Transport networks play a key role in the development of destinations, especially in the context of accessibility and connectivity.* The pattern and scope of tourism is ultimately governed by the degree of accessibility and connectivity within a transport network (e.g. Butler, 1997). New Zealand as a tourism destination, for example, benefits from long-haul, non-stop air services to the United States, one of its key markets. The Caribbean has historically received a significant proportion of its overseas visitors from the United States because of non-stop flights from major urban areas such as New York and Washington DC. Likewise, rural areas popular with second home owners depend on suitable road access. As a result, the importance of accessibility is such that the ability of a destination to attract tourists is largely contingent on the availability and efficiency of transport needed to travel to that destination.

5. *Growth in tourism and transport is bi-directional and reasonably symbiotic.* In some cases this may be true, but Bieger and Wittmer (2006) rightly note that transport growth is not the only determining factor in tourism development. They argue that favourable conditions of demand and supply in the origin and destination must also be present, with transport providing the vector by which each may be satisfied. The variability in tourism amenities, attractions and new forms of mobility, such as visiting friends and relatives (Duval, 2003), second homes (Hall & Müller, 2004) and return migration (Duval, 2002) have contributed to global and regional transport demand. Growth in both tourism and transport, of course, is not universally welcomed. For example, while the economic importance of tourism for the economy is critical (e.g. Domroes, 1999), the rapid development of tourism in the Maldives has brought with it several concerns over the impact of tourism on the environment and local populations (thus raising issues of tourism as a new form of dependency [see Bastin, 1984, for example]). According to official traffic statistics at Malé International Airport, passengers disembarkations more than doubled from 1986 to 1997 (Table 1.2).

Table 1.2 Passenger movements to Malé International Airport, Maldives

	Inbound	*Outbound*
1986	124,622	123,578
1987	144,254	123,578
1988	172,119	171,561
1989	179,488	178,994
1990	217,114	216,538
1991	220,720	220,450
1992	273,982	279,645
1993	305,071	299,626
1994	348,312	345,753
1995	371,055	373,368
1996	400,300	403,645
1997	447,823	443,311
1998	468,766	460,119
1999	505,919	513,010
2000	548,518	535,658
2001	538,576	533,985
2002	557,459	552,311

Source: http://www.airports.com.mv/pastyearspf.asp (accessed 26 September 2005)

7

The Maldives example is by no means unique. Several trends have emerged that have influenced the manner in which transport and tourism co-exist (Table 1.3). Some of these relate to operations, such as how transport firms manage the provision of transport relating to tourism (and leisure, for that matter), while others are associated specifically with markets. As well, the scope and scale at which transport providers operate has a strong bearing on their exposure to externalities and vulnerabilities. Externalities such as the price of crude oil can impact on transport providers at smaller spatial scales (e.g. regions) just as much as those which operate on larger scales (e.g. globally).

Table 1.3 Major trends in transport and tourism

Markets

- (Continued) tailoring of services and equipment for specific tourism-related needs and market demand (e.g., business-class only airlines, niche cruising, heritage rail packages)
- International transactions and flows are increasingly becoming easier through expansion of nodes and modes as well as deregulation of global distribution systems and networks
- Consolidation of service offerings, often through vertical and horizontal integration (e.g., charter airlines, rail package tours, cruise packages)
- Some modal services (e.g., airlines) moving towards service provisions that are truly global

Tourist motivation and demand

- Continued year-on-year growth of international arrivals since 2003, following a period of negative or stagnant growth in 2001 and 2002 (UNWTO, 2006)
- A general trend of increasing discretionary travel, both international and domestic
- Demand for unique, alternative tourist experiences (e.g., geotourism [Dowling & Newsome, 2005])

Barriers to mobility

- Economic pressures (unfavourable exchange rates) that can govern flows, and to which transport modes must adapt
- Political strife (either in the origin or destination)
- Terrorist activities (either actual or the threat thereof)

- War or conflict (origin or destination)

Transport supply

- Move towards direct selling of product/service by providers (e.g., airlines, rail)
- Consolidation in air, rail and personal transport modes, with the aim of streamlining service options and availability
- Technological advances designed to cut costs and improve service offerings
- Global alliances among major service providers with the aim of streamlining services and improving market access

Operations management

- Operations linked closely with marketing and sales
- Leasing (as opposed to outright ownership) of equipment for provision of services
- Information-driven organisational structures
- Sophisticated uses of yield management to set appropriate pricing levels to match fluctuating and complex demand

Government policies and regulation

- Deregulation continues to govern government-based policy on service provision in some, but not all, jurisdictions
- Increase in multilateral (or 'plurilateral' [Holloway, 2003]), bilateral and open skies service agreements worldwide governs air access and, by extension, tourist flows
- Increase in regulation for non-economic activities such as environmental compliance and safety/security measures
- Privatisation of infrastructure associated with air and rail networks and services, but at the same time increasing tensions between airlines and airport companies of the financing of new terminal developments

Externalities

- Volatility in fuel prices, largely due to related volatility in crude oil prices that affect transport operators' ability to hedge fuel costs
- Safety and security issues not in the control of transport providers and stemming from war or terrorism activities (see above)
- Environmental (negative) externalities and the consequential pressure to limit emissions

Source: Adapted, revised and expanded from Coyle *et al.* (1994)

INNOVATION AND TRANSPORT DEVELOPMENT

Historically, technological innovation in transport is directly associated with the scope and intensity of tourism and leisure activities (Table 1.4; Figures 1.1 and 1.2). According to Butler (1980), there have been five ways in which innovation in transport has affected tourism:

1. time reduction, where a reduction in travel time, if perceived as a cost, is a reduction in cost (although this is not always the case given yield management, demand and route structures, as demonstrated in Chapter 6 with respect to air travel);

2. a reduction in financial cost, especially on a per capita basis, of travel;

3. improvement in comfort and safety for passengers;

4. increased convenience (generally through increases in connectivity of destinations);

5. increased accessibility of destinations, and as Butler (1997: 40) notes: 'The innovation often becomes a type of tourism itself; for example, ocean cruising is both a means of transportation and a form of tourism, and so too are flying, driving for pleasure and sailing.'

Table 1.4 Technological innovations and their impact on tourism

Technological innovation	Tourism relationship
Wheeled wagons, roading systems (Minoan and Mycenaean civilisations, Greeks)	Spread of economic activities and associated travel; increased speed of travel
Introduction of extensive paved roads (Romans)	Annual holidays, itineraries, seaside resorts; network formation
Railway development, motorised vehicles (late 19th century, early 20th century)	Modern resort developments, organised tours (see Cocks, 2001)
Air travel, cruise tourism	Mass tourism, introduction of alternative and niche forms of tourism requiring lower intensity transport modes

Source: Adapted from Prideaux (2000b)

The demand for transport has fuelled innovations in transport design and provision, and likewise transport innovation has played an integral role in tourism development in many destinations. In the same way that rail travel opened up destinations in the 19th century (see Prideaux, 2000a, 2000b), the impact of low-cost air carriers has been similar in the past decade, with increased flows of travellers who otherwise may have not travelled due to price elasticities. Worldwide, there are several examples (e.g. China, India, the United States, Europe, Australia, New Zealand and Canada) where new low-cost air access has been beneficial to tourism overall. While LCCs have proliferated, some network or 'legacy' carriers have not fared as well. In the United States, where both domestic and international routes are offered across complex networks, some network carriers have shifted their focus to international routes since 11 September 2001 and reduced costs by culling employment levels (BTS, 2005a).

While the relationship between transport and tourism is, in one sense, practical and simple in principle, the reality is that transport is manifested both within and for tourism, as well as other forms of temporary mobility. As complex as 'tourism' as a phenomenon or mobile activity is, transport is equally diverse and multifarious. Air transport, because it is truly a global phenomenon and thus almost directly responsible for global growth in tourist arrivals, is given slightly more emphasis than other transport means. In other words, where rail and steam travel revolutionised tourism and leisure travel in the 19th century (see Figure 1.3), and personal automobiles achieved a similar impact beginning in the early 20th century, air travel has, since the 1950s and 1960s (Page, 1999), revolutionised global tourism in terms of frequency and volume previously unseen.

There are three critical aspects that frame the transport/tourism relationship:

1. *Tourists ultimately travel to and from a destination (or several destinations).* Given the most oft-cited definition of a tourist from the UNWTO (WTO, 1991) is one who 'travels to a country other than that in which he/she has his/her usual residence for at least one night but not more than one year, and whose main purpose of visit is other than the exercise of an activity remunerated from within the country visited", it is integral to understand how the travel portion of this process is manifested in order to understand the wider travel and tourism system. This realisation is, of course, not new, as most introductory tourist textbooks highlight how travel and transport fit within the wider tourism system (Page, 1999). Beyond wider scoping questions, however, questions arise such as: How and why is transport provided (raising issues of competition, government intervention, supply and demand)? To what extent can it be suggested that transport (or at least some modes of transport in certain situations) is almost entirely dependent on tourist use? Likewise, to what extent does tourism itself, as a phenomenon, rely on transport? How might one characterise tourist forms of transport versus non-tourist forms of transport, and does this distinction help or hinder a full understanding the relationship between transport and tourism?

2. *Understanding supply and demand characteristics in relation to tourism is critical in the planning and management of transport infrastructure.* Tourism is pervasive in numerous different environments, ranging from constructed or built environments such as urban cities (see Page &

11

DR. ALBERT SCHWEITZER, philosopher—musician—surgeon, and winner of the *Nobel Prize for Peace*, says:

"Friends I used to know only by mail, I now meet face to face!"

● Take a look at a map of Africa. —Along the line where the Equator cuts across the west coast of the "Dark Continent" you would hardly expect to find a hospital caring for 5,000 patients a year . . .

But there at Lambaréné, about 150 miles up from the mouth of the Ogowe River, a man dedicated to the service of other men, has established just such a healing mission.

This great man, Dr. Albert Schweitzer, was born in Alsace in 1875, and awarded the Nobel Prize for Peace in 1953 . . . In 1954, Pan American received a

letter, written in longhand, from Dr. Schweitzer. In it he said (translation from the French)—

"I now have the opportunity to receive friends at Lambaréné who are interested in my work. Many friends from America have arrived by Pan American Airways.

"They have been delighted with the way in which these planes have accomplished this long journey, and especially with the solicitude with which they have been received by the

company and lodged upon their arrival in Léopoldville until they continue their journey to Lambaréné.

"I am grateful to the Company Pan American Airways. Thanks to this company, it has been possible for me to meet personally friends from America, with whom I would otherwise have been in contact only by correspondence. With best wishes,

Your devoted,

Albert Schweitzer

The **only** U. S. airline flying the length of Africa is—

PAN AMERICAN
WORLD'S MOST EXPERIENCED AIRLINE

Figure 1.3 Historical snapshot of tourism/transport relationship: Pan American Airlines print advertisement, 1954

Hall, 2003) to natural environments. If it is recognised and accepted that there are clear (and often not so clear, as discussed in Chapter 2) distinctions between tourist forms of transport and non-tourist forms of transport, then it is vital to identify and measure the nature of demand for tourism-related experiences in order to allow for accurate and meaningful forecasting of transport demand. Further, shifts in preferences can have immediate and long-term impacts on transport provision, and such shifts are critical for transport planners to recognise.

3. *The dynamic nature of transport can have significant impact on tourism in a destination.* Because transport is an integral part of the tourist system, disruptions and changes to route structures (in the case of, for example, air access or shifts in cruise ship itineraries) can have a significant impact upon some destinations. Disruptions can be political (in the case of two or more countries negotiating access), natural (e.g. weather-related events that temporarily 'cut off' destinations to international or domestic traffic) or business- or operations-related (increased competition forcing some operations to close permanently or perhaps adopt new business models).

Kaul (1985, in Prideaux, 2000a) outlined several arguments that highlight how transport links with tourism (Table 1.5). Importantly, these postulates ultimately serve as the basis by which one is able to assess the *extent* to which transport has (and will likely continue to have) links with tourism, thus turning away from the question of *whether* this is indeed the case.

Table 1.5 Kaul's postulates

The evolution of tourism is greatly influenced by and is a function of the development of the means of transport.
Tourism is a mass phenomenon as well as an individual activity, which needs and calls for transport and other facilities suitable for each category.
Transport facilities are an initial and integral need for tourism and operate both as an expanding as well as a delimiting factor for traffic flows; the quality of transport services offered also influences the type of tourist flow.
The planned development, maintenance and operation of transport infrastructure under a well-conceived overall transport policy, to meet the present and future technology and demand requirements, is the key to the success of the transport system contributing to the growth of tourism.
Transport prices influence elasticity of demand for traffic and diversification of price structure, and competition has encouraged price reduction and qualitative improvements amongst modes of transport much to the benefit of tourism.
The integration of domestic and international transport systems, and parallel coordination with other countries, contributes to the ease of tourism flow and growth of domestic and international tourism.

Transport technological developments would exercise a deep influence on the means and patterns of transport in both developing and developed societies, with the result that a more efficient, faster and safer transport system, beneficial to the growth and expansion of tourism, would emerge and evolve.

Accommodation, as an essential ingredient of tourism development and success, must maintain comparative growth to meet the increasing and diverse demands and transport expansion.

The satisfactory development and equipping of terminal and en-route facilities, the systematic improvement in infrastructure, the absorption and adoption of new technology and appropriate mass marketing techniques in transport would have a pervasive impact in the continued growth of future world tourism.

Source: Kaul (1985) adapted from Prideaux (2000a: 55 [Table 1])

TRANSPORT IN THE TOURISM SYSTEM

The UNWTO (2005b) published a news release on 14 November 2005 suggesting that, despite record high oil prices, global tourism has not been affected significantly. This is perhaps the most telling example of how tourism is inextricably allied with transport. First, it suggests a relative price inelasticity of global tourism overall, although what the UNWTO statement does not indicate is the extent to which any shifts in travel behaviour and subsequent transport usage had been affected. Second, it also demonstrates the potential fragility of global tourist flows: high oil prices in 2005 and 2006 were expected to contribute to reduce demand for travel flows, and the question was raised as to how robust global tourism actually is in the face of increased costs for transport provision. In other words, what are the consequences for tourism when the cost of transport becomes too expensive for those travellers who have previously enjoyed lower transport costs and increased choice in destinations?

Positioning transport within the tourism system is useful in that it demonstrates how transport modes, nodes and networks interact to *facilitate* tourism (Page, 1999). As indicated earlier in this chapter, various external and internal elements can be identified in order to identify any potential shifts or changes. Figure 1.4 is a simplified graphical representation of a tourism system adapted from Page (1999) in which key areas of significant transport linkages are emphasised. For the sake of argument, it can be assumed that the users of this simplified system are tourists, even though, as discussed below (and more thoroughly in Chapter 2), many forms of transport utilised by tourists are also utilised by non-tourists. There are a number of salient features and assumptions within this model:

1. It suggests that specific flows of tourists utilise networks and routings that link origin and destinations (or nodes). The flows between these nodes are made possible by various

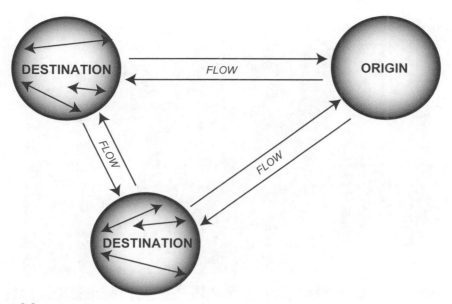

Figure 1.4 Model of the tourism/transport system

Source: Adapted from Page (1999)

modes of transport, such as commercial (or otherwise) airlines, rail or other forms of land-based transport, or even water-based transport. The operation of these flows are naturally variable and depend on numerous factors, including:

(a) the availability of specific modes of transport;

(b) cost-effectiveness of utilising various modes (discussed in Chapter 2 with respect to supply and demand) (see Figure 1.5);

(c) the motivation for travel, which is an important consideration for determining the feasibility of establishing new routes and networks or enhancing existing ones; and

(d) the time budgets associated with the potential users (or tourists) of these networks (Hall, 2005).

2. The model suggests that tourists might utilise various modes of transport within a particular destination, such as taxis, public transport, rail and air. What is important to remember, therefore, is that tourism occurs at a variety of spatial scales: air transport may be used to travel from origin to destination; rail travel may be utilised to travel within a particular country; bus services or taxis may be used to get around, for example, urban areas. Thus, the constraints and influences associated with the propensity to utilise various modes and transport can be influenced by several factors:

Figure 1.5 Reduced transport cost as a catalyst for tourism? Billboard at Exeter International Airport, UK, August 2004

(a) time-budgets whilst on holiday, such that the extent to which certain attractions or services are utilised could have an impact on the use of intra-destination modes of transport, and vice versa; and

(b) cost-effectiveness of specific modes of transport as governed by desire or motivation to undertake specific activities. One example is paying a cost premium for the opportunity to be transported by a more expensive mode that is rationalised by other motivations.

3. Finally, the model suggests that more than one destination is involved in any particular trip, and this ultimately has an impact on the utilisation of various modes of transport. For example, a family embarking upon a two-week holiday using a motor home will likely stop at numerous destinations and attractions. The flows of their travel will be influenced by the availability of infrastructure (i.e. highways and other roads), type of trip in the context of motivations (i.e. a family may elect to concentrate on destinations or attractions that are more oriented towards outdoor recreation) and the length of time available to them.

TRANSPORT SELECTION

Some studies (e.g. Ritchie, 1998) have examined the underlying motivation to travel in the context of transport, arguing that such information will allow planners and managers of tourism-related services to 'fine-tune' and 'tweak' services and products. An extension to this considers whether it is possible to suggest that different motivations to travel might have some impact on the particular mode of transport utilised. One might be inclined to think that common modes of transport are utilised concurrently by different 'types' of tourists. For example, a 747-400 travelling from Los Angeles to Sydney might have on-board numerous 'types' of tourists as described in the tourism literature. To some extent, then, the model depicted in Figure 1.4 certainly argues that the networks and flows of international tourism are inherently subject to transport provision (as argued earlier), but it inadvertently simplifies the matter in that it assigns tourism-related transport simply to an origin-destination pairing. As discussed above, transport in relation to tourism can be implemented on a number of spatial levels (i.e. within the destination, between destinations), and the extent to which transport may or may not function as part of the overall experience needs to be taken into consideration. Of equal importance, perhaps, is how the mode (or type) of transport is selected.

Mill and Morrison (1985) provide a model (roughly based on Sheth, 1975) that outlines the various elements and choices involved in transport mode selection (Figure 1.6). The importance of this model is that it captures elements of trip purpose, motivation, psychological and sociological characteristics (such as 'lifestyle') in the decision to select a particular mode or type of transport. At the same time, however, it also suggests that these variables connect into various characteristics (what Mill and Morrison call 'utilities') that ultimately govern the transport mode/type decision.

Mill and Morrison's model is important because it suggests that existing studies of travel/tourist motivations for visiting destinations or attractions need to be taken into consideration in establishing the role of transport in the wider tourism system. Perhaps what is missing, however, is a feedback mechanism whereby deficiencies in one variable can be compensated for by another. For example, less net income may result in the desire to acquire significant savings with the explicit purpose of, for example, using a particular form of transport whilst on holiday (e.g. flying on the Concorde or taking an expensive cruise). Similarly, mode accessibility may be sacrificed for mode design, such that an individual may elect to utilise a specific mode of transport because of, for example, the aesthetic qualities that it offers, even though that particular mode operates out of specific nodes that are, comparatively, inaccessible or uneconomical.

STRUCTURE OF THE BOOK

Structuring a book on transport and tourism presents several challenges. First, one is inclined to allow tourism to take 'centre stage' and weave transport into conceptualisations of the tourist system. Second, because of the complexity of the relationship (discussed in more detail in Chapter 2), it is difficult to organise the centralities and commonalities between different modes and tourism. Consequently, this book generally allows

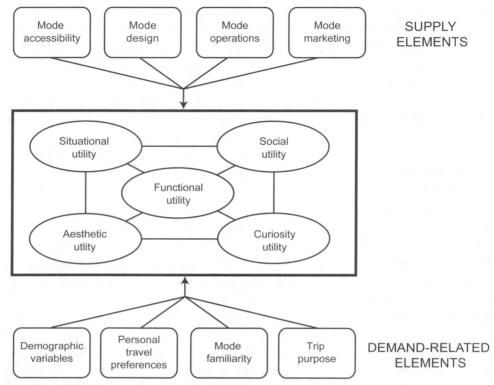

Figure 1.6 Transport mode selection model

Source: Adapted from Mill and Morrison (1985) and from Sheth (1975)

the nature of transport to take centre stage and it is therefore organised largely around the various modes and types that permeate tourism systems today. Third, while tourism as a field of enquiry is inherently multidisciplinary or transdisciplinary in nature, topics of interest to tourism development beg consideration from multiple disciplinary perspectives. In this case, the transport literature often takes centre stage throughout this book in an attempt to marry it with consideration for tourism (as well as, in some places, recreation and leisure).

Chapter 2 intentionally leaves many questions for the reader to consider. The intent of the chapter is to introduce the reader to the principles that guide this relationship. As such, the blurry distinctions between transport and tourism are outlined, with the suggestion that, quite often, delineating between tourist-focused transport and non-tourist-focused transport is problematic. Of course, much of this blurriness is a consequence of the definitional endeavour of characterising tourists. To this end, consideration is made of not only tourists but also recreation and leisure activities. Rather than enter into the debate of whether tourism is a subset of leisure (or vice versa), this book shall adopt the view that some modes and types of transport can be used in different contexts (leisure for some, tourism for others). In some ways, this amplifies the blurry distinctions discussed in Chapter 2. Chapter 2 also considers how transport is manifested within the tourist system, utilising the work of Mill and Morrison (1985) in the premise that touristic activities, and the provision for movement and mobility to facilitate these activities, are embedded within a complex system. The role of government is also discussed, primarily because the policy and planning measures and decisions rendered by national and local governments (and wider NGOs that span the global space) determine the extent of the relationship between tourism and transport. Thus, the extent to which government is involved (e.g. regulation and planning) is discussed. This gives rise to supply and demand issues and an important synopsis of models of elasticities.

As the book engages in a transport-centred focus, the third chapter reflects this in its discussion of the spatial aspects of transport networks. This is an important point because it means consideration is given to the physical manifestation of transport and, consequently, what that may mean for tourism at a variety of spatial levels (i.e. global, regional, local). Transport, quite simply, is rarely plotted outside of prescribed routes that are dependent on infrastructure. Passengers (and goods, for that matter) follow specific routes, most of which are pre-determined. Chapters 4 through 6 outline trends in each of the three main modes of transport (ground, marine, air). Each chapter examines critical issues associated with these modes and briefly interrogates the notion of sustainable modes of transport, a topic which is visited more broadly in Chapter 9. Chapter 7 highlights three critical areas of management with respect to transport management: nodal frameworks (using the example of airports), yield management, and safety and security issues. The chapter is inherently business-oriented in its presentation, but the three areas considered are critical in understanding (1) how networks govern tourism and mobility, and (2) how management considerations in tourism and transport need to consider auxiliary nodal elements (e.g. airports). Chapter 8 considers the marketing of transport in relation to tourism, and the nature of the 'product versus service' element of transport is considered. As well, various strategic marketing initiatives are discussed, including market penetration, market development and product development. Alliances are examined within a marketing context and a discussion on relationship marketing demonstrates how some transport providers use loyalty systems such as frequent flyer miles to understand their markets. Finally, Chapter 9 consider future trends in transport in two broad contexts: sustainability (particularly emissions control and peak oil) and space tourism, which may represent a fourth mode of tourism transport. Several future trends are discussed next with a view towards highlighting potential areas for further exploration and evaluation.

CHAPTER SUMMARY

Transport is tied to tourism and tourism development in a variety of ways. It functions as a means by which tourist flows are manifested, but it also plays a role in determining the success of tourism development and the financial viability of existing tourism services. This chapter has argued that, using modes, networks and flows as the central framework, transport and tourism relationships can be explored more fully. Importantly, these relationships are complex and in an almost constant state of flux. Transport provision worldwide is manifested on a variety of spatial scales using a variety of modes and types. As well, transport networks can range from being simple to complex. Importantly, the close relationship that is shared between transport and tourism ensures that neither is particularly immune from the externalities that each faces.

SELF-REVIEW QUESTIONS

1. Define mode, network and flow.

2. What is the general trend of world tourist arrivals and what does this mean for transport?

3. What are the key elements of a tourism system?

ESSAY QUESTIONS

1. Why are modes, networks and flows important in understanding the relationship between transport and tourism?

2. How has innovation in transport impacted upon tourist flows?

3. Tourism and transport have a uniquely symbiotic relationship. Write an essay that discusses this conclusion and provide examples to support your arguments.

KEY SOURCES

Page, S. (2005) *Transport and Tourism: Global Perspectives.* Harlow: Pearson Education.

A seminal work on transport and tourism, Page has succinctly woven issues of supply, demand and management together in an accessible text. The second edition (published in 2005) features an exhaustive reference list, useful for most students embarking upon assessments or theses.

Hall, C.M. (2005) *Tourism: Rethinking the Social Science of Mobility*. Harlow: Pearson Education/Prentice Hall.

Hall's book is an excellent introduction and background to some of the concepts introduced in this volume. The book is well situated to provide an introduction to such topics as mobilities, globalisation, production and consumption, and spatial interaction models. Hall also explores other critical issues of relevance to transport and tourism, including environmental change, security issues, geopolitics and tourism development.

CHAPTER 2:

TOURISM-TRANSPORT RELATIONSHIPS

LEARNING OBJECTIVES

After reading this chapter, you should be able to

1. Recognise and explain the blurry distinctions when investigating transport and tourism relationships.

2. Develop your own example of where transport and tourism have a symbiotic relationship.

3. Assess and differentiate transport development as a catalyst for tourism development from the development of tourism as a catalyst for transport initiatives.

4. Position and identify the role of government in transport and tourism relationships.

5. Understand the nature of supply and demand in relation to transport and tourism.

INTRODUCTION

The purpose of this chapter is to outline some of the salient issues that emerge when exploring the linkages between tourism and transport. These linkages, or 'interfaces' (Lumsdon & Page, 2004), are a useful point of departure because their sheer complexity would suggest that identifying and measuring a direct correlation between transport and tourism services and industries can often be difficult. Transport systems encompass numerous modes and types of transport. They feature complicated and dynamic routes determined by governmental policy and planning as well as underlying political factors (e.g. Nayar, 1995). Other factors include economic aspects, turbulent business operating environments and external issues of demand. It is, therefore, somewhat difficult to arrive at a final model or equation that definitely explains how transport fits within tourism and, conversely, how tourism fits within transport. Nonetheless, some top-line issues that highlight the tourism/transport relationship can be discussed, which is the intent of this chapter.

The shape of the chapter centres around three themes: 1) defining the transport/tourism relationship; 2) integration of transport within tourism systems; and 3) the nature of supply and demand. The chapter begins by considering the 'blurry distinctions' that characterise tourism and transport relationships, which roughly correlate to the perceived (and actual) difficulty in associating or establishing concrete relationships between modal forms/types of tourism and modes of transport. Following this, the integration of transport within the wider tourism system is considered, with a special emphasis on identifying transport as a particular (and often critical) element within the tourism system. Finally, consideration of supply and demand in the context of transport is examined.

BLURRY DISTINCTIONS

While the importance of transport to tourist flows (at a variety of spatial levels – e.g. international, domestic, local) was highlighted in the previous chapter, what remains to be considered is the *manifestation* of this relationship. In many ways, *how* transport and tourism are co-dependent is not always apparent. As such, it can be argued that there is a blurriness in the way transport and tourism co-exist. There are three reasons why the linkages and subsequent relationships between transport and tourism can be said to be blurry. First, a particular mode of transport can be both a facilitator of mobility (by tourists and/or recreationalists) as well as an attraction (Lumsdon & Page, 2004). Second, the provision of transport explicitly for tourist use is inherently rare (Hall, 1999), aside from perhaps explicit examples where the mode of transport is either the key attraction or the means by which an attraction is consumed or experienced (e.g. boat cruise around the fjords of Iceland). Thus, as Halsall (1992) points out, there is often very little to distinguish between tourist and non-tourist use of transport services. Third, the extent to which transport plays a role in tourism development, particularly in the development of destinations in international, national and local contexts, is often not entirely clear. Put another way, the question becomes as follows: does the presence of transport facilitate tourism growth in a destination, or must a destination be suitably developed in order to attract new transport provisions or enhance existing ones?

Transport as a facilitator and an attraction

For many tourists and recreationalists, transport is seen as merely utilitarian or functional. As an example, a business traveller flying from Singapore to London Heathrow may be interested primarily in securing a flight that is within his or her budget and immediately accessible at a particular time. A family taking a holiday from London to Singapore may use similar decision-making criteria. As a result, the decision-making criteria may be focused on the cost and efficiency of this particular mode of transport. A cruise passenger, on the other hand, certainly uses a large ship for transport to and from certain destinations or ports of call, but the ship itself may often be an attraction in its own right. To this end, many cruise companies are increasingly offering on-board shopping and activities, for a variety of reasons that will be discussed in Chapter 5. In these two examples, the functional aspect transport element is shared, but its use is quite different as are the motivations and key elements used by the traveller in ultimately deciding on the particular mode or type of transport. For some, transport facilitates travel/tourism/leisure experiences. In other situations, transport is deliberately part of (or is engineered to be) the experience.

BOX 2.1 The world's longest flight? EWR-SIN on SQ

The introduction of non-stop services between Newark, New York (IATA: EWR) and Singapore (IATA: SIN) by Singapore Airlines (using an Airbus A340-500 aircraft) in late 2004 is an example that illustrates how a mode of transport can also be the attraction. Billed as the world's longest non-stop flight (at 16,603km), the inaugural flight attracted a great deal of attention from aviation enthusiasts and frequent flyers (and has been accompanied by its own website, www.nonstop2newyork.com), with some purposely booking seats on the flight in order to quite literally be a part of history. One posting on an online discussion forum for travellers epitomises this desire: 'For me the chance to be on the historic first flight was reason enough – the miles, PPS sector credits and upgrade vouchers earnt [*sic*] along the way are just the icing on the cake!' If one was to profile those who took part in the inaugural flight from EWR to SIN, it would likely be possible to apply several leisure and tourism motivation theories to this kind of activity. Beard and Ragheb's (1983) competency-mastery component might go some way to explaining the desire of frequently flyers (some of whom regularly make 'mileage runs' for the explicit purpose of building up their frequent flyer account balances) to embark upon such a trip. For them, travelling such a distance on the inaugural flight might well be an achievement, and may serve to elevate status in an online community/discussion fora where issues relating to aviation, frequent flyer programmes and airlines are discussed. For others, the flight could be merely a novelty and offer a sense of prestige (Crompton, 1979; Dann, 1981). Finally, if Iso-Ahola's (1980, 1982) matrix of intrinsic rewards and interpersonal environments is adopted, it might highlight individuals who are keen to enhance their own ego but at the same time acquaint themselves with others (whom they may perceive as being similar to themselves) in interpersonal environments.

Questions for consideration

1. How might such long flights be marketed to potential travellers?

2. How might long distance travel, with fewer stops, affect global flows of people and some tourism destinations?

Tourist versus non-tourist use of transport services

Hall (1999: 182) suggests that there are three categories of transport users:

a) the host community (i.e. residents not directly involved in the tourism sector);
b) employees from the tourism sector;
c) tourists or excursionists.

Outside of the contested definition of a tourist and the relationship between travel and types of mobility, it can be suggested that there is a blurry distinction between non-tourist use and tourist use of certain modes and types of transport (see also Lumsdon & Page, 2004). There are few examples of a particular mode or type of transport reserved for the exclusive use of tourists. One could argue that examples such as light rail transit within a theme park or cruise ships might be designed exclusively for tourist use, but they may also be used by other people as well (e.g. employees or management executives associated with the operation itself), albeit in smaller proportions. The Rottnest Ferry in Western Australia, for example, carries both tourists and island employees to and from the city of Perth and Rottnest Island (Figure 2.1). But what of other modes of transport such as air travel or personal vehicles? It could be argued that these modes of transport may not be exclusively designed for and utilised by tourists. A country's road network, for example, is used by both residents (in day-to-day activities, or as excursionists and/or tourists), tourists and for commercial activities. Likewise, air travel is used by a variety of types of mobile individuals: tourists, migrants, excursionists, commuters, to name a few examples.

In recognising that there are, in fact, many different users of most modes of transport, it then becomes difficult for planners, policy-makers and, indeed, local and national governments to accurately measure the level of tourist use of these modes. Some destinations or regions, for example, may be inclined to charge a road toll for the use of specific road networks and, more often than not, these charges are designed to supplement declining funding for infrastructure renewal in the face of bourgeoning tourism activities. For example, a proposal was considered in 2002 by the Queenstown-Lakes District Council

Figure 2.1 Blurry distinctions: the Rottnest Express Ferry (Perth, Western Australia) carries both tourists and employees working on the island

in New Zealand, where specific road tolls would be implemented on scenic routes, thus directly targeting tourists and excursionists. This raises several questions: which tourists are being targeted? Domestic tourists might see this as a 'tax grab' and argue that their taxes already fund the road network, including upgrades, repairs and new developments. If targeted at international tourists, the question then becomes: to what extent, if any, will such tolls have a detrimental impact on visitation and visitor flows? Is it possible that the implementation of tolls might have a negative impact on demand? In 2004, the city of Edinburgh announced plans to implement road tolls on two key cordons in the city, but various members of the local tourism industry warned that such measures could result in tourists bypassing the city completely whilst visiting Scotland (Edinburgh News.com, 2004). What is important, then, is to recognise that transport is utilised by both tourists and non-tourists, yet within the 'tourist group', to use Hall's (1999) characterisation, multiple segments can be identified and it is not unreasonable to suggest that each have different needs with respect to transport.

Tourism for transport development or transport for tourism development?

Gauthier's (1970) review of the relationship between transport and economic development led him to characterise three ways in which the tourism development/transport relationship can be manifested: positive, permissive and negative (Table 2.1).

Table 2.1 Gauthier's (1970) transport/development characterisations as applied to tourism and transport

	Gauthier's economic development/transport relationship	The resulting tourism/transport relationship
Positive	Where transport has a direct and positive impact on economic development (i.e. providing transport directly influences economic development)	The use of transport to facilitate domestic and international mobility, linking origin and potentially several destinations to the benefit of the destinations in question, although it is recognised that this may also contribute to the economic well-being of the origin point (through positive balance of payment on services and retail sales associated with mobile residents). The management of transport industries in concert with tourism destinations, then, would seem to be critical. Partnerships and agreements should be established for the purpose of recognising the importance of gateways (e.g. Palhares, 2003).
Permissive	Where transport does not directly influence economic development (i.e. the provision of transport alone is not enough to influence economic development, thus it is relegated to a passive, but supportive role)	Transport itself may not be a significant contributing factor to tourism development, but other factors (e.g. shifting market trends and consumer preferences) may, in aggregate, shift demand and, ultimately, mobility flows, thus spawning a reaction from transport mode service providers.

| Negative | Where the provision of transport is fuelled by investment to the detriment of other economic development alternatives (i.e. transport hinders economic growth and productivity) | The overcapitalisation of transport flows and networks between multiple nodes usually results in the fragility of some operations. If and/when such operations become financially unviable, the reduction of routes along networks can have a negative impact, perhaps in the short term, for economies that may rely upon these modes of transport to bring tourists to them. |

As useful as Gauthier's (1970) characterisations are, it is necessary to consider the geographic scale of analysis in determining whether tourism has more of an impact on transport development than transport has on tourism development. There is no question that new forms of technology, as applied to transport services, have resulted in a 'globalising' effect of tourism. The road systems established by the Romans, for example, were used not only for military campaigns and maintenance of the empire but also for facilitating recreation and tourism by Roman citizens across modern Europe (Prideaux, 2000a). Further still, and as argued in the last chapter, it is evident that technological developments in transport have resulted in faster travel over further distances, perhaps even at a greater frequency (all other things being equal) and, as Prideaux (2000a) notes, in greater comfort. Thus, on a global scale, there is no question that transport has facilitated tourism development by 'opening up' new destinations or enhanced existing ones (Page, 1999).

BOX 2.2 Case study – Tourism development in the West Indies: Transport as a catalyst for tourism?

Tourism, it seems, may be one of the more significant economic sectors upon which stability in the West Indies is afforded. For centuries, agriculture (sugar and bananas, both of which are under threat because larger producers in other countries have argued to the WTO that the preferential markets for both contravene natural global trade practices) has been the mainstay of the region's economy. There are signs, however, that this is changing. St Lucia, for example, has all but abandoned sugar production in favour of tourism; indeed, tourists now ride the rail system that used to carry cane sugar. The wider West Indies region, comprised of a series of island states (and dependencies of varying size and stages of development), is often regarded as synonymous with conventional mass tourism. The region has hosted visitors from Europe and North America for centuries, but it was not until the development of the jet engine aircraft that tourism became an important social and economic force in some countries in the region. In the end, people from North America could get to the Caribbean and back again without spending significant portions of their vacations in transit. The result is that, starting in the 1950s, North America became the most important market for the region as a whole (Duval, 2004a).

While transport has led to significant development of tourism in the region, it has also contributed to specific forms of tourism. Cruise tourism, as discussed in Chapter 5, acts as both the means of transport and the attraction in the region, with 43% (2000 data) of all visitors to region arriving on pre-packaged cruise ships (CTO, 2002). The region is served by numerous international airlines (e.g. Air Canada, British Airways, Air France, United Airlines, US Airways, AA), although the recent financial crises surrounding US Airways, United Airlines and Air Canada highlight the rather fragile nature of existing routes and passenger mobility from North America. Of great concern when considering the United States market is the financial difficulties that have plagued AA since 2003. AA controls upwards of 70% of the market to the Caribbean from the United States (Smith, 2002). While regional carrier LIAT and BWIA continue to operate in the region, the reality is that adequate air access has recently become more dependent upon government involvement, either financially or logistically (Duval, 2004b).

Duval (2004b: 294) notes that 'it is likely that a formal emphasis on curtailing substantial competition from numerous, small airlines and subsequently shaping a regional transport plan of one or two strong RPT (Regular Passenger Transport) providers will transpire within the next five years'. Indeed, more recently BWIA may be re-branded as Caribbean Airlines in early 2007 and LIAT and Caribbean Star are exploring merger options.

As air transport was critical in helping the region develop into a premier tourism destination, it seems that the future of the region's tourism sector is still quite reliant on air access. In fact, Bahamian Premier Perry Christie suggested in 2002 that 'there can be no rejuvenation of Caribbean tourism without the simultaneous reinvention of Caribbean air transportation' (Smith, 2002). What is needed, according to Duval (2004b), is regional control over airlift, if only to secure the provision of transport in the hands of the countries that would benefit most. One step towards this was the 1996 Caribbean Community Air Services Agreement, which not only saw the liberalisation of air travel and access throughout the region, but also allowed for multi-nation investments in air transport operations (OECD, 1999). Although this solidified intra-regional travel, international access to the region has been, and still is for the most part, provided by foreign carriers, although the exception would be BWIA, which services Miami, New York, Washington DC, Toronto, Georgetown, Paramaribo, London and Manchester with nine aircraft. Recently, several Caribbean hotel owners have suggested that ownership of Caribbean-based airlines should perhaps be held across the region to address competitiveness and the importance of tourism overall to the region (Jamaica Gleaner, 2005).

Questions for consideration

1. Are there other areas of the world that have developed in a similar manner to the Caribbean with respect to transport?

2. Why would politicians and governments in general have a vested interest in ensuring that adequate airlift is maintained through the Caribbean?

On a more micro scale, however, there is room to suggest that tourism development, or more properly, the demand for particular services and/or attractions by tourists, can play a substantial role in facilitating or creating demand for either new modes of transport or enhancements to existing modes. A few examples:

1. *Firms offering specific modal services may elect to offer new services on routes where they perceive significant demand.* Air New Zealand, for example, announced in early 2004 the intention to offer direct flights between Auckland and Shanghai, largely because of increases in the number of Chinese tourists visiting New Zealand (New Zealand Herald, 2004), but also because of increasing migration-related connections between the two countries, such as permanent or temporary student migration. Similarly, a proposed high-speed rail line between Las Vegas and Los Angeles, at an estimated cost of US$1 billion, is meant to not only link two significant tourism centres but also stimulate travel between them (Las Vegas Sun, 2004; see also www.transrapid.de).

2. *There exists a synergy between new transport services and increases in demand.* The supply of transport can have some impact on demand (either in the positive or negative) through attempts to generate market interest or turn latent demand into actual demand. One example is the introduction of Kiwi Air International and Freedom Air in New Zealand, both of which began operating on routes between New Zealand and Australia in the mid-1990s. Consequently, a rise in the number of New Zealand residents visiting Australia was recorded (Table 2.2). Granted, the affordable fares on offer from both airlines (among other variables, of course) could very well have had some impact on encouraging travel, but it was the introduction of these new services that was the proximate cause of the 'fare war' (Duval, 2005c).

Table 2.2 Resident departures from New Zealand to Australia, 1993–2001

Year	Resident departures	Annual change	Percent change
1993	418,738	30,596	+7.9
1994	407,408	−11,330	−2.7
1995	460,266	52,858	+13.0
1996	587,488	127,222	+27.6
1997	598,612	11,124	+1.9
1998	616,743	18,131	+3.0
1999	620,027	3284	+0.5
2000	684,934	64,907	+10.5
2001	676,047	−8887	−1.3

Source: Statistics New Zealand (2002)

3. *Integration between transport providers and other tourism-related operations targets specific markets with the intent of stimulating latent demand.* The integration of transport and non-transport services allows for the possibility of numerous strategic management decisions, including the introduction of new products, enhancing market share or even facilitating market entry, reducing costs and increasing profitability (see, for example, Oum *et al.,* 2004). Although *horizontal* integration generally involves harmonising similar products across two or more firms (and airline alliances, in this regard, are discussed extensively in Chapter 6 as examples of integration), of particular interest is *vertical* integration, where transport can be linked and/or merged with tourism-related operations.

Vertical integration has the ability of generating efficiencies at the competitive level. By integrating product and service offerings across a value chain, future operations are more certain and the likelihood of competitor entries is somewhat diminished (Lafferty & van Fossen, 2001). Several airlines have interests in firms and operations outside of aircraft operations. For example, it can be said that Air Canada and Qantas have financial and operational extensions of their primary operations that include interests in hotels and

31

tour companies, thus enabling each to sell products and services in conjunction with their respective air services (Lafferty & van Fossen, 2001: Table 1). Likewise, Disney holds ownership and control over Castaway Cay in the Bahamas, where its own ships dock. Acknowledging and understanding vertical integration that features a transit or transport element is important for two reasons: 1) to control the sales and distribution of the means of travel and other associated services; and 2) to stimulate latent demand for profitable routes by capturing market interest in package holidays.

INTEGRATING TRANSPORT IN TOURISM DEVELOPMENT

Transport development, as a process, can occur at a variety of spatial levels and at varying degrees of integration with tourism development:

1. Global perspectives of tourism development generally examine the rate of tourist flows, north–south distinctions in the speed of development, pro-poor tourism development designed to empower less developed countries through tourist activities (and the associated debates that this brings), and wider consideration of the concept of mobility of which tourism is but one example. At the global level, transport is largely functional in the context of facilitating flows via prescribed networks, but there is some room to consider how some modes of transport can be utilised in branding and marketing exercises.

2. At the destination level, development includes, among other considerations, planning and policy measures including issues of implementation and monitoring; resource management and governance; physical landscape changes and any resulting impacts; indigenous peoples' and cultural impacts of tourism; and place promotion and marketing. Here, transport can be used not only as a facilitator (within smaller networks) but also an attraction (e.g. historic rail package tours). Transport should be integrated into destination development, planning and marketing decisions.

3. At the level of the attraction, micro-level business models of investment (sometimes foreign direct investment), financial viability of operations, seasonality and specific lifestyle factors, and organisational structures and behaviour are areas that have been investigated. Transport may not have an overt degree of integration at this level, but its importance cannot be overstated. The enterprise operator would undoubtedly have a strong interest in a transport operator's network development plans, marketing and overall successes (or otherwise).

More generally, the degree of transport integration can cross many spatial fields and involve multiple elements. These can include the availability of quality facilities relating to transport both within and outside the destination (Hall, 2004), appropriate routing to facilitate ease of flow (Halsall, 1992) and provision of adequate infrastructure for network development. For example, air transport on a global level is carefully monitored not only in the form of regulation and bilateral trade (see Chapter 7), but also destinations understandably form strong relationships with transport providers for the purpose of ensuring viable markets and a continuous (at least as much as possible) flow of tourists. Through destination marketing organisations, destinations will therefore work to ensure that they are accessible via one or more modes or types of transport.

An ideal model of the role of transport integration within tourism development would see three key stakeholders: tourists or travellers, destinations (including local stakeholders such as government and the community) and various relevant transport industries. Destinations have an interest in securing and maintaining market share. Transport providers will thus strive to ensure that their own market share and financial viability is maintained and will thus take great interest in the manner in which the destination undertakes development and marketing efforts. At the same time, destinations may attempt to entice transport providers to service particular places or locations, thus embarking on marketing to a different audience. Tourists and travellers, of course, form the primary user group and thus have expectations of the quality of the experience for both the mode of transport (and whether this is between origin and destination, or intra- or inter-destination transport) and within the destination itself.

The path of development, then, requires the considered coordination of how transport will fit within the tourist experience at two levels: a) the journey to and from the destination (or within the destination); and b) the extent to which transport provision can be made profitable through partnerships with destinations. Three areas of integration (although they are more) can be examined: the role of government, regulation and deregulation, and planning.

THE ROLE OF GOVERNMENT IN TOURISM/TRANSPORT RELATIONSHIPS

The tourism literature offers examples of the use of tourism by many governments as a form of economic restructuring (see, for example, Page and Hall [2003], in the context of urban tourism). The extent to which transport is positioned within such restructuring is, however, variable. As Hall (1993: 207–208) points out, there are several conditions that characterise how transport, tourism and economic restructuring are intertwined, some of which include:

(a) The national economic context: notably the availability of capital investment to develop the necessary infrastructure, not least transport and communications.
(b) Scale: small economies are more likely to depend upon imports.
(c) Level of development: lower levels of development, including that of domestic tourism, produce poor economies of scale for suppliers.
(d) The organisation of capital: the extent of the penetration of international capital may be critical in assisting development and/or leading to leakages of income abroad through payment of royalties, profits and dividends which the economy may ill afford.

The roles of foreign tour companies, carriers (notably airlines) and transport manu-facturers (of, for example, luxury tourist coaches), are significant here.

(e) Nature of tourism and background of tourists: tourists' contribution to eco-nomic development may vary considerably in terms of per capita spending power, infrastructural demands and the forms of tourism in which they participate.

Hall's observations are important for several reasons:

1. Broadly speaking, the extent to which governments are able to internalise transport provision for the benefit of tourism are vast, and can include (a) the creation of favoura-ble economic conditions or environments that encourage investment in transport services; (b) direct subsidies designed to offset unprofitable routes or operations (e.g. rail services in the United States – see Chapter 4); (c) direct regulation of services (discussed below and in Chapter 7); and (d) the establishment of policies and guidelines relating to opera-tional procedures.

2. The type(s) of tourism present (or under consideration) at a particular destination requires consideration of whether to invest or encourage private development of specific modes of transport. For example, Australia may be considered a long-haul destination for several of its non-Asian markets. Despite recent moves towards domestic liberalisation of air transport routes, the Australian government is likely keen to ensure the survival of Qantas in a crowded and competitive international environment as it represents at least some control of tourist flows to and from the country itself.

3. The varying size of destinations, and perhaps by extension the varying sizes of coun-tries and governments within which such destinations are located, can be critical when examining their ability to control how transport fits within economic restructuring. Smaller countries may not be able to afford to handle some aspects of tourism-related transport, and thus leave such operations to foreign-owned conglomerates or firms. The risk here, then, is that tourist mobility, most importantly to and from a destination, becomes an externality that is driven almost solely by profit as opposed to serving the greater economic good of the destination.

Given the complex relationship between transport and tourism and the economic frame-work within which both operate on a local, national and regional level, the wider role of government in the provision of transport as it relates to tourism can essentially be cap-tured in two broad ways: the regulation or deregulation of services, including the monitoring of competition, and the issuing of transport planning measures.

REGULATION AND DEREGULATION

A regulated transport environment refers to those instances where price and market access are tightly controlled by governments in the form of nationalised firms or local-level firms (Hoyle & Smith, 1998; Morrison & Winston, 1989) or through specific policy measures designed to influence terms of trade. In a deregulated environment, direct governmental controls are relaxed in favour of allowing market conditions to dictate operational success. While regulation and deregulation are often discussed in the context of aviation, a more general consideration would include issues relating to the facilitation (or otherwise) of competition and legislating through policy frameworks that speak to the overall economic importance of transport to national economies. Worldwide, governments must therefore decide whether to:

1. formally regulate the provision of transport services and access, including, of course, those blurry areas that could ultimately have some degree of impact on tourist flows. These actions would thus exert some control over routes and flows, pricing and frequency of access;

2. allow whole or partial market access to privately owned firms that may still need to meet standards of varying degrees with respect to routes and/or price; or

3. allow unfettered access to local or national markets without restriction.

As Button (1993: 244–245) outlines, paraphrased here, there are several arguments in favour of transport regulation:

1. Markets are, for the most part, somewhat imperfect and prone to failure, which could lead to high fares and dangerous service practices. In fact, the concern over safety and congestion became two of several reasons why, shortly after the 1978 deregulation of the United States aviation industry, some people were calling for the re-regulation of airline services (Morrison & Winston, 1989; see also Tretheway & Waters, 1998).

2. Regulation stifles what may otherwise be monopolistic operations within imperfect market structures.

3. Unregulated services could result in degradation of service quality through focused efforts on profitable route structures as opposed to a more general offering of services to multiple markets; to a large extent, this explains why some airlines which are government-owned offer services across networks which, if privately-owned, would likely be abandoned due to unprofitability.

4. Regulation is necessary in those instances where transport can be perceived as a public good; this may partially explain why the United States government chose to financially

protect and support many major airlines following the 11 September 2001 attacks in the United States as it was argued that the national infrastructure, as well as the flows of goods and people, must not be interrupted.

5. Government involvement is necessary in many forms of transport where the underlying infrastructure cost is high. Thus, the argument is that private-sector firms are less likely to be able (or willing) to direct significant capital into risky ventures where the bottom-line return on investment is years away.

6. A regulated market may result in certain externalities (such as environmental compliance measures) falling under government control and mandate, whereas such externalities may be ignored in a deregulated environment due to excessive cost and perceived lower returns-on-investment.

From the perspective of integration with tourism, deregulation can force destinations to become more competitive because the market is less restricted, and thus marketing and overall development plans become critical. It could even be argued that, in a deregulated environment, and particularly with respect to international air transport, tourism destinations must market to transport providers in much the same way as they advertise and promote their image(s) to tourists.

The benefits to passengers in a deregulated environment, especially with respect to air transport, are not necessarily a given. Morrison and Winston (1989) argue that the benefits of deregulation to the traveller should be matched by policies that encourage competition and efficient airport use, especially when some of the initial consequences of deregulation in the United States market (e.g. airport congestion, alliances) were found to be less beneficial to passengers. Further, McHardy and Trotter (2006: 87) argue that deregulation as it applies to air services may not, itself, provide passengers with benefits when other elements of the transport system (e.g. airports) may not be subjected to similar levels of competition. This element of competition is critical in a deregulated environment, where transport is based on the theory of contestable markets (Levine, 1987), although the context of such a deregulated environment itself technically pre-dates the introduction of this theory. The basis of the theory of contestable markets in the context of transport is that the free entry, or even the threat of entry, is enough to encourage efficient transport operations that would be adaptive in pricing to supply and demand vagaries. Put another way:

> Contestability theory was used to underpin the ideological moves to deregulate and privat e transport, which started in the USA and Great Britain at the end of the 1970s. This process then spread rapidly throughout the world and included many less-developed countries often at the instigation of the World Bank and the International Monetary Fund (Bell and Cloke, 1990). (Knowles & Hall, 1998: 76)

Under contestable markets, 'sunk costs, which a firm incurs in order to produce and which would not be recuperable if the firm left the industry, are not significant' (Sinclair & Stabler, 1997: 61). In such an environment, firms operate under the assumption that (continued) competition is inevitable as the barriers to entry are negligible. There are several examples of transport modes operating under deregulation that ultimately have some bearing on the shape of tourism and tourist flows:

1. The United States Airline Deregulation Act of 1978 facilitated the introduction of competitive air services, thus helping to establish a competitive market and subsequent growth in domestic travel (Adler, 2001).

2. Starting in the 1980s, the British government embarked upon a programme to privatise several transport-related services and operations, including Sealink Ferries, British Airways, the BAA, the National Bus Company and the Scottish Bus Group. The result is a fiercely competitive environment, especially in the context of air travel with the introduction of several new LCCs beginning in the 1990s (see Knowles & Hall, 1998 and Chapter 6).

3. Transport services serving third world countries (especially international air transport) were often affected by government reforms designed to deregulate the market in their own countries. Thus, with an increasing privatised transport market, coupled with the desire by many third world countries to encourage increases in visitation and, by extension, visitor expenditures, the deregulation or loosening of state controls over competition and transport operations in these countries has become somewhat inevitable. However, this can bring significant problems, not the least of which is the inability of third world-based operations to compete with large-scale services originating from developed countries. In the case of Air Zimbabwe, for example, Turton (2004: 75) notes that deregulation outside of the country in other jurisdictions was a factor in the restructuring of its own operations:

> In the 1990s Zimbabwe, in common with other developing states, embarked upon a program of economic structural adjustment. Many of the state undertakings, such as Air Zimbabwe, were subjected to a reappraisal by independent advisers and the report by a European consultancy recommended a policy of liberalisation for the airline and the loosening of constraints upon competition for traffic from other airlines. Within this competitive framework, long haul flights into Harare were introduced by Air Frances, KLM and Sabena and the national airline was ill-equipped to counter this with its limited financial resources and lack of aircraft suited to its various routes. However, the restructuring of Air Zimbabwe, with a loosening of state control, was viewed by the government as an opportunity for the airline to improve its performance on all routes and to compete more effectively in the tourism market.

In the past five years, Air Zimbabwe has faced rising operational costs and shrinking revenue. In September 2006, the airline was largely insolvent, despite injections of capital from the Reserve Bank of Zimbabwe designed to prevent a full collapse of the airline.

Regulation and deregulation policies may not be as 'clear cut' as they may seem. For example, a deregulated environment does not automatically mean the absence of regulatory structure. In the many countries, safety and operational procedures (such as pilot training) are heavily regulated, as are systems such as air traffic control. Road transport is regulated (largely in relation to speed) in most countries, as are the terms and conditions governing, for example, rental car contracts (i.e. mandatory third-party accident insurance, a critical issue in countries where tourists in rented vehicles can be responsible for a significant number of accidents). Ultimately, the deregulation of modes of transport has more to do with market access by competing firms than it does with operational standards and assessments. As a result, government role in transport planning, even in deregulated environments, can be critical.

TRANSPORT PLANNING

If the distinction between deregulation and regulation with respect to transport services as it relates to tourism can be considered a critical issue in transport policy, what remains is the *extent* to which government involvement is prevalent. With transport operations deregulated in many countries around the world (in many developing countries, some transport is heavily protected by government interests), it would be incorrect to assume that governments no longer have a financial or operational interest in the provision of transport services, both for tourists and non-tourists. Many national governments around the world have developed detailed transport plans that target areas of growth and shifts in demand. Banister (2002) outlines several agendas implicit in the relationship between markets and governments with respect to transport planning, two of which are highlighted here as they are integral in the specific context of tourism and transport planning:

1. 'There is a need for *intervention in the market* with new forms of regulation' (Banister, 2002: 229; italics in original). The issue here is the provision of a safe and stable business environment within which transport companies (and consortiums, if applicable) can operate. Destinations (on a wider spatial scale) and attractions (on a more micro level) are thus interested in how governments approach planning and, by extension, how it will impact on tourist flows and mobility patterns.

2. '*Environmental issues* must now be seen as integral to all transport policy decisions and investment proposals' (Banister, 2002: 229; italics in original). Clearly the sustainable operation of transport, from an environmental or biophysical perspective, is a moral and ethical idea (see Chapter 9), but this must be couched in the reality of externalities and

cost-benefits. Thus, by engaging in transport planning governments must provide the appropriate incentives to encourage the incorporation of appropriate environmental objectives without jeopardising the financial health of transport firms or the social benefits they provide.

While industries involved in the provision of tourism services, such as hospitality, may not have a direct and frequent impact on transport planning, government or state involvement in transport planning can have a significant impact on their performance. The question then remains: to what extent do governments recognise the impact of transport planning and policy-making on the tourism sector? The United States DOT recently released its 2003–2008 Strategic Plan (entitled 'Safer, Simpler, Smarter Transport Solutions') that is decidedly sector-wide in its focus. Interestingly, tourism is only mentioned twice in the entire Plan. It initially appears in a section in which future trends are discussed in relation to international transportation:

> Goal: To develop, coordinate and implement DOT's international transportation and trade policies and ensure that the U.S. transportation system supports the competitiveness of the U.S. transportation industry, and rapidly expanding global trade and *tourism*. (United States DOT, 2003; emphasis added)

This goal is linked to two desired strategic outcomes that are desired, namely 'Enhanced international competitiveness of US transport providers and manufacturers' and 'Harmon ed and standard ed regulatory and facilitation requirements'. The other mention of tourism in the Plan is in the context of domestic tourism, specifically:

> Investment in domestic and international transportation systems is central to survival in the global marketplace. Given the important role that transportation plays in commerce and *tourism*, if there is not greater private sector investment and improved coordination of public–private sector investment in domestic and international intermodal transportation connections, U.S. businesses will not be competitive in the global marketplace. (United States DOT, 2003; emphasis added)

Transport planning is closely tied to understanding the market for transport services. For example, the relationship between transport and domestic tourism is an important one as the ratio of domestic to international tourism can often be quite high. With existing constraints such as age, gender, income and social factors such as consumer culture and cultural context, the location of leisure and tourism activities can vary significantly. Georggi and Pendyala (2001), for example, note that older age segments and groups in lower income brackets are less likely to undertake long-distance travel when compared to younger population segments. In Canada, Statistics Canada estimates that almost 84 million non-business domestic trips were taken in 2003. A substantial number were same-day trips taken by automobile, thus suggesting that, spatially, many peoples' activity areas for same-day domestic tourism and recreational activities is very much local or regional. Table 2.3 shows the breakdown of domestic travel by mode of transport in Canada for 2003.

Table 2.3 Domestic travel in Canada by mode/type of transport (in thousands)

	Total	Same-day	OVERNIGHT/TRIP PURPOSE	
	Total	*Same-day*	*Non-business*	*Business*
Automobile	173,400	89,664	77,036	6700
Air	6807	515	3561	2731
Bus	4763	1717	2792	254
Rail	1479	240	938	301
Boat	589	135	416	38

Source: Adapted from Transport Canada (2004)

Despite the obvious size and economic importance of domestic tourism in Canada, a review of Transport Canada's 2001–2004 Business Plan (titled 'Looking to the New Millennium') reveals no mention of tourism, although it does discuss briefly safety and security issues. Similarly, Transport Canada's *Straight Ahead – A Vision for Transportation in Canada* (released in early 2004) makes no mention of the linkages between tourism and transport. The affiliated document, *Creating a Transportation Blueprint for the Next Decade and Beyond*, makes a somewhat generalist statement on the importance of transport in general: '…attention is…required to connect Canada's vast territory to our principal gateways by supporting corridors that are important to international trade and tourism' (Transport Canada, 2004: 8). It also makes reference to transport and rural areas: 'Rural and remote communities are often dependent on exporting resources to world markets, or on tourism, and transportation is a critical factor in the competitiveness of these products and services (Transport Canada, 2004: 10)'.

DEMAND AND SUPPLY

Tourism and transport has thus far been positioned as somewhat co-dependent, but what remains to be considered is how the relationships discussed above transfer to the actual use of transport by tourists. In other words, given either the deregulated or regulated environment of transport operations, what is the process by which people decide to travel on a certain mode or type of transport as tourists? The answer to this requires examination of transport demand and supply. A number of elements or variables effectively govern the extent to which modes of transport are selected. These can include:

1. *Family structure.* The role of family structures (which is associated with other lifestyle variables) in the selection of destinations is paramount, but it also raises the issue of the particular life-course of individuals utilising various transport services. For example, Thorton *et al.*'s (1997) travel diary study of tourists staying in Cornwall suggests that adults-only travel parties spent more time sightseeing by car or coach than travel parties that included children (see also Giuliano, 1997a). Such variables may also exert some influences on the choice of a particular transport mode or type. This has been raised in the transport geography literature (e.g. Giuliano, 1997a, 1997b), and the effect ageing populations will have some impact not only on the destination but also the choice of transport.

2. *Social and behavioural considerations.* These govern the ability to undertake travel (e.g. Wang, 2001). Cohen and Harris (1998), for example, suggest that British VFR travellers chose a particular mode based solely on economic reasons. Further, visitors to national parks in Britain who tend to utilise their own vehicle for transport purposes may be per-suaded to use public transport in order to keep pace with sustainable management of the parks system (which is growing) and, in theory, enhance the value of the experience (Eaton & Holding, 1996; see also Crabtree, 2000).

3. *The total cost of the trip.* The selection of a mode of transport needs to be considered in the wider context of the availability of the total trip budget. Thus, transport is one ele-ment within a series of variables that can include activities, accommodation and other expenditures. Prideaux (2000a) suggests that the demand for transport can be expressed as follows:

$$E_i = f(D_i, A_i, T_i)$$

where

E_i is the total holiday expenditure for destination i
D_i is the discretionary spending
A_i is the accommodation costs
T_i is the transport access costs

Ortuzar and Willumsen (2001) suggest that time, cost, reliability, convenience and com-fort that impact upon modal choice, with time and cost generally dominating in importance (cf. Crocket & Hounsell, 2005).

DEMAND FOR TRANSPORT

Although there are numerous variables involved, it is possible to generate models that illustrate the relationship they have with transport demand. Prideaux's (2004) transport cost model (Figure 2.2) not only neatly outlines how expenditure on transport cost is

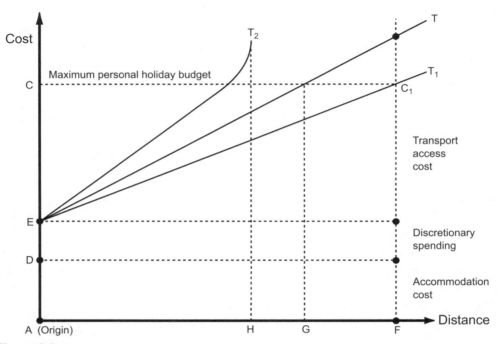

Figure 2.2 Prideaux's transport cost model

Source: From Prideaux (2004); reproduced with permission from Elsevier

affected by the function of distance, but it also highlights how other variables are also considered when selecting a destination. Prideaux's model suggests that trade-offs become necessary as an individual considers vacation destinations (H,G,F) further away from their point of origin (A). What is important to consider is the maximum personal holiday budget (CC_1) and the access cost for each destination depending on the mode of transport. For example, accessing destination H using transport mode/type T_1 is clearly within budget (given AD is accommodation cost, DE is discretionary spending and EC is the transport access cost). In fact, travel using mode T is also within budget. However, travel using mode T_2 is not within personal holiday budget. As destination G is further away from the point of origin, the model suggests that the cost of T and T_1 modes of transport will be higher. Selecting G as the destination will still be within budget, although note that selection mode T for destination G will result in maximising the total amount of money reserved for the entire trip.

A few issues with respect to how this model can be operationalised deserve consideration:

1. As Prideaux (2004: 83) notes, what appears as fixed costs for both accommodation (AD) and discretionary spending (DE) are, in reality, anything but fixed. Travellers may,

for example, opt to forfeit the cost of accommodation in favour of more expensive transport costs because of perceived value or comfort. Similarly, discretionary spending may
also be adjusted in favour of the variable transport access cost for similar reasons. Much
of this depends on the perceived value of the mode or type of transport, which is discussed more fully below.

2. There are situations where the transport access cost for some destination does in fact
increase the further away from the point of origin one travels. Prideaux (2004: 83–85)
uses this model to outline how peripheral regions can remain competitive in the face of
increasing access costs (which he breaks into three categories: fare cost, time spent travelling from origin to destination, and the 'cost of comfort'). In urban and peri-urban
situations, for example, modern road systems (e.g. motorways) may provide quick access
to destinations (or attractions) located along these routes (or zones of interaction, as Hall
[2005] refers to them). Attractions or destinations that are not as easily accessible may
suffer from higher access costs because of the increased time (due to the lack of motorways for transit) and the lack of value placed in the time taken to access. However, on a
much larger scale, the issues of supply, demand, competition and pricing structures
(among other elements) need to be taken into consideration. For example, to travel from
Dunedin, New Zealand to London is generally cheaper than to travel from Dunedin to
Toronto, which is shorter in both time and distance. Much of this has to do with the
supply and demand and the resulting pricing structures of airlines in both New Zealand
and North America, but it illustrates how distance is not always a factor in determining
access cost.

3. In some respects, the model treats transport as *'for'* tourism as opposed to *'as'* tourism,
and thus speaks to the earlier discussion on the blurry distinction between transport as a
facilitator and transport as the attraction. In fact, Lumsdon and Page (2004: 5) make this
distinction clear when they speak of 'transport for tourism' and 'transport as tourism'.

While models of transport expenditure, such as Prideaux's model, are useful for understanding the transactional nature of the holiday decision-making process, it is important
to understand how demand can be understood with respect to transportation. Transport
geographers and economists often distinguish between demand at the aggregate level (i.
e. examining flows and patterns in a particular zone) or the disaggregate level (i.e. at the
level of the individual). In the context of transport and tourism, the most useful manner
in which to approach demand for particular modes of transport is at the individual or disaggregate level, largely because it affords a more explanatory framework of analysis as
opposed to a generally normative one (Fischer, 1993). Below, a microeconomic approach
to analysing demand for tourism transport is discussed, as are general models relating to
decision-making processes that use the individual as their unit of analysis. Hoyle and

Knowles (1998) suggest that, as well, there are numerous elements that influence the provision and overall assessment of transport (Table 2.4).

Table 2.4 Factors relating to transport demand, provision and assessment

Demand	Demographic conditions	Structure, density/distribution/accessibility/connectivity, mobility
	Economic structures	Resource planning, land use, employment, other sectors
	Trade relations	Structure/flows, markets and market access, controls, regulations
Provision	Political structures	Planning, investment, regulations, partnerships
	Environmental constraints	Management, conservation
	Finance	Cost/revenue, investment, regulation
	Technology	Cost, distribution
Assessment	Usage	Cost/behaviour, trends, modal split
	Scales	Local, national/regional, international, global
	Dimensions	Spatial, temporal, structural
	Influences	Development, land use, marketing

Source: Adapted from Hoyle and Knowles (1998)

Generally, the demand for a particular good can be expressed as follows (Button, 1993: 54):

$$D_a = f\left(P_a P_1, P_2 ... P_w Y\right)$$

where

D = demand
P_a = price of the particular good
$P_1 ... P_w$ = price of other goods
Y = income

However, as Button (1993) points out, applying such a model to transport may not be entirely appropriate, largely because the factors involved, and as represented, tend to obscure the complex and important relationships between the factors themselves. The earlier discussion on the blurry distinctions of transport and tourism plays an important role here. Where the mode of transport is merely functional, price may play a pivotal role in measuring or assessing demand, yet when the mode of transport is also the attraction, such as a cruise experience, the price of the cruise is weighed up against the other benefits and services on offer. As a result, Button (1993) raises caution as to what product or service is actually under demand. Once this is recognised, the balance of price versus the price of other goods, as well as the degree to which other complex factors are involved, can be established.

A further point by Button (1993), with respect to the problem with applying a generalised model of demand for transport, relates to the costs incurred in order to utilise the service itself. Button (1993) argues that, for example, the cost of time whilst utilising a particular mode of transport needs to be taken into consideration (see also Preston, 2001). Thus, a particular mode or type of transport under consideration also plays a factor in deciding price versus the cost of time. For example, a business traveller deciding between taking the train or taking a plane may include in his or her decision the cost of parking or other forms of transport that are necessary. In essence, the argument here is that there is an opportunity cost that needs to be considered when a particular mode of transport is evaluated if the primary variable is price. For example, while the cost of transport mode A might be significantly lower than transport mode B, the amount of time spent travelling if one were to use mode B may be significantly less. Thus, for some travellers the added cost may be a justifiable expense and thus select mode B. Quinet and Vickerman (2004: 97) model this as follows:

$$C^i_f = p_f + h_i t_f$$

and

$$C^i_a = p_a + h_i t_a$$

where

C^i_f, C^i_a are the generalised costs of two modes of transport (e.g. commercial air carrier and rail, respectively)
p_a and p_f are the prices of the two modes
t_a and t_f are the travel times
h_i is the value of the time of the user

Thus, user i will likely choose to utilise a commercial air carrier (C^i_f) if $C^i_f \leq C^i_a$. Another way of representing this is as follows (Quinet & Vickerman, 2004: 97):

$$h_i \leq \frac{p_a - p_f}{t_f - t_a}$$

What this suggests is that a traveller could make a decision on the mode of transport on the basis of the amount of time necessary when using one mode of transport versus the other, but only if the value of time to that particular traveller warrants the additional cost incurred.

Transport economists recognise that the cost of transport and the time utilised 'in transit' are not the sole variables to consider in the demand for transport. There are numerous additional variables that have some bearing on the demand for a particular mode of transport. A few of the more obvious examples might include:

1. the cost of transport to and from the modal transport point. A good example is the cost to take a taxi to and from the airport from a place of residence or an office;

2. the amount of time necessary for transport from a place of residence or an office to the node (i.e. traffic congestion); and

3. the level of service provided by a particular mode of transport. For example, some travellers may be members of frequent flyer programmes that provide access to lounges and/or preferred check-in procedures.

By way of an example, and in order to illustrate the complex number and variety of variables involved in the demand for transport associated with tourism, assume that a couple are interested in a week-long holiday to Las Vegas. The city in which they live, Los Angeles, is a hub for a variety of transport options, not the least of which includes ground coach and commercial air carriers. They also have the option of using their own means of transport (i.e. a personal vehicle). All three modes of transport differ in terms of travel time, with air being the quickest and, for illustrative purposes in this example, the cheapest. In adopting a standard model of demand on the basis of price, the couple might be expected to be interested in pursuing this option solely because of cost. If, however, the couple live quite a distance away from the nearest airport that services their destination, the cost of travelling to the airport (both in terms of time and actual expenditures) may be seen to be too high to justify flying. Further, the couple may also not wish to subject themselves to the stress of proceeding through check-in and security, which has been substantially revamped and heightened as a result of the 11 September 2001 terrorist attacks in New York and Washington and again in August 2006 following the threats to aircraft originating in the United Kingdom but bound for the United States. The result is that the couple may decide to opt for one of the alternative transport modes (i.e. their own personal vehicle or a coach) to reach their destination, or they may decide not to travel to Las Vegas and, instead, embark upon another form of leisure or recreation closer to home.

This last point is critical and serves as a reminder as to why it is important to understand demand for transport and the numerous variables involved in selecting a particular mode of transport. Destinations are certainly interested in hosting visitors and ensuring their stay is enjoyable, but the argument here is that there are factors that are often beyond their control that govern whether they, as a destination, are even selected by potential tourists. In some cases, tourists may decide against visiting a particular destination when non-cost-related variables (e.g. security queues) are simply not strong enough to trump cost-related variables. Further, they may decide to travel to a destination at a further distance simply because the time and money required are potentially no greater than if they decided to travel to a destination closer to home.

Elasticity of demand

Elasticity of demand (or price elasticity) refers to the degree to which customers or users respond to shifts in prices. As a ratio, it is the 'percent change in quantity demanded to percent change in price' (Coyle *et al.*, 1994). As formula, elasticity is expressed as follows (Doganis, 2002):

$$\text{Price elasticity} = \frac{\% \text{ change in quantity}}{\% \text{ change in price}}$$

The relationship between price and quality of a good or product is generally referred to as either elastic or inelastic. If the demand for a product is elastic, the amount demanded is more than the total price change amount (thus resulting in a positive elasticity coefficient). If the demand for a product is inelastic, then the amount of product demanded is less than that the total change in price (thus resulting in a negative elasticity coefficient). An inelastic product is said, therefore, to be insensitive to price change. Understanding elasticity in relation to transport and tourism is important for two reasons:

1. It is not entirely clear in all cases whether the price of transport in relation to tourism is elastic or inelastic. In examining shits in demand and price, however, one also needs to take into consideration the length of the observation. Economists have recognised for quite some time that the cost of petrol at service stations is relatively inelastic because, quite simply, most consumers either genuinely need their personal vehicle (for example, to commute to and from their place of employment) or have no desire to give up the 'luxury' of personalised motor transport. Thus, over the long term, the price of petrol tends to be rather inelastic as shifts in consumption of other goods (e.g. dining out) may be affected in the first instance. In the short term, however, people may opt to not purchase petrol or reduce the frequency and duration of non-essential motorised travel. As a consequence, when examining the demand elasticity of travel, it may be necessary to measure the relatively elasticity over longer periods of time.

2. Where price is not a discriminating factor in either the selection of a particular mode or type of transport, or where competition exists to the point where price differentiation is negligible, then elasticity of service becomes important (Coyle *et al.*, 1994). In this case, what distinguishes one transport mode from another (or even two similar transport modes) ultimately becomes the more intangible service-related items as opposed to price (see Chapter 8). Competition between two modes of transport serving a particular route may, for example, result in very little difference in price. As a result, the competition for increased market share becomes based on levels of service. As Coyle *et al.* (1994: 33) point out:

> Assuming no price changes, the modal or specific carrier demand is much more sensitive to changes in service levels provided. Many air passengers monitor the 'on-time' service levels of the various air carriers and, when possible, will select the air carrier that provides the best 'on-time' service.

In relation to tourism, Doganis (2002: 203) argues that airlines (but this also applies to other providers of tourism-related transport) 'need to have a feel for the price elasticity of the various market segments on the route or routes they are dealing with. Without such a feel, they may make major planning and pricing errors.' In other words, different market segments will be more or less elastic/inelastic based on historic characteristics. Leisure travel, for example, may be perceived as more elastic than business travel or travel for emergency purposes (e.g. to a funeral). As a result, transport providers need to carefully consider the nature of the market when adopting pricing schemes for their product. As Doganis (2002: 204) points out, a market that is elastic may respond to a fare decrease with stronger demand, resulting in more people travelling, and thus higher revenues despite the fare decrease. Conversely, a market that is inelastic may respond to a fare increase with less demand, and the increase in fare in this case may not be enough to cover the drop in demand. A further discussion on pricing structures is considered in Chapter 7 when yield management (or price discrimination) is discussed.

ISSUES OF SUPPLY IN TOURISM AND TRANSPORT

The supply side of transport in relation to tourism is generally concerned with the ability of firms (sometimes engaged in public–private operational endeavours) to provide adequate levels of service to support nodes and affiliated networks. Supply issues can be examined from a macro perspective, where the structure of the market within which a mode of transport operates, or from a micro perspective where distribution characteristics are considered in the context of matching or meeting demand.

Macro determinant perspectives

The wider political environment within which transport is supplied for the purposes of tourism necessarily needs to consider issues of bilateral agreements (Chapter 7) and regulations of operations. As discussed, regulation and deregulation are efforts on the part of governments to exert some degree of control over market structures, either directly through regulation or the removal of control through deregulation. Whereas the previous discussion was concerned with the role of government in market structures or forms, further consideration is due regarding how deregulated market structures in transport have materialised and what impact this has on tourism. The shape of the macro operating environment is largely determined by the presence or absence of significant competitors. Various market forms exist that determine supply chains and distribution channels, but these largely exist as either imperfect or perfect competition models. Imperfect competition forms include pure monopolies, where a single firm is the only seller of a product. Contestable markets were emphasised earlier in the context of deregulation, but in some cases even deregulated environments can produce unbalanced supply of services. According to Sinclair and Stabler (1997: 81), deregulation of the air transport market has introduced competition where previously regulated environments would produce state-controlled or supported monopolies or oligopolies: 'In the international market some routes are competitive, being served by many carriers. Most of the others are served by at least two carriers, indicating an oligopolistic market, although a few routes are served by a single carrier which may be tempted to exercise monopoly powers.'

In a regional or national context, Graham (1997) and Goetz (2002) note that oligopolistic market structures in passenger air transport may be largely relegated to main trunk routes, perhaps to the detriment of regional feeder routes. In some markets, rail transport can exhibit market structures that are similar, with as few as two firms exerting oligopoly control (e.g. Knowles, 1998). Understanding macro-level market structures is critical for tourism because these can form supply landscapes to which demand elements are matched. The shape of tourism flows depends largely on the competitiveness of transport conveyance. Market structures that promote competition benefit the traveller, but quite often such structures can come at the expense of firms unable to compete. As Eccles and Costa (1996: 48) note, deregulation in the European market has led to considerable upheaval that may ultimately be of some concern to future tourist flows:

> ... many small European carriers will be swallowed up by the stronger, existing privat ed European airlines. If this is the case the consumer will have fewer airlines to choose from, the exact situation that has occurred in the USA. As airlines continue to strive for European dominance, the Asian carriers are seeking to link into the European network, and, to gain access, require strategic alliances, in particular with those carriers that are currently looking to control European aviation.

Micro determinant perspectives

Micro determinants in transport and tourism supply considerations can be said to focus on the transaction levied between the transport provider and the customer or user. To this end, the focus is on the product or service that is sold (see Chapter 8 for a discussion on products/services). In recent decades there has been a marked trend towards the use of information technology to facilitate this process, and often at the expense of more traditional distribution and supply chains, such as travel agents. In fact, many transport companies are utilising technology to target existing markets in an effort to consolidate distribution and acquire greater market penetration through innovation (Jarach, 2002). For Jarach (2002), a distinct difference exists between e-commerce (which focuses primarily on the manner by which outputs, or products, are sold) and e-business, which he classifies as broader value relationships. For airlines, Jarach (2002: 120) notes that '[t]his means satisfying the needs of consumers, as well as attracting, fascinating and tying the consumer to the airline in a creative and entertaining way'. Buhalis (2004) found that the airline industry utilises information technology to improve distribution efforts while at the same time reducing costs. While LCCs have generally pioneered the use of online sales, Buhalis (2004: 819) notes that some larger carriers have recently adopted similar distribution mechanisms in order to 'demonstrate the extra value they offer for comparable prices'. Many cruise companies now feature online booking, following a trend introduced by airlines. Royal Caribbean launched an online advertising campaign (utilising banners on web pages) that featured the tag-line: 'You can wait for warm weather or go find it. Get started now' (Van der Pool, 2004). Of interest here is what this means for the traditional distribution channels, such as the use of travel agents for ticket booking and sales.

When a passenger books a flight on a major carrier through a travel agent, it is not uncommon for the agent to use some form of CRS (e.g. Galileo, Sabre) to determine fare and routing options and pass along the options to the customer. In the 1970s and 1980s, many individual airlines operated their own CRS. CRS are designed to enhance information provision, such as offering instant choice on sales options for a particular carrier. However, that choice (or lack thereof) in product has not been without controversy:

> There has been concern about the market power given to operators of particular CRS and the partiality of systems both in the exclusion – rationalised on technical grounds – of other rival systems and the influence owners can exert of travel agents and other airlines … Allegations that six American airlines were using a CRS as a means of establishing a price fixing ring have been denied by following Department of Justice [US] pressure the practice has been discontinued (Tomkins, 1994) … Other forms of alleged abuse include the selective display of some airline flights to the detriment of alternatives. Initially CRS owners arranged for their own flights to be displayed first on possible flight listings and systems have also showed a display bias in favour of online over inter-line connections. (Driver, 1999: 135, 136)

Where this becomes significant is in human behaviour at the point of purchase. As Driver (1999) points out, customers may elect to refrain from searching for alternatives if their perception of the offer in front of them is deemed reasonable. Thus, an individual airline's CRS, coupled with a travel agent who is incentivised to book passengers with a particular carrier that offers higher commission rates, is a powerful tool. In the past few decades GDS, which are CRS affiliated with airlines (Buhalis & Licata, 2002; Page, 1999:

186) have become popular. These systems display several pricing offers from a variety of airlines, including schedules, availability, passenger information and fare rules (Page, 1999: 187). As efficient as these systems are, airlines are still paying travel agents commission on the sales they run through when utilising GDS. As many airlines have, for the past few decades, explored areas in which to cut costs as a means of boosting revenue, the commission paid to travel agents came under close scrutiny. For many, this means a fundamental re-think of the nature of the manner in which their product/service is distributed. Buhalis and Licata (2002) note that future distribution channels (which they call ePlatforms) will take three forms: online (internet) sales, interactive digital television and mobile devices. Online sales and e-ticketing are expected to be the dominant form of distribution for air travel by 2007 (O'Toole, 2002, referenced in Buhalis & Licata, 2002), yet the emergence of web portals (e.g. Yahoo) and online travel agents (e.g. Orbitz) has meant new challenges, particularly over the control of these systems by larger conglomerates (Field, 2005). Airlines are, of course, not the only mode to utilise online sales. Many railway operations and cruise companies offer the ability to book and pay for tickets online.

What do these new forms of distribution mean for traditional intermediaries such as travel agents? In 1998, the Guild of European Business Travel Agents ran a conference at which Kieron Brennan, a consultant, urged agents to develop 'journey management' businesses, where such intangible services such as tracking flight alerts, providing recommendation on routes, and utilising databases on customers' past purchases to, in the future, provide tailored options for travel (Travel Trade Gazetta Europa, 1998). The reduction in travel agent commission as a result of shifting distribution methods and new ePlatforms (Buhalis & Lacata, 2002) for generated sales is interesting for several reasons. First, at the same time many airlines were adopting online purchasing of tickets as a means of providing a direct service to their customers. While establishing online e-commerce activities came at a cost, airlines wanted to effectively set the price at which their seats were sold. At the same time, by adopting a model where direct purchase was possible, it achieved a degree of what has been termed by one industry observer as 'disintermediation' (Kennedy, 1996), where airlines were keen to cut out the middleperson in the distribution of travel sales and thus introduce a new distribution chain. Much of this started in the mid- to late 1990s when the global economy was relatively strong. However, following economic recessions (especially in the United States) caused some companies, airlines included, to re-think cost structures. Although the period since then has witnessed substantial fluctuations, many agents struggle to recover their costs in markets where direct purchasing (either online or over the telephone) is strong (although not at all dominant in most environments).

Second, many airlines also started to establish a strong online presence with booking capabilities as a means of getting closer to their customer. In fact, Ryanair is often regarded as one of the more successful carriers to implement an easy-to-use and highly successful online booking engine, which followed on the heels of a large telephone-based reservation system (which was subsequently dismantled for the purpose of cutting costs). By operating online booking engines themselves, airlines could track usage and itineraries as a means to help its yield management system in the future. Despite the simplicity of booking online, and thus an airline's ability to provide direct sales to customers, the systems are not without problems. Booking a series of flights that begin with domestic flights, follow through to international flights, and then back on domestic flights is problematic for most, if not all, airline online booking and reservation systems. In those cases, customers must either telephone the airline directly or utilise the services of a travel agent. Also, with the advent of cheaper fares by LCCs, many mistakes are made by customers when booking and purchasing online. When combined with the fact that the most inexpensive seats are often non-refundable, those customers who make mistakes often have little, if any, redress.

CHAPTER SUMMARY

This chapter has outlined some of the core elements of the tourism/transport relationship. It considered the blurry distinction between how tourism transport is actually conceptualised (especially with respect to tourist versus non-tourist use of transport services) and examined how transport can actually become the attraction rather than (or sometimes in addition to) the destination or attraction itself. The wider tourism system was also considered, and the nature of transport's position within this system was discussed. The model proposed (based on and adapted from Page, 1999) that various aspects of the tourism/transport relationship benefit from a systems approach, namely the flows of tourists, the mode of travel, the motivation to travel and the available time for travel. It also highlighted the fact that transport permeates many levels of the tourism experience. For example, many trips that involve the use of various modes of transport do so at various spatial levels. Transport therefore plays an integral role in tourist flows from origin to destination, from destination to destination, and within destinations.

The role of government is a critical area in which the tourism/transport relationship is manifested. Key among these is regulation and deregulation (or privatisation) and what impacts they have on tourist flows and the ability of modes to even offer services to tourists. Similarly, the planning for transport and whether tourism is a factor were considered, and it was found that tourism is often only given cursory consideration. This could be detrimental in the long run because it fails to consider the close relationship between economic development and tourism, and the important role that transport plays in facilitating tourism development at a variety of levels (both locally, regionally and nationally).

Issues of demand and supply were also considered, and it was noted that traditional models of demand for goods may not be adequate. As demand for transport is influenced by a number of factors (e.g. time, access, price), more comprehensive models are necessary in order to capture the nuances embedded within this reality. The cost of transport, for example, may not simply be the cost for the actual mode of transport, but also the cost in order access that particular mode. As well, cost is traditionally expressed in monetary figures, whereas the cost of time (e.g. time spent utilising and/or accessing a particular mode) must also be considered. The elasticity of transport demand was also considered in order to demonstrate the variability of such a concept as applied to tourism-related transport. In other words, demand elasticity for tourism transport may initially be somewhat elastic because new innovations or pricing structures may spawn increased travel. In the long run, however, it is not entirely clear whether this elasticity is maintained. To a large extent, it depends on the level of competition and the overall demand for the product or service. As a result, in a highly competitive environment, price elasticity may be replaced by service elasticity as more potential consumers opt to decide on travel based on variables other than price.

BOX 2.3 Case study – The Channel Tunnel: The right idea at the wrong time?

To a large extent, the rationale behind the construction of the Channel Tunnel was to provide fast, reliable and comfortable transit between two nodes, namely Britain and France. Generally, politicians in both countries argued that the overall economic benefit of going forward with a tunnel (the plans for which date back, in some form or another, to the 1960s [Gibb, 1994]) would bring significant economic benefits to both countries. What is significant for the development of tourism, as Essex (1994) points out, is the fact that 30 million people live within three hours travel of the Tunnel. Essex (1994) also suggested that the presence of the tunnel will have definitive impacts on tourism:

1. The Tunnel will 'remove the physical and psychological barrier of the Channel for some travellers, who perceive visits across the Channel as arduous and requiring careful organisation' (Essex, 1994: 81). This means that rail travel can now link continental Europe with the UK.

2. The Tunnel will substantially increase the carrying capacity between the two countries, and certainly from continental Europe to the UK.

3. The presence of the Tunnel, according to Essex (1994: 81), results in 'competition for the existing modes of passenger travel and so create greater choice and flexibility for the customer'. Essex uses the example of the London–Paris link: with the Tunnel, this would be a 3-hour service, compared to 7 hours by ferry and slightly less than 4 hours by air.

The Tunnel represents one of the largest privately funded infrastructure projects in the world (Tran, 2004), but the cost of development has been steep and the problems facing the operation have been numerous. First, and largely a function of high interest rates at the time of peak construction (early 1990s) as well as a total development cost of £10 billion, the Tunnel has struggled to encourage traffic (both passenger and freight) to a level where costs can be recovered. Second, Tran (2004) reports that shareholders are, as of early 2004, not entirely happy with how the Tunnel is managed. Third, competition from low-cost airlines operating throughout Europe (which may not necessarily have been foreseen during planning stages) have inhibited passenger travel using the Tunnel, especially given that Essex (1994) notes that price will be the deciding factor for most people when deciding on whether the Tunnel represents a suitable mode of transport. Overall, the future of the Tunnel seems somewhat turbulent, and it may be quite some time before the initial projections of use are realised. In recent years, the Tunnel's operators, Eurotunnel, have encountered financial problems due to lacklustre performance and problems with shedding costs. As of July 2006, Eurotunnel was actively seeking protection from creditors after negotiations to restructure the companies massive debt (some £6.2 billion) failed.

Questions for consideration

1. Why was the Channel Tunnel a good idea from the perspective of securing access between two countries?

2. Why are LCCs threatening the financial viability of the Tunnel?

SELF-REVIEW QUESTIONS

1. What are the three blurry distinctions that arise when describing tourism/transport relationships?

2. What are the key factors that influence demand for transport?

3. What is elasticity and how does it affect transport and, consequently, tourism?

ESSAY QUESTIONS

1. Why is it important to understand the principles of supply and demand when discussing the relationship between tourism and transport?

2. Compare and contrast two examples of where transport would fit within the tourism system.

3. Find an example of a local transport plan where you live and write an essay that evaluates it from the perspective of support for, and facilitation of, the local tourism sector.

KEY SOURCES

Lumsdon, L. and Page, SJ (eds) (2004) *Tourism and Transport: Issues and Agenda for the New Millennium*: Amsterdam: Elsevier.

The Lumsdon and Page volume explores significant issues revolving around the subject. Notable contributions are an update to Prideaux's transport cost model, Hall's discussion on sustainability and equity, and Freathy's discussion on future directions for airports. The lead chapter by the editors is also useful to capture a wider perspective on a variety of issues, and the notion of the transport/tourism 'interface' is addressed here.

Travel Industry Association of America – www.tia.org

Bureau of Transportation Statistics (US) – www.bts.gov

Department for Transport (UK) – www.dft.gov.uk

These three sites will generally offer recently available statistics and general measures relating to transport operations and use. In some instances, full Excel tables may be obtained.

Key journals that explore tourism and transport relationships include most of the existing tourism journals, but other transport industry-specific journals such as the *Journal of Air Transport Management, Journal of Transport Geography* and *Transportation Research* (Parts A, B and D) often feature articles relating to tourism and/or leisure and recreation.

CHAPTER 3:

TRANSPORT NETWORKS AND FLOWS

LEARNING OBJECTIVES

After reading this chapter, you should be able to

1. Describe and critically evaluate the importance of connectivity and accessibility of transport networks and their role in tourism development.

2. Recognise the important of networks in business-related decisions relating to transport provision.

3. Interpret the approach(es) of government versus the private sector with reference to connectivity and accessibility.

4. Describe various models of spatial interaction in transport and what this means for tourism flows and development.

5. Generate your own examples of connectivity and accessibility models and explain their structure.

INTRODUCTION

In Chapter 1 several of the key concepts that underpin much of the discussion in this book were outlined. Modes (and types), networks and flows were positioned within a wider tourism/transport framework, and it was suggested that these three elements, when combined, effectively determine the nature of tourist demand for transport products and services (although the exact distinction between transport products and services will be discussed in more detail in Chapter 8). By extension, much of the second chapter was economic (or at least business, management and politics) in format and presentation; it not only considered issues of supply and demand, but it also considered how governments are involved in transport planning. This chapter investigates the physical manifestation and spatial interactions surrounding tourism and transport. Here, the intent is to discuss the role of space and place, from a spatial geography perspective, in characterising the various *networks* of transport (Figure 3.1). In the context of tourism, the issue is the degree of complementarity between destinations and origins and, further, how transport flows and networks work to embed destinations or nodes and origins within the wider tourism system. This complementarity is related closely to demand characteristics and is essentially a form of 'time–space coordination' (Nutley, 1998). The purpose of this chapter is to suggest that the *mapping* of networks and tourists flows is integral to understanding how transport works with tourism. The central argument is that, through understanding the spatial relationships and spatial interaction within and across networks and flows, any analysis of supply, demand and government planning and policy-making becomes more meaningful. It is important to keep in mind, however, that the graphical representations of transport networks presented in this chapter are, in fact, heavily influenced by management, planning, marketing, demand and other external variables. In other words, this chapter is meant to introduce and position spatial concepts as complementary to the other forms of analysis (e.g. supply/demand, regulatory systems, environment, marketing, management) by which transport and tourism can be assessed.

Spatial processes have been adopted in recreation and leisure studies (e.g. Wolfe, 1952, 1966), but they have only recently been applied to tourism (e.g. Hall, 2005; although see van der Knaap, 1999 and McAdam, 1999 for an overview of GIS applications in tourism). Thus, in contrast with the chapters that follow, rather than focus on specific modes and types of transport, this chapter examines structures and activities associated with the flows of tourists and the networks of transport they utilise. More importantly, of interest here is determining *how* and *why* such networks are important to understand.

MOBILITY, SPACE AND PLACE: A BRIEF OVERVIEW

How do space and place, from a non-human/social geography perspective, relate to transport? Put simply, transport is the vector by which movement and mobility is facilitated. It represents the means by which people are shuttled from place to place, but more importantly it allows for some places to become accessible and connected across networks. Accessibility is perhaps the most critical aspect of understanding transport networks in the context of the layering tourist flows (e.g. multiple modes, multiple destinations, multiple routes). Aside from a few exceptions, there is usually more than one mode and associated route serving a particular destination, and most destinations are connected to large networks of modal and multi-modal transport services. As a result, understanding how accessible a destination is from the perspective of potential transport options is critical for destination planning and management.

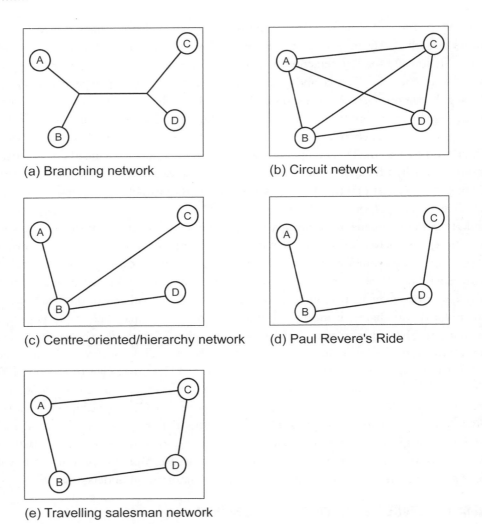

(a) Branching network

(b) Circuit network

(c) Centre-oriented/hierarchy network

(d) Paul Revere's Ride

(e) Travelling salesman network

Figure 3.1 A typology of networks

Source: Adapted from Fellman *et al.* (1992); Lowe and Moryadas (1975)

The fact that tourists and travellers are able to be whisked around the world in little more than 24 hours means that there are more places open and available to potential travellers, and thus represents a manifestation of globalisation (Hall, 2005). This is important because it points to what has been termed in the geography literature as time–space compression (Harvey, 1990) or time–space convergence (Janelle, 1969). At the beginning of the 21st century, increasing numbers of people have the ability to 1) travel further; 2) travel faster, given technological advances; and 3) experience and, most importantly, conceptualise more spaces and places. In short, mobility and the linking of places or nodes and spaces hinges on the provision of transport.

The importance of transport as it exists in conceptions of mobility and the extent to which individuals are mobile is not always apparent. It can be said, therefore, that transport provision is paramount for understanding mobility for five reasons:

1. Transport generally acts as the vector by which persons enter existing, or even non-existing (i.e. free form), networks and flows on a variety of spatial scales.

2. By extension, the spatial scales in which transport permeates is wide, ranging from local movement, within a relatively smaller geographic scale, to international, utilising modes such as air- and water-based transport to traverse large distances. In spatial geography, the extent to which people are mobile within a given area is referred to as their 'activity space' (Hägerstrand, 1970; see also Hall, 2005).

3. The range of transport modes available that facilitate mobility, and the fact that each generally features differing levels of speed for covering distances, also means that important decisions must be made with respect to personal time-budgets. Time-budgets refer to the amount of time an individual is willing to, or must, allocate to certain activities, in this case transport (see Chapin, 1966 and Hall, 2005 for a useful discussion on time-budget in relation to tourism). Building on the discussion from the previous chapter that considered travellers' choice of transport and its relationship to the value of time, the existence of multiple transport modes and corresponding types would suggest that decisions need to be made on whether a particular mode of transport is worth utilising given the often restricted amount of time available for leisure pursuits, including tourism.

4. Mobility is largely dependent on existing transport and related infrastructure in so far as it is allied with (a) the actual propensity for mobility (i.e. availability of existing networks, irrespective of demand in some cases), (b) the amount of time needed to travel from origin to destination (i.e. inaccessible destinations may require more time to travel to, such that sacrifices to other trip activities need to be made), and (c) the level of existing competition serving one or more destinations from a point of origin (i.e. the presence of competition can often result in lower costs to utilise transport, thus facilitating demand and ultimately the propensity for mobility).

5. In the context of transport and tourism, understanding mobility and the underlying structures of time–space utilisation, a complete picture of discretionary activities reflecting choice in participation, as opposed to activities that are more obligatory (Parkes & Wallis, 1978), is afforded. As such, time-budgets and activity spaces determine the spatial extent of mobility and accessibility (Ross, 2000) and may play an important role in determining tourist flows and flows for non-tourist purposes. Families, for example, may elect to go on holiday to locations that are convenient in a geographic sense and thus minimise travel time or expense (and stay confined to a particular activity space), but obligatory travel, such as visiting a sick relative, may not leave such choices open to alternatives.

Before discussing the mathematical foundations of spatial networks, it is important to consider a few of the wider social implications of movement and how it relates to 'space' and 'place'. The issue of how destinations function as places to be enjoyed and 'consumed' has been well researched both within the tourism literature (e.g. Meethan, 2001) and within other social science disciplines (e.g. Urry, 1995). Geographers have been interested in the spatial elements of places, but particularly in how place comes to be represented and juxtaposed with other places (see, for example, Hubbard *et al.*, 2004 for an excellent overview). Characterisations of space and place range from positivist constructions from the quantitative revolution in geography (e.g. Hägerstrand, 1967, 1970; Haggett *et al.*, 1977) to more behaviouralist approaches to spatial behaviour (e.g. Golledge, 1981) to the 'cultural turn' in human geography (e.g. Jackson, 1989).

The study of mobilities from a social perspective has only recently been appropriated by tourism studies for the purpose of cataloguing and explaining both individual and aggregate movements through time and space (e.g. Coles *et al.*, 2004, Hall, 2005). Characterising movement and mobility is, however, difficult and at times rather confusing. This is largely because of the numerous classifications of movement and the variability of the individuals undertaking that movement. The WTO, for example, recently started to classify day trips as a form of tourism, but what this highlights is the blurring of the distinction between tourism (defined as movement away from home for a particular period of time, but involving an overnight stay), leisure and even recreation. As Coles *et al.* (2004) argue, tourism should perhaps best be seen as a leisure-oriented form of mobility. Thinking of a range of mobilities, then, tourism is but one, and each of these manifestations of mobilities carries with them significant transport considerations (e.g. Box 3.1):

> Tourism [can be] seen as a leisure-oriented component of a continuum of mobilities that stretch from commuting and shopping through to what is usually categorised as migration. Such a representation of tourism clearly seeks to explicitly connect tourism not only with other discussions of mobility in the social sciences but also to integrate macro and micro scale understandings of mobility. Moreover, such a conceptualisation assists in further integrating research on the leisure dimensions of other forms of mobility such as second homes (e.g. Coppock, 1977; Hall and Müller, 2004), mobility of the highly skilled (OECD, 2002), travel for overseas work experience (Mason, 2001), and educational travel (Kraft *et al.*, 1994) with that of tourism mobility. (Coles *et al.*, 2004: 465–466)

BOX 3.1 Bottlenecks in connectivity and accessibility: Cottage country and weekend transport

The use of cottages and cabins (or holiday homes) can put enormous strain on highway networks during weekends (generally Friday afternoons/evenings and Sunday afternoon/evenings) and during extended holidays, especially when areas of cottage recreation (embedded within 'cottage landscapes' of rural recreation, Halseth, 2004) are within driving distance of major urban areas. Kremarik (2002) notes that approximately 823,000 Canadian households owned second homes or cottages, and approximately three-quarters of these were located within Canada. Svenson's (2004) research on cottage lifestyles shows that, while cottage owner-ship generally disfavours families, there is room to suggest that cottage use (as opposed to outright ownership) may be more family-oriented and thus used by various members of a particular family: 'The cottage, for many Canadians, is a place where extended family and friends gather together, where work is meaning-ful, where there is time for leisure and contact with nature, where community feels present' (Svenson, 2004: 73).

While studies of cottage use among urban residents has been conducted, little attention has been paid to the role of transport in these activities. One area where cottage use, as second homes (e.g. Hall & Müller, 2004), in relation to urban environments is significant is the metropolitan area of Toronto. The major highway (Highway 400) leading to an area of substantial cottage development north from Toronto (Muskoka) often becomes extremely congested on Friday afternoons in the summer as weekend recreationalists drive north to their cot-tages (see also Halseth, 2004). Anecdotal evidence from Toronto suggests that traffic congestion is even having an impact on decisions when to travel. Many opt to leave on either Thursday evening (thus taking Fridays as annual leave days over the summer until their leave is used up) or early on Saturday morning. In this case, transport has a strong impact on mobility patterns. It may also have an impact on how holidays are utilised; for example, occupants of cottages/cabins/second homes may elect to have multiple long weekends rather than one block of two or three weeks of annual leave. Svenson (2004) points out that driving times might be having some impact on decisions to purchase cottages in some areas of Canada. What this suggests is that access to cottage areas may be having significant impacts on second home recreational activities, although these assump-tions are currently in need of empirical validation:

1. Extensive traffic congestion may inhibit the enjoyment of second home/cottage properties if work/leisure flexibility is not realised (i.e. if an individual or family is unable to travel during a period of time where congestion is less onerous).

2. As Svenson (2004) notes, the time needed to travel from urban areas to areas of second home/cottage developments may ultimately have an impact on the overall attractiveness of the cottage as a suitable weekend-oriented recreational activity. Thus, in this case accessibility may in fact be responsible for altering recreational patterns.

3. Increasingly, accessibility may have an impact on the demographic profile of cottagers, such that cottage may cease to become weekend second home getaways and instead become locations of longer stays.

Questions for consideration

1. How has the congestion associated with major metropolitan areas such as Toronto influenced or changed mobility patterns of those with cottages?

2. What might the impact be of rising petrol/gas prices in a situation like the one described above?

SPATIAL ASSESSMENTS IN TOURISM AND TRANSPORT: CONNECTIVITY AND ACCESSIBILITY

With transport acting as a vector of mobility, there is a need to consider connectivity and accessibility between nodes, which are often referred to as 'vertices' in the spatial geography literature, as these two concepts underpin the ability of tourism destinations to exist. Broadly, there are several reasons for examining connectivity and accessibility in relation to transport and tourism:

1. for the purpose of establishing the role of government in public access to transport (including those modes of transport used by tourists);

2. assessing the priorities of private firms wishing to establish or expand current transport operations across a network; and

3. for use by other industries involved (to varying degrees) in the provision of tourism services in order to plan future expansion and/or diversification efforts.

As Chapman (1979: 209) notes, '[c]onnectivity indices provide useful aggregate measures of the spatial structure of a network'. Spatial analysis exercises in which connectivity and accessibility are measured can achieve several outcomes:

1. The ability to examine the relationship between different modes of transport and the wider networks within which they function. In other words, how well does a particular mode or type of transport service a particular region?

2. The ability to compare, between two places or nodes, the relative strength of a particular mode of transport to another mode of transport (i.e. the degree of connectivity or accessibility of air versus rail) and even by type. For example, in some heritage tourism destinations, this could mean comparing the utility and experiential benefits of certain rail services, such as an historic tram (e.g. Pearce 2001a, 2001b), with a guided bus trip.

3. The evolution of transport networks over time can be measured, including consideration for whether government policies designed to enhance or encourage transport innovation and service have been beneficial or detrimental. Fan (2006) found a remarkable increase in inter-city connectivity between the UK and Ireland and continental Europe between 1996 and 2004, largely attributable to the expanding networks created by LCCs (see also Dobruszkes, 2006).

The power of spatial assessments can even be used in making business decisions. For example, suppose a newly formed national coach company is interested in developing services across a specific network, incorporating several destinations. In the course of its planning, decisions need to be made with respect to which destinations could be served and where it might be best to establish an operational base (where routine maintenance and large repairs are carried out, and where a significant population base exists such that it can use the population base as its key market to service outlying destinations; this is commonly known as the hub-and-spoke concept and is discussed in Chapter 6 in relation to air transport). When determining which destinations are to be included, the company must carefully evaluate the overall value of servicing a particular node. This would be done not only in reference to the direct routes that it would bring, but also the integration of one node into the wider network and whether this would generate subsequent demand and a subsequent positive return on investment. By using connectivity and accessibility analysis, the company might be able to understand the true spatial value of the proposed network and, more importantly, institute pricing schemes or consider alternatives. Further, if certain routes along a proposed network (or the entire network itself) needed government approval (perhaps in order to satisfy that it was not being anti-competitive), the company could demonstrate the economic and social benefits of the proposed network structure by the fact that it is proposing to link destinations that may have otherwise been under-serviced or totally disassociated from connections to other nodes.

PUBLIC SERVICE CONSIDERATIONS: THE ROLE OF GOVERNMENT

From a government perspective, planning priorities can be established if demand for transport is known and the network along which that demand may be manifested is established and mapped (Werner, 1985). Governments have long been responsible for the provision of transport for the greater good of society, as Werner (1985: 12) notes:

> In a highly organised and diversified society such as ours, adequate transportation requires enormous resources (on the order of 20 percent of the gross national product) and sophisticated organisation and management. Such expenditures call for intelligent planning, which in turn requires that we understand the principles that govern transportation phenomena, their causes, their dynamics, their distribution, and their impact on space and time.

Yet governments are often also tasked with ensuring that transport networks are adequate in order to service tourists, both domestic and international. For example, most tourism destinations have multiple networks associated with them, largely because more than one mode of transport can be used for access. Various levels of government may therefore use information on the overall pattern of transport networks serving destinations in order to make decisions regarding, for example, incentives for upstart transport providers or gauging the extent to which public support for transport infrastructure is necessary. If a particular mode of transport is not adequately increasing the degree of connectivity between nodes, a government may wish to focus on supporting alternative means of transport through direct policies or subsidies. A good example is the global air services network, which is managed and regulated through a series of regulatory agreements and treaties (see Chapter 7). In some cases, governments may elect to liberalise access to its key nodes in order to enhance or increase the economic contribution that additional traffic may bring.

LOCATION, LOCATION, LOCATION: THE VIEW FROM THE PRIVATE SECTOR

From a private-firm perspective, potential destinations or nodes can be examined and assessed as to whether the existing population base is enough to warrant new service development given the additional costs needed in developing an expanded network (not to mention subsequent marketing costs). Analysing location is important as it allows for consideration of potential costs and risks for competitiveness (Daskin, 1995; Kidokoro, 2004). Examining accessibility and connectivity in these situations could help to address several questions:

1. Which routes would a private transport firm ideally select (i.e. what is the existing demand for services across a wide geographic area, such that specific profitable places can be identified)?

2. Given demand considerations, what are the key criteria involved in deciding whether to provide transport service to these places (i.e. cost of service, potential competition, future demand shifts and access to ancillary services would all enter into the equation)?

3. With respect to potential competition, private firms offering services across a network may also utilise connectivity and accessibility information to determine barriers to entry. For example, the coach company profiled above may decide to limit services along a specific route (or edge) and concentrate on a new destination in order to facilitate flow-on effects to other destinations. Alternatively, the same company may decide to operate services to a remote destination knowing that travellers will continue along the network using high-profit routes. In effect, incorporating some destinations may be financially detrimental to the overall operation, but necessary in that they demonstrate market presence and, as a result, cause potential competitors to closely evaluate the cost of entry. These kinds of decisions are common in the aviation industry. An airline, therefore, may service an intermediate destination solely for the purpose of getting customers integrated into their network and thus on more profitable routes. Some international airlines, such as Air Canada and Qantas, operate in a 'two tier' manner servicing both smaller domestic nodes and larger international hubs, and thus carefully monitor the extent to which their smaller domestic networks are able to feed their larger international networks. Other carriers, such as Virgin Atlantic, Singapore Airlines and Emirates, selectively fly between major hub airports and are not generally concerned with feeder traffic as these are handled by other airlines.

As tourism in general relies heavily on accessibility, other industries within the tourism sector can benefit from the knowledge gained from understanding connectivity and accessibility across multiple networks pertaining to specific modes and types of transport (see Hodge, 1997). For example, theme parks may decide to locate either immediately within or just outside of a particular vertex or destination. Such a decision may be made possible by examining the potential flows across a network of, for example, inter-regional motorways.

CONSTRUCTING CONNECTIVITY AND ACCESSIBILITY MATRICES

One of the more common means by which connectivity within a network is measured is graph theory. As Taaffe *et al.* (1996: 250; italics in original) note:

> Graph theory, a branch of topology, deals with abstract configurations of points and lines, or nodes and linkages. It does have considerable potential real-world usefulness, however, since it can provide empirical measures of the structural properties of any system once that system is translated as a set of nodes connected by a set of linkages. In graph theory terminology, *nodes* or points are usually referred to as *vertices*, and *linkages* or line segments are usually referred to as *edges*.

An example of a simple connectivity network is presented in Figure 3.2. In this particular network, five vertices (or nodes) (A, B, C, D and E) and six edges can be identified. The first step in examining this particular network is to determine its *overall* connectivity. This is important because it gives an indication (and numeric value) of the robustness of existing networks. A gamma index is calculated as one way of measuring overall connectivity (Scott *et al.*, 2006):

$$\gamma = \frac{e}{e_{max}}$$

where

e represents the total number of existing links in a network
e_{max} is the maximum (or potential) number of links in a network
e_{max} is calculated thus:

$$e_{max} = 3(v-2)$$

where

v represents the total number of vertices or nodes in a network.

In this hypothetical simple network from Figure 3.2, the value is as follows:

$$\gamma = \frac{6}{9} \text{ and thus } \gamma = 0.67$$

A gamma index will range from 0 to 1. Progressively higher gamma indices indicate more connected networks. The purpose of the index is to arrive at an aggregate measure, but one that is reasonably indicative of the overall connectivity of a network. Another measure of connectivity is the beta index, which is calculated by dividing the number of edges (e) by the number of vertices (v):

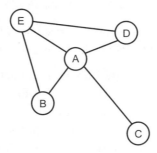

Figure 3.2 A simple connectivity network

$$\beta = \frac{e}{v}$$

In this hypothetical simple network from Figure 3.2, the value is as follows:

$$\beta = \frac{6}{5} \text{ and thus } \beta = 1.2$$

A higher beta index value means a network that is, overall, more connected. According to Chapman (1979: 206), it 'expresses the number of edges present in relation to the number of vertices to be connected and therefore may be regarded as indicating the average number of links leading into or out of each node'. If one were to remove one vertex and three edges, for example, the overall connectivity of the network would be reduced:

$$\gamma = \frac{3}{4} \text{ and thus } \gamma = 0.75$$

Once the overall connectivity value is known, it is possible to utilise other spatial analytical tools to help consider its connectivity and accessibility in relation to both the vertices and edges. For example, in considering the specific vertices within the sample network from Figure 3.2, it might be concluded that, upon visual inspection, vertex A seems to be the most connected as it has edges that connect it to vertices B, C, D and E. Vertex C, however, is only connected to vertex A, and is thus is not nearly as well connected as vertex A. To get a more precise measure of which vertex is the most *directly* connected within a particular network, the degree of connectivity can be plotted as a matrix (Figure 3.3[a]).

In Figure 3.3(a) matrix, any direct connection (that is, a connection where it is not necessary to pass through another vertex on an edge) receives a '1' in the corresponding cell. If no direct connection exists, a '0' is recorded. Thus, while there is a direct connection between A and B through a single edge, there is no direct connection between C and E using one single edge only, but it is certainly possible to reach E from C by going through A. This is referred to as a single step, and will be discussed below in the context of examining multiple steps. Initially, however, the idea is to establish the nature of the *direct* connections within the network. To arrive at a final numeric value that will help determine which vertex is the most connected, the rows for each vertex are summed. As a result, vertex A (with a score of 4) is the most *directly* connected as it has the highest number of direct connections (Figure 3.3[a]). The dispersion index is a relative measure of the overall connectivity of a network. It utilises the number of steps from each vertex to another vertex in the network. Thus lower dispersion indices reflect lower overall connectivity (Figure 3.3[b]).

As a result, the coach company may decide to set up its operations base at vertex A. In order to further help the company with this decision, and even to help schedule fleet

(a) Connectivity matrix

	A	B	C	D	E	
A	0	1	1	1	1	4
B	1	0	0	0	1	2
C	1	0	0	0	0	1
D	1	0	0	0	1	2
E	1	1	0	1	0	3

(b) Shortest path matrix

	A	B	C	D	E	
A	—	1	1	1	1	4
B	1	—	2	2	1	6
C	1	2	—	2	2	7
D	1	2	2	—	1	6
E	1	1	2	1	—	5

Dispersion index = 28
Mean dispersion index = 5.6

Figure 3.3 Connectivity and shortest path matrices

assignments, a further measure of accessibility can be measured. Figure 3.4 depicts the existing network with actual distances between the vertices indicated.

From this, it is possible to calculate an accessibility matrix that takes into consideration the *distances* (as opposed to the direct connectivity by presence/absence of a connection) throughout the company's network. To calculate, the required distances between vertices across the network are plotted in a matrix (Figure 3.5). Then, totals are summed and divided by the total number of vertices in the network. The result is that vertex A is spatially (by distance) central within the network, further supporting the decision by the coach company to locate its base of operations there (Figure 3.5).

From a simple spatial perspective, these measures may be useful, but there are issues with this kind of analysis that need to be considered before business decisions are considered:

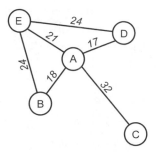

Figure 3.4 Connectivity network showing distance between vertices

	A	B	C	D	E	
A	0	18	32	17	21	17.6
B	18	0	50	35	24	25.4
C	32	50	0	49	53	36.8
D	17	35	49	0	24	25
E	21	24	53	24	0	24.4
	17.6	25.4	36.8	25	24.4	129.2

Figure 3.5 Measuring accessibility

1. In the case of land-based transport, topography is not considered when utilising connectivity and accessibility matrices. For example, in some small Caribbean islands, it can often take up to two hours to travel between two points that are, seemingly, geographically proximate to one another and thus appear to be relatively accessible. The reasons for this are the condition of the roads and the variable topography. Ultimately, these considerations can become diluted if they exist throughout the entire network, but the larger the spatial scale under consideration the more likely that these variables will have some degree of impact.

2. In measuring the connectivity of an overall network or the accessibility associated, individual vertices may be conceptually meaningful, but the *propensity* to utilise the network is not entirely clear. For example, two or three vertices may in fact be well connected from a transport perspective, but the demand to visit and thus utilise the network may not be present. Barriers to accessibility should be measured, as argued by Geurs and van Wee (2004), at the level of individual constraints in relation to time and distance. Somewhat related, and as discussed in Chapter 2, while transport links may indeed be present, the tourism product (or products) must be substantial enough to warrant travel and convert latent demand to actual demand. As a result, van Wee *et al*'s (2001) research into the nature of competition across networks (in relation to employment markets and competition for jobs) can be applied here because different destinations will have different marketing programmes, stakeholder planning networks (Hall, 2005) and levels of development that may influence choice.

MODELLING ACCESSIBLITY AND DEMAND

In Chapter 2, issues relating to supply and demand in relation to transport were highlighted. There, the strength of transport provision in relation to tourism was expressed primarily in economic terms, and it was noted that shifts in either supply or demand can be modelled and thus help inform propensity for travel. Building on this, other factors can be considered. Janelle (1969), for example, examined the function of transport innovation with respect to time–space affordability in his concept of location utility. Location utility

> is a measure of the utility of specific places or areas, which in this case is defined by the aggregate time-expenditure (cost or effort) in transport required for that place or area to satisfy its needs. Operational need refers to those natural and human resource requirements which permit the place or area to fulfil its functional roles in the larger spatial systems of places and areas.
>
> (Janelle, 1969: 349)

Put simply, a place experiences an increase in locational utility when transport innovations are captured positively in an individual's time-budget. Thus, the place has more value. Janelle's work was not tourism-specific, but it does introduce a central concept to this discussion: that of the perception of value as determined by cost, effort and time in relation to transport. Thus, innovation in transport allows for greater accessibility: 'As man speeds up his means of movement, it becomes possible for him to travel further in a given time, to increase his access to a larger area and, possibly, to more and better resources' (Janelle, 1969: 352).

Rather than focus on the propensity for travel, as Chapter 2 outlined, an alternative approach can be offered: spatial interaction modelling. The premise of this type of modelling is that space and the relationships between places can inform the *potential* for mobility. In other words, outside of the supply/demand arguments considered in the previous chapter, it is argued that a spatial consideration can be employed to help map potential flows and, indeed, may influence demand. Once a spatial system is understood, it is possible to arrive at a more coherent view of the relationship of places to each other and what bearing that may have on transport provision (see, for example, Werner, 1985).

There are several models of traffic growth that emerge from the spatial transport literature that are worthy of attention. The Growth Factor Model, for example, established by Martin *et al.* (1961) suggests that the growth of transport/traffic or movement between two locations will be roughly equivalent to growth across an entire area. This may be ideal in theory, but it does not consider future growth where transport does not already exist (Werner, 1985). Somewhat related, intervening opportunity models attempt to capture multiple choice assessment made on the basis of existing opportunities. Thus, they rely on the notion of Central Place Theory (see Christaller, 1972) where locations of services (i.e. tourism attractions or destinations) are established based on the nearest opportunity.

GRAVITY MODELS

Gravity models are commonly used in measuring the extent of spatial interaction (Taaffe *et al.*, 1996). A gravity model is spatial approximation that, in reality, can be directly correlated to demand, but in a more substantial and meaningful manner because it incorporates two key elements that support demand: population and distance (Taaffe *et al.*, 1996; see also Lowe & Moryadas, 1975s). The gravity model can be traced back to Carey (1858: 42), who stated: 'Man tends, of necessity, to gravitate towards his fellow man. Of all animals he is the most gregarious, and the greater in number collected in a given space the greater is the attractive force there exerted.' A gravity model is used to capture two characteristics (Haynes & Fotheringham, 1984: 11):

1) scale impacts: for example, cities with larger populations tend to generate and attract more activities than cities with small populations; and

2) distance impacts: for example, the farther places, people, or activities are apart, the less they interact.

Further, Chapman (1979: 196) notes that the gravity model allows for investigations of 'notions of complementarity, transferability, and intervening opportunity' with reference to spatial interaction.

A simplified equation of the model is as follows (Chapman, 1979: 196):

$$I_{ij} = \frac{P_i P_j}{d_{ij}^e}$$

where

I_{ij} is the interaction between place i and place j
P_i and P_j represents the population of places i and j
d_{ij} is the distance between i and j
e is a distance-decay function.

Expressed verbally, Chapman (1979: 196) suggests that the model 'implies that the amount of interaction between any two places will be directly proportional to the products of their populations and inversely proportional to some power of the distance between them'. In this sense, distance-decay can be interpreted as the relative power of a place

71

being inversely proportional to its distance from an origin. As tourism occurs between origin and (often multiple) destinations, the relationship in terms of distance between these points out to be of concern, especially if the model is suggesting the distance plays a critical role in determining the power of a destination (or destinations) to attract people from an origin rests with distance.

A few points of interest with respect to this model warrant elaboration. The first is that the distance between *i* and *j* as represented in the model is a strictly *geographic* distance. As discussed below, this can be a significant limitation to the gravity model if applied to tourism and transport relationships.

The second point is the distance-decay effect. Oppermann (1995) recognised the effect of distance in pleasure travel, and geographers with an interest in transport often focus on the effect of distance on the movement and mobility of goods. In other words, the volume of movement declines the further one moves away from their point of origin (Chapman, 1979). Expressed as an equation, the rate of decay of movement (*e*) further from an origin may be calculated using:

$$Q_{ij} = \frac{1}{d_{ij}^e}$$

where

Q_{ij} represents the quantity of movement between *i* and *j*
d_{ij} represents the distance between *i* and *j*.

From this equation, it can be seen that the smaller the value of *e*, the less distance-decay is experienced. As an integral part of the gravity model, it helps to model movement in the context of space and, more accurately, with causation related to distance. Problematic with the gravity model, however, is the extent to which it can be accurately applied to tourist movements between two places/nodes/destinations, or even touristic movements across multiple places (or destinations).

Figure 3.6 outlines an evolutionary model using the size and distance relationship and the potential flows of movement between four hypothetical urban areas using a gravity model function (with the thicker lines denoting larger flows and, thus, the strength of the relationship between two vertices). In this example, (re-drawn from Chapman, 1979: Figure 8.10), travel between A and C (Figure 3.6[b]) is substantial not only because of the relative sizes of their populations (which suggests that the greater the population, the higher the incidence for travel) but also because the distance between them is advantageous and supportive of substantial interactions. This explains the relatively smaller amount of interaction afforded between City A and City B. However, this stochastic model makes several assumptions that may not always be applicable in the context of transport and tourism:

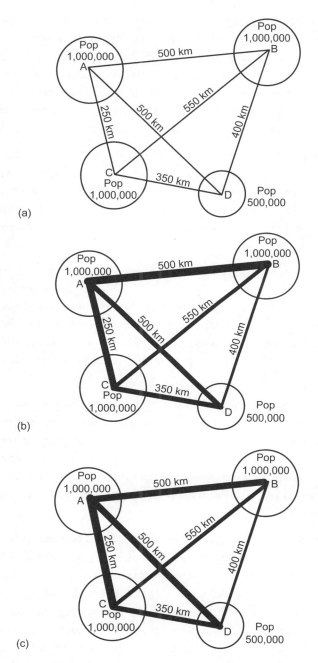

Figure 3.6 Size and distance relationships (a) and predicted movement flows (b) using gravity model

Source: Adapted from Chapman (1979)

1. It assumes that transport initiatives would not eventually be developed, thus enhancing travel between A and B, potentially to the detriment of A and C (assuming a finite amount of demand at City A) (Figure 3.6[c]). For example, B may be twice a far from A as C, but new transport infrastructure can effectively negate the affect of distance. Twinned motorways, for example, might reduce the travel time considerably. New airline upstarts may offer services that, in reality, significantly cut the time of travel between A and B to the point where it is quicker to get to B than C from A (see Figure 3.6[c]).

2. Somewhat related, the gravity model somewhat overstates the effect of distance (Taafe *et al.*, 1996) by assuming that the travel distance is roughly equal in perception between A and B and A and C. In other words, the perception might be that B is more than twice as far from A as C when in fact it is not if the effect of travel time is taken into account. Haynes and Fotheringham (1984: 12) suggest that this is one of the key modifications that are necessary to the basic gravity model:

> For example, the cost per mile of traveling may decrease with distance, as in air travel. Obviously the operational effect of distance would therefore not be directly proportional to airline miles and the negative aspect of distance would need to be reduced or dampened so that the model properly reflects its effects. On the other hand the effect of distance may be underestimated by mileage because the opportunity to know people in cities far away may be reduced by language, culture, and information.

What this means is that the *effects* of distance may not always be proportionate to distances travelled, especially with the introduction of transport services that may minimise such distances (as discussed in Chapter 1). As well, the perception of travel distance may be prone to the frequency of travel: 'frequent travelers to a certain destination are expected to perceive a destination as more accessible than those who do not have the chances to visit the destination often, even if the actual distance they have to travel is the same' (Hwang *et al.*, 2002: 53).

3. The gravity model also assumes that the type of travel between A and B and A and C is similar enough to warrant comparison. When measuring commodity flows, this may be entirely appropriate as similar forms of cargo transport tend to be used (e.g. truck, rail), but the nature of tourism and development is such that product development in two locations is rarely the same. As a result, markets can be substantially different, even if they are from a similar origin, thus the propensity for travel is considerably more complex than just being associated with distance. Heggie (1969) noted this deficiency in the gravity model concept by arguing that there is no limitation in supply, and no formulaic function to account for differentiation in supply. Further, the assumption made by the model is that demand is directly dependent on distance, thus ignoring economic realities, in this case, in either A, B or C (Heggie, 1969; see also Gutiérrez, 2001) and access to individual means of transport (Lanzendorf, 2000).

Given these limitations, a revised gravity model that would take into account issues of the amount of time necessary to travel from place to place can be formulated as follows:

$$I_{ij} = \frac{P_i P_j}{t_{ij}^e}$$

where

I_{ij} is the interaction between place i and place j
P_i and P_j represents the population of places i and j
t_{ij} is the normal travel time between i and j
e is a distance-decay function.

In this equation, the function of the distance-decay variable is related directly to the amount of time taken to travel between two places. In other words, decay becomes purely a function of time as opposed to distance. While this avoids some of the frictional effects traditionally measured in gravity models where distance is sometimes found to not be a strong factor in determining flows (Lösch, 1954; see also Huff & Jenks, 1968), it does not entirely dismiss the fact that distance plays some role. This relationship can be more accurately modelled, however, by taking accessibility measures into consideration. The result is as follows:

$$I_{ij} = \frac{a_{ij}}{t_{ij}^e}$$

where

a_{ij} is the degree of accessibility between i and j
t_{ij}^e is the distance-decay function in relation to the length of time it takes to travel from i to j

As such, it is possible to use the same four cities used in Figure 3.6 to demonstrate how new innovations in transport effectively reduce the distance-decay of time. Figure 3.7 represents another evolutionary depiction of movement. Figure 3.7(a) shows the existing travel times using ground transport (and for the sake of argument, personal automobiles are used for modelling purposes in this instance). In Figure 3.7(b) travel from B to C is longer, assuming the presence of natural barriers (e.g. mountains). Similarly, travel between A and C is generally quick because the mode of transport used facilitates rapid transit times. If, however, changes were made to the infrastructure (for example, twinning the motorway) such that travel from A to B was effectively halved, one could expect, all other things being equal, more flows between the two cities as a result (Figure 3.7[c]), and potentially to the detriment of flows between A and C. Similarly, if the travel time between

75

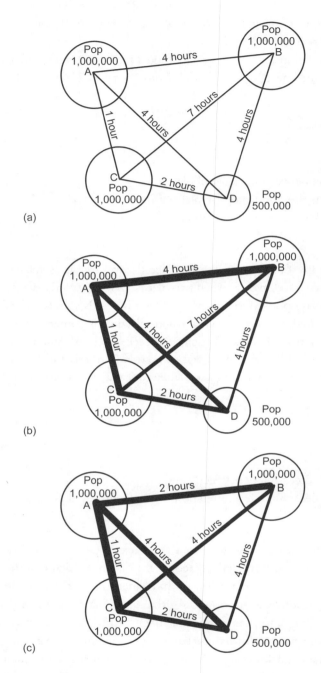

(a)

(b)

(c)

Figure 3.7 Gravity model application with length of time dependency

C and B were to be reduced through similar infrastructural development (or perhaps through the introduction of air transport), then one might expect to measure increased movement between them (Figure 3.7[c]).

The practicalities of examining accessibility and distance-decay with reference to tourism have been examined by McKercher and Lew (2003), who discuss the relationship between distance-decay and what they call ETEZ. These zones are areas where factors such as spatial incongruities, geomorphology and even political realities combine to limit and promote flows along certain routes and in certain directions: 'Collectively, these factors produce ETEZs, areas where little or no tourism activity occurs that is relevant to the source market while demand is concentrated at certain peak locations. In this way, ETEZs exert a distorting effect on the standard distance-decay curve' (McKercher & Lew, 2003: 161). The result of this is a revised distance-decay curve (Figure 3.8), where the standard decay exhibited as a result of diminishing distance is replaced by a secondary peak:

> Demand still peaks relatively close to the origin and declines rapidly with distance. However, the distance decay curve is shaped by expanses of ETEZs, secondary peaks

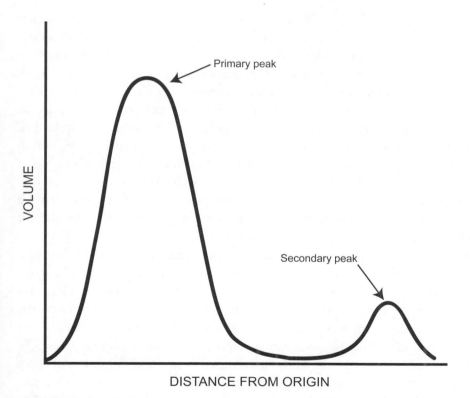

Figure 3.8 Primary and secondary peaks in tourism-related distance-decay curve

Source: Adapted and re-drawn from McKercher and Lew (2003)

are likely to occur at great distances from the origin, where a compelling pull of exceptional attractions overcomes the friction of travel. (McKercher & Lew, 2003: 161)

McKercher and Lew (2003) argue that there are several important factors that affect the flow of international tourism. Certainly the availability of transport modes to and from international destinations will affect flows, and will therefore affect the distance-decay curve indicated. For example, despite the fact that seasoned travellers may think nothing of embarking upon a 24-hour journey between New Zealand and the United Kingdom, some travellers may elect to travel to destinations that are closer to their point of origin. Thus, certain types of travellers may elect to ignore distance-decay effects. An important point made by McKercher and Lew (2004) is that the primary peak may, in fact, be extended in distance. Put another way, the initial peak may in fact be represented across a wider distance (as a plateau) and thus not be represented a narrow point as depicted in Figure 3.8. This may occur in situations where the draw of destinations or attractions along a route may be strong enough to warrant demand irrespective of distance. At some point, however, that demand would drop off as distance becomes a factor in the decision-making process.

Of course, and as mentioned briefly above, factors of distance and time are only part of a wider equation of demand for particular products/services/experiences in tourism. Another factor to be considered is the type of tourist. For example, using Cohen's (1974) typology of travellers, the explorer may be expected to visit destinations that are decidedly outside of more common transport routes or networks. Similarly, families may elect to travel to destinations that are closer, thus favouring more time at the destination as opposed to being in transit. Clearly, then, the distance-decay effect in relation to time spent travelling is an important consideration, but it is also one that may depend on numerous other variables. Also important is the degree of marketing that is undertaken by destinations around the world. As McKercher and Lew (2003) emphasise, no two destinations are alike and marketing efforts, combined with transport options that are available that support such efforts, can effectively serve to increase latent demand for their products and services (see, for example, Box 2.2).

The incorporation of distance-decay effects, in combination with accessibility and connectivity considerations, is, on the one hand, useful in order to obtain a snapshot of the position of destinations with networks of varying scales (international, national, local, for example), but, on the other hand, the dynamic nature of tourism and the complexity involved in developing tourism destinations can also suggest that modelling travel flows is difficult. It is possible, however, to construct a model that takes accessibility into consideration when attempting to profile the relationship between place, time and space (Figure 3.9). The model suggests that the number of trips may not always correlate precisely with high degrees of accessibility because such trips may be taken out of necessity or obligation. When thinking about the nature of mobility and its relation to transport, it

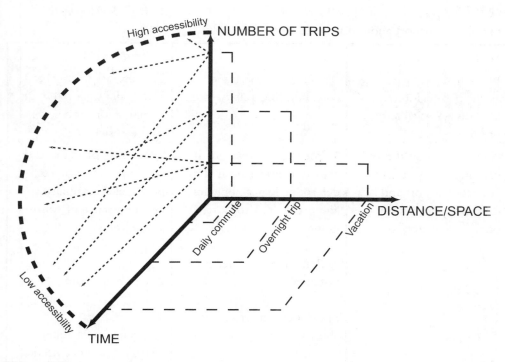

High accessibility NUMBER OF TRIPS

Low accessibility

Daily commute Overnight trip Vacation DISTANCE/SPACE

TIME

Figure 3.9 Time–space optimisation model in the context of accessibility

is not only the type of trip that needs to be considered, but also the frequency and duration of the mode of transport. As such, whilst numerically small, vacations and holidays
may incorporate both accessible (qualitatively evaluated or otherwise) and inaccessible.
Much of this accessibility depends on the availability of transport networks and thus their
ability to satisfy latent demand for a particular route. Similarly, daily commutes may be frequent, but the path followed from home to work may be inaccessible due to limitations in
the transport network (i.e. infrastructural limitations or temporary blockages). The fundamental concept underlying the model in Figure 3.9 is that accessibility is conditional and
continuous. While it can be measured in terms of actual modelling as discussed above, it
is also important to consider that perceived accessibility also plays a critical role. Thus,
whilst some individuals may consider a two-hour commute in a larger urban megacity to
be perfectly acceptable, others may feel otherwise.

Table 3.1 Application of spatial techniques to hypothetical business development options in transport and tourism

Scenario	Procedures	Output
Introduction of new airline to a region, ostensibly servicing three or more nodes	Model accessibility and demand using gravity model	Measure of potential accessibility; central node of operations can potential be designated
New public transit route carrying passengers to and from airport and key drop-off points throughout an urban area	1) Potential accessibility if choice of nodes needed to determine logical, practical and profitable drop-off points	1) Measure of demand in relation to location (i.e. potential accessibility given presence of tourists any/all sites)
	2) Beta index to determine potential routes	2) Optimal routing
	3) Connectivity matrix to show route plans	3) Optimal scheduling based on distance needed, but other factors (i.e. traffic) need to be considered

Table 3.1 outlines two scenarios of when the tools outlined in this chapter might be put to use. These situations reflect generic representations of real-world business opportunities, and while it is important to keep in mind that business decisions largely incorporate many other elements beyond that which is presented, it is argued that these issues should be considered initially before other considerations are given attention.

CHAPTER SUMMARY

This chapter has attempted to provide something of a spatial toolkit for the analysis of transport demand in relation to locations and places. It has shown how issues of connectivity and accessibility need to be carefully considered in establishing both the initial and long-term viability of transport operations. While spatial approaches in geography and transport studies have traditionally examined such issues in greater detail than what has been provided here, the intention is to gain a better understanding of the relationship between places and the potential interactions between them.

While this may seem somewhat out of place in a book on transport and tourism, understanding networks is important for several reasons:

1. Networks are inherently bounded by particular nodes and routes, and tracking movement through space and time allows for a clear understanding of how well positioned (or otherwise) a particular node is within a wider network (Figure 3.1). In the context of tourism and transport, this means that some destinations can spatially analyse the degree of connectivity and accessibility before examining market-based forces such as competition and regulation of routes and networks.

2. Furthermore, plotting accessibility and connectivity networks allows for a simplified view of accessibility and connectivity; in other words, the degree of accessibility and connectivity can ultimately play a key role in the success of a particular destination, especially when considerations of elasticity are involved.

3. Measuring connectivity along a network on a variety of levels can be a first step in determining a variety of business and operational decisions in transport, primarily those relating to barriers to entry and pricing/demand.

4. Above all else, the mobility of travellers (with tourists included in that characterisation) ultimately dictates the use of and demand for transport, and thus plays a significant role in destination development.

BOX 3.2 Case study – Practical examples of connectivity and accessibility concepts

The purpose of this case study is to demonstrate how spatial methods alone may not necessarily be adequate in understanding the relationship between tourism and transport. Several examples are shown. The first examines drive tourism in South Africa, while the second compares the route networks of jetstar Asia (based in Singapore) and Nok Air (based in Bangkok).

Drive tourism in South Africa
Although the concept of drive tourism has been addressed in the literature (e.g. Hardy, 2003; Laws & Scott, 2003; Olsen, 2003; Prideaux & Carson, 2003), what has yet to be fully assessed is the extent to which tourists make decisions regarding destinations during a self-drive holiday using spatial information. More importantly, the question remains as to how the tools discussed in this chapter might be used by those tourism operations with an interest in self-drive holidays (e.g. rental companies, attractions, accommodations, to name a few). In other words, how might strategic decisions regarding marketing and development make use of such information, and what problems are introduced in doing so?

Independent tourists represent a significant proportion of South Africa's travel market. Once in the country, many tourists opt to embark upon self-drive excursions. The impact of the internet in the distribution of tourist experiences in South Africa has been documented (Wynne *et al.*, 2001). www.drivesouthsfrica. co.za was established as a portal for visitors to rent a variety of personal vehicles (including campers and cars, as well as 4×4s), design tours, book accommodation and learn about festivals and events. South Africa is a sizeable country, so the extent to which it is connected comes into question. Table 3.2 outlines various distances of several key destinations in South Africa.

The modern roadway system assures almost full connectivity to most major centres, so generating a simple connectivity matrix may not be the most useful starting point. Instead, a full connectivity matrix with associated driving distances may provide some insight into the extent to which certain centres or places are more proximal to other areas. What is immediately apparent is that Kimberley, located close to the border of Northern Cape and Free State, is located the shortest distance within the network of locations and places in Table 3.2. This might imply that Kimberley should be the base of operations for any tourism business that features at its core the rental of vehicles for tourists on self-drive holidays. The problem with this conclusion is that, as indicated earlier in the chapter, this type of analysis ignores topography and actual travel time. Thus, while Kimberley may be spatially proximal to most other destinations, the actual travel time from Kimberley to other locations may be hindered by external variables such as poor roading (including surface type and speed limits), varying topography that can influence overall time irrespective of spatial distance. Thus, while connectivity matrices can be useful in establishing a theoretical spatial structure, they must be treated as the starting point only in terms of understanding how and why a network is constructed and how this information can be used in business decisions.

Comparing two route networks – jetstar Asia versus Nok Air

Based on the route network featured on jetstar's website (www.jetstar.com), a full connectivity matrix can be calculated (Table 3.3). This matrix is based on the ability of the passenger to book a complete ticket to the destinations listed. In many situations, where connectivity is not implied (e.g. an '0' is indicated) it is entirely possible for the passenger to travel between the two places but not on one single ticket.

Table 3.2 Distances (kms) between selected South Africa locations

	George	Bloemfontein	Cape Town	Durban	East London	Grahamstown	Johannesburg	Kimberley	Ladysmith	Mafikeng	Port Elizabeth	Umtata	Welkom	Messina	
George	0	773	438	1319	645	465	1171	762	1183	1203	335	880	926	1701	842.9
Bloemfontein	773	0	1004	634	584	601	398	177	410	464	677	570	153	928	526.6
Cape Town	438	1004	0	1753	1079	899	1402	962	1431	1343	769	1314	1156	1932	1105.9
Durban	1319	634	1753	0	674	854	578	811	236	821	984	439	564	1118	770.4
East London	645	584	1079	674	0	180	982	780	752	1048	310	235	737	1512	679.9
Grahamstown	465	601	899	854	180	0	999	667	932	1065	130	415	754	1529	677.9
Johannesburg	1171	398	1402	578	982	999	0	472	356	287	1075	869	258	530	669.8
Kimberley	762	177	962	811	780	667	472	0	587	380	743	747	294	1002	598.9
Ladysmith	1183	410	1431	236	752	932	356	587	0	597	1062	517	340	894	664.1
Mafikeng	1203	464	1343	821	1048	1065	287	380	597	0	1548	1003	451	808	787.0
Port Elizabeth	335	677	769	984	310	130	1075	743	1062	1548	0	545	830	1605	758.1
Umtata	880	570	1314	439	235	415	869	747	517	1003	545	0	718	1403	689.6
Welkom	926	153	1156	564	737	754	258	294	340	451	830	718	0	788	569.2
Messina	1701	928	1932	1118	1512	1529	530	1002	894	808	1605	1403	788	0	1125.0
	842.9	526.6	1105.9	770.4	679.9	677.9	669.8	598.9	664.1	787.0	758.1	689.6	569.2	1125.0	10465.3

Source: From www.places.co.za

Table 3.3 jetstar Asia connectivity matrix

	Singapore	Bangkok	Bangalore	Jakarta	Denpasar	Hong Kong	Phuket	Manila	Phnom Penh	Siem Reap	Yangon	Surabaya	Taipei	
Singapore	0	1	1	1	1	1	1	1	1	1	1	1	1	12
Bangkok	1	0	2	2	0	0	0	0	0	0	0	0	0	5
Bangalore	1	2	0	0	0	0	0	0	0	0	0	0	0	3
Jakarta	1	2	0	0	0	0	0	0	0	0	0	0	0	3
Denpasar	1	0	0	0	0	0	0	0	0	0	0	0	0	1
Hong Kong	1	0	2	0	0	0	0	0	0	0	0	0	0	3
Phuket	1	0	0	0	0	0	0	2	0	0	0	0	0	3
Manila	1	0	0	2	0	0	2	0	0	0	0	0	0	5
Phnom Penh	1	0	0	0	0	0	0	0	0	0	0	0	0	1
Siem Reap	1	0	0	0	0	0	0	0	0	0	0	0	2	3
Yangon	1	0	0	0	0	0	0	0	0	0	0	0	0	1
Surabaya	1	0	0	0	0	0	0	0	0	0	0	0	0	1
Taipei	1	0	0	0	0	0	2	0	0	2	0	0	0	5
	12	5	5	5	1	1	5	3	1	3	1	1	3	
												Dispersion		46
												Mean Dispersion		3.5

As shown, the jetstar Asia network is not particularly dense from a spatial perspective, but the power of the hub (see Chapter 6) in Singapore can be seen. As well, the airline uses Singapore as a stopover for several key routes, including Jakarta, Bangalore, Phuket and Taipei. The introduction of these routes is purely strategic, focusing on satisfying demand for travel to these destinations from origins such as Hong Kong, Manila and Phuket.

Compare this network with that of Nok Air (Table 3.4), operating out of Bangkok. Again, this matrix reflects the ability of a passenger to book a ticket from a place of origin to the destination indicated. Like the jetstar Asia example above, travel between two places is possible where connectivity is implied to be non-existent, but this would require two separate tickets.

Table 3.4 Nok Air connectivity matrix

	Bangkok	Udon Thani	Loei	Chiang Mai	Mae Hong Son	Phuket	Trang	Nakhon Si Thammarat	Hat Yai	
Bangkok	0	1	1	1	0	1	1	1	1	7
Udon Thani	1	0	1	1	0	0	0	0	0	3
Loei	1	1	0	0	0	0	0	0	0	2
Chiang Mai	1	1	0	0	1	0	0	0	0	3
Mae Hong Son	0	0	0	1	0	0	0	0	0	1
Phuket	1	0	0	0	0	0	0	0	0	1
Trang	1	0	0	0	0	0	0	0	0	1
Nakhon Si Thammarat	1	0	0	0	0	0	0	0	0	1
Hat Yai	1	0	0	0	0	0	0	0	0	1
	7	3	2	3	1	1	1	1	1	
								Dispersion		20
								Mean Dispersion		2.2

What is evident from the Nok Air connectivity matrix is that, first, the network itself is comprised of fewer vertices or nodes (9 versus 13 for jetstar Asia). The second feature of the matrix is that two distinct sub-networks are apparent. The first involves destinations that are north of Bangkok, including Mae Hong Son, Chiang Mai, Loei and Udon Thani. Among these destinations, including Bangkok, a considerably more connected network has been established when compared to the second sub-network, consisting of the remaining four destinations (Phuket, Trang, Nakhon Si Thammarat and Hat Yai). The second sub-group, all of which are located south of Bangkok, are considerably less connected among themselves and thus contribute to the lower dispersion and mean dispersion indicators for the entire network. To illustrate this, a graphical representation of the network appears in Figure 3.10.

The corresponding connectivity matrix, taking into account the distance depicted in Figure 3.10, is presented in Table 3.5.

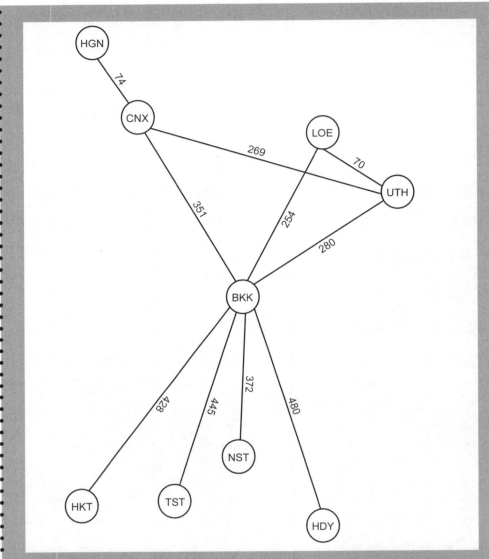

Figure 3.10 Nok Air network

Table 3.5 Nok Air connectivity matrix with distances

	Bangkok	Udon Thani	Loei	Chiang Mai	Mae Hong Son	Phuket	Trang	Nakhon Si Thammarat	Hat Yai	
Bangkok	0	280	254	351	0	428	445	381	480	290.0
Udon Thani	280	0	70	269	0	0	0	0	0	68.8
Loei	254	70	0	0	0	0	0	0	0	36.0
Chiang Mai	351	269	0	0	74	0	0	0	0	77.1
Mae Hong Son	0	0	0	74	0	0	0	0	0	8.2
Phuket	428	0	0	0	0	0	0	0	0	47.6
Trang	445	0	0	0	0	0	0	0	0	49.4
Nakhon Si Thammarat	372	0	0	0	0	0	0	0	0	42.3
Hat Yai	480	0	0	0	0	0	0	0	0	53.3
	290.0	68.8	36.0	77.1	8.2	47.6	49.4	42.3	53.3	672.7

Once again, this connectivity matrix has been constructed on the basis on how Nok Air actually offers sales of flights. If, however, the airline allowed for one ticket to cover, for example, Mae Hong Son through to Phuket or from Hat Yai through to Trang (via Bangkok), a very different matrix could be constructed (Table 3.6)

The result is that Bangkok continues to feature as the central hub, but there is room for the airline to consider future enhancements to allow the network to be more complete. For one, travel between Phuket, Trang, Nakhon Si Thammarat and Hat Yai requires a stop in Bangkok. Granted, an airline might be inclined to suggest that expanding the network to include flights between these four destinations would be beneficial to the traveller given that the stop in Bangkok would no longer be necessary, but the larger question is whether such routes would be profitable. In this particular case, Nok Air has decided that the opportunity cost of operating flights between these four destinations outweighs the gains from simply focusing on traffic from Bangkok down to each. It must also be remembered that Bangkok features as a major international gateway, and Nok Air has positioned itself as an LCC for travel to these southern tourism destinations.

Table 3.6 Nok Air connectivity network with distances (complete coverage)

	Bangkok	Udon Thani	Loei	Chiang Mai	Mae Hong Son	Phuket	Trang	Nakhon Si Thammarat	Hat Yai	
Bangkok	0	280	254	351	425	428	445	381	480	**337.2**
Udon Thani	280	0	70	269	343	708	728	652	760	**423.3**
Loei	254	70	0	339	413	682	699	626	734	**424.1**
Chiang Mai	351	269	339	0	74	779	796	723	831	**462.4**
Mae Hong Son	425	343	413	74	0	833	870	797	905	**517.8**
Phuket	428	708	682	779	833	0	873	800	908	**667.9**
Trang	445	728	699	796	870	873	0	817	925	**683.7**
Nakhon Si Thammarat	372	652	626	723	797	800	817	0	852	**627.6**
Hat Yai	480	760	734	831	905	908	925	852	0	**710.6**
	337.2	**423.3**	**424.1**	**462.4**	**517.8**	**667.9**	**683.7**	**627.6**	**710.6**	**4854.6**

Questions for consideration

1. Why might Nok Air have considerably less connectivity among its southern destinations?

2. How might a new entrant to the aviation market in Asia treat this information on the overall connectivity of jetstar Asia's network? How might this information be useful in deciding which routes to fly?

SELF-REVIEW QUESTIONS

1. Define connectivity and accessibility and explain how both are critical to understanding the relationship between transport and tourism.

2. In your own words, and with one example from your own experience, describe the distance-decay effect.

3. Describe the following equation in your own words and point out its importance for understanding flows between two nodes:

$$I_{ij} = \frac{P_i P_j}{t_{ij}^e}$$

ESSAY QUESTIONS

1. Outline some of the problems of the distance-decay model. When might such a model not be applicable in tourism?

2. Why is it important to even attempt to model demand from a spatial perspective? What can the tourism sector, and more importantly the numerous industries that comprise it, learn from spatial analyses?

3. Outline why mobilities and movement need to consider issues of transport.

KEY SOURCES

Chapman, K. (1979) *People, Pattern and Process: An Introduction to Human Geography*. London: Edward Arnold.

Chapman's text is a classic geography text published at a time when spatial methods in the discipline were popular. It covers network connectivity and accessibility, spatial distribution of activities, and movement and mobility.

Haynes, K.E. and Fotheringham, A.S. (1984) *Gravity and Spatial Interaction Models*. Beverly Hills, CA: Sage.

Following on from the Chapman text, this text examines further gravity models and interactions across geographic concepts of space.

Taaffe, E.J., Gauthier, H.L. and O'Kelly, M.E. (1996) *Geography of Transportation* (2nd edn). Upper Saddle River, NJ: Prentice Hall.

Taaffe *et al.*'s text is one of the key texts in the geography of transport. This text is particularly useful for understanding distribution of spatial elements and concepts, network form and structure as well as applied examples at regional and local levels.

CHAPTER 4:

GROUND TRANSPORT

LEARNING OBJECTIVES

After reading this chapter, you should be able to

1. Describe and interpret the importance of ground transport within the tourism system.

2. Explain the variances in scale and flows of ground transport.

3. Evaluate the differences and similarities in terms of international scope of various forms of ground transport in relation to tourism.

4. Differentiate, if possible, between recreation-based and tourism-based types of ground transport.

5. Understand recent advances in environmentally friendly forms of ground transport.

INTRODUCTION

In this chapter, several types of ground transport and their links with tourism (and the provision of tourist experiences) are discussed. First, the use of coaches (largely associated with packaged tours) is discussed. Rail travel is briefly profiled and linked to various forms of tourism (e.g. ecotourism, heritage tourism) that utilise this mode of transport to both add to the experience and as an effort towards maintaining some degree of sustainability. Following this, 'personal' types of transport (e.g. self-powered or motorised) in the context of tourism (and recreation) are discussed.

Because ground transport, and particularly personal automobile use, is so pervasive in many developed countries, it is difficult to render a clear assessment of tourism and ground transport relationships. Some of the standard definitions of 'a tourist' in the context of pleasure travel or holidaymaking are inherently limiting when discussing ground transport. Instead, the focus in this chapter will examine the use of ground transport that is inclusive of recreationalists, excursionists, commuters as well as tourists. This is partly to illustrate the blurry distinction between transport and tourism when discussing ground transport, but also to focus on those planning and development measures that, while ostensibly focusing on one particular type of user, may inevitably have an impact on other users.

GROUND TRANSPORT AND TOURISM

The various sizes and spatial scales in which ground transport operations operate play a significant role in the extent to which tourism and some recreational activities are facilitated. As a result, and for the purposes of simplifying this relationship, two broad types of transport under the ground mode that involve tourism can be identified:

1. Personal transport, including not only motor vehicles (which would generally be associated with tourist activities as means of transport) but also off-road, motorised 'quad' (four-wheel) vehicles and pedal-powered bicycles (which would be more properly associated with recreational pursuits and, thus, act as a focus of the experience itself).

2. 'Supplied' transport, including transportation relating to (a) package tours that, for example, make use of coaches or buses and (b) rail travel, including both intra-regional, inter-regional and local transport provision.

As complex as the various types of ground transport are, so too are the means by which they are measured. In urban environments, for example, transport is recognised as a key ingredient for economic development (e.g. Banister, 1995), leading to consideration of the relative cost of congestion, emissions and commuting time on overall productivity. Ground transport development can also be used for the purposes of urban revitalisation (Priemus & Konings, 2001). In the context of tourism, Page and Hall (2003) note that it also plays an important role in hosting visitors: not only is it often the most dominant means by which tourists enter a destination, it also represents a significant proportion of the mode of transport used within a destination. For example, of all the UK tourists travelling to Scotland, over two-thirds arrive by car (Tourism Scotland, 2003). Of course, the spatial proximity of destinations in the context of one's usual residence plays an important role in determining whether ground transport is used. Thus, as the majority of Canada's population lives along the international border with the United States, it is perhaps not surprising to learn that, in 2000, 97% of same-day and 56% of overnight travel by Canadians to the United States was by car (Transport Canada, 2001).

Perhaps unlike other modes of transport (such as air travel and marine transport), ground transport encompasses numerous types. In fact, one could argue that the provision of ground transport types is almost as complex and multi-faceted as the users of these systems. The provision of various types of ground transport is often governed by non-tourism related policies and planning measures. Thus, while the development of certain ground transport types may not be explicitly for the purposes of enhancing tourism, this does not mean that the overall provision of tourist-related activities and use is not possible. This at once raises the difficult question as to what actually can be classified as tourist-related transport provision. In Chapter 2, the blurry distinction between modes of transport and their association with tourism was shown to be problematic. This blurry distinction is perhaps most complicated when discussing various types of ground transport, primarily because it is difficult to separate out tourist use from non-tourist use of ground transport. There are several reasons for this. First, many recreational activities utilise the same mode of transport used for patterned, daily use (i.e. transport to and from work). As a result, the family car may be used as a means of transport for economic reasons (i.e. to and from one's place of employment), but may be used on weekends for family getaways or for afternoon trips to a local attraction such as the beach or a theme park. Trains and buses, for example, can be used not only by commuters, but also by tourists and local recreationalists. In one sense, the multi-purpose usage factor of various types of ground transport best highlights the problem of ascribing one particular type of ground transport almost exclusively to tourist use only. Most types of ground transport, therefore, service multiple functions both within and outside of the leisure/tourism/recreation realm. In many respects, this explains their pervasiveness in developed countries, and increasingly in some developing countries.

It is perhaps best to think of a continuum of association and use. At one end are those types of ground transport used almost exclusively by tourists. A good example is escorted coach tours, which are normally patronised by international tourists, although domestic coach package services can be found in some countries. The other end of the continuum is represented by those types of transport that are used by both tourists and non-tourists (e.g. taxis or other forms of public transportation). A second feature of ground transport that highlights the blurry distinctions involving tourism is the fact that travellers may elect to use, when available, multiple modes of ground transport. In the case of London, business travellers may well utilise a taxi service, the tube, and a city bus all in the same trip. The decisions made with respect to which types of transport are available for use can be based on a number of criteria, not the least of which may include the distance to be travelled, the cost of a particular type of transport (i.e. taxi versus the tube), and the particular time-budget available to the traveller.

A vacationing family to Disneyworld in California may utilise small shuttles around the park itself, or elect to use the park-specific train. For those visiting from nearby states such as Arizona or Oregon, they may elect to drive to the theme park along an interstate highway, while those visiting from further away may initially fly and then utilise ground transport for local mobility. Similarly, a traveller from Europe visiting family in Cairns,

Australia may find that renting a car is more convenient for getting around. The purpose of these examples is to demonstrate that characterising all types of ground transport as either tourist-focused or otherwise can be misleading.

A third and final consideration is the extent to which the motivations of travellers come into play when discussing ground transport. For example, the tourism literature is voluminous with theories of tourist motivation, but many of these are associated with making decisions in terms of which destination to visit. As shown in Chapter 2, the decision-set for modes of transport carries with it numerous elements, but it is the manifestation of that choice that is of interest. For instance, because most modes of ground transport are, in effect, multi-purpose, measuring the extent to which tourists utilise particular types of transport can be problematic. One example is the provision rail transport from Glasgow to Edinburgh in Scotland (Figure 4.1). As the trip is roughly one hour in duration, it is used by residents in both cities to commute, yet it is also used by tourists visiting Scotland as an inexpensive and reasonably convenient way to travel from one city to the other. With respect to managing a service such as this, what becomes critical is a functional assessment of the ridership. Planners tasked with managing types of ground transport need to incorporate tourism-related utilisation into long-range initiatives and operational

Figure 4.1 Multi-use ground transport: The Queen Street Station, Glasgow, is used by both tourists and commuters

decisions (such as seasonality, promotions, etc.). In August 2006 the recently appointed Director of the Glasgow–Edinburgh collaboration project announced that one of the project's goals over the next two years is 24-hour train access between the two cities. The Director noted: 'People coming from the US, from the continent, who are here as tourists, would just assume that, like other metropolitan centres, they would be able to get between the two much later at night. It is essential for tourism alone, as well as other travellers' (Johnston, 2006). By recognising the demand by tourists and other travellers for the nature of ground transport, governments and private companies will be in a better position to assess the incidence of use of specific modes of transport and thus tailor future growth appropriately.

Table 4.1 provides a ten-year overview of the various means of ground transport within the United Kingdom.

Table 4.1 Mode of passenger transport, UK (1992–2003) (in billions of passenger kilometres)

	Buses/ coaches	Cars, vans, taxies	Motorcycles	Pedal cycles	Rail
1992	43	583	5	5	38
1993	44	584	4	4	37
1993	44	607	4	4	37
1994	44	614	4	4	35
1995	43	618	4	4	37
1996	43	625	4	4	39
1997	44	632	4	4	42
1998	45	635	4	4	44
1999	46	641	5	4	46
2000	47	639	5	4	47
2001	47	654	5	4	47
2002	47	677	5	4	48
2003	47	678	6	5	49
2004	48	678	6	4	50
2005	48	678*	6	4	52

Source: Department for Transport (2006)

Note: * Preliminary results.

94

The important point from Table 4.1 is not necessarily the sheer number of passenger kilometres, but the variability and varying levels of growth in the use of ground transport within the United Kingdom. For example, the use of buses and coaches experienced steady growth over the ten-year period from 1992 to 2002, yet the use of pedal cycles for transport remained relatively flat. In the case of cycling, as will be discussed later, efforts are being made to encourage the use of bicycles for not only regular personal transport but also for recreational purposes. Table 4.2 expands on this and shows historic trend data on the average distance travelled for use of specific types of ground transport.

Table 4.2 Average distance travelled by selected modes of travel, UK (in miles per person per year)

	1975/ 1976	1985/ 1986	1991/ 1993	1996/ 1998	2002
Bicycle	51	44	39	38	33
Car only – driver	1849	2271	2993	3319	3356
Car only – passenger	1350	1525	1951	1973	2000
Motorcycle/moped	47	51	38	30	33
Surface rail	289	292	311	290	373

Source: Adapted from Department for Transport (2004b)

When examining Table 4.2 and Table 4.1 together, some interesting trends emerge. First, while the number of passenger trips by bicycle has remained steady during a ten-year period from 1992 to 2002, the average distance travelled has fallen. Similarly, while the number of rail trips has increased, the average distance travelled by rail has fluctuated. In the case of cycle tourism the increasing congestion of vehicular traffic on the UK roadway system may play a role in how far people journey.

In 2000 the UK government announced significant funding increases for transport infrastructure (BBC, 2000). This included:

- Rail – £60 bn:
  - investment to allow 50% more passengers, with faster and safer journeys;
  - £7 bn rail modernisation fund;
  - 6000 new carriages and trains.

- Roads – £59 bn:
  - £30 bn to eliminate backlog in road maintenance;

- 80 major trunk road schemes to improve safety and traffic flow at junctions;
- 100 new bypasses on trunk and local roads and 130 other full-scale local road improvement schemes;
- lower-noise surfaces for 60% of trunk roads;
- a 10% increase in bus passenger journeys and an extension of bus priority schemes;
- widen 360 miles of motorway and trunk road network.

• Local transport schemes – £26 bn:
- build 100 new bypasses;
- £20 bn for London, excluding roads – potentially including a cross-London rail link;
- up to 25 light railway schemes in urban areas;
- more cycle and walking routes and more 20 mph areas.

In November 2005 the Confederation of British Industry argued that £60 billion was needed to improve Britain's transport infrastructure in order to keep up with demand (Bloomberg News, 2005). Hidden within the data in Tables 4.1 and 4.2, however, and perhaps most importantly, are the reasons for the types of travel listed. Table 4.3 provides a breakdown of the trip purpose for UK travellers. What is remarkable is the growth in distance travelled for holidays, day trips and shopping, reflecting the provision of interconnectedness and accessibility of amenities relating to these activities. While not all of these relate directly to ground transport, it is important to position these figures in the context of government policy for transport infrastructure. Policy decisions need to be made with respect to the use and demand for infrastructure renewal and expansion, hence the reason that most national governments undertake comprehensive surveys and statistical modelling in order to identify probable causes of action.

Table 4.3 Distance per person per year by trip purpose, UK (in miles)

	1985/1986	*1991/1993*	*1996/1998*	*2002*
Commuting	1086	1207	1341	1294
Business	544	678	681	683
Education	161	183	190	195
Shopping	611	778	860	857
Visiting friends	1165	1357	1400	1364
Holiday: base	338	490	474	513
Day trip	307	373	343	368

Source: Adapted from Department for Transport (2004b)

COACH TRANSPORT

Coach transport is often associated with pleasure travel that encompasses numerous destinations (often in circuit routes, involving destinations or places that are usually geographically proximate to one another) over a specific period of time. As such, coach transport is unique in that it involves 1) multiple nodes or destinations; 2) prescribed flows and networks; and 3) highly structured itineraries. As such, one of the more common manifestations of coach travel is large buses shuttling tourists across a wide geographic region with stops at popular attractions and destinations (Figure 4.2). The length of these stops ranges from a few hours to several days.

Coach transport and its relationship to tourism can be significant in some areas and less so in others. In the Royal Borough (UK) (home to Windsor Castle and Legoland Windsor, two attractions that appear in the UK's overall top 20 attraction list) coach tourism is worth some £22 million per year (http://www.windsor.gov.uk/education/educat_index. htm; accessed 6 December 2005). By comparison, coach tours only account for 12% of arrivals to the city of York (www.cityofyork.com/econfact/keystats.htm; accessed 6 December 2005) and 3% of arrivals to Scotland (Tourism Scotland, 2003). The economic

Figure 4.2 Guided tours and coach transport: Tourists disembarking a coach at Te Anau, New Zealand

benefits of coach transport can be even less substantial for some smaller destinations or attractions that exist within a wider national network. These destinations, therefore, may experience regular visits from coaches bringing substantial numbers of tourists, but feature only as a brief stop within a larger itinerary. Without these stops, in some cases, visitor traffic at these destinations could, at best, be reliant upon pass-through traffic using personal modes of transport (i.e. passenger cars). In those destinations where the overall attraction and general infrastructure base is small, coach transport can often represent the most significant manner by which tourism is manifested. This is especially the case in rural destinations where other modes do not offer service, and especially smaller places along a prescribed route from one major destination to another. In the south island of New Zealand, for example, the small town of Gore sits almost half-way between Dunedin and Invercargill (Figure 4.3).

Coach tours make regular stops at Gore, allowing passengers the opportunity to use the toilets and purchase snacks. Despite the high numbers of coach visits, the overall eco-

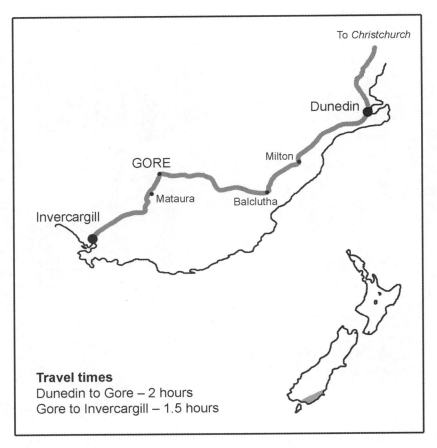

Figure 4.3 Location of Gore relative to Dunedin and Invercargill, New Zealand

nomic impact from these types of tourists is rather small, largely because most stops last little more than 30 minutes. As such, in those locations where coach tours make frequent 'rest stops' or 'tea breaks', it is not uncommon for local policy-makers to study different solutions designed to encourage visitors to stay longer. Yet this type of initiative does not solely rely on persuading coach tourists to stay longer. It requires fervent planning and decision-making processes to be in place and an understanding of how coach tour companies plan itineraries.

RAIL TRANSPORT

Rail transport played a significant role in the economic growth of many countries during the 19th century and, to some extent, the early 20th century (Turton & Black, 1998). In Romania, for example, the development of rail systems prior to the First World War resulted in new patterns of mobility between cities (Turnock, 2001). Rail travel in the United States was developed in a rather haphazard manner, with different gauges of track (i.e. different spacing between rails) being utilised and inefficient network planning that resulted in confusing (and laborious) itineraries for many travellers. As Cocks (2001) notes, 19th-century rail transport in the United States linked major urban areas and played a key role in their growth. For passengers using these early services, they had a choice between rather cramped and rudimentary carriage cars or more upmarket luxury coaches will full service. Using Pullman cars (specialised luxury travel rail coaches) for the luxury offerings, Cocks' (2001) historical research recalls how African-Americans were employed as porters, thus demonstrating how rail travel reflected a particular slice of social history of the time.

When examining how tourism can be linked with rail transport, two main sub-modes can be broadly identified:

1. Inter-destination rail transport (i.e. rail transport that links regions, cities, destinations and even attractions; this can be international or cross-border as well).

2. Intra-destination rail transport (i.e. rail transport that is designed to move passengers within a destination or attraction).

Of course, characterising rail transport this way may be problematic as there is often little to distinguish between these two from an operations/management perspective. For example, some organisations offer both intra-destination and regional rail transport. One example is the Loch Lomond area of Scotland, which lies just outside of the city of Glasgow. The area is frequented by tourists for the purposes of hiking and other outdoor recreational pursuits, and is accessible by car (40 minutes), by bus (40–45 minutes) or by train via services provided by ScotRail. The train service to the area involves a stop at Balloch after starting from downtown Glasgow. The service makes numerous stops in residential neighbourhoods and is primarily used, therefore, by residents to both enter and exit the city during the week. Because of the accessibility it affords, however, it can also be used by tourists as an alternative type of transport to the Loch area.

Many countries are turning to high-speed rail networks (using MAGLEV trains that can run at 500 km/h) to facilitate passenger and cargo movement. At present, Japan, France, Germany and Spain offer the service, although Korea recently launched the KTX service from Seoul to the port city of Busan (BBC, 2004a). A US$20 million study by the California High Speed Rail Authority recently suggested that 220 mph trains could be shuttling some 68 million passengers between San Francisco and Los Angeles by 2020 at a cost of US$37 billion (San Mateo County Times, 2004). Japan's high-speed rail network (Figure 4.4) is designed almost exclusively for the transport of passengers. While the network covers a significant portion of the country, it is designed primarily to link urban areas. Caution must be exercised, however, in determining how much of an impact high-speed rail can have. Unless the overall network is constructed such that rural or periurban areas are factored into the infrastructure, and thus connectivity, of the network, linking urban areas may serve to marginalise smaller regional centres. Gutiérrez *et al.* (1996: 238) suggested that the wider European high-speed network certainly helps link peripheral regions to urban centres, but potentially at the expense of the immediate urban 'hinterlands':

> Until the appearance of the high-speed train, ground transport systems shaped the space in a relatively continuous way: those places geographically located in the more peripheral regions were the least accessible. The high-speed train is changing this situation and is creating a space that is becoming more and more discontinuous (Plassard, 1992) in which the spatial distribution of accessibility depends less and less on the geographical location of the nodes and more and more on the type of infrastructures they are linked up to. Stations on the high-speed lines are at hundreds of kilometres distance from each other, thus creating 'islands' of greater accessibility and, in fact, a space that is becoming more and more discontinuous...

Hensher (1997) explored the demand for a high-speed rail network between Sydney and Canberra, a route that is dominated by the personal vehicle modes of transport, and noted that fierce competition between airlines with cheap airfares may affect profitability of the rail network (although see Chapter 8 for a discussion on Virgin Rail's efforts in the UK). Hensher's study found that varying levels of elasticity are evident in determining the demand for high-speed rail, yet the important lesson is the actual measurement of induced demand for such a product. As governments are more and more interested in funding profitable and efficient services, many will ask whether funding high-speed rail networks in this, an age of affordable air travel, is viable and, perhaps most importantly, politically popular. González-Savignat (2004) utilised experimental design techniques in demand modelling between

Figure 4.4 Moving passengers across extensive distances: High-speed train network in Japan

Source: By D.A. Follett, reproduced with permission

Barcelona and Madrid to answer this, and found that high-speed rail could impact on air travel markets as long as travel time is competitive between the two modes.

Demand for rail services must be measured along numerous variables, including convenience (i.e. factors relating to accessibility and connectivity; see Chapter 3) and price (see also Gutiérrez, 2001). Crockett and Hounsell's (2005) study of public rail transport in South Hampshire (UK) found that convenience related to access, station facilities, service frequencies and schedules, and interchange with other services. Bieger and Laesser (2001) found that factors such as safety, travel time, punctuality, flexibility and comfort were key when their 1999 survey of Swiss consumers considered journeys over 100 km. The advantage of rail transport as identified in Biefer and Laesser's study seems to rest primarily on lower costs, frequency and punctuality. This may be the case in some areas or countries, but with increasing competition from airlines in, for examples, Europe or the United States, the advantages of rail travel with respect to cost and frequency may be eroding. The issue, then, is one of viability. In New Zealand, the lack of demand (perhaps a result of poor marketing) for routes between regional urban centres such as Dunedin and Christchurch meant eventual closure. As the Washington Times reported in 2004, Russian President Putin is seeking to invest substantial amounts of capital in the railway

101

system, which is likely one of the largest in the world. Part of this is to disentangle the process of strong regionalism that has been at the centre of Russian politics for decades, but it could also be used as a means to move people for recreation or leisure purposes (Washington Times, 2004b)

Rail excursion/tour services can be packaged either by wholesalers or directly by the rail company itself. Both work closely with local service providers (primarily accommodations and, in some instances, restaurants and other attractions) to build all-inclusive rail holidays, some of which are escorted. One wholesaler, Maupintour, offers what it calls 'premier all-inclusive worldwide escorted packages' (Table 4.4), which represent a unique tour package in that the mode of transport is both the attraction as well as the key means of mobility. Canada's VIA Rail has long offered package trips across the country that more or less focus on the experiences on the train, but more recently has adopted a comprehensive package service that includes options for festivals, events, meetings and conventions, and adventure activities. In many ways, rail companies are seeking to build on the successes of air transport firms in providing packages and 'value-added' in order to drive business. Now that air transport options can often be just as cheap, if not cheaper, as rail transport, this represents a threat to ground transport provision.

RAIL TRANSPORT AND HERITAGE TOURISM

While the sub-modes of rail transport discussed above go some way to characterising the rail transport/tourism interface, there is another aspect of this interface that deserves mention. In recent years there has been a surge of interest in historical rail travel, where the means of transport also functions as the attraction itself (see Chapter 2). The growth in historic rail travel has, in a large part, been associated with the recognition of the importance of heritage tourism experiences (see Dann, 1994; Dickinson *et al.*, 2004). To this end, Halsall (2001: 152) suggests that '[p]reserved railways and tramways provide opportunities to view heritage transport in museum situations, and also to participate in the re-creations, accurate or otherwise'. Further, '[g]rowing numbers of people enjoy seeing and travelling on preserved historic transport modes, and are fascinated with steam propulsion, railways, and the images and emotions they stimulate…' (Halsall, 2001: 152).

To some extent, such interest is localised within the United States, where there is an abundance of little-used or completely abandoned track, but there has been growth in this area in the UK as well. Several examples from around the world highlight the growing interest in heritage rail travel:

- As an example of the integration of transport with heritage tourism development, in Pennsylvania excursions are utilised in tangent with 'battlefield tourism' as excursion trains wind through part of the Gettysburg battlefield site (Washington Times, 2004a).

- In Dunedin, New Zealand, the Taieri Gorge Railway (www.taieri.co.nz), jointly owed by the Dunedin City Council and the Otago Excursion Train Trust, shuttles day excursionists on The Taieri Gorge Limited along a 60 km route formerly operated by New Zealand Railways in the late 19th century. The railway is a popular choice for tourists as it introduces elements of the history of both the railway itself as well as its historic use in opening up Crown lands for development.

Table 4.4 Selected rail-based Maupintour journeys as at 2 September 2004

Journey	*Key features*
Europe Railway Journeys (8-day independent holiday)	• Private car airport transfers • 3 nights at the Thistle Marble Arch Hotel in London • Full-day London sightseeing • Transfer to Waterloo Station for first class Chunnel train to Paris • Private car transfer to Hotel Regina • 3 nights at the Hotel Regina in Paris
Rocky Mountaineer Escape (7-day escorted rail tour)	• 2 nights in Vancouver at The Sutton Place Hotel • 1 night in Kamloops at rail-assigned hotel • 2 nights at The Fairmont Banff Springs • 1 night at The Fairmont Chateau Lake Louise • Carriage ride through Stanley Park • 2-day rail journey aboard the *Rocky Mountaineer* • Visit Grouse Mountain Refuge for Endangered Wildlife • See Banff National Park • Sulphur Mountain gondola ride • Visit Columbia Icefield Parkway and take a Snocoach ride across Athabasca Glacier
Trans-Canada by Train (12-day escorted tour)	• 1 night at The Fairmont Royal York in Toronto • 2 nights aboard VIA Rail's *The Canadian* between Toronto and Jasper • 2 nights at The Fairmont Jasper Park Lodge • 1 night at The Fairmont Chateau Lake Louise • 2 nights at The Fairmont Banff Springs • 1 night in Kamloops at a rail-assigned hotel • 2 nights in Vancouver at The Sutton Place Hotel • 11 breakfasts, 7 lunches, 10 dinners

Source: www.maupintour.com (accessed 2 September 2004)

- Fostoria, Ohio was the first electric rail traffic control system to be demonstrated any-where in the world and was also the first place where centralised railroad traffic was established. Plans to revitalise a unique historical tower by the Fostoria Train Tourism Group follow from the recognition that accommodation accounts for only 11% of all visitor expenditures for Fostoria, thus leaving a significant amount (some US$8.5 million) that tourists spend in attractions, food and entertainment (Advertiser-Tribune, 2004)

These examples further demonstrate how a mode of transport can become closely inte-grated with the tourism experience, especially in an historical context. Mowforth and Munt (1998) captured this with their proclamation that tourism is now more concerned with travelling, trucking and trekking, as opposed to sun, sand and sea. This is an impor-tant consideration because it points to changing motivations for leisure and recreational activities, and in this particular case highlights how historic modes of transport get caught up in swaying tourist preferences.

The provision of historical train travel is often fraught with difficulties. First, decisions need to be made on how the project will be capitalised. Significant funding is often required to refit historic locomotives and refurnish passenger cars. In the case of the latter, this is often joined with enhanced safety protocols in order to meet modern safety regulations. In light of this significant investment, the other reality is simply whether enough demand can be realised for this type of experience.

PERSONAL TRANSPORT

Personal transport permeates numerous forms of human mobility, ranging from daily trips to supermarkets to lengthy family vacations, and features types of ground transport such as the personal automobile, motorcycle or bicycle (the latter of which is of course non-motorised). The range of personal transport available demonstrates the range of mobility that people have available to them. In other words, with motorised personal transport being made available at more affordable prices, the geographic scale of accessi-bility has grown. This section examines two particular personal transport types: the personal (or often 'family') automobile and the bicycle.

To a large extent, personal modes of transport can best be characterised and differenti-ated on the basis of provision or use:

1. Modes of transport provided by (or under legal ownership of) the individual; in rela-tion to tourism, this can mean the utilisation of personal automobiles for day or overnight trips at varying lengths.

2. Modes of transport that are provided to the individual at a set cost (i.e. through a rental or lease agreement); tourists may opt to rent a vehicle for transport to and from a destination or within a single, or between two or more, destinations.

Specific modes of personal transport used for leisure and recreation can fall into either category. Tourists in New Zealand may opt to rent 'Maui vans' and explore the country according to their own schedule, which is usually more flexible than packaged tours. These mobile caravans can be almost entirely self-contained for basic services (i.e. food preparation, showers and toilet), but this may also encourage the exploration of environmentally sensitive areas. Alternatively, individuals, couples and families may use their own personal vehicle for weekend or short-break holidays. The Dorset area of the United Kingdom, particularly Bournemouth and Weymouth, features as a popular vacation destination in the summer season. As such, congestion is not uncommon on the main motorway that stretches to London. Because of the popularity of utilising personal automobiles for the purposes of tourism, various road-side services are increasingly becoming available throughout the road networks of many countries. Throughout the UK, Canada and the United States, for example, 'services' (also known as 'rest stops' in North America) areas are common, where travellers are able to stop, use the toilet, stretch their legs, and purchase food and beverage items. In Canada, as in the United Kingdom, such rest areas are normally populated by retail or food and beverage chains. In the UK, RoadChef offers fast food, while in Canada Wendy's (fast food) and Tim Horton's (coffee and donuts) dominate most rest stops along the Trans-Canada highway (Figure 4.5).

Figure 4.5 Rest stop along the Trans-Canada Highway: Services for personal automobiles

PERSONAL AUTOMOBILES

Without question, the use of personal automobile for the purposes of tourism reflects, to a large extent, the proliferation of automobile use in developed countries. The growth of the use of personal automobiles in EU countries surpassed most other forms of transport between 1995 and 2002 (Table 4.5).

Table 4.5 Transport passengers per mode 1995–2002, EU (billions of passenger kilometres)

	Passenger cars	*Bus and coach*	*Railway*	*Tram and metro*
1995	3702.70	462.234	318.617	50.778
1996	3773.58	466.878	325.481	51.623
1997	3843.51	467.439	327.125	52.209
1998	3931.65	474.107	329.361	53.145
1999	4009.02	475.880	338.729	54.613
2000	4074.20	480.053	346.354	56.340
2001	4117.52	482.551	348.091	57.269
2002	4202.59	485.779	346.172	57.317
Percent change (1995–2002)	14%	5%	9%	13%

Source: European Union Road Federation (2005)

In the United Kingdom, the number of trips per person per year by mode and purpose varies considerably, but a pattern emerges that favours the use of personal automobiles for most forms of mobility. Table 4.6 demonstrates the pervasiveness of the automobile in personal mobility in the United Kingdom, with an average of 21 holidays or day trips per year being taken either as a driver or passenger.

In the United States, personal vehicles are used for more than 80% of long-distance domestic trips and over 90% of commuting trips to work, and the 2001 US National Household Travel Survey revealed that 90% of pleasure travel utilised personal automobiles (BTS, 2005c). As far back as 1996, 60% of American households already owned two vehicles, according to one survey (see Edmondson & Du, 1996). In the UK, that figure, as of 2002, was estimated to be only 22% (UK National Statistics, 2005), although two-thirds of all UK households own at least one car (European Commission, 2001). In 1998, over three-quarters (79%) of all passenger traffic in the EU is carried by some form of road transport.

Personal vehicles are used in many countries to access second home cottage areas (Weaver, 2005; see also Box 3.1). Cottage or cabins in North America, generally in wilder-

Table 4.6 Trips per person per year by mode and trip purpose, UK 1999/2001

	Bicycle	Car/van (as driver)	Car/van (as passenger)	Motorcycle	Other Private Vehicle
Commuting	6	89	18	2	1
Business	*	25	3	*	*
Education	1	3	18	*	3
Escort education	*	20	6	*	*
Shopping	2	81	49	*	*
Other escort	*	48	23	*	*
Other personal business	1	44	24	*	1
Visiting friends at home	2	50	43	*	*
Visiting friends elsewhere	*	12	14	*	*
Sport/ entertainment	1	25	22	*	1
Holidays/day trips	2	9	12	*	*
Other, includ- ing just walk	*	1	*	*	*
All purposes	15	407	232	2	6

Note: * No data available

Source: http://www.transtat.dft.gov.uk/tables/tsgb02/1/section1.htm#1.1

ness areas that are proximate to smaller communities that provide basic services such as food and petrol, are normally accessed via automobile as well. Dijst *et al.* (2005) note that personal automobiles are the dominant type of transport used to access second homes in the Netherlands and Germany, and Müller (2002a, 2002b) demonstrated empirically that proximity (and thus accessibility) played a key role in determining attractiveness of certain regions as weekend leisure zones in Sweden.

The use of personal transport for recreational purposes is also worthy of mention. Recent surges in sales of SUVs and light trucks might suggest that leisure activities and vehicle ownership have finally merged to the point where specific types of vehicles are being purchased with the intent of using them for specific recreational purposes, yet as Niemeier *et al.* (2001) point out, many owners utilise SUVs in much the same way as they would use regular passenger vehicles. See also Box 4.1 where Porsche Match production with tourism.

CYCLE TRANSPORT

Lumdson and Tolley (2001) make reference to UK General Household Survey research that suggests that Britons use a bicycle more for the purposes of leisure as opposed to a primary means of transport. What is interesting, however, is that this appears to be changing. The same survey suggests that more Britons are engaging with recreational cycling (Lumsdon & Tolley, 2001). What this means is that, as a mode of transport, the bicycle plays a key role in some tourism and recreational behaviour. Lumsdon *et al.* (2004) examined the NSCR, a 6000 km cycle trail that circles the North Sea, which was established in 1998 and officially launched in the year 2001. The project was funded by the European Union and local governments in Norway, Sweden, Denmark, Germany, the Netherlands, England and Scotland. The focus of the network is almost exclusively to generate multi-country touring:

> The tourism experience focuses on the North Sea, and an exploration of the rich maritime culture shared by the countries which border it, a theme which is recurrent throughout its entire length. These images are reinforced by a specific brand identity, which positions the route as a crossnational tourism offering where the use of transport is an integral part of the tourist experience. (Lumsdon *et al.* 2004: 13)

Using an intercept survey at key points along the route, the authors were able to profile the trip purpose of cyclists. Table 4.7 summarises the results of their survey. As shown, a significant number use the cycling route for recreational purposes, particularly for short trips.

Table 4.7 Purpose of journey (cycle trips), NSCR

	*Percentage**
Specific purpose (work, shopping)	8
Short, circular recreational trip (less than 3 hours total)	25
Short, out-and-back recreational trip	23
Day ride	10
Cycling short break (two or three days)	16
Other (including linear and circular touring holidays)	17

Source: Adapted from Lumsdon *et al.* (2004)

Note: * Numbers do not sum due to rounding.

BOX 4.1 Porsche AG weekend getaway: Matching production with tourism

In recent years, many auto manufacturers have sought to bridge the gap between the production process and their end customers. For example, BMW offers tours of its Spartanburg plant in the United States for potential Z4 owners, offering a glimpse of production lines and detailed presentations on product features. These are designed to enhance the experience of vehicle ownership and provide potential (and existing) customers with a value-added benefits and build relationships. It is, in effect, an attempt to build emotional ties to a brand (see Coles, 2004b).

Without question, Porsche automobiles straddle the border between luxury and performance and thus target a particularly exclusive corner of the automobile market. For many, the cost of outright ownership may be prohibitive, but one option available is to rent a Porsche for a weekend getaway. Porsche AG has taken this one step further by offering potential customers the chance to spend time with a product. Among other touring trips designed to acquaint customers with its product, Porsche offers a packaged, weekend trip from Ludwigsburg to Weyberhöfe in Germany, a package that includes a two-day test drive in a Porsche Boxster S (two persons per vehicle), one night's accommodation at the Schlosshotel Weyberhöfe Vital Resort, lunch on both days, a formal evening dinner, a complete tour pack with route map, and a Porsche Travel Club tour guide in German and English (other languages also available on request).

This example represents an interesting, and intentional, blending of lifestyle with tourism. In one sense, it is designed to offer potential buyers of a Porsche to have an extended test of the product before purchase. At the same time, however, it offers individuals who are not all likely to purchase a Porsche to experience an 'exclusive' vacation. It is one example where a particular mode of transport is used as the primary focus of a holiday or vacation.

Questions for consideration

1. Are there any other modes or types of transport that attempt to blend lifestyle with tourism?

2. How might this case study be used as an example of relationship marketing?

Management and marketing implications are apparent from a study such as this. As cycling often takes individuals or groups into areas where travel by motorised transport is otherwise less appealing, there is room to consider what the impact of a cycle route such as this may have on semi-rural areas (i.e. those areas in the near vicinity to larger urban areas). Lumsdon *et al.* (2004) suggest that marketing of the cycle route in urban and regional areas may bring added expenditures to smaller, fringe areas not normally included in day-trip itineraries using motorised transport:

> In overall terms, day visitation by the near market remains the most important seg-ment in terms of volume. The internal regional market is key to the success of this type of route. There is, therefore, a need to promote cycling on the route as a group activity, for example, to parties of family/friends living in residential areas on or near the NSCR. (Lumdson *et al.* 2004: 21)

In the UK, the 1996 National Cycling Strategy was launched with the intent of promot-ing the benefits of cycling. Immediately prior to this, Sustrans (a charity group) was awarded funding from the UK Millennium Commission (using lottery fund) to establish an NCN (Cope *et al.*, 2003). The network currently supports 8000 miles (or 14,400 km) of both cycling and walking routes, although this is projected to grow to approximately 18,000 km by 2005. According to Sustrans (www.sustrans.org.uk), almost one-third of the network is limited strictly to cycling and walking, and thus closed to vehicular traffic. The other two-thirds of the network shares smaller road networks that are open to vehicular traffic, as noted by Cope *et al.* (2003: 6):

> The NCN is a composite of over a thousand local sections ranging in length from a few metres to several kilometres. Each one is designed to be of benefit to local people, with on average two-thirds on minor or traffic-calmed roads and one-third on traffic-free paths. The sections are designed, built and signed by Sustrans and its part-ner bodies. There are over 400 active partners involved in the NCN project, including local authorities, countryside and utility bodies, landowners, central government, amenity groups and community groups.

The network was established both as a means to allow people the freedom to chose an alternative, and even sustainable, manner of transport to and from work, but also to encourage long cycle holidays and family rides that are shorter in duration. Many private companies affiliated with Sustrans offer full services for the traveller, including baggage care, accommodation booking along the route, and advice and tips on attractions. Some tours are even guided, thus bringing a wider package tour element to this mode of transport.

In discussing cycle tourism, an examination of the links between it and specific forms of tourism can be highlighted. For example, outdoor recreational activities and adventure tourism have become quite popular for many tourists. As such, examples such as bungy jumping and hiking highlight, once again, different motivations for undertaking such activities. With cycle tourism, some destinations utilise these outdoor activities for the purposes of reinvigorating tourism in the off-season. For example, in Whistler, British Columbia, off-road cycling (or 'mountain biking') is heavily promoted in the summer season as a recreational activity. In this particular case, tourists need not bring their own bike as many shops that rent skis during the peak winter season also rent mountain bikes. What this demonstrates is the further 'blurry distinction' (introduced in Chapter 1) of the mode of transport also being the central or core activity, but it also shows how a particular mode of transport, in this case a personal mode of transport, can be used to 'counter' seasonal affects of tourist flows. Box 4.2 provides another example of how cycle tourism is used to promote a destination, but at the same time offers tourists a simple mode of transport designed to enhance the experience of a destination.

Box 4.2 Enhancing the experience and vehicle for promotion: The Central Otago Rail Trail, New Zealand (by Sam Hepburn)

Many rural regions have successfully resorted to rural tourism as a way to preserve the rural community lifestyle from the demise of unemployment, urbanisation and development (see, for examples, Butler *et al.*, 1998, Sharpley, 2004). In recent years the transformation of abandoned railway lines into recreational rail trails has become an increasingly popular mechanism for attracting tourist expenditures and mending rural economies. The Otago Central Rail Trail (http://www.centralotagorailtrail.co.nz/) in the Central Otago region of New Zealand is an excellent illustration of a contemporary success story.

Once a vital link between Dunedin and New Zealand's major goldmines, the Otago Central Branch railway line generated a steady flow of commerce and activity to a number of towns and communities throughout Central Otago. However, as time progressed so did the evolution of modern transport, ultimately resulting in the slow demise of this 150 km stretch of railway. By the year 1990 the railway was permanently closed (Central Otago Rail Trail, 2004). The New Zealand Department of Conservation realised the potential of the redundant railway and subsequently acquired the line in 1993 with the vision of developing a unique recreational facility for walkers, cyclists and horse riders (Department of Conservation, 2004). After funding was granted by the Otago Central Rail Trail Trust, and extensive preparation and upgrading of the deteriorating railway was completed, New Zealand's first rail trail was opened in the year 2000 (Central Otago Rail Trail, 2004).

The landscape that the Otago Central Rail Trail traverses cannot be seen from the highways, thus providing a chance for users to enjoy the distinctive Central Otago environment from an exclusive perspective. The rail trail, which is steeped in a sense of history and remoteness, has played a significant role in preserving an important part of Otago's heritage (Otago Rail Trail, 2004). The rail trail now attracts thousands of visitors to the region every year, and although the trail is open to the public free of charge, it acts as a catalyst for economic development for those destinations and attractions spread along the trail (Cycling Advocates Network, 2004).

In conjunction with the Department of Conservation, Ross (1996) explored the types of people using the Otago Central Rail Trail and the activities the trail is used for. A total convenience sample of 47 New Zealand respondents was taken, with the majority being in large groups. Ross (1996) reported that the average age of those using the trail was 49 years, with 34% of the users indicating that they were between 60–69 years of age. The gender of the participants was skewed in favour of females, whom made up 62% of those interviewed.

According to Ross (1996), the vast majority (89%) of those surveyed revealed that they resided in the greater Otago region, with a total of 70% of these people indicating that they lived in Dunedin. The accommodation facilities most frequently used was private home followed by motel. A total of 40% of respondents indicated that they were not staying. Of those that stayed overnight, a high proportion specified that they were staying in either nearby towns such as Middlemarch or Hyde, which at the time of the survey were largely the only available accommodation options (Ross 1996). This has changed somewhat in recent years although anecdotal information provided by local residents and publicans near the rail trail suggests that accommodation provision is still a concern. Although the rail trail has benefited from significant exposure within New Zealand, and thus attracts a large number of residents, its international appeal is still rather limited, partially because of the lack of funding for the marketing of the trail, but also because the proportion of international visitors to the Central Otago region is small compared to domestic visitors.

Questions for consideration

1. How and why might one argue that all levels of government (i.e. local, regional, national) should be involved in the development and maintenance of attraction such as a rail trail?

> **2.** How might the concepts discussed in Chapter 2 benefit the development of a rail trail, particularly with respect to the strategic placement of ancillary attractions, accommodation and other features?

SUSTAINABLE GROUND TRANSPORT

The overall sustainability of ground transport necessarily means consideration not only for the actual environmental impacts, but also the degree to which transport can factor into the overall sustainable nature of tourism development. This includes the level of integration of transport within the tourism system and efficient (economically, as well as environmentally) movement of tourists. Much has been written in the transport literature on the benefits of adopting an overall sustainable approach to transport in general (e.g. Holden & Høyer, 2005). The economic benefits are paramount as costs can be reduced and efficiencies of network operations (whether goods-based or passenger-based) are established.

The degree of mobility offered by ground transport is staggering and relates to the concern over the sustainability of ground transport. In the EU, for example:

- the number of cars in the EU trebled over the 30 year period between 1970 and 2000, from 62.5 million to almost 175 million, with some 3 million cars per year growth;
- 10 hectares of land are covered by new roading each day;
- more than half of the oil consumed in the EU is from personal vehicles, and over two-thirds of the demand for oil is attributed to road transport in general (including transfer of goods);
- 84% of transport-related CO_2 emissions in Europe can be accounted for by general road transport. (Adapted from European Commission, 2001).

It is not entirely clear whether one particular type of ground transport is more sustainable than another type because the environment (and operating procedures, including the network served) varies considerably and may render direct comparison difficult. The use of private automobiles by tourists and recreationalists (either their own or rented) certainly can cause road congestion along main motorways and arterial routes in some countries. Alternatives include the provision of (light) rail in some urban areas or rail carriage in general to link regions and the promotion of other public services such as buses (Walton, 2003). Rail may be an option, but it shares many of the same physical environmental impacts with road travel (e.g. the use of non-renewable fuels and needs an infrastructure and network that is not unlike existing road networks), and varies depending on the level of integration that it has within national economies (see, for example, Plakhotnik *et al.*, 2005).

In Great Britain, Shaw and Farrington (2003: 108) note that rail travel is perhaps 'the most space and energy efficient way of moving large volumes of people and freight':

1. Rail may be up to four times more efficient per passenger kilometre than other types of ground transport, thus it has the ability to move more people at once as opposed to having one individual per personal vehicle on a roadway.

2. Increase in rail utilisation may mean less road traffic congestion, thus a more integrated means of transport between urban areas.

3. Rail is ostensibly safer than personally operated vehicles.

There has been some movement towards improving the environmental sustainability of rail transport. In October 2006, it was reported that Virgin Trains in the UK may have won concessions from the Treasury for the use of biofuels on the company's cross-country Penzance to Aberdeen franchise (Milmo, 2006). Between 1990 and 2005, VIA Rail Canada has cut greenhouse gas emissions by 11% and cut fuel consumption per passenger by almost 30% (Webwire, 2005). The World Bank (1996: 62) notes that a 'fully-loaded train requires only one-third of the energy per passenger-kilometre of a fully loaded car and little more than one-tenth as much as a fully loaded airplane...'. Electrically operated rail is, of course, an option, but this needs to be developed from sources that are renewable (e.g. wind, solar). As noted by the World Bank (1996), above anything else, the suitability of rail travel for passengers (including tourists) needs to be met from a satisfaction point of view before any ecologically friendly benefits are realised.

CHAPTER SUMMARY

The manifestation of coach transport in relation to networks, flows and the resultant user base is somewhat more straightforward. In this chapter, examples of coach transport being used on long excursions by tourists in particular destinations have been provided. In this sense, coach transport features as a particular mode of transport that is usually associated with intra-destination travel by pleasure travellers. At the same time, however, coach transport can be used to transport passengers from origin to destination, but as will be discussed later, this is proving to be less popular now that cheaper domestic airfares are being offered in many countries. In contrast to coach and rail transport, cycle transport is generally restricted to intra-destination or intra-attraction transport, largely because there are limits to which humans are able to supply transport under their own power (excluding, of course, professional athletes). To some extent, and as discussed above, cycle transport is somewhat more in line with recreational and leisure, although the example of the Otago Central Rail Trail shows that some tourist utilise bicycles both as a mode of transport and a recreational activity.

Although the general discussion in this chapter reflects the use of ground transport by tourists, the blurry distinctions introduced in Chapter 2 should be kept in mind with respect to the nature of transport provision not directly targeted at tourists. As such, urban and regional transport network planning also affects the scope of network and flows of tourists.

Box 4.3 Case study – The National Railroad Passenger Corporation (Amtrak)

In some form or another, various levels of government in the United States have been linked to the ownership and management of rail transport operations since the 19th century. The extent of this relationship has varied (i.e. outright ownership of operations and infrastructure or policy directives aimed at direct regulation) and depends largely on the level of government in question. In general, however, the Federal branch of government takes more of an interest in ensuring the overall viability of rail as a major mode of transport that is inherently tied to the wider manufacturing sector and is thus a significant means by which goods and raw materials are transported.

It is important to note, however, that the intense interest in rail operations by the United States is not unusual. As recently as June 2004, a secret report surfaced that suggested the British government is considering renationalising the rail industry in the face of increasing burdens (by some estimates, £3 billion a year) on the taxpayers to subsidise the industry (The Express, 2004). Page (1993) suggests that when government has a direct ownership role in rail transport, the resulting organisation charged with its management is characterised by:

- a close relationship with central government due to state ownership and the provision of operating subsidies;
- periodic changes in the political will of national governments to subsidise rail;
- constraints on investment planning and a forward-looking approach to development;
- a lack of management freedom prior to the 1980s;
- an inability to prevent loss of market share in rail travel in the 1970s and early 1980s. (Adapted from Page 1999: 84)

Although Page's example is somewhat specific to the European Union, a number of his listed characteristics can be applied to the role the US Federal Government has played in the corporate lifespan of the National Railroad Passenger Corporation, better known as Amtrak. Amtrak has been a formidable force in linking many places in the country. From a passenger operations perspective, it is an excellent example of the role of government in the provision of rail transport for the general population. It also serves to demonstrate the turbulent nature of rail transport provision, especially with regard to shifts in management structure and focus, combined with increasing competition from other modes of transport.

Amtrak services more than 24 million passengers a year in 46 states, utilising some 22,000 miles of track, which are mostly owned by independent freight railroad companies (Hoover's Company Profiles, 2004). Established in 1971 and funded by the US Federal government (a relationship that continues to this day), the 1990s were a turbulent time for the company, as it faced numerous external threats (Hoover's Company Profiles, 2004), including:

- flooding in the US Midwest;
- significant competition from airlines able to offer cheaper airfares; and
- ongoing safety concerns following severe, high-profile accidents.

Revamped strategic plans, including one that would result in the complete privatisation of the company in 2002, have generally been unsuccessful due to managerial 'bloat' along with declining revenues and, by extension, shrinking cash reserves. A bailout of US$300 million in 2002, following years of increased costs but shrinking revenues, helped, but it was the subsequent managerial reforms that allowed the railroad to cut costs and increase efficiencies. As of 2004, the company says it still needs significant amounts of funding to stay alive, but this is something the government is increasingly becoming wary of.

In July 2004, the US House Appropriations Committee approved an $89.9 billion fiscal 2005 spending package for the Transportation and Treasury departments, which included $900 million for Amtrak, a $300 million cut from 2004 funding, which was considerably less than the $1.8 billion Amtrak officials have sought. Ernest Istook Jr, a Republican congressman from Oklahoma and chairman of the House Appropriations transportation and treasury subcommittee, pointed to the problems with ongoing Federal government support for Amtrak:

> The administration believes, and I agree, that realistic Amtrak reform language must be enacted before we start putting more money into [the service], that includes acceptance of [financial] responsibility at the state and local level, which they have not been willing to have... Unfortunately, we have too many places in the country that say 'we want Amtrak, but we don't want to pay for it, we want Uncle Sam to be the only one to pay for it. (The Bond Buyer, 2004)

The company is facing heavy capital expenditures in the near future, not the least of which include replacing older carriage cars and locomotives and substantial infrastructure repairs and maintenance. To date, the government has injected some US$24 billion into the company (National Journal, 2004) and this has caused many to suggest several options to relieve the Government of the burden of running a massive transport operation such as Amtrak (see also www.saveamtrak.org):

- full privatisation, and at the same time encouraging competition;
- split the company into several companies (one of which would focus almost exclusively on passenger provision, while another would look after maintenance);
- transfer the operations of the company to individual states, although many states believe that the provision of interstate rail transport falls under Federal jurisdiction. (Adapted from National Journal 2004)

The future of Amtrak is very much in doubt, but it is unlikely any US Federal government will allow the company to completely cease operations. If anything, and not unlike many governments around the world, public transport is often heavily subsidised. In the US, the massive US interstate highway system and the airline industry receive substantial subsidies for operations, largely because the cornerstone of major economies is the ability to transport both people and goods.

Questions for consideration

1. Why do some people feel that a national rail network should be managed by the national government?

2. If a scenario of full privatisation is realised, how would competition be encouraged in such an environment? What would be the impacts for Amtrak in terms of operations?

SELF-REVIEW QUESTIONS

1. What are main types and key characteristics of ground transport in relation to tourism?

2. Why are some types of ground transport more likely to feature bi-directional flows than others?

3. Why can it be said that rail transport covers both national and local needs with respect to tourism-related transport?

ESSAY QUESTIONS

1. Why is it difficult to distinguish between tourist and non-tourist use of ground modes of transport?

2. Discuss the relationship between coach transport and touring holidays.

3. Give an argument outlining the importance of passenger rail transport in an age where relatively cheap air travel is available in most developed countries.

KEY SOURCES

Banister, D. (2002) *Transport Planning* (2nd edn). London: Spon Press.

Banister's book (although not really a textbook per se) is an excellent one generally outlining transport planning issues, including policy issues which inform plans. This book has a slight UK bias (despite the presence of a dedicated chapter on international experiences), but is nonetheless an excellent source.

Essex, S. (1994) Tourism. In R. Gibb (ed.) *The Channel Tunnel: A Geographical Perspective* (pp. 79–100). Chichester: John Wiley & Sons.

The entire Gibb volume provides an excellent overview of the development of the Tunnel itself. Essex's contribution is useful starting point, and should be read in conjunction with news items from early 2006 highlighting the financial problems the Tunnel is having. Readers should also consult news sites (e.g. Google News) for items on the Eurostar, particularly in relation to passenger loadings, markets and alliances with destinations/attractions such as EuroDisney.

Turton, B. and Black, W.R. (1998) Inter-urban transport. In B. Hoyle and R. Knowles (eds) *Modern Transport Geography* (2nd edn). Chichester: John Wiley and Sons.

The Hoyle and Knowles text is standard reading in many transport geography courses worldwide. In addition to Turton and Black's overview of inter-urban transport linkages, Page's chapter on tourism and transport is also worth a read as it encapsulates some of the salient issues.

CHAPTER 5:

MARINE TRANSPORT

LEARNING OBJECTIVES

After reading this chapter, you should be able to

1. Assess and evaluate the connections between globalisation and transnationalism and the global cruise industry.

2. Identify and describe various types of marine transport in the context of recreation and tourism.

3. Explain how certain marine tourism products are packaged and marketed.

4. Describe and critically assess models of market segments associated with cruise tourism.

5. Identify and evaluate the environmental impacts of marine transport.

INTRODUCTION

Much like the varying types of ground transport and their relationship to tourism, exploring the integration between marine transport and tourism also reveals significant variations and complexities. Marine transport, as a whole, can generally split between the transport of goods and the transport of people, which is, on the surface, not entirely dissimilar to a wider segmentation of the uses of ground and air transport (and, quite often, goods and people share transport in many situations). It also demonstrates many of the same blurry distinctions that were discussed in Chapter 2. Some island archipelagos rely on marine transport for the transfer of goods and people from island to island. Similarly, tourists often utilise various types (and forms) of marine transport for either functional reasons or directly integrated within a wider tourist experience.

The management of marine transport is difficult due the vast array of transport types that can be utilised for the purposes of recreation and/or tourism. In many cases, such as cruise tourism, international regulations may exist but are regularly seen to be lacking in the ability to be enforced because of lack of monitoring or policing at the international level. Much of this is related to environmental issues, but regulations relating to enterprise operations (business practices) are not overseen, generally, by international bodies to the extent where level playing fields exist (see Lester & Weeden, 2004, for example). Modern tourism is represented in marine environments in several ways, each of which is discussed in this chapter:

1. Cruise tourism, where worldwide growth in the past several decades has been substantial; growth post-11 September has also been significant, with the Cruise Line Industry Association reporting some 10.5 million cruise vacationers in 2005 (up 40% from 2001) (PE.com, 2005).

2. Functional marine transport mechanisms, such as ferries and other forms of propelled vehicles that move tourists (and non-tourists) from locality to locality.

3. Personal water transport, including powered and non-powered watercraft.

CRUISE TOURISM: RESORTS AT SEA

Mobility by sea is at the heart of human expansion. Early masted ships carried migrants and goods destined for newly colonised places. Prior to technological and economic realities that realised efficient, fast and (comparatively) cheap air travel, journeys were undertaken using ocean liners (in the tradition of *Titanic*). Such extended periods of holiday are comparatively fewer today, where it is not unusual for itineraries to begin and end at the same point, and often last little more than several weeks (Douglas & Douglas, 2001). 'Cruising', in other words, has become a commodity, and linkages to the predictability and routinisation of the experience have been made (Weaver, 2005). Douglas and Douglas (2001) outline a truncated history of cruise tourism:

- the initial offering of round-trip tickets from England to the Mediterranean onboard P&O ships in 1844;
- the first cruising yacht in operation in 1881 by the Oceanic Yachting Company in response to a British Medical Journal report suggesting that sea cruises provided significant health benefits;
- the first custom-built cruiseship, luxurious in ornamentation, launched in 1900 by the German company Hamburg–Amerika;

- the popularity of 'booze cruises' during the Prohibition Era in the United States in the 1930s;
- the conversion of migrant ships to cruise vessels to accommodate demand for cruising post-World War Two;
- the retrenchment of many line cruise companies during the 1950s and 1960s when air travel become more affordable, although this spawned increased popularity of package 'fly and sail' experiences.

As of early 2005, global cruise tourism shows few signs of stagnation, although annual and seasonal fluctuations continue to exist. The small Dutch island of Bonaire in the Caribbean reported an annual 6% growth in arrivals for the first six months of 2004 (Bonaire Department of Economic and Labour Affairs, 2004). The member companies of the CLIA (2005) carried 2,604,544 worldwide guests in the second quarter of 2004, representing an 11% increase over the same period the year previous.

Cruise tourism has, in recent years, also expanded internationally. The Indian cruise market has recently expanded to the point where the national government has opened up the sector to foreign direct investment (Express Travel and Tourism, 2005). In July 2006, Costa Cruises (part of Carnival) is scheduled to begin five-day cruises for Chinese travellers departing from Shanghai (Katz, 2006). Star Cruises, a Malaysian-based cruise line, has a number of large cruise ships visiting larger ports of call throughout Southeast Asia. Star Cruises ships are generally targeted at local Asia markets, but they also attract Australians, Britons and Americans (Gunderson, 2005).

The provision of cruise experiences is often measured in terms of the available berths, which is one way of describing total accommodation available on a ship. Berths can generally refer to individual bunks, and thus give a reasonably accurate indication of the total number of people that a ship is able to hold. As of 1 January 2004 there were 339 active ocean vessels plying water routes around the world, representing slightly less than 300,000 berths (Ebersold, 2004). The sizes of these vessels varies considerably, which can be somewhat explained on the basis of target market, ownership criteria and integration with other tourism attractions, destination and other forms of transport. Roughly one-third of ships have a total berth capacity of less than 500, and approximately 11% have berths of less than 100 (Ebersold, 2004). Larger ocean-going vessels often carry upwards of 2500–3500 people, whereas shorter, more coastal, cruise ships will carry far fewer and have nautical ranges which are considerably smaller (even though, by design, they may be able to traverse ocean waterways). Ships with fewer berths may also target a high-net income market segment, and thus offer more luxurious on-board amenities. As of 2003, the size of the global cruise market is said to be roughly 11 million to 12 million passengers (Ebersold, 2004: 2). Table 5.1 outlines the growth of worldwide cruise tourism over the course of the 1990s.

Table 5.1 Worldwide cruise demand (millions)

	North America	Europe	Rest of world	Total
1989	3.29	0.53	0.20	4.02
1993	4.48	0.88	0.25	5.61
1997	5.05	1.36	0.46	6.87
2000	6.88	1.95	0.78	9.61

Source: Adapted from WTO 2003a, based on data from CLIA (US and Canada), Passenger Shipping Association (Europe), GP Wild Ltd International (Rest of world)

Cruise demand is greatest in North America, and this is one of the more obvious reasons why regions such as the Caribbean have witnessed substantial cruise tourism growth over the past few decades (Wood, 2004a) (Table 5.1). Cruise companies have even diversified the products and ports/destinations served when targeting the North American market, with some companies (e.g. Cruise West – www.cruisewest.com) offering cruises up the west coast of the continent to Alaska and several tour companies in the United States marketing package tours that feature cruises to Antarctica. Although the cruise tourism product can be said to have been globalised as a consequence of substantial international demand for international cruise experiences (Wood, 2004a, 2004b), the North American market is currently served by three major companies (Carnival Corporation/Carnival PLC, Royal Caribbean Cruises, and Star Cruises), which account for over 80% of the cruise market capacity. These companies are simply keeping up with demand, and this demand has been fuelled by the desire of many North Americans (primarily United States residents, which account for 95% of all cruise passengers from North America) to holiday close to home rather than travel long distance (Travel and Tourism Analyst, 2004).

CRUISE MARKETS AND PRODUCTS

Cruise tourism has witnessed remarkable growth over the past few decades. The Caribbean, long popular with the North American market, carries the highest berth capacity (well over half) (Table 5.1), although there is significant growth in the European/Mediterranean area, Alaska, the trans-Panama canal route and Mexico (Dwyer & Forsyth, 1998; see also Ebersold, 2004). The largest source markets for cruise tourism are the United States and the United Kingdom; according to the UNWTO (WTO, 2003a) the United States alone makes up approximately three-quarters of the worldwide cruise market, although the main source markets in the United States are areas that are proximal to main base ports for many cruise companies (e.g. the Pacific, where Los Angeles and San Francisco serve as base ports, and the South Atlantic, as many cruise companies serving the Caribbean base ships in Florida). The city of New York, by its sheer size, also supplies a significant number of cruise tourists (WTO, 2003a). Post 11 September 2001, the popularity of cruise travel among United States residents waned slightly, largely due to fears of terrorism, although there are signs that this is improving (Conroy, 2004). As well, some peripheral countries that rely on US cruise tourists (such as New Zealand) have been worried that global unrest will result in US cruise tourists staying closer to home (New Zealand Herald, 2003).

BOX 5.1 Cruising with the cargo: A new segment in cruise tourism? (by Gregory S. Szarycz)

At present, the global cruise industry has approximately 40 new cruise ships on order worth around a total of $500 billion (Peisley, 2000: 12–13). The projection for the number of global annual cruisers is 16 million by 2009. This represents a 60% growth from 2000, an indication of a major boom in this sector of the tourism industry. In order to accommodate this growth the industry is building larger and fancier ships; Cunard recently celebrated the inauguration of the *Queen Mary 2*, the world's largest, most anticipated, and most expensive (at approximately US$800 million) ship ever constructed.

However, for a select group of discriminating travellers, opulent meals or movies on the deck with popcorn and a cocktail are not significant draw cards. Many former 'mass cruisers', dissatisfied with the artificiality and rigidity of these floating palaces, are turning to different 'kinds' of cruising experiences. One such alternative to the 'typical' cruise experience is travel aboard cargo ships. These 'freighter cruises' are essentially scheduled container vessels that have made available space for a limited number of passengers.

Freighters are one of the lifelines of the world economy; they acquire, transport and deliver a wide range of cargo across a global network of shipping routes, but of the 29,000 large ocean-going ships in the world, only about 1% carry both passengers and cargo. Freighters operate on tight schedules and, fundamentally, are not designed to accommodate tourist interest or demand. They are guided by where the cargo, not the passenger, needs to be. In terms of entertainment, there is not much social life, particularly on the freighters that take up to a maximum of 12 passengers. Nevertheless, although standardised, pre-packaged cruise holidays are still the norm, agencies booking freighter cruises are now appearing throughout the world, offering a variety of itineraries to match consumer interests.

The freighter market is a special niche serving those travellers with the time and temperament to sail long itineraries – anywhere from a few weeks to several months – and who don't mind doing without the amenities on a modern cruise ship. Passengers tend to be retired and well-travelled, but owing to trip length and usual lack of an on-board physician (on ships carrying fewer than 12 passengers), many vessels set an upper limit on passengers' ages – typically around 80 though sometimes as young as 75 – and passengers are required to present a doctor's note saying they are fit for this kind of travel.

So what motivates a tourist to choose a freighter over a luxury cruise ship, and where does this interest come from? Maybe it is bragging rights they are after – the trip nobody they know has taken. Or maybe cities at sea just remind them of cities at home, which is what they are looking to escape from. Passenger-carrying container vessels and their various itineraries appear to be in a favourable position from an overall consumer demand standpoint for many reasons. Preliminary investigations (Szarycz) into consumers' perceptions of freighter travel seems to indicate that travellers are actively seeking out freighters to experience 'real' ocean travel, providing novelty, adventure, challenge and insight about local peoples and their cultures in 'authentic' versus "over-touristified' (see Tucker, 2002) ports of call. Freighters also provide an ideal environment within which passengers can 'escape' from mass cruise tourism and the 'over-touristification' and commercialisation of the cruise experience.

Although it is very difficult to accurately define the size or scope of this market, all indicators show that it is expanding in size and becoming increasingly popular. In the United Kingdom, Germany and USA, an ever-increasing range of shipping companies are accepting paying passengers on board their ships. With rapidly growing numbers, this subculture may eventually represent a financially viable market in its own right.

Questions for consideration

1. How might an intermediary (such as a outbound tour operator) market these kinds of experiences?

2. It is noted above that the market segments targeted with these types of cruises are a 'subculture'. To what extent do you think other forms of cruise travel might be considered a subculture?

The UNWTO (WTO, 2003a) reports that the most rapid growth of cruise tourism was during the 1990s, when demand for international cruise trips grew at a cumulative rate of 7.9%, compared to 4.3% for overall world demand for international travel. Miller and Grazer (2002) note that the North American market alone has experienced an annual growth rate of over 8% since 1980. The CLIA, an organisation that represents companies that cover nearly all of the United States residents' marketable (i.e. influenced through advertising and promotion) cruise itineraries, claim that cruise tourism will be worth some US$85 billion in 2007 (Douglas & Douglas, 2004). The popularity of cruising certainly explains these increases, but the actual size of ships, which has increased as well, can also explain this growth. As Wood (2000) notes, economies of scale (i.e. larger ships = greater economies of scale) have translated into substantial profits for many cruise companies:

> These huge vessels have spawned a new category 'Post-Panama' ships because they are too big to go through the Panama Canal. Upping the ante further, Cunard has announced its project Queen Mary, to build the 'grandest and largest liner ever built' (Goodman, 1998). Further, in the wings although some doubt whether they will ever be realised are long-standing plans for the 250,000 ton America World City, which with three skyscraper-type towers on an aircraft carrier-style hull, would carry 6,200 passengers. (Wood, 2000: 349)

Traveltrade.com monitors the construction of new ships and reported several 'newbuilds' in January 2005 that feature massive size and berths (Table 5.2). Many of these newbuilds are of such a size that it raises issues of port suitability. Many are simply so big that manoeuvrability becomes difficult in ports that may have previously played host to numerous smaller ships. With bigger ships, however, cruise companies can reduce the cost per berth and, at the same time, maximise revenue per berth, but for some destinations larger ships may mean fewer ports of call. Some ports therefore have few options available to them when it comes to ensuring cruise lines continue to call. One is to ensure that harbour re-developments are adequate. Barbados, for example, has in recent years upgraded its harbour area, including the dredging of the inner basin to accommodate larger passenger and cargo ships (see www.barbadosport.com). However, with renewed dredging comes the problem of what to do with the material that is brought to the surface. In some instances, land reclamation can be undertaken, as in Barbados, or may simply be stored, as in the case of Tampa Bay, Florida. Even the regular maintenance of ship channels, often requiring dredging, is a challenge and a significant cost, both financially and in terms of adequate disposal of dredge materials.

Table 5.2 Cruise line newbuilds

Cruise line	Ship name	Tonnage	Berths	Launch date
NCL America	Pride of America	72,000	2000	June 2005
Carnival	Carnival Liberty	110,000	2974	July 2005
Princess	Crown Princess	113,000	3100	May 2006
Costa	Costa Concordia	112,000	3000	June 2006
Royal Caribbean	Freedom of the Sea	158,000	3600	April 2006

Source: From www.traveltrade.com (accessed 12 January 2005)

THE CRUISE TOURISM 'PRODUCT': EVOLUTION

Weaver (2005) applies the notion of 'McDonaldization' (where the core principles of production can be found in the elements of efficiency, calculability, predictability, control and the "irrationality of rationality') to the cruise experience. Interestingly, Weaver (2005) argues that the cruise experience exhibits characteristics that are more reminiscent of post-Fordist principles of customisation of experiences. Put another way, where Coles (2004a) notes the post-Fordist tendencies of resort production/consumption relationship in the Caribbean, Weaver (2005) points out that cruise companies recognise the shifts in their target markets worldwide:

> Indeed, some cruiseship companies own ships that are built to serve certain national markets. One owned by P&O Cruises, Oriana, can accommodate over 1,800 tourists and caters mostly to the British market. On board, the breakfast buffet features a number of popular British "delicacies": kippers, smoked haddock, and baked beans. That afternoon tea is served on board reinforces the ship's British extraction (Scull, 1996). The dinner menu features quite essentially British fare such as steak and kidney pie and roast beef. (Weaver, 2005: 359)

This represents, in many ways, the maturation of the cruise industry such that the common view of homogenous ships offering banal on-board experiences to similar groups of passengers may perhaps be outdated. Notwithstanding the question of whether cruise tourism is sold as a product or an experience (see Chapter 8 for a more detailed discussion of the complexity of the transport 'product'), in the past decade, cruise companies have certainly diversified the list and range of components that comprise the package or experience on offer, thus resulting in luxury-branded cruise options as well as budget cruises with fewer amenities. Wood (2004b) notes that three broad markets can be identified based on these variations of amenities: mass, niche and luxury. Ward (2005) notes that the current 'mass market product' that characterises modern cruise tourism can be divided into three categories (cf. Box 5.2):

1. The 'budget' segment: characterised by small companies (which may be operationally smaller but may also be tied to other distribution chains such as agencies or wholesalers) and the use of older ships.

2. The 'contemporary' segment: manifested in most major cruise lines (e.g. Carnival, Royal Caribbean, Disney, Star Cruises) and, as such, target 'the hedonistic orientation of the aging baby boomers'. Ships in use are generally larger and allow for significant economies of scale, and are thus akin to being described as 'floating destinations' or 'floating resorts' (Teye & Leclerc, 1998: 155) because of the wide variety of amenities, attractions and services on board.

3. The 'premium' segment: not unlike the contemporary segment in terms of operations (e.g. ships and perhaps price), but more or less targeted toward upscale markets (and perhaps older demographics) and may feature specific destinations in line with the demands of these markets [see Box 5.2].

Classifying cruise line companies and the products on offer is difficult because of the wide range of products, destinations (ports of call), market access and size of ships. The Berlitz Guide (www.berlitzpublishing.com; or internet search: Berlitz Guide), however, offers a classification system that is recognised as an industry standard. In examining variables such as the ship itself, the accommodation provided, the cuisine, the service and the programme (itinerary plus on-board activities), Berlitz assigns a star rating system to cruises, and not necessarily to actual ships or companies. The star system is not unlike standard accommodation ranking systems such as those used in North America and Europe: 5 star plus represents the highest rating, with 1 star the lowest. Related to this is Berlitz's lifestyle classification, which encompasses the following groups:

1. Standard: generally in the lower proportion of the price scale for cruises.

2. Premium: the middle band of the price scale, featuring better amenities such as accommodation and restaurants.

3. Luxury: the upper echelon of the price scale where amenities are considered to be excellent.

Niche markets

Beyond the mass market cruise profile is a more niche orientation in some of the product offerings. Wood (2004b) also outlines several of these, including multiple-mast ships (under sail), specialty destinations (e.g. Antarctica, the Arctic [see Marsh & Staple, 1995]), and other adventure-related products. Cartwright and Baird (1999) also identify 'freighter cruises' (sometimes referred to as merchant marine cruises; see Box 5.1), which use cargo vessels outfitted with a small number of passenger cabins, and 'river cruises' such as those along the Nile, the Danube and the Rhine, which generally do not feature accommodation on board.

The niche market segment, comprised of substantially more and often luxurious product components, is comparatively smaller and may perhaps not benefit from substantial economies of scale, but can be profitable nonetheless. The luxury cruise market is broadly characterised by higher prices as well as premium on-board products and services. To some extent, there is a blurring of this market with the 'premium' segment in Wood's (2004b) characterisation as many 'mass market' cruise ships may offer superior accommodations or additional hospitality at an extra cost. As a result, some of the larger cruise operations feature tiered service levels available on single ships. Each tier is targeted towards a distinct market that carries differing demand elasticities of price and service levels. Star Cruises in

BOX 5.2 *The World*: Luxury cruise ship or mobile residence?

One example of the luxury cruise segment is *The World*, introduced by ResidenSea in 2002 (Sometimes referred to as *The World of ResidenSea*). More of a permanent 'apartment complex' (Wood, 2004b: 136) than a cruise ship, it is marketed as floating resort complex where both permanent and temporary accommodation is available, thus calling into question whether the permanent residents on board are indeed 'tourists' (see Chapter 1). Services include, for example, a medical centre, concierge service, an art gallery and theatre, eight options for dining, a night club, a tennis court and conference rooms (see www.aboardtheworld.com). Apartment options, for purchase, include studios (beginning at US$725,000), one-bedroom units (starting at US$1,247,500) to three-bedroom units (starting at US$4,170,000). The target market to which *The World* is directed is clearly upscale, but the experience on offer is one that the company asserts is unlike other forms of cruise tourism. From the website, the company suggests: 'Because *The World* is our home – one of our holiday homes – it is a far cry from what people might imagine. It should be clear that *The World* differs from a cruise ship. Our travelers prefer an alternative to ordinary cruising or yachting.'

Questions for Consideration

1. To what extent could it be argued that *The World* is not, in fact, a cruise ship, but merely a permanent residence and/or second home?

2. Given the itinerary for *The World* (available on the website noted above), what similarities and differences are apparent when comparing to the itinerary/networks for major cruise lines such as, for example, Carnival?

India, for example, launched a specialised luxury cruise offering from Mumbai to Goa in 2005, designed specifically to target the domestic Indian market by offering distinct Indian features on board, including restaurants and brief stops to historic landmarks. Interestingly, and not generally in keeping with the typical profile of luxury cruise products, Star Cruises is marketing its product to multiple market segments, including middle-class and upper-class passengers as well as families (Hindustan Times, 2005).

A more recent 'step' along the evolutionary line of cruise provision is the close mirroring of some cruise operations to no frills air travel. easyCruise, launched in March 2005, operates a 'low-frills' service, with itineraries that are flexible and on-board facilities generally limited to one or two bars, a café, a shop and a gym. Compare this with some mass cruise experiences, which may feature multiple instances of each type of amenity. The target market for this kind of operation is, according to the company, 'independently minded' people in their 20s, 30s and 40s. Virgin also announced in October 2005 that it also plans to enter the cruise market.

TRANSNATIONAL CORPORATE REALITIES OF GLOBAL CRUISE LINES

The effect of globalisation on the status of multinational corporations such as those involved in cruise tourism has been noted (e.g. Wood, 2000, 2004a, 2004b). Wood (2004b) argues that cruise ships are themselves 'deterritorialised' on the basis of their transient routes and itineraries, but also with respect to ownership and substantive control of operations. The on-board experience is deterritorialised because, according to Wood (2004b: 140),

> [t]he mass-market cruise ship experience is deliberately manufactured to be detached from the region in which it cruises... Port information sessions are almost always exclusively about what things to buy and which shops to spend your money in. Entertainment is 'Las Vegas' style. Food and drink on board do not reflect the cruise region. By and large, generally with only minor exceptions, the regional culture where cruising takes places is almost invisible in terms of what is experienced onboard the mass market ships.

Further, ships are deterritorialised because of the multinational labour force on board. For most ships, the division of labour not only follows traditional descriptions (officers, staff, crew), but also the ethnicity within each is remarkable, as Wood (2000: 353) notes:

> On most vessels there is a clear ethnic cast to this hierarchy: Norwegian or Italian officers, Western European and North American staff (mainly the cruise director's, hotel management, entertainment, and business staff), and Asian, Caribbean, and Eastern European crew. While Eastern Europeans (with a significant proportion coming from areas of ethnic conflict) appear to occupy a somewhat ambiguous role in this hierarchy, there tends to be a quite sharp line between the first two groups and the third. Among 'the most common mistakes made', a cruiseship employment guide informs its intended audience of North Americans and Europeans, is 'applying for a job that is traditionally held by a Filipino or by someone from other "third world" countries' (Landon 1997: 48).

That cruise companies operate in multiple markets and service multiple international destinations is appropriate given that their companies themselves, and the organisational behaviour, are often situated in multiple jurisdictions (e.g. country of ship's registration, sales base, labour force). Unlike airlines, there is often little impetus to have a 'flag cruise company', and thus many companies have little formal association with any one single country. Not surprisingly, cruise companies are often incorporated in countries where corporate tax is minimal, if present at all (Wood, 2004b), or have relatively lenient employment laws and regulations (Carnival, for example, is registered in Panama, and Royal Caribbean is registered in Liberia, although both companies have offices in the United States). Unlike the airline industry, under the open-registry, or flag-of-convenience, structure of the global cruise industry, ships registered in countries where employment, health and safety laws are either absent or unchecked can hire crews at low wages (below minimum wage in the country of their home office [Wood, 2000]) and fewer benefits. As Wood (2004b) points out: 'The flag of convenience regime is at the heart of the cruise industry's economic competitiveness.' Cruise companies argue that such regimes allow for the negotiation of wage and compensation packages that are truly global, thus reflecting the global nature of the operation or enterprise, yet some, including Wood (2000: 351), recognise this as the manifestation of the very policies of globalisation as espoused by institutions such as the International Monetary Fund and the World Bank.

It is probably more accurate to speak of transnational corporate structures as there is considerable amount of horizontal international movement between large and small corporate enterprises (Table 5.3). Smaller companies and fleets are regularly purchased by larger companies, assets are sold or traded and networks, at which one time may have been concentrated within certain geographic area, are expanded. The nature of cruise company operations (largely in international waters) often means that national laws do not apply, and international regulations and governance are scarce. This becomes particularly significant in the context of waste dumping, which is discussed later in the chapter.

Table 5.3 Main companies/cruise lines (as at January 2002)

Group/cruise company	Number of ships	Gross tonnage	Berths
Carnival	46	2,323,110	61,597
RCC	23	1,841,244	47,184
Star Cruises Group	19	905,254	25,210
P&O Princess	18	1,083,062	27,420

Source: Adapted from WTO (2003a)

Interestingly, worldwide demand is being satisfied by a small number of companies. As Ebersold (2004: 1) notes, almost two-thirds of the global berth capacity is in the hands of ten companies. According to the WTO (2003a), four corporate groups of companies (multiple brands under a single corporate umbrella) hold nearly 80% of the world's supply of cruise berths: Carnival, Royal Caribbean Cruises, P&O Princess and Star Cruises. With market access and penetration being quite important, one assumption is that cruise companies are generally in competition with other companies. While this is true, most are, more accurately, in competition with ground tourist resorts as cruise ships are structured and operated to be not dissimilar to all-inclusive resorts: many contain casinos, shopping malls, libraries, meeting rooms, discos and nightclubs, jogging tracks, saunas, gyms, movies theatres, bars, a variety of restaurants (some with 24-hour service), beauty salons and a host of other activities designed to entertain guests. These larger ships, often classified as VLCV, then, are not only a means of transport *to* a destination, but are in many ways *the* destination itself. As well, all-inclusive cruise tourism and all-inclusive resort (or enclave) tourism feature heavy integration among all aspects of the production cycle. For example, not unlike enclave tourism, cruise companies will offer packages that feature integration and dependencies with other commercial operations, including airlines, hotels and various activities at certain ports of call. Such integration is also a feature of ground tourist resort products (Cartwright & Baird, 1999; Laws, 1997).

PROFILING CRUISE TOURISTS

While the issue of demand for various modes of transport was assessed in Chapter 2, there are several aspects that need to be considered when exploring the level of demand for cruise experiences. As cruise tourism is one of the fastest growing forms of leisure-based travel (WTO, 2003a), accurate forecasts are important for a variety of reasons:

1. Knowledge of future demand enables corporations to make more profitable decisions to be made, such as routing, port planning, alliances, ship development (and decommissioning) and corporate structure.

2. Coastal and island destinations that court cruise tourism are better able to plan for future (re)development of ports and their associated activities.

3. Horizontal corporate entities that are allied with cruise corporations will be able to act strategically in terms of the benefits and potential pitfalls of entering into alliances with these companies.

The most logical indicator of demand for cruise vacations would be the proportion of cruise vacations taken against the overall demand for leisure trips within a certain market. However, there are a number of problems with this:

1. Demand for leisure travel within a source market can be varied, and thus include international, national and local travel, thus complicating which market is of prime importance for assessing demand; with cruise lines offering multiple products, demand will need to be forecasted for each of these separate segments (i.e. budget travellers, luxury travellers, educational cruises, etc.).

2. Because cruise lines operate out of a base port (i.e. Miami for most major Caribbean lines), the cost of transport to and from Miami for those markets outside of the city itself must be built into the demand model. For instance, the relative cost of transport to and

from Miami for tourists on the northern part of the Eastern Seaboard (e.g. the Carolinas) must be factored into the demand for cruise vacations from this segment (especially given that many airlines that enter into arrangements to supply cruise companies with passengers through alliances often themselves embark upon marketing in the same market segments that encourage long-haul or short-haul travel that rivals cruise vacations).

Relating to demand, the motivation for cruise travel is complex, and thus not unlike the motivation for leisure or pleasure travel in general. Given that cruise tourism is a rapidly expanding segment of international tourism, considerable effort has been devoted to profiling potential cruise tourists, and indeed learning about those who already partake in this form of holiday or vacation. Indeed, Wood (2000: 349) notes that 'destinational cruising', where the ports of call often play a key role in potential customers' decisions, demonstrates how transport can assist with the promotion of destinations. This represents somewhat of a paradox: while cruise companies are certainly interested in generating as much on-board sales as possible, they are inextricably bound to offer itineraries that entice people to take a cruise. Not surprisingly, then, many cruise companies are quite interested in learning more about their markets (see, for example, Table 5.4).

Table 5.4 Selected demographic characteristics of Caribbean cruise tourists

		Percentage
Country of residence	United States	82.3
	Canada	8.5
	United Kingdom	5.5
	Others	3.7
Age	Under 25 years	17.6
	26–35 years	13.1
	36–45 years	18.7
	46–55 years	21.2
	56–65 years	16.7
	66 years and older	12.8
Annual income	Less than $25,000	6.7
(US$)	$25,000–$40,000	16
	$40,000–$60,000	17.3
	$60,000–$75,000	13.9
	$75,000–$100,000	22.6
	Over $100,000	23.4
Marital status	Single	17.2
	Married	76.3
	Widow(er)	3.2
	Divorced	3.3

Source: Adapted from WTO (2003a) based on data from Florida–Caribbean Cruise Association (2001)

Note: Not all figures total 100% due to rounding.

Market segmentation (often in relation to understanding motivation) in cruise tourism has been undertaken in numerous studies both by private associations and companies as well as scholars with a general interest in marketing and tourism. The CLIA (1995–2001), for example, identifies six segments of the United States and Canada cruise market:

- 'Restless baby boomers' – eager for novel experiences; represents approximately 33% of the total cruise market, with nearly 1 in 6 being first-time cruisers (WTO, 2003a).
- 'Baby boomer enthusiasts' – familiar with the potential cruise experience and use it as a break from routine; represents approximately 20% of the total cruise market with nearly half being first-timers.
- 'Lovers of luxury' – demand for high-cost, high-quality cruise experiences and opt for more specialised cruise operators; as expected, they only make up 14% of the total cruise market.
- 'Demanding buyers' – search for the optimal price-quality ratios, so discounts and specials are taken advantage of; represent 16% of the total cruise market; high degree of repeat customers (80%).
- 'Explorers' – high degree of travel experience, and thus perhaps more interested in the destinations along the itinerary; represent 11% of the market.
- 'Boat enthusiasts' – important repeat market with strong familiarity of cruise experience; nearly 90% are repeat buyers, but only represents approximately 6% of the total cruise market.

The WTO (2003a) has identified several niche markets for cruise tourism. The younger segments of the baby boomer population in several Western countries, for example, may actively search for modestly priced vacation experiences that can include the family. Thus, many cruise companies are encouraging children to partake in cruises. Not only does this capture the market for families, but it also introduces younger generations to the cruise experience, and thus companies are hopeful that they can eventually capitalise on this market as repeat customers. In Europe, one of the largest growing niche markets for cruising is the senior citizens market, primarily because of the strong purchasing power they hold. Another market that may hold considerable potential is one that focuses specifically on the conference and incentive market. MICE tourism is a rapidly growing segment worldwide, with many destinations actively involved in the promotion of their facilities and logistical/organisational arrangements to large corporations or organisations. Many newer ocean vessels feature the necessary conveniences and attributes, such as large halls with state-of-the-art audio/visual facilities, dining options and on-board accommodation.

Another niche market segment is one which is closely allied with adventure cruises. Tauck Tours (based in the United States), for example, was one of the first to offer regular chartered exploration cruises to the Antarctic. Such cruises are often hosted by experts and scientists. This segment is small, but it often commands a high price point for the services on offer (ranging from 'hard adventure' to 'soft adventure', Ryan & Trauer, 2003) because of the unique environments that are included on the itineraries. A related form is the utilisation of specialist ships for cruising. Not unlike heritage railways and their renewed popularity (see Chapter 4), sailing ships, designed to replicate historic ships, offer experiences not unrelated to those programmed under the wider characterisation of heritage tourism (e.g. museums). Further some specialist ships (e.g. Windjammer cruises) allow for passenger participation in the operation of the vessel itself.

Qu and Ping (1999: 241, Table 2), in their study of 330 residents of Hong Kong, found that key motivators for cruising included 'escape from normal life', 'social gathering', and 'beautiful environment and scenery'. Duman and Mattila (2005) examined several affective factors associated with the perceived value of cruise tourism to passengers. Using a mail panel in the United States to identify previous cruise passengers, their sample of 1500 residents found that hedonistic elements of cruising generating the strongest perceptions of value. This reinforces the perception held by some that cruise ships are often seen as resorts at sea, and thus demonstrates why cruise tourism is often in direct competition with enclave tourism.

Cartwright and Baird (1999: 94–101) surveyed 100 'cruisers' and found that the typical cruise profile consisted of seven elements that demonstrated the propensity to undertake a cruise:

- *Partygoer*: takes a cruise for the purposes of 'activities and nightlife' on board a ship and be 'less concerned with the higher density often associated with high-activity, intensive-destination oriented vessels' (Cartwright & Baird, 1999: 97).
- *Relaxer*: generally less concerned with ports of call, and thus may elect to spend minimal amounts of time in port partaking in activities or shopping; more content with lounging; this group is 'likely to be less comfortable with high-density vessels where private space may be at a premium' (Cartwright & Baird, 1999: 97).
- *Enthusiast*: high repeat visitation as this group typifies the type of cruiser who may be 'addicted' to cruising. Cartwright and Baird (1999) found that UK cruise travellers were more likely to stick with one company brand, which underlines the importance that cruise companies put on encouraging repeat visitation. Cruise enthusiasts are likely to be 'very knowledgeable about the industry and the cruise companies. The companies use this enthusiasm through their various loyalty schemes to ensure that the cruisers feel a part of the family...' (Cartwright & Baird, 1999: 97).
- *Stroller*: this group encompasses individuals for whom formalities (such as dressing for dinner on board) are important. It is likely, however, that few individuals would travel for the purpose of dressing up or experiencing formalities, but Cartwright and Baird (1999) point out that the characteristics of this group can be found in other groups. To

a large extent, this group represents a means by which passengers escape routine (see also Krippendorf, 1987).

- *Seeker:* this group represents individuals for whom cruises are perhaps not ideal. A seeker is one who is interested in learning about the destination visited, including cultures and history. To a large extent, 'mass' cruise ship itineraries do not typically allow for large amounts of time in ports of call, largely because it is in their interest to have passengers spend money on board rather than in duty-free areas in ports of call. Seekers, then, are likely disproportionately small compared to the other types listed above.

- *Explorer:* the explorer category is not dissimilar to the seeker category in that numerically they are small. However, there is evidence to suggest that many companies are catering for this particular grouping, who are interested in visiting places 'few have seen before' (Cartwright & Baird, 1999: 100). It is this grouping that is targeted with such cruises as those featuring Antarctica, for example.

- *Dipper:* this group represents the vast majorities of cruisers, and is characterised by Cartwright and Baird (1999: 100) as follows:

  > A little bit of culture, a small taste of a different lifestyle and then back to the welcoming cultural bubble of the ship. The dipper is truly the 'been there, seen that, experience this and bought the T shirt' person. The dipper will be, in the main, satisfied with an explanatory leaflet, a briefing from the port lecturer and a tour of the highlights.

EVALUATING THE ECONOMIC IMPACT OF CRUISE TOURISM

One of the most pertinent questions concerning cruise tourism is the overall economic impact of these activities. Dwyer and Forsyth (1998: 394) pose several questions that speak to these concerns:

> To what extent does foreign ownership of cruiseships limit the economic impacts of this form of tourism? Will these impacts be concentrated in stopover port areas or distributed nationally? What are the potential net benefits (as compared with economic impacts) of cruise tourism regionally and nationally?

Cruise passengers will normally spend on a variety of elements associated with their cruise experience, including air transport to and from the cruise base (where the ship is either stationed or where the cruise begins), food on board the ship itself (assuming that main meals are not covered in the overall cost of the cruise itself), and in port when a ship makes a temporary stop (Dwyer & Forsyth, 1998). Added to this is the money spent by the tourists before they leave for their holiday. For example, expenditures may be lodged on items needed for the trip itself, including clothing, toiletries, safety items (including medication) and assorted accessories.

Passenger expenditures exist within a delicate balance with the marine-related charges and fees levied against cruise companies. As a result, some will elect to utilise ports where such charges are comparatively small, thus reducing their operating costs. By extension, some ports may actively chase cruise business under the assumption that ships bring in tourists eager to spend money on souvenirs or other items. Finally, crew expenditures can include staff for ship maintenance, marketing of cruise offers and products in key market areas, and various taxes levied. In short, there are a variety of elements that need to be fully considered when examining the economic impact of cruise tourism, however many of these are difficult to calculate so a complete picture of that impact is often difficult, if not impossible, to ascertain. In many ways, this is not at all dissimilar to the challenges in measuring the economic impacts of tourism in general (e.g. Wagner, 1997)

What is perhaps most critical is the extent to which individual ports of call benefit from cruise tourism. Not all destinations benefit directly from cruise tourism and the expenditures of cruise tourists. Many cruise ships put into port for a limited time, often only a few hours (Dwyer & Forsythe, 1998). Thus, the window of opportunity for cruise tourists to generate a significantly beneficial economic impact on the destination is quite small, unlike those tourists who stay at least one night (often more) where expenditures are less concentrated and may be more significant. Further, the vast majority of cruise expenditures take place within duty-free areas or areas specifically controlled by local port authorities (Douglas & Douglas, 2004). Thus, the sale of goods (and prior distribution) may be highly regulated, and may only benefit certain retailers. Some port calls may include, however, short excursions outside of the port area, but because of the limited timeframe their economic impacts may be limited.

Overall, it is still not entirely clear whether cruise tourism is economically beneficial to many destinations. In the Bahamas, much like many other island states in the Caribbean, the number of cruise tourists as a proportion of all tourists is significant, but an important study by Wilkinson (1999) illuminated the very real financial impact of cruise tourists when compared to stayover tourists (i.e. those who stay at least one night). Wilkinson (1999) utilised real dollar expenditure data (calculated using the relative purchasing power of overall cruise tourist expenditures) and found that, between 1980 and 1996, visitor expenditures of cruise tourists declined almost 44%. Wilkinson (1999: 269) concluded that 'cruise visitors have little potential economic impact (in either current or real terms) on the average Bahamian compared to stayover visitors, even though the ratio between stayover and cruise real expenditures dropped from 17.5: 1 in 1980 to 13.2: 1 in 1996'. This is critical given that Wilkinson demonstrates that the average expenditure per person in port has risen. Wilkinson's study raises a important issue, and not just in the context of the Caribbean. Policy-makers and government officials need to carefully consider the real economic gain from cruise tourism not on its own, but rather in the context of whether ground FITs would be more lucrative for local business and the overall economy.

FUNCTIONAL MARINE TRANSPORT

The above section primarily considered those types of marine transport that acted, more or less, as both attractions and the mode of transport. However, there are examples of marine transport in which their function is more practical as opposed to operating for the purpose of providing entertainment or leisure value. Douglas and Douglas (2001: 331) refer to this kind of usage as 'line voyage', where the primary purpose is to travel from point A to point B.

Numerous examples of line voyages exist, although the geographic scope is somewhat more limited than it was in, for example, the 19th century when they were used for the transport of migrants from Europe to many areas around the world. Between the north and south islands of New Zealand several companies offer ferry services. One such company, the Interislander, offers a vehicle service where passengers board the vessel in their vehicle at Picton in the south island and disembark in Wellington in the North Island. This complements many touring holiday itineraries as it lessens the need to make separate arrangements for both islands. Other ferry services operate within the Mediterranean and provide a means by which regular labour mobility is facilitated between separate islands or an island and some mainland countries such as Italy and Greece. In all these cases, functional marine transport exists within a blurry distinction of transport-for-tourism and transport-and-tourism (Chapter 2), as both tourists and non-tourists can make use of these services.

In many areas of the world, watercraft are used as a functional means by which other tourism experiences are provided. Whale watching is an excellent example of this, although one of the key considerations is the impact on whales by the presence of marine vessels (e.g. Beach & Weinrich, 1989; Blane & Jaakson, 1995). Worldwide, concerns have been raised over the rapid over-crowding of near-shore waterways, which have significant impacts on whales and other aquatic species (Figure 5.1). Although visitor numbers to whale watch operations have been increasing, the concern is that increased interaction between boats and whales can have negative consequences for whale breeding and general welfare. In Boston harbour, the use of bigger and faster boats has certainly allowed more tourists, in greater comfort, to view whales, but accidents in which some whales are injured by these watercraft occur. Whale welfare concerns are not new. Japanese tour operators were concerned back in 1996 about growing numbers of tourists in boats and the impact this was having on local whale populations. In fact, some Japanese fishermen have turned to whale watching as an alternative economic activity in the summer, when available fishing stocks were traditionally low. In Iceland, it is hoped that promoting whale watching to domestic and foreign tourists may go some way to shifting attitudes towards the hunting of various species (Sykes, 1997) given international concerns over the Icelandic whaling industry. In September 1998, a boat carrying tourists from a whale watching expedition off the

Figure 5.1 Crowding at the attraction? A touring vessel in Milford Sound, New Zealand approaches a group of sea lions resting on shore

coast of Massachusetts struck a large Minke whale; tourists watched in horror as the body came to the surface in the wake of the boat (Bayles, 1998). The increase in popularity of whale watching means that consideration must be given to more appropriate forms of transport operations associated with the activity, including:

- the distance from boat to whales, with attention devoted to monitoring of chasing;
- the length of the trip/excursion (i.e. the length of time the mammals are exposed to watercraft);
- the most appropriate number of watercraft that can operate in an area (in effect, the carrying capacity);
- the type of watercraft used, and whether it is considered to be the most appropriate (i.e. number of engines, sound proofing);
- the behaviour of the boat in terms of direction, in order to minimise potential collisions and hardship caused to whales.

One answer to the problem of vessel proximity and presence is to completely remove the vessel from the experience. 'Wings over Whales' is a New Zealand-based company that offers flights for passengers to acquire a unique view of whales in their natural habitat. As their website (www.whales.co.nz) proclaims, passengers can observe several whales species, as well as other natural and man-made local features.

FERRY SERVICES

Also to be considered under the cruise product, but somewhat outside the traditional seg-mentation of cruise experiences based on amenities, is the role of hybrid cruise provision within multi-modal itineraries. Ferry systems are common in several parts of the world and offer transport for either practical reasons (i.e. to remote areas not easily accessible on land or air) or for other reasons (i.e. in order to allow people to sightsee whilst in tran-sit on a ferry). Intra-destination ferries, such as the Brisbane CityCat service, serve as alternative means of mobility within a destination. In other cases, ferry services are criti-cal for maintaining accessibility to more remote destinations. Along the north coast of British Columbia, Canada, the March 2006 sinking (in which two people lost their lives) of the *Queen of the North* (one of two ferries operated by BC Ferries to remote destina-tions along the coast) has meant that access to areas such as Prince Rupert has been cut in half (CBC, 2006).

Høyer (2000) notes that, in Norway, many Norwegians cross the Skagerak by ferry for leisure purposes. Preliminary data from Statistics Norway (2005) confirms the massive growth in marine transport for 2004. Car ferries can be used by FITs on self-directed hol-idays. One example is the Irish ferries systems offering ferry services to and from Britain under the slogan 'The Low Fares Ferry Company!' (http://www.irishferries.com/). In these examples, there is a marked departure from what is traditionally viewed as cruise tourism, but each feature amenities and distribution mechanisms that are not entirely dis-similar to more 'traditional' forms of cruising.

Challenges facing the ferry industry

Dunlop (2002) notes several challenges facing the ferry industry, particularly in Europe:

1. Safety issues will continue to be paramount after the Estonia disaster in the Baltic Sea in September 1994; since then regulations have been introduced governing stability and loadings, the cost of compliance to which, according to Dunlop (2002: 115), can be mil-lions of pounds.

2. The creation of fixed land links can render some ferry operations financially unviable. After the Channel Tunnel opened, prices for ferry services across the Channel fell but some operations were closed permanently (Dunlop, 2002).

3. The price of fuel is also a consideration for the financial viability of ferry services, but because, as a mode of transport, these would compete with other modes where fuel costs are also increasing, this is perhaps less of a challenge.

4. The biggest challenge, according to Dunlop (2002: 115–116), is loss of duty-free sales with the introduction of common markets across Europe:

Perhaps even more bizarre is the position of a ship that trades from the UK into two separate Continental countries. P&O's Pride of Bilbao trades to both Spain and France. In its shop one area displays items that can only be sold when the ship is on the Spanish route and another area displays goods that can only be sold when the ship is on the French route. No wonder the passengers are baffled.

Another issue that has arisen from ferry services is the environmental impact. In parts of Finland (especially Tallin Bay; see Andersson & Eklund, 1999) and New Zealand (the Foveaux Strait), concerns over wave damage from ferry crossings have been raised. In the New Zealand case, environmentalists claim that wave action is destroying sensitive underwater environments and contributing to erosion onshore. Other concerns with ferry operations include the dredging of harbour areas at ferry ports, pollution from ferries themselves (and thus not unlike cruise ships), and the safety of smaller vessels operating near larger, high-speed ferries. In Hawai'i, ferry services compete with inter-island air connections. Hawai'i Superferry Inc. (www.Hawaiisuperferry.com) recently announced high-speed ferry services between Kaua'i, O'ahu, and Mau'i beginning in 2007, with full daily services to the Big Island (Hawai'i) in 2009. According to the website:

> For half the price of flying, families can travel interisland with the convenience of their cars. School groups, hula halau, canoe clubs, and cowboys can travel to events with their vans, equipment, canoes, and horses in their trailers. Neighbor island farmers can deliver fresh produce and cattle to market daily. Hawai'i Superferry will soon be linking islands and connecting families ... economically, comfortably and with care for our environment.

In the early stages, however, the service has not been without its problems. In April 2006, state senators expressed concern over the lack of public input into the endeavour and have threatened to withhold public funds earmarked for harbour redevelopments (Star Bulletin, 2006). The battle for inter-island accessibility, however, is likely just beginning. Mesa Air Group Incorporated, responsible for the highly successful regional carrier Mesa Air in the continental United States, announced in March 2006 that it would launch a subsidiary airline (called 'go!') that would fly between Honolulu and airports on Kaua'i, Mau'i, and the Big Island for introductory fares of US$39 one way (Song, 2006). Compare this with the published fares (as of April 2006) on the Hawai'i Superferry website that show advanced, web-based fares of US$42 (US$52 during peak periods such as weekends) and it is clear that traditional 'fare wars' in Hawai'i have extended beyond single modes of transport.

PERSONAL WATER TRANSPORT

Outside of the formal aspect of tourism, it is important to identify where transport may fit in with leisure and recreation experiences as there may in fact be instances of cross-over (where a wide variety of recreationalists and tourists may participate in similar activities). Several examples of personal water transport are used in the context of leisure environments where factors such as safety, environmental sustainability and the quality of the experience are paramount:

1. Non-powered personal watercraft: Canoes are prime examples of non-powered personal watercraft currently used in a variety of leisure environments. In North America, recreational canoeing is common in seasonal cottage areas (see Box 3.1), where families may spend several weekends and perhaps one or two weeks a year on annual holiday leave. The British Canoe Union (www.bcu.org.uk), for example, indicates on its website: 'In an activity such as canoeing, safety and keeping people safe is all about risk assessment and minimising the risks involved at all levels of participation.' Canoeing, as with other forms of non-powered personal water craft, may cause comparatively fewer ecological impacts, but codes of conduct may also be in place in some areas that limit the potential for damage. For example, the presence of canoes can cause significant harm to nesting waterfowl. Due to the popularity of canoeing in some areas where canoes and their occupants must share the waterways with other recreational and non-recreational users, efforts are usually made to make people aware of the implications of actions.

2. Powered personal watercraft: This type is generally associated with motorised (or propelled) watercraft that can be used individually or to tow a rider behind using some other recreation device (such as an inner-tube, boogie board or waterskis). These types of watercraft can be dangerous to the operator due to the often high speeds involved, although many federal and local jurisdictions around the world have introduced mandatory operator certificates that are provided after short courses. In both Missouri and Pennsylvania, for example, a boating licence is not required, but operators of personal watercraft are required to obtain Boating Safety Education Certificate, which applies to personal watercraft (see www.boat-ed.com). Some concern over the impact of powered personal watercraft on waterfowl has been raised, and Burger and Leonard (2000) found that, because of their speed and agility, these craft can actually be more harmful than larger boats.

Regardless of the mode of power, codes of conduct, some of which are enforceable through legal means, can be found in many areas where outdoor water recreation activities are popular. For example, the New South Wales (Australia) personal watercraft code of conduct (http://www.maritime.nsw.gov.au/pwc.html) covers a significant array of issues, including operational elements (such as restricted zones), safety considerations and noise considerations. What is not mentioned, however, is whether certain areas, such as wildlife refuges, are de facto 'off limits' to operators, but local jurisdictions may require these areas to be clearly marked.

Personal watercraft can also be used as the mode of transport along specific trails. For example, in the Chesapeake Bay area in the United States (http://www.baygateways.net/watertrailtools.cfm), marine trails have been developed where recreational users are allowed to utilise personal watercraft for transport purposes. However, allowing these recreational pursuits means installing proper regulation and policy structures such that environmental damage, as well as social problems due to noise and perhaps trespassing, are managed. One of the problems this brings is the jurisdiction under which these trails may fall. In some cases, water trails may be contained within local or national parks, and thus their management may be comparatively easy, yet when these trails cross numerous jurisdictions, the management of recreation activity, and indeed the kinds of transport utilised (which may be a mix of terrestrial and marine transport options), trail-wide regulations become difficult (and the corollary to this is air transport emissions, which is explained in Chapter 9).

SUSTAINABLE MARINE TRANSPORT

Many of the environmental concerns over marine transport centre around the damage done to sensitive aquatic environments as a result of the presence of watercraft of varying sizes. Waste management on cruise ships is a concern for both cruise companies and the local jurisdiction in which they operate. They are a concern for the company because the handling of waste needs to be done in a manner such that the cost does not significantly impact upon the overall profitability of the operation (in other words, barring any social responsibility felt by the firm, if the cost of dumping waste is economically beneficial, it is likely to happen). Of course, some, if not most, companies wish to preserve the very environments in which they operate and thus act as responsible corporate citizens. On-board waste management is a concern for destinations, of course, because of the damage caused by pollution emanating in varying forms from cruise ships. The wider question, however, is one of monitoring. Johnson (2002) notes that the International Convention for the Prevention of Pollution from Ships (the 'MARPOL Protocol') has six annexes, of which four relate directly to ship waste, suggesting that is an important problem. Ocean Conservancy, an environmental NGO, has characterised ship pollution as 'unsolicited contributions', and can include:

1. Oil pollution resulting from groundings, collisions or the pumping of bilge water. Bilge water is a 'mixture of salt water and leaks from water cooling circuits, fuel, lubricating oil, drainage, from sedimentation tanks and particles of dirt and soot' (WTO, 2003a: 167). Cruise companies are generally required (or at the very least encouraged) to filter out impurities in bilge water before discharge.

2. Sewage, which is generally diluted with smaller amounts of water compared to sewage on land (largely because of limitations of space on a ship), and is thus more concentrated;

can carry bacteria and diseases which can affect aquatic wildlife and enter the local food chain.

3. Grey water, or waste water not from sewage sources (sinks, drains, showers, etc.), which can include 'fecal coliform, food waste, oil and grease, detergents, shampoos, cleaners, pesticides, heavy metals, and, on some vessels, medical and dental wastes' (Ocean Conservancy, 2002: 15).

4. Hazardous wastes can come from on-board photo processing chemicals, paints, solvents, printer cartridges, etc. Ocean Conservancy notes (2002: 16) that 'a typical cruise ship with 3,000 passengers and crew generates approximately 15 gallons of photo processing chemicals, one and a half gallons of PERC and other chemicals, and one and a half gallons of paint waste per day'.

5. Ballast water, which is often 'taken on' by some ships in order to balance the overall weight distribution of the vessel. Where this can become problematic is when a ship takes on water for this purpose in one area and releases it in another area, thus potentially introducing non-native aquatic species. As Ocean Conservancy (2002: 3) outlined, the legal implications of waste management for cruise operations are perhaps not as stringent as needed:

> Although cruise ships generate a tremendous amount of waste from the thousands of people on board, they are not subject to the same wastewater regulations that govern municipalities of comparable size. Under the Clean Water Act, cities must treat their wastes, limit the amount of pollution they discharge, and monitor and report on discharges from sewage treatment facilities. Yet cruise ships are not required to obtain Clean Water Act discharge permits, nor to monitor or report on their discharges. Gray water from on-board laundries, galleys, baths, and showers is essentially unregulated. And even where regulations are in place, enforcement is lax.

6. Solid waste: for 3000 passengers and crew, approximately 50 tons of solid waste is generated over a week-long cruise (Ocean Conservancy, 2002).

7. Air pollution is not normally thought of when discussing the environmental impact of cruise ships, but the reality is that diesel engines used to propel a large ship generate significant amounts of sulphur dioxide, nitrogen oxide and particulates.

8. Physical damage to aquatic ecosystems results from all of the above combined. This can include damage from anchors and the direct removal of habitats from dredging (in order to provide sub-surface 'space' for ship manoeuvres). In the Caribbean, for example, anchor damage has been known to be responsible for significant damage to coral reefs (Allen, 1992). In Tasmania, Ellis et al. (2005) developed a model that considered a range of variables (including boat length, draft, tonnage and propeller size) to predict the impact of turbulence from a ship on benthic marine habitats.

Local jurisdictions are increasingly putting tighter controls over cruise activities. In 2001, for examples, the state of Alaska became the first US state to impose pollution controls on cruise ships (Schulkin, 2002). Despite the tighter controls, infractions still occur. The Surfrider Foundation, a not-for-profit foundation, lists several instances of fines and infractions from the past decade:

- From 1993 to 1998, cruise ships were involved in 87 confirmed cases of illegal discharges of oil, garbage, and hazardous wastes into United States waters, and have paid more than $30 million in fines. Some of these cases involved multiple incidents of illegal dumping that numbered in the hundreds over the six-year period.
- In 2001, Royal Caribbean admitted in court it had installed special piping to bypass pollution control devices and pleaded guilty to dumping toxic chemicals. Royal Caribbean was levied fines and penalties totalling $33.5 million to settle dumping complaints that occurred between 1994 and 1998.
- In April 2002, Carnival Corporation pleaded guilty to falsifying records to cover up pollution by six ships over several years. They were assessed an $18 million fine and were placed on probation.
- In July 2002, Norwegian Cruise Lines paid a $1 million fine and agreed to pay $500,000 to environmental organizations in Florida for falsifying Coast Guard records regarding discharge of oily waste and hazardous waste into the ocean.
- In September 2002, a fired Carnival Cruise Lines executive filed a 'whistle-blower' lawsuit, alleging a host of environmental violations, including toxic chemical dumping.
- In October 2002, Carnival Corp. disclosed that officers from one of its ships had been subpoenaed to testify before a federal grand jury in Alaska regarding a 40,000-gallon wastewater release.
- In April 2003, a lawsuit filed by Bluewater Network, Environmental Law Foundation, San Diego Baykeeper and Surfrider Foundation against Carnival Corp., Princess Cruise Lines, Royal Caribbean, Holland America and others for illegal discharge of ballast water into shoreline waters was settled after the cruise lines agreed to pay $75,000 to research alternative ballast water management technologies. Carnival Corp. admitted to breaking the law. (http://www.surfrider.org/a-z/cruise.asp; accessed 18 October 2005)

Of course, the size and distribution of cruise activity needs to be considered. In Alaska, despite increasing concern from environmental groups, the proportion of pollution from cruise ships versus other ocean-going vessels and port-bound tugs is small (Crenson,

2001). In the Caribbean, where cruise tourism is more popular, concerns about environmental stability continue to grow as the number of ships and passengers either grows or remains constant. Ocean Conservancy (2002: 4) has outlined a series of recommendations for the United States cruise industry, although some of their recommendations could be applied in other jurisdictions:

- *Reducing and regulating cruise ship discharges to improve water quality*: Cruise ship discharges should be regulated under U.S. environmental laws just like similar sources of pollution. Consequently, Congress and the Environmental Protection Agency (EPA) should repeal the exemption of gray water discharges under the Clean Water Act and ban the discharge of untreated sewage from cruise ships in U.S. waters. In addition, treated sewage and gray water should be discharged only while the vessel is underway at a minimum of six knots speed and 12 miles from shore. No cruise ship discharges should be permitted within marine protected areas or other sensitive and important ocean habitats such as marine sanctuaries, refuges, or parks. Finally, the EPA should establish water quality standards and allow states to establish no-discharge zones to protect special ocean sites.
- *Improving monitoring and inspection*: Cruise ship wastes should be comprehensively monitored, sampled, and reported. Congress should increase U.S. Coast Guard funding for more aerial surveillance and surprise inspections, and the EPA's expertise should be used to ensure proper monitoring and testing of discharges and pollution control equipment. The data gathered should be made available to the public so that citizens can make informed choices about cruise ship operations in their communities.
- *Strengthening enforcement mechanisms*: The U.S. Justice and State Departments should take measures to ensure that cruise ships flying foreign flags – as all cruise ships in U.S. waters currently do – are not permitted by their governments to violate U.S. environmental laws. Penalties and fines for violations should be increased to effectively deter scofflaws. Moreover, passengers, crew, and the public should be encouraged to report violations through educational materials and rewards.
- *Improving air quality controls*: The EPA should issue regulations to reduce emissions from cruise ship smokestacks in U.S. waters, and cruise ships should be encouraged to use local electrical grids when in port to reduce emissions. The EPA and the Coast Guard should also work with states to develop air-sampling programs. To reduce air emissions from ships worldwide, the United States should ratify Annex vi of the MARPOL Convention [which addresses air pollution].
- *Developing education and training programs*: Cruise line companies should educate their passengers and crews on complying with U.S. and international anti-pollution laws, and develop 'green' training and education programs for onshore operators and guides. Portside waste reception facilities should be assessed, and where inadequate,

they should be improved to accommodate the large amount of trash generated by cruise ships.

- *Improving research and development*: All new cruise ships should be designed with the latest pollution control equipment to eliminate waste discharges into the marine environment. The cruise line industry should continue to research and develop state-of-the-art waste processing technologies and design and implement sampling programs to demonstrate that discharges are not harming the marine environment.

There are regulatory bodies that oversee activities such as cruise waste management systems. The IMO (a subset agency of the United Nations) has established two committees: the MEP and the Maritime Safety groups. Both oversee the regulatory environment within which cruise (and freight) traffic operate. As well, the ICCL promotes environmental awareness among its members. In recent years, the ICCL has worked towards establishing a series of waste management practices for ships. Revision 2 to Standard E–01–01 outlines many of these practices (ICCL, 2003):

1. Photo Processing, Including X-Ray Development Fluid Waste: Member lines have agreed to minimize the discharge of silver into the marine environment through the use of best available technology that will reduce the silver content of the waste stream below levels specified by prevailing regulations.

2. Dry-Cleaning Waste Fluids and Contaminated Materials: Member lines have agreed to prevent the discharge of chlorinated dry-cleaning fluids, sludge, contaminated filter materials and other dry-cleaning waste byproducts into the environment.

3. Print Shop Waste Fluids: Member lines have agreed to prevent the discharge of hazardous wastes from printing materials (inks) and cleaning chemicals into the environment.

4. Photo Copying and Laser Printer Cartridges: Member lines have agreed to initiate procedures so as to maximize the return of photo copying and laser printer cartridges for recycling. In any event, these cartridges will be landed ashore.

5. Unused and Outdated Pharmaceuticals: Member lines have agreed to ensure that unused and/or outdated pharmaceuticals are effectively and safely disposed of in accordance with legal and environmental requirements.

6. Fluorescent and Mercury Vapor Lamp Bulbs: Member lines have agreed to prevent the release of mercury into the environment from spent fluorescent and mercury vapor lamps by assuring proper recycling or by using other acceptable means of disposal.

7. Batteries: Member lines have agreed to prevent the discharge of spent batteries into the marine environment.

8. Bilge and Oily Water Residues: Member lines have agreed to meet or exceed the international requirements for removing oil from bilge and wastewater prior to discharge.

9. Glass, Cardboard, Aluminum and Steel Cans: Member lines have agreed to eliminate, to the maximum extent possible, the disposal of MARPOL Annex V wastes into the marine environment. This will be achieved through improved reuse and recycling opportunities. They have further agreed that no waste will be discharged into the marine environment unless it has been properly processed and can be discharged in accordance with MARPOL and other prevailing requirements.

10. Incinerator Ash: Member lines have agreed to reduce the production of incinerator ash by minimizing the generation of waste and maximising recycling opportunities.

11. Graywater: Member lines have agreed that graywater will be discharged only while the ship is underway and proceeding at a speed of not less than 6 knots; that graywater will not be discharged in port and will not be discharged within 4 nautical miles from shore or such other distance as agreed to with authorities having jurisdiction or provided for by local law except in an emergency, or where geographically limited. Member lines have further agreed that the discharge of graywater will comply with all applicable laws and regulations.

12. Blackwater: ICCL members have agreed that all blackwater will be processed through a Marine Sanitation Device (MSD), certified in accordance with U.S. or international regulations, prior to discharge. Discharge will take place only when the ship is more than 4 miles from shore and when the ship is traveling at a speed of not less than 6 knots.

Part of the problem with the management of cruise ship pollution or waste is the short-term economic forecasting undertaken by many destinations. Following on from some of the economic considerations of cruise tourism discussed earlier, it is not difficult to see that some destinations, such as those in the Caribbean, desire cruise tourism in some form for the foreign exchange that it brings. It also can be one of the more significant forms of tourism in some destinations, as access by other means (particular air) is difficult and expensive. Cruise tourism, then, and in some situations may represent the 'easiest' and economically logical form of tourism. Although Johnson (2002) calls for greater integration of policy and management between cruise companies and destinations in order to preserve local environments and thus escape setting goals that merely aim for short-term economic gain, this is often difficult in fragile economies where the planning for the long term is simply not feasible because of rapid shifts in existing economies and unforeseen externalities. The issue, then, is the price of sustainability. NGOs such as Ocean Conservancy undoubtedly have excellent suggestions for the management of waste and pollution from cruise ships, but part of the problem is the degree to which cruise companies serve destinations where alternative forms of tourism may be difficult to establish for a variety of reasons (e.g. initial development costs, foreign direct investment incentives, taxation and incentives, labour, market saturation due to nearby competition).

CHAPTER SUMMARY

Cruise tourism may be considered to be prevalent in a tourism context, but personal watercraft numbers have been growing (particularly in North America) and thus represent an important consideration of transport in recreation and leisure. Segmenting markets for cruise tourism is complex but the more common means include demand estimation, availability of transport alternatives or based on sub-type (such as 'budget' or 'luxury'). Assessing demand is equally complex and may depend on proximity to suitable source markets. Where these source markets exist outside of main ports, the factoring of additional transport (often manifested in cruise packages) needs to be considered. The economic impact of cruise tourism raises issues of adjusted or real dollar measurements of cruise activities in ports of call, and begs the question as to the real value of cruise tourism where other types may (or may not) achieve stronger social benefits. The environmental impact of cruise tourism is contentious, with many examples to found of both infractions and efforts to improve overall environmental responsibility.

Box 5.3 Case study – Corporate consolidation in the global cruise industry (with Adam Weaver)

There are several unique aspects of the global cruise industry that allow it to sit alongside other economic sectors (e.g. manufacturing and finance), thus demonstrating the extent to which global cruising for pleasure can be exceptionally profitable (Weaver & Duval, in press). The first is the massive amount of corporate consolidation that has taken place within the cruise industry since the 1980s, resulting in the creation of two substantial cruise companies: Carnival Corporation and Royal Caribbean Cruises Ltd. Together, they account for over 80% of total market share within the global cruise industry (Marti, 2005). Carnival Corporation, which owns Carnival Cruise Lines, acquired Holland American Line and P&O Princess Cruises in 1989 and 2003 respectively. In 2000, Carnival Corporation became the sole owner of Costa Cruises, an Italian-themed cruise line. Royal Caribbean Cruises Ltd, the company that owns Royal Caribbean International, acquired Celebrity Cruises in 1997. Efforts made by Royal Caribbean Cruises Ltd to merge with Princess in 2001 were thwarted by Carnival Corporation's successful takeover bid. The primary impetus behind these acquisitions and consolidation activities is the desire on the part of larger corporations to diversify. For example, each separate cruise line owned by Carnival Corporation intentionally serves a different market, and most acquisitions made by Carnival Corporation in the past decade have enabled it to serve specific markets previously untapped. The reasons large cruise conglomerates go through the process of acquiring other firms/companies is because acquisitions and mergers allow corporations to obtain less tangible assets, namely companies with reputable brand names. From a business standpoint, it is also seen to be very efficient in that it is often less expensive for a corporation to acquire an existing business than to start an entirely new product or service line itself.

Interestingly, in spite of the consolidation that has occurred within the global cruise industry, brand identities and ship names have often been preserved. For example, when Carnival Corporation acquired Holland America Line, ships within the Holland America fleet were not renamed. Initially, there were fears that Holland America would be 'Carnivalized' after the acquisition (Slater & Basch, 1989) because Carnival Cruise Lines markets its vessels as 'fun ships' and caters to consumers who enjoy a more festive environment on board. Holland America, however, actively markets to an older, more up-market clientele (Sarna & Hannafin, 2003). The reason Carnival has kept the Holland brand separate is primarily to retain existing market segments that are valuable and responsive to the brand itself.

As mentioned, the acquisition of different brands by a corporation may also be part of a strategy to serve different national markets. Some brands, for example, may only have value in certain national markets. A good example is when Carnival Corporation acquiring AIDA Cruises after the former consolidated with Princess Cruises in 2003. AIDA Cruises serves the German market, and the brand has been in existence since 1993. Carnival Corporation apparently plans to preserve the brand's current identity (Blenkey, 2005) in order to allow AIDA to preserve its market presence.

Questions for consideration

1. What variables might one company take into consideration when deciding whether to retain the brand name of a product/service produced by a company that it recently acquired?

2. To what extent could it be argued that such 'mega-mergers' are somewhat anti-competitive?

SELF-REVIEW QUESTIONS

1. What are the main forms of waste from cruise ships?

2. What are some of the more common cruise market segments?

3. Which areas have seen the biggest growth in cruise tourism?

ESSAY QUESTIONS

1. Write an essay that discusses why marine tourism, in general, may or may not be more likely to experience elasticity in demand among certain demographic segments.

2. Why could the argument be made that the environmental impacts of cruise tourism are more concentrated that land-based forms of tourism?

KEY SOURCES

Cartwright, R. and Baird, C. (1999) *The Development and Growth of the Cruise Industry.* Oxford: Butterworth-Heinemann.

This text is, in many ways, somewhat simplistic for university-level education, but it nonetheless offers a comprehensive overview of cruise ship operations, including pricing structures, markets and marketing, and itinerary construction. One criticism is the lack of acknowledgement of wider political or governmental influences.

Wood, R. (2000) Caribbean cruise tourism: Globalization at sea. *Annals of Tourism Research* 27 (2): 345–370.

Wood's article has acquired a certain status within the academic community in that it isolates regulatory and governmental considerations in the global cruise industry. Wood outlines how cruise tourism is effectively 'deterritorialised' in that it is manifested in global routes yet is based in countries where laws and governance are less than rigourous. A noteworthy angle of Wood's article is the nature of cruise employment and how this represents a true picture of globalisation of the industry.

Cruise Line International Association – www.cruising.org and International Council of Cruise Lines – www.iccl.org

CLIA and ICCL are large trade organisations representing the global cruise tourism industry. Both sites feature reports and recent facts/figures relating to the industry.

CHAPTER 6:

AIR TRANSPORT

LEARNING OBJECTIVES

After reading this chapter, you should be able to

1. Recognise the importance of air transport in global tourist flows.

2. Critically assess the extent to which air transport has contributed to tourism development both globally and in specific localities.

3. Appreciate the network structure of airline operations and how these relate to tourist flows.

4. Understand the nature of global airline alliances and the resulting marketing and operational considerations for tourism.

5. Identify and evaluate sustainable forms of air transport.

INTRODUCTION

Graham (1995) notes that the air transport industry has two discerning, but broad, characteristics: 1) returns are marginal on what is an extremely capital-intensive business; and 2) it is one of the most regulated transport industries, although this is slowly changing with the introduction of more liberalised air transport regimes worldwide. The economic uncertainty that follows global air transport may not be entirely unique (some rail operations, as discussed in Chapter 4, have experienced similar hardships), but it is followed closely in the international media because of the potential consequences for local and national economies if air services are culled due to negative financial performance. Immediately following the 11 September 2001 attacks in the United States, the United

States Federal government introduced the Air Transportation Safety and System Stabilization Act which provided some US$5billion in direct compensation and almost US$10billion in loan guarantees to assist carriers with the forecast slump in the air travel market (Guzhva & Pagiavlas, 2004). Unfortunately, the losses were too great. Almost four years later, almost to the day, Delta Air Lines and Northwest Airlines, two of the largest carriers in the United States, declared bankruptcy. According to both, one of the main reasons was the high cost of air turbine fuel (or jet fuel) prices, but some news reports also pointed to the fact that it is becoming increasingly difficult for many 'legacy carriers' (i.e. those airlines that have been operating for quite some time and operate under a model that is not necessarily 'low cost') to compete against LCCs or, perhaps more accurately, LCLF carriers. As a sign of turbulent times, Delta and Northwest were the third and fourth airlines to declare bankruptcy in the United States following the 11 September 2001 hijackings/terrorist attacks (the other two being United Airlines and US Airways), the immediate aftermath of which challenged airlines' operating profitability.

Without question, the operating environment for airlines in the early part of this century is contentious and fraught with uncontrollable externalities that are seemingly insurmountable. Examples that illustrate this are the rising cost of airline fuel and increased competition from other airlines (primarily LCLF carriers, as discussed in this chapter) with somewhat different business models. Curiously, some airlines have weathered recent world events without much trouble, and this is largely attributable to their existing financial health and ability to react to changes in the marketplace.

The chapter begins with an assessment of the role of aviation in tourism development. Following this, network structures (which should be read in conjunction with Chapter 3) are discussed. The nature of the LCC/LCLF 'revolution' is discussed next, followed by some consideration of the increase in mergers and alliances being formed worldwide. As is demonstrated, the issue of alliances is one in which the global map of mobility is demonstrated. The next section considers a very important aspect of global aviation operations, namely the nature of regulation and governance concerning, quite literally, who can fly where, how often, when and for what reason. These agreements effectively govern global mobility and thus play an enormous role in the ability of destinations to register themselves on potential tourists' perceptual 'radar screens'.

AIR TRANSPORT AND TOURIST FLOWS

Air transport is of interest to tourism development and tourist flows because it is a fundamental cog in the global tourism interaction sphere. The state of the global aviation sector is therefore important to understand as it can often single-handedly shape tourist flows where air access is part of the dominant network provision for accessibility and connectivity. This chapter, then, provides an overview of air services worldwide, with an emphasis on the nature of these services as they relate to tourism.

For the most part, two strands of services have emerged over the past few decades: FSAs (or network carriers, as they are sometimes called) and the value-based service option (often referred to as the LCC), which may often target the same markets as served by network carriers. There are other service offerings, however, including regional carriers and charter airlines, each of which can have different impacts on tourism flows (see, for example, Bieger & Wittmer, 2006) (Table 6.1). Charter airlines have been called the original LCCs (Buck & Lei, 2004) for they often opt for 'seat only' sales in conjunction with vertically-integrated alliances with tour operators. Papatheodorou (2002) notes that vertical integration is advantageous because the cost of marketing and promotion, commissions and commercial risk is generally borne by the tour operator, although in Europe as of late some charter operations have been replaced by LCC/LCLF carriers (Bieger & Wittmer, 2006).

Table 6.1 Air carrier typology and associated impact on travel flows

	Network carriers	*Regional airlines*	*LCC/LCLF airlines*	*Charter carriers*
Target market	Extensive coverage and attempt to increase market share; impact of formal alliances often critical in maintaining market share	Geographically smaller than network carriers, but often serves to feed larger networks; generally service geographically niche markets	Specific niche markets, perhaps where demand is price elastic	Tours and mass tourism flows to holiday resorts (e.g. UK to Mallorca).
Critical success factors	Market share	Share of niche market	Strong traffic growth that is almost self-generating	Relationships with tour operators; seasonal loadings
Network type	Generally hub-and-spoke	Several smaller hubs possible; some point-to-point routes	Generally point-to-point, but some smaller hubs can emerge	Generally point-to-point

Source: Adapted from Bieger and Wittmer (2006)

It is important to point out that the introduction of VBAs or LCCs (the terms are often used interchangeably, although they admittedly have slightly different meanings) has been significant in that it can explain much of the increased accessibility of some destinations worldwide (e.g. Forsyth, 2006). As outlined in Chapter 3, accessibility is one of the key factors in tourism development. As many destinations seek to target international markets, air transport has largely replaced other forms of long-distance transport (cruises or boats) and this has, in turn, literally opened up many destinations to multiple markets worldwide.

THE ROLE OF AVIATION IN TOURISM DEVELOPMENT

It is appropriate to begin with the potential role that aviation plays in tourism development. Several key points can raised at the outset:

1. The technological developments related to aircraft engineering, particularly with respect to efficiencies realised in power plant manufacturing and overall fuel efficiencies, but also in the area of improved aerodynamics, have resulted in overall reductions in operating costs. For the most part, this technological 'revolution' in air travel took place with the introduction of the jet engine technology, allowing aircraft to travel faster. This was a significant factor in explaining the increasing accessibility of some destinations to key markets. One particular example is the Caribbean, a region that has traditionally relied upon North American markets for the bulk of its tourist supply. With the introduction of jet-powered aircraft, many destinations in the Caribbean (particularly Hispaniola, Jamaica and Puerto Rico, but others as well) became more accessible to key urban markets in North America as a result of the reduced travel time. This was one factor that contributed to the expansion of Caribbean tourism in the 1950s and 1960s. Another example of the efficiencies brought about with the introduction of jet-engine technology was the ability to fly non-stop between two nodes in a network (with a good example being the introduction of non-stop services, for example, across the Pacific Ocean between Australia/New Zealand and the United States).

2. The ability of an airline (whether charter or RPT) to fly from one place to another is often carefully regulated by international bilateral agreements in air services (commonly called air service agreements). Although this is examined in more detail below, it is worthwhile to point out at this point that the political relationships between two or more countries (multilateral or plurilateral (Holloway, 2003), if more than two) can often dictate the flow of tourists between places, regardless of the physical ability of an airline to service a destination. In other words, an airport at a destination may be fully capable of servicing one or more international flights from an operations perspective, and a viable market may exist to justify a certain frequency of service, but the appropriate permissions and certifications at the government level must be in place before services are initiated.

This is an important consideration in that it is not always lack of demand that determines whether a carrier opts to run services on a particular network.

3. The expansion of air networks has meant the introduction of tourism to many non-Western countries. For example, Turton and Mutambirwa (1996) note that the government of Zimbabwe has needed to provide regular subsidies to Air Zimbabwe in order to ensure a regular flow (or as regular as possible) of tourists to the country (and certainly within the country). Not surprisingly, global economic conditions play an important role in the provision of flights to and from some destinations. Domestic and international travel in China has recently surged, largely a consequence of the country's strengthening economy. In 2004, some 28.5 million residents of China (PRC) travelled overseas (PATA, 2005). Data from 2003 indicate that the most popular destination was Hong Kong SAR, and, to meet this demand, China Airlines announced in October 2005 that it would be increasing flights frequency between Taipei and Hong Kong. Inbound international arrivals to China (PRC) have increased an average of almost 7% between 2000 and 2004 (PATA, 2005). In 2004, China (PRC) received almost 13 million international visitors by air, with the majority coming from Chinese Taipei, Japan, Korea and Hong Kong SAR (PATA, 2005) (Table 6.2), suggesting a largely regional market in terms of draw.

Table 6.2 Arrivals to China (PRC) by air, 2003 and 2004

	2003	*2004*	*Percent change*
The Americas	645,022	1,118,206	58
Europe	869,589	1,523,913	45.4
South Asia	71,058	122,733	30.6
Northeast Asia	5,265,475	7,653,418	16.5
Southeast Asia	872,127	1,575,039	54.6
Other Asia	157,795	293,600	54.2
Australia/New Zealand	151,013	246,418	52.6
South and Central Pacific	1176	1720	–0.1
Other areas	47,240	82,197	66.6
Total	8,080,495	12,617,244	19

Source: PATA (2005)

4. Air service expansion has also meant considerable expansion of domestic services in both developed and developing countries. In Mozambique, domestic passenger numbers have increased considerably in recent years, prompting the introduction of a new private

carrier, Air Corridor, serving Nampula to Maputo with regular low-fare service and nearly 100% loadings (Stevens, 2005). In New Zealand, Air New Zealand's introduction of its Express Class service, ostensibly a three-tier fare structure with the lowest fares being below NZ$100 has resulted in increases in domestic travel (New Zealand Herald, 2005).

NETWORK STRUCTURE: HUB-AND-SPOKE VERSUS POINT-TO-POINT/GRID NETWORKS

Airlines must make critical decisions as to where and how often they fly into and out of certain destinations. Much of this is based on demand, of course, but the cost of service also enters the equation. In other words, demand may be strong to serve particular origin–destination pairing (hereafter 'O–D pair'), but it may not be strong enough to warrant continuous service, taking into consideration seasonal fluctuations, economic fluctuations in both origin and destination, and the overall viability of tourism development at the destination. For example, an airline's market research may indicate that demand exists to service a particular O–D pair, but only at certain times of the week. Thus, in order to launch this service, the operations or scheduling department must decide which aircraft to use and, most importantly, what the aircraft will do when not serving that particular O–D pair. In other words, it may be entirely unprofitable for an airline, already sufficiently geared to meet its existing network, to purchase or lease new equipment to service a new O–D pair even if adequate demand exists. If, however, the new aircraft could be utilised efficiently in other routes during off-peak demand cycles on the new O–D pair, then it may be profitable. This goes some way to explaining decisions to reduce or eliminate services on some O–D pairs.

To some extent, the smart management of networks can help realise efficiencies of operation. As discussed in Chapter 3, networks are equated to potential accessibility and connectivity, which is a significant hurdle to ensuring that tourist flows are maintained and economically sustainable. As Bowen (2000: 27) notes: '…changes in the accessibility of a place within international airline networks can either enhance or detract from its ability to attract tourists'. What was not explored fully in Chapter 3, however, is the nature of networks and how they are involved in providing accessibility. There are three primary types of networks in passenger air transport:

1. Hub-and-spoke networks: this type of network involves a central hub into which traffic from outlying spokes feed the hub. Hub-and-spoke networks can exist in domestic networks (the United States also being an example as many airlines utilise hub operations at major US cities) as well as international networks (for example, Singapore Changi and London Heathrow are considered major international hubs) (Figure 6.1a). Since deregulation in the late 1970s in the United States, the use of hub-and-spoke networks has been increasingly popular (although Taneja (2003) points out that they were developed in the early 1950s).

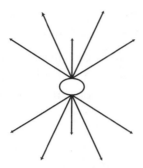

a) Hub-and-spoke network design

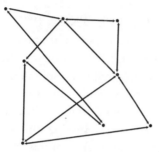

b) Grid network design

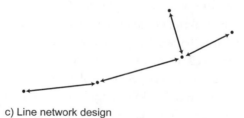

c) Line network design

Figure 6.1 Network options – air transport

Source: Adapted from Hanlon (1999)

2. Grid networks: generally a feature of domestic travel in some countries, particularly in larger countries such as the United States, this type of network has the advantage, according to Hanlon (1999: 84) such that 'they make it easier to achieve high rates of utilisation, of both aircraft and crews. Flights can be scheduled to operate on a number of different routes without backtracking, which helps to minimise the time for which aircraft are idle on the ground and which also means that crew stopovers and slippage can be minimised'

(Figure 6.1b). Fixed costs associated with this type of network are generally higher because of the cost of operating more links (Pels *et al.*, 2000).

3. Line networks: Hanlon (1999: 83) notes that a line network is realised if an aircraft 'sets out from its base airport and makes a number of intermediate stops en route through to its ultimate destination. The intermediate stops are made either to refuel or to pick up traffic' (Figure 6.1c).

THE HUB-AND-SPOKE CONCEPT

Air carriers, in recent years, have adopted hub-and-spoke networks for a variety of reasons. First, the nature of a hub-and-spoke network design (Figure 6.1a) is such that it allows for numerous permutations of O–D pairs served (Hanlon, 1999; see also Borenstein, 1989, Dresner & Windle, 1995, O'Kelly, 1998). In other words, when compared to a line network (Figure 6.1c), there is a substantial increase in the availability of O–D pairs that can be serviced (Hanlon, 1999). Nodes can be connected to only one hub (a single assignment model) or multiple hubs (a multiple assignment model) (Bryan & O'Kelly, 1999). As Taneja (2003: 39) notes, a hub-and-spoke system 'enabled an airline to increase frequency to thin markets by connecting the thin markets (the spokes) to a central airport (the hub)'. Hub-and-spoke systems became a popular way for airlines to manage their networks because the presence of a central hub meant the centring of operations. Passengers from the spokes would ultimately be routed at the hub, thus providing an increase in the potential market for the other spokes. The system meant airlines had the ability to service numerous markets, and is one of the reasons smaller aircraft (such as regional jets) are used on spokes and larger aircraft are used to move passengers from hubs to other hubs and internationally (Savage & Scott, 2004). American and United Airlines, for example, serve well over 100 smaller cities/markets using this system (Taneja, 2003). Some airports/cities now serve as critical hubs for specific airlines: American Airlines at Raleigh Durham and Nashville, Lufthansa at Frankfurt and Munich, and Singapore Airlines at Singapore. Dominance tends to be limited to the smaller regional or 'mid-size' urban centres. Thus, major international airports at London, Los Angeles or New York are not operated by airlines as market-capturing or network-enhancing hubs, rather, the network incorporates these as spokes in the wider network.

Second, the ability to market to wider segments must be considered when considering the power of a hub. Dresner and Windle (1995: 202), for example, found that hubbing by North American carriers resulted in increased passenger numbers across the Atlantic Ocean to Europe: 'A carrier with a strong hub at the home end of a trans-Atlantic route can expect to carry significantly more traffic than a carrier with a weak hub, all other things being equal.' Moreover, they (1995: 202) suggest: 'Combining regional and longer distance international traffic at a single hub airport would appear to be one policy that would facilitate hubbing and generate traffic.' Third, there may be significant cost efficiencies in routing traffic through a centralised hub airport in that the network can see profitable returns on operations if it is maintained and market demand is met. Aircraft utilisation efficiencies can also be realised in that inbound aircraft to a hub can be redeployed to other spokes. In the case of a line network, this is generally not as easily achieved, and aircraft can simply be relegated to flying back and forth between an O–D pair. This can result in considerable downtime on the ground between flights, which is an unprofitable exercise in that the aircraft, while not being used, is not earning revenue (Button, 2002).

In short, hubbing as a concept means that airlines have the opportunity to increase the utilisation of expensive aircraft. The reality, however, is not as simple as increased aircraft utilisation through hubbing. Doganis (2002) suggests that the economics of hubbing rests with the unit costs of flying short sector lengths between spokes and the hub: the higher frequency of short flights can be costlier because of additional aeronautical charges at airports through increased aircraft rotations (take-offs and landings) and the increased costs in handling passengers throughout the network must be considered.

What does hubbing mean for the passenger? In the positive, it means that the number of potential destinations served is exponentially greater. The hub concept can also reduce overall costs to passengers when compared to linear or point-to-point networks (Button, 2002). As discussed earlier, accessibility is critical in tourism development, and the ability of a carrier to integrate a destination with a series of other destinations utilising hubbing can be powerful in terms of marketing and the ability to secure positive market share. What it could also mean, however, and potentially as a negative consequence, is the dominance of one carrier at a particular hub. As Doganis (2002: 257) notes:

> Once airlines have established dominance at a hub through control of a disproportionate share of the flights offered and traffic uplifted, it is very difficult for another airline to set up a rival hub at the same airport, because it is unlikely to get enough runway slots to offer a similar range of destinations. In the United States the hub operator will also control most of the terminal gates. If the new entrant chooses to compete on just a few direct routes from the hub airport, it will face a competitive disadvantage *vis-à-vis* the hub airline in terms of ensuring adequate feed for its own services. Thence the notion of the 'fortress hub'.

The fortress hub can result in pricing that may not entirely favour the passenger at the hub airport, largely because there is little incentive to compete on price when the threat of competition is small (Borenstein, 1989). Although not a fortress hub in the strict sense of the definition, US Airways utilised Pittsburgh International Airport as a national hub for many years, but announced in late 2004 that it would no longer be doing so. The result was the introduction of new services from LCLF carriers and new services from existing network carriers, and fares for flights originating in Pittsburgh decreased dramatically (St Paul Pioneer Press, 2005).

Another problem highlighted by Doganis (2002) as well as Rietveld and Brons (2001) is that an efficient hubbing system must rely on precise frequencies of operations to and from the hub. If one flight is late there is a chance that other sectors and routes emanating from the hub can be negatively affected. In some cases, numerous flights may need to be held at the hub because an incoming flight from a spoke, carrying passengers en route to various other spokes via the hub, is delayed (Doganis, 2002). The power of hubs in creating increased accessibility (from a geographical perspective) across a particular network may, however, need to be carefully considered in the overall convenience of forcing passengers to transit through often congested airports. As Button (2002: 182) indicates, managing congestion is an exercise in economics:

> The issue is not about whether there should be no congestion at all, it would simply be wasteful of airline resources and airport capacity if congestion was zero, but rather of what is an optimal level of congestion. In economic terms, an optimal level of congestion is derived at that point where the benefits of an additional user just balance with the costs that the user imposes on the system (including those on other users). In the case of many transportation infrastructures, such as airports, the pricing system is not used to allocate resources but rather is used as a revenue-collecting device. As a result, it is argued, there will be excessive use of the infrastructure because users do not allow for the effects of their actions on other users.

Button goes on to note that the optimal scheduling of hub operations is generally a balance between the costs borne by the airline and by the passengers. The result is that scheduling through hubs is often done in 'banks'. These banks may result in periods of increased congestion at hub airports, but according to Button (2002: 183), they also mean lower fares and an increase in choices for services/routes as passengers can change aircraft at the hub and be on their way relatively quickly, or what Button (2002: 183) refers to as the 'convenient concentration of connecting services'.

Not all airlines operate a hub-and-spoke network. Southwest Airlines, for example, largely operates as a point-to-point network operator, and does so quite profitably. One question remains: When is an airline to adopt one network type over another? O'Kelly (1998: 176) helps answer this:

> Point-to-point systems have an advantage in short-haul market pairs with a dense level of demand, and work well provided the carrier does not try to offer service between all pairs of places. Hub-and-spoke systems in contrast seem to be the ideal solution (from the carrier's viewpoint) whenever the flows can be channeled through convenient switching points (such as Chicago or Atlanta).

In more recent years, the plethora of what have come to be known as 'sixth-freedom carriers' (e.g. Emirates, Etihad, Singapore Airlines) has meant substantial international point-to-point services being developed with less reliance on the hub. These carriers offer competitive fares over traditional legacy carriers with strong international networks, and their interest is primarily in shuttling passengers from major city to major city.

THE LCC/LCLF 'REVOLUTION'?

If recent worldwide press (but predominantly in Europe) is any indication, LCCs or LCLF carriers (which are sometimes even called simply 'no frills') seem to have limitless expansion possibilities. Francis *et al.* (2004: 508) explain this as follows:

> With the spread of deregulation of airline markets worldwide, low-cost carriers have begun to emerge in countries as diverse as Canada, Brazil, South Africa, Slovakia, Australia and New Zealand. There is little doubt that the growth in low-cost travel is the result of an innovative business model that has successfully reduced air fares to a point where they are often cheaper than surface transport alternatives (Doganis, 2001; Caves & Gosling, 1999; Barrett, 2000). Competitive price advantage is a key factor behind the low-cost carriers continuing to experience growth post-September 11, in stark contrast to many of the traditional scheduled carriers (Goodrich, 2002).

Traditional FSAs (or what are sometimes called 'network carriers' as they have armed themselves with expansive networks for maximum coverage and, thus, market share) have differentiated themselves on the basis of service and networks. Thus, an FSA may offer various classes of service (e.g. economy class, business class and first class, or any combination of the three) and serve major hub or international airports. In fact, the strategy that generally drove most FSAs was one of convenience and service, and thus many of the 'traditional' FSAs, or network carriers, boast enormous grid or hub-and-spoke networks with high levels of connectivity. A passenger on board an FSA could expect full meals (sometimes two if the sector length was long enough) and often free beverages. Often, alcohol is provided free on international flights. Other amenities provided include pillows, blankets, hygiene kits (including a toothbrush, toothpaste, socks; and these kits are often much more substantial in business and first class), complimentary newspapers and access to personnel at either the origin or destination to help with further travel arrangements.

Contrast this to a 'typical' LCC/LCLF (hereafter LCC) airline: services such as those listed above are reduced, if not completely withdrawn. Some aspect of service may still be emphasised, but this is more generally along the lines of non-aeronautical means of service provision, such as providing access to destinations not normally covered by the FSAs. Price, however, is the driving message in marketing and advertising (hence the designation of the VBA, and forms the basis of the service provision of these types of carriers. Some of the more common attributes by which LCCs are identified include:

1. *Cost control.* This is perhaps the single most effective means by which an LCC will compete with network carriers or FSA (Francis *et al.*, 2004). Profit is realised by cutting costs.

161

By keeping costs low, LCCs are generally in a position to turn higher profits or compete strongly along routes dominated by one or more FSA. Cost control encompasses a number of measures that can more or less be attributed as a means by which efficiencies are utilised. Costs are kept under control in a number of ways. One of the most common is the outright homogenisation of the fleet. A carrier such as Ryanair or easyJet, for example, may elect to utilise only Boeing 737 aircraft, thus enabling commonalities of crew training and rostering. B737s are extremely common (and thus financially successful for Boeing) and many LCCs utilise older aircraft that may be ex-lease from FSAs, and thus acquired at an attractive price. As well, this may mean that maintenance costs are kept low because only mechanics who can work on these type of aircraft are needed, although it should be pointed out that some LCCs (as well as FSAs) may elect to contract out maintenance procedures in a bid to save costs rather than keep permanent mechanics and service personnel on the payroll. It is, however, not entirely uncommon for an LCC to begin operations with new aircraft. Holloway (2003) notes that US LCC JetBlue initiated services with new Airbus A320 aircraft because of the aircraft's reputation for reliability and low maintenance costs. Another means by which costs are kept low is the almost constant utilisation of the aircraft. As aircraft are expensive and a significant part of the operating cost of an airline, an aircraft that is idle or parked at an airport waiting for the next flight is not earning revenue. As most LCCs tend to lease (or 'wet lease', meaning cockpit crew are contracted as well) aircraft, the cost of the lease applies whether the aircraft is flying or not. Thus, an LCC will endeavour to utilise an aircraft as much as possible such that it is able to maximise revenue generation.

One way to ensure maximum 'up time' in operations is to minimise the turn-around time at airports. It is not unusual, therefore, for LCCs (particularly in Europe) to have incredibly quick turn around times (some as short as 30 minutes) (Doganis, 2001). As Holloway (2003) cautions, however, the utilisation of aircraft may not necessarily help to control or reduce costs, but it does serve to minimise resource waste. Costs within the passenger cabin are also reduced as much as possible on LCCs, with the most common being the absence of free meals and most beverages. Most LCCs adopt what is termed a 'buy on board' policy, where passengers are offered snacks or sandwiches at a cost. Some beverages, such as tea and coffee, may continue to be offered free, but these are generally loss leaders in that the airline hopes that a biscuit or other snack item is purchased (perhaps at a substantial markup) to accompany the free beverage. More 'drastic' measures of cost control can occur. In 2005, for example, Ryanair removed the seat pockets from seats in order to save time and money in cleaning.

2. *Routing.* Like FSAs, LCCs generally do not rely upon any single model of network design. In many regional situations, such as the European Community, many LCCs opt to fly linear networks. Linear networks tend to allow for quick turnaround times (thus not needing to wait for other feeder aircraft from other spokes) and may help to serve a par-

ticular market pair with great frequency (see Box 6.1). Reynolds-Feighan (2001) examined the networks of LCCs in the United States and found that, rather than utilise hubs as a means to transfer passengers to other services, LCCs used instead nodes within their smaller networks as entry and exit points. Overall, Reynolds-Feighan (2001) noted the network density and degree of connectedness is smaller when compared to FSAs.

3. *Use of secondary airports.* The usage cost (e.g. aeronautical charges) at larger airports tends to restrict LCCs to regional airports, often at the expense of convenience for some passengers. LCCs will utilise secondary airports (some of which, such as London Stansted, have traffic growth rates such that they can be considered anything but a 'regional' airport) and thus incur lower aeronautical fees. Ryanair, for example, utilises Frankfurt Hahn airport, located approximately 120 km from Frankfurt itself, and Barcelona Girona, which is approximately 100 km from the city of Barcelona. Travel to and from cities like these to outlying airports is generally borne by the passenger (but provided, or at least organised, by the carrier), which raises the question of the actual savings in transport costs if this additional cost is factored in (Prideaux, 2000a, see also Chapter 2). Hall (2005: 241) notes that a French court decision in 2003 to stop Ryanair flights to Strasbourg (mounted as part of a legal challenge by Brit Air over subsidies paid to Ryanair by the Strasbourg Chamber of Commerce as an incentive to operate and thus generate tourist flows) could have a negative impact on accessibility for Britons owning second homes in France (although the airline did initiate flights to Baden-Baden, some 40 km outside of Strasbourg, following the court action).

4. *Single-class service.* It is not uncommon for an LCC to offer a single class of service (usually economy). Quite often, the seat pitch (which is the distance between a seat back and the seat back in front of it) is smaller than FSAs; it is not uncommon to find seat pitches of 32 inches, and sometimes even 30 inches. However, if one were to apply a cost-benefit analysis of smaller seat pitches, as most LCCs run on shorter routes passengers may be forgiving of less overall comfort if the price paid for the service is favoured. And in relation to seating, some LCCs may elect not to have pre-seating available, thus resulting in a first-on-board-first-selected seating arrangement. An added advantage of operating with a single class of service is that aircraft across the fleet are generally interchangeable, which is another example of efficient resource utilisation.

5. *Distribution channels.* Ryanair was one of the first LCCs to utilise call centres almost exclusively for a significant portion of its ticket sales (although its distribution channel in its early days still relied on travel agents to some extent). This served to minimise the cost of paying out commissions to travel agents on sales volumes, but it also allowed the airline to form direct relationships with its customers (Calder, 2002). In recent years, the internet has generally supplanted call centres for many airlines (not just LCCs), although LCCs generally embrace internet bookings as a means of controlling distribution costs (see also Box 7.1).

6. *No frequent flyer programme.* Most LCCs will neither operate their own, nor subscribe to others', frequent flyer programmes. These can be expensive to maintain and monitor, and thus generally do not figure into the 'low cost' model of the airline. There are, however, some exceptions. JetBlue in the United States, for example, offers TrueBlue points, which are earned on the basis of the length of flight (and when a passenger reaches 100 points on JetBlue, they are offered a free round-trip flight to any destination to which the airline flies):

- SHORT (2 pts): Flights from JFK to Buffalo, NY.
- MEDIUM (4 pts): Flights from Rochester, NY to Ft. Lauderdale, FL or from JFK to New Orleans, LA.
- LONG (6 pts): Flights from JFK to Oakland, CA or Burlington, VT to Long Beach, CA. (www.jetblue.com; accessed 2 November 2005)

In the Pacific region, Virgin Blue, Pacific Blue and Polynesian Blue reward passengers with points towards what they call the 'next generation' of loyalty programmes. In additional to teaming with a credit card provider, the airline's Velocity programme has partnered with several operations that have traditionally avoided linkages with other major loyalty programmes: Emirates, Virgin Airlines and Europcar.

BLURRY DISTINCTIONS BETWEEN LCCS AND FSAS

Despite what may seem to be clear differences between LCCs and FSAs, the question of what defines a 'typical' LCC airline was, at one time, quite easy to answer. Since 2002/2003, however, this delineation has become increasingly blurry. Part of this has to do with the economic realities facing legacy or FSAs following the 11 September 2001 attacks in the United States, but it also represents global economic realities as more and more aviation environments are deregulated and liberalised in terms of access. As a result, what used to differentiate an LCC from an FSA is now less clear. For one, as distinct as some of the features are that distinguish LCCs from FSA or network carriers, there have been recent changes to the industry that have brought about changes in FSA cost management structures that have led to service offerings that have more in common with traditional LCC carriers. In other words, at times it is difficult to identify a true full service carrier today because the nature of the product or service is changing and has become more and more like the typical LCC of the mid- to late 1990s. As Francis *et al.* (2004: 508) point out: 'Some of the major airlines have responded by lowering prices, simplifying their price structure and improving internet sales facilities.' For example, some FSAs have become somewhat truncated and serve only very selective routes where demand is strong. One way this is achieved is the decommissioning of certain routes structures, thus these traditional network carriers have networks that are less connected and thus not as accessible. As well, the price structures of airfares available from traditional carriers have changed to compete with LCCs. Indeed, Vowles (2000) found that the presence of low fare carriers in the United States had a statistically significant impact (in favour of the passenger) on air fares at hub airports.

Another means by which FSAs have sought to reframe their business strategy is to utilise a subsidiary or franchise airline to serve the shorter routes and effectively feed the hubs of the parent carrier (and example being the establishment of GO, a subsidiary of British Airways) (Pender, 1999). This serves two main purposes. First, it allows an existing carrier to compete in a particular market where its existing structure and operations profile may preclude it from doing so. Second, it protects the brand name of the parent enterprise should the LCC subsidiary face future financial problems (Pender, 1999; se also Holloway, 2003).

Cabin service among FSAs is also starting to closely mirror that of LCCs. Many FSAs have adopted a 'buy on board' approach to food items and services, particularly on domestic routes. In some cases, food services have been almost completely eliminated in favour of providing tea/coffee and a biscuit. In an effort to offset the cost of rising fuel, Air Canada announced in October 2005 that, on short-haul flights, the use of pillows and blankets will incur a charge (Airwise News, 2005a).

Table 6.3 outlines some of the similarities (and differences) between LCCs and FSAs. In some cases, it can be argued that there are few conceptual differences between the operating strategies of each, but what may be different is how these strategies are put in to practice or operationalised. For example, LCCs often state that where passengers are connected to another flight operated by the same airline, there is no guarantee that the second flight will be held for them if their initial flight is delayed. A passenger on Ryanair may purchase a ticket from Dublin to Luton and then another ticket from Luton to Milan (this is because Ryanair, like many other LCCs, will not issue a ticket from Dublin to Milan connecting at Luton). If the flight from Dublin to Luton is delayed for any reason, Ryanair may not necessarily guarantee that the flight from Luton to Milan will be held, even if there is more than one passenger on the Dublin–Luton flight destined for Milan. LCCs will do this because it introduces streamlined efficiencies into the system, even though some commentators claim it is at the expense of customer service. The airline will claim that its ability to offer low fares will come at a cost to convenience on some occasions, and thus cannot guarantee such interlining without impacting on fares. Contrast this, to some extent, with a traditional network carrier operating domestic flights as part of a wider network. In some situations, the Luton–Milan flight may be held for a specific length of time in order to capture late inbound Dublin–Luton passengers. Failing to do so may mean the airline, through its own policies, may be responsible for accommodating those late arriving passengers (either overnight or on a later flight).

Table 6.3 Similarities and differences in LCCs and FSAs

Product attributes	LCC	FSA
Branding	Generally limited to branding exercises associated with promoting low fare levels and resulting benefits to passengers (thus, advertising may feature pricing over other elements)	Generally extends to the brand of the airline as a service provider, but may also feature fare specials and, more recently, any overt fare structures introduced to compete with LCCs
Fare structure	Perhaps less complicated than an FSA, but yield management is still utilised	Moving towards a less complex model of fare structures as presented to the public (e.g. tiered based on permissible changes); yield management utilised
Distribution channels	Preference is online and direct sales	Increasing movement towards online and direct sales in order to reduce commissions paid to third-party channels (e.g. travel agents)
Check-in	Often utilises e-tickets as a cost-saving measure	Domestic operations of some carriers may utilise e-ticketing, but international travel or interlining (e.g. multiple carriers on one itinerary) may require paper tickets/coupons
Airport relationships	Secondary airports prevalent in order to keep aeronautical charges low	Focus still on major airports, although LCC subsidiaries of major carriers may opt to utilise secondary airports
Connections and connectivity	Primarily linear or point-to-point networks, with smaller hubs sometimes present	Hub-and-spoke connectivity models still present, but the main feature here is the ability to interline as a result of using major airports; membership to global alliances (and sometimes smaller alliance agreements) permits expansion of network

Product attributes	LCC	FSA
Class of service	Generally one class, but in some cases business class seating and (limited) amenities provided (e.g. Freedom Air in New Zealand)	Largely based on at least two classes of service (business and economy), but quite often first class service is offered on international or oceanic flights
Inflight service	Buy on board programmes; leather seats on some carriers (e.g. JetBlue in the United States)	Oceanic flights tend to offer full meal service(s), but some domestic services may be limited to complimentary tea/coffee/water with a light snack; improved seating, especially in business class (where the move toward 'lie flat' seating has been rapid in the past few years); buy on board programmes slowly being introduced
Utilisation of aircraft	High	Longer routes may mean different measures of utilisation; some domestic routes feature relatively high utilisation
Turnaround time	Fairly quick and efficient	Can often be just as quick, but may be hindered by scheduling that may not necessarily require quick turnarounds
Frequent flyer programmes	Becoming more common	Very common, and often linked with global programmes such as Star Alliance, OneWorld or Skyteam
Seating features	Often very dense, with 32 inch or 30 inch seat pitches common; some do not have pre-assigned seating	Varies by route: international routes may feature as much as 34 inches of seat pitch, while domestic services may offer less; pre-assigned seating dominates

Product attributes	LCC	FSA
Operational considerations	Expansion of service offerings to include ancillary products/ services such as accommodations and rental cars (and often part of branding initiatives)	Ancillary products/services remain, but also package deals with accommodation, rental cars becoming common

Source: Based on O'Connell and Williams (2005)

Using Table 6.3 as a reference point, the true differences between LCCs and FSAs are perhaps not as great as they were perhaps even five years ago. As discussed above, FSAs are emulating operational procedures (such as simplified fare structures, no frills service) that were once strictly within the operating domain of LCCs. As well, some LCCs have adopted service levels and procedures (e.g. frequent flyer programmes, comfortable seating) that were once limited to FSAs. The result is that even the comparison of LCCs versus FSAs is problematic in 2005, and will perhaps be increasingly blurry throughout the remainder of the decade.

BOX 6.1 Macau SAR and LCCs: Positive correlations between transport provision and tourism expansion (by Simon Rowe)

Macau is an SAR of the PRC with a total population of around 448,500 residents. Macau's tourism is based around its gambling industry which, when combined with general tourism, accounts for 40% of GDP. From July 2004, Macau has become a destination for several LCCs, such as Malaysia-based Air Asia and the Singapore Airlines' LCC subsidiary Tiger Airways. With the vast majority of Macau's tourists coming from Taiwan, China and Southeast Asia (DSEC, 2007), these LCCs play an important role in providing access and, consequently, the future of Macau as a tourism destination.

In July 2004, Air Asia was the first LCC to service Macau, and it now provides 7 scheduled flights per week (14 from December 2005) from Kuala Lumpur and 14 from Bangkok (21 from December 2005). Tiger Airlines began its scheduled daily service from Singapore to Macau in September 2004 and have subsequently added a daily flight from Manila effective from October 2005. Macau's national carrier, Air Macau, also services Bangkok and Manila.

As with many destinations where tourism is a dominant form of export earnings, Macau has been affected by externalities such as 11 September 2001, the bombings in Bali, and SARS. Table 6.4 shows the large reduction in visitor arrivals by air into Macau after 2002, possibly a consequence of the Bali bombings. It is interesting to note that, although arrivals by air were significantly reduced, total visitor arrivals still increased slightly. In 2004 when the two major LCCs began flying to Macau, visitor arrivals by air increased by 24% from 2003.

Macau is an attractive base for LCCs because of relatively smaller aeronautical charges at the main airport and its desirability as a tourism destination. For these reasons, two new Macau-based LCCs are planned to be launched in 2006. MEAS is planning to introduce a new LCC in May 2006. Golden Dragon Airlines is another Macau-based LCC being launched in 2006, with plans to fly to China, Vietnam and Laos. As a result, the ratio of air arrivals to total arrivals can also be expected to increase, as air travel becomes more affordable to Asian consumers. In effect, the continued growth in overall arrivals could spawn increased competition among LCCs servicing the destination.

Table 6.4 Arrivals to Macau SAR

Year	Total visitor arrivals (000's)	Visitor arrivals by air (000's)
2000	9162	834.2
2001	10,279	861.8
2002	11,531	905.4
2003	11,888	654.6
2004	16,673	861.8

Source: Adapted from (http://www.pata.org/patasite/fileadmin/docs/speeches_presentations/050311_Koldowski__PATA_ITB_Final.pdf) and (http://www.dsec.gov.mo/english/indicator/e_tur_indicator_2.html)

A major question here is whether the large increase in LCCs servicing Macau is sustainable. Australia's Virgin Blue was considering establishing a hub in Macau, but decided against it in May 2005. Although they did not provide an official reason for their decision, it is possible that they had concerns that the market was going to become saturated and overly competitive, leading to massive price wars and a subsequent loss of profitability. Price wars would, of course, be good news for the consumers, but also for the tourism industry of Macau, which will benefit greatly from the influx of tourists. If the increasing number of LCCs in Macau can be sustained without pricing each other out of the market, the future of tourism in Macau is very bright indeed.

Questions for consideration

1. What other regions or smaller countries have a strong reliance upon LCCs for the majority of their passenger airlift? Are there similar concerns regarding market saturation in that the total airlift is in the hands of one or two airlines (i.e. a duopoly or monopoly)?

2. To what extent could it be argued that tourism development in Macau is heavily dependent on the LCC model of airline operations?

What do LCCs mean for passengers? The reality is that many FSAs have lost business because of the price advantage, brought on by cost savings, introduced by LCCs. Writing in *The Times*, columnist Cath Urquhart (2005) noted that 'Ryanair has succeeded brilliantly in re-educating travellers as to what a short flight really is: something that is about as comfortable and basic as a bus journey.' This re-education effort has apparently been successful in some regions. In the UK, for example, one in three flights are operated by an LCC (This Is Money, 2005).

MERGERS AND ALLIANCES

Airline alliances have become extraordinarily common in the tight aviation market of the 21st century. Alliances can be global in scope (Table 6.6) or local with a focus on shared services. In many respect, alliances represent 'shortcuts' to otherwise out-of-reach (for aeropolitical reasons discussed below) markets. Indeed, the President and Chief Executive Officer of KLM, Leo van Wijk, once remarked that 'Alliances are … a reasoned response to an antiquated regulatory system … [They] permit indirect access to restricted markets' (Staniland, 1998). Tretheway and Oum (1992) have sketched out three types of airline alliances. These are:

- *Type I: a route-by-route alliance*. Such an alliance may involve coordination between two or more airlines on a specific route (i.e. reduction of 'wingtip' flights, where two flights from competing airlines leave from an origin bound for the same destination) or a combination of routes.
- *Type II: commercial alliance*. This type of alliance generally involves the 'coordination of flight schedules and ground handling, joint use of ground facilities, shared frequent flyer programs, code sharing, block seat sales, and joint advertising and promotion'

(Oum & Park, 1997: 138). In some cases, this can involve 'code sharing' where a passenger's ticket may indicate that they are flying with Airline Y when in fact the plane they board is operated by Airline Z. Airline Y, under a code-sharing agreement, is

Table 6.6 Major global alliances: key statistics

	Star Alliance	*OneWorld*	*SkyTeam*
Participating carriers*	Air Canada, Air New Zealand, ANA, Asiana Airlines, Austrian, bmi, LOT Polish Airlines, Lufthansa, Scandinavian Airlines, Singapore Airlines, Spanair, TAPPortugal, Thai Airways International, United Airlines, US Airways, Varig, SWISS, South African Airways	American Airlines, British Airways, Cathay Pacific, Finnair, Iberia, JAL, Malev, Quantas, Royal Jordanian	AeroMexico, Air France, KLM, Alitalia, Continental Airlines, Delta, Korean Air, Northwest Airlines, CSA Czech Airlines, Aeroflot
Global passenger share**	24.7	15.3	22.4
Global operating revenue share**	28.4	17.6	22.4
Jet aircraft in service**	2152	1574	2032

Source: Based on IATA (2004)

Notes: * As of August 2006; ** 2003 data. As part of the 'associate member' scheme (where airlines do not meet full entrance requirements) of SkyTeam, several airlines, including Air Europa of Spain, Panama's Copa Airlines, Kenya Airways, Romanian carrier Tarom, and Portugalia have been recruited; China Southern Airlines expected to join SkyTeam as a full member in late 2007; Turkish Airlines under discussions with Star Alliance in late 2006). MOUs signed between Air China and Shanghai Airlines in 2006.

allowed to sell a block of seats (agreed upon in the terms of the alliance) on a particular flight. This can be a powerful marketing tool for many airlines as such an alliance may serve to instantly expand its network in a virtual sense without the added cost of operations.

- *Type III: alliance of equity*. This type is typified by one airline obtaining a share of holdings in another airline, thus potentially leading to efficiencies of operations (perhaps initially financial, but ostensibly they have the opportunity to realise similar alliance benefits as identified in (I) and (II) above). This should not be confused with the outright share purchase agreements reached where no intention of alliance of operations features in the sale agreement. In other words, the selling of shares to another airline does not always proceed with the intent of forming some form of alliance. Glisson *et al.* (1996: 29) point out that equity alliances can actually be problematic in that they need to acquire regulatory approval in many jurisdictions:

> These equity holdings are looked on by some as a method of cementing the relationship between two airlines for the long run. However, they can be difficult to obtain because of severe restrictions and equity positions held by home governments. Those who oppose equity arrangements do not see the need for the investments, and feel they are nothing more than a waste of management time and an inappropriate use of investors' money. To many, equity alliances are becoming a system of airlines in distress. Others see them as defence postures.

All airline alliances are, in their own right, strategic in that they are usually designed to introduce operational efficiencies and markets to one or more existing carriers' networks (see Box 6.4). Oum and Park (1997) outline several reasons for strategic alliances, regardless of type, which I list here:

1. The expansion of networks can bring with it ease of transfers and integration: For example, passengers can 'interline' between two or more carriers who are members of the same alliance, primarily because of the agreement among them regarding passenger handling and booking (particularly in reference to customer reservation systems).

2. Feeding traffic between partners: An alliance between several carriers can mean an instant (often logarithmic) expansion of a network, although post-alliance business operations may need to be refined such that maximum efficiencies of network service are realised (e.g. decisions regarding which carrier shall remain on certain routes and which may not).

3. Efficiencies of cost: With the expansion of the network, airlines within an alliance can market themselves as being able to service, relatively seamlessly, numerous destinations, such that the cost of any one single airline achieving a network of this size would be prohibitive. Efficiencies of cost can also mean the sharing of maintenance and other personnel across an alliance.

4. Efficiencies of service: Relating to feed traffic discussed above, a good example of efficiency of services within an alliance is the conscious coordination of flight schedules across a network served by an alliance. This is one of the goals of a proposed alliance between several Arab airlines (Saudia, Egypt Air, Gulf Air, Middle East Airlines, Oman Air and Royal Jordanian) to be called Arabesk (www.ameinfo.com, 10 October 2005).

5. Wider choice of itineraries for passengers: Somewhat related, and by virtue of an expanded network and the accrued efficiency of service(s), itinerary choice can often be enhanced between multiple city pairs as passengers may have more than one airline choice.

The most visible alliances are those that are global in their operational outlook. The best known examples are Star Alliance, OneWorld and SkyTeam. Star Alliance captures the largest global passenger share and enjoys the highest operating revenue (Table 6.6). Tourists can often draw significant benefits from these types of alliances. For example, Star Alliance offers several round-the-world fares, the conditions for which are different but can often represent significant value for the passenger. For the Star Alliance, there are four fare levels: 26,000 miles, 29,000 miles, 34,000 miles or 39,000 miles, and in some cases there are no 'high season' surcharges (i.e. when some flights are generally more expensive due to higher demands in peak seasons). On these round-the-world tickets, journeys can be from ten days to one year in duration, and can include as few as 3 or as many as 15 stopovers (depending on the class of service), although there are limitations to the number of stopovers within a particular country or region. The normal conditions of such round-the-world tickets are that the outbound direction must be different from return trip; in other words, departing from Canada a traveller must travel in one direct (eastbound or westbound) and ultimately end up back home. Ticket prices are generally favourable and often fixed, and due to supply and demand for particular routes, quite often cheaper than simple O–D return trips.

   Where such global alliances were, at one time, primarily established and agreed to by partner airlines on the basis of enjoying the ability to market their own product as part of a seamless network of airlines around the world (discussed more extensively in Chapter 8), more recently attention has been directed towards the seamless operations across member airlines. Star Alliance, for example, has embarked upon new IT initiatives that would allow for joint electronic ticketing, which would allow passengers to receive an electronic ticket that covers a range of airlines across a substantial network.

REGULATORY ENVIRONMENTS

Worldwide, there are complex sets of arrangements, primarily political, that determine and dictate whether an airline has the ability to fly from one country to another and whether networks are indeed serviceable. Airlines are given permission to fly to destinations through ASAs, which can be considered more or less parallel with economic trade policies between countries. ASAs detail the extent to which air services may be allowed (or not) between two countries (and within countries by foreign airlines) and can include provision for the size of aircraft, the number of seats, and departure and arrival times. ASAs are sometimes referred to as aviation bilateral agreements (when two countries sign an agreement for air service) or multilateral agreements (when more than two countries are signatories), but this is more of procedural classification as bilateral and multilateral agreements themselves are not specific to air services and often include ASAs. Air services are governed ostensibly by what are referred to as 'freedoms of the air', of which there are nine (Figure 6.2).

The first five freedoms were established at a special conference held in Chicago in 1944, where the United States and 54 other countries sought to establish a common practice of regulating air routes. This was difficult given the number of countries involved, so it was resolved that individual nations could grant (or not) reciprocal rights to the use of their air space. Gradually, four more freedoms were added (http://www.icao.int/icao/ en/trivia/freedoms_air.htm; see also Doganis, 2001; Holloway, 2003). Using official ICAO descriptions, the nine freedoms are as follows.

First freedom – the right or privilege granted by one state to another state or states to fly across its territory without landing; as such, an airline registered in country A can fly to country B by freely flying over country C.

Second freedom – the right granted by one state to another state or states to land in its territory for non-traffic purposes (e.g. fuel or other technical/mechanic reasons); thus, an airline from country A has the right to land in country C en route to country B, but it cannot pick up or drop off passengers in country C.

Third freedom – the right or privilege granted by one state to another state to put down, in the territory of the first state, traffic coming from the home state of the carrier; that is, the right of an airline registered in country A to carry passengers from country A to country B.

Fourth freedom – the right or privilege granted by one state to another state to take on, in the territory of the first state, traffic destined for the home state of the carrier; that is, the right of an airline registered in country A to bring back passengers from country B (thus, the third and fourth freedoms are normally tied together).

Fifth freedom – the right or privilege granted by one state to another state to put down and to take on, in the territory of the first state, traffic coming from or destined to a third; in Figure 6.2, this means the right of a carrier registered in country A can fly to country C, drop off and pick up passengers, and continue on to country B. This will require an agreement between country A and country B as well as country A and country C. Holloway's (2003: 217) definition is as follows: '[A] privilege allowing an airline to uplift traffic from one foreign state and transport it to another state along a route which originates or terminates in that airline's home state.'

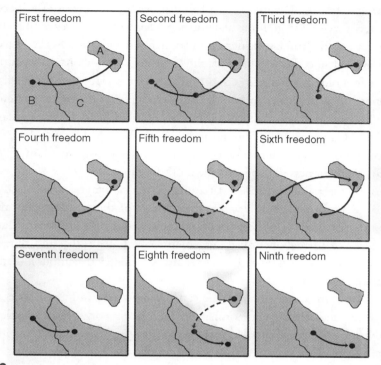

Figure 6.2 Freedoms of the air

Source: Based on Rodrigue (2006)

Sixth freedom – the combination of third and fourth freedoms, 'resulting in the ability of an airline to uplift traffic from a foreign state and transport it to another foreign state via an intermediate stop – probably involving a change of plane and/or flight number – in its home country (e.g. American carrying traffic from London to Lima over its Miami hub)' (Holloway, 2003: 218). Doganis' (2001: 227) definition is as follows: 'The use by an airline of country A of two sets of Third and Fourth Freedom rights to carry traffic between two other countries but using its base at A as a transit point.'

Seventh freedom – the right or privilege granted by one state to another state, of transporting traffic between the territory of the granting state and any third state with no requirement to include on such operation any point in the territory of the recipient state, i.e. the service need not connect to or be an extension of any service to/from the home state of the carrier. In Figure 6.2, this means that an airline registered in country A has seventh freedom rights to carry traffic between countries B and C without stopping in country A. If traffic was required to stop in country A, fifth freedom privileges would be enacted (or required).

Eighth freedom – the right or privilege of transporting cabotage traffic between two points in the territory of the granting state on a service which originates or terminates in the home country of the foreign carrier or (in connection with the so-called seventh freedom of the air) outside the territory of the granting state. 'Consecutive cabotage' is enacted when an airline registered in country A can have service that originates in country A, continues to a first port in country C, picks up and drops of passengers, and continues to another point in country C (Holloway, 2003, who uses the example of a international flight landing first in Hawai'i and then on-flying to Los Angeles). 'Full cabotage' 'is the operation by an airline of services within a single foreign country' (Holloway, 2003: 218), and is referenced by some as the ninth freedom.

Ninth freedom – the right or privilege of transporting cabotage traffic of the granting state on a service performed entirely within the territory of the granting state (also known as 'stand alone' cabotage). This freedom is somewhat rare (as are seventh and eighth freedoms) outside of formal open skies agreements, but it means that an airline registered in country A can operate entirely within, for example, country C without initiating or terminated a service in country A.

The provision of freedoms in air traffic can certainly have influence on competition and, by extension, accessibility and connectivity across networks. For example, the fifth freedom provision to allow airlines to pick up and drop off passengers at intermediate points often triggers discussions regarding protectionist policies of governments towards their own state-designated airlines. One of the most competitive fifth freedom markets in the world is the trans-Tasman route between New Zealand and Australia. Just after 11 September 2001, many fifth freedom carriers (including Thai, LAN, Aerolineas Argentineas, and several others) began flying from New Zealand (usually Auckland) and Australia (usually Sydney, Melbourne or Brisbane). Because these flights originated outside of either Australia or New Zealand, and benefited from the SAM established between Australian and New Zealand, stopping in either destination to drop off or pick up passengers meant access to new markets. Passengers benefited, with traffic across the Tasman growing significantly in the past few years. Overall, it is important to note that the Chicago Convention provided the ground work for the regulation of the airline industry, which was about to enter a period of significant growth. Coupled with this, of course, was the parallel growth in tourist traffic worldwide.

As the nine freedoms of the air demonstrate, governments are responsible for managing their airspace as well as the regulations by which airlines must abide in order to operate (for safety and tax reasons). Many are also responsible (or rather, hold themselves responsible) for managing the business environment in which airlines operate. Many bilateral agreements contain strict clauses governing substantial ownership and effective control regulations pertaining to airline operations between two countries. Airlines designated by a state are thus usually required to be substantially owned by nationals (usually a majority proportion), and effective control may be limited to a certain percentage of non-nationals. These provisions, as Holloway (2003) notes are perhaps the second-most important facet governing international aviation traffic flows and market entry (Holloway, 2003).

Ownership and effective control of a carrier leads to debate over whether they should adopt protectionist mechanisms that effectively protect national 'flag carriers' versus full liberalisation of the operating environment (thus opening up the market to competition). Flag carriers are those that have generally been certified to operate within a country and have thus met often very strict ownership and control provisions. Such provisions state that a certain percentage (often a majority) of ownership of the airline must be in the hands of national companies or citizens. As well, to be a flag carrier it is not uncommon for a percentage of effective control to be registered in the hands of nationals. Thus, it can be argued that by setting these kinds of regulations to which flag carriers must adhere, a certain degree of government protection is realised as they can act to control entry into the market by foreign carriers.

At one end of the protectionist–liberalisation spectrum is full liberalisation, in which governments allow foreign interests to operate or own a majority shareholding in an airline or allow foreign airlines unfettered access to local markets (perhaps even allowing them to operate domestically). In this case, airline operations are only impeded by logistic or infrastructural limitations (i.e. slot space at airports – see Chapter 7). At the other end of the spectrum is a protectionist policy in which a government may elect not to allow foreign carriers access to domestic markets or tightly restrict foreign ownership and control. In some instances, governments may be majority shareholders themselves in a particular airline (for a variety of reasons, but primarily to ensure services are available for the population and, thus, ensuring economic growth in peripheral regions), thus their own interest may dictate the extent to which protectionist policies are enacted. There are problems with a protectionist policy towards air services. As Hanlon (1999: 33) notes:

> Governments traditionally regarded air transport as, in some sense, a public utility. Strictly speaking, it is not. Economists prefer to reserve the term 'public utility' to enterprises that have characteristics of natural monopolies. Natural monopolies exist where the advantages of size are so great that a service can only be provided at least cost if it is supplied by one, and only one firm.

As such, Hanlon (1999) notes that airlines, unlike other service sectors such as telecommunications or electricity grids, have lower fixed-to-variable costs, thus fall outside of the traditional sense of needing full protection from competition.

For the most part, many countries are moving towards a more liberal form of government control of air services. In Europe, bilaterals after 1985 were largely 'open market' types, allowing open-route access and were generally unrestrictive in terms of capacity control (Doganis, 2001). Starting in the early 1990s, India, for example, has radically revised its policies towards competition and access by foreign airlines. Jet Airways was launched in 1993 and now holds a sizeable share of the domestic market.

As a result, Air India, owned fully by the government of India, launched an LCC spin-off, Air India Express, in April 2005. Other airlines, such as Kingfisher Airlines, SpiceJet, Go Airlines and Paramount Aviation also began operations in India in 2005, with two more (IndiGo and Indus Airways) initiated services in early 2006 (Manorama Online, 2005). With a population of over 1 billion, the introduction of competition has stimulated both domestic travel as well inbound and outbound travel (Travel Daily News, 2005).

Another example of the relaxing of protectionist policies is the increase in the number of open skies agreements that have been signed in the past few decades. One example is the SAM between Australia and New Zealand (see also Box 6.2). While not entirely a full open skies agreement, the SAM (established in the late 1990s) is designed to allow New Zealand-based and Australian-based airlines to operate within and between the two countries without barriers or restrictions. Such single market designations are important for two reasons. First, the economic benefits realised can be substantial. In the case of Australia and New Zealand, the SAM is couched in the wider closer economic relations policy that the two countries have adopted. Second, tourism can benefit because airlines, without government restriction, can elect to fly to an airport of their choice (although within capacity restrictions at the airport).

In the past few years, support for further liberalisation across regions and continents has been growing:

1. The European Union, for example, operates ostensibly as a wide, free market area (the EU single air market or more commonly known as the ECAA), designed to allow free movement of goods and peoples across borders. Prior to this, regulatory discretion was focused at the national level. Individual states within the EU continue to ratify bilateral agreements with external states, such as the case with India and the United Kingdom in 2005, which paved the way for increased air services that have been hugely beneficial for passengers in terms of accessibility and fares.

2. The Singaporean government has sought an open skies treaty with Australia for several years. Such an agreement would allow Singapore Airlines fifth freedom access to the United States via Australia. Already, Singapore has the rights to fly to the United States directly, but its fifth freedom traffic is limited to services to New Zealand. Understandably, Qantas, the Australian flag carrier, is concerned that this access could cut into its profitable Pacific routes between Australia and Singapore, particularly as Singapore Airlines is one of the launch customers for the Airbus A380 aircraft (although Singapore Airlines has hinted that it may not utilise the A380 on the Pacific route between Australia and the United States if an open skies agreement is reached, likely to the chagrin of Airbus, which may have hoped to use any operational successes of Singapore Airlines' utilisation in future marketing efforts). Qantas thus continues to urge the Australian government not

to ratify the agreement. Australia may, however, ultimately enter the agreement as part of a wider package of economic negotiations and bilateral agreements in an effort to secure strong relationships with Singapore.

3. Related to the EU's open skies agreement, discussions in November 2005 between the United States and the EU focused on the potential for free market access. New agreements would replace many of the bilateral agreements that the United States holds with many individual countries in Europe, some of which date to the 1970s. In fact, in November 2002 the European Court of Justice ruled that these multiple (and varied) agreements (covering routes, capacity, frequency and even fares in some instances) violated the EU Community Law. Many European nations, particularly Britain, have argued that the United States needs to eventually relax controls on its own domestic market, thus allowing foreign ownership and rights for foreign airlines to operate domestically. On 18 November 2005, a tentative agreement was reached (the first of several to come), allowing European carriers to depart from countries other than their own for the United States (ostensibly, fifth and seventh freedom rights). Some commentators (e.g. Firey, 2003) argue that a full open skies agreement would most likely benefit European carriers by way of mergers and alliances with American carriers as opposed to actually competing with them. However, given that a sizeable number of American carriers operating across the Atlantic are currently under bankruptcy protection, the attractiveness of such mergers with European carriers may be limited.

4. Also in November 2005, the United States and Canada ratified an updated version of their existing open skies agreement where airlines of each country will have complete fifth freedom access. In other words, a United States carrier can, for example, fly from Chicago to Toronto and then onward to London. However, the benefits to passengers may not be immediate as there is already in place numerous trans-Atlantic and Caribbean-bound flights from both countries so it is, at the time of writing, difficult to surmise what new routes may be added as a result of this revision.

Not all countries have embraced the liberalisation of air services. South African Airways, for example, has been attempting to negotiate the right to pick up passengers in Accra (Ghana) bound for the United States. At present, South African Airways flies to New York, Washington and Denver. The Ghanian government, however, is refusing access to the airline and the South African newspaper *Business Report* has suggested that protectionist policies are to blame, with Ghana worried that the airlines will capture, disproportionately, the Ghanian market at the expense of future Ghanian airlines (given that Ghana Airways ceased operations in 2003) (d'Angelo, 2005). A similar example revolves around the actions of the United States government with respect to Unites States designated carriers post-11 September 2001. In September 2005, British Airways PLC Chief Executive Rod Eddington suggested that the United States' protectionist policies of 'propping up' failing US-based airlines is unwise, noting: 'They're operating in protected markets, they're hoovering up public funds and still they can't make a profit' (Forbes, 2005). The implication is that US airlines operating under federal bankruptcy laws continue to operate at a loss across the Atlantic Ocean, thus preventing true competition from Europe-based carriers.

INTERNATIONAL REGULATORY FRAMEWORKS: INDUSTRY ORGANISATIONS

There are other international regulatory frameworks designed to represent common procedures. The most comprehensive of these is a series of articles and regulations established by NGOs such as the ICAO and the IATA. ICAO, a specialised agency of the United Nations, manages several aspects of aviation as agreed to by most world governments. It has recently adopted six strategic objectives for the period 2005–2010:

A. Safety – Enhance global civil aviation safety
B. Security – Enhance global civil aviation security
C. Environmental Protection – Minimize the adverse effect of global civil aviation on the environment
D. Efficiency – Enhance the efficiency of aviation operations
E. Continuity – Maintain the continuity of aviation operations
F. Rule of Law – Strengthen law governing international civil aviation. (www.icao.org)

IATA is a global industry association targeting air carriers by helping to 'ensure that Members' aircraft can operate safely, securely, efficiently and economically under clearly defined and understood rules' (www.iata.org). IATA acts to assist members with customs regulations, governmental regulatory policies and legal causes. It also operates the Simplifying Passenger Travel programme (www.simplifying-travel.org), which is a global programme that is designed to accommodate and promote efficiencies across the entire air travel experience (i.e. not just in the air). IATA's efforts are also designed to be of assistance to consumers/passengers, as stated on their website:

> For consumers, IATA simplifies the travel and shipping process. By helping to control airline costs, IATA contributes to cheaper tickets and shipping costs. Thanks to airline cooperation through IATA, individual passengers can make one telephone call to reserve a ticket, pay in one currency and then use the ticket on several airlines in several countries – or even return it for a cash refund. (www.iata.org)

Understanding the regulatory environment in which airlines operate is important for tourism because it dictates the networks and the performance of these networks. What can be concluded from this section is that tourist flows are highly political in that they are determined ultimately through the negotiations between two or more governments. As a result, it can be argued that the basis through which tourism exists at an international level, at least those tourist flows that rely on international air transport, is essentially an exercise in negotiations of access.

SUSTAINABLE AIR TRANSPORT

Several recent studies have outlined the environmental damage that air travel can cause. In 2000, the United States GAO published a report (GAO, 2000) that outlined the concerns with aircraft emissions and their impact on the atmosphere:

- Jet aircraft are the primary source of human emissions deposited directly into the upper atmosphere. The Intergovernmental Panel on Climate Change and experts noted that some of these emissions have a greater warming effect than they would have if they were released in equal amounts at the surface – by, for example, automobiles.
- Carbon dioxide is relatively well understood and is the main focus of international concern. According to the Intergovernmental Panel on Climate Change, it survives in the atmosphere for about 100 years and contributes to warming the earth. Moreover, as noted, global aviation's carbon dioxide emissions (measured in million metric tons of carbon) are roughly equivalent to the carbon emissions of certain industrialized countries.
- Carbon dioxide emissions combined with other gases and particles emitted by jet aircraft-including water vapor, nitrogen oxide and nitrogen dioxide (collectively termed NOx), and soot and sulfate – could have two to four times as great an effect on the atmosphere as carbon dioxide alone. According to the Intergovernmental Panel on Climate Change the atmospheric effects of these combined emissions will require further scientific study.
- The Intergovernmental Panel on Climate Change recently concluded that the increase in aviation emissions attributable to a growing demand for air travel would not be fully offset by reductions in emissions achieved through technological improvements alone. (GAO, 2000: 5)

The RCEP (UK) issued a report in 2002 that examines the impact of radiative forcing from aircraft emissions in the atmosphere. Radiative forcing is a 'convenient measure of the greenhouse effect of a change in a constituent is provided by the imbalance between solar and thermal radiation at the tropopause when the change in the constituent is suddenly imposed' (RCEP, 2002: Box 3A, 10; see also Egli, 1991). The tropopause is the distinct transition between the troposphere and the stratosphere. Aircraft generally travel between 9 km and 13 km above the Earth's surface, and very close to the tropopause which can vary depending on latitude. The RCEP (2002: 18) notes that '[t]he total radiative forcing due to aviation is probably some 3 times that due to the carbon dioxide emissions alone. This contrasts with factors generally in the range 1–1.5 for most other human activities.' The impacts of aircraft emissions, according to the RCEP's report, can

181

be different in the stratosphere and the troposphere, but the exact implications for the lower bands of the stratosphere are not exactly known. It has been suggested that water vapour from emissions may have some impact on cirrus cloud formations (Seinfeld, 1998), thus suggesting that the height at which aircraft travel could be altered depending on local climatic situations:

> Modern weather forecasting capabilities are increasingly such that the regions of likely supersaturation in the upper troposphere and the height of the tropopause in any region may be usefully predicted some days in advance. When there is more scientific understanding of the various elements involved in the climatic impact due to aviation, it should be possible to route individual aircraft so that, for example, they spend less time in regions where persistent contrails and enhanced cirrus cloud could be formed, or so that they almost always remained in the troposphere where the water vapour effects are negligible. (RCEP, 2002: 19).

In order to reduce the production of airborne particulates and emissions stemming from aircraft, some have advocated the use of an emissions tax, although such a tax was reasoned by Olsthoorn (2001) as having only a marginal impact on carbon dioxide levels. At Zurich airport, emissions charges are levied against aircraft based on the amount of pollutants they are known to emit; thus, larger aircraft are taxed at a higher rate than smaller aircraft. The European Commission is actively investigating the feasibility of introducing a region-wide emissions tax or, most significantly, extending carbon emissions trading to the aviation sector, which was being considered in mid-2004 (Wastnage, 2004; see also CE Delft, 2005) (see Chapter 9 for a discussion on Pigouvian taxes versus absolute emission reductions). The BBC reported in 2005 that aircraft are responsible for 3% of carbon emissions in the EU. Airlines would likely oppose the introduction of a new tax at a time when oil prices, and consequently jet fuel, are impacting upon profits.

The problem, however, is that these kinds of approaches do little to make the air transport industry more sustainable. Taxes or carbon trading may go some way to alleviating the burden of emissions on any one country, but true change may rest in alternatives brought on by technological innovation. One group, the Sustainable Aviation Group, comprised of British Airways, Virgin Atlantic, Airbus UK and the British Airports Authority, suggest that it is in fact technological innovations that are needed to stem emissions, yet some environmental groups (including the 'Green Sky Alliance' in the United Kingdom) and organisations point to the potential for rapid increases in greenhouse gases as a result of aircraft emissions and regardless of improvements made to engine technology (Webster, 2005). Virgin's Richard Branson was reported in November 2005 to be considering a new venture in which alternative aviation fuel can be developed. Using waste material from plants, the 'cellulosic ethanol' will be 100% environmentally friendly, but at the time of writing engine manufacturers such as General Electric and Rolls Royce had yet to speculate the amount of research and development needed to make alternative, sustainable aviation fuel a reality (ABC News [Australia], 2005).

Virgin Atlantic has arguably been at the forefront in environmentally friendly air transport activities. The company's website highlights several examples:

- Virgin Atlantic, the Group's flagship airline, has already developed its own Corporate Responsibility Policy and Strategy for Environmental Sustainability. Virgin Atlantic recognises the importance of minimising the impact of its operations on both the local and global environment through improving fuel efficiency, reducing emissions and noise.
- Virgin Atlantic has one of the youngest (and therefore more fuel-efficient) long haul fleets in the world.
- We have committed to meet the new EU limits on NO2 emissions which come into force on 1st January 2010.
- Over the past 30 years, the average fuel efficiency of an aircraft per passenger kilometre flown has improved by 50 per cent, thanks to improvements in airframe design, engine technology and increased load factors. Fuel represents a colossal proportion of operating costs, so using it efficiently is a commercial as well as environmental priority. Compared with its competitors, VAA's aircraft carry a higher number of passengers per air transport movement, and operate with a higher load factor – which means greater fuel efficiency.
- VAA's entire fleet complies with the ICAO Chapter 3 noise standards. VAA is monitoring its aircraft noise and seeking to set targets for its reduction. (http:// www.virgin.com/aware/future.asp; accessed 18 November 2005)

Given the obvious contribution of aircraft to pollution and greenhouse gas production, where does this leave tourism? Ironically, the very mode of transport that carries 'ecotourists' or 'green tourists' may in fact cancel out any gain from their immediate, on-the-ground activities designed to be sustainable, 'eco', or 'green'. Gössling et al. (2002: 210) sums this up appropriately:

> From a global sustainability and equity perspective, air travel for leisure should be seen critically: a single long-distance journey such as the one investigated in this survey requires an area almost as large as the area available on a per capita basis on global average. This sheds new light on the environmental consequences of long-distance travel, which have rather seldom been considered in the debate on sustainable tourism. Taking these results seriously, air travel should, from an ecological perspective, be actively discouraged.

CHAPTER SUMMARY

This chapter has outlined several contentious issues surrounding the provision of air services worldwide, including LCCs, airline alliances, the role of regulation (particularly bilateral ASAs) and environmental implications. Within the framework of networks, various network options were outlined, and it is important to note that no single network type is ideal in all circumstances. In Europe, for example, short flight sectors means linear networks can be made to be profitable. In other countries, hub-and-spoke domestic networks can be profitable by linking hinterland regions through spoke services.

Without question, airlines worldwide operate in 'turbulent' environments, both politically (with respect to bilateral and open skies agreements) as well as economic. Despite numerous bankruptcies since 11 September 2001, the airline sector is starting to show signs of (slow) recovery. Profits for some carriers have increased (although carriers such as Southwest and Ryanair generally prospered while network carriers, particularly in the United States, suffered immediately following 11 September 2001) and traffic levels are slowly recovering thanks to demand in China and India. Aviation fuel (also known as JET-A1) cost increases have meant an increase in the number of airlines applying fuel surcharges on top of ticket prices, leading some to suggest that the industry itself is quite unique in that very few other industries allow for the addition of surcharges to make up for operational costs. LCCs, or the LCLF, is spreading rapidly around the globe, having originated in the United States but fully expanded in Europe. The European adoption of LCLF carriers has, in part, been assisted by the dense network and strong connectivity possibilities throughout the region. In many cases, as discussed, it is difficult to distinguish between LCLF and FSAs as many FSAs have recently adopted drastic cost-cutting measures as a means of increasing profit.

SELF-REVIEW QUESTIONS

1. What is a hub-and-spoke network?

2. What are the nine freedoms of the air?

3. What are the key benefits, for both passengers and airlines, of airline alliances?

Box 6.2 Case study – The (failed?) Qantas/Air New Zealand SAA (based on Duval, 2005a).

In early December 2002, both Air New Zealand and Qantas (Air Pacific, based in Fiji, was also named on the application because Qantas held 46.32% of shares in the company; Air New Zealand held 1.9% and the Fijian government, as majority shareholder, held 51%) sought authorisation from the NZCC to ratify a 25 November 2002 SAA between the two parties that would, in effect, result in a JAO network across the Tasman Sea and, more generally, throughout the Pacific theatre. The proposed SAA included elements from all three of Tretheway and Oum's (1992) typology of airlines alliances. The applications filed by both Air New Zealand and Qantas to their respective governmental bodies were contextualised in several existing international policy environments, including:

1. the New Zealand-Australia closer economic relations trade agreement (established in 1983 and designed to harmonise trade relations between the two nations);

2. the SAM (created to foster cooperation in customs matters and ostensibly allowing commercial air carriers to designate their 'home market' as both Australia and New Zealand); and

3. the TTMRA (introduced in 1996 with the aim of allowing the free flow of goods and skilled personnel between the two countries).

The applicants (Air New Zealand and Qantas Airways Limited, 2002a, 2002b) argued that there were numerous benefits to the proposed alliance:

1. Cost savings: existing markets served under the SAM between Australia and New Zealand did not warrant the profitable operations of two FSAs.

2. Scheduling and direct services: it was argued that the alliance would effectively seek to tie customer and market bases together and allow for the management of inventory to be more efficient. One area in which customers/passengers would benefit was the code-sharing of some routes in order to allow feeder services into New Zealand from Australian domestic networks.

3. Tourism: the applicants argued that they were, quite literally, two of the largest organisations involved in the promotion and marketing of tourism for both

Australia and New Zealand. They argued that it would not be in their own best interests to jeopardise this through price collusion if the alliance were approved.

Assessing the impact of potential airline alliances is not easy. In the New Zealand context, several considerations were addressed by the NZCC:

1. What kind of impact would the proposed alliance have on domestic, trans-Tasman and trans-Pacific markets and operations; and

2. what would it mean to have Qantas own, as suggested by the Agreement, almost 25% of Air New Zealand? Under Section 67 of the New Zealand Commerce Act of 1986, Qantas was seeking to purchase 22.5% of shares in exchange for NZ$550million. There were, in effect, two options for the NZCC to consider:

(a) in the 'factual', allow Qantas to own nearly 25% of New Zealand's flag carrier, but at the same time recognise that some, if not all, of the arguments made in favour of the proposed Agreement (e.g. efficiencies, cost savings) would be passed on to the consumer; or

(b) in the 'counterfactual', allow Air New Zealand to operate on its own in an uncertain, global economic environment which, as discussed in this chapter, has already meant some airlines going bankrupt.

The decision was handed down in October 2003: the Agreement was rejected by the NZCC. This decision was appealed by Air New Zealand (on behalf of the applicants) in July 2004 to the High Court at Auckland, but the High Court endorsed the NZCC decision in September 2004. As of 2005, the airlines have not publicly discounted the possibility of attempting a merger or alliance of some sort in the future. While this case study has examined the New Zealand view of the proposed SAA, it is interesting to note that the ACCC, the Australian equivalent to the NZCC, also rejected the application on similar grounds, but the Australian Competition Tribunal, upon appeal, threw out the ACCC ruling and granted authorisation for the SAA to move forward. By this point, however, both airlines had moved on (and were still subject to the High Court ruling in New Zealand) and further options were being considered. One such option was the pursuit of an 'air share agreement' that would effectively allow both carriers to sell seats on either's aircraft.

One issue with respect to the timing of the alliance deserves some speculations. In a business environment, it is often said that one must keep a close eye on one's competition. At the time the SAA proposal was launched, the financial health of Air New Zealand was under question. It had recently been recapitalised by the New Zealand government and it was facing significant competition across the Tasman Sea by Qantas as well as numerous other 'fifth freedom' (discussed elsewhere in this chapter) carriers. Qantas had already established domestic operations along the main trunk routes in New Zealand through the operations of Jet Connect, who leased the Qantas brand. Qantas' financial health was strong. One theory that was floated in some aviation circles at the time was that the proposed SAA was one way for Air New Zealand to closely watch the operations of its major Pacific competitor. In so doing, Air New Zealand could be reasonably sure that any strategic or surgical move on the part of Qantas to the detriment of Air New Zealand (routes, fare structures) would be illogical given the pair were attempting to secure a strategic alliance. Granted, there were provisions in the SAA that would clearly benefit Qantas (i.e. easy access to the New Zealand market, greater control of the Pacific routes between New Zealand/Australia and the United States), but something to consider is whether, from the perspective of Air New Zealand, the SAA was more of an exercise or example of keeping a competitor at bay while internal re-organisation and operational efficiencies are improved.

Questions for consideration

1. Why did the NZCC claim that the SAA between Air New Zealand and Qantas was not in the public good?

2. Under what circumstances might the following react negatively against an alliance similar to the one discussed: (a) a major international airport; (b) a small regional airport?

ESSAY QUESTIONS

1. Justify the introduction of non-stop services between two places; why would an airline offer services non-stop when it could offer a segmented route that shuttles passengers between multiple destinations along a linear network?

2. Research a current bilateral agreement between two countries and determine whether there are any 'barriers to entry' for other carriers.

3. Why can it be said that many FSAs are not much different from LCCs?

KEY SOURCES

Doganis, R. (2002) *Flying off Course: The Economics of International Airlines.* London: Routledge.

This book is one of the more comprehensive and accessible examples of recent titles seeking to examine and explain the complexities of the modern global aviation system. Doganis covers several topics well, including route network planning, yield management, cost control and marketing.

Holloway, S. (2003) *Straight and Level: Practical Airline Economics.* Aldershot: Ashgate.

Holloway's text is superb in its treatment of the primary economic variables that shape airline operations. Particularly useful is his discussion on yield and revenue management, unit costs and scheduling. Although based in economics, the text is accessible to those who may not have formal training in advanced economic concepts.

International Air Transport Association – www.iata.org

IATA is an airline industry association that represents approximately 260 airlines around the world. The goal of the IATA is to essentially represent the interests of member airlines with respect to regulations, safety and security and passenger management, among others, but in a global context. The opinions from the IATA site should be compared to that of the Airports Council International (www.airports.org) site.

CHAPTER 7:

MANAGEMENT OF TRANSPORT FLOWS

LEARNING OBJECTIVES

After reading this chapter, you should be able to

1. Understand the history and importance of privatisation and liberalisation of transport infrastructure.

2. Appreciate the role of airports as hubs and nodes in the global transportation system.

3. Understand the principles of yield management in transport operations.

4. Recognise and evaluate recent advances in security and safety in relation to transport.

5. Assess the impact of external events on transport operations.

INTRODUCTION

Transport management incorporates several fields of enquiry, including, for example, transport economics (Button, 1993), international trade relationships and impacts of transport cost (Rauscher, 1997), business logistics and operations management (Gubbins, 2004), information systems, planning (Banister, 2002), and legal frameworks. While limitations in space prevent a thorough overview of each of these issues, the intent of this chapter, however, is to isolate three critical management applications in the context of tourism flows' relationship with transport.

First, the management of nodes within networks of travel are examined, with the modern airport used as an example of a node that acts as a conduit for travel and tourism. As shown, airports today function not only as hubs in order to facilitate the transfer of passengers from one place to another, but they also (and sometimes necessarily) function as centres of commerce. Second, the principle of yield management is outlined. Yield management is a complex method (yet reasonably simple in principle) by which airlines (and other transport-related industries) price their product/service. The third management application examines safety and security measures in transport. As is shown, a variety of industries associated with transport pay close attention to safety and security issues. The chapter, therefore, isolates specific examples where careful managing of transport-related procedures and management issues can overtly impact on tourism development and/or tourist flows. The selected three management functions described herein, and taken together, illustrate both the complexity of the transport/tourism relationship and the importance of understanding how tourism and travel in general can be impacted by fluctuations in the various components and transport operational factors.

PRIVATISATION AND LIBERALISATION: TRANSPORT INFRASTRUCTURE

In order to situate management implications, it is important to briefly note that, much like the actual modes of transport, the ownership and management of infrastructure, as a resource necessary for the provision of transport services, has undergone processes of liberalisation and privatisation in many countries. This is perhaps best exemplified through the increasingly popular process of liberalising and/or privatising airports, but can also apply to rail tracks once under the management of governments. Privatisation is meant to imply efficiencies and increased profitability, the latter of which generally focuses on increased commercialisation (Oum *et al.*, 2003; see also Chin, 1997). It also allows for access to more private investment to fuel growth, as in the case of the BAA, where capital expenditure before privatisation was constrained by government policy (Doganis, 1992). While the BAA often emerges as the bellwether by which the successes of airport privatisation can be identified (Doganis, 1992), throughout Europe airport competition and gradual privatisation has been heightened following the deregulation of the airline industry in the 1990s (Barrett, 2000). In Australia and New Zealand, airport privatisation was initiated at roughly the same time (Forsyth, 2002), while privatisation efforts in Asia have been comparatively slow as governments are concerned with possible monopolistic abuse (Hooper, 2002). (Their concern is not without foundation, as Gerber [2002] argues that sufficient regulation needs to pre-date any privatisation effort as it helps stimulate protection for user, balance for the various stakeholders involved and helps stimulate partnerships between government and private enterprise.)

In the United States, the privatisation of airports has not been as widespread as in Europe. Some US airlines are steadfastly opposed to such a move, largely because it would introduce competition at a level over which they may feel they have little control due to their own increasing operational costs. As well, airlines and airports in the United States have historically worked together under airport use agreements that govern the charges levied by the airport and prescribe the use entitled to the airlines (Graham, 2001). In fact, Graham (2001) notes that airlines have substantial input into future development at US airports. The argument could be raised that, in the case of major airports where one airline may account for a substantial amount of operating revenues, this kind of relationship or agreement is problematic: not only does the dominant airline have substantial control of route structures and pricing schemes, but it also may have considerable input in future development plans that may threaten its dominant status. Indeed, Doganis (1992: 30) points out that the risk of monopolies is possible as 'airport managers may reduce space for passenger and cargo shippers in order to maximize revenues from a variety of commercial activities'. The differences in liberalisation and privatisation of transport infrastructure and operations in the United States and the United Kingdom can be partially explained by the FAA mandate (and, by extension, the United States government) to ensure efficient operation of the nation's air transport system (Ellett, 2003). As well, in the UK it could be argued that there is more modal competition for travel and haulage of goods (Starkie, 2002), thus prompting some liberalisation of the transport infrastructure in order to ensure profitability.

What is the most appropriate level of ownership-management? This is difficult to state clearly, largely because there are few mechanisms in place to adequately compare the output of airports (Hooper, 2002). The situation with airports is somewhat mirrored in other transport modes. For example, Welsby and Nichols (1999) point out that the privatisation of the UK rail system perhaps overlooked future demand for infrastructure. As a result, and this situation is mirrored in New Zealand as well, governments may, in some cases, need to assume the responsibility for capacity enhancement through infrastructure maintenance and construction.

NODAL MANAGEMENT: AIRPORTS AS HUBS

Following on the discussion from Chapter 2, where the spatial distribution of transport in relation to tourism was discussed, the purpose of discussing nodal management is to highlight the issues involved in managing the flows of tourism traffic. Nodes can often act as hubs, and there are significant considerations for how transport provision is made possible (and profitable) by what occurs at these hubs. The majority of the following discussion focuses around airports, largely because they play an important role in global traffic, but also because they are integrated into the transport/tourism relationship on a number of levels, including facilitating traffic flows, impacting upon regional development, and securing other economic capital flows within the countries in which they reside.

One of the major areas in which the role of the airport contributes to tourist flows is the issue of capacity constraints, particularly as many existing airports, especially international hub airports such as London Heathrow, struggle to keep up with increasing demand.

As Starkie (1998) points out, as airports become popular (for reasons of geography) there is increasing demand for the services they offer. The magazine *Airline Business* argued in June 2005 that the crowded airports of Europe, for example, are currently facing a congestion crisis as they strive to meet increasing demand, especially where some (e.g. Airports Council International) are suggesting that demand is returning to pre-11 September levels (Airline Business, 2005a). In the United States, 35 of the nation's most crucial airports for managing the flow of air traffic are now operating at pre-2001 levels (Airline Business, 2005b). Additionally, the boom in air travel in India over the past few years is also affecting two of the country's biggest airports (New Delhi and Mumbai). The IATA has reportedly suggested that India will need to work fast to increase capacity at these hubs in order to facilitate the rapid projected growth in India's air markets (Mahapatra, 2005). What this means for tourism is that the networks that serve international tourist flows are becoming congested as the number of major nodes operating at peak capacity grows.

One way of alleviating capacity constraints and congestion at many airports is to construct new runways. The United States has opened eight new runways since 1999, with a further seven to be opened by 2009 (Airline Business, 2005b). The challenges to opening new runways, however, are enormous, despite the benefits towards alleviated congestion (adapted from McCartney, 2005):

- Atlanta's (Hartsfield Airport) fifth runway project has been in progress (planning through to the construction) for nearly 25 years. In that time, new housing developments near the airport have meant increasing community opposition.
- At Boston's Logan International Airport, a new runway specifically for turbo-props needing federal and local approval has taken almost 30 years because of community and legal battles.
- Environmental opposition to two new runways to be built on landfill at San Francisco has meant that the runway development has been scrapped.

Major international hub airports, such as JFK in New York or Heathrow in London, do not, of course, have the ability to handle unlimited traffic, even if new runways are constructed. All airports have a finite number of gates and internal (airside) capacity limits in the number of people they can service. Customs and immigration areas are also limited in their resource allocation. There are also capacity limits on the use of the runways themselves (Cao & Kanafani, 2000) as departures and take-offs need to be managed in accordance with existing international (and local) safety regulations (e.g. minimum distances of separation when landing and taking off). In short, most airports are 'capacity restricted' as well as capacity constrained, which is one way of suggesting that quick fixes are not always suitable solutions.

OPERATIONS MANAGEMENT: MANAGING CAPACITY THROUGH AIRPORT SLOT ALLOCATION

Capacity restrictions at airports mean that an airline cannot simply decide to start flying to a particular airport, arriving at a time of their choosing. Unlike ground tourist transport, which is comparatively free-flowing (i.e. bus tours, which may be governed by some time restrictions, often can show up at attractions with only a rough estimate given for arrival), air transport is highly scheduled and managed to maximise resource allocation and profit across the numerous operations that are involved (e.g. airports, airlines, ancillary services). The amount that any particular airline can utilise an airport is closely managed through the allocation of slots. Slot space is usually not allocated and governed entirely by the airports themselves. Instead, at most major airports around the world allocation is governed through a series of guidelines set out by the IATA, which functions as the global airline trade association. At the same time, however, certain 'grandfather' rights are recognised, so if a particular airline has historically (i.e. perpetually over a significant period of time) utilised a landing slot at a particular airport which has, very recently, suddenly become popular and in demand by other airlines, that airline has some rights to declare its use of the newly in-demand slot(s) on the basis of its grandfather rights. In some situations, 'historical' use of airport (or, more properly, runway) slots is based on use in the previous equivalent season (Starkie, 1998).

In order to secure slots at particular airports, many airlines regularly engage in slot trading at either one of the biannual conferences established by IATA (although it should be noted that not all world airlines are members of IATA). When slot space becomes available at a certain capacity-restricted airport, airlines can often bid large sums of money to acquire the rights/permission to fly there. In the United States, however, anti-trust regulations prohibit airlines from meeting to discuss mutually beneficial route structures and timings. As Starkie (2003: 53) outlines, market forces generally dominate the allocation of slots at US airports as

> there are few restrictions at US airports limiting the allocation of landing and take-off slots; for example, airline scheduling committees, which an important slot management outside the USA, do not operate at US airports. Airlines simply schedule their flights taking into account expected delays at the busier airport. Essentially, slots are allocated on a first come, first served basis, with the length of the queue of planes waiting to land or take-off acting to ration overall demand.

Because of capacity restrictions, airports carefully manage their operations (both airside and in general) in order to ensure that the amount of traffic coming in (and going out) is both manageable and profitable (from aeronautical charges). For example, aircraft rotations or movements (i.e. take-offs and landings) are generally relegated to daylight hours (usually as a result of zoning and noise restrictions), thus airport management can accurately plan for the most efficient use of specific resources. Baggage handling, for example, can be scheduled in accordance with incoming aircraft movements, so when multiple long-haul aircraft arrive at only certain times of the day or week, staffing can be allocated appropriately. Similar arrangements can be applied to customs officials, although this is usually embedded within an arrangement with national governments as customs and immigration fall under its purview.

Capacity restrictions on operations lead to slots or times that are inherently more valuable to airlines than others. Suppose an airline wishes to capture the business travel market with a flight that departs London Heathrow at 0800 and arrives at Charles de Gaulle (Paris) at 0910, a useful arrival time for business travellers who are perhaps only in Paris for the day. The problem, however, is that London Heathrow can be congested at this time of the morning, with numerous flights leaving for a variety of continental (and international) destinations. A slot for an 0800 departure may therefore not be available. Operating the flight at a later time in the morning, say 1100, may be possible due to available take-off slots, but it may not appeal to business travellers who may need a full day, for example, in Paris. It is not surprising, then, that capacity constrained airports, such as London Heathrow, actually act as a barrier to entry for some upstart airlines because the profitable and highly desirable slots are already occupied by established airlines. This is one of the reasons why many LCCs have moved to the use of secondary or regional airports (such as a London Luton or London Stansted), which may have slots available and may not be as capacity constrained. In general, the inability of new entrants to a particular market is made difficult by other factors, as Hanlon (1999) shows:

1. Airlines must acquire 'matching slots' at destinations. In other words, if a new upstart wishes to commence service from one particular airport, it must also acquire landing slots at the destination.

2. Slot trading is in place at several airports in the United States, where particular slots may be bought and sold. This raises the issue of the potential dominance of one or two airlines at a particular airport (sometimes called fortress hubs) thus limiting the ability of new entrants to initiate use.

3. Some incumbent or established carriers will utilise slots for the purpose of preventing new entrants even when policies regarding slot reallocation are introduced.

4. Slots that are reallocated (on the basis of non-use of existing slots or new slots) are often at times of the day that are not feasible and not as lucrative.

Not surprisingly, the value of slots, especially those at peak times, has not escaped the attention of airport operators. In April 2006, European Union transport commissioner Jacques Barrot hinted that congestion charges may be levied on airlines using European airports during the busiest periods (Minder, 2006). The real value, however, is in the slot itself. In 1993, the European Commission introduced Council Regulation 95/93 on 'common rules for the allocation of slots at community airports' (http://europa.eu.int/scadplus/leg/en/lvb/l24085.htm; accessed 31 August 2005). In the preamble to the regulation, the EEC (Council Regulation) stated:

> One of the main difficulties of the current system of slot allocation has been to find the right balance between the interests of incumbent air carriers and new entrants at congested airports so as to take due account of the fact that incumbent air carriers have already built up their position at an airport and have an interest to expand it further, while new entrants or air carriers with relatively small operations need to be able to expand their services and establish a competitive network.

To address this, the EEC (http://europa.eu.int/scadplus/leg/en/lvb/l24085.htm) established a series of procedures by which slots are allocated:

- A carrier using a time slot that has been cleared by the coordinator is entitled to claim the same slot in the next scheduling period. In a situation where all slot requests cannot be accommodated to the satisfaction of the air carriers concerned, preference is given to commercial air services and in particular to scheduled services and programmed non-scheduled air services.
- The coordinator also takes into account additional priority rules established by the air carrier industry and, if possible, the additional guidelines recommended by the coordination committee allowing for local conditions.
- If a requested slot cannot be accommodated, the coordinator informs the requesting air carrier of the reasons therefore and indicates the nearest alternative slot.
- Slots may be freely exchanged between air carriers or transferred by an air carrier from one route or type of service to another.
- A Member State may reserve certain time slots for regional services.
- The Regulation provides for the setting up of 'pools' containing newly-created time slots, unused slots and slots which have been given up by a carrier or have otherwise become available.
- Any slot not utilised is withdrawn and placed in the appropriate slot pool unless the non-utilisation can be justified by reason of the grounds of the grounding of a certain type of aircraft, or the closure of an airport or airspace or any other exceptional reason.
- Slots placed in the pools are distributed among applicant carriers. 50% of these slots are allocated to new entrants unless requests by new entrants are less than 50%.

Important within Regulation 93/95 is, as discussed earlier, the preservation of grandfather rights of incumbent airlines. Once allocated, carriers are required to utilise slots 80%

of the time in order to retain future grandfather rights. In doing so, an airline may utilise a particular slot solely for the purposes of creating a barrier to entry for a new upstart carrier and thus maximising their market share. (As discussed earlier, competitors have found a way around grandfathered slot allocations by establishing operations at secondary airports.) Indeed, Boyfield (2003: 34) has commented that many have seen the Regulation as 'antiquated' because it is actually centred around the concept of grandfather rights, so much so that '[c]arrriers have little incentive to hand back slots they hold at peak times, no matter how inefficiently they are used'.

Protests over the grandfathered slots have not gone unnoticed, however. Hanlon (1999) notes that a 1995 review of slot allocation by the UK Civil Aviation Authority recommended that all new slots or non-utilised slots should be turned over to new entrants. Although the system still exists in principle, it was not until 2004, when the EEC revised the regulations (EEC 793/2004; Commission of the European Communities, 2004) to widen the definition of new entrant airlines and established a list of priorities when allocating new or unused slots, that change was enacted. More significantly, the EEC later called for submissions exploring the possibility that commercialising the slot allocation system (through free-trading and auctions under the principle of liberalisation) might render the system more efficient (Paylor, 2005). Airlines, however, were concerned that the grandfather rights they hold to slots at major hubs might be jeopardised if such a system were introduced.

In fact, the commercialisation of slots has already begun, but it is far from transparent in many cases. A recent issue of *Airline Business* magazine characterised the 'grey' slot market at Heathrow as somewhat of a 'murky world'. In 2004 it was reported by the *Guardian* (Gow, 2004) that Qantas paid approximately £20 million each for two pairs of daily slots at Heathrow. The slots were previously held by LCC Flybe (formerly British European). Commercial transactions of slots, then, may ultimately favour larger carriers with access to large amounts of capital. With respect to the revised 2004 EEC regulations, the scarcity of slots at EU airports would be measured in monetary terms such that underutilisation of existing slots by incumbent carriers is financially compensated by local authorities, who would have the power to pull slot allocation(s) and reallocate to a new entrant who may promise to maximise utilisation. Although the slots themselves would be commercialised, financial compensation for incumbents, if they happen to underutilise, may be more preferable than allowing market forces to outright determine allocation. The reason for this is that new entrants would be restricted in their ability to acquire lucrative slots because of 1) incumbents refusing to sell slots or 2) local authorities unwilling to exercise authority (if any) of removing slots from incumbents and reallocating to new entrants.

Both the UK CAA and the UK government supported the introduction of the commercialisation of slots, noting that it would have an overall positive impact on the European aviation marketing (CAA, 2004; Department for Transport, 2004c), but this proposal to unleash slots to market forces has been concerning for some. The European Regions Airlines Association (*Flight International*, April 2004 issue) warned that such a system for slots may be detrimental for regional airports. It claimed that airlines operating out of larger hub airports (such as Heathrow, Frankfurt Main and Paris Orly) could shift their operations in favour of long-haul routes to the detriment of smaller regional routes. As well, smaller regional airlines may find servicing regional and major hub airports to be unprofitable, thus leaving some regions (and thus, travellers) without sufficient access to major hubs. Table 7.1 provides an overview of the concentration of airport activity throughout the UK. Critical within this table is the extent to which smaller regional centres such as Leeds/Bradford, Liverpool and East Midlands are proportionately smaller than larger airports such as Heathrow, Gatwick or Stansted.

Table 7.1 UK airport activity, 2002 (arrivals and departures at airports handling more than one million passengers)

	Domestic*	Scheduled	Non-scheduled	Total
Newcastle	1165	626	1597	3387
Manchester	2743	6463	9412	18,618
Leeds/Bradford	477	486	563	1526
Liverpool	736	1685	414	2835
East Midlands	548	1097	1588	3233
Birmingham	1222	3762	2928	7911
Luton	1745	3665	1064	6474
Stansted	2461	12,385	1203	16,049
Heathrow	6674	56,237	124	63,035
Gatwick	3427	15,029	11,062	29,518
London City	417	1184	1	1602
Bristol	925	1194	1296	3415
Cardiff	108	344	964	1416
Aberdeen	1613	407	529	2549
Edinburgh	5079	1418	415	6911
Glasgow	4297	1157	2315	7769
Belfast City	1886	1	3	1890
Belfast International	2683	182	686	3551
Other UK airports	3877	1587	1726	7190

Source: Adapted from CAA (2005)

Note: * *Domestic traffic is counted at airports on arrival and departure.*

There are other concerns with the slot system, regardless of whether it becomes fully (or even partially) commercialised, that are of concern to the flow of passengers. Chief among these is that potential for passengers having limited choice in air services, and indeed the congestion and hoarding of slots at smaller regional airports in the European

Union, was one of the reasons the initial 1993 slot allocation procedures were reviewed. In other words, when one or two airlines control the majority of the prime slots at an airport, prices for that particular market may not be at all competitive due to a lack of competition.

For tourism, the attention given to airport slot allocation (and trading, for that matter), is important for several reasons:

1. It remains to be seen whether profitable routes can be sustained if the cost of doing business on the ground is not justifiable to carriers. In some circumstances, slot trading, as an outright cost borne by a carrier to enter a particular market, may jeopardise connectivity within a network as carriers may decide not to service a particular node if the cost of gaining access to that node is prohibitive. Similarly, in such cases, tourism destinations that may rely on service from that node may suffer in terms of accessibility. Overall, then, where some nodes carry high slot costs, or where slots are at a premium, carriers servicing those nodes will only likely only fly on routes that are highly profitable, thus artificially creating travel flows that favour some destinations and disfavour others.

2. Somewhat related, slots (and their timing) are market drivers. Carriers will naturally attempt to streamline the timing of their aircraft operations in order to maximise profitability (e.g. rapid turn around times, which is an inherent feature of LCCs), yet their ability to command suitable and profitable market share can often depend on departure and arrival times at destinations or other nodes throughout a network. As air transport is undoubtedly part and parcel of the overall travel experience, suitable arrival and departure times therefore become critical. In this way, revenue can be impacted negatively if the ability of a carrier to service a market is restricted by the timings of take-offs and landings not only at the origin node, but also at the destination node as well. In essence, slot allocations need to be considered across the network, and a profitable and operationally efficient balance is maximised when a carrier retains appropriate network-wide slot access.

3. By extension, markets located in proximity to an airport at which a carrier is dominant because of grandfathering of slots or through saturation of services under the first come, first served rule (as in the United States) may find choices rather limited when it comes to holiday destinations. The implications for this are twofold: on the one hand, the economic impact of hubbing at a particular airport or node can be significant when one carrier is dominant; but on the other hand, this dominance comes at a price with respect to destination choice, as smaller carriers may not have the frequency and desirable destinations within their network. Again, the dominance of a carrier at a particular node may artificially determine travel patterns and, to an extent, demand as there is less of an incentive for the carrier to expand its network to other nodes if existing services are already profitable.

4. Finally, if market forces of slot allocation are adopted at a global level, then users (passengers, tourists) may find that increased competition could bring lower fares and more options for destinations served, thus enhancing tourism. In many respects, some LCCs have chosen to directly avoid the slot allocation issue in utilising regional airports for domestic and some international flights, particularly in Europe (e.g. Ryanair).

The issue of slots at airports is a worldwide concern, but particularly in Europe where competition has grown significantly in the past decade. Ostensibly it is an issue where balance is required between the interests of the travelling public (set and overseen by government policy) and the interests of shareholders of airlines who have great interest in retaining access to profitable markets (and, by extension, profitable stages or routes). As Paylor (2005) notes, consultation on the new policies targeted for enactment in the EU are ongoing, it may be some time before full implementation is realised.

OPERATIONS MANAGEMENT: AIRPORT SERVICES

On the subject of nodes and how air transport provision is affected by regulatory mechanisms that govern their inclusion in a carrier's network, it is also important to understand how the services rendered at nodes or airports can be characterised. This is important from a tourism perspective as airports function as vectors through which international travel often transpires. Airport revenue emanates from aeronautical or non-aeronautical operations (Graham, 2001). Aeronautical revenue sources can include landing fees, passenger fees, fees for parking aircraft (between flights or longer term for maintenance), and various handling fees if certain services (such as movement and management) are not provided by carriers. Non-aeronautical sources of revenue can include rents for spaces in the terminal affiliated with specific carriers, concessions, sales of products/services managed by the airport, and parking fees (Graham, 2001). The importance of the split can vary from airport to airport. For example, when Delta Air Lines declared bankruptcy in September 2005, Hartsfield-Jackson International Airport was immediately concerned for its own future revenue streams. The airport had recently approved an expansion plan worth approximately US$6 billion, and future revenue from Delta, which already accounts for 19% of the airport's revenue, was deemed critical for future profitability (Tagami, 2005). Indeed, many airports around the world manage ancillary, but often significant in terms of revenue, means of non-aeronautical sources of revenue. For example, Dunedin International Airport, in the South Island of New Zealand, owns several small farms in the immediate vicinity and approximately 500 head of cattle. The reason for this is largely practical; the airport is situated in a rural area (but still within the city boundaries) and by acquiring ownership of surrounding properties it can control any future development or expansion needs.

One way of counteracting the reliance upon aeronautical revenue streams is the development of non-aeronautical activities. Rather than rely upon the services of one or more airlines, airports around the world are instead turning to specific sources of revenue from passengers. For example, retail activities are increasingly becoming an important source of revenue for many airports, largely because passengers (both airside and landside) can be a captured market. The BAA's 2004 Annual Report (BAA, 2005) indicates that it generated nearly half a billion UK pounds from retail activities across the airports it manages (Heathrow, Gatwick, Stansted, Southampton, Glasgow, Edinburgh and Aberdeen). At Christchurch International Airport in New Zealand, concessions and lease rentals accounted for almost 40% of the total operating revenue in 2004, up from approximately 36% in 2003 (Christchurch International Airport, 2005). This reflects expansion activities that have resulted in many direct flights from the airport to Australian and other Pacific destinations.

Hanlon (2001) offers several reasons for the rapid growth in non-aeronautical or commercial activities at airports worldwide:

1. Commercialisation and privatisation has allowed many airports to effectively be run as commercial entities rather than publicly funded organisations managed at the local or national government level.

2. Airlines are 'exerting increasing pressure on the airport industry to control the level of aeronautical fees which are being levied' (Hanlon, 2001: 127), which means that airports must search for other means by which overall revenue and profit are realised.

3. The type of traveller utilising an airport has changed; where air travel at one time was reserved for those of high-net worth, advances in technology has meant that air travel is within reach for most people in industrialised countries, and this overall market is one which is demanding of (or at least responds to) retail opportunities.

4. Competition between airports, according to Hanlon (2001), may mean that, for some passengers, consideration of retail activities may be at least a secondary consideration for choosing air services (with the nature of those air services being the first).

Freathy and O'Connell (1998) argue that airports' concentration on non-aeronautical revenue reflects a change in the customers they service, and thus the role of the airport itself is somewhat blurred:

> There are those who remain close to the traditional view of an airport, i.e. that it exists to ensure the efficient movement of passengers between one destination and another. An alternative, and perhaps more eclectic approach, views airports within the framework of consumer change. In this context airports are seen not only as modal interfaces but also as leisure attractions and primary destinations in their own right. If airports are viewed as locations through which passengers are to be moved as quickly and as efficiently as possible, then the role of commercial activities within

airport operations will always remain limited. If however an airport is viewed as a primary leisure destination it itself, them it will remain possible to develop further the commercial opportunities within the airport. (Freathy & O'Connell, 1998: 16)

Freathy and O'Connell's comments are interesting in that they point to the challenge that airports face: on the one hand ensuring that customers/passengers are able to get to their aircraft efficiently, but on the other the realisation that, to remain viable, they must ensure revenue extraction from these same passengers is maximised. Freathy and O'Connell (1999) also proposed a typology of airport retailing: concessionaire-based retailing (the most widespread form of retail activity, and where the airport authority acts as the landlord), authority managed retailing (where the authority occupies retail space, although concessions may also be present), management contract (all operations handled by third or fourth party), and joint venture operations between multiple partners, some of whom may be overseas.

Without question, the means by which passengers are processed is critical to the overall efficiency of the airport (including customs controls and immigration), but airports can also maximise their physical layout to ensure that passengers are at the very least exposed to retail and other service opportunities. Doganis (1992) argues that there are three locational factors involved in relation to passenger flows: (1) position of shops; (2) the floor level; and (3) the split of available space between airside and landside areas. As Freathy and O'Connell (1998: 76–77) point out, there are several key factors that determine retail locations in airports:

- The logic of the passenger traffic flows: the location of shop units needs to mirror the direction in which the passengers are travelling. They should not be required to retrace their steps or go in a counter direction.
- Floor levels: retail outlets should be on the same floor as the departure gates and passengers should not have to ascend or descend stairs in order to shop.
- Distance: shops should be accessible without passengers having to traverse long distances. They should be sufficiently removed from the security and passport checks to allow the traveller to make the mental adjustment to a shopping environment.
- Visibility: before encountering the retail offer, passengers should have the retail outlets in their line of vision. This will help stimulate purchasing behaviour and possibly trigger impulse sales.

Retail activities have become increasing developed at many major global hub airports, incorporating elements of design strategies used elsewhere in retail environment planning (Crawford & Melewar, 2003; Rowley & Slack, 1999). At London Heathrow's Terminal 3, for example, the traveller is exposed to a wide range of retail services, ranging from distinctively up-market fashion to magazines and snacks. For the most part, the design of the shopping promenade in the terminal is meant to emulate a shopping mall. In fact, the design of Terminal 3 is such that, at almost any point, a clear view of the available shops is possible, a clear strategy in encouraging impulse purchasing (Crawford & Melewar, 2003). Some major international hub airports are moving beyond retail activities to include other activities aimed at passenger comfort and increasing revenue. At Changi International Airport in Singapore, the expansive nature of the passenger concourse (airside) in both Terminal 1 and Terminal 2 facilitates almost 25 million passenger movements (i.e. transferring or otherwise) per annum, and the airport features seven natural areas or gardens, a movie theatre, various napping areas, a fitness centre, a transit hotel, and over 100 retail outlets.

Many airports, especially those which have seen substantial increases in passenger traffic, fund their expansion activities through levies on passenger traffic. Whereas in the past airports have been able to fund airport expansion from the aeronautical revenues collected from carriers, many LCCs attempt to negotiate smaller landing and operational fees for aircraft handling and space rentals (Francis *et al.*, 2004), thus leaving airports with few options for revenue collection apart from retail activities. In 1997 Edmonton International Airport introduced an airport improvement fee (AIF) to fund capital expenditures and related financing costs for redevelopment and expansion of the terminal facilities. This new programme, however, has not entirely covered the cost of the redevelopment, according to the airport's most recent Annual Report (Edmonton Airports, 2005). As of 31 December 2004, total cumulative expenditures sat at CDN$357 million while the cumulative net AIF revenue was CDN$133 million.

In late August 2005, Ryanair announced that it was cutting 12 flights a week to and from Cornwall because of a recent decision by the Cornwall County Council to implement a £5 tax on departing passengers over the age of 16. Ryanair argued that it would cost the region over £10 million in lost revenue from visitors as approximately 100,000 fewer passengers per year would fly to the airport (Times Online, 2005). The airline also argued that an extra tax would be enough to dissuade people from flying to Cornwall, especially when passengers are 'price sensitive' (i.e. air travel is elastic) and may elect to chose a different destination simply because the amount of the tax, especially to an LCC, can amount to a substantial proportion of the cost of the ticket. As Graham (2001) points out, taxes levied by governments (at varying levels) are often used for airport improvements when they have some degree of ownership, but they are also used to fund destination marketing organisations and their marketing operations. For tourists, airports need to be functional as well as ergonomic (Caves & Pickard, 2001) and offer amenities and services that are both useful and efficient. The management of airport space, however, involves balancing the needs of several stakeholders: airlines want to be able to provide their transport service and make a profit, airports want to be able provide the departing (and incoming) passenger with a range of amenities to enhance their experience.

YIELD MANAGEMENT APPLICATIONS IN TRANSPORT

Related to the profitability and management issues associated with airports is how specific modes of transport manage their operations through yield management with the intent of maximising their revenue through a process of carefully managing supply and price in order to ensure that passengers pay the maximum possible price they are willing to pay. This concept relates to that of pricing. Pricing is strongly associated with economic concepts of value and scarcity, where individuals assess the value of a particular good or service in relation to its cost and/or availability. Price-sensitive consumers will react to higher prices by assigning a higher value to the money in their pocket (or for another good or service) than the good or service that it buys them. Non price-sensitive consumers may place a higher value on a good or service because it is convenient (or scarce). They are willing to pay more for that good or service. Thus, firms seek to offer their good or service at a cost that the market will bear; raising prices may or may not have an impact on sales. In the case of transport there are several markets to consider, each with its own sensitivity to price. As a result, transport operators consider how much each market segment would be willing to pay for what the transport operator is providing. This is roughly considered when discussing yield management, which is exactly that: the process by which overall yield is managed (or maximised) given different markets.

Yield management is perhaps one of the more important concepts when examining tourism and transport linkages because of its pervasiveness; both LCCs and network carriers use yield management systems, as do charter carriers, cruise lines, rail companies and car rental firms. In this section, the aviation industry is used, largely because it is the most common transport industry in which yield management practices are examined. Whereas Chapter 3 examined the network of operations and how, geographically, the extent and concentration (and connectivity) of that network needs to be carefully planned, yield management helps to understand the financial implications of providing services across a network to a diverse range of markets.

In the next chapter, the nature of the airline seat will be discussed from the perspective of what is actually marketed to the consumer. The question of concern here, however, is how an airline can adequately price a seat on an aircraft and still retain a profit. Does an airline make money on offering a seat at, for example, 10p? The short answer is 'no' as the cost of providing that seat for sale is likely more than 10p, but in the context of managing operations, achieving market share and maximising revenue, it may, in the long-term, be profitable and strategically advantageous for the seat to be sold at that price. Any business must cover its costs first and foremost before entertaining the possibility of posting a profit, and almost every business tracks their costs down to the most feasible unit. In the case of airlines, trains and cruise ships, this means a firm will know exactly how much it costs to transport someone from point A to point B.

For an airline, the total required to physically transport that seat from sector or stage (i.e. origin to destination) is what is called the seat-mile cost (O'Connor, 1978). The total revenue collected from that seat is referred to as the revenue passenger mile, which is the revenue collected transporting a passenger along a sector. A ratio between the two can be calculated as the load factor, which is the relationship between the passenger miles and seat miles (O'Connor, 1978). For example, an Air New Zealand ATR-72 aircraft, one that is used to regularly fly passengers between some of the smaller provincial centres, will hold 66 seats. The flight distance along the Dunedin and Christchurch sector is 204 miles (although this may differ slightly because of slight variations in the route due to other circumstances). This ATR-72 flight thus outputs 13,464 seat miles (66 seats × 204 miles). If, on a particular flight, 45 seats in the aircraft are filled, then the passenger miles are 9180 and the resulting load factor is thus 68% (seat miles divided by passenger miles).

Load factor calculations are not necessarily calculated by merely dividing the total seats available by the total seats occupied because airlines watch carefully the cost per seat mile, which is governed by several factors. For example, short-haul flights can often carry similar base costs to long-haul flights, such as baggage handling or check-in staff (O'Connor, 1978), yet short-haul flights are often more expensive to operate for an airline because, comparatively, landings and takeoffs consume more fuel than when cruising. As well, frequent rotations (i.e. the number of take-offs and landings) means higher costs through aeronautical charges at airports (O'Connor, 1978).

In general, airlines must carefully control their costs (which is why LCCs generally compete on the basis of lower costs per seat mile than traditional FSAs). Taneja (2003: 11) suggests that 75% of an airline's total costs are fixed costs (the actual aircraft, salaries and airport/maintenance facilities). As many airlines operate in a highly competitive environment, profit margins are thin and managing revenue is thus critical when fixed costs are high. The way an airline will manage its sales is through the process of yield management, which is a system by which airlines (and other service providers, such as hotels, cruise companies, rail companies, etc.) will attempt to match demand with supply and offer the product at a reasonable price. Doganis (2002: 283) notes that yield management

> involves the management of seat access through an airline's reservation control system in order to maximise the total passenger revenue per flight. This is not the same as ensuring the highest load factor or the highest average yield. In fact maximising revenue may in some cases mean that neither of these aims is achieved.

Doganis' point is that it is the revenue accrued from a flight that is of importance to an airline, and not whether the flight was full. The process of maximising revenue is complex and requires software that projects income based on a variety of factors (see Box 7.1). Human input is also provided as a means to inject certain relevant information (e.g. long-term marketing goals or unforeseen or non-trackable externalities) into the system that eventually determines how much the average tourist will pay for a flight from, say, Cairo

BOX 7.1 Overbooking: Managing passenger demand with restricted capacity

Holloway (2003) notes that there are two dependent areas or departments within an airline that control pricing and availability. A pricing department will 'create and administer the passenger fare and freight fare structures applicable to each market' and some larger international airlines will have several pricing departments worldwide that are charged with responding to local market competition and demand (Holloway, 2003: 113). A revenue management department will 'allocate the physical space available on each individual flight-leg (augmented by overbooking limits) between the different fare and rate bases available for sale on that leg' (Holloway, 2003: 115). The role of overbooking is really one of compensation for the operations of a particular sector or flight-leg. For example, a passenger that fails to show up at the airport can mean missed revenue opportunity if sufficient demand for the seat (in the form of late-booking or standby passengers) is low or non-existent. This is deemed as 'spoilage costs' (Holloway, 2003: 546). Similarly, if a passenger cancels a booking at a point in time where it becomes too difficult (or costly) to logistically fill that seat, lost revenue is incurred. A carrier may elect, in planning for no-shows or booking cancellation (with fare refund) in a number of ways:

1. Control of booking classes (see Chapter 6) to minimise cancellations or no-shows: for example, lower fares may carry restrictions on cancellation, ranging from non-refundable to only partially refundable, thus minimising last-minute cancellation by the passenger. Passengers booking on this fare are less likely to not show up for their flight.

2. Overbook in selected classes in order to contain lost revenue from no-shows or cancellations: for example, a flight may be 'overbooked' if there are more passengers than seats. Carriers will intentionally hedge their bets that not all passengers will show up for a particular flight, although this hedging will, to some extent, be managed by the revenue management department by alternating the fare classes sold in relation to demand in the market. For example, in a price sensitive (or elastic) market, a carrier may elect to offer more fare classes with fewer restrictions or penalties on cancellations, but at the same time overbook the flights in preparation for the historic trend of no-shows at the airport. Likewise, a carrier operating in a particularly inelastic market (or on a route where demand is particularly inelastic in relation to the city-pairs served or time of flight operation) may elect to offer fewer fare classes where cancellations are allowed without

penalty as the market will bear these fare types and demand is strong enough to warrant the minimal use of discounted fares or fare types allowed for free cancellation.

As Holloway (2003: 546) points out 'Airlines facing low yields and high break-even load factors have an incentive to overbook more aggressively', although this can be managed based on whether the carrier opts to restrict cancellation or refund opportunities. An RMS, then, is employed to minimise the spoilage costs, yet at the same time control what are known as 'denied boarding costs' (Holloway, 2003: 546). In reality, overbooking can sometimes mean more passengers with valid tickets than seats on the aircraft. This is why, and it usually happens at the gate immediately prior to boarding, airline officials will call for volunteers to wait and take a later flight to the same destination. The incentives offered to passengers willing to forfeit their seat for the flight are the denied boarding costs that a carrier must incur if their overbooking policy results in more passengers than seats. These incentives (to passengers) or denied boarding costs (to airlines) typically can include vouchers for food within the airport, certificates for use on future ticket sales (usually, if not always, with the same airline), or bonus frequent flier miles. These costs also include the cost of administration in situations of overbooking and denied boarding of some passengers, and as Holloway (2003) suggests, can even include the loss of value as held by the passenger and perhaps impact on whether or not future bookings are made with the same carrier.

In February 2005, the EU introduced new rules that compensated passengers if their flights were delayed or cancelled. If a flight is cancelled less than two weeks before flight time, passengers are to be offered a refund or re-routing to their destination, as well as meals, telephone calls and appropriate accommodation. Airlines (especially those represented by the European Low Fares Airline Association) argued that the cost of compensation (up to 600 euros) is often more than the cost of the ticket, and thus appealed the EU rules to the European Court of First Instance in late 2005. In a decision rendered in January 2006, the Court upheld the EU rules. It seems, then, that the practice of overbooking as an element of yield management may be more carefully managed in the future, at least in the EU.

Airlines are not the only transport mode to utilise overbooking procedures. Many rail operators will utilise overbooking strategies to manage supply and demand issues. For example, a large number of tickets sold for travel between cities in close proximity to one another may be last minute, but some may be sold as a 'book' of multiple-journey tickets that are valid for travel at any time. The rail operator, then, must carefully watch demand and loadings to account for the number of platform sales (sales immediately prior to departure) and advance sales. The one benefit that some rail operators have, however, is that the number of passengers can often exceed the number of seats in situations where commuter trains operate. For example, on a recent trip from Edinburgh to Glasgow, this author found himself standing for the entire journey because of unexpected demand for the service operating at the specified time. Throughout the train, passengers were standing in the aisle and the price they paid would have been the same whether or not they would have been able to get an actual seat. Although people were standing, operators still need to carefully manage occupancy rates of rail cars in order to keep within safety limits, which are usually imposed by governments. What some operators may argue, however, is that any train leaving without people standing means lost revenue, thus enforcing the idea as discussed in Chapter 8 that the 'product' on offer may not always be an actual seat.

Questions for consideration

1. To what extent can it be argued that overbooking constitutes a strategy for controlling yield?

2. How might a transport provider, accustomed to overbooking, decide to abolish this policy? What are the marketing and operational implications, including any potential impact on fares?

to London. Knowledge of the market is very important when determining fares. As Hanlon (1999: 190) notes:

> From their market research, airlines know that high-income travellers, business travellers and those travelling for urgent personal reasons (e.g. to attend a funeral) have relatively high price-inelastic demand. At the same time the airlines are aware that holidaymakers, those visiting friends and relations, students on vacation, etc. are all very sensitive in their demand to the fares charged. ... Differences between elastic and inelastic travellers in these respects are often rather wide and present airlines with good opportunities to segment the overall market by reason for travel and to use this as the basis for price discrimination.

Airlines will therefore attempt to maximise their profit by selling a seat at the right price to a particular market segment. As well, the time a ticket is purchased can also play a role, with some last-minute purchases often much higher than those tickets purchased months in advance (and vice versa as the marginal cost of adding an extra person on a flight is minimal).

Interestingly, some airlines will often price certain seats well below what it costs them to operate. As Taneja (2003: 11) points out, '[t]he high fixed costs combined with low marginal costs and the perishable aspects of the product have led managements to introduce some fare structures and levels during normal times that did not, and still do not, reflect the cost of equipment, let alone full-allocated costs'. This may seem somewhat illogical, but there are several justifiable reasons for this (Taneja, 2003). For one, and as indicated in the last chapter, aircraft costing between US$10 and US$300 million dollars do not accrue revenue if they are idle on the ground. As well, an airline may wish to acquire an increased market share. Thus, customers become familiar with the product/service and may chose to fly with the airline at another time. Finally, as Taneja (2003) points out, in the aviation industry the fixed costs tend to be quite high, and even with low fares the airline has an opportunity to generate some cash flow, however small.

Although low fares are quite common in the airline industry today, the reality is that few airlines will allow their flights to operate at a loss. There may be some circumstances where the offer of low fares may be justified. For example, 're-positioning' flights can be run when an airline needs to move one aircraft from one location to another outside of the existing schedule. As a result, the airline may offer extremely low fares which generate both cash flow and even a small profit, especially given that the aircraft needed to be re-positioned anyway. As well, some carriers may even elect to operate a route at a loss if they know that it feeds into a much more profitable (i.e. international) route. For example, consider the network in Figure 3.2. An existing carrier may know that the market for travel from A to B is too small to warrant direct services that would be profitable, so they elect to utilise a smaller aircraft (e.g. an ATR-72) and move passengers to C first, at which point they board a 737–800 and fly to B. This carrier may elect to run the A to B flight at a slight loss if they think that they are achieving significant market penetration in A to warrant. As well, they may price their seats from B to C in such a way as to make up for the losses accrued on the A to B sector. Of course, when competition enters into this mix, downward pressure on prices between any of the sectors may hinder profitability and even more so if a new entrant decides to offer direct services from A to C.

Providing real examples of the concept of yield management is almost impossible as airlines will closely guard their costs and revenue by sector. There are, however, some basic principles by which yield management works in relation to the pricing of aircraft seating. What is important to keep in mind, however, is that quite often airline seat sales or low fares in general are designed more as a marketing tool than a means to offer seats to customers. Airlines cannot continuously price all seats at below cost else the flight will not return a profit. As Doganis (2002) points out, Philippines Airlines fares between the Philippines and the United States, in the early 1990s, were low enough to capture 70% of

Table 7.2 Yield management and fare levels, example 1

Distance (km) from A to B			1050
Capacity (number of seats on the aircraft)			150
Available seat kilometres (ASKs)			157,500
Operating cost (estimated)			$18,000
Cost per ASK (cost per available seat kilometre, or unit cost)			$0.11
Loading (seats sold)			136
		Price per seat	
'Ultra saver' fare	10 seats	$109	$1090
'Super saver' fare	110 seats	$199	$21,890
'Try 'N' save' fare	16 seats	$299	$4784
Total flight revenue			$27,764

the market. Despite the fact their load factors were high, the airline lost money on the sector.

In the example in Table 7.2, a flight from point A to B (totalling 1050 kilometres) has the capacity of 150 seats, all of which are configured for economy class. This results in 157,500 ASKs (although available seat *miles*, or ASMs, are often used). With an estimated operating costs of $15,000 (the exact currency type is irrelevant for the purposes of this example), the cost per ASK (which is the unit cost) is $0.11. This is what it costs the airline to physically transport that seat on this particular route. Suppose, then, that 136 people are on this particular flight. When looking at the fare splits for all passengers (and three broad fare types are used to illustrate the point, but there are often, in reality, many more fare classes and prices), 10 passengers paid $109 (the ultra saver fare) for their seat, 110 paid $199 (the super saver fare) and only 16 paid $299 (the no saver fare). The total revenue for the flight (based on tickets only, not including any snacks or beverages for which the airline may choose to charge) is therefore $27,764. If the load (136 people) is multiplied by the distance (1050 kilometres), the result is 142,800, which is the total passenger kilometres flown on this particular flight. This figure can then be used to calculate the yield per seat kilometre (also known as the yield), which is simply the net revenue divided by the passenger kilometres flown. In this case, it is $0.19, which is compared to the cost per ASK of $0.11.

If the airline in this example was to sell all of the seats on that sector at the ultra saver fare, the results become quite interesting. In flight represented in Table 7.3, seats were sold at $109 which, because of strong demand at that price, resulted in a full aeroplane.

Table 7.3 Yield management and fare levels, example 2

Distance (km) from A to B			1050
Capacity (number of seats on the aircraft)			150
ASKs			157,500
Operating cost (estimated)			$18,000
Cost per ASK			$0.11
Loading (seats sold)			150
		Price per seat	
'Ultra saver' fare	150 seats	$109	$16,350
'Super saver' fare	0 seats	$199	0
'Try 'N' save' fare	0 seats	$299	0
Total flight revenue			$16,350
RPKs (revenue passengers multiplied by the number of kilometres flown)			157,500
Yield per seat kilometre (yield)			$0.10

The overall profitability of the flight, however, is negative, with the yield per seat kilometre now sitting at $0.10 when the cost per ASK is still $0.11. In other words, costs exceeded yield. Of course, another way of examining the profitability of this particular flight is to note that revenue ($16,350) versus costs ($18,000), but the point here is to illustrate how an airline might maximise revenue by selectively pricing seats. To be fair, this example and associated calculations are highly simplified, but the basic principle is that airlines will generally not consciously sell all seats on a flight at a low fare such as to jeopardise profitability of that flight. As indicated above, however, an airline may decide to operate a flight at a loss for a variety of reasons, and it may be perfectly reasonable from a business standpoint to operate a flight such as the one represented in Table 7.3.

Figure 7.1 demonstrates the principle of yield management in the context of consumer surplus, where the balance is set between what a consumer is willing to pay and the price at which an airline is willing to sell a seat in the context of marginal revenue it gains from selling that particular seat. Hanlon (1999: 192–194) notes that this price/cost versus output model aptly illustrates pricing strategies adopted by airlines. A fare at P1 would maximise profits as the amount of revenue (MR) is equal to the marginal cost (MC) of providing that seat. The airline may also sell some seats at cheaper fares (Q2 up to Qm, where the MC increases because demand would require introducing an additional flight). The shaded areas represent consumer surplus, where passengers are effectively gaining a net benefit because the price they pay is effectively below the level of demand. In other words, consumer surplus is present where the price paid is below what they would be willing to pay. Of course, an airline would like nothing better than to sell all of its seats at P1, but demand for seats is not constant at that price level. Thus, different pricing levels exist that are meant to reflect demand for seats at those prices. As Hanlon (1999: 194) notes

> By discriminating between passengers the objective of the airline is to expropriate as much as possible of what would otherwise be passenger consumer surplus if all seats were sold at MC (the shaded areas). The purpose of restricting the availability of the cheaper fares is inhibit passengers trading down from more expensive fares, or to limit what in airline parlance is called 'revenue diluation'.

For the average tourist, then, the big question is often 'When should I buy my ticket'? Given Figure 7.1, it might seem that purchasing in advance always results in the cheapest fares, but an airline may discover that advance purchasers on some rates have a higher willingness to pay than those who book and purchase closer to the time of departure. Figure 7.1 is simplified because it illustrates how an airline might approach fare prices, but

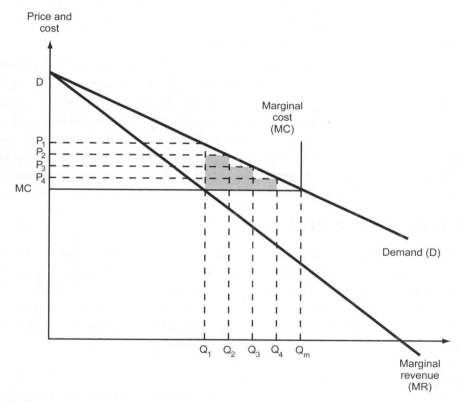

Figure 7.1 Yield management and consumer surplus

Source: Hanlon (1999) with permission from Elsevier.

211

in reality fares can change many times in the months or days leading up to departure. What is evident from the above discussion, however, is that the management of revenue in transport operations is paramount and often means that some travellers will pay more for a seat than other travellers, even when that physical difference between the seat itself and the service on offer is non-existent. For the passenger, the negatives of price discrimination (another term for yield management, although one with a somewhat negative overtone) can be outweighed by the value held of the good or service in question. As Botimer notes:

> Revenue management uses differentiated fare products priced at varying levels and booking limits to provide a flexible, flight-specific method of seat inventory allocation. To achieve efficiency in allocation, it is desirable to fill the aircraft with those passengers who value the service most *at departure* prompting a need to: (1) identify the passengers who value seats most; and (2) protect seats to accommodate those passengers. Airlines identify passengers by their values of willingness to pay by using price *discrimination* techniques. Airlines protect seats in their computer reservations systems for higher paying passengers through *seat inventory control* (or yield management) techniques based on forecasts of expected arrivals for different classes of service. (Botimer, 1996: 314; italics in original)

For airlines, yield management is an effective way of addressing fluctuations in demand and shifting costs. It is in use because, for the most part, it can be highly effective. For example, Belobaba and Wilson (1997) ran a simulation that showed that utilising effective yield management results in an overall increase in revenue. More importantly, they also were able to demonstrate that an airline who is first to utilise yield management in a competitive situation will benefit. The fact that the vast majority of carriers worldwide utilise an RMS or some form of yield management would suggest that its importance and success is meaningful.

SAFETY AND SECURITY MANAGEMENT

In many ways, safety and security are two separate issues, yet they remain inextricably linked. A secure transport environment is not necessarily a safe transport environment and vice versa. One could even argue that a totally secure transport environment is largely unattainable. For tourism, the perception of being safe and secure is often the price of entry for most destinations (Hall *et al.*, 2003). The need to incorporate safety and security measures in transport can be rationalised in several ways:

1. The perceived level of safety of a mode of transport can have significant impacts on a destination; for example, in January 2006 the EC established a blacklist of airlines (most of which are African) that were no longer permitted to fly into EU airspace because they lacked the ability to maintain aircraft to accepted international standards (Table 7.4). Such an action can have severe implications, not only for the airline(s) but also for those passengers who arrive in the EU as tourists and for those EU residents who might wish to utilise a blacklisted airline to travel to a foreign country.

2. Security levels have generally increased worldwide as a result of a combination of reasons: increased traffic overall, increased threats to security and an increased number of destinations served. Security issues are generally associated with airlines, but other forms of transport are involved in monitoring and establishing security and safety requirements. For example, British mainline railway stations are likely to soon introduce security screening procedures (x-ray scanning and frisking by security personnel) not unlike those found in airports (The Age, 2005).

3. Security is enhanced and made relevant both prior to and during transport. As such, it often falls under the purview of different government organisations as well as private enterprise. Following attacks on cruise ships by modern pirates around the Horn of Africa in 2005, there have been calls for regional governments to get involved in securing the waters and help the existing United Nations and Unites States patrolling warships (ABC News, 2005).

Table 7.4 List of carriers whose activities are banned within the EU

Legal name on air operating certificate (trading name, if applicable)	*Operating state*
Air Koryo	DPRK
Air Service Comores	Comores
Ariana Afghan Airlines2	Afghanistan
BGB Air	Kazakhstan
GST Aero Air Company	Kazakhstan
Phoenix Aviation	Kyrghizstan
Phuket Airlines	Thailand
Reem Air	Kyrghizstan
Silverback Cargo Freighters	Rwanda
Africa One	RDC
African Company Airlines	RDC
Aigle Aviation	RDC
Air Boyoma	RDC
Air Kasai	RDC
Air Navette	RDC

Legal name on air operating certificate (trading name, if applicable)	Operating state
Air Tropiques s.p.r.l.	RDC
ATO – Air Transport Office	RDC
Blue Airlines	RDC
Business Aviation s.p.r.l.	RDC
Butembo Airlines	RDC
CAA – Compagnie Africaine d'Aviation	RDC
Cargo Bull Aviation	RDC
Central Air Express	RDC
Cetraca Aviation Service	RDC
Chc Stelavia	RDC
Comair	RDC
Compagnie Africaine D'aviation	RDC
Co–za Airways	RDC
Das Airlines	RDC
Doren Aircargo	RDC
Enterprise World Airways	RDC
Filair	RDC
Free Airlines	RDC
Galaxy Corporation	RDC
Gr Aviation	RDC
Global Airways	RDC
Goma Express	RDC
Great Lake Business Company	RDC
I.T.A.B. – International Trans Air Business	RDC
JETAIR – Jet Aero Services, s.p.r.l.	RDC
Kinshasa Airways, s.p.r.l	RDC
Kivu Air	RDC
LAC – Lignes Aériennes Congolaises	RDC
Malu Aviation	RDC
Malila Airlift	RDC

Legal name on air operating certificate (trading name, if applicable)	Operating state
Mango Mat	RDC
Rwabika 'Bushi Express'	RDC
Safari Logistics	RDC
Services Air	RDC
Tembo Air Services	RDC
Thom's Airways	RDC
Tmk Air Commuter	RDC
Tracep	RDC
Trans Air Cargo Services	RDC
TRANSPORTS AERIENNES CONGOLAIS (TRACO)	RDC
Uhuru Airlines	RDC
Virunga Air Charter	RDC
Waltair Aviation	RDC
Wimbi Diri Airways	RDC
Air Consul SA	Equatorial Guinea
Avirex Guinee Equatoriale	Equatorial Guinea
COAGE – Compagnie Aeree de Guinee Equatorial	Equatorial Guinea
Ecuato Guineana de Aviacion	Equatorial Guinea
Ecuatorial Cargo	Equatorial Guinea
GEASA – Guinea Ecuatorial Airlines SA	Equatorial Guinea
GETRA – Guinea Ecuatorial de Transportes Ae5eos	Equatorial Guinea
Jetline Inc.	Equatorial Guinea
KNG Transavia Cargo	Equatorial Guinea
Prompt Air GE SA	Equatorial Guinea
UTAGE – Union de Transport Aereo de Guinea Ecuatorial	Equatorial Guinea
International Air Services	Liberia
Satgur Air Transport, Corp.	Liberia
Weasua Air Transport, Co. Ltd	Liberia

Legal name on air operating certificate (trading name, if applicable)	Operating state
All air carriers certified by the authorities with responsibility for regulatory oversight of Sierra Leone, including,	Sierra Leone
Aerolift, Co. Ltd	Sierra Leone
Afrik Air Links	Sierra Leone
Air Leone, Ltd	Sierra Leone
Air Rum, Ltd	Sierra Leone
Air Salone, Ltd	Sierra Leone
Air Universal, Ltd	Sierra Leone
Destiny Air Services, Ltd	Sierra Leone
First Line Air (SL), Ltd	Sierra Leone
Heavylift Cargo	Sierra Leone
Paramount Airlines, Ltd	Sierra Leone
Star Air, Ltd	Sierra Leone
Teebah Airways	Sierra Leone
West Coast Airways Ltd.	Sierra Leone
African International Airways, (Pty) Ltd	Swaziland
Airlink Swaziland, Ltd	Swaziland
Jet Africa	Swaziland
Northeast Airlines, (Pty) Ltd	Swaziland
Scan Air Charter, Ltd	Swaziland
Swazi Express Airways	Swaziland

Source: Adapted from http://europa.eu.int/comm/transport/air/safety/doc/flywell/2006_03_22_flywell_list_en.pdf (accessed 25 March 2006)

With respect to marine transport, Lois *et al.* (2004: 104) note that there are several points along the operational phase of a cruise ship in which passengers and crew are at risk: passenger boarding (fire in the terminal, gangway collapse, noise), leaving port (passengers falling overboard, collision), at cruise (collision, grounding, fire, engine failure), at dock (hard docking, fire) and disembarkation (slips and falls). Of course, marine transport is not the only mode to have safety risks. Janic (2000: 44) discusses the nature of risk and security in aviation and outlines five features of airline accidents that distinguish them from the impact of accidents involving other modes of travel:

216

1. Because flying may take place over long distances, accidents may occur at any point in time or space. Hence, there is exposure to individual and global hazard.

2. Passengers and aircraft crews are primal target groups exposed to risk of an accident but there are individuals on the ground who may be exposed to the same accidents albeit at a lower probability.

3. Although being a rare event in an absolute sense, aircraft accidents can have severe implications.

4. Conditionally, any aircraft movement is an inherently risky event, then, according to probability theory, aircraft accidents may be classified as highly unlikely (although possible) events.

5. With respect to time dependency, risk is always present during given time and space horizons (i.e. whenever a fight takes place). The effect is non-cumulative and particularly related to the separate exposures of the people on board.

Health safety on cruises has been the subject of much media attention, with the problems experienced by passengers ranging from 'simple' food poisoning to more series viral outbreaks. Not all incidents, however, can be definitively linked to poor sanitation efforts. In early October 2005, reports emerged suggesting that warming ocean waters in and around Alaska are thought to be responsible for the contamination of local shellfish with bacteria. These shellfish are subsequently consumed on-board ships cruising from the west coast of the United States up into the Alaskan region. Previously, the same waters were thought cold enough to thwart the proliferation of harmful bacteria in shellfish. Nonetheless, illness outbreaks on cruise ships do occur (see Table 7.5).

Despite air accidents frequently being shown on evening newscasts (to some extent, because they are relatively rare [Motevalli & Stough, 2004]), the ICAO reports that the fatality rate in aircraft accidents actually decreased between 1970 and 1993, even though the number of passengers increased some 500% (Janic, 2000). In fact, air travel is comparatively safe:

1. New aircraft designs have incorporated numerous safety measures, largely by virtue of international agreed specifications, but also because safer aircraft can be marketed by the manufacturer to potential customers (e.g. airlines).

2. Navigation systems have become sophisticated to the point where human error in the past can be mitigated through active on-board monitoring of environmental conditions and nearby aircraft movements. For example, many airlines have introduced collision-avoidance systems in some aircraft to minimise the risk of mid-air collisions (Kayton & Fried, 1997). Improvements in ground radar systems at major airports have also helped to mitigate ground incursions.

Table 7.5 Selected illness outbreaks on cruises for Q4 2004

December 16	*Golden Princess* (Princess Cruises)	A passenger reports there was a significant outbreak of illness (hundreds of passengers affected) on the Caribbean cruise, December 12–19. According to CDC [centre for disease control]: the ship reported that an unusual number of passengers and some crew members were experiencing GI [gastrointestinal] illness. The ship's medical staff reported that 84 of 2742 (3.06%) passengers and 15 of 1100 (1.36%) crew members were ill. Predominant symptoms are diarrhea and vomiting. The cruise ends in San Juan on December 19.
December 13	*Silver Shadow* (Silversea Cruises)	The ship reported that an unusual number of passengers and some crew members were experiencing GI illness. The ship's medical staff reported that 11 of 275 (4%) passengers and 20 of 291 (6.87%) crew members were ill. Predominant symptoms are diarrhea and vomiting. The cruise ends in San Diego on December 14.
December 10	*Norwegian Dream* (Norwegian Cruise Line)	The ship reported that an unusual number of passengers and some crew members were experiencing GI illness. The ship's medical staff reported that 73 of 1749 (9.37%) passengers and 9 of 744 (1.21%) crew members were ill. Predominant symptoms are diarrhea and vomiting. The cruise ends in New Orleans on December 12. According to a passenger, the numbers were significantly higher: 'Once the passengers realized that reporting gastrointestinal illnesses would result in a 48 hour quarantine, many just suffered and gutted it out (pun intended) in their rooms.'
December 10	*Norwegian Sea* (Norwegian Cruise Line)	The ship reported that an unusual number of passengers and some crew members were experiencing GI illness. The ship's medical staff reported that 44 of 1531 (2.87%) passengers and 4 of 683 (0.58%) crew members were ill. Predominant symptoms are diarrhea and vomiting. The cruise ends in Houston on December 11.
December 7	*M/V Explorer*	The ship reported that an unusual number of passengers and some crew members were experiencing GI illness. The ship's medical staff reported that 71 of 758 (9.37%) passengers and 1 of 195 (0.51%) crew members were ill. Predominant symptoms are diarrhea and vomiting. The cruise ends in Fort Lauderdale on December 8.

| November 2 | *Sun Princess* (Princess Cruises) | The ten-day cruise was struck with an outbreak of illness. According to one passenger: 'I was confined (quaren-teened) to my cabin for 5 days with the Norwalk Virus. I got it 4 days into the sailing and at the 1st port we arrived at. I never left the ship. We were later told that the service in the dining room was so poor because everyone was sick. Then we heard from the entertainer that she had the flu and a fever and the whole crew was given a vaccine (flu shot).' Representatives of the CDC boarded the ship, but no information has yet been released. |
| October 3 | *Veendam* (Holland America Line) | The ship reported that an unusual number of passengers and some crew members were experiencing GI illness. The ship's medical staff reported that 39 of 1230 (3.17%) passengers and 2 of 557 (0.36%) crew members were ill. Predominant symptoms are diarrhea and vomiting. The cruise began in San Diego and will end October 14. |

Source: Reproduced with permission from www.cruisejunkie.com

3. Air traffic control systems have undergone substantial technological improvements in the past several decades (Brooker, 2003), thus rendering aircraft movements in the sky and on the ground safer now than at any point in the history of civil aviation, despite rapid growth in the industry. Concern still exists, however, for the organisation and operation of aircraft in high-density air space, such as continental Europe where air traffic has increased over the past several decades and where individual airports often have their own traffic control centres. The concern generally relates to the rate at which aircraft are 'handed off' from one control centre to another when crossing multiple countries and control areas. Traffic across the Atlantic Ocean, from eastern North America to Europe, is handled by the OACC (operated by National Air Traffic Services, UK), which covers some 633,000 square miles:

> As radar only has a range of some 200 miles, controllers in the Oceanic Area Control Centre [OACC] use position reports and estimates passed from pilots to ensure aircraft are safely separated. This information is provided using high frequency radio and is transmitted and received via a radio communications station at Ballygireen, near Shannon in Ireland. To take account of passenger demands, time zone differences and airport noise restrictions, most North Atlantic flights operate in two time blocks – westbound in the late morning and afternoon and east bound during the night and early morning. Because of this and the limited height band for economical jet operations the airspace is comparatively congested. To safely accommodate as many aircraft a possible an organised track structure is created every 12 hours. This allows aircraft to be handled in an orderly and efficient manner. The OACC is respon-

sible for the day track system and the Gander Centre in Canada provides the night track system. After entering oceanic airspace, pilots are required to make position reports at every ten degrees of longitude. These reports are fed into the controllers' flight data processing system (FDPS) which automatically updates the controllers' traffic information displays. The FDPS alerts the controller if a report is overdue, or if the situation is other than that expected. Based on the time of the last reported position and the forecast winds the computer will work out an estimate for the next position. It will also warn the controller if the separation between any two flights is approaching the minimum allowed. (http://www.nats.co.uk/services/soacc1.html; accessed 27 September 2005)

4. Various international organisations have implemented safety monitoring programmes that cover technical and manpower elements. These include the United States' IASA, the Safety of Foreign Aircraft Programme from the European Civil Aviation Conference, and the Universal Safety Oversight Audit Programme established by the ICAO. The adherence to these, and many other, safety protocols is enshrined in international agreements and is often required before bilateral or multilateral agreements are signed and enacted. In general, organisations such as the ICAO have limited powers of enforcement (Button *et al.*, 2004). Instead, programmes such as IASA in the United States are designed to evaluate airline compliance with the codes established by ICAO.

5. Passengers are more aware of safety regulations and advice. Most, if not all, major international airlines feature on-board safety videos and demonstrations before take-off. They may also include safety information affixed to the back of seats or on cards in seat pockets. Like guests at hotels, passengers are often asked to note clearly the location of nearby exits in case of emergency.

An excellent example of the importance of passenger understanding of safety measures on board an aircraft was the crash of Air France Flight 358 on 2 August 2005 at Toronto's Pearson International Airport (IATA: YYZ). The aircraft involved was an Airbus A340–300 with 309 passengers and crew onboard. Preliminary accident analysis indicated that it may have skidded in wet conditions on the runway, possibly due to a microburst (a sudden downward wind blast), resulting in the aircraft coming to a rest in a small ravine and catching fire. Miraculously, no passengers were killed. The on-duty flight attendants successfully evacuated all passengers within minutes, and this obviously contributed to the lack of fatalities. Most modern aircraft are designed to be evacuated in as little as 90 seconds, regardless of the passenger loading. Likewise, crew are exhaustively trained in safety and evacuation procedures. Airport emergency services are also trained to respond to an accident within minutes, as was the case with AF358. Shortly after the crash, Transport Canada indicated that it would be reviewing safety procedures at airports, specifically new technologies that are designed to minimise aircraft damage and death and injury. One such measure is the use of soft end-point material at the end of runways to prevent massive overshooting such as the case with AF358.

POST-11 SEPTEMBER

The events of 11 September 2001 spawned radical changes in the securing of the infrastructure associated with transport around the world. In the United States, the Federal government instituted the Department of Homeland Security, the purview of which was the safety and security of the entire country but whose focus was publicly associated with the guardianship of air transport facilities. This meant that, almost overnight, the screening of air passengers was shifted out of the hands of private contractors at most airports in favour of the new TSA. For many travellers, the frequent consequence of the increased security was lengthy delays in security screenings at major airports, and a very detailed list of what could and could not be brought aboard an aircraft (see www.tsa.gov for the most recent list). Since its inception, the TSA has come under increasing scrutiny by the travelling public. On many online bulletin boards (e.g. www.flyertalk.com), travellers post stories about inconsistent screening procedures, failure to find and confiscate prohibited items and rude treatment by TSA staff.

In Australia, news reports in late 2005 suggested that the Australian national government is looking to spend upwards of AUS$200 million on upgrades to airport security programmes across the country. This follows a report, commissioned by the government to identify the security arrangements at major airports, which suggested that policing at the country's airports is largely inadequate and dysfunctional. As Australia has been involved in recent global conflicts and has been the victim of terrorist attacks overseas, the report is a severe indictment of the current state of affairs. Opposition parties in Australia have also been calling for a similar government department to oversee security throughout the country, not unlike the United States' Department of Homeland Security. Using PNRs, the United States acquires passenger information for flights entering US airspace and flights arriving from Europe. Although these data have been provided by the EU since 2003, the European Court of Justice recently indicated that handing over data to the United States government is potentially in breach of individual's privacy (RTE News, 2005).

The events of 11 September, and even the events that have followed (Bali bombings, the war in Iraq) have clearly ushered in a new era in safety and security management. At one point, it was once not unheard of for passengers to carry firearms on domestic flights in the United States (with the airline of course having full knowledge as they would have been declared prior to boarding). Today, the immediate confiscation of cigarette lighters is not uncommon in some airports, and significantly more passengers are subjected to secondary screening at security checkpoints prior to boarding. In some cases, such as Auckland International Airport in New Zealand, passengers departing New Zealand for the United States (either Los Angeles or San Francisco) are subjected to two screenings: once after check-in and again before entering the boarding lounge before being seating on the aircraft. For the airport, this has meant that certain areas (airside) are cordoned off for use by flights on these routes. The cost of this additional screening is generally borne by either the airport or the carrier (and sometimes both), which can result in increased fares or the application of security fees on top of fares.

OTHER SECURITY THREATS TO TRANSPORT

Between 1990 and 2003, over 52,000 animal strikes, 97% of which were bird strikes, were reported at United States airports. Aircraft components such as the nose (or radome in larger aircraft, where sensitive radar equipment is housed), windshields and engines bear the most brunt, and the results can often be catastrophic. Many bird species are attracted to airports as they are expansive and flat sections of land. As well, migratory birds such as Canada Geese were a factor in over 800 strikes at US airports between 1990 and 2003 (FAA, 2004). Canada Geese are not small, and as such they can do tremendous damage to aircraft components, but even smaller birds can cause engine failure and thus force pilots to abort either a landing or take-off and re-direct or re-attempt a landing or take-off. After an Aero Perlas de Havilland DCH-6 (Twin Otter) aircraft was affected by a bird strike in Central America, the aircraft was forced to ditch at sea and 20 people lost their lives.

Managing wildlife within airport boundaries can be challenging. At Dunedin International Airport in New Zealand it is not uncommon to see a vehicle speeding up and down the runway searching for birds in the immediately vicinity only minutes before an aircraft departs or arrives. If small groups of birds are found, the driver fires a small pistol (with blank bullets) in order to drive them away. At one time, the vehicle used to light up its orange safety lights which used to be enough to rid the runway area of birds. Over time, however, the birds became used to the lights and it was necessary to utilise loud noises to encourage them to move along. At Anchorage, Alaska, the problem is not so much with bird strikes but with moose wandering on to the runway. These mammals are by no means insignificant and can do incredible damage to an aircraft as they can typically weigh over 450 kilogrammes and stand almost 2 metres in height. In October 2005, this problem seems to have been solved with the introduction of a electric strip along the runway which gives wandering moose a short electric jolt (along with a loud snapping sound) if they are about to cross onto the runway itself (Reuters, 2005).

Other safety and security issues relate to those modes of transport operated by tourists themselves. Tourists travelling to foreign countries may only need an International Driving Permit (IPD) to legally operate a motor vehicle. The IPD was established by the 1949 UN Convention on Road Traffic (after an earlier Convention in 1926) that allowed holders of valid driving licences in their home country to receive the IDP without any further testing, although in many countries there are restrictions in place for holders of IDPs. In New Zealand, many tourists elect to rent smaller motor homes (called 'Maui vans') and tour around the country. Some of them may hold IDPs while others may hold permits from their country of origin that may be recognised as valid in New Zealand. The problem, however, is that it is incumbent upon tourists to learn the rules of the road whilst visiting. For North American visitors, rental agencies constantly remind tourists to 'keep left', yet on more than one occasion this author has encountered Maui vans pulling into the wrong lane onto a major highway (in New Zealand, a major highway is often a bi-directional, two-lane highway). This illustrates that there are safety issues with managing tourist flows where they utilise personal transport in their mobility. It is therefore incumbent upon destination marketing organisations to work closely with automobile associations, rental agencies and even publishers of guidebooks worldwide to ensure that rules of the road are available to tourists.

While transport is the vector for passengers and tourists, it can also be the prime vector for the spread of disease. The speed with which passengers can move across the globe is ultimately the speed at which viruses and disease can spread. Governments, airlines and the public can be forgiven for being scared at the potential economic and social upheaval the threat of airborne particulates can bring from overseas destination. Kenyon *et al.* (1996) found that passengers seated on an aircraft within approximately two rows of an infected person with tuberculosis were in danger of getting infected themselves. The SARS scare in Asia in 2003 wreaked havoc with many airlines, including American Airlines and Singapore Airlines, both of which had extensive route networks that included many Asian destinations. Passengers were either simply afraid to fly or local governments ordered flights cancelled. On 11 April 2003, a 48-year-old Hong Kong businessman tested positive for the SARS coronavirus after a flight from Hong Kong. Before confirmation of SARS was established, this particular passenger travelled on seven flights within continental Europe. Using passenger manifests of the seven flights on which the patient flew, Breugelmans *et al.* (2004) tested the capacity of SARS to be transmitted within an aircraft cabin by conducting tests on a sample of passengers (although all passengers were contacted, not all agreed to participate in the study). None of the passengers tested were infected with the SARS coronavirus, and the researchers concluded that efficient transmission in an aircraft cabin was not likely. Breugelmans *et al.* (2004) note that their results are consistent with other studies that had similar conclusions.

Although SARS is not easily vectored in closed environments such as aircraft cabins, the public perception was that it was dangerous to board aircraft to and from the Asian region (Mason *et al.*, 2005). Almost immediately after the presence of SARS was announced, the impact on tourism in the Asian region was swift and, unfortunately, catastrophic. According to the WTTC (2003), tourism arrivals fell by at least 70% across the Asian region. McKercher and Chon (2004, referencing a news article that appeared in the *London Evening Standard* newspaper) note that media coverage showing airline passengers falling ill had severe repercussions of how the Asian region was perceived as a tourism destination.

More recently, attention has been directed at the potential impacts of the H5N1 subtype of the avian bird influenza virus. Once again, airlines and certainly other transport firms, are carefully watching the situation and considering the impact in several ways. The impact on their operations, largely in the form of considerable drop in demand, could be significant if a global flu epidemic strikes, especially if it is found that the virus can easily spread in, for example, an aircraft cabin (unlike SARS). In late 2005, some major international hub airports, for example Los Angeles International Airport, were already developing plans for quarantining passengers if necessary (Mercury News, 2005). The lessons learned from SARS, and even from H5N1 (it is still unclear as to the real danger it poses), suggest that modern transport in all its efficiencies of mobility that it provides can be responsible for the rapid spread of disease and viruses. What is necessarily is for organisations such as the ICAO and the IATA to carefully consider any new policies of disinfecting and cleaning that may be required when future epidemics or pandemics occur.

CHAPTER SUMMARY

The shape of management of transport operations can have significant impacts on tourism. For example, the decision of one or two airlines to cease operations out of a particular airport can have negative implications for the destinations served by the carriers addressing these markets; on the other hand, in the short term there may be an increase utilisation of coach or other forms of ground transport (perhaps even personal cars) for the purposes of recreation or tourism closer to home. Revisiting Prideaux's transport cost model (2000a, 2004; see also Chapter 2), the form of transport can, in some situations, dictate travel flows. Similarly, pricing can be quite erratic in some markets due to competition and efforts by a transport provider to stimulate demand. In some cases, the decision might be made to 'open up' certain fare classes and/or utilise yield management to ensure maximised revenue.

This chapter has utilised air transport heavily in its explanation of yield management largely because the stability of air transport is, at the time of writing, a concern that is worldwide. Finally, safety and security is paramount not only in the destination but also in the form of transport. In some preliminary research conducted by this author in New Zealand across a representative sample of residents, safety and security was found to be one of the top three travel motivators that determine whether people choose to fly or not. In effect, safety and security are the price of entry. In many situations, countries are no longer willing to risk their very public reputations as safe destinations when competition for global tourist traffic is immense. This may be one reason why several countries around the world are closely examining the safety records of both airlines and manufacturers.

Box 7.2 Case study – Airport expansion: Heathrow's Terminal 5

The ongoing construction of the new terminal at London's Heathrow airport is seen as necessary by many because London functions as one of busiest international airports in the world. In 2004, 67 million passengers passed through the airport, representing an increase of over 6% from the previous year (ATW, 2005b). Terminal 5's construction was approved in 2001. From May 1995 until March 1999, the longest public inquiry in the UK's history was held, totalling some 525 days. The inquiry focused on a number of subjects, including the overall economic need of the new terminal, land use policies, access to the terminal itself, and noise and air quality concerns. The project is being funded by the BAA (with some help from British Airways) at a cost of £4.2 billion. Construction started in September 2002 and the first phase of the project is to be completed by April 2008. The new terminal will undoubtedly be a marvel of mobility, with fully integrated road and rail transport (including tunnels for rail service along the Piccadilly Line and the Heathrow Express Line) and a full automated people mover to shuttle passengers from the main terminal to the satellite buildings. Other facts about the new terminal:

- The site of the new terminal is 260 acres, roughly the size of Hyde Park in London.
- The terminal building will be 400 m long and have five full floors.
- It has provision for an additional 60 aircraft stands, with approximately 15 of these designed to be used by the new Airbus A380.
- It has the capacity to serve 30 million passengers per year, which will mean Heathrow overall will serve some 90 million per year (www.baa.com).
- Two rivers have already been diverted around the new development.

The planning and development of Terminal 5, however, has been somewhat controversial. Many opponents to the new terminal point to the likely increase in noise and air pollution, and suggest that congestion at the airport and the immediate area will be substantial. As the airport is located in the London Borough of Hillingdon, residents there have continued to voice opposition to the development. Friends of the Earth argue that Heathrow already causes pollution in the South East from air and road traffic emissions, and the noise levels from existing flight operations already 'disrupt the sleep of half a million people' (Friends of the Earth, www.foe.co.uk/campaigns/transport/case_studies/ heathrow.html). The controversy surrounding the expansion of Heathrow will likely continue, however, as there have been recent calls for the construction of a new runway (which will mean demolition of certain areas) and a future Terminal 6. This announcement (from 2003) was met with similar consternation. The HACAN recently suggested that the expansion will be a detriment to the communities surrounding the airport (Trivedi, 2003). As BBC News reported (Trivedi, 2003), the government has several 'conditions' that the new terminal will need to address with respect to the overall sustainability of an additional terminal beyond Terminal 5, including the use of clean fuels for service vehicles and the introduction of charges for driving to the airport.

Questions for consideration

1. Make a list of all stakeholders that would need to be consulted regarding the expansion of the largest airport in the country in which you live.

2. To what extent could it be argued that airports constitute a 'public good' and thus need to be allowed to operate without intrusion from external interests?

SELF-REVIEW QUESTIONS

1. Describe, in your own words, RPKs and ASKs.

2. Define yield management in relation to consumer surplus.

3. What are the differences between aeronautical and non-aeronautical charges in the context of airport management?

ESSAY QUESTIONS

1. What impact can terrorism have on travel flows (both domestic and international) and the operations of airlines or other forms of transport?

2. Is a slot a piece of real estate available for an airport to sell (or for an airline to trade) or is it a right of access to which governments must attribute rules and regulations?

3. Why has there been a difference in approaches to privatisation and liberalisation of transport infrastructure and operations in the United States and the UK?

KEY SOURCES

Doganis, R. (1992) *The Airport Business.* London: Routledge.

Graham, A. (2001) *Managing Airports: An International Perspective.* Oxford: Butterworth-Heinemann.

These two titles offer excellent explorations of the structure of modern airports. It is useful to juxtapose them to understand how the study and analysis of airports has changed somewhat over the nearly a decade that separates their publication. Where Doganis' volume concentrates on overall structure, including cost structures, scheduling, operations and relationships with customers (e.g. airlines), Graham's text captures the privatisation and liberalisation of modern airports in depth (owing to nature of the operational environment of many airports during which the text was written) and outlines the move towards non-aeronautical revenue streams.

ACI – www.airports.org

ACI is an international organisation representing the interests of airports worldwide. The website provides various publications and position papers relating to issues in global air transport and airport management. To compliment the views from ACI, the IATA website should be visited as well (www.iata.org).

CHAPTER 8:

TRANSPORT AND TOURISM MARKETING

LEARNING OBJECTIVES

After reading this chapter, you should be able to

1. Appreciate the importance and complexity of transport marketing in relation to tourism.

2. Understand and explain the differences and similarities between treating transport as a service and as a product.

3. Recognise that transport marketing can often involve the marketing of destinations.

4. Appreciate the various forms of strategic marketing in transport and their relationship to tourism marketing and development.

5. Understand how service quality is assessed in transport operations.

INTRODUCTION

One of the more intriguing aspects of transport marketing is that, quite often, the marketing of transport is critical to the overall development and viability of attractions, destinations and countries. In other words, it could be argued that transport marketing in association with tourism fulfils a dual role: 1) that of marketing the product/service (a distinction to be debated later in this chapter) in its own right in order to drive business; and 2) the secondary destination marketing that transport providers ultimately provide, such that a transport operation may elect to promote and advertise a destination itself for the purpose of driving its own business or operations. The second point is critical as it demonstrates how the marketing of transport operations is often closely allied with other

228

marketing efforts as established or implemented by destinations or attractions. Thus, while distribution systems feature strongly in the sales of transport products/services, perhaps more consistent and meaningful characterisation would rest with the multi-line, often integrated marketing efforts where a single marketing strategy is adopted yet ultimately serves the purposes of more than one organisation or enterprise.

The purpose of this chapter is to dissect the nature of transport marketing as it relates to tourism. The chapter does not address strictly 'advertising/promotion' elements in the marketing of transport, although these are considered, but rather considers the numerous factors that determine the markets for transport (e.g. segmentation) and the consequential marketing efforts in a Maslowian sense designed to address the needs, wants and desires of these markets. Just as important in understanding the markets for transport, what also must be discussed is the nature of the transport product. More specifically, the question remains as to whether transport, especially the type relating to tourism, is a product or a service.

Marketing is a key ingredient in any tourism experience as it links desire and latent demand with conversion into actual holiday experiences. Thus, markets and marketing are key areas where transport providers need to be as aware as possible, especially when part or much of their core business is involved in the servicing of passengers who are embarking on travel for personal, pleasure or business reasons. The purpose of this chapter, then, is to draw attention to the complex nature of marketing efforts designed by transport enterprises around the world and position these in the context of the consequences this can have for tourism development. As will be shown, transport firms have engaged in multiple strategic and tactical marketing programmes designed to entice passengers, not least of which include pricing strategies in relation to yield management strategies as discussed in the last chapter, frequent flyer programmes as established by many airlines, alliances (including mode-specific and multi-mode integration programmes) and traditional advertising.

MARKETING 101: RELATIONSHIPS TO TRANSPORT

Traditional marketing texts, and even those written for the purpose of isolating key strategies in use by the global tourism sector, tend to isolate several key factors when discussing marketing and tourism. Seaton and Bennett (1996), for example, discuss the nature of the marketing mix in tourism, pointing out that tourism is comprised of multiple sectors, including accommodation, transport, attractions and even the wider destination. Each of these sectors features core, tangible and augmented tourism products. For example, Seaton and Bennett (1996: 122, Table 5.4) argue that the core product of an airline is simply transport, and the basic need function is to transport customers from point to point. The tangible products, then, include the airline name, lounges, the quality of in-flight service and perhaps the comfort of the seats. Tangible products are 'the specific features and benefits residing in the product itself; styling, quality, brand name, design, etc' (Seaton & Bennett, 1996: 121). Shaw (2004) argues that the aviation industry's product is intangible and is thus 'instantly perishable and cannot be stored'. Middleton and Clarke (2001: 373), however, suggest that

> most airline marketing focused on product augmentation, corporate images and the quality of service provided by staff. Apart from obvious distinctions between first-class, business-class and economy-class, and with limited but important exceptions such as Concorde, the traditional approach to marketing airline products was rather sterile and unimaginative. Seats on transport are just commodities in the eyes of most consumers.

The augmented product of an airline, according to Seaton and Bennett, could be elements such as the chauffeur to the airport, any add-ons to the flights, such as hotels or other car services, and frequent flyer programmes. These augmented products represent 'add-ons that are extrinsic to the product itself but which may influence the decision to purchase' (Seaton & Bennett, 1996: 121). An airline, in an attempt to understand the specific product that its customers may require, really has numerous levels of product to consider. Augmented products may, for some customers, be a primary influence on the decision to purchase, perhaps even more so than tangible products. For example, rather than chose an airline on the basis of tangible elements such as seat pitch or seat quality, a frequent traveller may elect to travel with a certain air carrier over others because of the ability to collect points towards future air travel. In other words, and depending on the market segment, some tangible elements may not be part of the decision-set criteria when selecting an airline. Graham (2001) notes that the composite nature of airports almost precludes the concept of the augmented product from being applied, and this may perhaps be extended to airline operations as well.

The core, tangible and augmented product differentiation can also be applied to other modes of transport. Cruise companies, for example, may offer, by virtue of external linkages to other services and products, ground transport at specific destinations. Such augmented products can often determine itineraries and market demand. Tangible products relating to cruise tourism can include the décor of the ship itself, with more and more ships, as noted in Chapter 5, being outfitted as luxury vessels in an effort to segment the cruise tourism market. With cruise tourism, even the core product can be questioned. For example, using the blurry distinctions discussed in Chapter 2, one question that arises is whether a cruise company's core product is even transport. Cruise tourism is complex from the perspective of transport in that the ship itself functions as a mode of transport as well as an attraction. With more and more cruise companies offering on-board shopping and other amenities, the fact that the ship moves from port to port is, to some extent irrelevant. Cruise companies would prefer passengers spend their money on-board as opposed to the duty-free areas in port at the next destination. Thus, perhaps the core product of many cruise operations is not transport, but rather service and amenities relating to the experience on offer.

PACKAGING

Middleton and Clarke (2001: 372) describe what they call 'passenger transport bundles', which are comprised of:

- Service availability and convenience (reflecting routes offered, schedules and capacity).
- Cost in comparison with competitors on the same routes.
- The design and performance of the vehicle (comfort and speed).
- Comfort, seating, ambience and any services offered during the journey.
- Passenger handling at terminals and car parks.
- Convenience of booking and ticketing arrangements.
- Contact with staff and their roles in contact with customers.
- Image and positioning of each operator. (Middleton & Clarke, 2001: 372)

The importance of these bundles is that they highlight what is available to marketers. As the core product remains largely undifferentiated, it is the tangible and even augmented elements that are promoted in order to help potential customers differentiate one firm offering passenger transport from another. There are, of course, significant relationships between core, tangible and augmented products relating to a particular mode of transport, as shifts in one can have significant impacts on the other. For cruise tourism, it could be argued, the tangible benefits on offer for cruise tourists have slowly become core products for some cruise tourists. The same could be said for airlines. At the beginning of the aviation revolution, which saw the world conceptually shrink in time and space (Hall, 2005), airlines provided a basic core product of transport, but some might argue that stiff global competition has resulted in the core product of an airline shifting from transport to service. This raises the issue as to whether transport itself, particularly in relation to tourism, is a product or a service.

PRODUCT OR SERVICE? POSITIONING TOURISM TRANSPORT

Exploring the distinction between tourism transport as a product or service necessarily involves examining the concepts of tangibility, heterogeneity, perishability and separability (Bitner et al., 1993; Hartman & Lindgren, 1993). These differences are critical in understanding exactly what is being marketed when considering the relationship between transport and tourism, but also because it calls into question the nature of the transport experience and where it is situated in the wider tourism experience.

1. *Tangibility*. Products are often physical entities; that is, one is able to handle and inspect them before purchase. Services, on the other hand, cannot be directly handled, but they can be inspected. For instance, an individual is able, if they wish, to observe the behaviour of restaurant staff before deciding to dine there, on the assumption that the information gleaned from observation will provide an indication of the level of service on offer. Services are therefore intangible, and must adopt affiliated marketing schemes that should create a sense of what that service is like in the mind of the customer (Seaton & Bennett, 1996). In relation to transport, the question is whether a seat purchased from British Rail from Exeter to London constitutes the purchase of product (in this case, transport from one place to another) or a service. When one purchases a ticket, they are not purchasing the seat itself. The sale, rather, involves a contract that states that the passenger has permission to board the train, sit in an assigned seat (or not, depending on the level of service purchased – and the irony is noted here), and disembark at the appropriate end point. In other words, there is very little that is tangible about the journey.

2. *Separability*. Unlike most products, services are effectively consumed and produced at the same time (Onkvisit & Shaw, 1991). The journey is happening as you experience it, and for this reason, it can be argued that the production and consumption of transport is, for the most part, inseparable.

3. *Perishability*. As a service, transport cannot necessarily be stored or carried forward for consumption at a later date, although some purchase options may allow this to happen. Generally, empty seats or berths represent lost revenue opportunity.

4. *Heterogeneity*. For the most part, services are difficult to standardise simply because they are fluid offerings that differ from one encounter to the next due to the variable nature of human behaviour. Unlike physical products, the service encounter is highly erratic (Onkvisit & Shaw, 1991). Once again the question is raised whether tourist-related transport has as its core product the simple notion of being transported from one place to another or whether it is the tangible products that form the transport experience and are the elements by which potential customers are converted into actual customers. There will exist a standard level of service on a train from, from example, Exeter to London: passengers will be offered coffee, they will be allocated to a seat which is roughly similar to the other seats in the same class, and they can expect a degree of service quality at either end of the journey in the form of, for example, check-in and baggage retrieval. In some situations, delivery of standard service may not be possible. Coffee services may be withdrawn if technical problems arise or baggage may be lost. More importantly, as standard as this service offering may be, passengers will experience them differently and thus hold differing levels of satisfaction. One passenger may find the seats uncomfortable, while another, perhaps a businessperson, may find that the constant motion of the train itself unsuitable for reading or working on his/her laptop. As standard as the service offering may appear, how that service is perceived and received is highly variable.

STRATEGIC MARKETING IN TOURISM TRANSPORT

Strategic marketing focuses on the available processes designed to introduce new consumers to existing products or develop new products for existing consumers. It also incorporates the mission and goals of a corporation or firm and how these can be reoriented towards proving the right product or service to the right markets (Kerin & Peterson, 1998). Transport operators, like many other companies, can engage in various means of strategic marketing, including market penetration strategies, market development strategies and product development strategies. Each of these is examined below.

MARKET PENETRATION STRATEGIES

A typical market penetration strategy 'dictates that an organization seek to gain greater dominance in a market in which it already has an offering' (Karin & Peterson, 1998: 7). A common means of achieving this is through promotion or advertising, but particularly increasing brand recognition. In fact, many modes of transport utilise indirect forms designed to increase awareness of a particular brand. For example, Dragonair, an airline based in Hong Kong, painted new 'livery' (decorative elements on the exterior of aircraft) to celebrate it's twentieth year of operation. The livery design featured Chinese motifs on one side of the aircraft and Hong Kong motifs on the other. Ryanair is known for some of the more 'creative' advertising in the airline industry. Shortly after the bombings on the London Underground in July 2005, the airline developed a print campaign that ran in the Independent and the Telegraph and featured a likeness of Winston Churchill calling for people for visit London regardless of the potential for renewed attacks. In a deliberate play on the words of Churchill's famous speech during the Second World War, the ad features the byline: 'We shall fly them to the beaches; we shall fly them to the hills; we shall fly them to London.' The ASA in Britain received 318 complaints about the ad on the basis that 1) 'the advertisement was offensive and distressing, because it sought to use the recent terrorist attacks in London for commercial advantage'; and 2) 'the use of Winston Churchill's image and the parody of his famous speech were offensive and disrespectful to the memory of Winston Churchill and to those who lost their lives during World War two' (ASA, 2005). In their adjudication, the ASA chose not to uphold the complaints:

> The Authority acknowledged that the complainants had found the approach extremely tasteless, but noted many media commentators had, in the days that immediately followed the terrorist attacks, commented on the positive and determined response of Londoners to continue with life as normal. Because it noted that response was a source of strength and pride to many, and the advertisers had restricted the theme of the advertisement to the stoical response that followed the attacks, the Authority concluded that the advertisement stopped short of causing serious or widespread offence or promoting further distress... The advertisers believed the use of Winston

Churchill's image and the parody of his speech were neither offensive nor disrespect-ful; they pointed out that his response to the bombings during World War 2 was one of defiance and 'business as usual'. The advertisers believed they had captured the spirit of Churchill and the Blitz mentality of Londoners in the days that followed the terrorist attacks. (ASA, 2005)

Peattie and Peattie (1996) note that price-based promotions are the most popular form of promotions in travel and tourism. This is largely because the use of specific modes of transport for the purposes of leisure and tourism is largely elastic; that is, the higher the cost of transport, the less likely a customer is to utilise that mode of transport without making sacrifices for the nature and quality of their overall experience assuming a fixed budget.

Segmenting the market

As some passengers are more price sensitive than others, different segments of markets can be isolated and targeted. Segmentation is 'the process of portioning markets into seg-ments of potential customers with similar characteristics who are likely to exhibit similar purchase behavior' (Weinstein, 1987: 4). It builds on the nature of the decision-making process that customers undertake, which involves innate needs and motivations, percep-tions or ontologies of the world, demographic characteristics (e.g. lifestyle attributes), the overall awareness of the product, and purchasing behaviour (Weinstein, 1987). If a firm is able to understand this particular segment properly, it can use this to its advantage over its competitors by tailoring and promoting a product or service that is targeted towards this segment. Segmentation, then, is a powerful means by which firms come to 'know their market' and excel in a highly competitive market.

Transport firms offering services to tourists, including business tourists, utilise segmen-tation to ensure that their product and service offers are relevant and in demand. Airlines, for example, use segmentation analysis as a means of relationship marketing processes to target specific travellers and thus increase market share. For example, those who fly on business may do so more frequently than those who travel for the purposes of leisure. As a result, business travellers may have an affinity towards more comfortable environments whilst travelling and 'in transit', hence the use of business class and first class, as well as airport lounges, targeted towards this type of traveller. Leisure travellers, however, may be less demanding of such amenities, and may respond more favourably to cheaper fares, although recent research by Dresner (2006) noted that business and leisure passengers expected similar levels of service at airports. Mason (2000) found price to be the most important determinant in business travellers' decisions to fly with particular low-cost airlines.

Some cruise companies target specific segments of the population in an effort to build market share. Stelios Hadji–Ioannou, the founder of easyJet in Europe, announced easy-

Cruise in March 2005, which, according to Hadji–Ioannou, will target 'younger crowds, in their 20s and 30s, rather than wealthy older people who like more traditional cruises' (Carassava, 2005). What is interesting about easyCruise is that the emphasis is on the destination rather than the on-board amenities that most cruise companies emphasise. In targeting younger markets, easyCruise is making various ports in the French and Italian Riviera the primary attractions. At each port, passengers will disembark and enjoy the nightlife 'scene' before re-boarding and moving on to the next destination (Carassava, 2005). Other cruise companies, such as Princess Cruises, are utilising advertising to target people who have never taken a cruise. Carnival Cruises is doing the same, with its tagline, introduced in late 2002, of 'So much fun. So many places' (Griswold, 2002).

Rail companies are also keen to tap into new markets in an attempt to re-package their produce/service and lure people away from the popular low-cost airline alternative to transport. The American Orient Express was developed to combine luxury ambience with a heritage tour of national parks such as Grand Canyon, Grant Telton and Yellowstone. The rail cars used for the trip are refurbished 1940s and 1950s models (Mulrine, 2002). As Mulrine (2002) reports, interest in the American Orient Express surged after the 11 September 2001 attacks on the United States, with the owner noting that 'we began getting more calls from people who wanted to travel but didn't want to get on a plane' (Multine, 2002: np).

With the popularity of, and often exceptional value provided by, low-cost air travel across Europe, it has been increasingly difficult for rail companies to compete. Virgin Trains recently launched an aggressive campaign across England in order to increase modal market share. Television ads featured cinematic music (from the 62-piece London Metropolitan Orchestra) against modern visual shots of passenger rail cars. Intriguingly, the passengers in the ads feature modern travellers juxtaposed with some of Hollywood's famous celebrities from the past:

> Margaret Lockwood and May Witty order a pot of tea, asking the waiter to make sure the water's boiling. Cary Grant tries to chat up Eva Marie Saint. And (rather strangely, since the train has already been racing through the fields) Tony Curtis and Jack Lemmon hobble down a Euston platform in high heels and make it on to the train just in time. The advert – a full minute long – reaches its climax (to the kind of orchestral soundtrack one might expect from a Hollywood epic) with Cary Grant declaring: 'Beats flying, doesn't it.' (BBC, 2004d)

Clearly, an ad as such as this was designed to be interesting to the viewer from an historical perspective, but it is also follows many of the key criteria that Morgan and Pritchard (2001: 46) argue constitute good advertising: simplicity, relevance, uncomplicated and long term. On the BBC website, however, readers were invited to post their comments, and one reader challenged the veracity of what was being promoted in the television spot:

I absolutely cannot fault this very well crafted short film. Unfortunately, it doesn't work as an advert, because it is rather let down by the reality it promises to deliver. If only the trains in the UK were really this nice! It is a fantasy film therefore, to be enjoyed on only that level, and not to be regarded as reflecting the reality of train travel in the UK today anymore than 'The Lord of the Rings' films reflected the reality of life in New Zealand. (BBC, 2004d)

Air New Zealand in early 2005 announced a revamped long-haul 'product', the advertising for which had substantial reach and frequency throughout New Zealand. Print ads (Figures 8.1 and 8.2) were run in major daily newspapers (thus reaching most of the country) and television adverts were featured in key advertising time periods (for example, television prime time, from roughly 7 pm to 9 or 10 pm). With this particular advertisement, what is being promoted are the many improvements in the service intangibles and produce tangibles associated with flying long-haul routes on the airline. New Zealand as a country is somewhat geographically peripheral to most of the world (save for perhaps Australia), and as such Air New Zealand must be seen to offer a higher degree of comfort on its long-haul flights versus its competitors. In this particular print ad, what is

Figure 8.1 Print run example (2005) from Air New Zealand showing new business premier service (reproduced with permission)

Figure 8.2 Print run example (2005) from Air New Zealand (typical third of a page newspaper run (reproduced with permission)

shown is the upgrading of the 'in-flight' experience for all classes of travel. The re-vamped long-haul product being advertised is intended to be a value driver; that is, short of purchasing or leasing yet-to-be-developed faster aircraft, many airlines now focus on particular elements of the in-flight experience that help drive the perception of value in the mind of the customer/passenger. Contrast this with Figure 8.2, where the objective is to highlight fares and destinations. Indeed, it is an example of the tight integration that airlines have with tourism, and how airlines themselves have a keen interest in ensuring the viability of destinations worldwide (consider, for example, the line in the ad in Figure 8.2: 'So whether you want to admire the iconic Mt Rushmore, experience theme park thrills in California, or relax on the sun kissed beaches of Hawai'i, the best way to see the great sights is with our great prices.'). What is not mentioned in the ad in Figure 8.3 is the services and conveniences with flying Air New Zealand, even though this advertisement ran in local newspapers throughout New Zealand. It contains several critical elements for ensuring that potential travellers have several ways of purchasing tickets: a toll-free 'Freephone' number (NZ only), mention of the Air New Zealand Travelcentre (with locations throughout the country) and the main website. What is clear is that the airline is

237

interested in having a strong amount of control over how its service/product is distributed.

MARKET DEVELOPMENT STRATEGIES

Market development strategies generally involve attempts at securing market share in markets not currently being served (Kerin & Peterson, 1998). For example, LCCs (or VBAs) have often sought to enter new markets using price as the means of generating business. Mason (2001) discusses how some VBAs (or LCLF carriers, from Chapter 6) in the European Union have begun targeting business travellers. Mason compared the travel habits, but particularly the importance placed on specific attributes or tangible products, of business travellers that originated from London's Luton Airport and London Heathrow. Mason's study attempted to determine whether there was a difference between those business travellers who utilise a VBA out of Luton and those who utilise a network carrier (or FSA) out of London Heathrow. Mason's hypothesis was that business travellers who utilise a VBA fundamentally act as a different market segment than those who use a FSA. The results of Mason's research suggest that, among short-haul business travellers, there are not enough commonalities between those who utilise VBAs and those who use FSAs:

> The profile of business travellers using low-cost airlines seems to be different in the size of the company that they work for, the booking process used, the channel used to book flights, and the importance placed on the price of travel, in-flight service, frequent flier schemes, and business lounges. While there are differences between the two groups there was also much common ground, particularly in the proportion of travellers who select their own flights, the opinion travellers have about the value for money of business class products, and the importance of airline punctuality, flight frequency and ticket flexibility. (Mason, 2001: 108)

Mason found that price sensitivity was paramount for those business travellers utilising both VBAs and FSAs. He notes that business travellers working for small- or medium-sized companies were more likely to utilise VBAs because 1) 'people working for smaller companies are likely to see a clearer delineation from travel costs to the profits made in their businesses than travellers working for larger companies' and 2) larger companies may be in a better position to negotiate more lucrative travel deals based on potential volume of sales (Mason, 2001: 109; see also Mason, 2000).

In some instances, LCLF carriers have sought to unseat traditional full service or network carriers by competing directly at the price point, but also in the development of new markets. The case of Ryanair (IATA: FR) and Aer Lingus (IATA: EI), two Irish airlines, is particularly interesting as it demonstrates how an upstart VBA can generate new business for a variety of destinations through market development. Ryanair generally succeeded as a VBA for two reasons (Kangis & O'Reilly, 2003). First, significant competition in the beginning was primarily Air Lingus, which operated out of Dublin Airport and targeted specific niche markets which, according to Kangis and O'Reilly (2003) exposed the airline to the vagaries of the international aviation environment. Air Lingus' operations were essentially value-added (Kangis & O'Reilly, 2003: 106), which entailed providing seamless service throughout the experience of flying with the airline. Ryanair, on the other hand, adopted a 'focus on core activities', which became its key strategy for success (Kangis & O'Reilly, 2003: 106). This entailed providing a low-cost, low-frills service in order to maximise sales (Kangis & O'Reilly, 2003: 106). The result has been an almost 20-year 'battle for the skies' that has seen Ryanair become one of the largest, if not the largest, VBA in Europe. In order to achieve this, Ryanair adopted a business model (use of secondary airport and a generally a point-to-point or linear network configuration, see Chapter 6) that features cautious expansion principles without the risk of jeopardising inflated costs.

These two elements combined meant that Ryanair was able to introduce low-costs flights to new markets. As a result, '[t]he Ryanair policy is one of market creation where fares and frequencies are attractive to contingent or fringe travellers, such as those who would not normally make the journey or who would travel by another form of transport' (Kangis & O'Reilly, 2003: 107). Hanlon (1999: 179) has argued that while point-to-point travel and a directive of reduction in costs may have allowed for increase travel, 'successful operation of point-to-point routes owes at least something to the unusually high proportion of ethnic demand in the particular city pair markets serviced and also to the fact that the only surface competition comes from a sea crossing'. As well, Ryanair generally paid lower commissions to travel agents, preferring instead to sell seats to customers through Ryanair Direct (Barrett, 2000). More recently, the airline has primarily sought to sell tickets through its website. It also does not have a frequent flyer programme, nor does it make use of extra frills at the airport such as lounges. Air Lingus, on the other hand,

> employs traditional arrangements with travel agents and pays normal rates of commission. Aer Lingus markets on the strength of its image, and has tried to create brand loyalty. It operates a 'gold circle' club, providing luxury lounges at all the airports that it is servicing. It also has a frequent flier programme for its most loyal customers. (Kangis & O'Reilly, 2003: 108)

PRODUCT DEVELOPMENT STRATEGIES

Product development strategies involve the introduction of new products to existing (and with the potential of development of new) market segments. These efforts usually extend beyond the addition of value-added components, which are designed to enhance existing products; instead, the focus is on the recognition of a need for new offerings. Such strategies have been prevalent in cruise tourism in the past few decades with the increase in global competition. In many ways, cruise ships have ceased being modes of transport and, as discussed in Chapter 5, now feature a range of on-board amenities designed to appeal to numerous market segments. For example, on the *Voyager of the Seas*, a passenger can go ice skating, practice their rock climbing skills, and be entertained in movie theatres. The president of the CLIA in 2002 remarked that '[y]ou could spend a whole week on a ship and you wouldn't know you're on a ship' (Elliot & Silver, 2002). What this marks is a fundamental shift in the product that is purchased. Cruise ships have effectively diversified their product offering and, as a result, tapped into the all-inclusive market segment in countries such as the United States.

New product development is somewhat more limited when it comes to aviation, but the industry is not without examples. In mid-2005, two new airlines were launched offering business-class travel between the United States and the UK. Eos is a privately held company hoping to compete directly with high-quality and well-received business-class offerings from Virgin Atlantic and British Airways. The airline will use Boeing 757 aircraft with 48 seats rather than the usual 200 in double-class (economy and business) configuration. The second, MAXjet, is also a privately held company and will offer return services from New York to London Stansted using Boeing 767-200 aircraft with 102 seats (whereas the aircraft is normally configured in approximately 200-seat configurations). On the website for MAXjet, it states that the airline 'was founded to bring the low-cost carrier revolution to the international market. It will be the first.' This may not be entirely correct, depending on how 'international' is defined. Ryanair has been flying internationally (or transnationally) for quite some time, but MAXjet was the first to offer trans-Atlantic business class-only services in an LCC format. Both Eos and MAXjet will offer standard business-class amenities: large seat-pitch (the distance between the front of one seat to the same point on the seat ahead) and full meals and beverage services. The product that MAXjet and Eos have each developed is a business class-only airline, and the intent is to use the produce to target business class travellers who generally prefer comfort and amenities to cheap prices, but this is an interesting example in product development in that the airline industry normally attempts to offer two or three class service offerings on most flights, thus catering to multiple markets on a single flight. Over time, the test will be to see if Eos and MAXjet are able to secure enough of a market share to ensure ongoing financial viability. There may be several factors that may hinder profitable performance, however:

1. Downturns in economies (either in the United States or the UK) may mean a reduction in corporate spending on travel. Traditional multi-class carriers may not be as vulnerable in these situations, but a strictly business class airline will need to offer price points that are competitive as perhaps the average economy class fares of its competitors. On the website, however, MAXjet is promising fares that they claim are often what one would pay to fly economy (and use the example of £599 one-way).

2. Some business travel may be seasonal (for example, generally less travel during Christmas holidays), so it is not clear whether sufficient transactions will be realised in order to be profitable during the off-peak periods.

3. As evidenced by some online travel discussion boards (e.g. www.flyertalk.com), some business travellers undoubtedly select airlines on the basis of accruing frequent flyer miles and privileges. These two business class-only airlines, for now, will not be part of a formal global alliance, nor is it clear whether they will offer any type of frequent flyer reward programme.

4. The use of London Stansted as the primary airport reflects the restrictions on slot space (discussed in Chapter 7) at larger airports such as London Heathrow, and it remains to be seen whether passengers on business place a higher premium on using an airport closer to the central city to which they are travelling.

Alliances as marketing tools

As discussed in Chapter 6, code-sharing and schedule coordination is a common alliance format for airlines. This type of tactical alliance (or 'mode-specific alliance' as the concentration of market benefits sit within a specific mode of transport) often has significant benefits for marketing because it allows airlines to tap into new markets that would have otherwise necessitated the introduction of their own services and, therefore, consuming substantial amounts of capital investment (Glisson *et al.*, 1996). Table 8.1 highlights the strength of the major airline alliances operating in the summer of 2006, including the extent to which each alliance is in competition with another as measured by the duplicate destinations served. The table also indicates that over one-half of all global destinations are served by at least one airline alliance using some 60 billion ASKs.

Global airline alliances are of course not the only means by which different airlines link networks. Oum *et al.* (1996: 187) note that code-sharing agreements 'are used to enhance

Table 8.1 Comparison of alliance network strength based on weekly scheduled operations in (northern hemisphere) summer 2006

	Total Destinations	Duplicate Destinations	Total countries served	Capacity (available seat kilometres)	Proportional share
Star Alliance	873	318	147	22.6 billion	20.6%
Oneworld	591	163	128	15.9 billion	14.5%
SkyTeam	730	366	141	20.4 billion	18.6%
Total				58.9 billion	53.7%

Source: Adapted from Airline Business (2006b)

services and to create a marketing advantage of on-line connecting services'. Code-shares are the means by which one airline can be seen to offer 'seamless' service across a substantial network that it otherwise would not have been able to service itself due to the prohibitive cost (Beyhoff, 1995):

> Codesharing is a marketing arrangement between two airlines whereby one airline's designator code is shown on flights operated by its partner airline. Two letter designation codes are provided by the International Civil Aviation Organisation (ICAO) to identify the airlines on passenger tickets, computer reservation systems (CRS), airline guides and airport information boards. Under a codesharing agreement the connecting flights being operated by two separate airlines may be listed as bring a 'single carrier' service, which gives substantial marketing advantages. (Oum *et al.*, 1996: 188)

The effects of codesharing have been scrutinised by Brueckner (2001), who found that passengers from interhubs (i.e. those city-pairs that serve a major hub) are somewhat financially disadvantaged when a code-share alliance is established for the purpose of serving two or more major hubs. However, Brueckner (2001) also found that there was an overall gain in consumer and total surplus following the formation of a code-share alliance. What this suggests is when selecting a potential code-share partner, an airline would think carefully about the potential market gain from servicing major hubs using such an arrangement, and thus sharing the revenues in an interline market, versus the total costs for operating in the network alone.

RELATIONSHIP MARKETING

Relationship marketing can come in a variety of forms, from direct sales marketing to the establishment of an online presence designed to remove distributors from the total transaction. Within the last decade, many transport firms have utilised IT to form ongoing relationships with their customers (Bejou & Palmer, 1998). Many airlines, for example, employ direct marketing in the form of regular (or erratic) email announcements to members of their frequent flyer programme. These can be highly effective in targeting specific and multiple segments, as Roberts and Berger (1999: 167) argue:

> [T]he airline can manipulate the information it already has to help it better understand the behavioral patterns of its frequent customers. It can also collect and store additional information, which may be attitudinal as well as behavioral. This additional information can either be general (request of all or most of the frequent fliers) or specific (requested of only those who have not flown the airline for the past three months, for example).... It can then promote these programmes directly to the fliers who have a high probability of responding instead of wasting its promotional dollars on those who have a low probability of response.

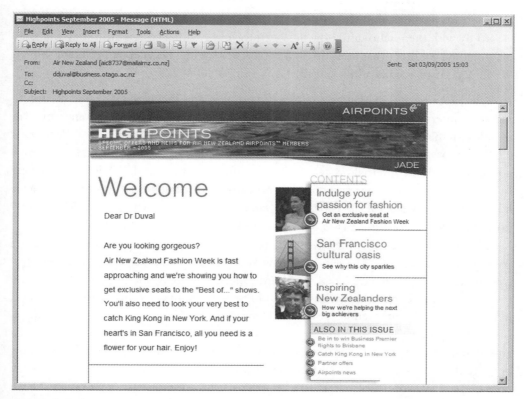

Figure 8.3 Direct marketing gone slightly askew or lack of segmentation?

For example, in a bid to enhance its relationship with this author, Air New Zealand sent an email (Figure 8.3) in early September 2005 that at once exemplifies non-directed relationship marketing. Everyone listed as a frequent flyer member for Air Points is likely to have received the email, which illustrates how direct marketing should perhaps be segmented. Of course, the intent of the email was to showcase the range of destinations that one might be interested in, but by providing it via this medium (the email included links to the airline's online portal and booking engine) it is attempting to form a relationship. Relationship marketing is a means by which firms put as much effort into retaining existing customers as they do seeking new ones. In doing so, firms seek to gain a competitive advantage and foster a long-lasting relationship with a customer (Gilbert, 1996). What is involved is rather simple in principle, but somewhat difficult given strong competition, as Shaw outlines in the context of airlines:

> Once someone has decided on a particular airline, that airline only has the task of persuading them to continue to make the same choice. This should be relatively easy, because it will be a question of reinforcing in their mind the correctness of

243

their original decision. If on the other hand, a carrier needs to persuade someone to fly with them who until now has been traveling with a competitor, they will need to convince them that their original choice was wrong. Human nature being what it is, few of us readily admit our mistakes. (Shaw, 2004: 229)

In reality, relationship marketing is far more complex, and involves a wide range of sub-markets (internal, referral, supplier, recruitment and influence markets) and involves establishing plans and strategies to shift the focus of a particular enterprise (Peck *et al.*, 1999). It is at once concerned with service issues and customer satisfaction, but it is also concerned with the internal processes that are often just as critical. While the full scope of relationship marketing is vast and thus only briefly discussed here, it is raised because it has significant analytical and explanatory value when it comes to the marketing of transport in relation to tourism (Bejou & Palmer, 1998; Long & Schiffman, 2000).

Although there are other means of securing relationships with customers, one of the more prevalent examples of relationship marketing in tourism transport is an administrative tracking programme designed to reward loyalty. Loyalty is not an unusual means of relationship marketing as many businesses utilise specific practices to increase retention in purchase behaviour (Hennig-Thurau & Hansen, 2000). Celebrity Cruises, for example, offers a Captain's Club programme where frequent cruisers can enjoy specific rewards and upgrades depending on the number of times they have cruised. 'Classic' status members are those who have accumulated 1–5 'cruise credits', and can enjoy a 'one-category upgrade' or have access to an 'exclusive' Captain's Club party on their next cruise. Those who have 11 or more cruises to their name are known as 'Elite' status members and can enjoy, among other things, private shipboard departure lounge access and an invitation to the Captain's or Officer's table for dining.

Cruise companies are not the only form of transport to offer a loyalty-based programme that rewards frequent use of a service. Via Rail Canada runs their VIA Préference programme, where a member earns one point for every dollar spent on rail travel along VIA's network across the country and on some services to the United States. As with most other programmes, as a passenger spends more money on services within a particular qualifying period (usually a 12-month period), they receive higher status in the programme, which consequently brings more privileges and benefits.

Most airlines offer some form of mileage accrual programme to its customers (see Long *et al.*, 2003; Yang & Liu, 2003). These programmes are relatively simple in their construction: the more a passenger flies, the more 'miles' or 'points' become accrued that can be used at a future date for fare-free/'reward travel' or other services (as of late, some airlines offer redemption of points or miles in exchange for new electronic goods or full holidays). The points accrued through travel can be used in the future when a certain threshold has been reached, for reward travel. The amount of miles accrued is largely dependent on the level of service (e.g. economy, business, first) and, to some extent, on

BOX 8.1 Tax implications for loyalty programmes/relationship marketing

The frequent flyer miles that some businesspeople accumulate on business trips are often used (and not always legally) for personal travel. Some national governments, however, would suggest that using miles in this manner constitutes a taxable benefit, a move not unsurprising given that, as a global currency, frequent flyer miles have a value which far surpasses many of the world's major monetary currencies (Clark, 2005). In Canada, the CRA has made it explicit under the Employees' Fringe Benefits section of the Income Tax Act that such benefits are indeed taxable. According to Section 14 under Part A (Amounts To Be Included In Income):

> Under this program, which is usually sponsored by an airline, a frequent air traveller can accumulate credits which may be exchanged for additional air travel or other benefits. Where an employee accumulates such credits while travelling on employer-paid business trips and uses them to obtain air travel or other benefits for the personal use of the employee or the employee's family, the fair market value of such air travel or other benefits must be included in the employee's income. Where an employer does not control the credits accumulated in a frequent flyer program by an employee while travelling on employer-paid business trips, the comments in Paragraph 3 above will not apply and it will be the responsibility of the employee to determine and include in income the fair market value of any benefits received or enjoyed. (http://www.cra-arg.gc.ca/E/pub/tp/it470r-consolid/it470r-consolid-e.html#P128_12793; accessed 10 August 2005)

Upon seeing this, some business travellers may think twice before cashing in their frequent flyer miles for a trip to MedSun destination with their family. This guideline, however, introduces several issues:

1. What is the cost-benefit for the CRA to undertake regular audits of business travellers to determine whether there is failure to report additional income based on the 'fair market value' of the points accumulated? Presumably, however, cases of tax evasion of this sort are sorted during regular audits.

2. What is 'fair market value' when, as discussed in Chapter 6, airfares are volatile and extremely dynamic? Would a capacity-dump situation, where airlines unload excess capacity on certain flights, count? Or, would a mean fare value be more appropriate? If so, what period of time should be established in order to generate a mean baseline fare (months, weeks, days)?

3. On reward travel, the customer normally must pay the taxes and surcharges, and it is unclear whether these can be deducted from the fair market value of the reward flight(s) given that the value of the ticket itself is to be treated as income which, eventually, is subjected to certain levels of tax.

Questions for consideration

1. What are the ethical implications for booking a reward flight for personal travel using frequent flyer miles generated from travel for business?

2. To what extent is the root of this problem based on the fact that frequent flyer miles are bestowed on the individual on the plane as opposed to the individual or corporation responsible for paying for the ticket? How might this be rectified yet still retain the sense of 'loyalty' claimed by airlines?

the particular fare class. For example, some airlines will not allow accrual on low-fare tickets (e.g. N fare class, but this designator is not uniform across all airlines) but will on full-fare or mid-fare tickets (e.g. Q or Y fare class). Some airlines even offer up to 1.5 times as many miles if a passenger purchases a business- (e.g. J class) or first-class (i.e. F class) fare.

Gilbert argues that airlines need to consider three critical elements to the micro-marketing features inherent in frequent flyer programmes:

(1) There must be a greater emphasis on the database information held so as to slice and portion it to provide improved aspects of individual or group service delivery.

(2) The essence of relationship marketing needs to be the provision of differentiated communication and services. These have to be customized based on the researched characteristics of potential and current customers.

(3) There is a need to track and monitor each member of FFPs to ensure there is an assessment of the lifetime value and retention history of the individual. (Gilbert, 1996: 582)

Gilbert is advocating the use of frequent flyer programmes to offer members' personalised services. In one sense, this accurately represents a key reason for the establishment of almost any loyalty programme: the company has access to the purchasing habits and service/product usage of as many programme members that are in its database. This is a powerful tool for tailoring marketing and promotional activities. For example, an airline may discover that residents of a particular city regularly undertake travel to another regional centre for the purposes of onward travel to a foreign destination. Specific marketing (such as ad buys in newspapers or television spots) can be created for distribution in that particular market. Put another way, the existence of loyalty programmes such as those outlined above are examples of a means by which customer-specific data are acquired for the eventual purpose of market segmentation and the specific database marketing (Robinson & Kearney, 1994) examples mentioned.

Although some may argue that these programmes are designed to induce loyalty to a particular airline, with the introduction of global alliances between airlines (see Chapter 6), the value of loyalty has, in some cases, shifted from the individual airline towards a global alliance that recognises frequent flyer benefits across a number of airlines (although Bruning, 1997, notes that, on the whole, price followed by an airline's country-of-origin were key purchase determinants in his study of Canadian travellers). Passengers flying on any Star Alliance member carrier can earn (and burn) points on any carrier that is also a member of the alliance. First, however, it is important to note that each Star Alliance member programme has its own status tiers (often three or more). The higher tiers correspond to the Star Alliance-branded higher tiers recognised across the Star Alliance network, thus resulting in an almost global recognition of status and access to benefits and privileges. For example, Air Canada's Aeroplan has three tiers: Basic, Prestige (Star Alliance Silver) and Elite (Star Alliance Gold). Air New Zealand's Airports Programme has three levels as well: Silver (Star Alliance Silver), Gold (Star Alliance Gold) and Gold Elite (Star Alliance Gold as well). Those who achieve Gold Elite on Air New Zealand's programme benefit from Air New Zealand-specific benefits, such as valet parking and hotel or rental car vouchers. The general benefits of Gold status, as indicated on the Star Alliance website, generally include:

- Priority Reservations Waitlisting – when there aren't any seats left on your preferred flight, gives you priority should a seat become available.
- Priority Airport Standby – gives you the flexibility to change plans at the last minute when you don't have a reservation.
- Priority Airport Check-in – avoid long lines regardless of paid fare or class of service.
- Priority Baggage Handling – like you, your bags get priority treatment and are among the first to be unloaded.
- Extra Baggage Allowance – an additional 20kg (44 pounds) or one additional piece of luggage which means you can check in three bags instead of two.
- Priority Boarding – enjoy the freedom of boarding at your convenience along with First and Business Class passengers.

- Airport Lounge Access – available worldwide for you and a friend when you travel with any Star Alliance airline regardless of your class of travel. (http://www.staralliance.com/star_alliance/star/content/status.html; access 25 July 2005)

Like most loyalty programmes, status is awarded based on the number of flights in a qualifying period. Passengers achieve status through an annual measure of the amount of miles accrued during a particular qualifying period on any Star Alliance airline, yet the amount of miles or points required to achieve status recognition by the Star Alliance network varies from programme to programme. Air Canada, for example, will award Gold status if a passenger accrues 35,000 miles through eligible flights operated by any Star Alliance carrier. With United Airlines' Mileage Plus Programme, however, 50,000 miles are needed to reach Premier Executive status, which brings with it Gold status across the Star Alliance network. What this discrepancy demonstrates is that, despite the nature of a global alliance designed to foster loyalty to a global group of airlines, the means by which that loyalty is awarded and recognised is not entirely uniform.

A further aspect of global alliances in the airline industry is that the type of customer that they have effectively 'produced' has almost erased the need for individual airline frequent flyer programmes. As such, the global nature of frequent flyer programmes, coupled with the alliance networks that have been formed, now means that one's place of residence is almost irrelevant. This has interesting implications for individual airline loyalty programmes. For example, the author of this book, as a resident of New Zealand but Canadian citizen, has chosen to accrue miles through the Air Canada Aeroplan Programme (although he is also a member of several other airline programmes for 'research purposes', including the discovery in 2002 that, in fact, one flight can be credited to two separate programmes, a revelation that came as quite a surprise to both airlines concerned when it was pointed out to them). However, at present the vast majority of his flights are on Air New Zealand and Singapore Airlines aircraft. As a result, this author has accumulated a substantial number of miles that have been credited to his Aeroplan account, but less than 30% were actually accumulated on Air Canada metal. Put another way, in this particular case miles are being rewarded onto Air Canada's frequent flyer programme yet the bulk of revenue has gone to Air New Zealand and Singapore Airlines. However, Aeroplan carries the contingent liability (i.e. the possibility that Air Canada may be asked by this author for redemption of those miles in the form of a reward ticket for travel on an Air Canada-operated flight). Contingent liabilities are rarely reported (Bennett, 1996), which means it is difficult to determine how many outstanding points are being held by customers. However, because Air Canada is part of the Star Alliance, this author's miles can be redeemed on any Star Alliance airline. As members of this particular alliance, the individual airlines would hope that the network-wide redemption eventually balances out any contingent liability of its own programme, which means that the entire network has contingent liability for all frequent flyer miles/points accrued by all member airlines.

A commonly held belief is that the contingent liability of existing air miles held in frequent flyer programmes is problematic for many airlines in that they may not be able to provide seats to match demand without realising a significant drop in marginal revenue. The reality, however, is somewhat different. First, the manner in which air miles are collected by the public is often not from flying. The most common means of collecting miles is through credit card purchases. In this arrangement, a bank will reward air miles to a customer's frequent flyer programme according to a set ratio (charges:miles awarded). To do this, banks purchase miles from airlines or the often separate companies that airlines have established in order to manage their frequent flyer programmes. According to the *Economist* (2005), this arrangement is worth some US$10 billion to airlines around the world. The airline's marginal cost to provide seats to those who request a reward seat is relatively small. As a result, given that more frequent flyer miles are being accumulated from non-flight activities (Economist, 2005), and that airlines are being paid a considerable amount for miles by banks in order to allow the latter to use them for promotional purposes, airlines actually make money from their frequent flyer programmes, and sometimes even when the airline itself may be running at a loss. The second reason why air miles, as a contingent liability, are not necessarily a threat to airline solvency rests with their ability to alter the value of reward miles themselves. In other words, an airline may elect to introduce certain blackout periods where reward travel is not possible or increase the number of miles or points needed to redeem reward seats.

Airlines regularly use global network alliances and frequent flyer programmes as means of promotion. Each may feature specific offers for vacation packages, upgrades and hotel discounts to its members. For some passengers, particularly business tourists, the value of the specific frequent flyer programmes is high enough such that the selection of the airline they chose to fly can be based almost purely on whether reward miles can be accrued or status levels can be maintained. For example, a businessperson wishing to travel from Chicago to Auckland may elect to purchase a ticket with a carrier who is aligned with a particular global alliance such as One World or Star Alliance. The businessperson may chose to fly from Chicago to Los Angeles with United Airlines, and then Air New Zealand for the flight from Los Angeles to Auckland. Using these two carriers guarantees (again, depending on the fare type, but most international flights will accrue some miles) mileage accrual. As well, if the businessperson travels enough on an annual basis to be considered Gold in status, he or she will be able to utilise specified lounges in Chicago, Los Angeles and Auckland. Specified Star Alliance Gold Lounges are frequented by business travellers because they offer free alcohol and other beverages, free food (in some lounges), free wireless internet access, showers and a comfortable atmosphere. In many lounges, small conference rooms and business centres are available.

Shaw (2004) points to several lingering problems with the use of alliances to differentiate products in a strongly competitive environment. For one, alliances represent a particular 'mindset' by which airlines, in the face of competition, will form marketing and service alliances with other airlines rather than engage in competitive behaviour:

> When faced with a tough competitor, it has nearly always been the airlines' instinct to form a collusive, rather than competitive relationship... Without the challenge of strong competition, airlines do not work sufficiently hard to control their costs, particularly their labour costs. They therefore quickly eat up all the guaranteed revenues which collusive behaviour gives them, leading to calls for a further diminution of competition. (Shaw, 2004: 111)

Another problem that Shaw points to is the fact that the financial performance of many air carriers in alliances varies considerably, and points to the example of Lufthansa (a carrier that enjoys comparatively strong financial health) and United Airlines (which has been in financial trouble for years). This leads to some serious questions about the uniformity of product/service delivery across any alliance. For example, and as pointed out by Shaw (2004), how can United be expected to finance future service availability (or, rather, limit the erosion of service quality) on its own network when it belongs to an alliance where partners such as Lufthansa are capable of retaining existing service levels? To this end, Shaw (2004: 112) asks: '[H]ow can the Star Alliance carriers generally engage in strategic discussions about developing their long-term co-operation, when they must all know the possibility exists that United will not survive?'

SERVICE QUALITY CONSIDERATION IN TRANSPORT AND TOURISM

Regardless of whether transport is considered a product or a service, the quality of delivery must be considered. In transport research, considerable attention has been devoted to the issue of service quality and how it is to be measured (see, for example, Chen & Chang, 2005; Gursoy *et al.*, 2005; Tsaur *et al.*, 2002). Tripp and Drea (2002) found, in a study of over 2500 Amtrak passengers in the United States, on-board conditions, café car conditions and on-time performance were considerations in both overall attitudes towards Amtrak and whether passengers intended to re-purchase. In air transport, service quality has been examined with respect to the impact it can have on passenger behaviour (e.g. Park *et al.*, 2004), passenger expectations (Gilbert & Wong, 2003) and safety perceptions (Rhoades & Waguespack, 2000). Suzuki *et al.* (2001) and Suzuki and Tyworth (1998) have modelled the important relationship between service quality and airline market share utilising a weighted average of on-time performance, over-sales, mishandled baggage and in-flight food quality when measuring an air carrier's overall attractiveness. Notably, Suzuki *et al.* (2001: 786) argue that 'if an airline's service quality falls below the market reference point (median service quality of the industry at time t), the airline's market share will decrease significantly, but the service increase from the reference point may not increase an airline's market share'.

One of the more popular measures of service quality is the gap method introduced by Parasuraman *et al.* (1985). In essence, this method measured the difference between customer's expectations and perceptions. Based on a specific instrument (SERVQUAL), Parasuraman *et al.* (1988) measured service perceptions in various organisations (bank, credit card company, repair and maintenance company, and a telephone company) and arrived empirically at a list of service dimensions (Parasuraman *et al.*, 1988: 23, 1991), which I paraphrase here:

1. Tangibles, including facilities, buildings and staff appearance.

2. Reliability, which relates to the ability of the service to be performed consistently and accurately.

3. Responsiveness, or the ability of the organisation or service provider to respond to customer needs.

4. Assurance, or the extent to which staff exude confidence and trust.

5. Empathy, which refers to the ability of the organisation to be caring and attentive when necessary.

Competition on the basis of service levels is a feature of some modes of transport. Airlines and many rail services (particularly in the UK) position themselves (via business models) on the basis of service. As seen in Chapter 6, the LCLF and FSA concepts differ on a number of elements, including service provision. Interestingly, with the lack of service provision generally attributed to LCLF carriers (in an effort to reduce cost), one might be inclined to think that this would have a negative impact on revenue and profits. O'Connell and Williams (2005), however, found that passengers travelling on LCLF carriers generally placed price ahead of other considerations, but those travelling on FSAs may tolerate higher fares in return for some service provision. Even more interesting was that O'Connell and Williams (2005) found that preference for the LCLF concept of low fare and minimal service was international as they surveyed passengers in both Asia and Europe.

Service level considerations extend beyond actual modes of transport. Tam and Lam (2004), for example, explore passenger wayfinding in airports in the context of service provision. In the context of airport design, such considerations are critical as airports are increasingly relying upon non-aeronautical revenue (see Chapter 7). Overall, the service encounter (Bitner, 1990) in the context of transport and tourism can occur at several points:

1. Pre-travel interactions between the traveller and the transport provider, including booking (online or through direct call centres).

2. During travel, including customer evaluation and experience of core and ancillary products and services.

3. Post-travel, including quality of post-sales service and attention (e.g. lost baggage, correct credit of frequent flyer miles).

CHAPTER SUMMARY

The marketing environment for transportation is constantly changing. Although these changes can be said to reflect the dynamic (some may even argue turbulent) environment in which competition for patronage is intense, many of the more significant changes are in the media through which advertisements and promotions are delivered. The example of direct marketing using email has already been mentioned above, but it is perhaps the internet that is providing the means through which substantial interest in marketing has taken place. As discussed, Virgin's internet advertising campaign for its UK train service was extensive and utilised the latest in imbedded advertising on web pages. Google searches are often peppered with 'google ads', which are meant to bear resemblance to the search term you inputted. Those involved in advertising are always conscious of where people get their information, and transport operations are no different. Where television advertising used to mean a captive audience, the introduction of hard disk recorders (such as TIVO in the United States) now means that consumers can time-shift their television programmes automatically and even omit commercial advertisements.

The marketing of transport operations in relation to tourism is more comprehensive, of course, than the means by which the product is advertised. What is important is how consumers perceive the advantages of the type and level of service being offered. This is particularly paramount in air transport, especially in a domestic environment where, quite often, LCCs offer cut-throat fares in a bid to drive traffic and enhance their presence in a market. With the increasing concerns over the cost of oil, however, it remains to be seen whether air travel, in some situations, will be seen as economically feasible for most travellers (see, for example, the discussion of Prideaux's transport cost model [2000a, 2004] discussed in Chapter 2).

Box 8.2 Self-check-in: New service experiences in airports

The *Airline Business* IT trends survey from 2006 reported that an average 27% of all passengers are using self-service kiosks at check-in (Airline Business, 2006a). Roughly one-half of all airports around the world employ some form of self check-in kiosk, and this is predicted to rise to 75% over the next two years (SITA, 2006). The importance of these data cannot be understated: passenger growth is predicted to rise exponentially in many regions around the world. The UNWTO's World Tourism Barometer reported in July 2006 that preliminary numbers indicate an increase of 10 million more tourist arrivals worldwide for the first four months of 2006 over the similar period in 2005. Managing these flows is becoming critical, and airports and airlines are both seeking ways of managing passenger throughput more efficiently. Whereas many airports will see a rationale for improving customer 'throughput' during peak hours of a given day, airlines may wish to utilise IT to enhance the passenger experience or as a means to reduce costs. Regardless of the strategic rationale, technological advances have helped with this process.

Passenger activities in airports generally consist of check-in, customs and security, shopping and then boarding. Although there are variants at many airports (including the introduction of enhanced retail and service activities, as discussed in Chapter 7), many airports, and airlines, have sought ways to speed up the process of passenger check-in. Check-in represents a significant time when passengers queue, although in an increasingly security conscious world, queues can also be found at customs and security checkpoints (of which there may be more than one). Many airlines and airports have sought to decrease the time spent checking-in for most passengers.

Self-check-in kiosks are becoming increasingly common at many airports (Figure 8.4). The benefits for airports are clear: they improve passenger movement and could facilitate growth in passenger numbers without a corresponding increase in foot congestion. A downside for airports, however, is that faster throughput may mean less time actually in the airport. Given the increasing reliance on non-aeronautical revenue, some airports may be reluctant to move towards more kiosks. For airlines, self-check-in kiosks can be financially lucrative. Ground staff numbers can be reduced, and thus ground operational costs shrink. For passengers, having access to multiple kiosks as opposed to proportionately fewer ground check-in staff can mean faster processing of travel documents and acquiring boarding passes more quickly. A few examples from airline press releases:

Continental Airlines (NYSE: CAL) announced on Tuesday (18 April) that it has installed its 1,000th Self Check-in Kiosk in Bogota, Colombia. According to Continental the carrier now offers more kiosks per customer than any other airline. The kiosks, which offer service in English, Spanish, French and German, enable travellers to print their boarding passes at the airport. In addition domestic passengers can select or change their seat, upgrade or

Figure 8.4 Service efficiency: Self-check-in kiosks at Dunedin International Airport, New Zealand

stand by for First Class, verify or input their OnePass number, and change their flight for same-day travel by using a Self Check-in Kiosk, the airline said. (http://www.findarticles.com/P/articles/mi_m0CWU/is_2006_April _19/ai_n16126991)

easyJet is transforming the airline industry once again with its plans to introduce self-check-in across all airports, a process which is currently in place at Nottingham East Midlands, Geneva and Berlin airports. Some airlines have offered self-check-in for passengers with hand luggage for a number of years and a very small number allow self check-in for those with hold baggage. However, all these airlines allow passengers to check-in using either kiosks or traditional methods. Keeping two channels open is an unnecessary duplication and increases, rather than decreases, costs. Ultimately dual processes keep fares unnecessarily high. This major initiative is part of easyJet's drive to reduce costs by using technology to simplify processes and reduce complexity, which in turn will help keep your fares low. It will also help to increase airport capacity by using space more efficiently. You should also find that the check-in process is much faster, with less time spent queuing! (http://www.easyjet.com/ EN/Flying/leapcheckininfo.html)

Emirates ensures that each step of your journey is a unique experience in itself. The 24-hour Self Check-in facility at Dubai International Airport helps make checking in faster and more convenient than before. So whether you are travelling light with hand baggage only, or off on a longer journey with baggage to check in, this is the easiest way to fly. This service allows you to check in, select your seat, register your Skyward Miles and even obtain your First or Business Class lounge invites. (http://www.emirates.com/TravellerInformation/airport/SelfCheckin/selfcheckin.asp)

The caveat with self-check-in kiosks, however, is that passengers still be required to queue to 'drop off' check-in baggage. In other words, queue congestion is transferred from the check-in area to other areas, although it could be argued that is more efficient overall in terms of moving passengers throughout a terminal. For business travellers and those who travel only with carry-on luggage, kiosks can dramatically save time.

Other improvements in the check-in process have been made by several airlines. Many airlines are turning to the internet to facilitate the check-in process. Singapore Airlines, for example, offers passengers with a valid KrisFlyer (their frequent flyer programme) membership account to check-in for most international flights online. During online check-in, the passenger has the ability to change his or her seat. They are also able to confirm details such as passport identification and preferred frequent flyer programmes for mileage credit. In some instances, a boarding pass can even be printed. Such a service helps the passenger in that less time is spent at the airport check-in counter. It also helps the airline because it confirms who is meant to show up for a flight, thus allowing for planning of last-minute sales.

Overall, self-check-in represents another example of self-service trends in many economic sectors. Supermarkets, petrol stations and online shopping are good examples of how the customer's interactions with the service provider or manufacturer can be minimised. In the case of air transport, this trend in self-service is yet another means of reducing costs when margins are getting thinner and thinner. In many respects, this is ironic in that, through relationship marketing, many airlines are making conscious efforts to form relationships with customers and potential customers, yet the self-service paradigm ensures that customers are far removed from interactions with staff.

> **Questions for consideration**
>
> 1. What problems are associated with self-check-in procedures for air travel?
>
> 2. What other forms of transport have begun to utilise self-check-in?

SELF-REVIEW QUESTIONS

1. What are frequent flyer programmes and to whom are they targeted?

2. How is tangibility defined in the context of transport products and services?

3. Define core, tangible and augmented products in relation to tourism and transport.

ESSAY QUESTIONS

1. When your purchase an airline ticket from Copenhagen to London, what are the possible core, tangible and augmented products that you are purchasing?

2. Why do airlines engage in frequent flyer programmes? Compare the programme structure, qualification levels and reward procedures for two airlines within the same alliance. Why are they both different *and* similar?

3. How has the market for cruise tourism shifted? What new product/service offerings have been introduced, and why?

KEY SOURCES

Shaw, S. (2004) *Airline Marketing and Management* (5th edn). Aldershot: Ashgate.

This is an excellent introductory text for understanding the nuances and complexities with airline marketing. Shaw links concepts from the marketing literature and ties these together with the uniqueness of airline marketing activities. The chapter on relationship marketing is particularly strong, but the author also discusses distribution models, revenue management, and advertising and promotional strategies.

Bennett, M.M. (1996) Airline marketing. In A.V. Seaton and M.M. Bennett *The Marketing of Tourism: Concepts, Issues and Cases* (pp. 377–398). London: International Thomson Business Press.

Bennett's contribution to the Seaton and Bennett volume is particularly useful in that it shows how concepts discussed in the wider volume can be applied to airline environments. While the text itself is set as an undergraduate/graduate level offering, Bennett's discussion of products and strategic marketing is excellent, if not slightly dated given recent changes.

CHAPTER 9:

FUTURE TRENDS IN TOURISM AND TRANSPORT

LEARNING OBJECTIVES

After reading this chapter, you should be able to

1. Understand the complexity of sustainable transport in relation to taxation and regulation.

2. Understand the relationship between the Kyoto Protocol and transport.

3. Explain the relationship between the peak oil hypothesis and transport and tourism.

4. Evaluate the development of space tourism as a new mode of transport for tourism.

5. Critically assess future trends in transport that may have significant impacts on tourist flows and tourism development worldwide.

INTRODUCTION

Having considered the salient issues in the scope of tourism/transport relationships over the past eight chapters, attention can now be devoted to potential future trends. It is important to begin with broad trends that resist mode-specific or industry-specific 'predictions'. One of the more salient topics that has received significant media attention internationally since the early part of this century is the nature and feasibility of sustainable transport provision. With the growing threat of global warming, critics are pointing to the transport sector (but in particular aviation) as contributing significant emissions. Unfortunately, global capital flows, and indeed some countries' GDP strength, rely on air transport networks. This makes the question of sustainable tourism not merely one of protecting the environment but recognising the economic importance of transport. This is discussed in the context of juxtaposing command-and-control emission control measures versus natural competitive frameworks. Embedded within this is how 'global' agreements such as Kyoto impact upon on transport and, by extension, tourism.

One other significant trend in the development and relationship between transport and tourism is space tourism. As discussed, there are regulatory and management implications for such activities. Even the environmental implications are, as of the time of writing, still somewhat unknown given that space tourism as a viable commercial means of tourism transport has not yet been extensive due to logistical and financial realities. The chapter concludes with several key issues relating broadly to future trends in transport provision and tourism.

SUSTAINABLE TRANSPORT?

Transport has been extensively considered in the context of environmental impacts in the academic literature (e.g. Hayashi *et al.*, 1999). Lumsdon (2000: 372) outlines a series of stages when developing a sustainable tourism transport network:

> The first stage involves an analysis of existing policy frameworks, in relation to an audit of existing infrastructure and available data on the market. In the second stage, it will be necessary to re-appraise existing land use and assess future proposals for tourism development against, for example, core sustainability indicators. In terms of the likely criteria to be adopted, proposals for new tourism attractions, for example, would be assessed in relation to access on foot and by cycle in contrast to the current trend towards extensive car park provision. The third stage would include a synthesis of work undertaken in stage two, in the form of policy guidance or documentation. The aim would be to secure an appropriate balance in the tourism transport system, which might be different according to local conditions at each destination. In devising a tourism transport network, priority would be given to modes of travel which enhance the visitor experience, but the process would involve a weighting of this gain in relation to social and environmental impacts on residents. The final stage involves implementation and continuous monitoring in terms of both software and hardware requirements of the tourism transport network.

Lumdson's characterisation of sustainable transport planning is useful in that it highlights the extent of integration between transport and tourism. In some situations, sharp integration may be needed where transport provision is necessary for economically feasible tourism development. In other cases, less integration may be more appropriate given overall tourism development plans and policies.

The issue of sustainable transport is reaching the agendas of intergovernmental commissions and committees struck to gauge future impacts. The First International Conference on Tourism and Climate Change (http://www.world-tourism.org/sustainable/climate/brochure.htm), held in Tunisia in 2003 with representatives from IOC,

UNESCO, IPCC, UNCCD, UNEP, UNFCCC, WMO, and UNWTO, concluded with a Declaration that addresses key considerations in the balance of climate change with global tourism. The Declaration outlines specific levels of agreement relating to transport. For example:

- To encourage the tourism industry, including transport companies, hoteliers, tour operators, travel agents and tourist guides, to adjust their activities, using more energy efficient and cleaner technologies and logistics, in order to minimize as much as possible their contribution to climate change.
- To call upon governments to encourage the use of renewable energy sources in tourism and transport companies and activities, by facilitating technical assistance and using fiscal and other incentives. (Djerba Declaration on Tourism and Climate Change, http://www.world-tourism.org/sustainable/climate/brochure.htm)

The conference paid close attention to the role of transport in affecting change to climate, noting that

[w]hile concern about tourism's polluting effects covers all aspects of a tourist's activity, there was a consensus that the primary issue relates to travellers' consumption of transport services, notably road and air transport. In the former case, there is clear evidence from major tourism destinations such as France, that the use of road transport by travellers contributes significantly to greenhouse gas (GHG) emissions. The conference clearly felt that the tourism industry shares some of the responsibility for road transport pollution and thus also shares a responsibility to minimise harmful emissions by encouraging sustainable, carbon-neutral road transport solutions.

Air transport, although currently contributing substantially lower levels of GHGs than road transport, was also raised as a cause for concern. The proportionate contribution made by air transport to total GHG emissions was agreed to be rising rapidly. Schemes to achieve carbon neutral air transport by the introduction of voluntary levies have already been described. There is evidence from countries such as the UK and New Zealand that carbon taxes of one kind or another are increasingly being placed on the political and environmental policy agenda. It seems inevitable that, at some future date, serious consideration will be given to additional environmental taxes or levies targeting the air transport sector specifically. The conference was concerned that the tourism industry acknowledge the polluting effects of air transport and take steps to minimise its impact. When considering the control of the air transport sector for its emissions, the socio-economic impacts of the control measures on destinations should also be examined, as it can affect local economies especially in long-haul destinations in developing countries. (WTO, 2003b)

Broadly, the concern with sustainable transport can be sketched in two ways: 1) the control and regulation of emissions; and 2) the availability of alternative means of power in light of the peak oil problem.

EMISSIONS CONTROL: KYOTO AND BEYOND?

The Kyoto Protocol (negotiated in 1997, but enacted in 2005) was/is designed to produce mechanisms and incentives to cut the production of GhGs produced as a result of human productivity and industries whose by-products reduce the health of the atmosphere and, as a result, the biosphere. It is important to note, however, that not every country in the world ratified the Kyoto Protocol (although over 140 did): the United States and Australia (both of which signed the original Protocol but have not ratified the Agreement) have generally refused because the internationally regulated reduction of GhG emissions could have serious impacts on their respective national economies. Both have argued that national- or region-based programmes would be more efficient.

The Kyoto Protocol states that '[t]he Parties included in Annex I shall pursue limitation or reduction of emissions of greenhouse gases not controlled by the Montreal Protocol from aviation and marine bunker fuels, working through the International Civil Aviation Organization and the International Maritime Organization, respectively'. This is an important point because the international aspect of aviation is not mentioned. Article 2 of the Protocol states specifically that, in order to promote sustainable development practices, countries should '[i]mplement and/or further elaborate policies and measures in accordance with its national circumstances, such as ... [m]easures to limit and/or reduce emissions of greenhouse gases not controlled by the Montreal Protocol in the transport sector' (http://unfccc.int/resource/docs/convkp/kpeng.html). (The Montreal Protocol, signed initially in 1987, was instrumental in generating incentives towards removing several noxious elements from the stratosphere, including CFCs, carbon tetrachloride, halons and methyl chloroform by 2000.)

The Protocol states clearly that those countries who have voluntarily bound themselves to the Protocol must work towards reducing aviation emissions in their own countries, but of course aircraft operations are not restricted only to domestic operations. The transnational nature of aircraft operations makes it somewhat difficult to affix emissions violations or curtailment successes to one particular country. In fact, the closest form of an 'emissions tax' seems to be one based on, or embedded within, aeronautical charges levied by airports (as is the case with some German airports). In the absence of international agreements (and incentives) to cut emissions, however, the impact of aviation-related emissions will have difficulties with establishing meaningful management.

Although Kyoto may not have been the success that some economists and environmentalists may have wished for (particularly with respect to transport), there are examples of regional approaches to emissions reductions. For example, the European Commission introduced in July 2006 legislation proposals that address the exponential growth in air traffic and the resultant emissions. Specifically, the EU Parliament called for airlines to be brought in to the carbon trading schemes already in place in the EU as well as pay a tax on aviation fuel. The intent of these suggestions is to introduce incentives to curb emissions. Such a plan is not without its critics, however. The IATA suggests that regional schemes do little to curb emissions overall, and that a global solution is necessary. Writing in *The Times* (UK), columnist Carl Mortishead argues that, while it is admirable to want to curb emissions, all evidence points to the fact that demand for air travel is increasing in spite of fuel surcharges and that the airline industry is 'so inefficient that it can absorb more fuel costs as it eliminates chronic waste and subsidies' (Mortishead, 2006).

The EU Parliament proposal is not the only regional effort. In 2005, a new vision for pollution reduction and energy efficiencies was agreed to in principle by Australia, China, India, Japan, Korea and the United States. The Asia–Pacific Partnership on Clean Development and Climate is designed to sit next to Kyoto as opposed to outright replacing it, with the major difference being that the signatories will be allowed to set their own emissions reductions and not be penalised for missing the targets. Although non-binding, however, and with very little mention of transport issues, there may be some consolation in that the countries involved are some of the biggest developed-nation polluters in the world. The Worldwide Fund for Nature, however, cast doubt the on the pact, suggesting that '[a] deal on climate change that doesn't limit pollution is the same as a peace plan that allows guns to be fired' (BBC, 2005).

A series of meetings of countries from around the world was held in Montreal in December 2005 with the intent of paving the way for a new international focus on climate change and emissions. Some gains were made, particularly in the area of future talks that would extend climate control beyond Kyoto, although no specific mention was made with respect to transport emissions (at least not publicly nor in the final statements at the wrap-up of the conference). Importantly, however, one noteworthy event transpired at the Montreal meetings that raises the question of who is to pay for the cost of achieving sustainable transport through emissions reductions. Stephen Byers, the former environment secretary in Britain, suggested (Independent, 2005) that, if the United States would not opt in to a new agreement, regulations should be imposed on United States-registered aircraft entering and using European airspace and landing at European airports. This model of emissions control is one where absolute cuts are enforced. If the European Union enforced an absolute cut in emissions by United States-registered carriers, the cost of compliance by an American carrier could well be higher than the returns or profits realised. For some there may be little economic incentive to continue operations to Europe. As the trans-Atlantic routes are some of the most profitable for many United States major airlines, reduction in services in order to comply with absolute emissions cuts could further destabilise the United States air industry.

A popular means (as measured by support from governments and environmentalists) by which aircraft emissions may be reduced is through Pigovian taxation (Pigou, 1920). A Pigouvian tax effectively requires a polluter to internalise the cost of pollution through the imposition of a tax that represents the cost to society as a consequence of the pollution generated. Thus, if the European Union were to impose an emissions tax (per quantity of some particulate released into the air, but usually through the amount of GhG emitted) on United States-registered airlines flying to and from Europe, the cost to those carriers effectively becomes a set amount based on emissions. Thus, the airline would have to determine the cost of its operations at present with the tax versus the cost to cut emissions. In other words, the airline would need to determine what the opportunity cost is to continue operating on the route where emissions taxes would be imposed, particularly if other routes to other destinations may not attract similar taxation.

Taxation to cut emissions places the cost of reducing emissions firmly in the hands of airlines. Of course, the cost of adopting newer operational procedures designed to cut emissions will likely not be the same for all airlines, and this illustrates one problem with the option of taxing emissions on international aviation. Some airlines, for example, may be able to adopt processes that cut emissions even further than one-half of current amounts if significant tax savings are realised, while others may find that the cost in tax is cheaper than adopting more efficient operations. In essence, the principle at work here is that, for a cost-effective reduction in emissions, particularly for transport, the marginal cost of abatement for each airline (or cruise company, or car manufacturer) is the same, but the problem is setting a tax rate where the maximum cut in emissions is realised. This is difficult because the cost of reducing pollution is unknown for all companies, and will naturally vary. However, with the taxation approach, as opposed to absolute cuts, firms will cut emissions as cheaply as possible (i.e. they will select the best option where profits are maintained, and the cost to society is minimised). In fact, absolute emission cuts can be politically dangerous, as those firms whose costs rise substantially may be forced to trim workforce size (thus society may incur some cost for absolute emissions cuts). In an international context, this could lead to strained relations between trading partners.

Pigouvian taxes, abatement and Coase's Theorem

Whether Pigouvian taxes or absolute emissions cuts are enacted, an argument could be made that the compliance costs should be borne by those who are directly affected by unsustainable activities, especially when the direct and tangible benefits of those activities is important enough to maintain. This argument is derived from the Coase Theorem (Coase, 1960; see also Millimet & Slottje, 2002):

> Given free bargaining and low transaction costs, voluntary actions of individuals in the market will allocate property rights to the most highly valued and efficient use. Both parties in a dispute over property rights have an incentive to move to this posi-

tion. Such allocation occurs automatically without regard to how property rights are initially or legally assigned. Judicial action to allocate them generates a superfluous social cost and is itself a negative externality. (Cobin, 1999: 380)

Coase essentially argued that direct regulation was inefficient in the context of addressing externalities (Hillman, 2003). Coase's Theorem has already been considered roughly in an environmental context (e.g. Hanley *et al.*, 1997; Pearson, 2000), and its principle argument can thus be considered subsequently when discussing aircraft emissions. In the example above, it is a given that the presence of United States-registered carriers covering the Atlantic route is important for both tourism and overall commerce and trade in Europe. A call for an absolute reduction in emissions may adversely affect those carriers who account for a substantial amount of the capacity between the United States and Europe. Airlines, faced with mandatory restrictions on emissions, would have two primary options: 1) reduce emissions as required through potentially costly means (i.e. newer, more efficient engines); or 2) completely stop flying to Europe. There are, of course, options within these, such as modifying some aircraft for specific use to and from European airspace. The problem with option 1 is that it would likely mean the costs are off-set to passengers. Classic supply/demand curves and price elasticities would suggest that passengers, facing increased ticket costs to Europe, may elect to travel elsewhere (although some business travel would, perhaps, be less elastic). In this scenario, the result could be a hugely diminished market for travel to Europe. Opting for option 2 could mean a hugely retrenched airline, with job losses and, perhaps as well, diminished traffic to Europe because of the subsequent decrease in capacity.

In applying the Coase Theorem, however, both the airlines and the European Union (acting on behalf of the public) would negotiate any subsidies or levels of absolute emissions cuts to the point where the social cost to both parties is effectively minimised. In other words, the question becomes whether the costs involved in introducing absolute emissions cuts should be borne by those calling for the emissions cuts or by those responsible for the emissions. The most appropriate solution, of course, is to adopt absolute emissions cuts in such a way as to minimise the social cost as much as possible. The problem, however, is how social cost can be measured internationally, especially given that Carlsson (2002) noted that different markets (especially the nature of imperfect competition) and networks would undoubtedly produce differing levels of emissions. In other words, would the social costs to Europe outweigh those in the United States, or would the robustness of the totality of both economies be maintained if the social cost is borne by, for example, the United States? It is plausible that countries that rely heavily on tourist traffic arriving by air would not likely call for absolute emissions cuts from the airlines that service it because the potential social cost to their own economy (assuming airlines decide to cease operations) may be too significant in the immediate term. In other words, airlines are less likely to absolutely cut emissions if, for example, the marginal cost of doing so is prohibitive.

At its most basic level, a Coasian approach used in addressing international aviation emissions would assume that bargaining between the polluters (airlines) and the 'victims' (individual nations or supranations, acting on behalf of its citizenry) would result in a mutually agreeable level of emissions. In adopting a Coasian framework, however, a number of issues are raised (Duval, 2006):

1. *The role of aeropolitics.* Nations and supranational entities (e.g. trading blocs) negotiate ASAs that effectively allow flag carriers to establish routes and connections between several points within a service network. Bilaterals are negotiated on basis of the economic benefits brought to a country through the provision of these services, and the move towards open skies (Canada/United States, Australia/New Zealand and potentially the US/EU) demonstrates the relative importance placed in air access for the purposes of economic growth and global connectivity of markets. The imposition of a Pigouvian tax or some form of Coasian approach at a national or supranational level may call into question the reciprocal rights of airline whose initial air operating certificate is from a foreign country. In fact, a 1999 report from the European Commission considered two options for the introduction of an excise duty on aviation fuel: option A involved taxation of all routes departing any Community airport and option B focused purely on intra-European routes:

> The results show clearly that the environmental effectiveness of imposing kerosene taxes is significantly higher where all routes departing from EU airports are taxed. Moreover, the ratio between environmental effectiveness, on the one hand, and economic and competitive impact on the European airline industry, on the other hand is, from a European view, significantly better where all air carriers are taxed, at least as long as circumvention practices by means of taking fuel in third countries is not widespread. Finally, in relation to cost-benefit considerations, it is at least questionable whether a reduction in all transport-related CO_2-emissions of just 0.26% (as calculated for an EU 2005 scenario with 1992 a base year on the basis of applying option B) and of NO_x-emissions by 0.12% would justify considerable pressure on the competitiveness of the European aviation industry which would have to compete head-on with third country air carriers enjoying intra-Community traffic rights, as a side-effect of the cumulative effects of so-called open-sky agreements concluded by Member States.

> Consequently, any effective approach would necessitate a system that allows for taxing/charging all carriers operating out of Community airports (Option A). Such an approach, however, if applied in the field of kerosene taxation would require fundamental changes to existing policies at ICAO-level and, in particular, to existing bilateral Air Service Agreements (ASAs) that allow for the imposition of taxation only in case of a reciprocal agreement. These changes will be difficult to achieve

without considerable concessions in other fields. For these reasons, the Commission considers that the approach suggested in its 1996 report should be maintained, for the time being, pending progress in international fora. The alternative (Option B), though legally feasible, is unacceptable in the Commission's view. It would not strike the delicate balance between environmental, economic and internal market requirements which is necessary for a coherent policy in this area. The conclusion reached as to the relative attractiveness of options A and B also applies to lower tax levels even though these may reduce the economic burden for Community air carriers. (Commission of the European Communities, 1999)

2. *Should the consumer be responsible for emissions abatement?* The benefits of airlines servicing a destination can be calculated through manufactured goods (from cargo) and tourist receipts, including the magnitude of the multiplier and any leakages present in respective service sectors. The full and direct impact of emissions, however, is not as clear. As a result, an airline (or the wider industry) might argue that the full cost of emissions production should be borne by the destination, given that the *known* social benefits of its services outweigh the (generally) *unknown* social costs of its emissions (see, for example, Duval, 2006; Vlek & Vogels, 2000). If a Pigouvian tax or a command and control (CAC) measure were introduced, the airline may cease services, thus rendering not only a reduction in emissions (a social benefit) but also a social cost to the destination because the sudden drop in the financial impact of the services provided indirectly by the presence of the airline. In this instance, the question is whether the net social benefit of emissions reduction is *greater* than the social cost endured as a result of the reduction of those services.

3. *Power structures and transaction costs.* Under a Coasian framework, where both parties would negotiate and bargain towards a level of pollution acceptable to both, the social and environmental costs are evaluated against economic benefits of the indirect and direct services provided by airlines. There is, however, a significant problem with the implementation of a Coasian approach. Negotiating or bargaining might work in a constrained environment, such as a factory emitting pollution, which has as a negative effect on local residents, but international aviation presents significant problems because of its size and transnational/globalised nature. As a result, an airline and a particular nation might well negotiate an equilibrium point given the marginal net private benefits and marginal external costs, but if this is not implemented on a global scale it provides an immediate disincentive for airlines to service a particular destination such that their marginal external costs are disproportionately allied to a specific nation or region (Duval, 2006).

Where does this leave sustainable transport? In one sense, sustainable transport as a concept needs to be thought of beyond strict environmental measures; it needs to take into account financial and social sustainability, and nowhere is this more critical than with respect to international aviation and tourist travel. More importantly, the level of measurement and analysis must be considered. If global units of analysis are not feasible, regional interpretations (e.g. Haynes *et al.*, 2005) must be developed in order to capture in aggregate as much data within a wide spatial scope.

Box 9.1 Pigouvian taxes – who pays? (based on Duval, 2006)

Ryanair announced in July 2006 that services from Prestwick, Ayrshire, Luton and Stansted to various Swedish destinations would be cut if a new general aviation tax proposed by the Swedish government is to be formally implemented. Under the tax, passengers flying within Europe will pay an additional SKR94 (approximately 10 euros) and SKR188 if travelling internationally (Forbes, 2006). However, the European Commission is, at the time of writing, currently investigated the tax (The Local, 2006). Commentators have argued that the tax may not be legal on the grounds that it stifles competition, particularly when some smaller regional airports would not be required to collect the tax on the basis that it would stimulate travel to these destinations.

Ryanair argued that the tax would add an extra 30% to the average cost of the fares on offer from the airline (Evening Times, 2006). Michael Cawley, deputy chief executive of Ryanair, argued that '[t]he introduction of this tax will make Swedish tourism uncompetitive when compared with cheaper alternatives in Spain, Italy and elsewhere in Europe' (Evening Times, 2006). This example demonstrates a potential response by an incumbent carrier to the introduction of a new tax or levy. Prior to this announcement, Ryanair had been reporting healthy profits for its operations (although in August 2006 it was announced that rising fuel costs would cut into projected profits significantly), and as such the rationale for the threat of flight cuts to Sweden was not likely on the basis of shrinking financial efficiencies of its network.

With the introduction and proliferation of LCCs throughout Europe, including low cost subsidiaries of larger FSAs, many are susceptible to the introduction of additional levies because of inherent business models that favour stringent management of marginal costs. Indeed, as outlined in Chapter 6, the success of LCCs is largely attributed to the management of costs. Naturally, any new cost from a new tax or levy can be passed onto the passenger, but when other destinations are deemed as being relatively accessible and where transport costs (and thus ticket prices) are lower, the viability of the network segment with the additional tax or levy will be questioned from a strategic management perspective. Indeed, if it is accepted that airfares are somewhat elastic (see Chapter 2) when compared to other goods and services, then the cost of any tax or levy will likely be covered by the airline in the face of significant competition for other services.

Figure 9.1 provides an idealised and hypothetical model of the impact of a tax or levy upon a particular route where high degrees of elasticity are realised. The model is useful in that it demonstrates the strategy an airline may employ in making business decisions regarding the financial feasibility of a particular route within a larger network. The model does not incorporate the complicated nature of yield management (see Chapter 6), which would suggest that, when the cost base is altered, varying fares would be offered in order to cover that new cost level. The model, then, assumes a fixed price for the product on offer, or in this case a seat on an aircraft.

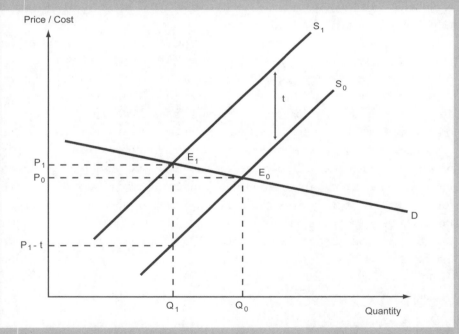

Figure 9.1 Theorised elasticity of airline seat prices (not under yield management) and impact of tax

Source: Adapted from Turner *et al.* (1993) based on Duval (2006)

In the model, the equilibrium price prior to the introduction of tax (t) is achieved at E_0, given D and S_0. The introduction of a new tax or levy shifts the supply curve to S_1, thus reflecting an increase in the cost of production, or in this case the cost of operating a particular flight. This shift results in a new equilibrium point (E_1) given that the quantity demanded subsequently falls. As a result, where P_1 to P_1-t represents the tax enforced, P_0 to P_1 represents the total cost of the new tax borne by passengers and P_0 and P_1-t the amount borne by the producer, in this case the airline. Once again, it is important to remember that this model assumes that fares are uniform and yield management systems are not in place. In reality, an airline would have the option, through yield management, of reducing the number of cheaper fares in an effort to increase their RPK. Depending on the actual monetary value of the tax itself, the airlines' ability to recover the tax from P_0 and P_1-t may not be entirely possible.

An airline facing increased costs on a particular route will undoubtedly re-evaluate the strength of the route from a return-on-investment perspective. In other words, it may decide that rather than fly that particular route to a destination that has imposed a tax on its operations, it could instead utilise its aircraft on other routes where similar taxes are not present and thus the overall operational cost base is lower. The nature of the elasticity can be used to establish how producers might respond with alternate pricing schemes. For instance, where the market for products/services (in this case, seats on an aircraft) exhibit significant inelasticity, producers will likely be able to recover increased costs as a result of an introduction of a tax or levy. Travellers who utilise air services out of necessity will bear the increase cost through higher fares. Where demand is suitably elastic, competition between producers can continue on the basis of a uniform increase in cost, but the consequential increase in price (or in this case, fares) may not be uniform. In the example above concerning Ryanair's flights into Sweden, if all airlines were charged the new tax (and indeed this is what was proposed) and if travel to Sweden on holiday was deemed to be comparatively elastic, demand for holidays to Sweden would likely fall and thus shift to other destinations. Arguably, such a simplified model does not take into account holiday cost models that feature the cost of transport as part of the overall trip cost (see Chapter 2 for a discussion of Prideaux's transport cost model). It can, however, be argued that transport cost, as part of the overall cost of travel, can be relatively inelastic while the cost of other components (such as discretionary spending, accommodation, activities, etc.) may be fully elastic. As a consequence, the imposition of the tax by Sweden, if successful, may not necessarily result in a drop in visitor numbers if those visitors were willing to sacrifice costs in other aspects of their travels.

Questions for consideration

1. What kinds of travel can be considered elastic/inelastic and how might they be affected by the introduction of new taxes that raise the cost of transport?

2. How might the cost of transport be affected if a tax or levy (or any aspect of the overall cost base) is reduced or removed? Use Turner *et al.*'s model from Figure 9.1 to explain your answer.

PEAK OIL: TOURISM TRANSPORT IMPLICATIONS

The problem of emissions may not be as much of a problem in the (near?) future if the peak oil hypothesis, which has been at the forefront of many environmental discussions in the popular press since the early part of the current century, becomes reality. According to the IEA (2002), transport is the fastest-growing economic sector in terms of energy consumption. The rapid growth in mobility of people and cargo worldwide has been supported in the past two to three decades by both the increasing liberalisation of transport markets and the provision of cheap oil (Greene & Wegener, 1997), although some might argue that this 'bubble' may be set to burst with the increasing recognition of the reality that oil, upon which this exponential growth in mobility is based, is definitely finite and, more importantly, may be at its peak in terms of efficient production. In fact, geologists' claims (which are not recent) that the world may be approaching a peak in oil production are starting to receive considerable attention by mainstream media, and thus more attention by people and governments worldwide. Peak oil could have severe implications for countries that have a high reliance on oil for base forms of energy. As the vast majority of transport (and not just tourist transport) relies upon cheap, refined oil/petroleum, the impact of peak production could very well be staggering.

If the remaining 50% of the world oil reserves are difficult to extract and refine, the cost of petrol, diesel and aviation fuel will likely increase significantly, thus transforming the nature of mobility (both domestically and internationally) as the cost of transport could well be out of reach for many individuals. The issue is not so much the lack of oil, but how much the remaining oil will cost to refine. As the cost of refinement rises, the cost of fuel product will also rise to maintain existing margins. As a result, it is entirely unclear what the exact repercussions might be for tourism as the cost of refining oil rises after peak production, but several arguments can be made:

1. If the cost of transport increases substantially and thus occupies a higher proportion to personal income, shifts in mobility patterns are likely. Some destinations may become inaccessible because of the high cost of transport. Others' network positions, and thus accessibility, could default to positions where transport costs are the least likely to dissuade markets. Some long-haul destinations, for example, could see falling arrivals if the cost of transport from their key markets becomes too great.

2. Transport networks may spatially constrict because the fixed and marginal cost of operations precludes any possibility of securing market share, particularly if wages do not increase to match proportional increases in transport costs. Transport modes may opt to offer services only where sufficient demand (and net personal benefit) is maximised. As such, the connectivity of existing networks may shrink, with cuts to services or frequencies due to a combination of higher fuel costs and depressed demand.

3. Non-essential travel may be at risk if the cost of transport is too high. Indeed, current ITs already exist that may soften the economic implications of rising transport costs. For example, some business travel, perhaps deemed non-essential, could be replaced by internet telephony (such as VOIP).

The problem is much larger than tourism, and it is of course necessary to position tourism within a wide global system of input/output processes that may be affected adversely from peak oil. While recent increases in the price of crude oil (Figure 9.2) have helped publicise the peak oil hypothesis (although it is more a fact than a hypothesis, but what is hypothetical is when the 50% mark will be reached), there have been steps taken to reduce global dependency on oil and fuel in the transport sector. To avoid rising aviation fuel costs, or at least their wide variability, some airlines have adopted operations policies that are more sustainable (e.g. use of more fuel efficient engine technologies, reduction of noise pollution), even though many are currently (as of December 2005) charging an extra fuel surcharge on top of ticket prices (e.g. Malaysian Air and Singapore Airlines, as of 1 November 2005, were both applying a $50 one-way fuel surcharge). The question, however, now becomes: what alternative modes of transport are available that do not rely upon oil?

Greene and Wegener (1997) note that there are three fields of policy and planning that can influence sustainable transport: technology, supply and demand. Technological innovation has brought several alternatives to motorised transport, particularly in the area of powerplants:

1. The introduction (and constant improvement) of fuel-efficient jet turbine engines, particularly in concert with new aircraft from Boeing and Airbus. Additionally, GE introduced its GEnz engines for use in the Boeing 787 (Dreamliner), the 747 Advanced, and the new Airbus A350. New materials and design help increase overall efficiency, but GE

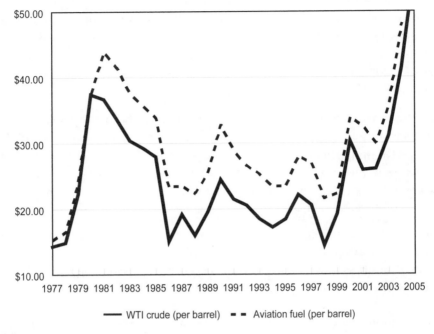

Figure 9.2 Crude oil costs and aviation fuel costs

Source: http://www.airlines.org/econ/d.aspx?nid=9336; accessed 6 January 2006

Note: Crude oil WTI, and aviation fuel costs represented by major, national and large regional United States passenger and cargo carriers.

claims that the engine is more fuel efficient (by 15%) and will reduce emissions significantly. According to the company's website (http://ge.ecomagination.com/@ v=312005_0548@/index.html): 'If all of today's fleet of 200–300 passenger aircraft had GEnx engines, annual carbon dioxide emissions would be reduced by an amount equal to removing more than 800,000 cars from the road for a year, or the carbon dioxide absorbed by 1.2 million acres of forest in a year.' Further innovations may include so-called 'zero-emissions' aircraft fueled by hydrogen and under development/study by NASA (Becken & Simmons, 2005), but these are likely several decades away from being adopted into regular use. Indeed, not everyone believes that increased air traffic and travel will result in irreversible changes to the global climate. The UK aviation technology group Greener by Design suggested recently that aviation emissions will actually be quite a bit less in 2050 than currently thought, largely because of advances in aircraft operational efficiencies, such as reducing drag coefficients (Szodruch, 2001) and new engine technologies (Airline Business, 2005c).

2. The introduction of hybrid automobiles (battery-powered/petrol combinations) in some countries (including the United States and Europe) offers owners an opportunity to engage in short-distance trips without burning petrol. The question, of course, then becomes how the power used to charge the batteries is supplied (and whether its ecological footprint favours its use).

Other aspects of technological innovation include new forms of transport that harness alternative forms of mobility, including:

1. Solar-powered ground transport: for the most part, still in the testing phase, and to some extent hampered by the small size of the vehicles (usually one occupant).

2. Electric-powered ground transport: with the introduction of hybrid automobiles, if the source of electricity is, for example, nuclear, an argument could be made the ecological footprint is still impacted, even though reliance upon a non-renewable source of energy such as oil is reduced. If it is hydro-electric, increased demand on power grids can have serious implications for a country or region's ability to meet demand (as in the case of New Zealand and parts of California).

As Holden and Høyer (2005) argue, the potential for reducing the ecological footprint of transport will soon be based on the use of both conventional and alternative fuel technologies, however this path may not be easy to follow:

> Hydropower has a very low ecological footprint, but is not a global resource with sufficient volumes to support the ever increasing transport systems. Natural gas also has a low ecological footprint but does not have these resource volume limitations, at least not for several decades. But it is not a renewable energy resource, and it does not fulfil the long-term requirements of a sustainable energy system. Biomass is globally available in large volumes and is a renewable resource, but would lead to unacceptable increases in ecological footprints if used extensively. Therefore, it seems that only a combination of more efficient use of resources, substitution to less environmentally harmful fuels, and reduced transportation will meet long-term sustainability objectives.

Demand for transport provision is ostensibly geared for existing forms of available transport. As Greene and Wegener (1997: 182) suggest:

> Medieval cities were built for walking, and this required that living and working were close together. The railway made spatial division of labour possible and so opened the way for the growth of cities. Rapid transit and the cars have facilitated the expansion of metropolitan areas over wider and wider territories with the consequence of ever longer trips and greater volumes of traffic with all their problems of congestion, traffic accidents, energy use, pollution and land consumption.

Tourism, then, has ridden this wave of expansion of transport networks fuelled by the availability of cheap oil. Shifts in the ability to provide transport due to the problem of 'peak oil' will undoubtedly be exacerbated by the layout of the existing network as they were planned and constructed at a time when concerns over peak oil had not yet reached mainstream media. If the era of cheap oil is truly in the past, then the spatial realm of people and goods may be severely constricted in the future if the expense of transport is outside the ability to rationalise its necessity. In aggregate (i.e. globally), oil prices have not had the same impact on global tourism traffic as events such as 11 September 2001 or conflict in the Middle East, but over time the cost of travel may become too burdensome, and the ability of suppliers to rationalise lower costs may be limited without having an impact of profitability.

The sustainability principle in tourism has certainly achieved strong consideration in the academic literature, and has also garnered considerable attention from government and agencies such as the UNWTO. Measurement units have been studied and disseminated in units such as MJ (energy use), emissions (such as GhGs) and carbon dioxide equivalents (CO2–e). As well, the displacement of land can also be measured. Rather than adopting site-specific or micro-level measurements of sustainable practices in tourism (e.g. certification schemes showcasing compliance or minimising environmental impacts through select visitor management techniques), one benefit of examining the sustainability principle of tourism through the lens of transport is that a wider view of sustainability is afforded. Gössling *et al.*'s comments (2005: 418) serve as a useful starting point to adopting a broader approach to sustainability:

> First, whether using energy consumption, greenhouse gas emissions or area-equivalents as basis for calculations, a substantial share of tourism needs to be seen as unsustainable. Second, the use of fossil fuels and related emissions of greenhouse gases is, from a global point of view, the most pressing environmental problem related to tourism (cf. Graßl *et al.*, 2003; Sala *et al.*, 2000; Thomas *et al.*, 2004). Third, transport contributes overproportionally to the overall environmental impact of leisure-tourism; this is between 60% and 95% at the journey level, and including local transport, accommodation, and activities.

What this means is that efforts at achieving sustainability practices 'on the ground', while useful, do little to address the larger issue of the global climate change, and thus radical shifts in quality of life in some areas of the globe. Gössling and Hall (2006: 315) perhaps best address this fundamental misguided attempt to parley sustainability into a 'feel-good' action:

> [T]he reality is that concentrating on tourism alone, and by that we mean the tendency to focus just on what is happening at the destination, is one of the great problems with sustainable tourism. For tourism to really contribute towards security

and sustainable development it needs to be placed within the bigger picture of human mobility, lifestyle, consumption and production. The consumption and production system that seeks to use 'pro-poor tourism' by those from the developed countries to help those in the developing world is the same consumption and production system that has often led to the situations that have contributed to inadequate development practices and poverty in the first place. The most sustainable forms of tourism in many cases may well be no tourism at all, rather focusing on other dimensions of development and a full consideration of alternatives.

Becken (2002) noted that one-way travel to New Zealand by all international tourists resulted in 1900 kilotonnes of CO_2 being emitted into the atmosphere. Put into context, it seems somewhat futile for a country such as New Zealand, to portray itself as '100% pure' (the current marketing slogan) when the very act of travelling to New Zealand is surprisingly (or not, to some) environmentally harmful.

SPACE TOURISM: NEW FRONTIER(S)?

One might be inclined to think that space travel is perhaps the best way of minimising the environmental impacts of commercial air transport, but even space transport comes with its own set of environmental issues. First, however, it is necessary to position space tourism development in the wider context of transport. As of the end of 2005, three individuals have already been in earth orbit as 'passengers' (i.e. not as members of a scientific crew): Dennis Tito became the first in 2001 thanks to a Russian Soyuz capsule that docked with the International Space Station (ISS), Mark Shuttleworth became the second in 2002 with a similar itinerary (and both each paid US$20 million for the privilege), and Greg Olsen also visited the ISS in late 2005. The future of tourism and transport, it seems, involves space. In fact, it may even involve other planetary bodies. In September 2005, the United States announced that it will once again go to the moon, and a few months later reports emerged that China will head to the moon by 2017. Budgeted at US$104 billion, something The *Economist* dubbed as 'suspiciously precise', NASA plan's include the use of a Crew Launch Vehicle (CLV), which will dock with the ISS, as will a second vehicle, the Crew Exploration Vehicle (CEV). The CEV will be tasked with propelling its occupants directly to the moon. All of this, including a replacement shuttle vehicle due in 2010, is targeted for 2018.

Outside of the scientific realm, space tourism is quickly becoming the latest niche product involving transport. Richard Branson's Virgin Galactic will transport tourists in from origin to destination in record times using sub-orbit flight trajectories, much higher than traditional aircraft. Significantly, some 38,000 people have already paid a deposit for travel on some of the first flights (Wardell, 2005). This is not surprising considering polls from the late 1990s suggest that space travel would be welcomed by the public (CNN, 1998). Both NASA and the Space Transport Association have long suggested that space as a frontier for travel could be developed, and a series of recommendations from 1998 established the importance of joint industry–government partnerships and support:

- National space policy should be examined with an eye toward encouraging the creation of space tourism.
- The expansion of space camps, space-themed parks and other land-based space tourism should be encouraged.
- The federal government should cooperate with private business to reduce the technological, operational and market risks – much as it has done with aviation and satellite communications.
- The government should sponsor research and development to dramatically lower the cost of space travel and demonstrate ways to reduce the effects of space sickness. (CNN, 1998)

Crouch (2001) argues that there are several forms of space tourism:

1. *Near-earth orbit:* This has yet to reach the tourist masses, although several 'ordinary' citizens have already paid for the privilege. Dennis Tito was the first 'tourist' in space, spending some US$20 million for the opportunity to ride a Russian Soyuz rocket and capsule that eventually docked with the ISS. Critics of this endeavour were quick to point out that only individuals of high-net worth could afford such adventures, and it will likely be some time before weekend trips around the world in space are realised.

2. *Low-earth orbit, high-speed aircraft:* Boeing announced its Sonic Cruiser, designed to fly at supersonic speeds, in March 2001 (see http://www.boeing.com/news/feature/concept/background.html). By flying in the upper limits of the atmosphere, and much higher than 'traditional' jumbos such as the Airbus A340 or the Boeing family of large jets, the aircraft would minimise the time spent travelling from origin to destination, and thus further compressing the time-based perception of distance first seen with the development of long-haul aircraft in the mid-19th century. Ultimately, Boeing opted out of fully producing the Sonic Cruise and instead poured its energy into the development of the Boeing 787, or Dreamliner, which favoured efficiency in operations over speed. As noted by Duval (2005b), there is potential for future development of low-orbit or sub-orbit aircraft, but travellers would need to consider the overall transport cost of the trip. For some essential travel, such as business trips, the cost-benefit could be acceptable. For leisure travel, however, unless a trend of 'massification' is realised, as it was with long-haul travel in the later part of the last century, sub-orbit travel will remain available for those individuals of high-net worth. Further still, and in relation to the sustainability of sub-orbit transport, further studies will need to consider the increased environmental damage to sensitive atmospheric layers (see also Chapter 6 for a discussion of air transport and environment).

3. *Terrestrial-based space tourism activities*: Including attractions and events such as space shuttle launches and tours to locations around the world where recent solar eclipses would be visible. Carlson Wagonlit (through www.eclipsetours.com), refers to such activities as 'astro-tourism'.

At the end of 2005, the FAA within the United States government released a series of proposed rules to regulate space tourism (www.faa.gov/regulations_policies/rulemaking/recently_published/media/ai57.pdf). Among the more notable regulations issued by the FAA (ratified in December 2006) includes the requirement that companies inform potential 'space flight participants' of the risks involved with space travel. It is also suggested that companies require tourists sign a written consent form and be fully trained in safety procedures. Technological developments in vehicles designed to travel to and from space will undoubtedly push space tourism to the point where many companies and governments are involved. As discussed, however, the management of this new mode of transport will need to be carefully considered (Duval, 2005b) (see also Box 9.3).

FUTURE TRENDS AND ISSUES IN TOURISM AND TRANSPORT

Identifying future trends in an industry as varied and dynamic as this is somewhat problematic. To some extent, the prevalence of a mode of transport in the current media can be assessed somewhat on the basis of its presence in mainstream media (and in the informal media such as blogs and discussion forums). The airline industry seems to change on an almost daily basis (reports of bankruptcies, new routes being introduced, new open skies agreements being debated, security screening systems introduced), while rail transport tends to move slightly slower (with the exception of the concerns raised over troubled firms such as Amtrak). A quick search of Google News on 8 December 2005 revealed, at the very top of the list, a report (from Newsday, New York) of family who is considering suing Royal Caribbean because their newly married relative disappeared without a trace whilst on holiday in the Mediterranean (see http://tinyurl.com/8qvhr). Outside of the current focus of the global media, several trends and issues can be identified that can help position where transport and tourism might evolve.

LCCS: EXPANDING INTERNATIONAL NETWORKS

LCCs (or LCLF carriers, see Chapter 6) could well begin servicing international markets within five to seven years, particularly as new fuel-efficient aircraft (e.g. Airbus A350 or Boeing's 787) enter service (Tretheway & Mak, 2006). To some extent, some low-frill airlines already serve destinations within a five- to six-hour catchment (e.g. JetBlue serving the continental United States or Freedom Air serving Australia from New Zealand across the Tasman Sea), but it remains to be seen whether a truly low-cost format will be utilised between major hubs internationally. Already, there have been suggestions (based on hints given by its president in the April 2005 edition of *Airline Business* magazine) that Emirates may be looking at establishing an Emirates Express brand that would utilise the new Airbus A380 in an all-economy, high-density layout (Airline Business, 2005d). LCCs will also likely begin to grow in the Middle East, with National Air Services already planning an LCC out of Saudi Arabia sometime in 2006 (Arab News, 2005).

Although the networks of LCLF airlines may shift, low-cost as a concept will likely come to dominate the airline industry. In many ways, this is a safe forecast as, for the most part, most air carriers worldwide already focus on cutting costs as a means to maximise revenue. This may have, though, little impact on destinations and tourism development as the costs offset by removing frills and ancillary services only covers increases in operating costs relating to, for example, fuel. In other words, rising aviation fuel prices, and any corresponding increase in ticket prices, may result in stagnant or slightly depressed demand for travel. This is especially the case for short-haul travel, where fuel efficiencies may not be as great. In the United States, many traditional network carriers (or FSAs) seem to have significant problems with achieving profitable operations (Table 9.1). In 2004, for example, several large network carriers reported significant losses, while LCCs such as Southwest, AirTran and JetBlue reported positive profit margins (Table 9.2). The United States BTS reported that fourth quarter results of airline performance show regional domestics carriers (as opposed to the larger LCCs and the larger network carriers) generally performing well (BTS, 2005b).

Table 9.1 Operating profit/loss of US network carriers as a percentage of total operating revenue

	Q1 2004	*Q2 2004*	*Q3 2004*	*Q4 2004*
US Airways	−11	2	−14.3	−10.1
Northwest	−2.9	4.3	1.6	−11.7
Alaska	−11.2	1	6.9	−11.7
American	−8.3	−4.6	−8.2	−14
Continental	−9.9	−4.4	−7	−15.4
Delta	−13.1	−6.3	−13	−17.7
United	−12.2	−4.7	−7.7	−22.7

Source: Adapted from US BTS, Form 41, Schedule P1.2

RAIL TRAVEL: LIMITED TO NICHE MARKETS?

Rail travel will likely continue to appeal to specialist or niche markets, but may face difficulties with any attempt to re-establish itself as a prime mode of transport for tourists

Table 9.2 Operating profit/loss of US LCCs as a percentage of total operating revenue

	Q1 2004	Q2 2004	Q3 2004	Q4 2004
Southwest	3.1	11.5	11.4	7.2
JetBlue	11.3	14.1	7.1	3.7
AirTran	4.3	11.3	−4.9	1.3
America West	2	2.6	−4.7	−6.9
Frontier	−8	−3.8	−0.3	−7.3
Spirit	2	−3	−13.3	−31.6
ATA	−14.8	−9.1	−12.5	−187

Source: Adapted from US BTS, Form 41, Schedule P1.2

between origin and destination. The presence of air service is often comparable in price or, if it is not, has the benefit of time in its favour. There is, however, some room for consideration that smaller, regional services may be profitable and attract some tourist traffic. Virgin Trains, for example, has developed advertising campaigns designed to shift the perception of train travel in the UK. Such services could be utilised by weekend recreationalists, thus avoiding congested roads.

SHIFTING DEMOGRAPHICS

The Population Division of the Department of Economic and Social Affairs of the United Nations recently (2005) released projections regarding aging populations worldwide (Table 9.3). The implications for rapidly ageing populations are certainly economic, including shrinking GDP, loss of economic influence and general market malaise. Hall (2005: 285) noted that

> the demographic shift in Western countries is also accompanied by changed employment patterns, particularly the increase in part-time, casual and contract employment in relation to permanent employment. Such changes in social structures have a number of flow-on effects in the tourism and leisure sectors, including the increase of short breaks as opposed to longer holidays.

As tourist flows often take place between 'advanced' or Western countries (Ryan & Trauer, 2004), some (e.g. Dwyer, 2004: 540) suggest that 'many older people wish to enjoy the activities and entertainment that they enjoyed in their youth, and they have more disposable income to spend on those activities'. As a result, it is quite likely that the heterogeneity found in current tourist flows with respect to desired experiences and holiday locations will continue, although Hall (2005) rightly notes that the spatial scale of those travels may be more limited. Coupled with ageing are overall population levels. In less developed countries (Africa, Asia [excluding Japan], Latin America and the Caribbean plus Melanesia,

Micronesia and Polynesia), population levels are predicted to rise at a much faster rate than more developed countries (Europe, Northern America, Australia/New Zealand and Japan) by 2050 (DESA, 2005b) (Figure 9.3). Given the concentration of international traffic within and between developed countries, this could change dramatically over the next 50 years (DESA, 2005b). Tourist and migration traffic between less developed countries and more developed countries will likely increase, and traffic between more developed countries may be relatively less robust.

Table 9.3 Actual and projected population growth of 65+ years age category by percentage

	1950	1975	2000	2025	2050
Africa	3.2	3.1	3.3	4.1	6.9
Asia	4.1	4.2	5.9	10	16.7
Europe	8.2	11.4	14.7	21.5	29.2
Latin American and the Caribbean	3.7	4.3	5.4	9.6	16.9
Northern America	8.2	10.3	12.3	18.7	21.4
Oceania	7.4	7.4	9.9	14.4	18

Source: DESA (2005a)

CRUISE TOURISM: RIDING THE WAVE OF SHIFTING DEMOGRAPHICS

Cruise tourism will likely continue to enjoy growth (whether moderate or high will depend on the economic conditions in the markets served), but as noted in Chapter 5, and coupled with shifting demographics in some countries as noted above, changing trends in cruise markets have meant some companies have targeted specific markets, as in the case of easyCruise and younger passengers. The major growth areas in cruise tourism will likely not be traditional regions such as the Mediterranean or the Caribbean, however. Rather, growth in Asia and the Gulf region (e.g. India, Bahrain) will likely surpass these traditional cruising regions within the next decade. Reports from late 2005 suggest 2006 will see some 11 million cruise passengers, and one of the new efforts at attracting market share will be branding exercises that cruise companies form with other companies (e.g. Royal Caribbean's partnership with Fisher-Price toys) (Asbury Park Press, 2005).

NON-WESTERN DOMESTIC TOURISM AND TRANSPORT GROWTH

In recent years several countries around the world have capitalised on global economic growth by enhancing internal (and outward-connecting) transport modes. In the past few years, and as noted in Chapter 6, China's domestic and regional aviation market has grown rapidly on the back of substantial domestic economic growth in the past five years. This

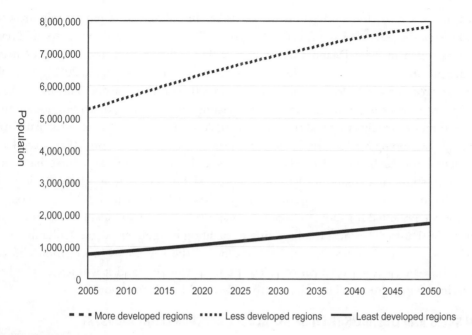

Figure 9.3 Global population forecast

Source: DESA (2005b)

has meant increases in the number of outbound Chinese tourists and a general push towards transport infrastructure renewal. Inbound tourism is also expected to grow at a healthy rate. China's integration into the global economic system is not only benefiting airlines. In 2004, for example, the Chinese government awarded contracts to three foreign firms to upgrade the country's crowded rail system (BBC, 2004c). Although SARS had an impact on China's internal travel demand in 2003, travel volumes rebounded in 2004 and 2005. By one estimate, from the General Administration of Civil Aviation of China, some 130 million Chinese people travelled on Chinese airlines in 2005, second only to the United States in terms of outbound travel. The rebound has resulted in airlines capitalising their operations with new aircraft. China Southern Airlines, in 2004, agreed to purchase 15 A320 and 4 A319 Airbus aircraft, adding to its fleet of 125 aircraft. The new planes will likely serve domestic markets, but also regional Asian centres, particularly Japan (BBC, 2004b). Overall, another 500 to 600 passenger planes (in addition to the existing 900 already in service) will be introduced by 2010, and that number is expected to reach 3000 by 2020 (People's Daily Online, 2005). There are some concerns over possible over-capacity given several major carriers plan to expand their fleets: in late December 2005 the Shanghai Securities News reported significantly slower growth (15%, compared to 33% in 2004 and 20% in 2005) in China's travel market for 2006 (Airwise News, 2005b).

Not unlike China, India's aviation market is in the middle of a remarkable growth period: domestic air travel is expected to grow 25% over the next five years (it grew almost as much in 2005 [Manorama Online, 2005]) following the Indian government allowing private companies to provide air services as 'air taxis' (Bhaumik, 2002). As well, Boeing is predicting deliveries of almost 500 aircraft to Indian carriers and the Indian government is investing in huge upgrades to existing infrastructure to accommodate the huge amount of mobility planned (Unnikrishnan, 2005). Carriers in India, particularly Air India, are also hoping for increased demand for travel following the April 2005 open skies agreement between India and the United States. Such agreements of course have the potential to stimulate demand for leisure-based travel, but they may also have the impact of stimulating demand for expatriate Indians to travel back to India. Another consequence is the potential for India to become a major hub in the region, although Sri Lanka (through Sri Lankan Airlines) is attempting to position its main airport at Columbo as a major regional hub (Airwise News, 2005c). One of the key issues facing India's rapid growth, however, is the provision of adequate infrastructure, and it is unclear whether growth in infrastructure will match growth in demand for air transport.

OPEN SKIES AND LIBERALISATION OF THE GLOBAL AIR TRANSPORT INDUSTRY

With an increasingly globalised economic climate, open skies agreements will continue to increase in number, with liberalisation efforts extending beyond simple scheduling and capacity elements to include ownership and effective control. Holloway (2003) notes that the liberalisation of existing bilateral agreements and the move towards open skies reflects general dissatisfaction with the current international regulatory regime in aviation traffic rights. Holloway (2003) also suggests that a move towards multilateral systems will continue to grow. Morocco, for example, announced in early 2006 an open skies pact with the European Union in an effort to boost its international tourism arrivals and receipts. It is likely that other countries close to the EU will adopt similar policies with the hope of capitalising on their proximity and ease of network integration. Similarly, strategic alliances of business operations (e.g. code-sharing or commercial alliances) will continue, particularly Asia and the Middle East (e.g. Qatar and Saudi Arabian Airlines announced a code-share agreement at the end of 2005).

CAPACITY CONCERNS

Capacity is likely to be a key issue in the economic sustainability of international transport (Tarry, 2004). Growing capacity without permanent reduction in costs, as Tarry (2004) suggests, may result in future capital losses for the air transport industry as investors see fewer returns. What this can mean in the future for tourism mobility is not clear due to unforeseen externalities, but for the time being global airline passenger traffic is increasing: in 2005, global RPKs were 7.5% above 2004 levels, and ASKs (capacity) only slightly increased. Together, this means that load factors were healthier in 2005 than they were in 2004 (ATW Online, 2005). Manufacturers are responding with vigour, with two the main equipment firms, Boeing and Airbus, expanding their fleet choice options (see Box 9.2).

BOX 9.2 Battle of the jumbos: The business of air transport equipment provision

Operating global networks requires significant equipment. Given that one of the largest sunk costs in establishing an airline is the cost of the aircraft, it is important to understand what is happening in the global arena of aircraft manufacturing. Our concern here is primarily with large, 'jumbo jet' aircraft because it is these that are responsible for shuttling passengers across the globe. There are two primary manufacturers for large civilian aircraft: Boeing and Airbus. Each has their own strategy and view of how civil aviation will evolve over the next few decades. Airbus recently began test flights of its new A380 superjumbo. With a maximum passenger load of 840 persons (although most options will be fitted for around 500–600 passengers in a multiple-class layout), four engine producing 77,000 lbs of thrust, and orders from airlines including Lufthansa, Singapore Airlines, Air France, Emirates, Etihad Airways, Qantas, the A380 is designed primarily as a aircraft to service international hubs. The announcement of the A380 (or A3XX as it was known during initial project design phases) ushered in a phase of excited competition between Airbus and Boeing, the world's two largest aircraft manufacturers. In one sense, the A380 was a response to the Boeing 747, which has been a global workhorse for numerous airlines around the world. Like the 747, it has been suggested that the A380 will revolutionise air travel, particularly because of the low cost per seat that could be realised by transporting more people on a single aircraft. The A380, then, represents efficiencies of scale in the air. Critics point to the problems that passengers could face: 1) queues for boarding and disembarkation; 2) costs incurred by airports in order to ensure their services are 'A380 compliant'; and 3) safety concerns with respect the time it may take to evacuate 550+ passengers (although separate evacuation tests in 2006, where 853 passengers and 20 crew left the aircraft in 78 seconds, meant the plane received approval from the European Aviation and Safety Agency and the United States FAA to carry its maximum of 853 passengers). The last point was addressed in late March 2006 when over 850 passengers, during a trial run, exited the aeroplane in less than 90 seconds with only one half of the 16 available emergency exits available, although approximately 30 passengers were injured (BBC, 2006).

On the one hand, the Boeing's response has been to introduce a replacement for the '76' family of aircraft and one that would compete with Airbus' A330 aircraft. Most importantly, Boeing wanted to develop an aircraft that was fuel efficient and generally more environmentally friendly than existing aircraft. The result was the introduction of Boeing's Dreamliner aircraft, also known as the 7E7 and, more recently, and officially (as of April 2005), the Boeing 787. Current orders for the aircraft are strong (Table 9.4).

The 787 was only part of Boeing's late 1990s/early 2000s strategy for new aircraft development. Introduced in March 2001, the 'Sonic Cruiser' was a unique aircraft designed primarily for speed. According to Boeing, it would hold '200 to 250 passengers, fly between 6,000 and 9,000 nautical miles, and travel at a speed between Mach 0.95 and Mach 0.98 – 15 to 20 percent faster than what currently is possible' (http://www.boeing.com/news/feature/concept/background.html; accessed 26 October 2005). This was distinctly different from the proposed A380 project by Airbus, which was ostensibly designed to transport more people at similar speeds to existing aircraft. According to the Boeing website:

> With its huge speed advantage, the new airplane will cut travel times by approximately 20 percent, or one hour for every 3,000 miles travelled. And because it can travel at altitudes well above today's commercial airplanes, the airlines will be less impacted by traffic congestion, an emerging industry concern. Environmental performance is very important to the Sonic Cruiser program. Because it is being designed for the environment from the earliest stages, the Sonic Cruiser will be able to deliver its speed advantage with about the same fuel burn per passenger as conventional aircraft with similar seating capacity – a level of performance that was previously thought impossible. (http://www.boeing.com/news/feature/concept/background.html; accessed 26 October 2005)

Boeing estimated travel times hitherto unheard of with conventional aircraft: Singapore–Los Angeles (2.5 hrs); Los Angeles–Sydney (2 hrs); Tokyo–Los Angeles (2 hrs). Ultimately, Boeing scrapped the Sonic Cruiser programme in December 2002 (due to lack of interest from major carriers) and concentrated development activities on the 787 discussed above.

Table 9.4 Cumulative orders for the Boeing 787 Dreamliner (January to December 2006)

Airline	Country	Order date	Total
Aeromexico	Mexico	August 2006	2
Air Pacific	Fiji	April 2006	5
Boeing Business Jet	USA USA	August 2006	1
Boeing Business Jet	USA	November 2006	1
Boeing Business Jet	USA	July 2006	2
Boeing Business Jet	USA	September 2006	1
C.I.T. Leasing Corporation	USA	September 2006	5
Continental Airlines	USA	June 2006	13
First Choice Airways	United Kingdom	September 2006	2
Icelandair	Iceland	March 2006	2
ILFC	USA	July 2006	2
Jet Airways	India	December 2006	10
Kenya Airways	Kenya	March 2006	6
Kenya Airways	Kenya	December 2006	3
Monarch Airlines	United Kingdom	August 2006	6
Nakash	USA	December 2006	2
Pegasus Aviation Finance	USA	July 2006	2
Qantas	Australia	March 2006	15
Qantas	Australia	March 2006	30
Singapore Airlines	Singapore	October 2006	20
Unidentified customer	Unidentified	July 2006	2
Unidentified customer	Unidentified	September 2006	11
Unidentified customer	Unidentified	September 2006	6
Unidentified customer	Unidentified	October 2006	10
Unidentified customer	Unidentified	March 2006	1

Source: Adapted from http://active.boeing.com/commercial/orders/userdefinedselection.cfm

More recently, the Boeing 747ADV (Advanced), or the 747-800 as it has become to be called, was was introduced at the Paris Air Show in 2003. It is set to become the new form of the highly successful 747 (itself introduced in the 1970s) that will seat 440 passengers in a standard three-class configuration. Using the existing 747 schematics, an additional two to three rows (roughly 30 seats) will be added, as will tips to the wings, which help improve fuel efficiency. The aircraft will likely have a range of 14,800 km or 8000 nautical miles.

Not to be outdone, Airbus recently introduced the new widebody A350 (officially known as the A350 XWB) after an earlier design for the same model did not find favour with major customers. With a range of 8500 nautical miles, the 'new design' long-haul, twin-engine A350 is due to begin service in 2010 and will compete specifically against Boeing's 777 and 787 aircraft. It will be produced in three variants (A350-800, A350-900 and A350-1000) and will seat 270, 314 and 350 passengers respectively. In 2006, however, Airbus faced significant challenges with its A380 programme. Initial delays on the installation of cabin wiring pushed the delivery schedule back some six months, and later in the same year the schedule was pushed back a full year due to other production problems. Many industry observers have suggested the Airbus is in financial trouble as a result of these delays, and launch customers Singapore, Qantas and Emirates may need to search for other solutions to the problem of securing suitable equipment for their operations.

Clearly, the battle of the jumbos rests in the hands of two manufacturers, Boeing and Airbus, and the success (and design) of the aircraft produced over the next few decades will shape the trajectory of air transport as well as tourism. Equally important for consideration, however, is the fact that these companies operate in global environments and face significant externalities in much the same way that their customers do.

Questions for consideration

1. Although airlines (both passenger and cargo) are generally seen as the true 'customers' for Airbus and Boeing (as well as other manufacturers), to what extent could it be argued that the traveller is also a key stakeholder? How might each company target those customers?

2. Other than the major airlines listed above, what other airlines or routes might benefit from the introduction of the A380, regardless of whether the ground-level infrastructure (i.e. airports) is capable of handling such an aircraft?

INFORMATION TECHNOLOGY

IT trends in the transport industry will continue to evolve to the benefit of the passenger. Already, IT infrastructure has altered distribution channels within all modes of transport (particularly through GDS), and this will undoubtedly extend towards providing wireless internet access during a journey. Already, some airlines and cruise ships have installed wired or wireless internet access for on-board passengers, and with the evolution of long-range wireless networks such as WiMAX, many types of ground transport could well offer similar services. The more common IT initiatives in transport generally revolve around service provisions for passengers (e.g. web check-in or purchase, on-board entertainment) but there are other initiatives that are slowly becoming pervasive: supply management applications, customer relationship management software/applications, and knowledge or content management initiatives.

CONCLUSION

Transport will undoubtedly continue to be a central feature in tourism. Changing trends in travel will continue to have a significant impact on transport provision. Increased air accessibility may often be the impetus for securing greater market shares, especially for those destinations that enjoy limited market share or are peripheral to existing key markets. In the case of Bermuda, air carriers such as USA 3000 and Spirit Airways already provide service from the United States, but government and industry representatives on the island are hopeful that JetBlue will initiate (low-cost) services sometime in 2006. As well, flights to Bermuda from London (Gatwick) on British Airways are set to increase to seven times a week in March 2006. This has coincided with a planned marketing push in the UK market of Bermuda as a holiday destination, with the hope of securing a larger portion of the Caribbean-bound UK travel market (Walters, 2005). The scope of travel may change, due to peak oil, emissions standards that limit long-haul travel or any number of other externalities, but movement and mobility will always feature in travel and tourism as activities that take place outside of familiar spaces and places. Cheaper airfares, renewed interest in alternative forms of transport (such as heritage), and the tight integration that transport has with international travel and tourist experiences would suggest that demand will not abate through shifts in market forces alone.

What may hamper demand, however, and as discussed above, is the proportion of fuel and oil costs to tourism expenditure. It has already been suggested above that, with continuing decreases in the efficiency of oil extraction and refinement, the cost of transport could continue to rise, thus some forms of transport could be reserved for individuals of high net worth, or at least those who can afford. Some might argue that the increase in oil prices in the past four to five years has resulted in a new interest in alternative modes of transport, but to some extent this may ignore a fundamental principle international economics and finance. International firms, such as airlines, and especially those operating as

287

privately held companies, are responsible to shareholders and thus any desire to increase overall efficiencies will not be allowed to transplant potentials increases in profits. There is a social benefit to introducing sustainable means of transport, but the question remains as to who will be responsible for encouraging companies to follow this path.

The nature of tourism, and wider human mobility, naturally depends on many modes and types of transport. As well, transport is inherently linked within the business environment of tourism, and thus has an interest in the marketing of destinations, how tourism is managed and the overall viability of tourism development. As tourism development is very much concerned with issues of accessibility, and given that transport provides the networks through which tourists flow, it is integral that each pays close attention to the wider economic, social and biophysical environments within which each operates.

Box 9.3 Case study – Tourist spaceports: Environmental considerations

In Chapter 7, we considered how airports act as hubs and vectors of air transport worldwide. In this chapter, the increasing interest shown in future types of space transport was demonstrated. Indeed, it was even suggested that space tourism, or more properly extra-terrestrial vehicles, could be considered as a fourth mode of transport. While there are environmental and operational considerations of future space tourism endeavours, the ground-level support and infrastructure network is worthy of similar attention.

Several examples of the future development of spaceports have been proposed since mid-2005. Virgin Galactic entered into a partnership agreement with the State of New Mexico to construct a spaceport in the state at a cost of US$225 million. The Southwest Regional Spaceport was the first purpose-built example of a spaceport (see www.edd.state.nm.us/index.php?/about/category/locate_at_new_mexicos_spaceport/). Space Adventures (www.spaceadventures.com) announced plans to construct a commercial spaceport in the United Arab Emirates (and thus close to Dubai, which enjoys substantial air traffic from around the world), and is apparently planning further ports in Singapore and North America (Aljazeera, 2006). Currently, Space Adventures operates training facilities at the Gromov Flight Research Institute, located at the Zhukovsky Air Base near Moscow. Rocketplane (www.rocketplane.com) is closely eying the use of the former Clinton–Sherman Air Force Base (now the Clinton–Sherman Industrial Airpark) in Oklahoma that was recently granted permission from the FAA to operate as a spaceport. There are several other spaceports that have ties to space tourism. Spaceport Systems International (www.calspace.com) operates a spaceport at Vandenberg Air Force Base in California. The Mojave Airport and Civilian Aerospace Test Center (www.mojaveairport.com) operates as a spaceport and was the site of the test of SpaceShipOne, designed by Burt Rutan, which completed the first privately funded human flight into space in June 2004. Not unlike other private aerospace companies, Blue Origin (www.blueorigin. com), owned by Amazon.com-founder Jeff Bezos, operates a testing centre in Texas, although unmanned test flights have not been planned until late 2006.

Spaceports face significant challenges that are not unlike modern commercial airports designed for commercial aircraft. For example, a proposed commercial spaceport along the Gulf Coast in Texas was met with concerns from local residents over noise, potential harm to local wildlife and general loss of quality of life (Lozano, 2006). As seen in Box 7.2 these concerns are similar to those expressed in the (re)development of airports. In the case of the Clinton–Sherman Industrial Airpark, a website dedicated to the environmental impact assessment has been established (www.okspaceporteis.com).

The Southwest Regional Spaceport under construction for use by Virgin Galactic was subjected to a number of environmental considerations. According to a poster prepared by the FAA (2006) in the United States and posted on the EIS website, the agency considered several variables:

- Air Quality – launch emissions; levels of criteria pollutants; emissions from potential accidents.
- Airspace – use of airspace; impacts to other operations; changes to flight routes.
- Biological Resources – critical habitat and protected areas; wildlife movement corridors; threatened, endangered, or sensitive species; wetlands.
- Cultural Resources – historic and cultural structures; archaeological sites; Native American sites.
- Geology and Soils – mineral depletion; soil erosion; geologic hazards; hydrology and drainage patterns.
- Hazardous Materials and Waste – releases, transport, storage, use, and disposal of hazardous materials and waste.
- Land Use and Section 4(f) – conversion of farmland; existing land use plans; parks and recreational facilities.
- Noise – existing ambient noise levels; exposure of sensitive receptors to excessive noise; sonic booms.
- Health and Safety – launch operations hazards; spills, fires, and explosions; traffic and mechanical accidents.

- Socioeconomics and Environmental Justice – employment; demographics; disproportionate and adverse effects on minority and low-income populations.
- Transportation and Infrastructure – vehicular traffic and roadways; air traffic patterns; parking; utilities.
- Visual Resources – scenic vistas and resources; aesthetic quality of sites and sources of light and glare.
- Water Resources – surface water; ground water; waste water treatment facilities; floodplains; riparian issues.
- Cumulative Impacts – past, present, and foreseeable actions with potential for environmental impacts.
- Induced Impacts – impacts that could arise from activities associated with proposed action and alternatives.

It is almost certain that extra-terrestrial vehicles as a mode of transport will be developed in congruence with space tourism, but what is not certain is the extent to which terrestrial infrastructure, such as spaceports, will act in similar capacities as modern airports. One question remains as to whether the operation of spaceports will follow similar guidelines as airports themselves. While many industry-level airport associations exist worldwide, national governments impose detailed security and operational measures. It is not clear at this point whether spaceports will be governed in much the same way.

Questions for consideration

1. In thinking about the activities in modern airports, which of these may or may not be easily ported over to the operation of spaceports?

2. In addition to noise and impacts on wildlife, what other environmental hazards might need to be considered in the operation of a spaceport?

SELF-REVIEW QUESTIONS

1. What is peak oil and why is it important to tourism and transport?

2. Define Pigouvian taxes and provide an example of how they are used in transport.

3. What are some of the key issues for the future of tourism and transport?

ESSAY QUESTIONS

1. You are the manager of a major international airline and one of your destinations has just imposed a surcharge or tax of US$100 for every passenger you bring to that destination. Write a one-page briefing document to your shareholders that outlines the purpose of such taxes/surcharges.

2. Write an essay that compares the safety considerations of space travel with the three other modes of transport discussed in this book.

3. Write an essay that considers the increasing cost of fuel and the impact that may have on peripheral tourism destinations around the world.

KEY SOURCES

Gössling, S., Peeters, P., Ceron, J.-P., Dubois, G., Patterson, T. and Richardson, R.B. (2005) The eco-efficiency of tourism. *Ecological Economics* 54, 417–434.

An excellent overview of the ecological footprint of tourism activities, this article is a must-read in order to appreciate the environmental implications for tourism.

Gössling, S. and Hall, C.M. (eds) (2006) *Tourism and Global Environmental Change: Ecological, Social, Economic and Political Interrelationships.* London: Routledge

An excellent (and recent) overview of environment change concerns stemming from tourism activities. The book is unique in that it introduces the political underpinning for (in)action relating to climate change. The concluding chapter by the authors is particularly insightful and should serve as a starting point for those interested in the topic.

Flight International – www.flightglobal.com

Flight International is a leading weekly trade publication that often features extensive information on extra-terrestrial vehicles and the business of transport. It is also an excellent source of up-to-date information on trends in global air transport.

SELECTED SOURCES OF FURTHER INFORMATION

The internet provides numerous sources of information relating to transport issues in general and in the context of tourism. Listed below are several key academic and trade journals relating to transport. As well, a selection of websites by topic is provided. These sources may be used as a starting point in searching for additional information. Most of the popular internet search engines can be used as well.

ACADEMIC JOURNALS

Journal of Air Transport Management (www.elsevier.com)
Journal of Transport Geography (www.elsevier.com)
Transportation Research (particularly Parts 'A' through 'E') (www.elsevier.com)
Journal of Transport Economics and Policy (www.jtep.org)
Transport Review (www.tandf.co.uk)

TRADE JOURNALS

Airline Business (www.airlinebusiness.com)
Airport Business (www.airportbusiness.com)
Flight International (www.flightglobal.com)
Air Transport World (www.atwonline.com)
Aerlines Magazine (www.aerlines.nl) – Free, quarterly e-zine

COMMERCIAL MAGAZINES

Airliner World (www.airlinerworld.com)
Airways (www.airwaysmag.com)
The Railway Magazine (www.countrylife.co.uk/subscriptions/railway.php)
Porthole Cruise Magazine (www.porthole.com)
Cruise Magazine (www.cruisemagazine.com)

AIR TRANSPORT-RELATED WEBSITES

www.iata.org – International Air Transport Association
www.icao.int – International Civil Aviation Organization
www.eraa.org – European Regions Airline Association
www.aea.be – Association of European Airlines
www.elfaa.com – European Low Fares Airline Association
www.raaa.com.au – Regional Aviation Association of Australia
www.ebaa.org – European Business Aviation Association
www.iapa.com – International Airline Passengers Association
www.afraa.org – African Airlines Association
www.aapairlines.org – Association of Asia Pacific Airlines
www.airlines.org – Air Transport Association of America
www.airlinebusiness.com – *Airline Business* magazine
www.airportbusiness.com – *Airport Business* magazine
www.airlinemeals.net – comprehensive listing and evaluation of on-board meals by various airlines
www.faa.gov – Federal Aviation Administration (US)
www.aviation.dft.gov.uk – Department for Transport (Aviation) (UK)
www.wirelessairport.org – Wireless Airport Association
www.routesonline.com – Annual airlines and airports event/trade show
www.cate.mmu.ac.uk – Centre for Air Transport and the Environment (Manchester Metropolitan University, UK)
www.flyaow.com – Class availability for many global flights
www.airlinecrew.net – Bulletin board for airline crew
www.airliners.net – Bulletin board and an excellent source of copyrighted photos
www.flyertalk.com – Bulletin board focusing primarily on frequent flyer programmes and air travel in general
www.johnnyjet.com – An incredible amount of air transport-related links

GROUND TRANSPORT-RELATED WEBSITES

www.eriksrailnews.com – Erik's Rail News
www.railtimes.com – Rail times
www.railnews.net – Rail news
www.railcan.ca – Railway Association of Canada
www.ara.net.au – Australasian Railway Association
www.aar.org – Association of American Railroads
www.riagb.org.uk – Railway Industry Association (UK)
www.ukhrail.uel.ac.uk – Heritage Railway Association (UK)
www.irfca.org – Indian Railways Fan Club Association

www.traininc.org – Tourist Railway Association
www.railjournal.com – *International Railway Journal*

MARINE TRANSPORT-RELATED WEBSITES

www.cruising.org – Cruise Lines International Association
www.iccl.org – International Council of Cruise Lines
www.f-cca.com – Florida–Caribbean Cruise Association
www.atlanticcanadacruise.com – Atlantic Canada Cruise Association
www.medcruise.com – The Association of Mediterranean Cruise Ports

MISCELLANEOUS BLOGS, WIKIS, ORGANISATIONS AND OTHER SITES

http://wiki.jeffsandquist.com/default.aspx/AirPower/HomePage.html – AirPower Wiki
(locate power outlets at airports around the world)
www.seatguru.com – Locate the best seats on a variety of aircraft types (sorted by airline)
www.atrsworld.org – Air Transport Research Society
www.irtsociety.com – The Society of International Railway Travelers
www.thirtythousandfeet.com – Aviation directory

REFERENCES

ABC News (US) (2005) Attack on ships show pirates emboldened, 7 November 2005 (http://abcnews.go.com/International/print?id=1286496). Accessed 11 November 2005.

ABC News (Australia) (2005) Branson looks to plant waste for jet fuel, 17 November 2005 (http://www.abc.net.au/news/newsitems/200511/s1508526.htm). Accessed 18 November 2005.

Adler, N. (2001) Competition in a deregulated air transportation market. *European Journal of Operational Research* 129: 337–345.

Advertiser-Tribune (2004) Train tourism planned for Fostorias economic future, 29 February 2004 (http://www.advertisertribune.com/news/story/0229202004_new01trains2-29.asp)

The Age (2005) UK rail stations to get airport-style security, 31 October 2005 (http://www.theage.com.au/news/world/uk-rail-stations-to-get-airportstyle-security/2005/10/30/1130607151927.html#). Accessed 31 October 2005.

Airbus S.A.S. (2005) Global market forecast, 2004–2024. (http://www.airbus.com/en/myairbus/global_market_forcast.html). Accessed 30 December 2005.

Airline Business (2005a) Capacity crunch, 6 June 2005 (www.airlinebusiness.com/Articles/Article.aspx?liArticleID=198195). Accessed 7 June 2005.

Airline Business (2005b) Concrete plans, 6 June 2005 (www.airlinebusiness.com/Articles/Article.aspx?liArticleID=198193). Accessed 7 June 2005.

Airline Business (2005c) Saving the planet, 3 November 2005 (http://www.bizbuzzmedia.com/blogs/airline/archive/2005/11/03/678.aspx). Accessed 9 November 2005

Airline Business (2005d) Low-cost A380 services – imagine that, 16 December 2005 (http://www.bizbuzzmedia.com/blogs/airline/archive/2005/12/16/915.aspx). Accessed 26 December 2005.

Airline Business (2006a) IT trends survey 2006, July 2006, 42–49.

Airline Business (2006b) Stellar orbit, September 2006, 46–48.

Air New Zealand and Qantas Airways Limited (2002a) Commerce Act 1986: Restrictive Trade Practice, Section 58: Notice Seeking Authorisation, 9 December 2002. Public version accessed via New Zealand Commerce Commission website (since removed).

Air New Zealand and Qantas Airways Limited (2002b) Commerce Act 1986: Business Acquisition, Section 57: Notice Seeking Authorisation, 9 December 2002. Public version accessed via New Zealand Commerce Commission website (since removed).

Airwise News (2005a) Air Canada puts a price on comfort, 15 October 2005 (http://news.airwise.com/story/view/1129294309.html). Accessed 15 October 2005.

Airwise News (2005b) China's air traffic growth to slow in 2006, 27 December 2005 (http://news.airwise.com/story/view/1135689408.html). Accessed 27 December 2005.

Airwise News (2005c) Sri Lankan Airlines targets regional hub, 19 December 2005 (http://news.airwise.com/story/view/1135027423.html). Accessed 19 December 2005.

Aljazeera (2006) Spaceport comes to UAE, 18 February 2006 (http://english.aljazeera.net/NR/exeres/BFCD648C-FE21-498B-921A-324AC5D7EE28.htm). Accessed 28 July 2006.

Allen, W.H. (1992) Increased dangers to Caribbean marine ecosystems: Cruise ship anchors and intensified tourism threaten reefs. Bioscience 42 (5), 330–335.

Andersson, K. and Eklund, E. (1999) Tradition and innovation in coastal Finland: The transformation of the archipelago sea region. *Sociologica Ruralis* 39 (3), 377–393.

Arab News (2005) First low-cost airline planned in the Kingdom, 22 November 2005 (http://www.arabnews.com/?page=6&section=0&article=73519&d=22&m=11&y=2005). Accessed 25 November 2005.

ASA (2005) Non-broadcast adjudication. (http://www.asa.org.uk/asa/adjudications/non_broadcast/Adjudication+Details.htm?Adjudication_id=40129). Accessed 10 August 2005.

Asbury Park Press (2005) Cruise trends for 2006: Themed trips and six new ships, 12 December 2005 (http://www.app.com/apps/pbcs.dll/article?AID=/20051204/LIFE02/512040321/1006/LIFE). Accessed 12 December 2005.

ATW Online (2005) World RPKs rise 7.5% in 2005, passengers top 2 billion, 19 December 2005 (http://www.atwonline.com/news/story.html?storyID=3466). Accessed 21 December 2005.

ATW (2005a) The world's top 25 airlines 2004. July 2005, 33.

ATW (2005b) Europes biggest airports. July 2005, 120.

BAA (2005) Success through innovation: Annual Report 2004/2005. BAA.

Banister, D. (1995) *Tourism and Urban Development*. London: Spon Press.

Banister, D. (2002) *Transport Planning* (2nd edn). London: Spon Press.

Bastin, R. (1984) Small island tourism: Development or dependency? *Development Policy Review* 2 (1), 79–90.

Barrett, S.D. (2000) Airport competition in the deregulated European aviation market. *Journal of Air Transport Management* 6, 13–27.

Bayles, F. (1998) Accidents shadow whale-watching industry. *USA Today*, 21 September, 03A.

BBC (2000) Transport 2010 at a glance, 20 July 2000 (http://news.bbc.co.uk/1/hi/uk_politics/843129.stm). Accessed 7 March 2004.

BBC (2004a) South Korea launches high speed train, 1 April 2004 (http://news.bbc.co.uk/2/hi/asia-pacific/3589591.stm). Accessed 14 May 2004.

BBC (2004b) Airbus wins $1.2b China order, 12 April 2004 (http://news.bbc.co.uk/go/pr/fr/-/2/hi/business/3619353.stm). Accessed 12 April 2004.

BBC (2004c) China to modernise rail routes, 29 August 2004 (http://news.bbc.co.uk/go/pr/fr/-/1/hi/business/3610200.stm). Accessed 29 August 2004.

BBC (2004d) Love train, 1 July 2005 (http://news.bbc.co.uk/1/hi/magazine/4640947.stm). Accessed 25 July 2005.

BBC (2005) US agrees climate deal with Asia, 28 July 2005 (http://news.bbc.co.uk/2/hi/science/nature/4723305.stm). Accessed 9 December 2005.

BBC (2006) Volunteers injured in A380 drill, 26 March 2006 (http://news.bbc.co.uk/2/hi/business/4847344.stm). Accessed 27 March 2006.

Beach, D.W. and Weinrich, M.T. (1989) Watching the whales. *Oceanus* 32 (1), 84–88.

Beard, J.G. and Ragheb, M.G. (1983) Measuring leisure motivation. *Journal of Leisure Research* 15 (3), 219–228.

Becken, S. (2002) Analysing international tourist flows to estimate energy use associated with air travel. *Journal of Sustainable Tourism* 10 (2), 114–131.

Becken, S. and Simmons, D.G. (2005) Tourism, fossil fuel consumption and the impact on the global climate. In C.M. Hall and J. Higham (eds) *Tourism, Recreation and Climate Change* (pp. 192–208). Clevedon: Channel View Publications.

Bejou, D. and Palmer, A. (1998) Service failure and loyalty: An exploratory empirical study of airline customers. Journal of Services Marketing 12 (1), 7–22.

Bell, P. and Cloke, P. (1990) *Deregulation and Transport: Market Forces in the Modern World*. London: Fulton.

Belobaba, P.P. and Wilson, J.L. (1997) Impacts of yield management in competitive airline markets. *Journal of Air Transport Management* 3 (1), 3–9.

Bennett, M.M. (1996) Airline marketing. In A.V. Seaton and M.M. Bennett *The Marketing of Tourism: Concepts, Issues and Cases* (pp. 377–398). London: International Thomson Business Press.

Beyhoff, S. (1995) Code-sharing: A summary of the German study. *Journal of Air Transport Management* 2 (2), 127–129.

Bhaumik, P.K. (2002) Regulating the domestic air travel in India: An umpires game. *Omega* 30, 33–44.

Bieger, T. and Laesser, C. (2001) The role of the railway with regard to mode choice in medium range travel. *Tourism Review* 56, 33–39.

Bieger, T. and Wittmer, A. (2006) Air transport and tourism – Perspectives and challenges for destinations, airlines and governments. *Journal of Air Transport Management* 12, 40–46.

Bitner, M.J. (1990) Evaluating service encounters: The effects of physical surroundings and employee responses. *Journal of Marketing* 54, 69–82.

Bitner, M.J., Fisk, R.P. and Brown, S.W. (1993) Tracking the evolution of the services marketing literature. *Journal of Retailing* 69 (1), 61–103.

Blane, J.M. and Jaakson, R. (1995) The impact of ecotourism boats on the St Lawrence beluga whales. *Environmental Conservation* 21 (3), 267–269.

Blenkey, N. (2005) New ships, new thinking. *Marine Log* 110 (2), 23–26.

Bloomberg News (2005) UK transport needs extra 50 bln pounds, business group says, 27 November 2005 (http://www.bloomberg.com/apps/news?pid=10000102&sid=a 3axm4YI54PQ&refer=uk#). Accessed 29 November 2005.

Boeing (2005) World demand for commercial airplanes, 2005 (http://www.boeing.com/commercial/cmo/). Accessed 30 December 2005.

Bonaire Department of Economic and Labour Affairs (2004) Cruise tourism statistics (http://www.bonaireeconomy.org/tourism_statistics/cruise_statistics.html). Accessed 24 May 2005.

The Bond Buyer (2004) House appropriations approves new spending package. 349 (31932), 23 July 2004.

Borenstein, S. (1989) Hubs and high fares: Dominance and market power in the US airline industry. *The RAND Journal of Economics* 20 (3), 344–365.

Botimer, T.C. (1996) Efficiency consideration in airline pricing and yield management. *Transportation Research Part A* 30 (4), 307–317.

Boyfield, K. (2003) Who owns airport slots? A market solution to a deepening dilemma. In K. Boyfield (ed) *A Market in Airport Slots* (pp. 21–50). London: The Institute of Economic Affairs.

Bowen, J. (2000) Airline hubs in Southeast Asia: National economic development and nodal accessibility. *Journal of Transport Geography* 8, 25–41.

Breugelmans, J.G., Zucs, P., Porten, K., Broll, S., Niedrig, M., Ammon, A. and Krause, G. (2004) SARA Transmission and commercial aircraft. Letter to editor. *Emerging Infectious Diseases* 10 (8), 1502–1503.

Brooker, P. (2003) Control workload, airspace capacity and future systems. *Human Factors and Aerospace Safety* 3 (1), 1–23.

Brueckner, J.K. (2001) The economics of international codesharing: An analysis of airline alliances. *International Journal of Industrial Organization* 19, 1475–1498.

Bruning, E.R. (1997) Country of origin, national loyalty and product choice: The case of international air travel. *International Marketing Review* 14 (1), 59–74.

BTS (2005a) Airline travel since 9/11. (http://www.bts.gov/publications/issue_briefs/number_13/html/entire.html). Accessed 30 December 2005.

BTS (2005b) Fourth quarter 2004 airline financial data: Regional passenger airlines only group to report domestic profit (http://www.bts.gov/press_releases/2005/bts022_05/html/bts022_05.html#table_01). Accessed 31 October 2005.

BTS (2005c) 2001 National Household Travel Survey (http://www.bts.gov/publications/highlights_of_the_2001_national_household_travel_survey/). Accessed 6 December 2005.

Buck, S. and Lei, Z. (2004) Charter airlines: Have they a future? *Tourism and Hospitality Research* 5 (1), 72–78.

Buhalis, D. (2004) eAirlines: Strategic and tactical use of ICTs in the airline industry. *Information and Management* 41, 805–825.

Buhalis, D. and Licata, M.C. (2002) The future of eTourism intermediaries. *Tourism Management* 23, 207–220.

Burger, J. and Leonard, J. (2000) Conflict resolution in coastal waters: The case of personal watercraft. *Marine Policy* 24, 61–67.

Butler, R. (1980) The concept of a tourist area cycle of evolution: Implications for management of resources. *Canadian Geographer* 24, 5–12.

Butler, R. (1997) Transportation innovations and island tourism. In D.G. Lockhard and D. Drakakis-Smith (eds) *Island Tourism: Trends and Prospects* (pp. 36–56). London: Pinter.

Butler, R., Hall, C.M. and Jenkins, J. (1998) *Tourism and Recreation in Rural Areas*. Chichester: John Wiley and Sons.

Button, K.J. (1993) *Transport Economics* (2nd edn). Aldershot: Edward Elgar.

Button, K.J. (2002) Debunking some common myths about airport hubs. *Journal of Air Transport Management* 8, 177–188.

Button, K., Clarke, A., Palubinskas, G., Stough, R., and Thibault, M. (2004) Conforming with ICAO safety oversight standards. *Journal of Air Transport Management* 10, 251–257.

Byran, D.L. and O'Kelly, M.E. (1999) Hub-and-spoke networks in air transportation: An analytical review. *Journal of Regional Science* 39 (2), 275–295.

CAA (2004) Introducing commercial allocation mechanisms: The UK Civil Aviation Authority's response to the European Commission's staff working paper on slot reform (http://www.caa.co.uk/docs/5/SlotReform-theUKCAAFinalResponse.pdf). Accessed 31 August 2005.

CAA (2005) (http://www.statistics.gov.uk/STATBASE/ssdataset.asp?vlnk=7819). Accessed 18 November 2005.

Calder, S. (2002) *No Frills: The Truth Behind the Low-cost Revolution in the Skies*. London: Virgin Books.

Cao, J.-M. and Kanafani, A. (2000) The value of runway time slots for airlines. *European Journal of Operational Research* 126, 491–500.

Carassava, A. (2005) Easy does it on the high seas. *Time*, 25 April 2005, 165 (17), A3.

Carey, H.C. (1858) *Principles of Social Science*. Philadelphia: J.B. Lippincott Company.

Carlsson, F. (2002) Environmental charges in airline markets. *Transportation Research Part D* 7, 137–153.

Cartwright, R. and Baird, C. (1999) *The Development and Growth of the Cruise Industry*. Oxford: Butterworth-Heinemann.

Caves, R. and Gosling, G. (1999) *Strategic Airport Planning*. Oxford: Pergamon.

Caves, R. and Pickard, C.D. (2001) The satisfaction of human needs in airport passenger terminals. *Transport* 147 (1), 9–15.

CBC (2006) Ferry uncertainty could cost northern BC, 20 April 2006 (http://www.cbc.ca/bc/story/bc_ferry-jobs20060420.html). Accessed 23 April 2006.

CE Delft (2005) Giving wings to emission trading: Inclusion of aviation under the European emission trading system (ETS): Design and impacts, reported commissioned by European Commission, DG Environment, Number 05.7789.20 (http://europa.eu.int/comm/environment/climat/pdf/aviation_et_study.pdf). Accessed 2 January 2006.

Central Otago Rail Trail (2004) (http://www.centralotagorailtrail.co.nz/index.htm). Accessed 9th May 2004.

Chapin, F.S. Jr (1966) The use of time budgets in the study of urban living patterns. *Research Previews* 13, 1–6.

Chapman, K. (1979) *People, Pattern and Process: An Introduction to Human Geography*. London: Edward Arnold.

Chen, F.-Y. and Chang, Y.-H. (2005) Examining airline service quality from a process perspective. *Journal of Air Transport Management* 11, 79–87.

Chin, A.T.H. (1997) Implications of liberalisation on airport development and strategy in the Asia Pacific. *Journal of Air Transport Management* 3 (3), 125–131.

Christaller, W. (1972) How I discovered the theory of central places: A report about the origin of central places. In P.W. English and R.C. Mayfield (eds) *Man Space and Environment* (pp. 601–610). London: Oxford University Press.

Christchurch International Airport (2005) Christchurch International Airport Annual Report. CIA Limited.

Clark, A. (2005) Frequent flyer miles soar above sterling. *The Guardian*, 8 January 2005 (http://www.guardian.co.uk/print/0,3858,5098772-103676,00.html). Accessed 9 January 2005.

CLIA (1995–2001) *The Cruise Industry: An Overview*. New York: CLIA.

CLIA (2005) Cruise news (http://www.cruising.org/CruiseNews/news.cfm?NID=174). Accessed 24 May 2005.

CNN (1998) NASA says space tourism is on its way but skeptics doubt it, 25 March 1998 (http://www.cnn.com/TECH/space/9803/25/space.tourism/#1). Accessed 25 March 1998.

Coase, R.H. (1960) The problem of social cost. *Journal of Law and Economics* 3, 1–44.

Cobin, J.M. (1999) *A Primer on Modern Themes in Free Market Economics*. Parkland, FL: Universal Publishers.

Cocks, C. (2001) *Doing the Town: The Rise of Urban Tourism in the United States, 1850–1915.* Berkeley: University of California Press.

Cohen, A.J. and Harris, N.G. (1998) Mode choice for VFR journeys. *Journal of Transport Geography* 6 (1), 43–51.

Cohen, E. (1974) Who is a tourist? A conceptual clarification. *Sociological Review* 22, 527–555.

Coles, T. (2004a) What makes a resort complex? Reflections on the production of tourism space in a Caribbean resort complex. In D.T. Duval (ed.) *Tourism in the Caribbean: Trends, Development, Prospects* (pp. 235–256). London: Routledge.

Coles, T. (2004b) Tourism and retail transactions: Lessons from the Porsche experience. *Journal of Vacation Marketing* 10 (4), 378–389.

Coles, T., Duval, D.T. and Hall, C.M. (2004) Tourism, mobility and global communities: New approaches to theorising tourism and tourist spaces. In W. Theobald (ed.) *Global Tourism: The Next Decade* (3rd edn) (pp. 463–481). Oxford: Butterworth-Heinemann.

Commission of the European Communities (1999) Communication from the Commission to the Council, the European Parliament, the Economic and Social Committee and the Committee of the Regions – Air transport and the environment: Towards meeting the challenges of sustainable development. Brussels, 1 December 1999 COM (1999) 640 final.

Commission of the European Communities (2004) Commission staff working document: Commercial slot allocation mechanisms in the context of a further revision of Council Regulation (EEC) 95/93 on common rules for the allocation of slots at Community airports (http://europa.eu.int/comm/transport/air/rules/competition2/doc/2004_09_17_consultation_paper_en.pdf). Accessed 31 August 2005.

Conroy, M. (2004) Upbeat developments in the state of the cruise industry. Business Briefings: Global Cruise 2004, May 2004 (http://www.bbriefings.com/cdps/cditem.cfm?NID=858&CID=6&CFID=3992128&CFTOKEN=96594492). Accessed 6 January 2005.

Cope, A., Cairns, S., Fox, K., Lawlor, D.A., Lockie, M., Lumsdon, L., Riddoch, C. and Rosen, P. (2003) The UK National Cycle Network: An assessment of the benefits of a sustainable transport infrastructure. *World Transport Policy & Practice* 9 (1), 6–17.

Copock, J.T. (ed.) (1977) *Second Homes: Curse or Blessing?* Oxford: Pergamon.

Coyle, J.J., Bardi, E.J. and Novack, R.A. (1994) *Transportation.* St Paul/Minneapolis: West Publishing Company.

Crabtree, R.M. (2000) A system dynamics model for visitors choice of transport mode to and from national parks. *Countryside Recreation* 8 (3), 2–5 (www.countrysiderecreation.org.uk/journal/journal2000.asp). Accessed 6 December 2004.

Crawford, G. and Melewar, T.C. (2003) The importance of impulse purchasing behaviour in the international airport environment. *Journal of Consumer Behaviour* 3 (1), 85–98.

Crenson, S.L. (2001) Cruise ship pollution under fire. *AP Online*, 7 April 2001.

Crockett, J. and Hounsell, N. (2005) Role of the travel factor convenience in rail travel and a framework for its assessment. *Transport Reviews* 25 (5), 535–555.

Crompton, J.L. (1979) Motivations for pleasure vacation. *Annals of Tourism Research* 6, 408–424.

Crouch, G.I. (2001) The market for space tourism: Early indications. *Journal of Travel Research* 40, 213–219.

CTO (2002) *Caribbean Tourism Statistical Report: 2000–2001 Edition.* St Michael: CTO.

Cycling Advocates Network (2004) DoC recreation opportunities review (http://www.can.org.nz/submissions/CAN-subm-040131-DoC-Review.pdf). Accessed 10 May 2004.

D'Angelo, A. (2005) Ghanian protectionism thwarts SAA, 25 October 2005 (http://www.businessreport.co.za/index.php?fArticleId=2964617). Accessed 9 November 2005.

Dann, G.M.S. (1981) Tourist motivation: An appraisal. *Annals of Tourism Research* 8 (2), 187–219.

Dann, G.M.S. (1994) Travel by train: Keeping nostalgia on track. In A.V. Seaton (ed.) *Tourism: The State of the Art* (pp. 775–782). Chichester: John Wiley and Sons.

Daskin, M.S. (1995) *Network and Discrete Location: Model, Algorithms, and Applications.* New York: John Wiley & Sons.

Department of Conservation (2004) The Otago Central Railway (http://www.doc.govt.nz/Conservation/Showcase-Areas/Otago-Central-Rail-Trail.asp). Accessed 11 May 2004.

Department for Transport (2004a) Transport statistics for Great Britain 2004 edition (http://www.dft.gov.uk/stellent/groups/dft_transstats/documents/page/dft_transstats_031999.hcsp). Accessed 21 October 2004).

Department for Transport (2004b) Transportation statistics bulletin: National travel survey 2002 (revised July 2004) (United Kingdom National Statistics) (http://www.dft.gov.uk/pgr/statistics/datatablespublications/personal/mainresults/nts2002/nationaltravelsurvey2002revised). Accessed 20 March 2007.

Department for Transport (2004c) UK response to European Commission's slot allocation consultation (http://www.dft.gov.uk/stellent/groups/dft_aviation/documents/pdf/dft_aviation_pdf_033272.pdf). Accessed 31 August 2005.

Department for Transport (2005) Transport trends 2005 (http://www.dft.gov.uk/stellent/groups/dft_transstats/documents/page/dft_transstats_026292.xls). Accessed 18 May 2006.

Department for Transport (2006) Transport statistics for Great Britain 2006 edition (http://www.dft.gov.uk/pgr/statistics/datatablepublications/tsgb/2006edition/transportstatisticsforgreatb1856). Accessed 11 March 2007.

DESA (Population Division) (2005a) World population ageing: 1950–2050 (http://www.un.org/esa/population/publications/worldageing19502050/regions.htm). Accessed 9 January 2006.

DESA (Population Division) (2005b) World population prospects: The 2004 revision and world urbanization prospects: The 2003 revision (http://esa.un.org/unpp). Accessed 9 January 2006.

Dickinson, J.E., Calver, S., Watters, K. and Wilkes K. (2004) Journeys to heritage attractions in the UK: A case study of National Trust property visitors in the south west. *Journal of Transport Geography* 12, 103–113.

Dijst, M., Lanzendorf, M., Barendregt, A. and Smit, L. (2005) Second homes in Germany and The Netherlands: Ownership and travel impact explained. *Tijdschrift voor Economische en Sociale Geografie* 96 (2), 139–152.

Dobruszkes, F. (2006) An analysis of European low-cost airlines and their networks. *Journal of Transport Geography* 14 (4), 249–264

Doganis, R. (1992) *The Airport Business*. London: Routledge.

Doganis, R. (2001) *The Airline Business in the 21st Century*. London: Routledge.

Doganis, R. (2002) *Flying Off Course: The Economics of International Airlines*. London: Routledge.

Domroes, M. (1999) Tourism in the Maldives: The resort-concept and tourist-related systems. *International Journal of Island Affairs* 8 (3), 7–14.

Douglas, N. and Douglas, N. (2001) The cruise experience. In N. Douglas, N. Douglas and R. Derrett (eds) *Special Interest Tourism: Context and Cases* (pp. 330–354). Brisbane: John Wiley & Sons Australia.

Douglas, N. and Douglas, N. (2004) Cruise ship passenger spending patterns in Pacific Island ports. *International Journal of Tourism Research* 6, 251–261.

Dowling, R. and Newsome, D. (eds) (2005) *Geotourism: Sustainability, Impacts and Management*. Oxford: Butterworth-Heinemann.

Dresner, M. (2006) Leisure versus business passengers: Similarities, differences, and implications. *Journal of Air Transport Management* 12, 28–32.

Dresner, M. and Windle, R. (1995) Are US air carriers to be feared? Implication of hubbing to North Atlantic competition. *Transport Policy* 2 (3), 195–202.

Driver, J.C. (1999) Developments in airline marketing practice. *Journal of Marketing Practice: Applied Marketing Science* 51 (5), 134–150.

DSEC (2007) Results of the vistor arrivals for February 2007 (http://www.dsec.gov.mo/e_index.html). Accessed 22 March 2007.

Duman, T. and Mattila, A.S. (2005) The role of affective factors on perceived cruise vacation value. *Tourism Management* 26, 311–323.

Dunlop, G. (2002) The European ferry industry – challenges and changes. *International Journal of Transport Management* 1, 115–116.

Duval, D.T. (2002) The return visit-return migration connection. In C.M. Hall and A.M. Williams (eds) *Tourism and Migration: New Relationships between Production and Consumption* (pp. 257–276). Dordrecht: Kluwer Academic Publishers.

Duval, D.T. (2003) When hosts become guests: Return visits and diasporic identities in a Commonwealth Eastern Caribbean community. *Current Issues in Tourism* 6 (4), 267–308.

Duval, D.T. (2004a) Trends and circumstances in Caribbean tourism. In D.T. Duval (ed.) *Tourism in the Caribbean: Trends, Development, Prospects* (pp. 3–22). London: Routledge.

Duval, D.T. (2004b) Future prospects for tourism in the Caribbean. In D.T. Duval (ed.) *Tourism in the Caribbean: Trends, Development, Prospects* (pp. 298–299). London: Routledge.

Duval, D.T. (2005a) Public/stakeholder perceptions of airline alliances: The New Zealand experience. *Journal of Air Transport Management* 11 (6), 355–462.

Duval, D.T. (2005b) Small steps, giant leaps: Space as the destination of the future. In M. Novelli (ed.) *Niche Tourism: Contemporary Issues and Trends* (pp. 213–222). Oxford: Butterworth-Heinemann.

Duval, D.T. (2005c) Tourism and air transport in Oceania. In C. Cooper and C.M. Hall (eds) *Oceania: A Tourism Handbook* (pp. 321–334). Clevedon: Channel View.

Duval, D.T. (2006) Coasian economics and the management of international aviation emissions. *International Journal of Innovation and Sustainable Development* 1 (3), 201–213.

Dwyer, L. (2004) Trends underpinning global tourism in the coming decade. In W. Theobald (ed.) *Global Tourism: The Next Decade* (3rd edn) (pp. 528–545). Oxford: Butterworth-Heinemann.

Dwyer, L. and Forsyth, P. (1998) Economic significance of cruise tourism. *Annals of Tourism Research* 25 (2), 393–415.

Eaton, B. and Holding, D. (1996) The evaluation of public transport alternatives to the car in British national parks. *Journal of Transport Geography* 4 (1), 55–65.

Ebersold, W.B. (2004) Cruise industry in figures. Business briefings: Global cruise 2004, (http://www.bbriefings.com/cdps/cditem.cfm?NID=858&CID=6&CFID=39921 28&CFTOKEN=96594492). Accessed 6 January 2005.

Eccles, G. and Costa, J. (1996) Perspectives on tourism development. *International Journal of Contemporary Hospitality Management* 8 (7), 44–51.

Economist (2005) Funny money. 377 (8458), 104–105.

Edinburgh News.com (2004) Chiefs fear Edinburgh tolls will drive away tourists, 6 April 2004 (http://edinburghnews.scotsman.com/index.cfm?id=390612004). Accessed 21 October 2004.

Edmondson, B. and Du, F. (1996) Who needs two cars? Automobile ownership statistics. *American Demographics*, December 1996 (http://www.findarticles.com/p/articles/mi_m4021/is_n12_v18/ai_18894247). Accessed 6 September 2004.

Edmonton Airports (2005) Edmonton Airport annual report 2004 (www.edmontonair-ports.com). Accessed ???.

Egli, R.A. (1991) Climate: Air-traffic emissions. *Environment* 33 (9), 2–5.

Ellett, T. (2003) Airport privatization after the Bush executive order (http://www.rppi. org/apr2003/airportprivatizationafter.html). Accessed 28 September 2005.

Elliot, C. and Silver, M. (2002) Cruise-a-palooza, *US News and World Report*, 18 March 2002, 72.

Ellis, C., Barrett, N. and Schmieman, S. (2005) Wilderness cruising: Turbulence, cruise ships, and benthic communities. *Tourism and Marine Environments* 2 (1), 1–12.

Essex, S. (1994) Tourism. In R. Gibb (ed.) *The Channel Tunnel: A Geographical Perspective* (pp. 79–100). Chichester: John Wiley & Sons.

Express Travel and Tourism (2005) Cruise industry: Future is bright, November 2005 (http://www.expresstravelandtourism.com/200511/lookout08.shtml). Accessed 15 April 2006.

European Commission (2001) White paper: European transport policy for 2010: Time to decide (http://europa.eu.int/comm/energy_transport/en/lb_en.html). Accessed 4 December 2005.

European Union Road Federation (2005) 2005 road statistics (http://www.erf.be/images/ stat/ERF_stats.pdf). Accessed 18 May 2006.

Evening Times (2006) Airline cuts Sweden flights over tax row, 12 July 2006 (http://www. eveningtimes.co.uk/print/news/5054657.shtml). Accessed 3 August 2006.

Express (2004) New rail hell. 14 June 2004.

FAA (2004) Wildlife strikes to civil aircraft in the United States, 1990–2003, Serial Report Number 10, June 2004.

FAA (2006) Environmental impact statement scoping topics (http://ast.faa.gov/files/ pdf/EIS%20Scoping%20Topics_Scoping%20Poster.pdf). Accessed 28 July 2006.

Fan, T. (2006) Improvements in intra-European inter-city flight connectivity: 1996–2004. *Journal of Transport Geography* 14 (4), 273–286.

Fellmann, J., Getis, A. and Getis, J. (1992) *Human Geography: Landscapes of Human Activities* (3rd edn). Dubuque, IA: Wm. C. Brown Publishers.

Field, D. (2005) Online charge. *Airline Business*, December 2005.

Firey, T. (2003) Nothing to fear from open skies with European Union. CATO Institute (http://www.cato.org/research/articles/firey-030924.html). Accessed 15 November 2005.

Fischer, M.M. (1993) Travel demand. In J. Polak and A. Heertje (eds) *European Transport Economics* (pp. 6–32). Oxford: Blackwell.

Florida–Caribbean Cruise Association (2001) *Cruise Industry's Economic Impact on the Caribbean*. Florida: PriceWaterhouseCoopers.

Forbes (2006) Ryanair slashes services to Sweden ahead of new passenger tax on Aug 1, 11 July 2006 (http://www.forbes.com/finance/feeds/afx/2006/07/11/afx2870654. html). Accessed 3 August 2006.

Forbes (2005) BA's Eddington says US protectionism props up failing airlines – September 2005 (http://www.forbes.com/markets/feeds/afx/2005/09/22/afx2.   ɔ4. html). Accessed 9 November 2005.

Forsyth, P. (2002) Privatisation and regulation of Australian and New Zealand airports. *Journal of Air Transport Management* 8, 19–28.

Forsyth, P. (2006) Martin Kunz memorial lecture. Tourism benefits and aviation policy. *Journal of Air Transport Management* 12, 3–13.

Francis, G., Humphreys, I. and Ison, S. (2004) Airports perspectives on the growth of low-cost airlines and the remodeling of the airport–airline relationship. *Tourism Management* 25, 507–514.

Freathy, P. and O'Connell, F. (1998) *European Airport Retailing: Growth Strategies for the New Millennium*. London: Macmillan Business.

Freathy, P. and O'Connell, F. (1999) A typology of European airport retailing. *Service Industries Journal* 19, 119–134.

GAO (2000) Aviation and the environment: Aviations effects on the global atmosphere are potentially significant and expected to grow. GAO/RCED-00-57.

Gauthier, H.L. (1970) Geography, transportation and regional development. *Economic Geography* 46 (4), 612–619.

Georggi, N.L. and Pendyala, R.M. (2001) Analysis of long-distance travel behaviour of the elderly and low income. In *Personal Travel: The Long and Short of It, Conference Proceedings* (28 June–1 July 1999), Transportation Research Circular E-C026. Washington, DC: Transportation Research Board.

Gerber, P. (2002) Success factors for the privatisation of airports – an airline perspective. *Journal of Air Transport Management* 8, 29–36.

Geurs, K.T. and van Wee, B. (2004) Accessibility evaluation of land-use and transport strategies: review and research directions. *Journal of Transport Geography* 12, 127–140.

Gibb, R. (1994) The Channel Tunnel project: origins and development. In R. Gibb (ed.) *The Channel Tunnel: A Geographical Perspective* (pp. 1–30). Chichester: John Wiley & Sons.

Gilbert, D.C. (1996) Relationship marketing and airline loyalty schemes. *Tourism Management* 17 (8), 575–582.

Gilbert, D. and Wong, R.K.C. (2003) Passenger expectations and airline services: A Hong Kong based study. *Tourism Management* 24, 519–532.

Giuliano, G. (1997a) Family structure and travel demand. *Journal of Transport Geography* 5 (1), 43.

Giuliano, G. (1997b) Age and trip-making. *Journal of Transport Geography* 5 (1), 44.

Glisson, L.M., Cunningham, W.A., Harris, J.R. and Di Lorenzo-Aiss, J. (1996) Airline industry strategic alliances: marketing and policy implications. *International Journal of Physical Distribution & Logistics Management* 26 (3), 26–34.

Goetz, A.R. (2002) Deregulation, competition, and antitrust implications in the US airline industry. *Journal of Transport Geography* 10, 1–19.

Golledge, R.G. (1981) Misconceptions, misinterpretations, and misrepresentations of behavioural approaches in human geography. *Environment and Planning A* 13, 1315–1344.

González-Savignat, M. (2004) Competition in air transport: The case of the high speed train. *Journal of Transport Economics and Policy* 38 (1), 77–108.

Goodman, J. (1998) Untitled. *Cruise News* (email newsletter), 12 June, 1.

Goodrich, J.N. (2002) September 11, 2001 attack on America: A record of the immediate impacts and reactions in the USA travel and tourism industry. *Tourism Management* 23 (6), 573–580.

Gössling, S. and Hall, C.M. (2006) Conclusion: Wake up…this is serious. In S. Gössling and C.M. Hall (eds) *Tourism and Global Environmental Change: Ecological, Social, Economic and Political Interrelationships* (pp. 305–320). London: Routledge.

Gössling. S., Hansson, C.B., Hörstmeier, O. and Saggel, S. (2002) Ecological footprint analysis as a tool to assess tourism sustainability. *Ecological Economics* 43, 199–211.

Gössling, S., Peeters, P., Ceron, J.-P., Dubois, G., Patterson, T. and Richardson, R.B. (2005) The eco-efficiency of tourism. *Ecological Economics* 54, 417–434.

Gow, D. (2004) BA outbid for Heathrow slots. *Guardian*, 21 January 2004 (http://www.guardian.co.uk/print/0,3858,4840673-103676,00.html). Accessed 7 March 2004.

Graßl, H., Kokott, J., Kulessa, M., Luther, J., Nuscheler, F., Sauerborn, R., Schellnhuber, H.-J., Schubert, R. and Schulze, E.-D. (2003) *Climate Protection Strategies for the First Century: Kyoto and Beyond*. Special Report. Berlin: WBGU.

Graham, A. (2001) *Managing Airports: An International Perspective*. Oxford: Butterworth-Heinemann.

Graham, B. (1995) *Geography and Air Transport*. Chichester: John Wiley & Sons.

Graham, B. (1997) Regional airline services in the liberalized European Union single aviation market. *Journal of Air Transport Management* 3 (4), 227–238.

Griswold, A. (2002) Carnival Cruise Lines beefs up campaign buy: Cooper & Hayes ads get new tagline, target, to increase exposure. *ADWEEK New England Edition*, 4 November 2002, 39 (44), 3.

Greene, D.L. and Wegener, M. (1997) Sustainable transport. *Journal of Transport Geography* 5 (3), 177–190.

Gubbins, E.J. (2004) *Managing Transport Operations* (3rd edn). London: Kogan Page Limited.

Gunderson, A. (2005) Cruise lines set their sights on Asia. *New York Times*, 2 October 2005, 5.3.

Gursoy, D., Chen, M.-H. and Kim, H.J. (2005) The US airlines relative positioning based on attributes of service quality. *Tourism Management* 26, 57–67.

Gutiérrez, J. (2001) Location, economic potential and daily accessibility: An analysis of the accessibility impact of the high-speed line Madrid–Barcelona–French border. *Journal of Transport Geography* 9, 229–242.

Gutiérrez, J., González, R., and Gómez, G. (1996) The European high-speed train network. *Journal of Transport Geography* 6, 227–238.

Guzhva, V.S. and Pagiavlas, N. (2004) US Commercial airline performance after September 11, 2001: Decomposing the effect of the terrorist attack from macroeconomic influences. *Journal of Air Transport Management* 10, 327–332.

Hägerstrand, T. (1967) *Innovation Diffusion as a Spatial Process*. Chicago: University of Chicago Press.

Hägerstrand, T. (1970) What about people in regional science? *Papers of the Regional Science Association* 24, 7–21.

Haggett, P., Cliff, A.D. and Frey, A. (1977) *Locational Analysis in Human Geography* (2nd edn). London: Arnold.

Hall, D.R. (1993) Transport implications of tourism development. In D.R. Hall (ed.) *Transport and Economic Development in the New Central and Eastern Europe* (pp. 206–225). London: Belhaven Press.

Hall, D.R. (1999) Conceptualising tourism transport: Inequality and externality issues. *Journal of Transport Geography* 7, 181–188.

Hall, D.R. (2004) Transport and tourism: Equity and sustainability issues. In L. Lumsdon and S.J. Page (eds) *Tourism and Transport: Issues and Agenda for the New Millennium* (pp. 45–55). Amsterdam: Elsevier.

Hall, C.M. (2005) *Tourism: Rethinking the Social Science of Mobility*. Harlow: Pearson Education/Prentice Hall.

Hall, C.M. and Müller, D.K. (2004) (eds) *Tourism, Mobility and Second Homes: Between Elite Landscape and Common Ground*. Clevedon: Channel View.

Hall, C.M., Timothy, D.J. and Duval, D.T. (2003) (eds) *Safety and Security in Tourism: Relationships, Management, and Marketing*. Binghamton, NY: Haworth Hospitality Press.

Halsall, D.A. (1992) Transport for tourism and recreation. In B.S. Hoyle and R.D. Knowles (eds) *Modern Transport Geography* (pp. 155–177). London: Belhaven.

Halsall, D.A. (2001) Railway heritage and the tourist gaze: Stoomtram Hoorn-Medemblik. *Journal of Transport Geography* 9, 151–160.

Halseth, G. (2004) The cottage priviledge: Increasingly elite landscapes of second homes in Canada. In C.M. Hall and D.K. Müller (eds) *Tourism, Mobility and Second Homes: Between Elite Landscape and Common Ground* (pp. 35–54). Clevedon: Channel View.

Hanley, N., Shogren, J.P. and White, B. (1997) *Environmental Economics: In Theory and Practice*. New York: Oxford University Press.

Hanlon, P. (1999) *Global Airlines* (2nd edn). Oxford: Butterworth-Heinemann.

Hanlon, P. (2001) *Managing Airports: An International Perspective*. Oxford: Butterworth-Heinemann.

Hardy, A. (2003) An investigation into the key factors necessary for the development of iconic touring routes. *Journal of Vacation Marketing* 9 (4), 314–330.

Hartman, D.E. and Lindgren, J.H. Jr (1993) Consumer evaluations of goods and services: Implications for services marketing. *Journal of Services Marketing* 7 (2), 4–15.

Harvey, D. (1990) Between space and time: Reflections on the geography of imagination. *Annals of the Association of American Geographers* 80, 418–434.

Hayashi, Y., Button, K. and Nijkamp, P. (eds) (1999) *The Environment and Transport*. Cheltenham: Edward Elgar Publishing.

Haynes, K.E. and Fotheringham, A.S. (1984) *Gravity and Spatial Interaction Models*. Beverly Hills, CA: Sage.

Haynes, K.E., Gifford, J.L. and Pelletiere, D. (2005) Sustainable transportation institutions and regional evolution: Global and local perspectives. *Journal of Transport Geography* 13 (3), 207–221.

Heggie, I.G. (1969) Are gravity and interactance models a valid technique for planning regional transport facilities? *Operational Research* 20 (1), 93–110.

Hennig-Thurau, T. and Hansen, U. (2000) *Relationship Marketing: Gaining Competitive Advantage Through Customer Satisfaction and Customer Retention*. Berlin: Springer-Verlag.

Hensher, D.A. (1997) A practical approach to identifying the market potential for high-speed rail: A case study in the Sydney–Canberra Corridor. *Transportation Research A* 31 (6), 431–436.

Hillman, A.L. (2003) *Public Finance and Public Policy: Responsibilities and Limitations of Government*. Cambridge: Cambridge University Press.

Hindustan Times (2005) Super luxury cruises, Indian tourism circuits latest fad, 1 December 2005 (http://www.hindustantimes.com/news/181_1561808,0011000200 13.htm). Accessed 27 December 2005.

Hodge, D. (1997) Accessibility-related issues. *Journal of Transport Geography* 5 (1), 33–34.

Holden, E. and Høyer, K.G. (2005) The ecological footprint of fuels. *Transportation Research Part D* 10, 395–403.

Holloway, S. (2003) *Straight and Level: Practical Airline Economics*. Aldershot: Ashgate.

Hooper, P. (2002) Privatisation of airports in Asia. *Journal of Air Transport Management* 8, 289–300.

Hoover's Company Profiles (2004) National Railroad Passenger Corporation, 5 August 2004; accessed via Factiva.

Høyer, K.G. (2000) Sustainable tourism or sustainable mobility? The Norwegian case. *Journal of Sustainable Tourism* 8 (2), 147–160.

Hoyle, B. and Knowles, R. (1998) Transport geography: An introduction. In B. Hoyle and R. Knowles (eds) *Modern Transport Geography* (2nd edn) (pp. 1–12). Chichester: John Wiley and Sons.

Hoyle, B. and Smith, J. (1998) Transport and development: Conceptual frameworks. In B. Hoyle and R. Knowles (eds) *Modern Transport Geography* (2nd edn) (pp. 13–40). Chichester: John Wiley and Sons.

Hubbard, P., Kitchin, R. and Valentine, G. (2004) *Key Thinkers on Space and Place*. London: Sage.

Huff, D.L. and Jenks, G.F. (1968) A graphic interpretation of the friction of distance in gravity models. *Annals of the Association of American Geographers* 58 (4), 814–824.

Hwang, Y.-H., Gretzel, U. and Fesenmaier, D. (2002) Multi-city pleasure trip patterns: An analysis of international travelers to the US. In K. Wöber (ed.) *City Tourism 2002: Proceedings of European Cities Tourisms International Conference in Vienna, Austria, 2002*. Wien: Springer Economics.

IATA (2004) World Air Transport Statistics (48th edn) (for 2003).

IATA (2005) Passenger traffic growth slows, freight remains flat, 30 November 2005 (http://www.iata.org/pressroom/pr/2005-11-30-02.htm). Accessed 31 December 2005.

ICCL (2003) ICCL Environmental Standard E-01-01 (Revision 2), 12 December 2003 (http://www.iccl.org/policies/environmentalstandards.pdf). Accessed 18 October 2005.

IEA (2002) IEA reports on ways to achieve sustainability in urban transport (http://www.iea.org/dbtw-wpd/Textbase/press/pressdetail.asp?year=%25&keyword=4121&Submit=Submit&PRESS_REL_ID=65). Accessed 8 December 2005.

Independent (2005) Bush must not stand in the way of new Kyoto deal (http://news.independent.co.uk/environment/article331973.ece). Accessed 9 December 2005.

Iso-Ahola, S. (1980) *The Social Psychology of Leisure and Recreation*. Dubuque, IA: Wm. C. Brown Company.

Iso-Ahola, S. (1982) Toward a social psychological theory of tourism motivation: Rejoinder. *Annals of Tourism Research* 9 (2), 256–262.

ITA (2005) World & US International Arrivals & Receipts 1984–2004p (http://tinet.ita.doc.gov/outreachpages/inbound.world_us_intl_arrivals.html). Accessed 19 November 2005.

Jackson, P. (1989) *Maps of Meaning*. London: Unwin Hyman.

Jamaica Gleaner (2005) Hoteliers call for Caribbean airline, 12 November 2005 (http://www.jamaica-gleaner.com/gleaner/20051112/business/business1.html). Accessed 13 November 2005.

Janelle, D.G. (1969) Spatial reorganization: A model and concept. *Annals of the Association of American Geographers* 59 (2), 348–364.

Janic, M. (2000) An assessment of risk and safety in civil aviation. *Journal of Air Transport Management* 6, 43–50.

Jarach, D. (2002) The digitalisation of market relationship in the airline business: The impact and prospects of e-business. *Journal of Air Transport Management* 8, 115–120.

Johnson, D. (2002) Environmentally sustainable cruise tourism: A reality check. *Marine Policy* 26, 261–270.

Johnston, J. (2006) Late-night train plan to forge Glasgow–Edinburgh link, 6 August 2006 (http://www.sundayherald.com/57001). Accessed 6 August 2006.

Kangis, P. and O'Reilly, M.D. (2003) Strategies in a dynamic marketplace: A case study in the airline industry. *Journal of Business Research* 56, 105–111.

Katz, R. (2006) Carnival plunges into cruise market. *China Daily*, 8 March, 11.

Kaul, R.N. (1985) *Dynamics of Tourism: A Trilogy (Volume III: Transport and Marketing)*. New Delhi: Sterling.

Kayton, M. and Fried, W. (1997) *Avionics Navigation Systems*. New York: John Wiley & Sons.

Kennedy, G. (1996) Airlines new buzzword cuts out tickets – and high costs. *National Business Review*, 5 July 1996.

Kenyon, T.A., Valway, S.E., Ihle, W.W., Onorato, I.M. and Castro, K.G. (1996) Transmission of multidrugresistant Mycobacterium tuberculosis during a long airplane flight. *New England Journal of Medicine* 334, 933–938.

Kerin, R.A. and Peterson, R.A. (1998) *Strategic Marketing Problems: Cases and Comments* (8th edn). Upper Saddle River, NJ: Prentice Hall.

Kidokoro, Y. (2004) Cost-benefit analysis for transport networks: Theory and application. *Journal of Transport Economics and Policy* 38 (2), 275–307.

Knowles, R. (1998) Passenger rail privatization in Great Britain and its implications, especially for urban areas. *Journal of Transport Geography* 6 (2), 117–133.

Knowles, R. and Hall, D. (1998) Transport deregulation and privatization. In B. Hoyle and R. Knowles (eds) *Modern Transport Geography* (2nd edn) (pp. 75–96). Chichester: John Wiley and Sons.

Kraft, R.M., Ballantine, J. and Garvey, D.E. (1994) Study abroad or international travel? The case of semester at sea. *Phi Beta Delta International Review* 4, 23–61.

Kremarik, F. (2002) A little place in the country: A profile of Canadians who own vacation property. *Canadian Social Trends* 65, 12–14.

Krippendorf, J. (1987) *The Holiday Makers: Understanding the Impact of Leisure and Travel*. London: Butterworth-Heinemann.

Lafferty, G. and van Fossen, A. (2001) Integrating the tourism industry: Problems and strategies. *Tourism Management* 22, 11–19.

Landon, M. (1997) *Cruise Ship Crews: The Real Truth About Cruise Ship Jobs*. London: Mark Landon.

Lanzendorf, M. (2000) Social change and leisure mobility. *World Transport Policy and Practice* 6 (3), 21–25.

Las Vegas Sun (2004) High-speed Vegas-LA train pitched to public, 22 June 2005 (http://www.lasvegassun.com/sunbin/stories/text/2004/jun/22/517058927.html). Accessed 25 June 2004.

Laws, E. (1997) *Managing Package Tourism.* London: International Business Press.

Laws, E. and Scott, N. (2003) Developing new tourism services: Dinosaurs, a new drive tourism resource for remote regions? *Journal of Vacation Marketing* 9 (4), 368–380.

Lester, J.-A. and Weeden, C. (2004) Stakeholders, the natural environment and the future of Caribbean cruise tourism. *International Journal of Tourism Research* 6, 39–50.

Levine, M.E. (1987) Airline competition in deregulated markets: Theory, firm strategy, and public policy. *Yale Journal on Regulation* 29, 393–494.

The Local (2006) EU gives negative signals over flight tax, 6 July 2006 (http://www.the-local.se/article.php?ID=4270&date=20060706). Accessed 3 August 2006.

Lois, P., Wang, J., Wall, A. and Ruxton, T. (2004) Formal safety assessment of cruise ships. *Tourism Management* 25, 93–109.

Long, M.M. and Schiffman, L.G. (2000) Consumption values and relationships: Segmenting the market for frequency programs. *Journal of Consumer Marketing* 17 (3), 214–232.

Long, M.M., Clark, S.D., Schiffman, L.G. and McMellon, C. (2003) In the air again: Frequent flyer relationship programmes and business travelers quality of life. *International Journal of Tourism Research* 5, 421–432.

Lösch, A. (1954) *The Economics of Location.* New Haven: Yale University Press.

Lowe, J.C. and Moryadas, S. (1975) *The Geography of Movement.* Atlanta: Houghton Mifflin Company.

Lozano, J.A. (2006) Residents concerned about environmental impact of spaceport, Star Telegram, 11 July 2006 (http://www.dfw.com/mld/dfw/news/state/15017006.htm). Accessed 27 July 2006.

Lumdson, L. (2000) Transport and tourism: Cycle tourism – A model for sustainable development? *Journal of Sustainable Tourism* 8 (5), 361–377.

Lumsdon, L. and Page, S.J. (2004) Progress in transport and tourism research: Reformulating the transport–tourism interface and future research agendas. In L. Lumsdon and S.J. Page (eds) *Tourism and Transport: Issues and Agenda for the New Millennium* (pp. 1–28). Amsterdam: Elsevier.

Lumdson, L. and Tolley, R. (2001) The National Cycle Strategy in the UK: To what extent have local authorities adopted its model strategy approach? *Journal of Transport Geography* 9, 293–301.

Lumdson, L., Downward, P. and Cope, A. (2004) Monitoring of cycle tourism on long distance trails: The North Sea Cycle Route. *Journal of Transport Geography* 12, 13–22.

McAdam, D. (1999) The value and scope of geographical information systems in tourism management. *Journal of Sustainable Tourism* 7 (1), 77–92.

McCartney, S. (2005) As airports try to add runways, many hurdles loom, *Wall Street Journal,* 31 August 2005 (http://www.post-gazette.com/pg/05243/563083.stm). Accessed 1 September 2005.

McHardy, J. and Trotter, S. (2006) Competition and deregulation: Do air passengers get the benefits? *Transport Research Part A* 40, 74–93.

McKercher, B. and Chon, K. (2004) The over-reaction to SARS and the collapse of Asian tourism. *Annals of Tourism Research* 31 (3), 716–719.

McKercher, B. and Lew, A. (2003) Distance decay and the impact of Effective Tourism Exclusion Zones on international travel flows. *Journal of Travel Research* 42, 159–165.

McKercher, B. and Lew, A. (2004) Tourist flows and the spatial distribution of tourists. In A. Lew, C.M. Hall and A.M. Williams (eds) *A Companion to Tourism* (pp. 36–48). Oxford: Blackwell.

Mahapatra, R. (2005) India must increase airport capacity. Associated Press, 18 October 2005. (www.usatoday.com/travel/news/2005-10-18-india-airports_x.htm). Accessed 1 December 2005.

Manorama Online (2005) Aviation 2005: Sky is not the limit, 27 December 2005 (http://www.manoramaonline.com/servlet/ContentServer?pagename=manorama/MmArticle/CommonFullStory&cid=1135260645119&c=MmArticle&p=10021948 39100&count=10&colid=1002258272843&channel=News). Accessed 27 December 2005.

Marsh, J. and Staple, S. (1995) Cruise tourism in the Canadian Arctic and its implications. In C.M. Hall and M.E. Johnston (eds) *Polar Tourism: Tourism in the Arctic and Antarctic Regions* (pp. 64–72). Chichester: John Wiley & Sons.

Marti, B. (2005) Cruise line logo recognition. *Journal of Travel & Tourism Marketing* 18 (1), 25–31.

Martin, B.V., Memmott, F.W. and Bone, A.J. (1961) *Principles and Techniques of Predicting Future Demand for Urban Area Transportation*. Cambridge, MA: MIT Press.

Mason, K.J. (2000) The propensity of business travellers to use low cost airlines. *Journal of Transport Geography* 8, 107–119.

Mason, K.J. (2001) Marketing low-cost airline services to business travellers. *Journal of Air Transport Management* 7, 103–109.

Mason, P., Grabowski, P. and Du, W. (2005) Severe acute respiratory syndrome, tourism and the media. *International Journal of Tourism Research* 7, 11–21.

Meethan, K. (2001) *Tourism in Global Society: Place, Culture, Consumption*. Basingstoke: Palgrave.

Mercury News (2005) LA airport officials race to develop bird flu quarantine plan, 18 October 2005 (http://www.mercurynews.com/mld/mercurynews/news/local/states/california/northern_california/12930857.htm). Accessed 19 October 2005.

Middleton, V.T.C. and Clarke, J. (2001) *Marketing in Travel and Tourism* (3rd edn). Oxford: Butterworth-Heinemann.

Mill, R.C. and Morrison, A. (1985) *The Tourism System: An Introductory Text*. Englewood Cliffs, NJ: Prentice Hall.

Miller, A.R. and Grazer, W.F. (2002) The North American cruise market and Australian tourism. *Journal of Vacation Marketing* 8 (3), 221–234.

Millimet, D.L. and Slottje, D. (2002) Environmental compliance costs and the distribution of emissions in the US. *Journal of Regional Science* 42 (1), 87–105.

Milmo, D. (2006) Branson asks Brown to cut duty on fuel to power green trains, 16 October 2006 (http://business.guardian.co.uk/story/0,,1923153,00.html). Accessed 21 October 2006.

Minder, R. (2006) Airlines face peak-hour congestion charges, *Financial Times*, 5 April 2006 (http://news.ft.com/cms/s/9cfda466-c4c3-11da-b7c1-0000779e2340,_i_rss Page=1dffe558-c989-11d7-81c6-0820abe49a01.html). Accessed 6 April 2006.

Morgan, N. and Pritchard, A. (2001) *Advertising in Tourism and Leisure*. Oxford: Butterworth-Heinemann.

Morrison, S.A. and Winston, C. (1989) Airline deregulation and public policy. *Science (New Series)* 245 (4919), 707–711.

Mortishead, C. (2006) Carbon tax on airlines would never fly. Times Online (UK), 21 June 2006 (http://business.timesonline.co.uk/article/0,,13130-2234987,00.html). Accessed 6 July 2006.

Motevalli, V. and Stough, R. (2004) Aviation safety and security: Reaching beyond borders. *Journal of Air Transport Management* 10, 225–226.

Mowforth, M. and Munt, I. (1998) *Tourism and Sustainability: New Tourism in the Third World*. London: Routledge.

Müller, D.K. (2002a) Reinventing the countryside. German second home owners in southern Sweden. *Current Issues in Tourism* 5 (5), 426–446.

Müller, D.K. (2002b) Second home ownership and sustainable development in northern Sweden. *Tourism and Hospitality Research: The Surrey Quarterlt Review* 3 (4), 345–355.

Mulrine, A. (2002) A grand land cruise. *US News and World Report*, 21 October 2002, pd2.

National Journal (2004) Working on the railroad. 17 July 2004.

Nayar, B.R. (1995) Regimes, power, and international aviation. *International Organization* 49 (1), 139–170.

New Zealand Herald (2003) Cruise industry expects fall, 20 November 2003 (http://www.nzherald.co.nz/storyprint.cfm?storyID=3535087). Accessed 14 February 2004.

New Zealand Herald (2004) Air NZ plans San Francisco venture, 20 January 2004 (http://www.nzherald.co.nz/storyprint.cfm?storyID=3544434). Accessed 14 February 2004.

New Zealand Herald (2005) Airways profits dips slightly (http://www.nzherald.co.nz/section/story.cfm?c_id=3&ObjectID=10351386). Accessed 26 October 2005.

Niemeier, D., Redmond, L., Morey, J., Hicks, J., Hendren, P., Lin, J., Foresman, E. and Zheng, Y. (2001) Redefining conventional wisdom: Exploration of automobile ownership and travel behavior in the United States. Transportation Research Circular E-C026, 207–219 (http://wwwcf.fhwa.dot.gov/exit.cfm?link=http://trb.org/trb/publications/ec026/07_niemeier.pdf). Accessed 5 March 2004.

Nutley, S. (1998) Rural areas: The accessibility problem. In B.S. Hoyle and R.D. Knowles (eds) *Modern Transport Geography* (pp. 185–215). London: Belhaven.

Ocean Conservancy (2002) Cruise control: A report on how cruise ships affect the marine environment (http://www.oceanconservancy.org/site/DocServer/cruisecontrol.pdf?docID=141). Accessed 18 October 2005.

O'Connell, J.F. and Williams, G. (2005) Passengers perceptions of low cost airlines and full service carriers: A case study involving Ryanair, Aer Lingus, Air Asia and Malaysia Airlines. *Journal of Air Transport Management* 11, 259–272.

O'Connor, W.E. (1978) *An Introduction to Airline Economics*. New York: Preager Publishers.

OECD (1999) OECD workshop on regulatory reform in international air cargo transportation, Paris, 5–9 July 1999 (www.oecd.org/dataoecd/1/28/1821288.pdf). Accessed 27 November 2005.

OECD (2002) *International Mobility of the Highly Skilled*. Paris: OECD.

O'Kelly, M.E. (1998) A geographer's analysis of hub-and-spoke networks. *Journal of Transport Geography* 6 (3), 171–186.

Olsen, M. (2003) Themed tourism routes: A Queensland perspective. *Journal of Vacation Marketing* 9 (4), 331–341.

Olsthoorn, X. (2001) Carbon dioxide emissions from international aviation: 1950–2050. *Journal of Air Transport Management* 7, 87–93.

Onkvisit, S. and Shaw, J.J. (1991) Is services marketing really different? *Journal of Professional Services Marketing* 7 (2), 3–17.

Oppermann, M. (1995) A model of travel itineraries. *Journal of Travel Research* 33, 57–61.

Ortuzar, J. De Dios and Willumsen, L.G. (2001) *Modelling Transport* (3rd edn). Chichester: Wiley.

Otago Rail Trail (2004) Your accommodation and transport guide to the Rail Trail (http://www.otagorailtrail.co.nz/). Accessed 9th May 2004.

O'Toole, P. (2002) IT Trends Survey 2002. *Airline Business*, August 2002.

Oum, T.H. and Park, J.-H. (1997) Airline alliances: Current status, policy issues, and future directions. *Journal of Air Transport Management* 3 (3), 133–144.

Oum, T.H., Park, J.-H. and Zhang, A. (1996) The effects of airline codesharing agreements on firm conduct and international airfare. *Journal of Transport Economics and Policy* 30 (2), 187–202.

Oum, T.H., Yu, C. and Fu, X. (2003) A comparative analysis of productivity performance of the worlds major airports: Summary report of the ATRS global airport benchmarking research report 2002. *Journal of Air Transport Management* 9, 285–297.

Oum, T.H., Park, J.-H., Kim, K. and Yu, C. (2004) The effect of horizontal alliances on firm productivity and profitability: Evidence from the global airline industry. *Journal of Business Research* 57, 844–853.

Page, S.J. (1993) European rail travel. *Travel and Tourism Analyst* 1, 19–39.

Page, S.J. (1999) *Transport and Tourism*. Harlow: Prentice Hall.

Page, S.J. and Hall, C.M. (2003) *Managing Urban Tourism*. Harlow: Prentice Hall.

Palhares, G.L. (2003) The role of transport in tourism development: Nodal functions and management practices. *International Journal of Tourism Research* 5, 403–407.

Papatheodorou, A. (2002) Civil aviation regimes and leisure tourism in Europe. *Journal of Air Transport Management* 8, 381–388.

Parasuraman, A., Berry, L.L. and Zeithaml, V.A. (1991) Refinement and reassessment of the SERVQUAL scale. *Journal of Retailing* 67 (4), 420–450.

Parasuraman, A., Zeithaml, V.A. and Berry, L.L. (1985) A conceptual model of service quality and its implications for future research. *Journal of Marketing* 49 (4), 41–50.

Parasuraman, A., Zeithaml, V.A. and Berry, L.L. (1988) SERVQUAL: A multiple-item scale for measuring consumer perceptions of service quality. *Journal of Retailing* 64 (1), 12–40.

Park, J.-W., Robertson, R. and Wu, C.-L. (2004) 'The effect of airline service quality on passengers' behavioural intentions: A Korean case study. *Journal of Air Transport Management* 10, 435–439.

Parkes, D. and Wallis, W.D. (1978) Graph theory and the study of activity structure. In T. Carlstein, D. Parkes and N. Thrift (eds) *Human Activity and Time Geography* (pp. 75–99). London: Edward Arnold.

PATA (2005) *Annual Statistical Report 2004*.

Paylor, A. (2005) The slots game. *Air Transport World*, April 2005, 52.

PE.com (2005) Hawai'ian cruise industry booming, 3 December 2005 (http://www.pe.com/business/local/stories/PE_Biz_D_cruisebiz04.2921837.html). Accessed 12 December 2005.

Pearce, D.G. (2001a) Tourism and urban land use change: Assessing the impact of Christchurch's tourist tramway. *Tourism and Hospitality Research* 3 (2), 132–148.

Pearce, D.G. (2001b) Tourism, trams and local government policy-making in Christchurch, New Zealand. *Current Issues in Tourism* 4 (2–4), 331–354.

Pearson, C.S. (2000) *Economics and the Global Environment*. Cambridge: Cambridge University Press.

Peattie, K. and Peattie, S. (1996) Promotional competitions: A winning tool for tourism marketing. *Tourism Management* 17 (6), 433–442.

Peck, H., Payne, A., Christopher, M. and Clark, M. (1999) *Relationship Marketing: Strategy and Implementation*. Oxford: Butterworth-Heinemann.

Peisley, T. (1995) The North American cruise market. *Travel & Tourism Analysis*. London: Travel and Tourism Intelligence.

Pels, E., Nijkamp, P. and Rietveld, P. (2000) A note on the optimality of airline networks. *Economics Letters* 69, 429–434.

Pender, L. (1999) European aviation: The emergence of franchised airline operations. *Tourism Management* 20, 565–574.

People's Daily Online (2005) Number of Chinese airline passengers to be world's no. 2, 17 October 2005 (http://english.people.com.cn/200510/17/eng20051017_214812. html). Accessed 18 October 2005.

Pigou, A.C. (1920) *The Economics of Welfare*. London: Macmillan.

Plakhotnik, V.N., Onyshchenko, Ju. V. and Yaryshkina, L.A. (2005) The environmental impacts of railway transportation in the Ukraine. *Transportation Research Part D* 10, 263–268.

Plassard, F. (1992) Limpact territorial des transports a grande vitesse. In P.-H. Derycke (ed) *Espace et dinamiques territoriales* (pp. 243–261). Paris: Economia.

Preston, J. (2001) Integrating transport with socio-economic activity – A research agenda for the new millennium. *Journal of Transport Geography* 9, 13–24.

Prideaux, B. (2000a) The role of the transport system in tourism development. *Tourism Management* 21, 53–63.

Prideaux, B. (2000b) Links between transport and tourism – Past, present and future. In B. Faulkner, G. Moscardo and E. Laws (eds) *Tourism in the Twenty-first Century: Reflects on Experience* (pp. 91–109). London: Continuum.

Prideaux, B. (2004) Transport and destination development. In L. Lumsdon and S.J. Page (eds) *Tourism and Transport: Issues and Agenda for the New Millennium* (pp. 79–92). Amsterdam: Elsevier.

Prideaux, B. and Carson, D. (2003) A framework for increasing understanding of self-drive tourism markets. *Journal of Vacation Marketing* 9 (4), 307–313.

Priemus, H. and Konings, R. (2001) Light rail in urban regions: What Dutch policymakers could learn from experiences in France, Germany and Japan. *Journal of Transport Geography* 9, 187–198.

Qu, H. and Ping, E.W.Y. (1999) A service performance model of Hong Kong cruise travelers motivation factors and satisfaction. *Tourism Management* 20, 237–244.

Quinet, E. and Vickerman, R. (2004) *Principles of Transport Economics*. Cheltenham: Edward Elgar.

Rauscher, M. (1997) *International Trade, Factor Movements, and the Environment*. Oxford: Oxford University Press.

RCEP (2002) The environmental impacts of civil aircraft in flight (http://www.rcep.org. uk/avreport.htm). Accessed 12 July 2004.

Reuters (2005) Landing in Alaska? Fear moose collisions no more, 21 October 2005 (http://today.reuters.com/news/newsArticle.aspx?type=oddlyEnoughNews&storyI D=2005-10-21T151442Z_01_ARM154815_RTRUKOC_0_US-MOOSE. xml&archived=False). Accessed 29 October 2005.

Reynolds-Feighan, A. (2001) Traffic distribution in low-cost and full-service carrier networks in the US air transportation market. *Journal of Air Transport Management* 7, 265–275.

Rhoades, D.L. and Waguespack Jr, B. (2000) Judging a book by its cover: The relationship between service and safety quality in US national and regional airlines. *Journal of Air Transport Management* 6, 87–94.

Rietveld, P. and Brons, M. (2001) Quality of hub-and-spoke networks: The effects of timetable co-ordination on waiting time and rescheduling time. *Journal of Air Transport Management* 7, 241–249.

Ritchie, B.W. (1998) Bicycle tourism in the South Island of New Zealand: Planning and management issues. *Tourism Management* 19 (6), 567–582.

Roberts, M.L. and Berger, P.D. (1999) *Direct Marketing Management*. Upper Saddle River, NJ: Prentice Hall, Inc.

Robinson, R. and Kearney, T. (1994) Database marketing for competitive advantage in the airline industry. *Journal of Travel and Tourism Marketing* 3 (1), 65–81.

Rodrigue, J.P. *et al.* (2006) The geography of transport systems, Hofstra University, Department of Economics and Geography (http://people.hofstra.edu/geotrans). Accessed 20 March 2007.

Ross, N. (1996) Otago central rail: Who's using it? Dissertation, Postgraduate Diploma in Tourism, University of Otago, Dunedin, New Zealand.

Ross, W. (2000) Mobility & accessibility: the yin & yang of planning. *World Transport Policy and Practice* 6 (2), 13–19.

Rowley, J. and Slack, F. (1999) The retail experience in airport departure lounges: Reaching for timelessness and placelessness. *International Marketing Review* 16 (45), 36–37.

RTE News (2005) Overturn data sharing law, says EU law officer, 22 November 2005 (http://www.rte.ie/news/2005/1122/eu.html?rss). Accessed 22 November 2005.

Ryan, C. and Trauer, B. (2004) Aging populations: Trends and the emergence of the nomad tourist. In W. Theobald (ed.) *Global Tourism: The Next Decade* (3rd edn) (pp. 510–528). Butterworth-Heinemann.

Ryan, C. and Trauer, B. (2003) Involvement in adventure tourism: Toward implementing a fuzzy set. *Tourism Review International* 7 (3–4), 143–152.

Sala, O.E., Chapin III, F.S., Armesto, J.J., Berlow, E., Bloomfield, J. *et al.* (2000) Global bio-diversity scenarios for the year 2100. *Science* 287, 1770–1774.

San Mateo County Times (2004) Bullet train system will lead the future. 28 January 2004.

Sarna, H. and Hannafin, M. (2003) *Frommer's Caribbean Cruises & Ports of Call*. Hoboken, NJ: Wiley Publishing, Inc.

Savage, I. and Scott, B. (2004) Deploying regional jets to add new spokes to a hub. *Journal of Air Transport Management* 10, 147–150.

Schulkin, A. (2002) Safe harbors: Crafting an international solution to cruise ship pollution. *Georgetown International Environmental Law Review* 15 (1), 105–132.

Scott, D.M., Novak, D.C., Aultman-Hall, L. and Guo, F. (2006) Network robustness index: A new method for identifying critical links and evaluating the performance of transportation networks. *Journal of Transport Geography* 14, 215–227.

Scull, T. (1996) Ship lives up to P&O's standards. *Travel Weekly*, 5 December, C3.

Seaton, A.V. and Bennett, M.M. (1996) *The Marketing of Tourism: Concepts, Issues and Cases.* London: International Thomson Business Press.

Seinfeld, J.H. (1998) Clouds, contrails and climate. *Nature* 391 (26), 837–838.

Sharpley, R. (2004) Tourism and the countryside. In A.A. Lew, C.M. Hall and A.M. Williams (eds) *A Companion to Tourism* (pp. 374–386). Oxford: Blackwell Publishing.

Shaw, J. and Farrington, J. (2003) A railway renaissance? In I. Docherty and J. Shaw (eds) *A New Deal for Transport?* (pp. 108–134). Oxford: Blackwell.

Shaw, S. (2004) *Airline Marketing and Management* (5th edn). Aldershot: Ashgate.

Sheth, J.N. (1975) A psychological model of travel mode selection. In *Advances in Consumer Research* (Volume 3) (pp. 425–430) (Proceedings of the Association of Consumer Research, Sixth Annual Conference).

Sinclair, M.T. and Stabler, M. (1997) *The Economics of Tourism.* London: Routledge.

SITA (2006) Airport IT trends survey (http://www.sita.aero/News_Centre/Airport_IT_Trends/webconference_launches_Airport_IT_Trends_Survey.htm). Accessed 29 July 2006.

Slater, S. and Basch, H. (1989) Carnival buys up Holland America. *Los Angeles Times*, 12 February, 7.

Song, J. (2006) A new Hawaiian airline sparks inter-island fare war with $39 one-way flights, *The Seattle Times*, 24 March 2006 (http://seattletimes.nwsource.com/html/traveloutdoors/2002887504_webhawaiiair24.html). Accessed 29 March 2006.

Smith, M. (2002) Caribbean mulls merging airlines. Associated Press Online, 12 November 2002.

Staniland, M. (1998) The vanishing national airline? *European Business Journal* 10 (2), 71–77.

Star Bulletin (Hawai'i) (2006) State funds obligate ferry to heed concerns (Editorial), 14 April 2006 (http://starbulletin.com/2006/04/14/editorial/editorial02.html). Accessed 24 April 2006.

Starkie, D. (1998) Allocating airport slots: A role for the market? *Journal of Air Transport Management* 4, 111–116.

Starkie, D. (2002) Airport regulation and competition. *Journal of Air Transport Management* 8, 63–72.

Starkie, D. (2003) The economics of secondary markets for airport slots. In K. Boyfield (ed.) *A Market in Airport Slots* (pp. 51–79). London: The Institute of Economic Affairs.

Statistics New Zealand (2002) Tourism and Migration 2001, Table 3.01 (http://www.stats.govt.nz/domino/external/web/prod_serv.nsf/htmldocs/Tourism+and+Migration+2001). Accessed 25 April 2003.

Statistics Norway (2005) Substantial growth in water transport (http://www.ssb.no/english/subjects/10/12/stranskom_en/). Accessed 18 May 2006.

Stevens, A. (2005) Air corridor: Mozambique's channel to competition. *Airways*, August 2005, 28–33.

St Paul Pioneer Press (2005) Loss of airline hub can be a boon for travelers, 6 November 2005 (http://www.twincities.com/mld/twincities/business/13084956.htm). Accessed 7 November 2005.

Suzuki, Y., and Tyworth, J.E. (1998) A theoretical framework for modeling sales-service relationships in the transportation industry. *Transportation Research Part E* 34, 87–100.

Suzuki, Y., Tyworth, J.E. and Novack, R.A. (2001) Airline market share and customer service quality: A reference-dependent model. *Transportation Research Part A* 35, 773–788.

Svenson, S. (2004) The cottage and the city: An interpretation of the Canadian second home experience. In C.M. Hall and D.K. Müller (eds) *Tourism, Mobility and Second Homes: Between Elite Landscape and Common Ground* (pp. 55–74). Clevedon: Channel View.

Sykes, L. (1997) Watch a whale. *Geographical*, September 1997.

Szodruch, J. (2001) Aircraft drag reductions as an answer to global challenges. *Air & Space Europe* 3 (3/4), 93–97.

Taaffe, E.J., Gauthier, H.L. and O'Kelly, M.E. (1996) *Geography of Transportation* (2nd edn). Upper Saddle River, NJ: Prentice Hall.

Tagami, K. (2005) Whats it mean for the airport?, 13 September 2005 (www.ajc.com/news/content/business/delta/0905/deltaharts.html). Accessed 28 September 2005.

Tam, M.-L. and Lam, W.H.K. (2004) Determination of service levels for passenger orientation in Hong Kong International Airport. *Journal of Air Transport Management* 10, 181–189.

Taneja, N.K. (2003) *Airline Survival Kit: Breaking Out of the Zero Profit Game*. Aldershot: Ashgate.

Tarry, C. (2004) The difficult part is yet to come: Profit rather than traffic alone remains they key to airline prosperity. *Tourism and Hospitality Research* 5 (1), 79–83.

Teye, V. and Leclerc, D. (1998) Produce and service delivery satisfaction among North American cruise passengers. *Tourism Management* 19 (2), 153–160.

Times Record (2004) Fate of excursion train remains to be decided, 2 September 2004 (http://www.swtimes.com/archive/2004/September/02/business/fate.html). Accessed 6 September 2004.

This Is Money (2005) Budget airline growth continues, 10 October 2005 (http://www.thisismoney.co.uk/money-savers/article.html?in_article_id=404245&in_page_id=5). Accessed 11 October 2005.

Thomas, C.D., Cameron, A., Green, R.E., Bakkenes, M., Beaumont, L.J. *et al.* (2004) Extinction risk from climate change. *Nature* 427, 145– 148.

Thorton, P.R., Shaw, G. and Williams, A.M. (1997) Tourist group holiday decision-making and behaviour: The influence of children. *Tourism Management* 18 (5), 287–298.

Times Online (2005) Cornwall flights cut by Ryanair, 31 August 2005 (http://travel.times-online.co.uk/article/0,,10295-1758709,00.html)

Tomkins, R. (1994) Six airlines agree not to use 'price fixing system'. *Financial Times*, 19 March.

Tourism Scotland (2003) Tourism in Scotland 2003 (www.scotexchange.net/tourism_in_scotland_2003.pdf). Accessed 6 December 2005.

Tran, M. (2004) Q&A: Eurotunnel. *Guardian*, 7 April 2004 (http://www.guardian.co.uk/print/0,3858,4897368-103630,00.html). Accessed 22 April 2004.

Transport Canada (2004) *Creating a Transportation Blueprint for the Next Decade and Beyond: Defining the Challenges* (http://www.tc.gc.ca/aboutus/straightahead/challenges/menu.htm). Accessed 14 October 2004.

Transport Canada (2001) Transportation in Canada, Annual Report 2001 (http://www.tc.gc.ca/pol/en/Report/anre2001/tc0100ae.htm). Accessed 6 December 2005.

Travel and Tourism Analyst (2004) Cruises: North America and the Caribbean, No. 9, June 2004.

Travel Daily News (2005) The skies open up over India (http://www.traveldailynews.com/makeof.asp?central_id=894&permanent_id=33). Accessed 9 November 2005.

Travel Trade Gazetta Europa (1998) Agents must by ready for urgent action over fees. 9 April 1998, 9.

Tretheway, M. and Mak, D. (2006) Emerging tourism markets: Ageing and developing economies. *Journal of Air Transport Management* 12 (1), 21–27.

Tretheway, M.W. and Oum, T.H. (1992) *Airline Economics: Foundation for Strategy and Policy*. University of British Columbia: The Centre for Transportation Studies.

Tretheway, M.W. and Waters, W.G. II (1998) Reregulation of the airline industry: Could price cap regulation play a role? *Journal of Air Transport Management* 4, 47–53.

Tripp, C. and Drea, J.T. (2002) Selecting and promoting service encounter elements in passenger rail transportation. *Journal of Services Marketing* 16 (5), 432–442.

Trivedi, C. (2003) Mixed views on Heathrow growth, BBC News, 16 December 2003 (http://news.bbc.co.uk/go/pr/fr/-/1/hi/england/london/3324710.htm). Accessed 10 September 2005.

Tsaur, S.-H., Chang, T.-Y. and Yen, C.-H. (2002) The evaluation of airline service quality by fuzzy MCDM. *Tourism Management* 23, 107–115.

Tucker, H. (2002) Welcome to Flintstones-Land: Contesting place and identity in Goreme, Central Turkey. In S. Coleman and M. Crang (eds) *Tourism: Between Place and Performance* (pp. 143–159). New York: Berghahn Books.

Turner, R.K., Pearce, D. and Bateman, I. (1993) *Environmental Economics: An Elementary Introduction*. Baltimore: The Johns Hopkins University Press.

Turnock, D. (2001) Railways and economic development in Romania before 1918. *Journal of Transport Geography* 9, 137–150.

Turton, B. (2004) Airlines and tourism development: The case of Zimbabwe. In L. Lumsdon and S.J. Page (eds) *Tourism and Transport: Issues and Agenda for the New Millennium* (pp. 69–78). Amsterdam: Elsevier.

Turton, B. and Black, W.R. (1998) Inter-urban transport. In B. Hoyle and R. Knowles (eds) *Modern Transport Geography* (2nd edn). Chichester: John Wiley and Sons.

Turton, B.J. and Mutambirwa, C.C. (1996) Air transport services and the expansion of international tourism in Zimbabwe. *Tourism Management* 17 (6), 453–462.

UK National Statistics (2005) (www.statistics.gov.uk/STATBASE/Expodata/Spread sheets/D8066.xls). Accessed 12 November 2005.

United States DoT (2003) Strategic Plan, 2003–2008: Safer, simpler, smarter transportation solutions (http://www.dot.gov/stratplan2008/strategic_plan.htm). Accessed 3 September 2004.

Unnrikrishnan, M. (2005) Indias aviation market surges on strong domestic and international demand, *Aviation Daily*, 3 November 2005 (http://aviationnow.com/avnow/news/channel_aviationdaily_story.jsp?id=news/INDINT.xml). Accessed 21 December 2005.

UNWTO (2005a) *Tourism Highlights, 2005 Edition*. World Tourism Organization.

UNWTO (2005b) High oil prices yet to impact on tourism says WTO, 14 November 2005 (http://www.world-tourism.org/newsroom/Releases/2005/november/oil.htm). Accessed 14 November 2005.

UNWTO (2006) International tourism up 4.5% in the first four months of 2006, 28 June 2006 (http://www.unwto.org/newsroom/Releases/2006/june/barometer.html). Accessed 29 July 2006.

Urquhart, C. (2005) Why I don't like Ryan Air. *The Times Online*, 17 September 2005 (http://business.timesonline.co.uk/article/0,,9077-1782464,00.html). Accessed 17 September 2005.

Urry, J. (1995) *Consuming Places*. London: Routledge.

van der Knaap, W. (1999) GIS oriented analysis of tourist time–space patterns to support sustainable tourism development. *Tourism Geographies* 1 (1), 56–69.

Van der Pool, L. (2004) Royal Caribbean battles winter blues. *ADWEEK Southeast*, 28 December 2004.

van Wee, B., Hagoort, M. and Annema, J.A. (2001) Accessibility measures with competition. *Journal of Transport Geography* 9, 199–208.

Vlek, S. and Vogels, M. (2000) AERO – Aviation emissions and evaluation of reduction options. *Air & Space Europe* 2 (3), 41–44.

Vowles, T.M. (2000) The effect of low fare air carriers on airfares in the US. *Journal of Transport Geography* 8, 121–128.

Wagner, J.E. (1997) Estimating the economic impacts of tourism. *Annals of Tourism Research* 24, 592–606.

Walters, T. (2005) Tourism has real potential in 2006, 19 December 2005 (http://www.theroyalgazette.com/apps/pbcs.dll/article?AID=/20051220/NEWS/112200174). Accessed 27 December 2005.

Walton, W. (2003) Roads and traffic congestion policies: One step forward, two steps back. In I. Docherty and J. Shaw (eds) *A New Deal for Transport?* (pp. 75–107). Oxford: Blackwell.

Wang, D. (2001) Impacts of institutional policies on individuals participation in non-work activities. *Journal of Transport Geography* 9, 61–74.

Ward, D. (2005) *Ocean Cruising and Cruise Ships 2005* (15th edn). London: Berlitz Publishing.

Wardell, J. (2005) Virgin spaceport to be built in NM, 13 December 2005 (http://news.yahoo.com/s/ap/20051213/ap_on_sc/britain_space_tourism&printer=1;_ylt=A9 FJqZP8fp9Ds4UBGhRxieAA;_ylu=X3oDMTA3MXN1bHE0BHNlYwN0bWE-). Accessed 14 December 2005.

Washington Times (2004a) Traveling the rails to picturesque sites, 2 September 2004 (http://www.washingtontimes.com/weekend/20040901-100727-2446r.htm). Accessed 6 September 2004.

Washington Times (2004b) Russian railways plans for future, 31 May 2004 (http://www.washtimes.com/upi-breaking/20040531-094033-5911r.htm). Accessed 4 June 2004.

Wastnage, J. (2004) EC considers airlines and airports in new emissions trading scheme. *Flight International* 9–15 November: 10.

Weaver, A. (2005) The McDonalization thesis and cruise tourism. *Annals of Tourism Research* 32 (2), 346–366.

Weaver, D. (2005) The distinctive dynamics of exurban tourism. *International Journal of Tourism Research* 7, 23–33.

Weaver, A. and Duval, D.T. (in press) International and transnational aspects of the global cruise industry. In C.M. Hall and T.E. Coles (eds) *Tourism and International Business*. London: Routledge.

Webster, B. (2005) Aircraft emissions to double by 2030 despite hi-tech jets, 21 June 2005 (http://www.timesonline.co.uk/article/0,,2-1662662,00.html). Accessed 15 November 2005.

Webwire (2005) VIA Rail exceeds Kyoto targets, 12 April 2005 (http://webwire.com/ViewPressRel.asp?SESSIONID=&aId=6440). Accessed 6 December 2005.

Weinstein, A. (1987) *Market Segmentation: Using Niche Marketing to Exploit New Markets.* Chicago: Probus Publishing Company.

Welsby, J. and Nichols, A. (1999) The privatisation of Britain's railways. *Journal of Transport Economics and Policy* 33 (1), 55–76.

Werner, C. (1985) *Spatial Transportation Modeling.* Beverly Hills, CA: Sage.

Wilkinson, P. (1999) Caribbean cruise tourism: Delusion? Illusion? *Tourism Geographies* 1 (3), 261–282.

Wolfe, R. (1952) Wasaga Beach: The divorce from the geographic environment. *Canadian Geographer* 1 (2), 57–65.

Wolfe, R. (1966) Recreational travel: The new migration. *Canadian Geographer* 10 (1), 1–14.

Wood, R. (2000) Caribbean cruise tourism: Globalization at sea. *Annals of Tourism Research* 27 (2), 345–370.

Wood, R. (2004a) Global currents: Cruise ships in the Caribbean Sea. In D.T. Duval (ed.) *Tourism in the Caribbean: Trends, Development, Prospects* (pp. 152–171). London: Routledge.

Wood, R. (2004b) Cruise ships: Deterritorialised destinations. In L. Lumsdon and S.J. Page (eds) *Tourism and Transport: Issues and Agenda for the New Millennium* (pp. 133–145). Amsterdam: Elsevier.

World Bank (1996) *Sustainable Transport: Priorities for Policy Reform.* World Bank.

WTO (1991) *Resolutions of International Conference Travel and Tourism, Ottawa.* Madrid: WTO.

WTO (2003a) *Worldwide Cruise Ship Activity.* Madrid: WTO.

WTO (2003b) Climate Change and Tourism: Proceedings of the 1st International Conference on Climate Change and Tourism Djerba, Tunisia, 9–11 April 2003 (http://www.world-tourism.org/sustainable/climate/brochure.htm). Accessed 8 December 2005.

WTTC (2003) *Special SARS Analysis: Impact of Travel and Tourism.* London: WTTC.

Wynne, C., Berthon, P., Pitt, L., Ewing, M. and Napoli, J. (2001) The impact of the Internet on the distribution value chain: The case of the South African tourism industry. *International Marketing Review* 18 (4), 420–431.

Yang, J.-Y. and Lui, A. (2003) Frequent flyer program: A case study of China airlines marketing initiative – Dynasty Flyer Program. *Tourism Management* 24, 587–595.

INDEX